Lecture Notes in Computer Science   4672

Commenced Publication in 1973
Founding and Former Series Editors:
Gerhard Goos, Juris Hartmanis, and Jan van Leeuwen

T0181156

Keqiu Li   Chris Jesshope   Hai Jin
Jean-Luc Gaudiot (Eds.)

Network and Parallel Computing

IFIP International Conference, NPC 2007
Dalian, China, September 18-21, 2007
Proceedings

 Springer

Volume Editors

Keqiu Li
Dalian Maritime University
E-mail: keqiu_01@163.com

Chris Jesshope
University of Amsterdam
E-mail: Jesshope@science.uva.nl

Hai Jin
Huazhong University of Science and Technology
Wuhan, 430074, China
E-mail: hjin@hust.edu.cn

Jean-Luc Gaudiot
University of California
E-mail: gaudiot@uci.edu

Library of Congress Control Number: 2007934763

CR Subject Classification (1998): C.2, F.2, D.2, H.4, H.5, D.4, K.6

LNCS Sublibrary: SL 1 – Theoretical Computer Science and General Issues

ISSN   0302-9743
ISBN-10   3-540-74783-4 Springer Berlin Heidelberg New York
ISBN-13   978-3-540-74783-3 Springer Berlin Heidelberg New York

Springer is a part of Springer Science+Business Media

springer.com

© IFIP International Federation for Information Processing 2007
Printed in Germany

Typesetting: Camera-ready by author, data conversion by Scientific Publishing Services, Chennai, India
Printed on acid-free paper   SPIN: 12119219   06/3180   5 4 3 2 1 0

Preface

Welcome to the proceedings of the 2007 IFIP International Conference on Network and Parallel Computing (NPC 2007) held in Dalian, China.

NPC has been a premier conference that has brought together researchers and practitioners from academia, industry and governments around the world to advance the theories and technologies of network and parallel computing. The goal of NPC is to establish an international forum for researchers and practitioners to present their excellent ideas and experiences in all system fields of network and parallel computing. The main focus of NPC 2007 was on the most critical areas of network and parallel computing: network applications, network technologies, network and parallel architectures, and parallel and distributed software.

In total, the conference received more than 600 papers from researchers and practitioners from over 20 countries and areas. Each paper was reviewed by at least three internationally renowned referees and selected based on its originality, significance, correctness, relevance, and clarity of presentation. Among the high-quality submissions, only 53 regular papers were accepted by the conference. All of the selected conference papers are included in the conference proceedings. After the conference, some high-quality papers will be recommended to be published in a special issue of several international journals.

We were delighted to host four well-known international scholars offering the keynote speeches: Tharam Dillon from Curtin University of Technology, Australia, Takashi Nanya from University of Tokyo, Japen, Guang R. Gao from University of Delaware, USA, and Zhiwei Xu from Chinese Academy of Sciences, China.

We would like to take this opportunity to thank all the authors for their submissions to NPC 2007. Many of them travelled some distance to participate in the conference. We also thank the Program Committee members and additional reviewers for the efforts in reviewing the large number of papers. Thanks also go the local conference organizers for their great support.

Last but not least, we would like to express our gratitude to all of the organizations who have supported our efforts to bring the conference and workshops to fruition. We are grateful to IFIP Working Group 10.3 on Concurrent Systems, Institute of Computing Technology of the Chinese Academy of Sciences, Dalian Maritime University, Huazhong University of Science and Technology, and Central Queensland University for their sponsorship and assistance.

September 2007

Keqiu Li
Chris Jesshope
Hai Jin
Jean-Luc Gaudiotium

Organization

Honorary Chair

Zuwen Wang, Dalian Maritime University (DLMU), China

General Co-chairs

Jean-Luc Gaudiot, University of California, Irvine, USA
Hai Jin, Huazhong University of Science and Technology, China

Steering Committee Chair

Kemal Ebcioglu, Global Supercomputing Corporation, USA

Program Co-chairs

Chris Jesshope, University of Amsterdam, Netherlands
Keqiu Li, DLMU, China

Program Vice-Chairs

Rudolf Eigenmann, Purdue University, USA
Skevos Evripidou, University of Cyprus, Cyprus
Susumu Horiguchi, Tohoku University, Japan
Zhaohui Wu, Zhejiang University, China

Publication Co-chairs

Minyi Guo, University of Aizu, Japan
Mingyu Lu, DLMU, China

Publicity Co-chairs

Wenbin Jiang, Huazhong University of Science and Technology, China
Alex Shafarenko, University of Hertfordshire, UK

Organization Co-chairs

Yuqing Sun, DLMU, China
Weishi Zhang, DLMU, China
Bo Jiang, DLMU, China

Workshop Chair

Yang Xiang, Central Queensland University, Australia

Finance Chair

Ruixue Xu, DLMU, China

Registration Co-chairs

Zhenjun Du, DLMU, China
Chunli Wang, DLMU, China

Industry Sponsorship Chair

Bo Jiang, DLMU, China

Local Arrangement Chair

Guanyu Li, DLMU, China

Internet Chairs

Zhihuai Li, DLMU, China
Jianping Jiang, DLMU, China

Conference Secretariat

Zhiying Cao, DLMU, China
Hong Ye, DLMU, China

Program Committee Members

Ajith Abraham, Chun-Ang University, Korea
Ishfaq Ahmad, University of Texas at Arlington, USA
Shoukat Ali, University of Missouri-Rolla, USA
Makoto Amamiya, Kyushu University, Japan
Ramon Beivide, University of Cantabria, Spain
Jacir L. Bordim, University of Brasilia, Brazil
Luc Bouge, IRISA/ENS Cachan, France
Pascal Bouvry, University of Luxembourg, Luxembourg
Wentong Cai, Nanyang Technological University, Singapore
Jiannong Cao, Hong Kong Polytechnic University, Hong Kong
Ralph Castain, Los Alamos National Laboratory, USA
Rong Chen, DLMU, China
Xueqi Cheng, Institute of Computing Technology, CAS, China
Zhongxian Chi, Dalian University of Technology, China
Jong-Deok Choi, IBM T. J. Watson Research Center, USA

John Morris, Auckland University, New Zealand
John Morrison, University College Cork, Ireland
Yoichi Muraoka, Waseda University, Japan
Koji Nakano, Hiroshima University, Japan
Jun Ni, The University of Iowa, USA
Lionel Ni, Hong Kong University of Science and Technology, Hong Kong
Stephan Olariu, Old Dominion University, USA
Jong Hyuk Park, Hanwha S&C Co., Ltd., Korea
Andy Pimentel, University of Amsterdam, Netherlands
Depei Qian, Xi'an Jiaotong University, China
Wenyu Qu, University of Tokyo, Japan
Felix Rauch, NICTA and University of New South Wales, Australia
Wolfgang Rehm, TU Chemnitz, Germany
Arnold Rosenberg, University of Massachusetts at Amherst, USA
Ulrich Rude, University Erlangen-Nuremberg, Germany
Frode Eika Sandnes, Oslo University College, Norway
Stanislav G. Sedukhin, University of Aizu, Japan
Selvakennedy Selvadurai, University of Sydney, Australia
Franciszek Seredynski, Polish Academy of Sciences, Poland
Xiaowei Shen, IBM T.J. Watson Research Center, USA
Sven-bodo Sholz, Hertfordshire University, UK
Ivan Stojmenovic, University of Ottawa, Canada
Yutaka Takahashi, Kyoto University, Japan
Makoto Takizawa, Tokyo Denki University, Japan
El-Ghazali Talbi, University of Lille, France
Domenico Talia, University of Calabria, Italy
Guozhen Tan, Dalian University of Technology, China
David Taniar, Monash University, Australia
Guoku Teng, DLMU, China
Mitchell D. Theys, University of Illinois at Chicago, USA
Xinmin Tian, Intel Corporation, USA
Theo Ungerer, University fo Augsberg, Germany
Cho-Li Wang, The University of Hong Kong, Hong Kong
Guojun Wang, Central South University, China
Hongjun Wang, Dalian Naval Academy, China
Xiangyang Wang, Liaoning Normal University, China
Xicheng Wang, Dalian University of Technology, China
Xingwei Wang, Northeastern University, China
Xingyuan Wang, Dalian University of Technology, China
Ian Watson, Manchester University, UK
Paul Werstein, The University of Otago, New Zealand
Weng-Fai Wong, National University of Singapore, Singapore
Di Wu, Dalian University of Technology, China
Nong Xiao, National University of Defense Technology, China
Qin Xin, The University of Bergen, Norway
Cheng-Zhong Xu, Wayne State University, USA
Deqin Yan, Liaoning Normal University, China

Chao-Tung Yang, Tunghai University, Taiwan
Laurence T. Yang, St. Francis Xavier University,Canada
Qing Yang, University of Rhode Island, USA
Xun Yue, Shandong Agricultural University, China
Lixin Zhang, IBM Austin Research Laboratory, USA
Zixiang Zhao, DLMU, China
Weimin Zheng, Tsinghua University, China
Si Qing Zheng, University of Texas at Dallas, USA
Bing Bing Zhou, University of Sydney, Australia
Hai Zhuge, Institute of Computing Technology, CAS, China
Albert Y. Zomaya, The University of Sydney, Australia

Additional Reviewers

Christopher Ang
Alvaro Arenas
Faruk Bagci
Ayon Basumallik
Sourav S. Bhowmick
Gavin Brown
Bernd Burgstaller
Tom Cai
Linchun Cao
Eugenio Cesario
Jed Kao-Tung Chang
Sanjay Chawla
Hanhua Chen
KaiKai Chi
Hyung-Kyu Choi
Youngkyu Choi
Chun-Tung Chou
Carmela Comito
Luke Dalessandro
Gregoire Danoy
Ali Elghirani
Markus Esch
Katrina Falkner
Alan Fekete
Jacek Gajc
Qi Ge
Patrick Gratz
Jose Angel Gregorio
Clemens Grelck
Xiaoming Gu
Faisal Hasan
Luc Hogie

Sung Hyun Hong
Qihang Huang
Ka-Shun Hung
Satoko Itaya
XiaoHong Jiang
Dong Heon Jung
Tomasz Kaszuba
Ashok Argent Katwala
Kirk Kelsey
Chris Kirkham
Florian Kluge
Irena Koprinska
Dominique Lavenier
Je-Hyung Lee
Jaemok Lee
Seyong Lee
Bo Li
Xiaofei Liao
Godfrey van der Linden
Kai Liu
Na Liu
Ren Ping Liu
Shaoshan Liu
Yi Liu
Zhi Liu
Malcolm Yoke Hean Low
Mikel Lujan
Guangyu Ma
Kevin Maciunas
Omer Mahmood
Virendra Marathe
Carmen Martinez

Andrea Matsunaga
Torsten Mehlan
Rodrigo Mello
Stefan Metzlaff
Frank Mietke
Jose Miguel-Alonso
Jörg Mische
Hong Son Ngo
Xiaomin Ning
Marek Ostaszewski
Linfeng Pan
Xuan-Hieu Phan
Marek Pilski
Apivadee Piyatumrong
Cheryl Pope
Louis-Noël Pouchet
Li Qi
Weizhong Qiang
Philippe Robert
Nathan Rountree
Sergio Ruocco
Krzysztof Rzadca
Liria Matsumoto Sato
Christoph Schommer
Seung-Woo Seo
Marcin Seredynski
Zhiyuan Shao
Ke Shi
Xuanhua Shi
Jeremy Singer
Jaroslaw Skaruz
Meiping Song
Samia Souissi
Christopher Stewart
Thomas Stricker
Masaya Sugawara
Piotr Switalski
Miroslaw Szaban
Andrea Tagarelli
Javid Taheri
Jiakui Tang
Huan-ling Tang
Cuihua Tian

Yuchu Tong
Sid Touati
Ken C.K. Tsang
Sascha Uhrig
Jothi vasudevan Nathella Vijayakumar
Bao-feng Wang
Hsiao-His Wang
Qiang Wang
Tao Wang
Kan Watanabe
Ulf WEHLING
Tien-Hsiung Weng
Adam Wierzbicki
Bryan Wong
Zhengyu Wu
Jun Wu
Song Wu
ChangMing Xing
Naixue Xiong
Ye Yan
Weiyu Yang
Chao-Tung Yang
Qinyun Yang
Yan Yang
Yanqin Yang
Kazuto Yano
Rami Yared
Yijiao Yu
Yong Yu
Zhihang Yu
Pingpeng Yuan
Aijun Zhang
Chengliang Zhang
Daqiang Zhang
Gw Zhang
Jian Zhang
Jun Zhang
Li Zhang
Ming Zhao
Yuanzhen Zhao
Huiyuan Zheng
Tanveer Zia
Deqing Zou

Table of Contents

Network Applications

Cluster and Grid Computing

Internet Computing

Optical Networks

Peer-to-Peer Computing

Ubiquitous Computing

Wireless Computing

Network Technologies

Communication Technology

Network Algorithms

Network Reliability, Security, and Dependability

Network Storage

Network and Parallel Architectures

Multicore Design Issues

Network and Interconnect Architecture

Nontraditional Processor Technologies

Performance Modeling and Evaluation

System Design Issues for Low Power and Energy Efficiency

Parallel and Distributed Software

Data Mining

Parallel Programming Tools, Models, Languages and Compilers

Keynote Speeches

On a High-Order Compact Scheme and Its Utilization in Parallel Solution of a Time-Dependent System on a Distributed Memory Processor

Okon H. Akpan

Bowie State University, Bowie MD 20715, USA
oakpan@cs.bowiestate.edu

Abstract. The study resulting in this paper applied a parallel algorithm based on a fourth-order compact scheme and suitable for parallel implementation of scientific/engineering systems. The particular system used for demonstration in the study was a time-dependendent system solved in parallel on a 2-head-node, 224-compute-node *Apple Xserve G5* multiprocessor. The use of the approximation scheme, which necessitated discretizing in both space and time with h_x space width and h_t time step, produced a linear tridiagonal, *almost-Toeplitz* system. The solution used p processors with p ranging from 3 to 63. The speedups, s_p, approached the limiting value of p only when p was small but yieldd poor computations errors which became progressively better as p increases. The parallel solution is very accurate having good speedups and accuracies but only when p is within reasonable range of values.

1 Introduction

Finite difference methods are among the commonest approximation schemes used for numerical solution of ordinary and partial differential equations, mainly, because of their simplicity of use and the fact that they lend themselves quite easily to the Taylor series analysis of any incurred errors. Other approximation methods exist, and they include *finite elements*, *finite volumes*, and *spectral* methods. While there are a number of problems, for example, *elliptic* systems, which can be solved with low-order approximation methods (second or lower) with reasonable accuracies, there is also a large class of problems, including those of *acoustics* [1,2,3], and of *fluid dynamics* [5,6,7,9,13,14], the solutions of which typically require higher order approximation solution schemes for higher levels of accuracy.

A solution method is said to be of order h^n, where h is the mesh size of the problem domain, when its truncation error varies as h^n. In a second order approximation scheme, for instance, where error $\approx h^2$, halving the mesh size (h) reduces the error by a factor of approximately four. Low order approximations generally require *compact stencils* which utilize three nodal points in any direction. Thus 1-D, 2-D, or 3-D compact stencils require 3, 3×3, or $3 \times 3 \times 3$

K. Li et al. (Eds.): NPC 2007, LNCS 4672, pp. 1–12, 2007.

grid nodes respectively. Any approximation method which involves grid nodes outside those of a compact stencil is said to be *non-compact*. Higher order finite difference approximations (that is, those with approximation error $\approx h^n$, where $n > 2$) are possible but these methods typically require non-compact stencils, and application of non-compact stencils at or near boundaries of the problem domain usually requires inclusion of fictitious nodes thus complicating the resulting numerical formulations, and the usual consequences of those complications include increases in the overall number of grid points as well as increases in the bandwidths of the resulting system matrices. The latter problem, namely, increases in the bandwidths, precludes the use of implicit methods for solution of the resulting systems because those systems are usually not of *tridiagonal* form. Lastly, non-compact approximation methods do not easily allow for approximations with non-uniform grids thus excluding solution of certain problems notably *boundary-layer*, *driven-cavity*, and *turbulent flow* problems which typically involve wide ranges of space and time scales.

Approximation schemes which must retain a high accuracy without incurring most of the complications of non-compact methods must of necessity be compact, although they too must somehow deal with the problems imposed by having to apply the stencils at or near the problem boundaries and to come up with a numerical formulation with a high accuracy result. Gustafsson [15,16] has demonstrated that such a compact method must have *boundary closures* in which the boundary- and near-boundary points have about the same accuracy as that of the interior points or at most one order less. Abarbanel and Chertock [17] have successfully used a five-order *boundary closure* in their solution of hyperbolic initial boundary value problems in 1-D and 2-D spatial domains using a sixth-order compact difference scheme. In summary, a compact differencing scheme requires more work per grid point, but the result is higher approximation accuracy, a few grid points to compute with, and less computer memory requirements to store the computed result. As a result, compact approximation schemes are more efficient than both non-compact methods of the same order and also than low-order solution methods in general [18,19,20]. As stated by Orszak [21], at the cost of slight computational complexity, fourth-order compact schemes can achieve results in the 5% accuracy range with approximately half the spatial resolution in each space direction when compared with the second-order schemes.

The compact difference approximation methods that treat the approximated function and its derivatives as unknowns at grid points are fourth-order and they produce tridiagonal systems. These compact schemes generally fall into two classes. The first class consists of those solution methods which are best suited for uniform grids, and they include the Kreiss and Oliger's approximating scheme [18,4], and the Mehrstellen's scheme [1]. The second class consists of methods that allow for variable grids. These include the cubic spline methods of Rubin and Khosla [23,24] and the hermitian finite difference methods of Adam's [25,26]. Also belonging in this class are the fourth-order compact schemes for solution of *incompressible viscous flow* problems the most notable of which being the fourth-order, three-nodal stencil compact scheme of Gupta [27,28] useful for solution of convection diffusion equations. Gupta's compact scheme, which does not seem to suffer excessively from the spurious oscillatory behavior as do other methods, has been applied by Yavneh to solve *convection-diffusion problems* [29], and also by Weinan to solve unsteady viscous flow problems [30].

While over the years there have been a large number of approximating schemes constructed for solution of many classes of scientific problems, the literature has reported relatively a few successful solution paradigms designed to fully exploit the capabilities of modern supercomputers for efficient solution of problems with these approximating schemes. The reported paradigms all attempt to solve complicated scientific problems in parallel harnessing the supercomputing resources in the process, and, if all goes well, the result is often an efficient solution in terms of both time (speed) and space (memory) requirements. The earliest parallel solution methods were designed for solution of *fine-grained* problems, that is, problems with $n \approx p$, where n is the size of the problem and p the number of processors (of a supercomputer), and, also, the methods were based on high-speed solution using tridiagonal solvers. The most known of these methods include the *recursive-doubling reduction* method of Stone [31] and its improved version [32], the *odd-even* or *cyclic reduction* technique of Hockney [33,34], and recently, the *prefix* scheme by Sun [35,36], which is a variation of the *cyclic reduction* method. Each of the cited parallel solution method is capable of solving n-dimensional tridiagonal system in $\mathbf{O}\log(n)$ time using n processors. More recent efforts are geared toward problem solution in various parallel computing environments, not just *fine-grained*. These include the methods of Lawrie and Sameh [37], Wang [38] designed for *median-* (that is, $p < n$) to *course-grained* (that is, $p \ll n$).

The thrust of this study is to apply the Kreiss and Oliger's fourth-order compact scheme to solve in parallel a time-dependent parabolic differential equation with Neumann boundary conditions. The focus is strictly computational. It is not concerned with developing another solution methodology, nor with modification of an existing one to solve any problem. Given the dearth of utilization of supercomputing resources to solve the kinds of problems mentioned here, the study clearly and painstakingly demonstrates the steps needed to numerically solve a given problem in parallel on a supercomputer in full consideration of both the inherent parallel properties of the problem and the architecture of the supercomputer involved.

2 Kreiss and Oliger's Fourth Order Compact Scheme

Kreiss and Oliger [18] suggested a fourth-order compact difference method in which the first (f') and second (f'') derivatives for constant mesh size (h_x) are approximated by

$$f_n' = \left(\frac{D_o}{1 + \frac{1}{6}h_x^2 D_+ D_-} \right) f_n, \tag{1}$$

and

$$f_n'' = \left(\frac{D_+ D_-}{1 + \frac{1}{12} h^2 D_+ D_-} \right) f_n, \tag{2}$$

where

$$D_o f_n = \frac{1}{2h_x} (f_{n+1} - f_{n-1}),$$

$$D_+ f_n = \frac{1}{h_x} (f_{n+1} - f_n),$$

$$D_- f_n = \frac{1}{h_x} (f_n - f_{n-1}).$$

Multiplying equations (1) and (2) with the respective denominators and simplifying yields

$$\frac{1}{6} f_{n-1}' + \frac{2}{3} f_n' + \frac{1}{6} f_{n+1}' = \frac{1}{2h_x} (f_{n-1}), \tag{3}$$

$$\frac{1}{12} f_{n-1}'' + \frac{5}{6} f_n'' + \frac{1}{12} f_{n+1}'' = \frac{1}{2h_x^2} (f_{n+1} - 2f_n + f_{n-1}). \tag{4}$$

Each of the above approximations utilizes a 1-D 3-node *compact* stencil

$$\left\{ 1 \quad a' \quad 1 \right\}$$

where $a' \in \{4, 10\}$. When (3) and (5) are correctly applied to approximate first or second order partial derivatives respectively, the system

$$\begin{bmatrix} c_0 & 1 & & & \\ 1 & c & 1 & & \\ & \ddots & \ddots & \ddots & \\ & & 1 & c & 1 \\ & & & 1 & c_0' \end{bmatrix} \mathbf{x} = \mathbf{A} x = \mathbf{k}, \tag{5}$$

results in which c_0, c_0' result from boundary conditions, and $x \in \{f', f''\}$, $c \in \{4, 10\}$, whereas the conventional fourth-order scheme results in systems with larger bandwidths. A conventional fourth-order scheme approximating the same system with, for instance,

$$f_n'' = \frac{1}{12h_x^2} (-f_{n-2} + 16f_{n-1} - 30f_n + 16f_{n+1} - f_{n+2})$$

applies a *non-compact* stencil (5-node stencil:

$$\{-1 \quad 16 \quad -30 \quad 16 \quad -1\} \tag{6}$$

in this case).

3 Parallel Solution

There are a number of parallel algorithms for solution of system (5). The most known among them are the *cyclic reduction* algorithm by Hockney, [34], the *recursive doubling* by Stone [32], and the *prefixed* method by Sun [36]. In this study, we used the *cyclic reduction* method as we found this algorithm to be very easily implementable on our supercomputing system.

A parallel *cyclic reduction*, which assumes availability of p processors where p and n (the system's order) need not be equal, uses l reduction levels, $1 \leq l \leq log2(n')$. Every process, p_i, has 3 4-vectors, *myVec*, *leftVec*, and *rightVec*, where for any such vector (*vec*), $vec[0] \leftarrow$ d, $vev[1] \leftarrow$ e, $vec[2] \leftarrow$ f, and $vec[3] \leftarrow$ k, where d, e, f are the row components of **A** and k of (5). At a reduction level l, there is data transfer to process p_i from 2 processes with ranks *fromLProc* and *fromRProc*, and from p_i to 2 processes with ranks *toLProc* and *toRProc*. The interprocessor data transfers can be facilitated with the use of data structure:

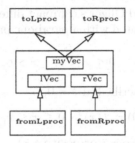

Another data structure is the array **D** which holds rows $\boxed{d|e|f|k}$ of **A** and **k** of (6). In this implementation, the first row of **D** contains a special vector $\boxed{0|1|0|0}$, the second row of **D** contains the first row of **A** and of **k**, and so forth. Without the first row of **D** containing the special vector, the inter-process data transfers may not be correct or, if correct, at an unacceptable cost.

4 Computational Environment

The computational environment used for all parallel computations in this study is the Bowie State University's supercomputer facility locally dubbed *Xseed*. At the core of *Xseed* is Mac OS X Server operating system running a cluster configuration presently consisting of 2 ultradense, 1U rackmount XServe G5 servers and 224 G5 compute nodes each of which a dual, 64-bit, 2.0 GHz processor with 2 GB RAM and local store of 80 GB capacity. The 224 G5 compute nodes are clustered into shared-memory nodes with dual gigabit Ethernet on the motherboard which, in combination with the high bandwidth system control, effectively reduces contentions in both the network and i/o traffics. The 2 servers are the *XSeed's* administrative nerve center which is responsible for coordinating all computations and data routings, as well as managing data storage. *XSeed* is capable of theoretical performance rate of 2.104 Tflops and has a combined work storage space of over 6 TB.

XSeed is ideal for scientific and high performance computing as well as image rendering operations. Each G5 processor's superscalar, super-pipelined architecture supports up to 215 simultaneous instructions with a high-bandwidth execution core offering over 12 discrete functional units, including dual floating-point units and dual integer units, to process an immense number of instructions in parallel with 64-bit precision on 64-bit wide paths! Also *XSeed* is fully grid-enabled running a complete package of functioning *Globus Alliance*'s Globus Toolkit middleware (version 4.0.1). Thus packed with enormous floating-point computational muscle, plenty of memory for work space, and updated Grid infrastructure, *XSeed* is truly a distributed, self-contained, net-centric computing environment primed to harness (and share) federated computational resources globally for parallel solution of any type of scientific and engineering problems.

5   Application

An application of the Kreiss and Oliger's compact difference scheme for approximation solutions was demonstrated with a parabolic partial differential equation

$$\frac{\partial u}{\partial t} = \kappa \frac{\partial^2 u}{\partial x^2}, \quad 0 \le x \le \widehat{x}, \quad \widehat{x} > 0, t \ge 0, \tag{7}$$

having an initial condition prescribed at $t = 0$,

$$u(x, 0) = f(x), \quad 0 \le x \le \widehat{x}, \tag{8}$$

and Neumann boundary conditions (for positive κ)

$$\frac{\partial u}{\partial x}\bigg|_{x=0} = g_1(0, t), \tag{9}$$

$$\frac{\partial u}{\partial x}\bigg|_{x=\widehat{x}} = g_2(\widehat{x}, t). \tag{10}$$

To solve (7) computationally, discretization in both time and space is needed. Discretization in time is done by performing the Taylor's series expansion of (7) in time to obtain

$$u_x^{n+1} = u_x^n + \kappa h_t \frac{\partial^2 u_x^n}{\partial^2 x^2}, \tag{11}$$

in which n corresponds to a time level, and x a spatial location. Introducing a spatial mesh width, h_x, obtainable by dividing the given interval $[0, \widehat{x}]$ into N sub-intervals, that is, $h_x = \frac{\widehat{x}}{N}$ (where $N > 0$ is some integral value), and also the notations

$$x_i = ih_x, \quad t_j = jh_t, \tag{12}$$

where $i = 0, \cdots, N$, and $j = 0, 1, \cdots$, then (11) can be rewritten as

$$u_i^{j+1} = u_i^j + \kappa h_t \frac{\partial^2 u_x^j}{\partial^2 x^2}\bigg|_{x=ih_x}. \tag{13}$$

The solution of (13) involves discretizing the spatial derivative $\frac{\partial^2}{\partial x^2}$ with the compact second-derivative operator provided in (2) to obtain the tridiagonal system (5), solving the resulting system by the parallel cyclic reduction whose code design and implementation are detailed above, substituting that solution into (13), and, finally, solving the resulting system to obtain u_i^{j+1}.

6 Experiments and Results

We solved (13) for case of $\hat{x} = 2$, $g_1(0,t) = g_2(2,t) = 0$ using $0 < \kappa\frac{h_t}{h_x} \le \frac{1}{2}$ (to avoid onset of instabilities in order to focus on the numerical solution, the objective of this study) for several h_x. A solution with a given value of p required time marching, and each time-step advance required a single compact solve in parallel. In order to be able to compare the parallel solutions to sequential solutions, we also solved (13) at the same time step, h_t, using the best sequential method, the LU decomposition:

$$\mathbf{L}g = k, \tag{14}$$

$$\mathbf{U}u = g, \tag{15}$$

where $\mathbf{L}$ and $\mathbf{U}$ are the lower and the upper triangular matrices respectively. Lastly, to compare approximate solutions to the *true* solutions, we first solved (7) analytically to obtain

$$u = 800 \sum_{n=0}^{\infty} \frac{1}{n^2(2n+1)^2} \cos\frac{(2n+1)(\pi(x-1)}{2} e^{-0.3738(2n+1)^2 t},$$

and, second, we encoded and then solved the equation at time levels t to obtain analytical (*true*) results, u_{actual}. Executions were carried out with the number of processors, p, equal to 3, 7, 15, 31, and 63. All codes – parallel cyclic reduction and LU decomposition – were appropriately *instrumented* for execution parameters notably time. The results are given in Figure 4, Figure 5, and Figure 6 below. The parameters in the the solution figures are explained as follows:

1. p is the number of processors, n the order of the system, hence, $p = n = n'-1$, $n' = \frac{\hat{N}}{h_x}$.
2. s_p is *speedup* given as $s_p = \frac{t_1}{t_p}$ $(1 \le s_p \le p)$, where t_1 is the time it took to execute the resulting tridiagonal system by the LU decomposition, t_p the time of solution of the same system with the parallel cyclic reduction with p processors.
3. ϵ_p is *efficiency* computed as $\epsilon_p = \frac{s_p}{p}$ $(\frac{1}{p} \le \epsilon_p \le 1)$.
4. Given h_x, the corresponding time step, h_t, is computed as $h_t = \frac{1}{2}\frac{h_x^2}{\kappa}$.
5. *Max.E_p* is the *maximum relative error* determined from all solutions, u, during a system solve with p processors at a given time level. Here, $E_p = \frac{u_{actual} - u_{approx}}{u_{actual}}$, where u_{actual}, u_{approx} are the analytical solution and approximate solution respectively.

8   O.H. Akpan

h_x	h_t	p	s_p	ϵ_p	$Max.E_p$
0.2500	0.8250	3	2.9103	0.9701	0.072
0.2500	0.2063	7	6.5727	0.9390	0.051
0.1250	0.0515	15	13.6581	09105	0.020
0.0625	0.0129	31	27.2871	0.8802	0.001
0.0313	0.0032	63	54.1605	0.8597	0.000

Fig. 1. Execution results for $p = 3, 7, 15, 31,$ and 63

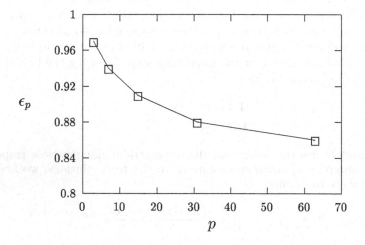

Fig. 2. Results for $p = 3, 7, 15, 31,$ and 63

7 Observations

1. The Kreiss and Oliger's fourth order compact scheme produced very accurate solution results only when solved with reasonably small spatial and time steps and when the solution was within the *stability* regimes, that is, $\kappa \frac{h_t}{h_x^2} \leq \frac{1}{2}$, but inaccurate results with error as large as 10% when the steps in time and space became large. More specifically, when h_x became large (implying small p because $p = \frac{\hat{N}}{h_x} - 1$), the results at all time levels were unacceptably poor with the worst errors occuring at $h_x = 0.5$ or $p = 3$, that is, $Max.E_3 \approx 10\%$. But as h_x became small, the errors became correspondingly small until perfect results occured at about $h_x = 0.0313$ with $p = 63$, that is, $Max.E_{63} \approx 0\%$).

2. When $p \leq 7$, the speedups s_p were very high approaching their limiting values of p, but as p increased (with decreasing h_x), the speedups became smaller tending to a limiting (but acceptable) value of about 82.5%.

3. For $n > 15$, the parallel cyclic reduction completed reduction computation, (that is, with every process i obtaining its final vector, $\boxed{d}\boxed{e}\boxed{f}\boxed{k}$, at $\log_2 n - 1$ levels, that is, one level short of the theoretical maximum of $\log_2 n$.

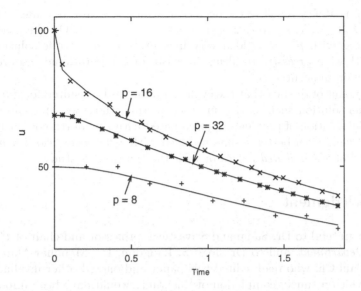

Fig. 3. Efficiency versus *Time*

8 Conclusion

1. Solution of the tridiagonal system resulting from application of the Kreiss and Oliger's compact appromation scheme produced very high speedups but very inaccurate results at small values of p, and produced low speedups but very accurate results at high value of p. The reason for this is that, although the parallel cyclic reduction exhibits 100% load balance at every reduction level,
   (a) there is no parallelism between reduction levels, that is, level-level computation is purely *sequential* supported by *MPI_Barrier* and similar freeze commands which ensure completion of all reduction operations by all processes at the current level before the same operations are started at the next reduction level,
   (b) even at a reduction level where computation is parallel at 100% load balance, the interprocessor inter-communication is quite high
   thus contributing to low speedups and corresponding low efficiencies.
2. The time for inter-process communication (for data exchanges), t_{comm}, which was quite significant when p was high, dominated the actual computation time, t_{calc}, at all reduction levels and this accounted for low speedups and efficiencies at high p, but, at low p, t_{calc} dominated t_{comm} thus resulting in high speedups but at the expense of accuracy.
3. The solution methods used in this study are highly recommended for parallel solution of time-dependent systems provided such solutions use reasonable number of processors and appropriate steps in time and space whose range can be determined from observations. (For the system used in the study,

solutions at $7 \le p \le 31$ were deemed reasonable with error range of $10\% \le Max.E_p1 \le 1\%$, speedup range of $95\% \le s_p \le 88\%$). On the other hand, solutions with $p < 7$ yielded very inaccurate results, while solutions with $p \ge 31$ were _excessive_ resulting in waste of computational resources with little gain in accuracy.)

4. On account of the fact that the cyclic reduction is best suited for _fine-grained_ parallel solution such as the one used in this study, we conclude that the parallel solution of problems approximated with the fourth compact scheme would yield even better results if solved with a _massively parallel processor_ instead of a _distributed processor_ as is the case in this study.

Acknowledgment

I am very grateful to Dr. Sadanand Srivastava, professor and chair of _Computer Science Department_, and to Dr. Joan S. Langdon, Dr. Manohar Mareboyana, and Dr. Paul Chi who read, edited this paper and offered other invaluable help without which a timely completion of this study would have been impossible. I am also indebted to Dr. Mark A. Matties, director of the _Xseed_ project, whose technical support and suggestions significantly propelled this study to its successful completion.

References

1. Krause, E., Kordulla, W.: Fourth-Order Mehrstellen Integration for Three-Dimensional Turbulent Boundary Layers. In: AIAA Comp. Fluid Dyn. Conf. (1973)
2. Gustaffsson, B.: Time Compact Difference Methods for Wave Propagation in Discontinuous Media, Tech. Reports., Dept. of Inf. Tech., Uppsala Univ., 2003-023 (2003)
3. Cohen, G., Joly, P.: Construction and Analysis of Fourth-Order Finite Difference Schemes for the Acoustic Wave Equation in Nonhomogeneoues Media. SIAM J. Num. Anal. 33 (1996)
4. Hirsh, R.: Higher Order Accurate Difference Solutions of Fluid Mechanics Problems by a Compact Differencing Technique. J. Comp. Phys. 19, 1 (1975)
5. Tolstykh, A.I.: Higher Order Accurate Non-Centered Compact Difference Schemes for Fluid Dynamics Applications. Series on Adv. in Math. for Appl. Sc. 21 (1994)
6. Ratnesh, K., Shukla, S.: Derivation of High-Order Compact Finite Difference Schemes for Non-Uniform Grid Using Polynomial Interpolation. Jour. Comp. Phys. 204, 2 (2005)
7. Joslin, R., Streett, C., Chang, C.: Validation of Three-Dimensional Incompressible Spatial Direct Numerical Simulation Code, NASA Tech. Report, TP-3025, NASA Langley Research Center (1992)
8. Spotz, W., Garey, G.: High-Order Compact Scheme for the Stream-function Vorticity Equations. Int'l J. for Num. Method. in Eng. 38, 20 (1995)
9. Haiwei, S., Kang, N., Zhang, J., Carlson, E.: A Fourth-Order Comapct Difference Scheme on Face Centered Cubic Grids with Multigrid Method for Solving 2D Convection Diffusion Equation. Math. and Comp. in Simul. 63, 6 (2003)

10. Lambiotte, J., Voigt, R.: The Solution of Tridiagonal Linear Systems on CDC Star-100 Computer. ACM Trans. Math. Soft. 10 (1984)
11. Ortega, J., Voigt, R.: Solution of Partial Differential Equations on Vector and Parallel Computers. SIAM Review (1985)
12. Spotz, W.: Accuracy and Performance of Numerical Wall-Boundary Conditions for Steady 2D Incompressible Stream-Function Vorticity. Int'l J. for Num. Meth. in Fluids 28, 4 (1998)
13. Berikelashvili, G., Gupta, M.M., Mirianashvili, M.: Convergence of Fourth Order Compact Difference Schemes for Three-Dimensional Convection Diffusion Equations. SINUM (SIAM Jour. on Num. Anal.) 45, 1 (2007)
14. Spotz, W., Garey, G.: Formulation and Experiments with High-Order Compact Schemes for Nonuniform Grids. Int'l J. for Heat & Fluid Flow 8, 3 (1998)
15. Gustafsson, B.: The Convergence Rate for Difference Approximations to Mixed Initial Boundary Value Problems. Math. Comp. 29, 396 (1975)
16. Gustafsson, B.: The Convergence Rate for Difference Approximations to General Mixed Initial Boundary Value Problems. SIAM J. Numer. Anal. 18, 179 (1981)
17. Abarbanel, S., Chertock, A.: Strict Stability of High-Order Compact Implicit Finite Difference Schemes: The Role of Boundary Conditions for Hyperbolic PDEs. J. of Comp. Phys. 160 (2000)
18. Kreiss, O., Oliger, J.: Methods for the Approximate Solution of Time-Dependent Problems, GARP Report, No. 10 (1973)
19. Zhang, J.: Multigrid Solution of the Convection-Diffusion Equation with High Reynolds Number. In: Proc. Copper Mountain Conf. on Iter. Meth. (1996)
20. Zhang, J.: On Convergence and performance of iterative Methods with Fourth-Order Compact Schemes. Num. Meth. for Partial Diff. Eqns. 14 (1998)
21. Orszak, S., Isreal, M.: Numerical Simulation of Viscous Incompressible Flows. Annual Rev. of Fluid Mech. 6 (1974)
22. Hirsh, R.: Higher Order Accurate Difference Solutions of Fluid Mechanics Problems by a Compact Differencing Technique. J. Comp. Phys. 19, 1 (1975)
23. Rubin, S., Khosla, P.: High-Order Numerical Solutions Using Cubic Splines, NASA CR-2653 (1976)
24. Rubin, S., Khosla, P.: High-Order Numerical Methods Derived from Three-Point Polynomial Interpolation, NASA CR-2735 (1976)
25. Adam, Y.: A Hermitian Finite Difference Method for the Solution of Parabolic Equations. Comp & Math. Appl. 1 (1975)
26. Adam, Y.: Highly Accurate Compact Implicit Mehods and Boundary Conditions. J. Comp. Phys. 24 (1977)
27. Gupta, M., Manohar, R., Stephenson, J.: A Single Cell High Order Scheme for the Convection-Diffusion Equation with Variable Coefficients. Int'l J. Num. Meth. Fluids, vol. 4 (1984)
28. Gupta, M.: High Accuracy Solutions of Incompressible Navier-Stokes Equations. J. Comp. Phys. 93 (1991)
29. Yavneh, I.: Analysis of Fourth-Order Compact Scheme for Convection-Diffusion. J. Comp. Phys. 133 (1997)
30. Weinan, E., Liu, J.: Essentially Compact Schemes for Unsteady Viscous Incompressible Flows. J. Comp. Phys. 126 (1996)
31. Stone, H.: An Efficient Parallel Algorithm for the Solution of a Tridiagonal Linear System of Equations. J. of ACM 20 (1973)
32. Stone, H.: Parallel Tridiagonal Solvers. Assoc. Comp. Mach. Trans. Soft 1 (1975)
33. Hockney, R.: A Fast Direct Solution of Poisson's Equation using Fourier Analysis. J. of ACM 12 (1965)

34. Hockney, R., Jeshoppe, C.R.: Parallel Computers 2: Architecture, Programming, and Algorithm, 2nd edn. Inst. of Physics Pub., Bristol, Philadelphia (1988)
35. Sun, X., Joslin, R.: A Parallel Algorithm for Almost-Toeplitz Tridiagonal Systems. Int'l Jour. of High Speed Comp. 4 (1995)
36. Sun, X., Gustafson, J.: Toward a Better Parallel Performance Metric. Par. Comp. 17 (1991)
37. Laurie, D., Sameh, A.: The Computation and Communication Complexity of a Parallel Banded System Solver. ACM Trans. Math. Soft. 10 (1984)
38. Wang, H.: A Parallel Method for Tridiagonal Equations. ACM Trans. Math. Soft. 7 (1981)

Dynamic Multi-resource Advance Reservation in Grid Environment

Zhi-Ang Wu and Jun-Zhou Luo

School of Computer Science and Engineering, Southeast University,
210096 Nanjing, P.R. China
{zawu,jluo}@seu.edu.cn

Abstract. How to guarantee user's QoS (Quality of Service) demands becomes increasingly important in service-oriented grid environment. Current research on grid resource advance reservation, a well-known and effective mechanism to guarantee QoS, fails to adapt to dynamic variability of grid resource, and imprecise deny of user's reservation request often happens. For this, new system architecture for advance reservation is proposed. SNAP (Service Negotiation and Acquisition Protocol) is extended to support this architectture. Then VRC (virtual resource container) is adopted to alleviate negative effect resulted from resource performance variability, and QDD (QoS deviation distance) based logical resource selection algorithm is addressed to decrease imprecise reject rate of reservation. At last, this new architecture is deployed to campus grid, and two illustrative experiments are conducted in campus grid too. Preliminary results show that it can alleviate negative influence of grid resource dynamic fluctuation and avoid imprecise reject of advance reservation request effectively.

1 Introduction

Services provide higher-level applications for large-scale, open environment. Thus, services can be used to implement and configure software applications in a manner that improves productivity and application quality [1]. With the emergence of OGSA (Open Grid Services Architecture) and WSRF (WS-resource framework), grid begins to be a use case for Web Services [2, 3].

QoS (Quality of Service) encompasses important functional and non-functional service quality attributes, which is the key issue in service-oriented grid. Since delivering end-to-end QoS is a critical and significant challenge, how to guarantee QoS becomes a hot issue in this area. Advance reservation is a well-known and effective mechanism to guarantee QoS. GRAAP(Grid Resource Agreement and Allocation Protocol) work group of GGF(Global Grid Forum) has defined advance reservation as [4]: an advance reservation is a possibly limited or restricted delegation of a particular resource capability over a defined time interval, obtained by the requester from the resource owner through a negotiation process.

K. Li et al. (Eds.): NPC 2007, LNCS 4672, pp. 13–22, 2007.

In this study, we propose enabling system architecture for multi-resource advance reservation, which can adapt to dynamic variability of grid resource. Efficient logical resource selection algorithm is designed and implemented. Preliminary experimental results indicate that dynamic multi-resource advance reservation strategy proposed in this paper can avoid negative influence of grid resource dynamic fluctuation and imprecise reject of advance reservation request effectively.

The contribution of our research is as follows:

1. We overview related work of multi-resource advance reservation in grid environment. Concept and possible states of advance reservation are concluded. Advance reservation states transition is analyzed.
2. New system architecture for multi-resource advance reservation is proposed. VRC (virtual resource container) is proposed firstly and embedded in this architecture too. It aggregates same kind of logical resource and binds reservation request with resource dynamically. Consequently, it can solve negative influence of grid resource dynamic fluctuation effectively, and enhance stability of grid system.
3. QDD (QoS deviation distance) based logical resource selection algorithm is implemented in our architecture. QDD describes distance between user's desired QoS requirements and resource QoS properties, and QDD calculation method is improved newly in this paper. Then, QDD based logical resource selection algorithm is proposed. It avoids imprecise reject of reservation request, which exists widely in previous reservation negotiation strategies.

2 Related Work

The draft document of advance reservation established by GRAAP surveys advance reservation functionality in batch scheduling system [4]. It considers advance reservation from the client's perspective, where the client may be a user or a super-scheduler. Advance reservation is defined as a possibly limited or restricted delegation of a particular resource capability over a defined time interval, obtained by the requester from the resource owner through a negotiation process. Possible states of advance are also proposed in this document.

SNAP (Service Negotiation and Acquisition Protocol) is proposed in [5], which provides lifetime management and an at-most-once creation semantics for remote SLAs (Service Level Agreements). Three different types of SLAs are included in SNAP. They are Task service level agreements (TSLAs), Resource service level agreements (RSLAs) and Binding service level agreements (BSLAs). BSLA associates a TSLA with the RSLA and the resource service capabilities should satisfy the task's requirements. BSLA binds a task with a certain resource statically. This static binding is good for systems without supporting advance reservation, because this binding does not consider resource status at job's runtime. When applying this static binding to support advance reservation, the availability of this bond resource at runtime cannot be guaranteed, for resource may join or quit dynamically and the workload also varies dynamically in grid environment. So, this performance fluctuation of grid resource will increase reject rate of advance reservation in great extent. Aiming at this deficiency, new architecture for advance reservation is proposed in this paper. VRC in this new architecture binds task with resource dynamically. And by using queuing theory, it is proved virtual resource container can improve service ability without degrading quality of service.

A lot of negotiation strategies for advance reservation have been presented in previous research. Backup resource selection is added to reservation to guarantee quality of service [6], which clusters same type resource and selects backup resource according to resource availability. Priority based reservation strategy is proposed in [7]. QoS and contention-aware multi-resource reservation is addressed in [8]. Though these reservation strategies mentioned above are able to solve some problems in grid environment, there are at least two deficiencies. First, user's QoS requirements are rarely considered. And these few existing consideration on QoS is short of good representation and classification of grid QoS. Second, the criterion of denying user's reservation request is coarse granularity. Imprecise deny of request often happens. In fact, not satisfying some provisional QoS requirements should not result in deny of user's request. Our proposed resource selection algorithm considers multi-dimensional QoS parameters and tries to avoid this imprecise deny of request based on detailed research on grid QoS in our early work.

R. Al-Ali, etc. classify the service QoS properties into five QoS domains in [9]. From performance perspective, grid QoS should include accounting QoS, service reliability and service security. And from guarantee mechanism perspective, grid QoS includes service QoS and provisional QoS. Our early research classifies grid QoS parameters newly from performance perspective and hierarchical structure model is proposed [10]. It can represent QoS parameters very well and reflect the intuition of the grid QoS. Grid QoS indeed can also be divided into service QoS and provisional QoS according to guarantee mechanism. Service QoS includes all the QoS parameters which must be guaranteed during reservation process. Its values can not be degraded. But QoS parameters belong to provisional QoS can be degraded within a range during negotiation process. Service QoS and provisional QoS are considered respectively to avoid imprecise deny of user's reservation request.

3 States of Advance Reservation

The possible states of advance reservation are addressed in [4] as table 1 shows. It is seen that the lifecycle of advance reservation starts from Requested and ends in either of following four kinds of state: Declined, Cancelled, Terminated and Completed. An advance reservation that ends in Completed state is a successful reservation and that ends other three state is unsuccessful reservation which may be resulted from scheduler's refuser or user's canceler.

Table 1. States of Advance Reservation

State	Description
Requested or In Negotiation	A user has requested, or is negotiating, a set of resources for a reservation. If the reservation is accepted/agreed, it goes to being booked. Otherwise, it becomes declined.
Declined	The reservation is not successfully allocated for some reason.
Booked	A reservation has been made, and will be honoured by the scheduler. From here, the reservation can become active, or be cancelled by the user or system, or be altered.
Booked, change requested/in renegotiation	A user is trying to alter the resources for the reservation prior to its starting. Goes back to booked state on success or failure.
Cancelled	A user or scheduler cancels the reservation prior to beginning.
Active	The reservation has started, but not ended.
Terminated	A user, or possibly the system, terminates an active reservation before the end-time.
Completed	The reservation continued until its end-point.
Active, change requested/in renegotiation	A user is trying to alter the resources for the reservation after the reservation has become active. Goes back to active state on success or failure.

4   Multi-resource Advance Reservation Architecture

In order to support dynamic advance reservation, enabling system architecture is introduced, which is illustrated in figure 1. Logical resource encapsulates service ability providing to remote tasks. This service ability varies with local workload, however, the capability of resources is fixed. Various logical resources can be divided into different kinds according to their function. VRC is proposed in this paper to aggregates the same kind of logical resource to be a computing pool. When user submits reservation request, advance reservation interface provided by VRC negotiates with user broker. If this negotiation is successful, advance reservation queue is established in VRC. VRC is responsible for maintaining and scheduling advance reservation queue, and renegotiating when negotiation is booked. It also collects available logical resource information and refreshes dynamically.

Figure 1 shows two kinds of logical resource: computing resource and device resource. Two kinds of VRC aggregate these two kinds of logical resource. User broker submits advance reservation request to advance reservation interface, and then advance reservation queue is established. When an advance reservation element in queue arrives at its start time, VRC selects appropriate logical resource by logical resource selection manager. And it binds this reservation with selected logical resource dynamically. Then this advance reservation process is invoked and switches to active state.

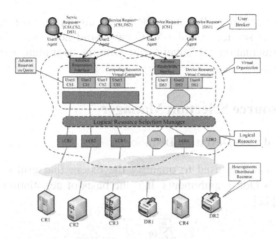

Fig. 1. Architecture for Advance Reservation

In this architecture, the key part is VRC, which aims to solve dynamic fluctuation of grid resource. So, the performance of VRC determines the performance of this advance reservation architecture.

By using of queuing theory, a computing pool including c distributed supercomputers is proved that: while keeping the same average waiting time, the throughput of each supercomputer can be significantly improved by increasing the rate of receiving user's applications [11]. We assumed that the advance request arrival process is a Poisson process and a server has a service time which is an exponentially distributed random variable. A computing pool including c distributed supercomputers is modeled as $M/M/c$ queuing system. The average waiting time of $M/M/c$ is deduced in queuing theory, and Wq_c can be calculated by formula (1).

$$W_{q_c} = \frac{C(c,a)}{\mu_c(c-a)} \tag{1}$$

In formula (1) a is workload ratio and $C(c,a)$ is the probability of all supercomputers are busy when an application arrives. These two parameters are derived from formula (2) and formula (3).

$$a = \frac{\lambda_c}{\mu_c} = \frac{c\lambda_1}{\mu_1} \tag{2}$$

$$(0 \leqq a < c)$$

$$C(c,a) = \frac{\frac{a^c}{c!(1-a/c)}}{\sum_{n=0}^{c-1}\frac{a^n}{n!} + \frac{a^c}{c!(1-a/c)}} \tag{3}$$

A $M/M/c$ queuing system has the following properties: Wq_c is the monotonic increasing function of λ_1, and Wq_c is the monotonic decreasing function of c. So, a balanced condition exists: Wq_c kept unchanged, while λ_1 can be increased with the growth of c. It is said that kept Wq_c unchanged (means non-degraded quality of service), the rate of receiving user's application λ_1 (means service ability) will be increased with the growth of number of supercomputers aggregated by computing pool.

This result can be used to illuminate the VRC can improve service ability without degrading quality of service. So, the VRC can avoid negative influence of grid resource dynamic fluctuation effectively, but without degrading the performance of advance reservation.

5 Logical Resource Selection Manager

5.1 Calculation of QoS Deviation Distance

QoS deviation distance is used to quantify the extent that grid resource satisfy or dissatisfy the user's QoS requirements. It is the basis of negotiation and is calculated by formula (4) in [12].

$$\varepsilon = \sqrt{\sum_{i=1}^{m}(q_i - r_i)^2} \tag{4}$$

Where:
User request vector is : $Q=\{q_1,q_2,.......q_m\}$
Resource property vector is: $R=\{r_1,r_2,.......r_m\}$

This calculation by method reflects the distance between user's QoS requirements and resource QoS properties, but it is not appropriate for all kinds of QoS parameters. To provisional QoS, smaller QoS deviation distance denotes user is satisfied more. But to service QoS, once no resource can meet user's QoS requirement, this user's request should be denied, no matter how small QoS deviation distance is. When applying formula (4) to advance reservation negotiation algorithm, it selects resource with minimum QoS deviation distance. But once one service QoS parameter can not be satisfied, this resource can not satisfy this user's request actually, even QoS deviation distance is so minimum. Then renegotiation should be executed, and the efficiency of negotiation process will be decreased in great extent. So we have to improve on the calculation method of QoS deviation distance.

Grid application is represented as a set of grid service requests and grid resource in one VO can be abstracted to a set of logical resources [10]. Grid application $A=\{S_1,S_2,...,S_m\}$, SNAP establishes TSLA for each grid service, which can be seen as a vector of QoS parameters, $S_i=\{q_1,q_2,...,q_l\}$. Grid resource $R=\{R_1,R_2,...,R_n\}$, RSLA is also established by SNAP, $R_i=\{r_1,r_2,...,r_l\}$. We assume there exists k service QoS parameters and namely l-k provisional QoS parameters. So, TSLA and RSLA can be represented as : $S_i=\{q_1,q_2,...,q_k,q_{k+1},...,q_l\}$, $R_i=\{r_1,r_2,...,r_k,r_{k+1},...,r_l\}$.

QoS parameters are divided into negative criterion and positive criterion [13]. Negative criterion denotes the higher value the lower quality, such as response time. Positive criterion denotes the higher value the higher quality, such as CPU cycle and memory size. We define characteristic value c_j to represent whether user's j-th QoS parameter is satisfied. $c_j=1$ represents it is satisfied perfectly, or $c_j=0$. c_j of negative and positive criterion are calculated by formula (5) and (6) respectively.

$$c_j = \begin{cases} 1 & r_j - q_j \le 0 \\ 0 & r_j - q_j > 0 \end{cases} \tag{5}$$

$$c_j = \begin{cases} 1 & r_j - q_j \geq 0 \\ 0 & r_j - q_j < 0 \end{cases} \tag{6}$$

$$h_i = \prod_{j=1}^{k} c_j \tag{7}$$

h_i denotes whether all service QoS parameters of the i-th grid service request are satisfied perfectly. We calculate h_i by formula (7). If $h_i=1$, it shows that all $c_j=1$, $1 \leq j \leq k$, namely each service QoS parameter can be satisfied. And if $h_i=0$, it shows that at least one service QoS parameter can not be satisfied and this user request will be denied. After all service QoS parameters were satisfied, QoS deviation distance is calculated to determine the distance between resource performance and requirement. So, QoS deviation distance calculation formula is redefined as follows.

$$\varepsilon = \begin{cases} +\infty & h_i = 0 \\ \sqrt{\sum_{j=k+1}^{m} (q_j - r_j)^2} & h_i = 1 \end{cases} \tag{8}$$

5.2 QDD-Based Logical Resource Selection Algorithm

Logical resource selection manager is used to select current appropriate logical resource to complete reservation request in queue. Our selection algorithm is based on QoS deviation distance, which tries to select logical resource with minimal QoS deviation distance.

A successful reservation is abstracted to three tuple: advance reservation request ID, logical resource ID and a time interval in the future. We assume Re_{mn} is reservation matrix, $Re_{mn}[i][j]=t_{ij}$ denotes the completed time t_{ij} that resource R_j is delegated to S_i. So, the main purpose of this selection algorithm is finding a near optimal reservation matrix. The input of this selection algorithm is advance reservation requests queue, named as AR_Queue, and logical resource set, named as LR_Set. The element of AR_Queue should include necessary parameters of advance reservation, and it is defined as a triple $< t_i^{start}, t_i^p, Q_i >$, in which t_i^{start} is the start time of reservation, t_i^p is duration of this reservation and Q_i is QoS parameters of this reservation request. The output is reservation matrix Re_{mn}. The selection algorithm is described as follows.

```
(1) While AR_Queue is not null
(2) Si=AR_Queue.out()
(3)    If tcur==tstart
(4)       For j=1 to j=n
(5)          Determiningεij using formula (8)
(6)          Qdmn[i][j]=εij
(7)       End for
(8)       For each eligible resource in increased order
    according toε
(9)          Assume current resource is LRj
```

$$(10) \qquad If \ \bigcap_{k=1}^{i-1}(t_{kj} < t_i^{start})$$

(11) $\qquad\qquad Re_{mn}[i][j]=t_i^{start}+t_i^{\,p}$
(12) $\qquad\qquad Break$
(13) $\qquad\qquad End \ if$
(14) $\qquad End \ for$
(15) $\quad End \ if$
(16) $End \ While$

The advance reservation requests queue *AR_Queue* is ordered by start time of requests. When the queue head arrives at its start time, it calculates QoS deviation distance matrix Qd_{mn}, which denotes the QoS deviation distance between grid service request S_i and logical resource LR_j. Then available resource for each request is of in increasing order according toε. And available resource is delegated to service request whose ε is small as possible as we can. Reservation matrix $Re_{mn}[i][j]$ records completed time of this reservation request, which is designed only to be convenient to confirm the availability of resource and start time can be gained from advance reservation request triple.

6 Experimental Results

Our experiment is conducted in SEUGrid(Southeast University Grid), which is developed based on Globus Toolkit. SEUGrid is designed for AMS-02(Alpha Magnetic Spectrometer) experiment. The AMS experiment is large-scale international collaborative project, and it is the only large physics experiment on the international space station [14]. Before AMS-02 is launched, SEUGrid is mainly used to process mini-type vast data in the MC (Monte Carlo) production. MC production is a kind of typical parameter sweep application, which is executed with a distinct set of parameters. There are also no inter-task communication or data dependencies in MC production.

Because to execute a MC production job requires large mount of computational and storage resource, resource advance reservation mechanism is needed to guarantee QoS. System architecture for advance reservation proposed in this paper is implemented in SEUGrid. And QoS oriented logical resource selection algorithm is applied to SEUGrid too. We use part of computational resources in SEUGrid to conduct our experiments.

In this experiment reservation requests include HPL (High Performance Linpack) testing jobs and MC production jobs. HPL jobs are much smaller than MC production jobs. According to adjusting HPL problem size, executing time is limited from 10min to 30min. And the executing time of MC production job is often limited from 1 hour to 4 hours. In order to simulate the fluctuation of grid resource, all grid nodes produce local HPL request randomly. We assumed that once CPU execute local HPL testing job, this CPU is seen as unavailable, which cancels accepted remote reservation request in this time interval and will not accepts any other remote reservation request at all. We produce 2400 reservation requests spreading over 24 hours, namely 50 requests per 30 minutes. The success rates of reservation with VRC and without VRC is compared in figure 2 – each point represents the success rate in a 30 minutes interval.

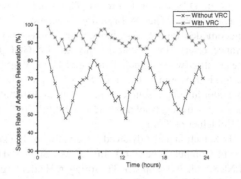

Fig. 2. Comparison of Reservation Success Rate

During one day, the average success rate with VRC reaches 92%, while without using VRC is only 66%. This result shows that VRC constantly achieves higher overall success rate, though resource performance varies dynamically in grid environment. And the range of curve without VRC is 35.3%, but using VRC reaches 12.9%. This result indicates that using VRC results in good stability of grid system.

7 Conclusion and Future Work

In the work described in this paper, main research focuses on alleviating negative influence of grid resource dynamic fluctuation and avoiding imprecise reject of advance reservation request. Two solutions, which are VRC and QDD-based selection, are embedded in advance reservation architecture. Performance evaluation and experimental results all indicate that dynamic multi-resource advance reservation strategy proposed in this paper can solves these two difficulties mentioned above effectively.

Workload balance and more flexible QoS supports for advance reservation will be researched and implemented in near future.

Acknowledgement

This work is supported by National Natural Science Foundation of China under Grants No. 90412014 and 90604004 and Jiangsu Provincial Key Laboratory of Network and Information Security under Grants No. BM2003201.

References

1. Huhns, M.N., Singh, M.P.: Service-oriented Computing: key concepts and principles. Internet Computing 9(1), 75–81 (2005)
2. Foster, I., Kesselman, C., Nick, J.M., Tuecke, S.: The physiology of the grid: An open grid services architecture for distributed systems integration (2002), http://www.gridforum.org/ogsi-wg/drafts/ogsa_draft2.9_2002-06-22.pdf

3. Czajkowski, K., Ferguson, D.F., Foster, I., Frey, J., Graham, S., Seduknin, I., Snelling, D., Tuecke, S., Vambenepe, W.: The WS-resource framework (Version 1.0) (2004), http://www-106.ibm.com/ developerworks/library/ws-resource/ws-wsrf.pdf
4. MacLaren, J.: Advance reservations: State of the Art. In: GGF GRAAP-WG (August 2003), See Web Site at: http://www.fz-juelich.de/zam/RD/coop/ggf/graap/graap-wg.html
5. Czajkowski, K., Foster, I., Kesselman, C., et al.: SNAP: A protocol for negotiating service level agreements and coordinating resource management in distributed systems. In: Feitelson, D.G., Rudolph, L., Schwiegelshohn, U. (eds.) JSSPP 2002. LNCS, vol. 2537, pp. 153–183. Springer, Heidelberg (2002)
6. Li, C., Xiao, N., et al.: Selection and Advanced Reservation of Backup Resources for High Availability Service in Computational Grid. In: Li, M., Sun, X.-H., Deng, Q.-n., Ni, J. (eds.) GCC 2003. LNCS, vol. 3033, pp. 26–33. Springer, Heidelberg (2004)
7. Min, R., Maheswaran, M.: Scheduling Co-Reservations with Priorities in Grid Computing Systems. In: Proceedings of the 2nd IEEE/ACM International Symposium on Cluster Computing and the Grid (CCGRID.02), May 2002, pp. 266–266. ACM Press, New York (2002)
8. Xu, D., Nahrstedt, K., Viswanathan, A., Wichadakul, D.: QoS and Contention-Aware Multi-Resource Reservation. In: High-Performance Distributed Computing, 2000. Proceedings, August 2000, pp. 3–10 (2000)
9. Al-Ali, R., ShaikhAli, A., Rana, O., Walker, D.: Supporting QoS-Based Discovery in Service-Oriented Grids. In: International Parallel and Distributed Processing Symposium (IPDPS'03), Nice, France (2003)
10. Wu, Z., Luo, J., Song, A.: QoS-Based Grid Resource Management. Journal of Software 17(11), 2264–2276 (2006)
11. Liu, P., Shi, Y., Li, S.: Computing Pool—a Simplified and Practical Computational Grid Model. In: GCC 2003. LNCS, Springer, Heidelberg (2003)
12. Zhu, S., Du, Z., Lam, W.K.: Design and Application of Contractual Computing Meta-Service in Grid Environment. Chinese Journal of Computers 28(4), 487–494 (2005)
13. Jin, H., Chen, H., Lu, Z., Ning, X.: QoS Optimizing Model and Solving for Composite Service in CGSP Job Manager. Chinese Journal of Computers 28(4) (April 2005)
14. Luo, J., Song, A., Zhu, Y., et al.: Grid Supporting Platform for AMS Data Processing. In: Pan, Y., Chen, D.-x., Guo, M., Cao, J., Dongarra, J.J. (eds.) ISPA 2005. LNCS, vol. 3758, pp. 276–285. Springer, Heidelberg (2005)

A Novel Adaptive Proxy Certificates Management Scheme in Military Grid Environment*

Ying Liu, Jingbo Xia, and Jing Dai

Telecommunication Engineering Institute, Air Force Engineering University,
Xi'an, shanxi, 710077, P.R. China
yying_liu @126.com

Abstract. Proxy Certificates (PCs) is one of key mechanisms in Grid Security Infrastructure (GSI). Users need PCs to access grid service. But there is no effective mechanism to manage the PCs in GSI. In order to apply GSI in Military Grid, a novel adaptive Proxy Certificates management scheme is brought forward based on the hierarchical one-way hash chains. The hierarchical one-way chain consists of two or more levels of chains, where values of a first-level chain act as roots of a set of second-level chains and each PC is protected by a hash value, so the PCs' available time can be controlled adaptively and safely. The experimental results indicate that the scheme more adapt to the Military Grid environments.

Keywords: Military Grid, GSI, proxy certificate, hash value, hierarchical one-way chains.

1 Introduction

The Military Grid(MG) is a huge and complex undertaking that is intended to integrate virtually all of military information systems, services, and applications into one seamless, reliable, and secure network. MG's overall concept is to enable data access for a variety of systems and users in the network no matter which military service owns a weapon system or where a user might be located around the world. MG is designed to form the basis of a network-centric or "netcentric" way of fighting wars and to create a decisive advantage over adversaries. With such a large number of nodes unproven, MG require enhanced security mechanisms[1].

The Grid Security Infrastructure (GSI) [2] that is the portion of the Globus Toolkit [3] has been developed to support Grid environments, and widely used in Grid deployments worldwide. Our MG security Infrastructure is based on GSI. GSI uses public key cryptography (also known as asymmetric cryptography) as the basis for its functionality. GSI provides a delegation capability by using a proxy certificate that is derived from, and signed by, a normal X.509 Public Key [4] End Entity Certificate or by another proxy certificate for the purpose of providing restricted proxy and delegation within a PKI based authentication system. If a Grid computation

---

* This research is supported by Shaanxi Provincial Natural Science Foundation of China under Grant No. 2004F14.

K. Li et al. (Eds.): NPC 2007, LNCS 4672, pp. 23–30, 2007.

requires that several Grid resources be used (each requiring mutual authentication), or if there is a need to have agents (local or remote) requesting services on behalf of a user, the need to re-enter the user's password can be avoided by creating a proxy. But there is no effective mechanism to manage the proxy certificates if GSI is implemented in MG. So, a new adaptive proxy certificates management scheme is brought forward in this paper. We focus on the problem to manage proxy certificates [5] available time and improve the success rate of Grid tasks.

The rest of this paper is organized as follows: Section 2 brief analyzes MG security platform and the existing proxy certificates mechanism. In Section 3 we present an adaptive proxy certificates management scheme based on the hierarchical one-way chains and describes it in detail. Experimental results and conclusions of the scheme are discussed in Section 4.

2   MG Security Platform Based on GSI

A central concept in GSI authentication is the certificates. Every user and service on the Grid is identified via a certificate, which contains information to identifying and authenticating the user or service. The GSI uses public key cryptography as the basis for its functionality. So the MG security platform is based on digital certificates. Six main components are described in Fig.1: Security Authenticate Sever Security Control Server, Security Management Server, Security Manager, User Register Database and User Access Database. The platform has the speciality of logical centralized management and physical distributed control and can ensure MG resources security. The communications in the security platform between severs and databases or users are transmitted by the encrypted safe channels.

This paper addresses the security problems of proxy certificates in MG. In GSI, a proxy consists of a new certificate and a private key. The key pair that is used for the

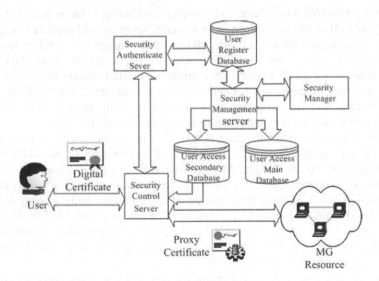

Fig. 1. MG security platform

proxy, i.e. the public key embedded in the certificate and the private key, may either be regenerated for each proxy or obtained by other means. The new certificate called proxy certificate contains the owner's identity, modified slightly to indicate that it is a proxy. The new certificate is signed by the owner, rather than a CA. The proxy certificate also includes a time notation after which the proxy should no longer be accepted by others. Proxy certificate have limited lifetimes.

When proxies are used, the mutual authentication process differs slightly. The remote party receives not only the proxy's certificate (signed by the owner), but also the owner's certificate. During mutual authentication, the owner's public key (obtained from his certificate) is used to validate the signature on the proxy certificate. The CA's public key is then used to validate the signature on the owner's certificate. This establishes a chain of trust from the CA to the proxy through the owner.

Existing proxy certificates scheme can achieve the requirement of dynamic delegation, dynamic entities and repeated authentication. But this approach has two drawbacks. First of all, in order to enable single sign-on, the proxy certificate's private key is stored in a local storage system without being encrypted. If an attacker can get the file by some ways, he may imitate the operation of the user. It may bring some security leaks. Secondly, GSI provides weak control on proxy certificates without a revocation mechanism. Available time of proxy certificates can not be dynamically changed by the owners of certificates or managers of the Grid. If over long available time of a proxy certificate is defined, it might bring some security problems because of the naked personal key of the proxy certificate. If over short available time is defined, it may be disabled while the task have not finished yet. As we know, it is difficult to forecast the completion time of a task correctly in a large-scale and dynamic MG environment.

3 Proxy Certificates Management Scheme

In this section we present a new adaptive proxy certificates framework in which the maximum lifetime of a certificate is divided into short periods and the certificates could expire at the end of any period under the control of the Grid user. Our scheme is based on Hierarchical one-way hash chains we proposed. One-way chains are an important cryptographic primitive in many security applications. As one-way chains are very efficient to verify, they recently became increasingly popular for designing security protocols. And the constructions for one-way hash chains is simple, a low-powered processors can compute a one-way function within milliseconds.

3.1 One-Way Hash Chains

Hash chains are based a public function H that is easy to compute but computationally infeasible to invert, for suitable definitions of "easy" and "infeasible". Such functions are called one-way functions (OWF) and were first employed for use in login procedures by Needham [6]. If the output of a one-way function is of fixed length, it

is called a one-way hash function (OWHF). The definition of OWHF is given in [7]
Definition:

A function H that maps bit strings, either of an arbitrary length or a predetermined length, to strings of a fixed length is an OWHF if it satisfies three additional properties
Given x, it is easy to compute $h(x)$
Given $h(x)$, it is hard to compute x
It is hard to find two values x and y such that $h(x) = h(y)$, but $x \neq y$.
A hash chain of length N is constructed by applying a one-way hash function H ( ) recursively to an initial seed value s.
$$H_N(s) = H (H (H (...H(s)...))) \ (N \text{ times})$$

The last element $H_N(s)$ also called the tip T of the hash chain resembles the public key in public key cryptography i.e., by knowing $H_N(s)$, $H_{N-1}(s)$ can not be generated by those who do not know the value s, however given $H_{N-1}(s)$, its correctness can be verified using $H_N(s)$, This property of hash chains has directly evolved from the property of one-way hash functions.

3.2 Hierarchical One-Way Hash Chains

Here we bring forward hierarchical one-way Chains. A hierarchical one-way chain consists of two or more levels of chains, where values of a first-level chain act as roots of a set of second-level chains. The secondary chain rooted in the ith value of the primary chain as the ith secondary chain. Here, all the values of the ith secondary chain are released before any of the values of the $i + 1^{st}$ chain is released; the primary chain value H_i is released in between. As Fig. 2 shows, to set up the hierarchical chain, the generator picks H_0 at random and computes the primary chain H_1, $H_1...H_n$, then choose $H_0, H_1, ... , H_n$ as the seed to generate n hash chains respectively.

3.3 Proposed Adaptive Proxy Certificates Scheme

We discuss the generation of proxy certificates from two aspects as follows: one condition is that Grid nodes have much better computing and communication capability,

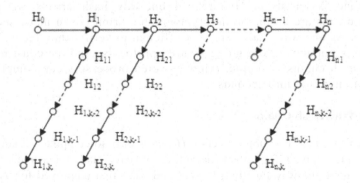

Fig. 2. Hierarchical one-way chains

such as personal computer, workstation and so on. The other is that the nodes have worse computation and communication capability, and can not afford the overhead of proxy certificate generation and management, Such as hand-held devices, wireless devices and so on.

In actual Grid environments, such classification is reasonable and indispensable. About the first condition, all operations of proxy certificates run on local nodes. A proxy certificates with an extensible expiry date could be generated in the following way:

(1) Forecast prospective proxy certificate path of length n, and generate first-level chains $H_0(r)...H_n(r)$, $H_0(r)=r$ is a random value which is known to the user only.

(2) Generate the first proxy certificate.

(a) User U generate a pair of keys:

SK_p – private key

PK_p – public key

(b) Define the proxy certificate parameters:

T – maximum lifetime (the most common available time period of proxy certificates is 12 hours in traditional schemes, but we can revoke the proxy certificate at any time in our schemes, so proxy certificate's maximum lifetime can be long enough according to Grid application)

D – starting valid date

L – time period for refreshing validity of the proxy certificate

Suppose $k = T/L$ is an integer. The refreshing points are denoted as $D_1 = D+L$, $D_2 = D+2*L... D_k = D+k*L$.

(c) Generate the first proxy certificate = $SIGN_U(U, PK_p, D, H_{n,k}(r), k, L)$ of nth chain, then User signs this proxy certificate with his private key.

(d) Generate other proxy certificates of this chain. Like the first proxy certificate, generation process of others need not the user's the signature but the previous proxy's.

(e) Issue of the hash value. At the starting valid date of jth proxy certificate that belong to this chain, U release $H_{j,k-1}(r)$ to initialize the validity of proxy certificate, which then has an expiry date $D = D_j +L$. Suppose the next refreshing point of proxy certificate is D_e. User will release $H_{ji}(r)$, where $i = k - (D_e-D)/L$. The value of T, D and L in each proxy certificate may be same, or different according to requirements. In our scheme, suppose they are same. Then, at each refreshing point, corresponding hash value should be released.

(3) Generate the other proxy certificate chains according to the Grid Tasks. This process like(2). After the entire Grid task have finished, a confirmation is return and all the proxy certificates' available time end automatically.

(4) Verification to proxy certificate. When a resource or another user V wants to verify this proxy certificate, it or he can take the following steps to check its status.

(a) V verifies the user's signature on $(U, PK_p, D, H_{jk}(r), k, L)$. If true, V is sure that proxy certificate's public key is PK_p. The starting valid date is D, the maximum lifetime is $T = k*L$, the refreshing time period is L, and the last hash value for j^{th} proxy certificate in the one-way hash chain is $H_{jk}(r)$.

(b) V checks that $0 \leq i < k$ and $H_{j,k-i}(H_{ji}(r)) = H_{jk}(r)$. If true, V believes that $H_{ji}(r)$ is a valid hash value in the one-way hash chain ended with $H_{jk}(r)$.

(c) V checks that $D \leq D + (k-i)*L$. If true, V concludes that proxy certificate is valid now, and remains valid until $D = D + (k-i)*L$. In such a way, U can control the validity of proxy certificate by releasing the corresponding $H_{ji}(r)$.

In the second condition, proxy certificates servers must be set up in Grids as Fig. 3.

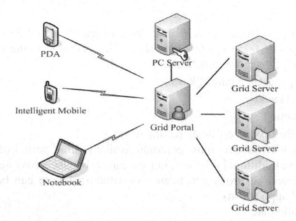

Fig. 3. Proxy certificates servers

The proxy certificates server may accept Grid nodes' request and replace all operations of the proxy certificates, include generation of the proxy certificates and the hash chain and issue of the hash value.

3.4 Protection of Hash Chain Root

For the first condition, the proxy certificate owner U relies on the hash chain root r to control the expiry date of the proxy certificate. There is an advantage on the use of a separate secret r to protect the private key SK_p. The system remains secure. The proxy certificates should also include an identifier of the hash function used to generate and verify the hash chain, as long as either r or SK_p is not compromised. If SK_p is compromised, U could destroy r then proxy certificates will expire shortly at the next refreshing point. Similarly, if r is compromised, U could destroy SK_p and stop using it. It might be at the same risk, however, if r and SK_p are stored in the same computer system. If the system is broken, both r and SK_p will be compromised. Then, a hacker holding r and SK_p can always generate valid signatures by refreshing the validity of the proxy certificate until its maximum lifetime T. Therefore we need to protect them separately or destroy r after memorize it.

For the condition that there are the proxy certificates servers, because all operations of the proxy certificates are completed by the proxy certificates server, the security of the server seems very important. So the servers must be managed by a trusted third party and has some security contracts with its users.

4 Experiments and Conclusions

The experiments were conducted in the MG platform of which each node provides the different types information in five military departments. The hardware configuration and operating systems used in the nodes are given in the Table 1. Grid middleware Globus Toolkit 4.0.3 is installed on each Grid node and the 100M switch and 100M transmission line are used in the network.

Table 1. The Small Grid environment

Name	Number	CPU	Memory	Operating system
LenovoE3 PC	$p_1 \ldots p_{100}$	Intel P4 2.8G Processor	512M	Win XP
IBM X455 Server	I_1, I_2	Intel Itanium 2 Processor 1.5G*4	56G	Win2003 Server
LenovoT630 Server	L_1, L_2, L_3	Intel Xeon Processor 2.0G *2	10G	Win2003 Server

In order to monitor the network flows, network flow monitoring software OnlineEye Pro V1.6.0 are installed on each server and ten personal computers. The information of five different military departments is saved on five servers respectively. A MG task is to inquire about the information simultaneously on one computer as a MG node in the certain department and record the every time. Let the maximum length of proxy certificates be 100, the largest life-cycle be one hour and the updating cycle be one minute. Our experiments select two situations as example: one is visiting I_1, I_2, L_1, L_2, L_3 directly by a random workstation, the other is visiting indirectly $p_2, \ldots p_{100}$ and I_1, I_2, L_1, L_2, L_3 by the agent on p_1.

The studies indicated that in the first situation when visiting the database directly, our improved the system could operate normally and the flows would not obviously changed, the running time only 0.01s; in the second one our system also could operate normally, but the flows increased a little but not evident, the running time 1.93s. Considerating the dynamic join of other nodes and network delay, the burden of computation and communication in our scheme can be ignored.

The paper addresses the security problems of GSI proxy certificates applied in MG. A novel adaptive proxy certificates management scheme is brought forward based on the hierarchical one-way hash chains. Every certificate is protected by a hash value, so the proxy certificate's available time can be controlled adaptively and safely. According to theory analysis and experiments result, it can improve the security of proxy certificates and the success percentage of MG tasks, and don't debase the performance of the system obviously. Our future work is to implement and test our schemes in large scale MG environments.

References

1. Buda, G., Choi, D., Graveman, R.F., Kubic, C.: Security standards for the global information Grid. In: Proceeeding of Military Communications Conference 2001. Communications for Network-Centric Operations: Creating the Information Force, vol. 1, pp. 617–621. IEEE Computer Society, Los Alamitos (2001)

2. Welch, V., Siebenlist, F., Foster, I.: Security for Grid Services. In: Twelfth International Symposium on High Performance Distributed Computing (HPDC-12), IEEE Press, Los Alamitos (2003)
3. Foster, I., Kesselman, C.: Globus: A Metacomputing Infrastructure Toolkit. Int. J. Supercomputer Applications, 115–129 (1997)
4. Kocher, P.: On Certificate Revocation and Validation. In: Hirschfeld, R. (ed.) FC 1998. LNCS, vol. 1465, pp. 172–177. Springer, Heidelberg (1998)
5. Tuecke, S., Welch, V., Engert, D.: Internet.509 Public Key Infrastructure Proxy Certificate Profile. In: IETF RFC 3280 (2004)
6. Wilkes, M.V.: Time-Sharing Computer Systems. Elsevier, New York (1972)
7. Berson, T.A., Gong, L., Lomas, T.M.A.: Secure, Keyed, and Collisionful Hash Functions. Technical Report. SRI-CSL-94-08. SRI International (1994)

A Scheduling Model for Maximizing Availability with Makespan Constraint Based on Residual Lifetime in Heterogeneous Clusters*

Xin Jiang, Chuang Lin, Hao Yin, and Yada Hu

Department of Computer Science and Technology,
Tsinghua University, Beijing, P.R. China
jiangx05@mails.tsinghua.edu.cn,
{clin,hyin,yadandaner}@csnet1.cs.tsinghua.edu.cn

Abstract. A notable requirement of clusters is to maximize its processing performance. Lots of work in this area has been done to optimize the system performance by improving certain metric such as reliability, availability, security and so on. However, most of them assumes that the system is running without interruption and seldom considers the system's intrinsic characteristics, such as failure rate, repair rate and lifetime. In this paper, we study how to achieve high availability based on residual lifetime analysis for the repairable heterogeneous clusters with makespan constraints. First, we provide an availability model based on addressing the cluster's residual lifetime model. Second, we give an objective function about the model and develop a heuristic scheduling algorithm to maximize the availability the makespan constraint. At last, we demonstrate these advantages through the extensive simulated experiments.

Keywords: Scheduling strategy, Availability, Residual lifetime, Cluster, Makespan.

1 Introduction

With the advent of new high-speed networks, it is now possible to link together a collection of distributed, cost-effective and possibly heterogamous resources in the form of a cluster [1]. Heterogeneous cluster is the coordinated use of different types of computers, networks and interfaces to meet the requirements of widely varying application. In fact, most components of such system are different in many aspects such as total running time, processing performance, expected residual lifetime and other physical conditions with respect to circumstances. These differences have a strong impact on the task processing performance for clusters. In order to achieve high performance, some metrics, which can affect system availability, must be considered carefully. Our work is to improve the

* This work is supported by the National Natural Science Foundation of China (No.90412012, 60473086 and 60673184) and the National Grand Fundamental Research 973 Program of China (2006CB708301).

K. Li et al. (Eds.): NPC 2007, LNCS 4672, pp. 31–40, 2007.

availability of clusters without sacrificing conventional system quality of services (QoS) metrics. With QoS constraints, we address a novel scheduling strategy to endeavor to maximize the availability from the system residual lifetime's point of view.

For a job consisting of m tasks $t_1, t_2, ..., t_m$, how to allocate these tasks to each computing node is a critical problem. Some previous researches focus on the conventional measures about system qualities of service, such as the response time, finishing time, load balancing, etc. In an actual computing environment, however, it seems that how to complete the entire job successfully is more important than how to finish the job as quickly as possible. That is, the availability of system to processing tasks maybe a more important performance metric than the system's response time. For example, consider the residual lifetime of each computing node for cluster at time t, see Fig. 1. The time interval $R_i, (i = 1, 2, ..., n)$ is the residual lifetime of corresponding node at time t. For a task assignment scheme with the goal to maximize the system performance, intuitively, it may be better to allocate the task with longer execution time to the node which has longer residual lifetime. That is, under such task assignment, there's a decrease in the number of the worse cases that the node failed before the task processed by the node is finished.

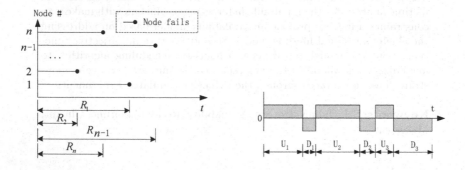

Fig. 1. Residual lifetime distribution of cluster at time t   **Fig. 2.** A typical evolution of a failure-repair progress for a computing node

In this paper, we propose a novel model to describe the availability for repairable heterogeneous cluster based on its expected residual lifetime with the tasks' *makespan* constraints. Then we employ the model to put forward a task scheduling strategy, which can minimize the cluster availability, by allocating the tasks with longer execution time to the nodes with longer expected residual lifetime. At last, we conduct a series of simulated experiments to illustrate our task distribution strategy which is efficient to balance the availability and the *makespan* of heterogeneous clusters.

The rest of this paper is organized as follows. In section 2, we briefly introduce related work. Section 3 extends the availability model based on analyzing the residual lifetime and then gives the objective function for optimization. We provide a scheduling algorithm to maximize the availability and with the *makespan* constraint for the cluster in section 4. Section 5 presents the simulation results of the algorithm and gives the experimental results. Section 6 concludes the whole paper and presents our future work in this field.

2 Related Work

Scheduling Strategies for cluster have been extensively studied in previous work both experimentally and theoretically. Besides widely investigated task allocations that improve system performance by optimizing the conventional performance measures, such as *makespan* or completion time [2], a few established task allocation models attach importance to system reliability, availability, safety and robustness, etc. Shatz et al deal with the task allocation with the goal of maximizing the system reliability [3]. Srinivasan et al describe a method to determine an allocation that introduces safety into a heterogeneous distributed system and at the same time attempts to maximize its reliability. Xie and Qin integrate tasks' availability requirements into stochastic scheduling so as to achieve a good balancing between system availability and throughput measured as average response time [4]. Schmidt [5] reviews results related to deterministic scheduling problems where machines are not continuously available for processing. [6] and [7] refers to a resource allocation's tolerance to uncertainty as the robustness of that resource allocation. It presents a stochastic robustness metric suitable for evaluating the likelihood that a resource allocation will perform acceptably. In [8], Dogan and Ozguner present two different cost functions which can guide a matching and scheduling algorithm to produce task assignments so that failures of the network resources will have less effect on the execution of application. Topcuoglu et al introduce two scheduling algorithms for a bounded number of heterogeneous processors with an objective to simultaneously meet high performance and fast scheduling time [9]. In [10], Hariri and Raghavendra provide two optimization algorithms for allocating the functions of a given distributed task so that the reliability is maximized and the communication delay is minimized.

   In these researches introduced above, more attention is put on the metrics of reliability and availability. For instance, the maximum reliability is achieved by straightly optimizing the system reliability function, $e_{-\lambda t}$, with respect to the accumulative execution time and the intertask communication cost in [3] and [11]. An availability deficiency is defined which represents the discrepancy between the availability of a node and the availability requirements of tasks allocated to the node. By balancing the availability discrepancy and the *makespan*, a stochastic scheduling scheme is developed [4]. Our work is different from these methods above. We try to find a task allocation scheme to optimize the system availability by maximizing the objective function based on nodes' expected residual lifetime as much as possible. Furthermore, the heterogeneous cluster we considered is repairable which has been neglected by most researches above. That is, we believe that the computing node is a failure-repair system, and alternates times and again between the up state and down state. Objectively, such failure-repair system is suitable in most actual cases.

3   Scheduling Strategy Model

3.1   Assumption and System Model

In this paper, cluster is assumed to consist of a set of heterogeneous computing nodes, $N = \{n_1, n_2, ..., n_k, k = 1, 2, ..., n\}$, connected via a high-speed interconnection network. The computing nodes only have local memory and do not share any global memory. We assume every computing node has different failure and repair rate. During an interval, all nodes might have undergone one or more failures inevitably, including either instantaneous failures or permanent failures. We suppose when the instantaneous failure occurs the node can auto-resume by re-configuring the system parameters or rebooting the machine. While the permanent failure occurs, the failed nodes are made operational by repairing or replacing. Therefore, it can be described as a Poisson stochastic process. See section 3.2. We also assume that a task can be interrupted at any time when failure occurs and continued after repair is finished.

Given a job consists of m independent tasks $T = \{t_1, t_2, ..., t_m\}$ arriving at the scheduler of cluster, it is the duty for the scheduler to allocate each task to one of the n computing nodes. Different task assignments have diverse efficiency of task processing for cluster. Successful implementation of a job requires every task of it to be finished reliably by corresponding computing nodes. At the same time, some QoS constraints, for example the *makespan*, must be considered. In our study, we present an objective cost function with the *makespan* constraint for the cluster availability. The main notations and definitions will be used in the rest of paper specified as Table 1.

Clearly, we have the equation $\tau_k = \sum_{i=1}^{m} p_{ik} e_{ik}$, and the job finishing time, *makespan*, is $Max\{\tau_k | k = 1, 2, ..., n\}$. Now, our goal is to find an optimal task

Table 1. Main notations and definitions

t_i	ith task of a job
n_i	ith computing node
X	A $m \times n$ matrix corresponding to a task assignment
p_{ij}	An element of X. It equals 1 if t_i is assigned to n_j; otherwise it equals 0
e_{ij}	Accumulative execution time for task t_i running on processor n_j
τ_k	The total computing time of node k for all tasks allocated to it
λ_i	Failure rate of the ith node
μ_i	Repair rate of the ith node
U_k	The length of the kth operation period
D_k	The length of the kth repair/replacement period
$B(\tau)$	$Prob.$(node is up, residual lifetime $> t$) at time τ
$A(\tau)$	Availability function of cluster

assignment X, under which we can maximize the system availability function $A(\tau)$ and minimize the value of *makespan*.

3.2 Residual Lifetime Modeling

In the reliability engineering [12], the expected residual lifetime is a random variable representing the remaining life of a system at time t. Considering one repairable node k of the heterogeneous cluster, each node has two-states and is assumed to undergo random failures with time elapsing independently. Simultaneously, each failure entails a random duration of repair before the node is put back into service. Also, we assume that the duration of the failing node is independent of the states of other nodes. Due to the random nature of the component failures, the Poisson process is an appropriate model to employ. Let $U_k, k \in N$ represents the length of the kth operation period, and let $D_k, k \in N$ represents the length of the kth repair/replacement time for the node as shown in Fig. 2. We denote $H(t)$ and $Y(t)$ as the probability distribution function of U_k and D_k, respectively, and λ and μ are the failure rate and the repair rate of the node respectively. As is known, $1/\lambda$ is the mean time to failure (MTTF) of the node while $1/\mu$ is the mean time to repair (MTTR) of the node. In our study, we assume that $H(t)$ is exponential distribution, then we have the lifetime distribution function of the node, $H(t) = 1 - e^{-\lambda t}$, and the survival function, $\overline{H}(t) = 1 - H(t) = e^{-\lambda t}$.

Let S_n denote the nth failure time, then $S_n = U_1 + \sum_{k=1}^{n-1}(U_k + D_{k+1})$. Obviously, the S_n sequence generates a delayed renewal process $N(t)$. The U_1 has the distribution function H. All other interarrival times have the same distribution function $H * Y$ with mean $1/\lambda + 1/\mu$, where $*$ represents convolution. Given that the node is up at time t, the residual lifetime $W(t)$ represents as follows:

$$W(t) = S_{N(t)+1} - t. \tag{1}$$

The probability that node is up and residual lifetime is greater than ω, $\omega > 0$, at time t is given as:

$$B(t, t+\omega) = P(node\ is\ up, W(t) > \omega) = \overline{H}(t+\omega) + \int_0^t \overline{H}(t-x+\omega)dm(x). \tag{2}$$

where $m(x) = \sum_{n=1}^{\infty}(H * Y)^{(n)}(x)$, and (n) is the n-fold convolution of $H * Y$ with itself. The proof of equation (2) can be seen in [12].

From the Key Renewal Theorem [13], we can give the equation:

$$B(\omega) = \lim_{t \to \infty} P(node\ is\ up, W(t) > \omega) = \frac{\int_\omega^\infty \overline{H}(x)dx}{1/\lambda + 1/\mu}. \tag{3}$$

with $\overline{H}(x) = e^{-\lambda t}$, we can calculate the probability:

$$B(\omega) = \frac{\mu e^{-\lambda \omega}}{\lambda + \mu}. \tag{4}$$

3.3 Objective Function

We define the model for each node according to equation (4), indexed by "k". Then for the node k, we have the probability that the node is up and its expected residual lifetime at time t is greater than τ_k which is given as follows:

$$B_k(\tau_k) = \frac{\mu_k e^{-\lambda_k \tau_k}}{\lambda_k + \mu_k}. \tag{5}$$

where τ_k is the total computing time of node k for all tasks allocated to it, and λ_k, μ_k are the failure rate and repair rate of node k respectively.

Now we define availability function $A(\tau)$ as the geometric mean of all $B_k(\tau_k)$, so $A(\tau)$ represents the average probability that every nodes' residual lifetime is longer than corresponding τ_k. Then, we have the equation:

$$A(\tau) = \sqrt[n]{\prod_{k=1}^{n} B_k(\tau_k)} = \sqrt[n]{exp(-\sum_{k=1}^{n} \lambda_k \tau_k) \prod_{k=1}^{n} \frac{\mu_k}{\lambda_k + \mu_k}} \tag{6}$$

Clearly, $A(\tau)$ reflects the cluster's availability of performing all tasks based on the node's residual lifetime property. We regard $A(\tau)$ as the objective function. Thus, our goal of scheduling is to find a task assignment $X = \{p_{ij} | 1 \leq i \leq m, 1 \leq j \leq n\}$ to make the value of $A(\tau)$ maximum and simultaneously reduce the *makespan* of cluster as much as possible. Without question, maximizing $A(\tau)$ is equivalent to minimizing the function $RLcost(\tau) = \sum_{k=1}^{n} \lambda_k \tau_k$, since λ_k and τ_k are constant for every node. Now, what we will do is to find a task assignment X, which can maximize the cluster performance as follows:

$Min\ RLcost(\tau) = \sum_{k=1}^{n} \sum_{i=1}^{m} \lambda_k p_{ik} e_{ik};$
$Min\ makespan = max\{\sum_{i=1}^{m} p_{ik} e_{ik} | 1 \leq \lambda \leq n\};$
$s.t. \begin{cases} \sum_{k=1}^{n} p_{ik} = 1, 1 \leq i \leq m \\ p_{ik} = 0\ or\ 1, \quad 1 \leq i \leq m, 1 \leq k \leq n \end{cases}$

It is a multi-object optimization problem (MOP). Finding a optimal solution of the problem is known as a NP-hard problem [14], since the optimizing objects conflict each other when optimizing them. Therefore, we develop a heuristic algorithm to find a trade-off solution which minimizes the function $RLcost(\tau)$ as well as the function *makespan*.

4   Scheduling Algorithm

In order to determine probability vector X, which corresponds to a task scheduling policy, we propose a heuristic algorithm to achieve a trade-off solution. In respect that our preferred goal is to maximize the availability, our heuristic algorithm finds the minimum value of $RLcost(\tau)$ first and then tries to satisfy the need of *makespan* constraint. The full algorithm is depicted in Table. 2.

Table 2. Trade-off algorithm

---

1. $p_{ij} \leftarrow 0$, for all i and j;
2. Arbitrarily order the tasks of a set $T = \{t_1, t_2, ..., t_m\}$;
3. Arbitrarily order the computing nodes of a set; $N = n_1; n_2, ..., n_n$
4. Create a set ST (ST will hold the tasks that have been allocated to nodes);
5. While ($T \neq \phi$) do
6.   Get task t_i from T in turn, move it into ST;
7.   Find node n_j in N, whose value of is the minimization among all of nodes';
8.   if ($\sum_{s=1}^{i-1} p_{s1}e_{s1} = \sum_{s=1}^{i-1} p_{s2}e_{s2} = ... = \sum_{s=1}^{i-1} p_{sn}e_{sn}$) then Goto 10
9.   if (($\sum_{s=1}^{i-1} p_{sj}e_{sj} + e_{ij}) > max(\sum_{s=1}^{i-1} p_{s1}e_{s1}, ..., \sum_{s=1}^{i-1} p_{sn}e_{sn})$) then
      $j \leftarrow \{k | (\sum_{s=1}^{i-1} p_{sk}e_{sk} + e_{ik}) = min(\sum_{s=1}^{i-1} p_{s1}e_{s1} + e_{i1}, ..., \sum_{s=1}^{i-1} p_{sn}e_{sn} + e_{in})\}$;
10. $p_{ij} \leftarrow 1$;
11. End While;
12. Output X.

The algorithm has m rounds calculation. In each round, Pareto efficient solution is chosen and reserved for the next turn calculation, so the algorithm converges at the overall optimal solution [15].

At first, for every task t_i, step 7 endeavors to minimize the value of corresponding $RLcost(\tau)$ through finding the node n_j which has the minimum value of $\lambda_j e_{ij}$. In succession, step 8 and 9 decide if the choice of n_j can make all allocated tasks' execution time (*makespan*) minimum. If it does, we believe that n_j is the best choice for task t_i. Otherwise, we have to find a node n_j', which corresponds to the minimum *makespan* if allocate t_i to it. What must be noticed is that *makespan* here is the executing time for all the tasks that has been allocated. Note that step 8 ensures getting the maximum availability when all nodes *makespan* are equal. After doing that, node n_j' will be selected, and then task t_i will be ultimately allocated to it. It's worth noting that n_j' and n_j may be one and the same at some occasions.

Time complexity of this algorithm is $O(m^3 n)$. However, it can be improved by sacrificing some space complexity. If we conserve the value of $\sum_{s=1}^{i-1} p_{sk}e_{sk}$ in memory for the next round computing at ith round, i.e. if we can use the ith round computing result to calculate the value of $(i+1)$th round, time complexity of the algorithm will be reduced to $O(m^2 n)$.

5 Experiment and Discussion

In this section, we will use some experiential data to compute the values of $A(\tau)$ and *makespan* by a simple example. In this example, the repairable heterogeneous cluster has three computing nodes and their failure rates and repair rates are shown as Table 3. The matrix of execution times is given in Fig. 3, whose entity e_{ij} represents the execution time of t_i on node n_j. We must point out that all the data we use in our simulation are not actual figures but approximate values chosen empirically. It does not affect the simulation results, because the

$$E = \begin{bmatrix} 0.3000 & 0.1000 & 0.5000 \\ 0.7000 & 1.2000 & 0.6000 \\ 0.2000 & 0.2000 & 0.5000 \\ 0.3000 & 0.6000 & 0.8000 \\ 0.9000 & 1.0000 & 1.3000 \\ 1.2000 & 0.9000 & 1.7000 \end{bmatrix}$$

Fig. 3. Matrix of execution time for all tasks

algorithm is independent of the input figures. Our aim is only to evaluate the algorithm's performance for the proposed model.

The trade-off algorithm introduced above is running with the parameters and we achieve a task assignment X_1, as shown in Fig. 4(a). We calculate the *makespan* and $A(\tau)$ using the model introduced in section 3 under the assignment X_1. In order to identify the validity of the algorithm, we also figure out the extremes of *makespan* and $A(\tau)$ respectively. The former, X_2 (Fig. 4(b)), is achieved by maximizing the availability without considering *makespan*. And the latter, X_3 (Fig. 4(c)) is achieved by exhaustively enumerating all task assignment to find the minimum *makespan* without considering $A(\tau)$. See Table 4.

$$X_1 = \begin{bmatrix} 0 & 1 & 0 \\ 0 & 0 & 1 \\ 1 & 0 & 0 \\ 1 & 0 & 0 \\ 0 & 1 & 0 \\ 1 & 0 & 0 \end{bmatrix} \qquad X_2 = \begin{bmatrix} 0 & 1 & 0 \\ 1 & 0 & 0 \\ 1 & 0 & 0 \\ 1 & 0 & 0 \\ 0 & 1 & 0 \\ 0 & 1 & 0 \end{bmatrix} \qquad X_3 = \begin{bmatrix} 0 & 1 & 0 \\ 0 & 0 & 1 \\ 0 & 0 & 1 \\ 1 & 0 & 0 \\ 1 & 0 & 0 \\ 0 & 1 & 0 \end{bmatrix}$$

$\qquad\qquad$ (a) $\qquad\qquad\qquad\qquad$ (b) $\qquad\qquad\qquad\qquad$ (c)

Fig. 4. Tasks assignment with different preferences . (a) The trade-off solution (b) Maximizing the availability without considering *makespan* (c) Minimizing the *makespan* without considering availability.

Compared with X_2, the assignment X_1 reduces the availability of cluster 0.058% and improves the *makespan* about 15%. Contrarily, X_1 raises the availability 0.012% and degrades the *makespan* about 42% than X_3. We take note of that the variation range of availability is very small and reverse happens to *makespan*. The reason is that the failure rate of cluster we choosed is very small, i.e. the cluster is reliable enough and it is difficult to improve its availability, just as cluster shows in most practical situations. On the contrary, *makespan* is interrelated with the number of tasks and their execution time, which result in

Table 3. Failure rate and repair rate for all computing nodes

	n_1	n_2	n_3
λ	0.0050	0.0030	0.0070
μ	1.1900	1.2410	1.1100

Table 4. Simulation results

	$RLcost(\tau)$	$makespan$	$A(\tau)$
X_1	0.0160	1.7000	0.8665
X_2	0.0120	2.0000	0.8670
X_3	0.0167	1.2000	0.8664

the distinct fluctuation of the execution time for cluster under different task assignment.

Furthermore, we address the effect on the tradeoff algorithm by varying the numbers of nodes and tasks, and compare it with the algorithm which only maximizes availability without considering $makespan$. We suppose that the value of availability and $makespan$ computed by using the tradeoff algorithm are A_1 and m_1 respectively, and corresponding values are A_2 and m_2, which computed by using the algorithm without taking into account the $makespan$, respectively. We denotes A_1/A_2 as the ΔA and $(m_2 - m_1)/m_2$ as Δm. Thus, we can acquire the variety of ΔA and Δm, as Fig. 5 and Fig. 6 shows.

Fig. 5 illustrates the variation of ΔA and Δm with the tasks number increasing from 1 to 1000, while there are 3 computing nodes. Fig. 6 illustrates the variation of ΔA and Δm with the nodes number increasing from 1 to 50, while there are 1000 tasks.

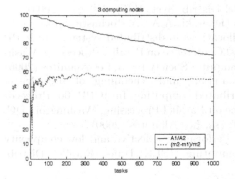 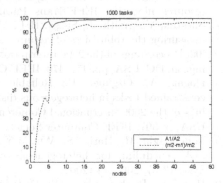

Fig. 5. 3 nodes, ΔA and ΔM vary with the number of tasks increasing

Fig. 6. 1000 tasks, ΔA and ΔM vary with the number of nodes increasing

6   Conclusion and Future Work

The residual lifetime is a very important factor for cluster availability. In this paper, we have presented task allocation to maximize availability with the $makespan$ constraint. We have analyzed the residual lifetime of the computing node and addressed the stochastic model for cluster availability. In order to incorporate availability and $makespan$ into task scheduling, we have proposed a trade-off scheduling algorithm. Our algorithm can improve the performance in availability as much as possible with the *makespan* constraint. At last we have given some experimental results and simple analysis about that.

In the future, we will improve our availability model through considering the effects of tasks inter-communication channel's lifetime model which have not been involved in this paper. By applying the model and algorithm to the real cluster systems, we can evaluate its performance and improve it. We will also make use of existing algorithms, such as genetic algorithm and evolutionary algorithm, to find the solution of our model. Based on those, a more efficient algorithm would be proposed, since the algorithm represent here is not efficient enough for large scale clusters.

References

1. Alhamdan, A.A.: Scheduling Methods for Efficient Utilization of Clusters Computing Environments. PhD thesis, University of Connecticut (2003)
2. Chu, W., Holloway, L., Lan, M.T., Efe, K.: Task allocation in distributed data processing. IEEE Mag. Computer 13, 57–69 (1980)
3. Shatz, S.M., Wang, J.P., Goto, M.: Task allocation for maximizing reliability of distributed computer systems. IEEE Trans. Comput. 41(9), 1156–1168 (1992)
4. Xie, T., Qin, X.: Stochastic scheduling with availability constraints in heterogeneous clusters. IEEE Proc. Cluster Computing 9, 1–10 (September 2006)
5. Schmidt, G.: Scheduling with limited machine availability. International Computer Science Institute Technical Report (TR-98-036) (1998)
6. Ali, S., Maciejewski, A.A., Siegel, H.J., Kim, J.K.: Measuring the robustness of a resource allocation. IEEE Trans. Parallel Distrib. Syst. 15(7), 630–641 (2004)
7. Shestak, V., Smith, J., Siegel, H.J., Maciejewski, A.A.: A stochastic approach to measuring the robustness of resource allocations in distributed systems. In: ICPP '06: Proceedings of the 2006 International Conference on Parallel Processing, Washington, DC, USA, pp. 459–470. IEEE Computer Society Press, Los Alamitos (2006)
8. Dogan, A., Özgüner, F.: Reliable matching and scheduling of precedence-constrained tasks in heterogeneous distributed computing. In: ICPP '00: Proceedings of the 2000 International Conference on Parallel Processing, Washington, DC, USA, p. 307. IEEE Computer Society Press, Los Alamitos (2000)
9. Topcuouglu, H., Hariri, S., Wu, M.Y.: Performance-effective and low-complexity task scheduling for heterogeneous computing. IEEE Trans. Parallel Distrib. Syst. 13(3), 260–274 (2002)
10. Hariri, S., Raghavendra, C.S.: Distributed functions allocation for reliability and delay optimization. In: ACM '86: Proceedings of 1986 ACM Fall joint computer conference, Los Alamitos, CA, USA, pp. 344–352. IEEE Computer Society Press, Los Alamitos (1986)
11. Srinivasan, S., Jha, N.K.: Safety and reliability driven task allocation in distributed systems. IEEE Trans. Parallel Distrib. Syst. 10(3), 238–251 (1999)
12. Aven, T., Jensen, U.: Stochastic Models in Reliability. Stochastic Modelling and Applied Probability. Springer, Heidelberg (1999)
13. Kallenberg, O.: Foundations of Modern Probability. Springer, Heidelberg (2001)
14. Papadimitriou, C.H.: Comuputational Complexity. Addison-Wesley, Reading (1993)
15. Goldberg, D.E.: Genetic Algorithms in Search, Optimization, and Machine Learning. Addison-Wesley, Reading (1989)

A VO-Based Two-Stage Replica Replacement Algorithm

Tian Tian and Junzhou Luo

School of Computer Science and Engineering, Southeast University,
210096 Nanjing, P.R. China
{tian_tian,jluo}@seu.edu.cn

Abstract. Due to high latency of the Internet, it becomes a challenge to access large and widely distributed data quickly and efficiently on data grids. Replication is a process to address this issue, by storing data in different locations to reduce access latency and improve data locality. However, because of the limited storage capacity, a good replica replacement algorithm is needed to improve the efficiency of the access to the replicas. In this paper, a VO-based two-stage replica replacement algorithm is proposed, which provides a good solution to deal with the relations between value and cost. In a VO, replica value is determined according to popularity to make sure which replica will be replaced, and the bandwidth is predicted to make replacement cost as low as possible. Experiments show that compared with traditional replacement algorithms our new replica replacement algorithm shows better performance and efficiency of the data access on Data Grids.

Keywords: Data Grid, Replica Replacement.

1 Introduction

Data Grid [1] is a new kind of data management infrastructure to manage large amounts of data produced by some large-scale data-intensive science research. It enables geographically distributed data to be accessed and analyzed by different communities of researchers which are always geographically distributed. The main challenge Data Grid faced with is how to well support efficient data access and sharing, which is hindered mostly by the high latency of Wide Area Networks. Therefore, large amounts of data need to be replicated at several distributed sites, to make data access as quick as possible.

As the study on Data Grid becoming more popular, techniques of replica management become increasingly well into research [2, 3]. Replica management service discovers the available replicas and selects the best replica that based on some selection criteria. However, because of the limited storage capacity, an efficient replica replacement algorithm is needed to replace low value replicas with high value replicas.

The more popular replica replacement algorithm now is based on an economic model. In the algorithm, a grid is recognized as a market, and the eventual purpose of the algorithm is to maximize the profits gained by the storage sites and to minimize the cost paid by the computing sites. However, this kind of model just considers the

K. Li et al. (Eds.): NPC 2007, LNCS 4672, pp. 41–50, 2007.

value factor well during the replacement. In real circumstances, cost factors such as network latency and bandwidth consumption should be taken into account.

Such kind of research work has also been done in Southeast University. A prediction-based and cost-based replica replacement algorithm was proposed in [7], which combined prediction factor and cost factor together. The product of the prediction factor and the cost factor is considered to be a new replacement factor. The main disadvantage of this algorithm is that a replica with high predicted value may be replaced because of its too much cost. Therefore, how to find a point at the best combination of value and cost is the key in replica replacement algorithms.

Moreover, all prediction methods for replica value are based on some particular file access patterns [4] and the content similarity between files. The access pattern itself is a variation. A method adaptive to one access pattern may not perform well if access pattern changes. In addition, the content similarity between files is still an open problem, which has great difficulties in implementation. Therefore, the prediction methods do not have good performance in real grid systems even if they perform well in simulation.

A VO-based two-stage replica replacement algorithm is proposed in this paper. In the first stage, replica value is calculated according to popularity, and higher value replicas are confirmed to replace low value replicas. In the second stage, replacement cost can be made as low as possible through the prediction of network bandwidth periodically.

The rest of the paper is structured as follows. In section 2, related work is discussed briefly in the research field of replica replacement. In section 3, a detailed description is made about our new replica replacement algorithm. Section 4 is the experiments and results of the algorithm. Section 5 gives a conclusion and discusses shortly about future work.

2 Related Work

A definition of replica replacement algorithm was made at the first time in [5].

In [6], a marketplace interaction model was used to optimize access and replication of data on a Data Grid. Optimization is obtained via interaction of the actors in the model, whose goals are maximizing the profits and minimizing the costs of data resource management. The model consists of four kinds of actors: Computing Element, Access Mediator, Storage Broker and Storage Element.

A cost-driven replication algorithm was proposed in [8], which can dynamically replicate data on the Grid. Replica decisions were driven by the estimation of the data access gains and the replica's creation and maintenance costs that based on some factors such as replica size and bandwidth. However, its bandwidth factor doesn't change dynamically.

In order to make the replica replacement cost as low as possible, a proper choice of prediction is crucial. Currently, a number of prediction approaches have been used in many fields. In [9], the authors constructed two component models, network and disk access, and then combine these performance models for a prediction of I/O performance. However, this approach may not be practical, because in a shared environment the performance may be dynamic.

Another approach for predicting is to use observations on the whole system. The Network Weather Service [10] provides the TCP/IP throughput forecasts based on observations from past end-to-end network performance. This approach of forecasting end-to-end behavior from historic performance of the entire system has been applied to predict file transfer time in some applications.

There are also some Grid simulators for study dynamic data replication algorithms. OptorSim [4] is such a simulator, which uses a prediction function to make decisions of replica replacement. The disadvantage is that in OptorSim bandwidth and replica size are fixed. As a result the cost factor is not taken into account carefully.

3 The VO-Based Two-Stage Replica Replacement Algorithm

3.1 Scenarios

A local storage site may receive several file requests from computing sites. A request may request only one file or more. All the files requested form a requested file list $(F_1,...,F_n)$. Excluding those files which have already been stored in the storage site, the rest should be transferred from other storage sites to local storage site in the form of replicas, and these files also form a file list $(f_1,...,f_m)$. Replica replacement will be triggered if there is not enough space left for all the new files. As a result, a selection should start in the file list $(f_1,..., f_m)$.

3.2 The First Stage: Value Determinations

First, we need to give a definition of replica value in this algorithm. As we know, request patterns for the files can exhibit various locality properties [5], including:

Temporal Locality: Recently accessed files are likely to be accessed again.

Geographical locality (Client locality): Files recently accessed by a client are likely to be accessed by nearby clients.

Spatial Locality (File Locality): Files near a recently accessed file are likely to be accessed.

The definition of Spatial Locality was used in [11] to put forward a prediction method of replica value. In that paper, replica value is defined as the number of times that a replica will be requested in a fixed future time window. The method has two assumptions, one is sequential correlation between file requests, which means that, if a file f0 was accessed last time, files have bigger content similarity to f0 (what "near" means exactly in the definition of Spatial Locality) will be accessed more likely next time. The content similarity is reflected by the difference of file identifiers. Assuming that there are two files f_1 and f_2 with identifiers ID_1 and ID_2 respectively, the smaller the difference $|ID_1-ID_2|$, the bigger the content similarity between file f_1 and f_2 is.

However, in the real implementation of a Data Grid, the file identifier is no more than a sign that makes a file be unique in the grid. The identifiers can not reflect the content similarity well, because they are generated randomly. For example, in European DataGrid, the UUID is a long string composed of numbers and letters, which can be obtained by some particular algorithm [15].

As mentioned above in section 1, prediction methods for replica value are based on some particular file access pattern, which itself is a variation. A method adaptive to one access pattern may not perform well if access pattern changes. And it is very hard to confirm access patterns before the replacement starts. Therefore, the prediction method of replica value based on content similarity does not have good performance in real circumstances.

In this paper, replica value is defined as something like popularity in different virtual organizations (VO). A virtual organization is a set of individuals and/or institutions defined by some sharing rules [16]. It could be, for example, consultants engaged by a car manufacturer to perform scenario evaluation during planning for a new factory, or members of an industrial consortium bidding on a new aircraft and members of a large and international high-energy physics collaboration.

From the definition we can know that members in a VO are more likely to be interested in the same content or similar content. As a result, the jobs they submit may request files that have similar content more probably. Then a definition of replica popularity is given. Replica popularity reflects how popular a file is in a VO. In a grid system, it can be expressed by the total times of requests in a fixed time period. The initial value of popularity of a file and all its replicas is zero. And the popularity will increase by one unit every time a file or its replica is requested. Meanwhile, the popularity of all files is reduced periodically, in order to prevent some disturbance from replicas that is just very popular in the past. In addition, replicas can't be replaced if their ages are smaller than a pre-configured value of age, since some relative new replicas which can show high value in future may be replaced because of their current low value. The age of a replica is the time a replica has been stored in a storage site.

Replica value in this paper can be measured by replica popularity. The bigger the replica popularity, the higher the replica value is. In a VO where members have similar interests, files with bigger replica popularity may also be requested more times in the future. So files of bigger popularity should be kept, and files of smaller popularity should be replaced when the storage capacity is out of limit.

In fact, the formation of VOs reflects Geographical locality (Client locality) well. Files recently accessed by a client in a VO are likely to be accessed by another client in the same VO. Although clients may be physically distributed, they logically form a VO with similar interests. In addition, the popularity also reflects the Temporal Locality. Recently accessed files are likely to be accessed again in the future.

According to the results in our former research, a rule was made by us that the value factor is more important than the cost factor. Storing a replica with high value will be helpful to improve the speed of data access. However, a replica with low value does no good to the rise of data access speed, even if it has a low replacement cost. That's because it won't be requested much times in the future.

3.3 The Second Stage: Prediction of Bandwidth

At the beginning, we also give a definition of replacement cost factor, which is the quotient of replica size and bandwidth. Cost factor is an important factor during the whole process of replica replacement. Replicas with a variety of sizes have different replacement cost, even replicas of the same size may have difference in replacement cost due to different bandwidths. Our purpose is to decrease the cost factor, so the jobs will spend shorter time in waiting for replicas they need. Consequently, the grid computing will have a better performance, especially for some real-time applications. In a word, the lower the cost factor is, the better is the performance of replacement algorithm.

In the first stage, replicas which will go to the second stage have been conformed, so the size factor is fixed. Therefore, the bandwidth should be considered carefully. Algorithms employed previously do not pay much attention to dynamic bandwidth changes. Instead, bandwidths between sites are all configured as constants, which do not conform to real circumstances. There are also some algorithms predicting the bandwidth. For example, mean-based techniques, the general formula of which is the sum of previous values over the number of measurements. Another method is based on evaluating the median of a set of values. These two prediction methods are all based on historical data. However, they do not have good accuracy.

In order to improve accuracy, a new prediction method is proposed here, which is also based on historical data. By prediction, a network link with the biggest predicted bandwidth will be chosen to transfer the replica. Of course, the source site should have the replica requested.

As we know, the bandwidth of every network link changes dynamically in a range, which has a max value and a min value. As a result, the bandwidth of a link could be recognized as a random variable.

For every network link, the total traffic every time interval D is measured. Then the bandwidth of the link during the interval D can be figured out. After measuring for N times, we have a time series of bandwidth $f(1),...,f(N)$. To improve the prediction precision, we calculate the average bandwidth $f_m(1),...f_m(n)$ by

$$f_m(i) = \sum_{(i-1)m}^{im} f(j) \bigg/ m \qquad (1)$$

Then we predict the future network bandwidth based on this averaged time series of bandwidth. The method applied in the prediction is the minimum mean square error (MMSE) method. Assuming that the real bandwidth in the future time interval mD is $F_m(n+1)$ and the predicted bandwidth is $f_m(n+1)$, so $f_m(n+1)$ could be expressed as

$$f_m(n+1)=a_1f_m(1)+a_2f_m(2)+...+a_nf_m(n)+b \qquad (2)$$

By the way, $a_1,...a_n$ and b are the coefficients to minimize the mean square error of the prediction, which could be expressed as $E[\{F_m(n+1)-f_m(n+1)\}^2]$. Detailed solutions to this function could be referenced by [12]. Thus, we get the predicted bandwidth of every network link in a future time window mD.

In our former research, we just chose the best one——the one with the largest bandwidth to transfer the needed replica at the beginning of the transfer. However, some problems happened in real circumstances. The network link we chose could become slower than others, which would cause the whole replacement to be delayed greatly. To the contrary, some network link that is slow previously may become faster than others. In order to address these problems, a little change was made to our algorithm. We divided the whole replica into several equal parts. At the beginning, a best network link is chosen to transfer one part of the replica.When the transfer of one part is finished, the algorithm chooses a new best link to transfer another part also based on the prediction results. The algorithm does not go to an end until all the parts of all needed replicas have been transferred to local storage site.

4 Evaluation

4.1 Experimental Setup

SEU-SOC [13] is a grid system built for the AMS (Alpha Magnetic Spectrometer) project. The AMS project [14] is an experiment with the goal of searching for antimatter and dark matter in space, which will be carried out in the year of 2008. Currently, large amounts of simulation data have been produced for storage and analysis. The computing part of the SEU-SOC consists of three virtual organizations. One is for Monte Carlo simulation, one is for data processing and the left one is for data analysis.

Our evaluation testbed is deployed on the VO for data analysis. Some machines have been chosen to do this evaluation and the topology of these machines is show in Figure 1. The jobs for data analysis are submitted to CEs (computing element), and a CE can get all files needed from the SEs (storage element). In order to make the evaluation easier, we make a rule that every CE has the same priority and processing ability as well as a storage space of 1GB. Every SE has a storage space of 2GB. A job may need only one file or more and the file size ranges from 1M to 1000M. Moreover, all machines have been installed Globus toolkit 4.0 including GridFTP server configured for data transfer.

4.2 Results and Discussion

Some traditional replica replacement algorithms are introduced first for a comparison. For example, least frequently used algorithm (LFU), least recently used algorithm (LRU) and random replacement algorithm.

Table 1. Some parameters in the experiment

CE numbers	3
SE numbers	8
Max Bandwidth	100Mb/sec
Workloads	10 jobs、50 jobs、100 jobs

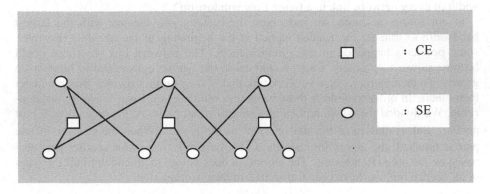

Fig. 1. Topology of the experiment

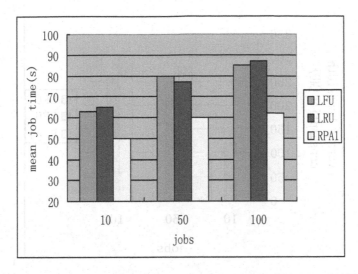

Fig. 2. Mean job time of RPA1, LRU and LFU for 10 jobs, 50 jobs and 100 jobs

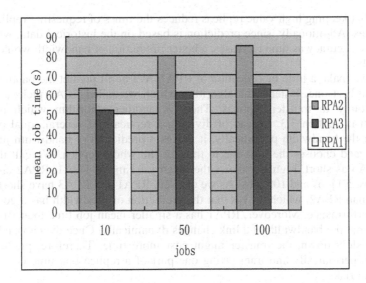

Fig. 3. Mean job time of RPA1, RPA2 and RPA3 for 10 jobs, 50 jobs and 100 jobs

The purpose of the research of replica replacement algorithm is to improve the grid performance, which can be best evaluated by the parameter of mean job time. As Table 1 shows, we submitted 10 jobs, 50 jobs, 100 jobs separately in order to have a look at the performance of our new replica replacement algorithm (RPA1) under different levels of workloads. We also made a comparison of mean job time among RPA1, LFU and LRU. The results depicted by Figure 2 indicate that RPA1 algorithm has a smaller mean job time and shows better performance as workload increases. It is

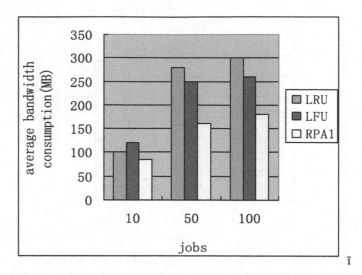

Fig. 4. Average bandwidth consumption for 10 jobs, 50 jobs and 100 jobs

because that keeping high value replicas reduces the times of requesting replicas from distant sites. Additionally, since prediction is based on the historical data, which will show more accuracy as time increases, a better prediction of bandwidth would happen more likely.

Next, we make a little modification of RPA1. We don't predict the bandwidth and choose the best one. Instead, the algorithm which we called RPA2 picks a network link randomly to transfer replicas. There is another algorithm which has been introduced in section 3.3. Instead of dividing a replica into several equal parts and predicting the bandwidth periodically, it makes a prediction of bandwidth just at the beginning and chooses the best one to transfer the whole replica. We call this algorithm RPA3 as short. Figure 3 shows the mean job time of RPA1, RPA2 and RPA3 for 10 jobs, 50 jobs and 100 jobs. As we can see, RPA1 and RPA3 have shorter mean job time than RPA2, which proves that the prediction of bandwidth has a good effect on grid performance. Moreover, RPA1 has a smaller mean job time than RPA3. The reason is that the bandwidth of a link changes dynamically. Once the chosen best link begins to slow down, the transfer might cost more time. Therefore, predicting the bandwidth periodically and transferring one part of a replica one time could reduce this kind of risk.

The results shown in Figure 4 indicate that RPA1 decreases the bandwidth consumption. It is mainly because the increase in replica value reduces the times of replica replacement. Of course, the prediction of bandwidth also contributes to it.

In all, our promising results demonstrate that our new algorithm improves the grid performance.

5   Conclusion

A VO-based two-stage replica replacement algorithm is proposed in this paper. We find it is very hard to make a prediction of replica value in real grid systems, for the file access pattern can't be easily determined. Therefore, replica value is calculated according to popularity in the first stage, and high value replicas are fixed to replace low value replicas. In the second stage, replacement cost can be made as low as possible through the prediction of network bandwidth periodically. The experiment results demonstrate that our new algorithm contributes to better grid performance.

In future work, we plan to use multiple replicas to improve the speed of data transfer during the replacement process, and design a new mechanism to meet QoS requirements in parallel transfer if needed.ïï

Acknowledgement

This work is supported by National Natural Science Foundation of China under Grants No. 90412014 and 90604004 and Jiangsu Provincial Key Laboratory of Network and Information Security under Grants No. BM2003201.

References

1. Chervenak, A., Foster, I., Kesselman, C., Salisbury, C., Tuecke, S.: The Data Grid: Towards an Architecture for the Distributed Management and Analysis of Large Scientific Datasets. Journal of Network and Computer Applications 23, 187–200 (2001)
2. Guy, L., Kunszt, P., Laure, E., Stockinger, H., Stockinger, K.: Replica Management in Data Grids., Technical report, GGF5 Working Draft (July 1, 2002)
3. Cameron, D., Casey, J., Guy, L., Kunszt, P., Lemaitre, S., McCance, G., Stockinger, H., Stockinger, K.: Replica Management in the European DataGrid Project. Journal of Grid Computing 2, 341–351 (2005)
4. Bell, W.H., Cameron, D.G., Capozza, L., Millar, A.P., Stockinger, K., Zini, F.: OptorSim - A Grid Simulator for Studying Dynamic Data Replication Strategies. International Journal of High Performance Computing Applications 17(4), 403–416 (2003)
5. Ranganathan, K., Foster, I.: Identifying Dynamic Replication Strategies for a High Performance Data Grid. In: Lee, C.A. (ed.) GRID 2001. LNCS, vol. 2242, Springer, Heidelberg (2001)
6. Carman, M., Zini, F., Serafini, L., Stockinger, K.: Towards an Economy-Based Optimization of File Access and Replication on a Data Grid. In: Proceedings of the 2nd IEEE/ACM International Symposium on Cluster Computing and the Grid (CCGRID.02), May 2002, ACM Press, New York (2002)
7. Teng, M., Junzhou, L.: A Prediction-based and Cost-based Replica Replacement Algorithm Research and Simulation. In: Proceedings of the 19th International Conference on Advanced Information Networking and Applications, vol. 1, pp. 935–940 (2005)
8. Lamehamedi, H., Zujun Shentu Szymanski, B., Deelman, E.: Simulation of Dynamic Data Replication Strategies in Data Grids. In: Parallel and Distributed Processing Symposium, 2003. Proceedings. International, p. 100.2 (2003)
9. Shen, X., Choudhary, A.: A Multi-Storage Resource Architecture and I/O, Performance Prediction for Scientific Computing. In: Proceedings of 9th IEEE Symposium on HPDC, IEEE Computer Society Press, Los Alamitos (2000)
10. Wolski, R., Spring, N.T., Hayes, J.: The Network Weather Service: A Distributed Resource Performance Forecasting Service for Metacomputing. The Journal of Future Generaton Computer Systems, 757–768 (1999)

11. Capozza, L., Stockinger, K., Zini, F.: Preliminary evaluation of revenue prediction functions for economically effective file replication. In: DataGrid-02-TED-020724 (July 24, 2002)
12. Ludeman, L.C.: Random Processes: Filtering, Estimation, and Detection, p. 608. John Wiley&Sons, New Jersey (2003)
13. Junzhou, L., Aibo, S., Ye, Z., Xiaopeng, W., Teng, M., Zhiang, W., Yaobin, X., Liang, G.: Grid Supporting Platform for AMS Data Processing. In: Pan, Y., Chen, D.-x., Guo, M., Cao, J., Dongarra, J.J. (eds.) ISPA 2005. LNCS, vol. 3758, pp. 276–285. Springer, Heidelberg (2005)
14. Fisher, P., Klimentov, A., Mujunen, A., Ritakari, J.: AMS Ground Support Computers for ISS mission. AMS Note 2002- 03-01 (March 12, 2002)
15. Stockinger, H., Hanushevsky, A.: Http Redirection for Replica Catalogue Lookups in Data Grids. In: Proceedings of the 2002 ACM symposium on Applied computing, pp. 882–889 (2002)
16. Foster, I., Kesselman, C., Tuecke, S.: The Anatomy of the Grid: Enabling Scalable Virtual Organizations. International Journal of High Performance Computing Applications 15(3), 200–222 (2001)

Grid Scheduling Optimization Under Conditions of Uncertainty

Zeng Bin, Luo Zhaohui, and Wei Jun

Department of management, Naval University of Engineering,
Wuhan, China
zbtrueice@163.com

Abstract. One of the biggest challenges in building grid schedulers is how to deal with the uncertainty in what future computational resources will be available. Current techniques for Grid scheduling rarely account for resources whose performance, reliability, and cost vary with time simultaneously. In this paper we address the problem of delivering a deadline based scheduling in a dynamic and uncertain environment represented by dynamic Bayesian network based stochastic resource model. The genetic algorithm is used to find the optimal and robust solutions so that the highest probability of satisfying the user's QoS objectives at a specified deadline can be achieved. It is shown via a simulation that the new methodology will not only achieving a relatively high probability of scheduling workflow with multiple goals successfully, but also be resilient to environment changes.

Keywords: workflow scheduling, grid computing, genetic algorithm, optimal scheduling scheme.

1 Introduction

A Grid's ability to produce an efficient plan or schedule for its task execution is critical to its service performance. Given the dynamic nature of a complex resource environment [1], an effective resource management system is to create the robust schedules at the right nodes and at the right time. Therefore, environmental conditions affect the feasibility of Grid's schedules, making some schedules more likely to succeed than others.

There are some approaches that try to solve the problem. The multicriteria resource selection method implemented in the Grid Resource Management System (see [2] and [3]) has been used for the evaluation of knowledge obtained from the prediction system. Nevertheless, due to incomplete and imprecise information available, results of performance prediction methods may be accompanied by considerable errors (to see examples of exact error values please refer to [4] and [5]). Another aid to avoid uncertain problems comes in the form of contracts ([6],[7]). In the simplest contracts, clients use initial estimates of job completion time to bind Grid resources, and then monitor job progress during execution to determine if the contract will be met for reacting swiftly and appropriately to

K. Li et al. (Eds.): NPC 2007, LNCS 4672, pp. 51–60, 2007.

recover if it is not. However, the contract based work is limited to the system where estimates may be gathered a priori and where clients may monitor runtime progress. Some research such as FailRank [8] try to monitor the Grid sites with the highest potential to feature some failure. Thomas model the Grid scheduling system as a collection of queues where servers break down and are subsequently repaired to investigate the penalty of prolonged delays in information propagation to the scheduler [9]. Anyhow, current distributed service scheduling research has not presented a complete solution that incorporates uncertainty.

This paper introduces a framework for devising a robust Grid scheduler to maximize the probability of successfully achieving the QoS objectives, while minimizing its variability. A normative model of the stochastic Grid resource environment, based on a dynamic Bayesian network [10], to infer indirect influences and to track the time propagation of schedule actions in complex Gird environment is developed. For a user specified QoS requirements and resource constraints, a near-optimal Grid scheduling strategy is obtained via genetic algorithms, where the DBN serves as a fitness evaluator for candidate schedules.

2   DBN Model for Job Scheduling Optimization

The stochastic scheduling problem faced by an uncertain Grid system can be defined as follows: given an initial system state, determine optimal scheduling strategy that will bring the system to a specified objective state at a specified time with a relatively high probability. The objective, in our case, is the set of desired QoS objectives. The process to solve this problem is to:

1. Represent the joint dynamics of the jobs and its assigned resources;
2. Optimally select appropriate scheduling strategy;
3. Assess the probability of successfully achieving the desired QoS objectives under resources constraints.

A dynamically evolving DBN-based scheduling model $G_k = G(t_k) = (V, E, P_k)$, which can be viewed as a Bayesian network at time t_k, combines knowledge about the jobs and its execution environment. G_k is a directed acyclic graph consisting of a set of nodes V and a set of directed edges E with a fixed structure. Every node is considered as a random variable and can assume Boolean values. For each node $v_i \in V$, we define a probability mass function (pmf) $P_k(v_i) = P\{v_i(t_k)\}$ to characterize the environment uncertainty at time t_k.

The dynamic evolution of the DBN-based scheduling model unfolds through a finite horizon timeline as in shown in Fig. 1, which is discretized into T time steps (from t_1 to t_T). The solid arcs are used to represent the causal relationship in a single time step, and the dashed edges are used to show the temporal evolution of the model between neighboring time steps.

Based on Fig. 1, The definition of our DBN model for scheduling jobs is described below:

1. System state: A state consists of current execution tasks, execution time and current location, with $S(t_k) = \{P_k(v_i)|v_i \in V_k\}$ to portray the overall state of the Grid at time t_k;

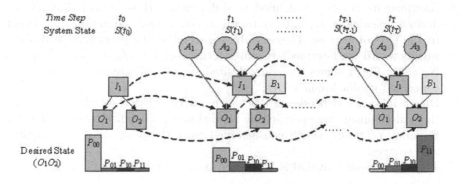

Fig. 1. Time evolution of scheduling model as a DBN

2. Objectives: Objectives are regarded as desired states of DBNs. $O = \{O_n | 1 \leq n \leq N_O\}$ specified by the desired probability of QoS satisfied ('1' or '0') and the corresponding terminal time t_{O_n} for each QoS objective: $O_n(t_{O_n}) = 1$ or $O_n(t_{O_n}) = 0$. Here $N_O = |O|$ is the total number of QoS objectives specified by users;

3. Critical system events: regarded as noise factors, whose occurrence is beyond the control of the Grid resource management system, but will affect the resource dynamics: $B = \{B_j | 1 \leq j \leq N_B\}$. $N_B = |B|$ is the total number of system events in the environment. In many cases, one has partial knowledge of the statistical properties (e.g., means and variances, probability distributions) for these events. For instance, if event B_1 in Fig. 1 occurs with a probability that is uniform between [0.2,0.6] at time t_k, then $P_k\{B_1 = 1\} = p_1$, $P_k\{B_1 = 0\} = 1 - p_1$, where $p_1 \sim U[0.2, 0.6]$. The prior pmfs in the model are normally acquired from domain experiences or analysis of Grid feedback sources [8]. Note that some events may have inhibiting effects in that they reduce the probability of achieving certain desired QoS objectives;

4. Actions: An action in the model is to allocate a time slot on a service or node resource to a task. Actions are regarded as control factors, which can be employed by an Grid scheduling system to influence the state of the environment: $A = A_q | 1 \leq q \leq N_A$, where $N_A = |A|$ is the total number of feasible actions. Each action will take a value of "true" or "false" at each time step once the scheduling system determines a strategy. That is, $P_k\{A_q = 1\} = 1$ if action A_q is activated at time step t_k; otherwise, $P_k\{A_q = 1\} = 0$. Without loss of generality, we assume that $(r_q + 1) \ll 2^T$ feasible choices for action A_q from a domain $\Omega_{A_q} = \{a_q^0, a_q^1, a_q^2, \wedge, a_q^{r_q}\}$ are available. Each element $a_q^i (0 \leq i \leq r_q)$ in this set maps to a time series based actions '$a_q^i(t_1) \wedge a_q^i(t_T)$' with $a_q^i(t_k) \in \{0,1\} (0 \leq k \leq T)$ which representing task q is mapped to resource node i at time t_k. Let C_{a_q} be the cost of selecting schedule a_q for action A_q. A strategy under a given initial environment state $S(t_0)$ is a set of series for all the actions: $R = \{(a_1, a_2, \wedge, a_{N_A}) | a_q \in \Omega_{A_q}\}$, Thus, the cost of the strategy is $C_R = \sum_{q=1}^{N_A} c_{a_q}$.

5. Intermediate states are defined to differentiate those states that are not desired finishing state, but are useful in connecting the actions and events to the QoS objectives. They can be regarded as the predefined states of a workflow. All the intermediate states form a set $I = \{I_m | 1 \leq m \leq N_I\}$ with $N_I = |I|$. Fig. 1 shows that only desired states and intermediate states are connected by diachronic edges;

6. Direct influence dependencies between all the objects of the system and their mechanisms are specified by conditional probability tables (CPTs) in Bayesian networks, which can attained from the priori analysis of system feed sources.

7. The total resource available for the Grid is constrained by C_{budget}.

Conceptually, the problem is to achieve the desired objective states $\{O\}$ with a high probability at specified times. The mathematical formulation of the scheduling strategy optimization problem is as follows:

$$\max_S(P\{O(t_k)|S(t_0), R\}) = \max_S(P\{O_1(t_{O_1})O_2(t_{O_2}) \wedge O_{N_O}(t_{O_N})|S(t_0), R\})$$

$$= \max_S\left(\prod_{n=1}^{N_O} P\{O_n(t_{O_n})|S(t_0), R\}\right) \quad (1)$$

Subject to:

$$C_R = \sum_{q=1}^{N_A} C_{a_q} \leq C_{budget} \quad (2)$$

3 Applying DBNs to a Robust Scheduler

3.1 Framework of the Solution Approach

As shown in Fig. 2, We combine concepts of robust design, DBNs and genetic optimization algorithms to solve the scheduling optimization problem. DBNs integrated with probability evaluation algorithms are used to model the dynamics of the Grid resources and to calculate the probability of desired QoS objectives at specified deadline. Monte Carlo runs are made to account for uncertainty in system parameters in the inner loop of DBN. That is, disturbances are introduced by randomly choosing DBN parameters (prior pmfs of events and conditional probabilities). In each Monte Carlo run, DBN will evaluate the joint probability of achieving the desired QoS objectives. The histogram provided by the results of Monte Carlo runs is approximated as a Gaussian density (based on the Central Limit Theorem) with sample mean and sample variance. Using the sample mean and variance and following robust design techniques, a signal-to-noise ratio (SNR) is computed; this criterion maximizes the probability of achieving the desired QoS objectives while minimizing its variability. A genetic algorithm is employed in the outer loop to optimize the scheduling strategies.

Conceptually, the probability of achieving the desired QoSs is a function of actions A, exogenous events B and time t_k, that is $P(O) = f(A, B, t_k)$. In iterations of the genetic algorithm, since we choose candidate scheduling strategies,

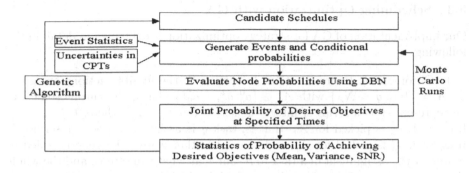

Fig. 2. Framework Overview

thereby fixing the values of A, the probability will be a function of events B and time t_k, that is, $P(O|A) = g(B, t_k)$. Then, in each Monte Carlo run of DBN inference, for the given sequences of actions A, we estimate the occurrence probabilities of exogenous events B. Consequently, from a single Monte Carlo run, we have $P(O|A, B) = h(t_k)$. We can see that Monte Carlo runs inside the DBN inference makes it possible to measure the robustness of a schedule in an uncertain environment in terms of the signal-to-noise ratio.

3.2 Probability Propagation Through DBN

Based on the DBN of Fig. 1, we extended from the initial static Bayesian Network by introducing dummy nodes for all the intermediate and desired states. Dummy nodes are defined as: $V_i^0 = \{v_i^0 | v_i \in I \cup O\}$ with $P_{k+1}\{v_i^0\} = P_k\{v_i\}$. The probability will propagate vertically from causal nodes to effect nodes, and propagate horizontally from one time step to the next as follows:
(1) Set the initial pmfs of nodes:$P_1\{v_i^0\} = P_0\{v_i\}$ based on known $S(t_0)$;
(2) Let $k = 1$;
(3) Select an action strategy: $R = \{(a_1, a_2, \cdots, a_{N_A}) | a_q \in \Omega_{A_q}, 1 \leq q \leq N_A\}$, where if $a_q(t_k) = 1$, set $P_k(A_q = 1) = 1$;else $P_k(A_q = 1) = 0$;
(4) Randomly select probability mass functions of exogenous events $P_k\{B_j\}$;
(5) Calculate probability mass functions of the intermediate and desired objectives using Bayesian model averaging:

$$P_k\{v_i\} = \sum_{\pi(v_i), v_i^0} P\{v_i|\pi(v_i), v_i^0\} \cdot P_k\{\pi(v_i)\} P_k\{v_i^0\}, v_i \in I \cup O$$

Where $\pi(v_i)$ is the possible instantiation of the parent nodes of v_i;
(6) Propagate the current probability mass functions to the next time step:
$$P_{k+1}\{v_i^0\} = P_k\{v_i\};$$
(7) Let $k = k + 1$. If $k \leq T$, go back to step (3); otherwise, stop.

3.3 Scheduling Optimization with GA

Our implementation of GA for strategy optimization is explained in detail in the following.

1) Chromosome Representation: In section 2, the feasible actions are given by $A = \{1 \leq q \leq N_A\}$ with $A_q \in \{a_q^0, a_q^1, \wedge, a_q^{r_q}\}$. Thus, the chromosome can be represented as a series of integer genes $= (\omega_1 \omega_2 \cdots \omega_q)$, where $0 \leq \omega_q \leq r_q$. If $\omega_q = 1$, a_q^1 is picked for A_q, that is, task q is assigned to node or service 1, If $\omega_q = 2$, a_q^2 is picked for A_q, and so on. In other words, the gene is coded to represent the assignment of a task to resource at what time steps, and the whole chromosome is a code representing a schedule [11,12].

2) Population Initialization: It is the first step in GA. In our problem, we generate the initial schedule randomly. Thus, for any individual $\omega = (\omega_1 \omega_2 \wedge \omega_q)$, in the initial population, $\omega_q (1 \leq q \leq r_q)$ satisfying the constraints of cost and resource budgets is selected from $\{0, 1, \wedge, r_q\}$.

3) Fitness function: DBN performs the inner loop inference to compute the evaluation function for GA. The evaluation function will map the population candidate into a partially ordered set, which will be input to the next step, i.e., population selection. DBN is used to obtain the probability of achieving the desired effects at certain time slices for a given strategy $P\{O_1(t_{O_1})O_2(t_{O_2}) \wedge O_{N_O}(t_{O_N})|S(t_0), R\}$. In a noisy environment, this probability is a random variable because of the uncertainty in the statistical description of exogenous events B. In the DBN loop, we generate a histogram of this probability via Monte Carlo runs, the sample mean and variance are computed via:

$$\mu = \frac{1}{M} \sum_{i=1}^{M} P_i\{O_1(t_{O_1})O_2(t_{O_2}) \wedge O_{N_O}(t_{O_N})|S(t_0), R\} \tag{3}$$

$$\sigma^2 = \frac{1}{M-1} \sum_{i=1}^{M} (P_i\{O_1(t_{O_1})O_2(t_{O_2}) \wedge O_{N_O}(t_{O_N})|S(t_0), R\} - \mu)^2 \tag{4}$$

Signal-to-noise ratio (SNR) provides a measure of goodness or fitness of a strategy. SNR is computed via:

$$SNR = -10 log_{10} \left[\frac{1}{\mu^2} \left(1 + 3 \frac{\sigma^2}{\mu^2} \right) \right] \tag{5}$$

The optimized evaluation function, SNR, corresponds to a schedule that has high probability of success, and that is also robust to changes in the environment (unforeseen events, uncertainty in parameters, etc.).

4) Selection function: Since SNR is negative in our case, we use the normalized geometric ranking method as follows. When population is $\{S_i | 1 \leq i \leq N_P\}$, the probability of selecting S_i is defined as:

$$P(\text{select } S_i) = \frac{q(1-q)^{r-1}}{1-(1-q)^{N_P}} \tag{6}$$

Where q is a specified probability of selecting the best individual, r is the rank of the individual with the best individual ranked at '1'.

5) Genetic operators: Mutation and crossover are basic operators to create new population based on individuals in the current generation. Since our chromosome is a series of integers, we employ the following genetic operators to generate individuals for the new strategy:

$$\text{Uniform mutation: } \omega_q' = \begin{cases} U(0, r_q), & \text{if the } q^{th} \text{ gene is selected for mutation} \\ \omega_q, & \text{otherwise} \end{cases}$$

(7)

Integer-valued simple crossover generates a random number l from $U(1, N_A)$, and creates two new strategies ω_i' and ω_j' through interchange of genes as follows:

$$\omega_i' = \begin{cases} \omega_i, & \text{if } (i < l) \\ \omega_j, & \text{else} \end{cases} \qquad \omega_j' = \begin{cases} \omega_j, & \text{if } (i < l) \\ \omega_i, & \text{else} \end{cases} \tag{8}$$

6) Termination criteria: We Define a maximum number of generations and stop at a predefined generation.

4 Experimental Results and Analysis

To validate our work, we conducted experiments in a small eight-node Grid of which includes 2 sensors (sen1, sen2), one storage server (st1), two IBM X260 servers (ws1 ,ws2) and three workstations (ws3, ws4, ws5). We simulate a simple workflow job including four tasks tk1, tk2, tk3, tk4.

The feasible actions of the workflow are to schedule tasks to perform their work: A_1— tk1 execute FFT1 algorithm on the signal data read from sen1; A_2— tk2 execute FFT2 algorithm on the signal data read from sen2; A_3— tk3 execute correlation analysis algorithm on the frequency data read from tk1 and tk2 and save the result to st1; A_4— tk4 read the result from st1 and transfer it to a remote monitor.

We generate three exogenous events, where: B_1—network channel to sen1 is congested; B_2—network channel to sen2 is congested; B_3—storage server st1 is overloaded. Each event has an approximate probability, based on the result

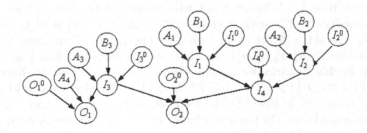

Fig. 3. Workflow Scenario

of benchmark software on the network and computers if in real application. However, the time at which the events happen is unpredictable.

Desired QoS objectives are defined as: O_1— the result is transferred to remote monitor; O_2—keep the measurement error to a minimum.

The following intermediate states are designed to connect actions or events to the desired objectives: I_1 —measure from sen1; I_2 —measure from sen2; I_3 —store the correlation result to st1; I_4 — the error in FFT algorithm. Since the events may happen at arbitrary times, the problem is, given a pos-

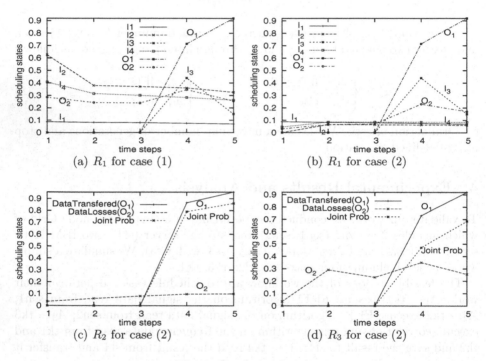

(a) R_1 for case (1)

(b) R_1 for case (2)

(c) R_2 for case (2)

(d) R_3 for case (2)

Fig. 4. Simulation Result

sible combination of events, which schedule will maximize the probability of achieving the desired objectives. Consider two cases: (1) sen1 and sen2 are congested at time t_1. Whenever tk4 will transfer data, the storage is overloaded immediately; (2) sen1 is congested at time t_1 and sen2 is congested at time t_2; the st1 will act as in case (1). The results from these two cases under schedule $R_1(a_1^1, a_2^2, a_3^2, a_4^1)$ are illustrated in Fig. 4(a) and Fig. 4(b), respectively. In this scenario, we assumed the probabilities of events happen are: $P\{B_1 = 1\} = 0.8, P\{B_2 = 1\} = 0.7, P\{B_3 = 1\} = 0.8$. Since sen1 and sen2 are separately congested in case (2), the FFT algorithm will be under a moderate packet loss probability. On the other hand, in case (1), the combination of two events may put the tk1 and tk2 in the measurement under severe loss probability. Thus, the computation error will be higher in case (1).

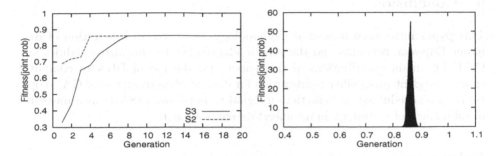

Fig. 5. Schedule Optimization through GA   **Fig. 6.** 1000 Monto Carlo Runs for R_2

Now, we focus on case (2) to see which action strategy will be better. Comparing R_1 with $R_2(a_1^1, a_2^2, a_3^1, a_4^1)$ and $R_3(a_1^1, a_2^3, a_3^2, a_4^1)$, we can see from Fig. 4(c) and Fig. 4(d) that R_2 is the best among these three schedules because all the data are immediately processed. As a consequence, the computation error due to packet loss is low. Fig. 4(c) and Fig. 4(d) depict the joint probability of achieving both of the desired objectives: $P\{O_1(t_k) = 1, O_2(t_k) = 0\}$. Fig. 5 is the result from genetic algorithm, where we use $P\{O_1(5) = 1, O_2(5) = 0\}$ as a fitness measurement.

Table 1. Potential Actions for GA

Action	A_1					A_2					A_3		A_4	
	a_1^1	a_1^2	a_1^3	a_1^4	a_1^5	a_2^1	a_2^2	a_2^3	a_2^4	a_2^5	a_3^1	a_3^2	a_4^1	a_4^2
t1	1	0	0	0	0	1	0	0	0	0	0	0	0	0
t2	0	1	0	0	0	0	1	0	0	0	0	0	0	0
t3	0	0	1	0	0	0	0	1	0	0	0	0	0	0
t4	0	0	0	1	0	0	0	0	1	0	1	0	1	0
t5	0	0	0	0	1	0	0	0	0	1	0	1	1	1

Additionally, we consider a scenario where the data from benchmark is noisy. We suppose $P\{B_1(t_1) = 1\} = P_1$, $P\{B_2(t_2) = 1\} = P_2$, $P\{B_3(t_4) = 1\} = P_3$, where P_1 is uniformly distributed between $[0.6,1]$, P_2 is uniformly distributed between $[0.5,0.9]$ and P_3 uniformly distributed between $[0.7,0.9]$. Results of $P\{O_1(5) = 1, O_2(5) = 0\}$ from 1000 Monte Carlo runs are shown in the histograms of Fig. 6, with the Gaussian distribution superimposed. The sample mean and standard deviation are 0.8641 and 0.0089, respectively. The two-sided 95% confidence region of this schedule is (0.8467, 0.8816). A narrower confidence region means better control of the environment.

5 Conclusion

This paper introduced a general methodology, based on an integration of dynamic Bayesian networks and the genetic algorithms, to optimize schedules for Grid. The main contributions of this paper are: the use of DBN to compute time-dependent probability propagation for desired objectives; use of GA to optimize job scheduling; introduction of signal-to noise ratio (SNR) as a measure of robustness of a strategy in an uncertain environment.

References

1. Real, R., Yamin, A., da Silva, L., Frainer, G., Augustin, I., Barbosa, J., Geyer, C.: Resource scheduling on grid: handling uncertainty. In: Proceeding of the Fourth International Workshop on Grid Computing, pp. 205–207 (2003)
2. Kurowski, K., Nabrzyski, J., Oleksiak, A., Weglarz, J.: Multicriteria aspects of Grid resource management. Grid resource management: state of the art and future trends table of contents, 271–293 (2004)
3. Domagalski, P., Kurowski, K., Oleksiak, A., Nabrzyski, J., Balaton, Z., Gombás, G., Kacsuk, P.: Sensor Oriented Grid Montoring Infrastructures for Adaptaive Multicriteria Resource Management Strategies. In: Proceedings of the 1st CoreGrid Workshop, pp. 163–173 (2005)
4. Smith, W., Taylor, V., Foster, I.: Using Run-Time Predictions to Estimate Queue Wait Times and Improve Scheduler Performance. In: Proceedings of the IPPS/SPDP '99 Workshop on Job Scheduling Strategies for Parallel Processing, pp. 202–219 (1999)
5. Smith, W., Foster, I., Taylor, V.: Predicting Application Run Times Using Historical Information. Lecture Notes on Computer Science, pp. 122–142 (1998)
6. Sample, N., Keyani, P., Wiederhold, G.: Scheduling under uncertainty: planning for the ubiquitous grid. In: Proceedings of the 5th International Conference on Coordination Models and Languages, pp. 300–316 (2002)
7. Li, J., Yahyapour, R.: Learning-Based Negotiation Strategies for Grid Scheduling. In: Proceedings of CCGRID'06, pp. 576–583 (2006)
8. Zeinalipour-Yazti, D., Neocleous, K., Georgiou, C., Dikaiakos, M.: Managing failures in a grid system using failrank. Technical Report TR-2006-04, Department of Computer Science, University of Cyprus (2006)
9. Thomas, N., Bradley, J., Knottenbelt, W.: Stochastic analysis of scheduling strategies in a Grid-based resource model. IEEE Proceedings Software 151, 232–239 (2004)
10. Santos, L., Proenca, A.: Scheduling under conditions of uncertainty: a bayesian approach. In: Proceedings of the 5th International Conference on Coordination Models and Languages, pp. 222–229 (2004)
11. Kim, S., Weissman, J.: A genetic algorithm based approach for scheduling decomposable data grid applications. In: Proceedings of 2004 International Conference on Parallel Processing, pp. 406–413 (2004)
12. Di Martino, V., Mililotti, M.: Sub optimal scheduling in a grid using genetic algorithms. Parallel Computing 30, 553–565 (2004)

A Dynamic Adjustment Strategy for File Transformation in Data Grids*

Chao-Tung Yang**, Shih-Yu Wang, and Chun-Pin Fu

High-Performance Computing Laboratory
Department of Computer Science and Information Engineering
Tunghai University, Taichung, 40704, Taiwan
ctyang@thu.edu.tw

Abstract. In this paper, we propose a dynamic file transfer scheme with co-allocation architecture, called Dynamic Adjustment Strategy, a dynamic file transfer scheme with co-allocation architecture that reduce the file transfer times and improves the performance in Data Grid environments. Our approach reduces the idle time faster servers spend waiting for the slowest server, and decreases file transfer completion time. We also present a new toolkit, called Cyber-Transformer, with a friendly graphical user interface interface running on the client side that makes it easy for inexperienced users to manage replicas and download the files in Data Grid environments. We also provide an effective scheme for reducing the cost of reassembling data blocks.

1 Introduction

The term "Data Grid" traditionally represents the network of distributed storage resources from archival systems to caches and databases, which are linked using a logical name space to create global, persistent identifiers and provide uniform access mechanisms [4]. Data Grids aggregate distributed resources to resolve large-size dataset management problems [1, 2, 3, 5, 6, 7, 8, 9, 29, 30]. Increasingly, large collections of measured and computed data are emerging as important resources in many data-intensive applications.

Certain data-intensive scientific applications entail huge amounts of data that require data file management systems to replicate files and manage data transfers and distributed data access. Data grid infrastructure integrates data storage devices and data management services in grid environments consisting of scattered computing and storage resources, perhaps located in different countries/regions yet accessible to users [12].

Replicating popular content in distributed servers is widely used in practice [14, 17, 21, 30]. Recently, large-scale, data-sharing scientific communities such as those described in [1, 5] used this technology to replicate their large datasets over several

---

* This work is supported in part by the National Science Council, Taiwan R.O.C., under grants no. NSC95-2221-E-029-004 and NSC95-2218-E-007-025.
** Corresponding author.

K. Li et al. (Eds.): NPC 2007, LNCS 4672, pp. 61–70, 2007.

sites. Downloading large datasets from several replica locations may result in varied performance rates. Bandwidth quality is the most important factor affecting transfers between clients and servers since download speeds are limited by the bandwidth traffic congestion in the links connecting the servers to the clients.

One way to improve download speed is to use replica selection techniques to determine the best replica locations [21]. This method selects the servers most likely to provide optimum transfer rates because bandwidth quality can vary unpredictably due to the sharing nature of the Internet. Another way is to use co-allocation technology [17, 21, 23, 24, 25, 26, 27, 28, 30] to download data. Co-allocation of data transfers enables the clients to download data from multiple locations by establishing multiple connections in parallel. This can improve the performance over single-server downloads and alleviate the Internet congestion problem [17]. Several co-allocation strategies were presented in our work [17]. An idle-time drawback remains since faster servers must wait for the slowest server to deliver its final block. Thus, reducing the differences in finish times among replica servers is important.

In this paper, we propose a dynamic file-transfer scheme with co-allocation architecture, called the Dynamic Adjustment Strategy, which reduces file-transfer times and also improves data transfer performance in Data Grid environments. Our approach can reduce file server idle times and decrease file-transfer completion times. We also present a new toolkit, called Cyber-Transformer, with a friendly client-side GUI interface integrated with the Information Service, Replica Location Service, and Data Transfer Service [25]. And we provide an effective scheme for reducing the cost of reassembling data blocks. Experimental results show that our approach is superior to previous methods and achieves the best overall performance. We also discuss combination cost and provide an effective improvement.

2   Background Review

2.1   Data Grid and Grid Middleware

In Data Grid environments, access to distributed data is typically as important as access to distributed computational resources [1, 2, 3, 4, 5, 6, 30]. Distributed scientific and engineering applications require transfers of large amounts of data between storage systems, and access to large amounts of data generated by many geographically distributed applications and users for analysis and visualization, among others.

The Globus Project [9, 11, 16] provides software tools collectively called The Globus Toolkit that make it easier to build computational Grids and Grid-based applications. Many organizations use the Globus Toolkit to support their applications. The composition of the Globus Toolkit can be pictured as three pillars: Resource Management, Information Services, and Data Management. Each pillar represents a primary component of the Globus Toolkit and makes use of a common foundation of security. GRAM implements a resource management protocol, MDS implements an information services protocol, and GridFTP implements a data transfer protocol. They all use the GSI security protocol at the connection layer [10, 11, 13, 16].

2.2 Replica Management and Selection

Replica management involves creating or removing replicas in data grid sites [21]. A replica manager typically maintains a replica catalog containing replica site addresses and file instances. The replica management service is responsible for managing the replication of complete and partial copies of datasets, defined as collections of files.

Data Grid may contain multiple replica catalogs. The purpose of the replica catalog is to provide mappings between logical names for files or collections and one or more copies of objects in physical storage systems. The catalog registers three types of entries: logical collections, locations and logical files. Despite the benefits of registering and manipulating collections of files using logical collection and location objects, there may be a need for users and applications to characterize individual files. For this purpose, the Replica Catalog includes optional entries that describe individual logical files. Logical files are entities with globally unique names and one or more physical instances. The Catalog may optionally contain one logical file entry in the Replica Catalog for each logical file in a collection.

Replica selection [16] is used to select replicas from among the sites in a Data Grid [21]. The selection criteria depend on application characteristics. This mechanism enables users to efficiently manage replicas of data sets at their sites. The replica selection process commonly consists of three steps: data preparation, preprocessing and prediction. Applications then select replicas according to their specific attributes.

3 The Dynamic Adjustment Strategy

3.1 The Co-allocation Architecture

Candidate replica locations are passed to the replica selection service [21], which was presented in a previous work [23, 24, 25]. This replica selection service provides estimates of candidate transfer performance based on a cost model and chooses appropriate amounts to request from the better locations. The architecture proposed in [17] consists of three main components: an information service, a broker/co-allocator, and local storage systems. The co-allocation architecture [7] is shown in Figure 1, which is an extension of the basic template for resource management. Applications specify the characteristics of desired data and pass the attribute description to a broker. The broker queries available resources and gets replica locations from an information service [6] and a replica management service [21] creates a list of the desired files physical locations. The co-allocation agent then downloads the data in parallel from the selected servers.

Data grids consist of scattered computing and storage resources located in different countries/regions yet accessible to users [8]. We used the grid middleware Globus Toolkit [16] as our data grid infrastructure. The Globus Toolkit provides solutions for such considerations as security, resource management, data management, and information services. One of its primary components, MDS [6, 11, 16, 26], is designed to provide a standard mechanism for discovering and publishing resource status and configuration information. It provides a uniform and flexible interface for data collected by lower-level information providers in two modes: static (e.g., OS,

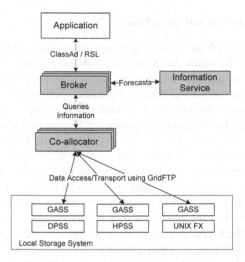

Fig. 1. The Co-Allocation Architecture in Data Grids

CPU types, and system architectures) and dynamic data (e.g., disk availability, memory availability, and loading) [15, 22]. And it uses GridFTP [1, 11, 16] to provide efficient management and transfer data in a wide-area, distributed-resource environment. We use GridFTP [1, 11, 16] to enable parallel data transfers.

As datasets are replicated within Grid environments for reliability and performance, clients require the abilities to discover existing data replicas, and create and register new replicas. A Replica Location Service (RLS) [4] provides a mechanism for discovering and registering existing replicas. Several prediction metrics have been developed to help replica selection. For instance, Vazhkudai and Schopf [18, 19, 20, 21] used past data transfer histories to estimate current data transfer throughputs.

In our previous work [23, 24], we proposed a replica selection cost model and a replica selection service to perform replica selection. In [17], the author proposes a co-allocation architecture for co-allocating Grid data transfers across multiple connections by exploiting the partial-copy feature of GridFTP. It also provides Brute-Force, History-Based, and Dynamic Load Balancing for allocating data blocks.

- Brute-Force Co-Allocation: Brute-Force Co-Allocation works by dividing files equally among available flows. It does not address bandwidth differences among the various client-server links.
- History-based Co-Allocation: The History-based Co-Allocation scheme keeps block sizes per flow proportional to transfer rates predicted by previous results of file transfer results.
- Conservative Load Balancing: One of their dynamic co-allocation is Conservative Load Balancing. The Conservative Load Balancing dynamic co-allocation strategy divides requested datasets into "k" disjoint blocks of equal size. Available servers are assigned single blocks to deliver in parallel. When a server finishes delivering a

block, another is requested, and so on, until the entire file is downloaded. The loadings on the co-allocated flows are automatically adjusted because the faster servers will deliver more quickly providing larger portions of the file.

These co-allocation strategies do not address the shortcoming of faster servers having to wait for the slowest server to deliver its final block. In most cases, this wastes much time and decreases overall performance. Thus, we propose an efficient approach, called the Dynamic Adjustment Strategy, and based on the co-allocation architecture. It improves dynamic co-allocation and reduces waiting time, thus improving overall transfer performance.

3.2 The Dynamic Adjustment Strategy

Dynamic co-allocation is the most efficient approach to reducing the influence of network variations between clients and servers. However, the idle time of faster servers waiting for the slowest server to deliver its last block is still a major factor affecting overall efficiency, which Conservative Load Balancing and Aggressive Load Balancing [17] cannot effectively avoid. The approach proposed in the present paper, a dynamic allocation mechanism, called Dynamic Adjustment Strategy, can overcome this, and thus, improve data transfer performance.

Co-allocation technology [17] enables the clients to download data from multiple locations by establishing multiple connections in parallel. In our previous work [23], we proposed a replica selection cost model and a replica selection service to perform replica selection. We now propose a new data transfer strategy based on this model. It consists of three phases: initial phase, steady phase, and completion phase.

- Initial phase: We assign equal block sizes to all GridFTP servers. In this phase, our system determines the next block size for each replica server.
- Steady phase: As job transfers are completed, servers are assigned their next jobs. Jobs sizes are determined by multiplying the client bandwidth by the weighting.
- Completion phase: To avoid the generating excessively small job sizes, we set an end condition such that if the remaining target file size is smaller than the initial block size, it is transferred immediately.

To determine the initial block size, we set an upper bound that is dependent on the relation between the client's maximum bandwidth and the number of replica sources. Though multiple replicas can be downloaded in parallel, the gathered portions of files from different links must be transferred to the client in a single link. It is clear that the client's bandwidth could be bottleneck in co-allocation architecture. The formula for upper bound is:

$$initialPT \leq ClientMaxBandwidth\ /Number\ of\ Replica\ Source \qquad (1)$$

In our previous work [23, 25, 26, 27, 28], we proposed a replica selection cost model in which we defined a formula for calculating the weighting. First, we get a score based on the states of the various server devices:

$$Score_i = P_i^{CPU} \times R^{CPU} + P_i^{Mem} \times R^{Mem} + P_i^{BW} \times R^{BW},\ and\ R^{CPU} + R^{Mem} + R^{BW} = 1 \qquad (2)$$

The parameters are:

- $Score_i$: the score for server i such that $1 \leq i \leq n$.
- P_i^{CPU}: percentage of server i CPU idle states [15]
- R^{CPU}: CPU load ratio defined by the user
- P_i^{Mem}: percentage of server i memory free space [15]
- R^{Mem}: memory free space ratio defined by the user
- P_i^{BW}: percentage of bandwidth available from server i to client (user node); current bandwidth divided by highest theoretical bandwidth [22, 24]
- R^{BW}: network bandwidth ratio defined by users.

After getting the scores for all server nodes, the system calculates the $weighting_i$:

$$weighting_i = Score_i / \sum_{k=1}^{n} Score_k \qquad (3)$$

The weighting is then used to determine the size of the next job:

$$newPT_i = ClientBandwidth \times weighting_i \qquad (4)$$

Where $newPT_i$ denotes the next job size for server i, and $ClientBandwidth$ denotes the current client bandwidth.

When server i finishes transferring of a block, it gets a new job whose size is calculated according to the real-time status of server i. Each time, our strategy dynamically adjusts a job size according to source device loading and bandwidth. The lighter the loading a source device has, the larger job size it is assigned. We show experimental results and analyses that confirm our strategy in the next section.

4   Experimental Results and Analysis

In this section, we discuss the performance of our Dynamic Adjustment Co-Allocation strategy in a real data grid. We evaluate four co-allocation schemes: (1) Brute-Force (Brute), (2) History-based (History), (3) Conservative Load Balancing

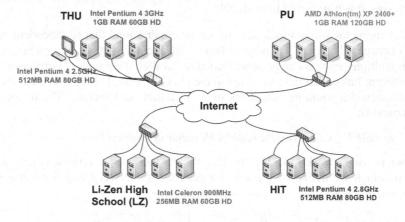

Fig. 2. Our Data Grid testbed

Table 1. GridFTP end-to-end transmission rates from THU to various servers

Replica Server	Average Transmission Rate
HIT	61.5 Mbits
LZ	49.5 Mbits
PU	26.7 Mbits

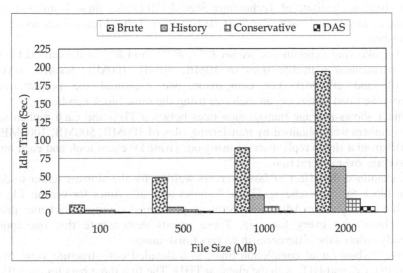

Fig. 3. Idle times for various methods; servers at PU, LZ, and HIT

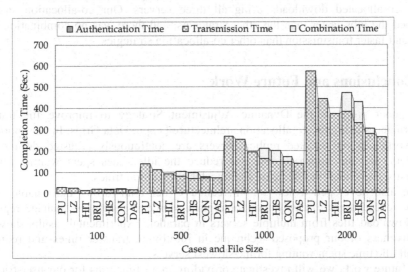

Fig. 4. Completion times for various methods; servers are at PU, LZ, and HIT

(Conservative) and (4) Dynamic Adjustment Strategy (DAS). We analyze the
performance of each scheme by comparing their transfer finish times, and the total

idle time faster servers spent waiting for the slowest servers to finish delivering the last block. We also analyze overall performances in the various cases.

We performed wide-area data transfer experiments using our GridFTP GUI client tool. We executed our co-allocation client tool on our testbed at Tunghai University (THU), Taichung City, Taiwan, and fetched files from four selected replica servers: one at Providence University (PU), one at Li-Zen High School (LZ), and the other one at Hsiuping Institute of Technology School (HIT). All these institutions are in Taichung, Taiwan, and each is at least 10 Km from THU. Figure 2 shows our Data Grid testbed.

In the following experiments, we set R^{CPU}, R^{MEM}, and R^{BW} in the ratio 0.1:0.1:0.8. We experimented with file sizes of 10MB, 50MB, 100MB, 500MB, 1000MB, 1500MB, and 2000MB. For comparison, we measured the performance of Conservative Load Balancing on each size using the same block numbers.

Table 1 shows average transmission rates between THU and each replica server. These numbers were obtained by transferring files of 100MB, 500MB, 1000MB, and 2000MB from a single replica server using our GridFTP client tool, and each number is an average over several runs.

We examined the effect of faster servers waiting for the slowest server to deliver the last block for each scheme. Figure 3 shows total idle times for various file sizes. Note that our Dynamic Adjustment Strategy performed significantly better than the other schemes on every file size. These results demonstrate that our approach efficiently reduces the differences in servers finish times.

Figure 4 shows total completion times in a detailed cost-structure view. Servers were at PU, LZ, and HIT, with the client at THU. The first three bars for each file size denote the time to download the entire file from single server, while the other bars show co-allocated downloads using all three servers. Our co-allocation strategy finished the jobs faster than the other strategies, and there was no combination time cost, and faster transmission than other co-allocation strategies.

5   Conclusions and Future Work

This paper proposes the Dynamic Adjustment Strategy to improve file transfer performances using the co-allocation architecture [17] in Data Grids. In our approach, the workloads on selected replica servers are continuously adjusted during data transfers, and our approach can also reduce the idle times spent waiting for the slowest servers, and thus decrease file transfer completion times.

We also developed a new toolkit, called Cyber-Transformer that enables even inexperienced users to easily monitor replica source site statuses, manage replicas, and download files from multiple servers in parallel. Experimental results show the effectiveness of our proposed technique in improving transfer times and reducing overall idle time spent waiting for the slowest servers.

In future work, we will investigate providing more functions for our user-friendly interface, for example, auto parameters input, and auto scan to find better replica servers for downloading. We also plan to improve replica management, especially on the problem of replica consistency.

References

1. Allcock, B., Bester, J., Bresnahan, J., Chervenak, A., Foster, I., Kesselman, C., Meder, S., Nefedova, V., Quesnel, D., Tuecke, S.: Data Management and Transfer in High-Performance Computational Grid Environments. Parallel Computing 28(5), 749–771 (2002)
2. Allcock, B., Bester, J., Bresnahan, J., Chervenak, A., Foster, I., Kesselman, C., Meder, S., Nefedova, V., Quesnel, D., Tuecke, S.: Secure, efficient Data Transport and Replica Management for High-Performance Data-Intensive Computing. In: Proceedings of the Eighteenth IEEE Symposium on Mass Storage Systems and Technologies, pp. 13–28 (2001)
3. Allcock, B., Tuecke, S., Foster, I., Chervenak, A., Kesselman, C.: Protocols and Services for Distributed Data-Intensive Science. In: ACAT2000 Proceedings, pp. 161–163 (2000)
4. Chervenak, A., Deelman, E., Foster, I., Guy, L., Hoschek, W., Iamnitchi, A., Kesselman, C., Kunszt, P., Ripeanu, M.: Giggle: A Framework for Constructing Scalable Replica Location Services. In: Proceedings of Supercomputing 2002, Baltimore, MD (2002)
5. Chervenak, A., Foster, I., Kesselman, C., Salisbury, C., Tuecke, S.: The Data Grid: Towards an Architecture for the Distributed Management and Analysis of Large Scientific Datasets. Journal of Network and Computer Applications 23, 187–200 (2001)
6. Czajkowski, K., Fitzgerald, S., Foster, I., Kesselman, C.: Grid Information Services for Distributed Resource Sharing. In: Proceedings of the Tenth IEEE International Symposium on High-Performance Distributed Computing (HPDC-10'01), August 2001, pp. 181–194 (2001)
7. Czajkowski, K., Foster, I., Kesselman, C.: Resource Co-Allocation in Computational Grids. In: Proceedings of the Eighth IEEE International Symposium on High Performance Distributed Computing (HPDC-8'99) (August 1999)
8. Donno, F., Gaido, L., Ghiselli, A., Prelz, F., Sgaravatto, M.: DataGrid Prototype 1. In: Proceedings of the TERENA Networking Conference (June 2002), http://www.terena.nl/conferences/tnc2002/Papers/p5a2-ghiselli.pdf
9. Foster, I., Kesselman, C., Tuecke, S.: The Anatomy of the Grid: Enabling Scalable Virtual Organizations. International Journal of Supercomputer Applications and High Performance Computing 15(3), 200–222 (2001)
10. Foster, I., Kesselman, C.: Globus: A Metacomputing Infrastructure Toolkit. International Journal of Supercomputer Applications and High Performance Computing 11(2), 115–128 (1997)
11. Global Grid Forum, http://www.ggf.org/
12. Hoschek, W., Jaen-Martinez, J., Samar, A., Stockinger, H., Stockinger, K.: Data Management in an International Data Grid Project. In: First IEEE/ACM International Workshop on Grid Computing - Grid 2000, December 2000, Bangalore, India (2000)
13. IBM Red Books, Introduction to Grid Computing with Globus, IBM Press, http://www.redbooks.ibm.com/redbooks/pdfs/sg246895.pdf
14. Stockinger, H., Samar, A., Allcock, B., Foster, I., Holtman, K., Tierney, B.: File and Object Replication in Data Grids. Journal of Cluster Computing 5(3), 305–314 (2002)
15. SYSSTAT utilities home page, http://perso.wanadoo.fr/sebastien.godard/
16. The Globus Alliance, http://www.globus.org/
17. Vazhkudai, S.: Enabling the Co-Allocation of Grid Data Transfers. In: Proceedings of Fourth International Workshop on Grid Computing, November 2003, pp. 41–51 (2003)

18. Vazhkudai, S., Schopf, J.: Using Regression Techniques to Predict Large Data Transfers. International Journal of High Performance Computing Applications (IJHPCA) 17, 249–268 (2003)
19. Vazhkudai, S., Schopf, J.: Predicting Sporadic Grid Data Transfers. In: Proceedings of 11th IEEE International Symposium on High Performance Distributed Computing (HPDC-11 '02), July 2002, pp. 188–196 (2002)
20. Vazhkudai, S., Schopf, J., Foster, I.: Predicting the Performance of Wide Area Data Transfers. In: Proceedings of the 16th International Parallel and Distributed Processing Symposium (IPDPS 2002), April 2002, pp. 34–43 (2002)
21. Vazhkudai, S., Tuecke, S., Foster, I.: Replica Selection in the Globus Data Grid. In: Proceedings of the 1st International Symposium on Cluster Computing and the Grid (CCGRID 2001), May 2001, pp. 106–113 (2001)
22. Wolski, R., Spring, N., Hayes, J.: The Network Weather Service: A Distributed Resource Performance Forecasting Service for Metacomputing. Future Generation Computer Systems 15(5-6), 757–768 (1999)
23. Yang, C.T., Chen, C.H., Li, K.C., Hsu, C.H.: Performance Analysis of Applying Replica Selection Technology for Data Grid Environments. In: Malyshkin, V. (ed.) PaCT 2005. LNCS, vol. 3606, pp. 278–287. Springer, Heidelberg (2005)
24. Yang, C.T., Shih, P.C., Chen, S.Y.: A Domain-based Model for Efficient Network Information on Grid Computing Environments. IEICE Trans. Information and Systems, Special Issue on Parallel/Distributed Computing and Networking E89-D(2), 738–742 (2006) (accepted and to appear)
25. Yang, C.T., Wang, S.Y., Lin, C.H., Lee, M.H., Wu, T.Y.: Cyber-Transformer: A Toolkit for Files Transfer with Replica Management in Data Grid Environments. In: Proceedings of the Second Workshop on Grid Technologies and Applications (WoGTA'05), December 2005, pp. 73–80 (2005)
26. Yang, C.T., Yang, I.H., Chen, C.H., Wang, S.Y.: Implementation of a Dynamic Adjustment Mechanism with Efficient Replica Selection in Co-Allocation Data Grid Environments. In: Proceedings of the 21st Annual ACM Symposium on Applied Computing (SAC 2006) - Distributed Systems and Grid Computing Track, April 23-27, 2006, pp. 797–804 (2006)
27. Yang, C.T., Yang, I.H., Li, K.C., Hsu, C.H.: A Recursive-Adjustment Co-Allocation Scheme in Data Grid Environments. In: Hobbs, M., Goscinski, A.M., Zhou, W. (eds.) Distributed and Parallel Computing. LNCS, vol. 3719, pp. 40–49. Springer, Heidelberg (2005)
28. Yang, C.T., Yang, I.H., Li, K.C., Wang, S.Y.: Improvements on Dynamic Adjustment Mechanism in Co-Allocation Data Grid Environments. The Journal of Supercomputing (December 2006) (accepted and to appear)
29. Zhang, X., Freschl, J., Schopf, J.: A Performance Study of Monitoring and Information Services for Distributed Systems. In: Proceedings of 12th IEEE International Symposium on High Performance Distributed Computing (HPDC-12 '03), August 2003, pp. 270–282 (2003)
30. Venugopal, S., Buyya, R., Ramamohanarao, K.: A Taxonomy of Data Grids for Distributed Data Sharing, Management, and Processing. ACM Computing Surveys 38(1), 1–53 (2006)

Spatial Map Data Share and Parallel Dissemination System Based on Distributed Network Services and Digital Watermark

Dong Zhang[1,2], Depei Qian[1], Weiguo Wu[1], Ailong Liu[2],
Xuewei Yang[2], and Pen Han[2]

[1] Department of computer science, Xi'an Jiaotong University, Xi'an, China
Navgrid@163.com
[2] Xi'an Research Institute of Surveying and Mapping, Xi'an, China

Abstract. A distributed map data parallel dissemination system, which can be used to distribute spatial map data to remote users through different networks, is presented. The paper first defines spatial map data, associated metadata and network resource nodes with graphic formalization definition. Then, the relations between map data and network resources are established. Based on formalized definition to the whole system, a map data dissemination framework and a series of essential distributed CORBA services, conditions input methods based on three querying conditions are presented. We also explore network map copyright validating in dissemination course, and present an improved adaptive watermarking algorithm for vector digital maps whose data is the most difficult and necessary to watermark. Different from other methods, we compare the watermarked map with the original watermarked map, not with the primitive map, before extraction. The results show that compared with Direct Copy, our dissemination system can delivery spatial map data effectively. The transfer performance of CORBA services mode is almost equal to Direct Copy. The system can approach the biggest transfer rate more quickly but dependents on data amount weakly. And, the improved watermarking algorithm has better robustness.

Keywords: Map data, Metadata, Network services, Watermarking.

1 Introduction

The Map Data Network Dissemination system (MDND) is dissemination of Spatial Map Data (SMD) to remote users under network environment. The SMD data have such characteristics as storage in distributed form, high precision, mass data, multi-scales, which is suitable to be applied in the network environment [1]. Meanwhile, network has become the main mean to obtain SMD today and in future. The statistics data in developed countries show that more than half information search is correlative to spatial position. However, due to limited resources and developing technical means, the map data dissemination services through network lie in a relatively lower level in China. There are several technical issues lied in SMD dissemination process.

K. Li et al. (Eds.): NPC 2007, LNCS 4672, pp. 71–80, 2007.

They are SMD and map metadata management and application modes, network services design and configuration, whole data security technique, network transferring course and user ends [2]. Data security involves many research subjects. In this paper, we mainly research copyright validating algorithm being essential in dissemination. As the primary copyright validating approach, watermarking technology is difficulty and emphases, especially for vector map data focused in relative research fields.

2   Review of Correlative Technologies

Special dissemination systems in main developed countries have been realized and, some of them in America and England have been used in real dissemination although with simple functions and narrow application fields. Not only in developed countries, but also in developing countries, map dissemination systems are researched widely. For example, Surveying and Mapping Authority of the Republic of Slovenia has done a lot of work in the field of elaboration of the reference data sets [3].

In china, however, research on special map data dissemination system supporting all map types has just begun. Although there are vast map applications cases via internet, the map data type and quantity in the cases are limited and the area is always local.

At the same time, SMD is difficult to be processed in real time and employed in real demands from remote server nodes effectively without special dissemination system. Metadata is essential in remote SMD data access [4].

A static map may exist as a predefined image or a customized image created by a CGI Server-side utility program [5]. [6] has analyzed distributed module service technology. [7] studied data sharing and visualization based on ActiveX and Dcom. [8] gave out a JAVA network map access and display engine. [9] presented a method to implement data share by using Web Service frame. As a whole, the disadvantages through above technologies to implement SMD share and dissemination lie in the following aspects, which make a special dissemination system in urgent need:

(1) Weak for complex computation, high precision and discrete distribution;
(2) Weak for virtual computation, 3-D visualization in SMD dissemination;
(3) Limited data types;
(4) Low repetitive use efficiency for software codes and resources.

In network dissemination system, digital map copyright could not be ignored. Digital watermarking is definitely one of the most successful solutions. Vector maps, the most important type in SMD, are constructed by coordinates of points, lines and polygons whose format have the characteristic of flow data not raster data [10]. The algorithms for vector maps need to consider the robustness under revisions. Therefore, most classic watermark embedding and detection algorithms could not be applied directly to vector maps [11]. Probably due to these difficulties, we know of only a few published works on watermarking of vector digital maps. [12] subdivided a vector map into some rectangular blocks of adaptive sizes according to the density of vertices and embedded each bit by displacing the vertices in a block. [13] and [14] proposed the Fourier descriptors for watermarking of graph images. [15] divided a vector map into rectangular blocks with the uniform area.

We have constructed an experimental MDND system based on CORBA Visibroker framework and an improved adaptive watermarking algorithm for vector digital maps.

3 Dissemination Method

3.1 SMD Resources in Network Environment

Definition 1: Network Resources (NR) is defined as a relax Graph, G= (N, A), where N is the network nodes set classified as SMD resources nodes N_r and metadata information nodes N_i, and A is the connections set. $|N|=n'$ is the nodes number, and the ith node is represented by n_i, and the W-n_i is the weight of time cost for searching n_i. $|A|=m$ is the sides number, and the ith side is represented by arc$_i$, and the W-arc$_i$ is the weight of time cost for searching arc$_i$.

Definition 2: R stands for network resources NR, and $|R|$ represents the resources number. We define the relations between resources r and resources nodes (n_i) as In (n_i, r), $n_i \in N_r$. In(n_i,r)=1 represents r is on the resource node n_i.

Definition 3: SMD Metadata is classified to six classes such as MRas, MIma, MVec, MEle, MBen and MGeo, which present the metadata of raster, image, vector, elevation, benchmark and geodesy orderly. Simply they are presented as M_{sub}^i. We define content entity and element set as follows. SVec (k,r) represents the element r of entity k in MVec.

$$M_{ent} = \{ SRas\ (k,r),\ SIma\ (k,r),\ SVec\ (k,r),\ SEle(k,r),\ SBen(k,r),\ SGeo\ (k,r) \} \qquad (1)$$

Definition 4: Define Metadata base M-DB as (2). Sub-databases B_M^i can be defined as (3) corresponding to M_{sub}^i and data dictionary B_i'. The database establishment rules are denoted as C_i. Here, B_i' is relative to comparison table of data, data field, and other tables.

$$BM = \{ BRas,\ BIma,\ BVec,\ BEle,\ BBen,\ BGeo \} \qquad (2)$$

$$B_M^i = C_i\ (\ M_{sub}^i\ ,\ B_i'\ ) \qquad (3)$$

Definition 5: The relationships among metadata-set, metadata-base and information nodes n_i: Logically, Set (B_M^i), including one or several B_M^i, is defined as a network information node $n_i \in N_r$, here In (n_i, r)=1, and r= Set (B_M^i).

3.2 MDND and CORBA Distributed Services

According to method for entity and relation, define D= (E, R') , as follows:

Definition 6: The entity of MDND is a five-elements set. Here, U, BM, B, c, s stand respectively for users, metadata and SMD base, query condition, and network service.

$$E = \{U, BM, B, c, s\} \tag{4}$$

Definition 7: The relations in MDND are $R' = \{R_{sub}^i, 1 \leq i \leq 6\}$, R_{sub}^i represents the all relations within entities. How to design the correlative services depends on MDND entity relations. Several entity relations and services are designed as Table 1. It should be pointed out that the given services S3-S10 (S4 exception) are formalization services, which must be changed to different service contents due to different data types [16].

There are also many other absolute computations in the system called absolute services and loosely connected with network, shown in Table 2.

Table 1. Corresponding table between entity relations and distributed services

R'	Entity/ relation	Meaning	IDL definition for CORBA Service	Service content
R_{sub}^1	(U, c)	Acquisition term input	S1:UserManagment() S2:IORService()	User management service IOR service
R_{sub}^2	(c, BM)	For metadata	S3:Metalocate()	Search for metadata-bases
R_{sub}^3	(BM, s)	Metadata bases services	S4:RightPro() S5:MetaDataQuery() S6:MetaDataGet()	Data authorization service Metadata searching service Metadata acquisition service
R_{sub}^4	(BM, B)	SMD bases location	S7:Maplocate()	SMD route pointing service
R_{sub}^5	(B, s)	SMD bases distributed services	S4: RightPro() S8:DataQuery() S9:DataPreDisplay() S10:DataGet()	SMD contents searching Pre-display and confirming SMD acquisition service
R_{sub}^6	(U, B)	DownloadSMD	S11:DailyRecord()	Log service

Table 2. Absolute services table

Absolute Service in Servers (before transferred from servers)	Absolute Service in Client (after received on clients)
S12:DataCompression() S13:DataEncrypting() S14:WatermarkEmbedding() S15:DataEncapsulation()	S16:DataDe-compression() S17:DataDe-encrypting() S18:WatermarkDetection() S19:DataBackuping() S20:CoherenceChecking() S21:CacheManagement() S22:DisplayEngine()

3.3 MDND Architecture Based on Distributed Services

The dissemination system architecture based on CORBA ORB is shown as Fig. 1. Here, only a part of main data operation services, which can reflect dissemination flow, are given. Metadata and SMD are distributed in server ends. For SMD, it is logically comprised of several bases according to the data types. The SMD Data operation services include data query, pre-display, acquisition of S8-S10 and authorization service S4. Moreover, a series of complex algorithms without close relations with network operations, such as data encryption, data compression, watermarking, etc, are designed as absolute services, which are essential to dissemination. Similar to SMD, metadata is supported mainly by the data query service S5, the acquisition service S6 and the authorization S4.

The client end shows the whole dissemination flow, including logical demands presentation, data de-compression and de-encryption, watermark detection, pre-display and display of metadata and SMD, user and log management (S11, S16-22), etc. This paper mainly research network operation services and absolute services S14, S18.

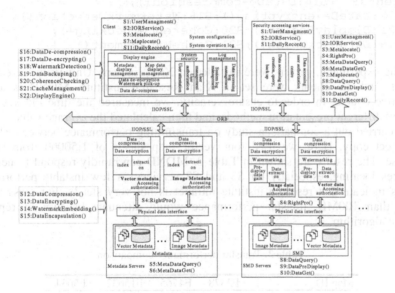

Fig. 1. Distributed CORBA services chart in MDND

3.4 Realization of MDND

From users' demands to object data, the operation steps are as follows:

(1) Demands logical presentation: There are three query methods related to R^1_{sub} to build correlative query condition α, they are fulfilled based on catalog tree, visualization map window, and blurry restriction condition query.

(2) Metadata and SMD retrieving services: Compared with reference [16], this paper designed metadata centralization query service Metalocate() and SMD route

pointing service Maplocate(). The searching procedure can be considered as a path in graph G from start resource node n_0 to the node n_i. The dissemination flow shows as:

Dissemination (data type: Mvec, Bvec, Input: α, Mvec,Bvec, Output: SMD-Vector Map)

```
{Input Conditions(α);
Servers: S3:Metalocate(Nᵢ,α);
If (S4:RightPro())then { S5:MetaDataQuery();
  S12:DataCompression(); S13:DataEncrypting();
  S6:MetaDataGet();   }
S7:Maplocate(Nᵣ,Mⁱsub(k,r));
If (S4:RightPro())then{ S8:DataQuery();
  S9: DataPreDisplay(); S12:DataCompression();
  S13:DataEncrypting(); S14:WatermarkEmbedding();
  S15:DataEncapsulation();S10: DataGet(); }

Clients:  {S16:DataDe-compression();
  S17:DataDe-encrypting();S18:WatermarkDetection();
  S22:DisplayEngine();S20:CoherenceChecking();
  S19:DataBackuping();S21:CacheManagement(); } }
```

In the experiment, servers were installed in Xian Jiaotong University linked with internet, and the clients were set in Xian Research Institute. MDND is a user interactive course. In order to ensure veracity, we measured the time indexes three times by different presentation methods, and then calculated the average value.

We carried out a comparison study on transmitting performance between MDND and direct copy. Here, we used four vector map sheets of 1:50000 from Oracle database. The results are shown in Table 3. MDND can rapidly respond to network resources locating, especially for S3 and S7 services. A few instable performance indexes indicate that research institute intranet is not very steady. For mass image bigger than 100MB, transfer performance would attenuate because of repeated iterative algorithm.

Table 3. Transfer performance comparison

Map ID	F2378	F4765	F15632	F5634
Map data (MB)	19.0	22.0	17.9	18.9
S3:Metalocate() (ms)	32	15	16	16
S7:Maplocate() (ms)	16	31	16	32
S10:DataGet() (KB/s)	573	450	498	525
Copy (KB/s)	626	513	564	567

4   Copyright Validating

4.1   Embedding and Extraction

Embedding algorithm should explicitly make use of perceptually significant features in the data [17]. In the algorithm introduced here, the embedded intensity of watermark will be modulated adaptively according to the corresponding density of vertices. After the subdivision, according to the corresponding density of vertices, the embedded intensity of watermark in each block will be modulated adaptively as formula (5) and formula (6);

$$\alpha_s = (1-\gamma) \times \alpha_{max} + \gamma \times \alpha_{min} \tag{5}$$

$$\gamma = [\max(NP_s) - NP_s] / [\max(NP_s) - \min(NP_s)] \tag{6}$$

α_s $(s = 1, 2, \cdots k * l)$ is the embedded intensity of rectangle blocks, α_{max} is the maximum of embedded intensity, and α_{min} is the minimum of embedded intensity. α_{max} is chosen within the range of the maximal mapping error so that the displacement won't affect visual qualities of maps. NP_s is the vertex numbers of rectangle blocks, $\max(NP_s)$ is the maximum of NP_s, and $\min(NP_s)$ is the minimum of NP_s.

According to the corresponding embedded intensity, the watermark is embedded into the vector map by displacing the vertices in the rectangles. Repeatedly, embedding each bit c times increases resiliency of the watermark against additive random noise. Formula (7) gives the method to compute c. NP is the number of vertices in the map.

$$c = [NP/n] \tag{7}$$

When extraction, different from other methods we compare the watermarked map with the original watermarked map, not with the primitive map. The original watermarked map, published to the users, is the unrevised watermarked map directly derived from the primitive map and has the same record order with the primitive map. If we align the watermarked map with the primitive map directly, it is very possible to make mistakes because there are two types of noises (watermark data and random noises) between the two types of map data. This bas been done by minimizing the Euclid distance between vertices in the watermarked and the original watermarked map.

When extracting the watermark image, we use mean-value detection, different from the double-threshold combinative detection used by Reference [15]. The algorithm can get the valid embedding times and the total embedding bits of each pixel in the two-value watermark image through the alignment and comparison mentioned. Then the mean value of the total embedding bits of each pixel can be easily computed and converted to the corresponding pixel value of the two-value watermarking image.

4.2 Experiments and Results

In the experiment, we used a 1:50000-scale vector map which has 10 feature layers and 380368 vertices, partly shown in Fig. 2, and its size is 9.85 MB. The two-value watermark image used here is a 128x128 Bmp file, shown in Fig. 2, and the size is 10.0 KB. The maximum of embedded intensity is set to 2.5m, and the minimum of embedded intensity is set to 1m. The map is divided into 30x3020 blocks. The watermark image was embedded into abscissa of vertices.

   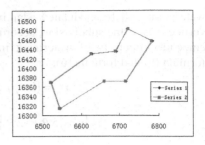

Fig. 2. Map and watermark image in experiment   **Fig. 3.** Visual difference after zooming in

We compared the coordinate of watermarked map with the primitive map to observe the change of coordinate made by watermarking. The range of coordinate change is within ±2m, and the watermarked result is satisfied with mapping demand. In Fig. 3, the visual difference between the two data is still very little after zooming in many levels. Here, Series 1 denotes primitive data and Series 2 denotes watermarked data.

Table 4 shows the results of the attack experiments under random noise, vertices insertion, vertices deletion, etc.. The advantage of the improved algorithm is especially presented in random noise of amplitude 28m. Fig. 4 gives the results of both algorithms against random noise attacks. (1) is the improved algorithm, (2) is [15] algorithm. The improved algorithm slightly outperformed the one in Reference [15] when we deleted 371527 vertices from the map data. From the experiments, we also found both algorithms withstand vertices insertion and random noise of amplitude 8m.

Table 4. Performance in various attacks

Attacks		Improved algorithm	[15] algorithm
Random	8 m	1.00	1.00
noise	28 m	0.90	0.29
vertices insertion		1.00	1.00
vertices deletion		0.98	0.96

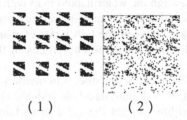

(1)   (2)

Fig. 4. Results of random noise attack

5   Conclusion and Future Work

The experiment results indicate that: ①Remote user can get SMD conveniently with integrated SMD and network environment, which expands data application channel. ②The services have excellent performances in metadata and SMD management, SMD location and accessing, and SMD transmitting, etc. ③User is able to access SMD data in real time only after registration, authorization, request, download, and configuration. ④The architecture is better for expanding servers, services, SMD resources, and overcomes other systems' disadvantage of bad expansibility. Furthermore, the system supports C++ environment, complex SMD computation and mass data. At the same time, an improved watermarking algorithm for vector digital map presents the concept of original watermarked map in extraction. Experiments show that the improved algorithm is more resilient against many types of attacks.

In the future, we will study user dynamic customization technology and the re-developing capability on the existing system.

References

1. Tsou, M., Buttenfield, B.: Client/Server components sand Metadata objects for distributed Geographic Information Services. In: Proceedings of GIS/LIS'98, November 1998, pp. 590–599 (1998)
2. Futrelle, J.: Developing metadata standards for science data reuse in NCSA's distributed Grid architecture, pp. 1217–1219. IEEE, Los Alamitos (2000)
3. Azman, I., Peter, T.: Data dissemination and pricing policy for spatial data at the Surveying and Mapping Authority of the republic of Slovenia. In: 8th EC-GI & GIS work shop ESDI-A work in Progress Dublin, Ireland, July 2002, pp. 3–5 (2002)
4. Cromley, R.G., McGlamery, P.: Integrating spatial metadata and data dissemination over the internet. In: IASSIST Quarterly Spering, pp. 13–16 (2002)
5. Kobben, B.: Publishing maps on the web. In: Kraak, M.J., Brown, A. (eds.) Web Cartography, Taylor and Francis, New York (2001)
6. Wang, Y., Ge, L., Rizos, C., et al.: Spatial data sharing on GRID. Geomatics Research Australia (81), 3–18 (2004)
7. Zhang, D.: Map data visualization browser technology on network environment. Zhenzhou: Institute of Surveying and Mapping, Information Engineering University (2005)
8. Laszewski, G.v., Foster, I., Gawor, J., Lane, P.: A Java Commodity Grid Kit. In: Concurrency and Computation: Practice and Experience, vol. 13(8-9), pp. 643–662 (2001)
9. Wang, F.: A distributed Geographic Information System on the common object request broker Architecture (CORBA). Geoinformatic, 89–115 (2000)
10. Obelheiro, P.R., Fraga, J.S.: Role-based Access Control for CORBA Distributed Object System. In: Proceedings of the 7th International Workshop on Object-oriented Real-time Dependable Systems (2002)
11. Chung, H.-H., Chen, T., Kun, K.-S.: Watermarking 2D/3D Graphics for Copyright Protection. In: Proceedings of IEEE International Conference Acoustics, Speech, and Signal Processing, vol. 4, pp. 720–723 (2003)
12. Ohbuchi, R., Ueda, H., Endoh, S.: Robust Watermarking of Vector Digital Maps. In: Proc ICME2002, Lausanne, vol. 1, pp. 577–580. IEEE Computer Society Press, Los Alamitos (2002)
13. Nikolaidis, N., Pitas, I., Solachidis, V.: Fourier descriptors watermarking of vector graphics images. In: Proceedings of XIII Brazilian Symposium on Computer Graphics and Image Processing vol. 3, pp. 9–12 (2000)
14. Solachidis, V., Nikolaidis, N.: Watermarking Polygonal Lines Using Fourier Descriptors. In: IEEE 2000 ICASSP, pp. 1955–1958 (2000)

15. LI, Y.-Y., XU, L.-P.: Copyright protection of the vector map using the digital watermark. Journal of Xidian University 31(5), 719–723 (2004)
16. Krauter, K., Buyya, R., Maheswarn, M.: A taxonomy and Survey of Grid resource management systems for distributed computing. In: Software Practice and Experience, vol. 32(2), pp. 135–164 (2002)
17. Kutter, M., Bhattacharjee, S.K., Ebrahimi, T.: Towards Second Generation Watermarking Schemes. In: IEEE 1999 ICIP, vol. 1, pp. 320–323 (1999)

Managing Email Overload with an Automatic Nonparametric Clustering Approach

Yang Xiang[1], Wanlei Zhou[2], and Jinjun Chen[3]

[1] School of Management and Information Systems, Central Queensland University
Rockhampton, Queensland 4700, Australia
y.xiang@cqu.edu.au
[2] School of Engineering and Information Technology, Deakin University
Burwood, Victoria 3125, Australia
wanlei@deakin.edu.au
[3] Faculty of Information & Communication Technologies, Swinburne University of
Technology, Hawthorn 3122, Australia
jchen@ict.swin.edu.au

Abstract. Email overload is a recent problem that there is increasingly difficulty people have faced to process the large number of emails received daily. Currently this problem becomes more and more serious and it has already affected the normal usage of email as a knowledge management tool. It has been recognized that categorizing emails into meaningful groups can greatly save cognitive load to process emails and thus this is an effective way to manage email overload problem. However, most current approaches still require significant human input when categorizing emails. In this paper we develop an automatic email clustering system, underpinned by a new nonparametric text clustering algorithm. This system does not require any predefined input parameters and can automatically generate meaningful email clusters. Experiments show our new algorithm outperforms existing text clustering algorithms with higher efficiency in terms of computational time and clustering quality measured by different gauges.

Keywords: Email, overload, text clustering, knowledge management.

1 Introduction

As part of daily life, email has made significant changes to the way of exchanging and storing information. According to the estimate in [1], the number of worldwide email messages sent daily has reached 84 billion in 2006. On one side, email can be an effective knowledge management tool that conveniently enables fast and accurate communication. On the other side, the increasing volume of email threatens to cause a state of "email overload" [2] where the volume of messages exceeds individuals' capacity to process them. This is because of the fact that the majority of email users use email as an archival tool and never discard messages [3]. As this gradual congestion of a user's mailbox with messages ranging from working related documents and personal information, users are becoming unable to successfully

K. Li et al. (Eds.): NPC 2007, LNCS 4672, pp. 81–90, 2007.

finding an important archived message hidden in their mailbox without any structure. We urgently need an effective managing tool to solve the email overload problem.

Recently people realize that categorizing email messages into different groups can significantly reduce the cognitive load on email users [4]. If an email system can present messages in a form that is consistent with the way people process and store information, it will greatly help them in comprehending and retrieving the information contained within those groups [5]. Currently categorizing email messages often involves manually creating folders in users' mailbox and setting up rules to dispatch incoming emails [6, 7]. This requires heavy cognitive load of creating the folder structure and the rules, which can be difficult for normal users.

In this paper, we propose a new automatic nonparametric clustering approach to manage email overload. We implement this system with a client-side prototype application. It can automatically generate email clusters according to emails' content (title and body) by a new text clustering algorithm. It does not require users to input any predefined parameter and therefore it is especially useful for non-technical users. The evaluation shows our approach achieves good clustering results with high efficiency and high clustering quality.

2   System Design

The system design goal of the automatic email clustering system is to automatically categorize emails into different meaningful groups and thus to alleviate human cognitive load to process emails. The emails in clusters the system produced must be of same relative group. We also notice a fact that most actual email users manually create 1-level folders in their mail box, rather than create multi-level hierarchical folders because exploring the multi-level hierarchical structure is also burdensome. Therefore, we choose 1-level folders containing emails as the output in this system. We implement the system by a client-side prototype application. It first read email messages from an email client's data file, then it converts email texts into vector matrix and generate similarity matrix. The details regarding algorithms will be introduced in section 3. After the matrices are generated, they are input into our new nonparametric text clustering algorithm. The algorithm produces email clusters. Finally the application outputs 1-level email clusters in a user interface. The flow chart can be found in figure 1.

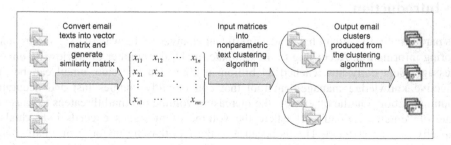

Fig. 1. System flow chart

3   A New Nonparametric Text Clustering Algorithm

3.1   Cluster Validity

To validate a cluster analysis solution, there are many validation techniques such as Hubert's Γ statistic [8, 9], significance tests on variables (MANOVA) [10], and Monte Carlo procedures [9]. We use Hubert's Γ statistic which does not require predefined parameters to validate the cluster structures. The underlying idea is that our algorithm aims at evaluating the degree of agreement between a predetermined partition and the inherent clustering structure. Therefore, our algorithm combines the cluster optimization and clustering itself together, which produces high quality clusters and achieve high efficiency.

First let us define an $N \times N$ proximity matrix $Y = [Y(i, j)]$, where

$$Y(i, j) = \begin{cases} 1, \text{if emails } i \text{ and } j \text{ are clustered in the same cluster} \\ 0, \text{if emails } i \text{ and } j \text{ are not clustered in the same cluster} \end{cases} \tag{1}$$

Consistently, the inherent clustering structure can be represented by using an $N \times N$ proximity matrix $X = [X(i, j)]$, to observe correlation coefficient of emails i and j, which means the proximity of point i to point j in the whole email space.

The Hubert's Γ statistic then can be obtained by measuring the correlation between these two symmetric matrices $X = [X(i, j)]$ and $Y = [Y(i, j)]$ as follows

$$\Gamma = \frac{1}{n(n-1)/2} \sum_{i=1}^{n-1} \sum_{j=i+1}^{n} \left(\frac{X(i, j) - \overline{X}}{\sigma_X} \right) \left(\frac{Y(i, j) - \overline{Y}}{\sigma_Y} \right) \tag{2}$$

Where $\overline{X}$ and $\overline{Y}$ are the means of the values in X and Y, and σ_X and σ_Y are the standard deviations. The value of Hubert's Γ statistic scaled from -1 to 1, and a large absolute value of the normalized statistic implies well separated and compact clusters. (2) can be further written as

$$\begin{aligned} \Gamma &= \frac{\sum_{i=1}^{n-1} \sum_{j=i+1}^{n} (X(i, j) - \overline{X})(Y(i, j) - \overline{Y})}{\sqrt{\sum_{i=1}^{n-1} \sum_{j=i+1}^{n} (X(i, j) - \overline{X})^2} \sqrt{\sum_{i=1}^{n-1} \sum_{j=i+1}^{n} (Y(i, j) - \overline{Y})^2}} \\ &= \frac{\sum_{i=1}^{n-1} \sum_{j=i+1}^{n} (X(i, j)Y(i, j) - \overline{X}Y(i, j) - X(i, j)\overline{Y} + \overline{X}\overline{Y})}{\sqrt{\sum_{i=1}^{n-1} \sum_{j=i+1}^{n} (X(i, j) - \overline{X})^2} \sqrt{\sum_{i=1}^{n-1} \sum_{j=i+1}^{n} (Y(i, j) - \overline{Y})^2}} \end{aligned} \tag{3}$$

The Hubert's Γ statistic has twofold meanings. First, the proximity matrices X and Y measures are generic to cover both inter-class and intra-class statistics. Second, when the product of $X(i, j)$ and $Y(i, j)$ is large, it is very likely that the email points are apart and assigned to different clusters with distant mean vectors. Therefore we can see that the larger the Hubert's Γ statistic means stronger evidence there are compact clusters generated. To this end, we use the maximum Hubert's Γ statistic as our cluster validation measure as follows

$$Validity = \arg(\max(\Gamma)) \tag{4}$$

3.2 Vector Space Model for Text Clustering

Before emails can be classified into different clusters, they must be represented by a numerical form. In this paper we adopt the vector space model [11], which has been used in Information Retrieval to compute the degree of similarity between each text document stored in the system. In this model, each email is converted to a vector e, in the term space, as follows.

$$e = \{tf_1, \cdots, tf_i, \cdots, tf_K\} \tag{5}$$

Where tf_i is the frequency of the ith term in the email. In the vector space model, Intra-similarity is quantified by measuring the raw frequency of a term t_i inside a email document e_i. tf_i is usually normalized as formula (6) to prevent a bias towards longer emails (which may have a higher term frequency regardless of the actual importance of that term in the email) to give a measurement of the importance of the term t_i within the particular email.

$$tf_i = \frac{n_i}{\sum_k n_k} \tag{6}$$

Where n_i is the number of emails in which the index term t_i appears, and the denominator is the number of occurrences of all terms.

Inter-cluster dissimilarity is quantified by measuring the inverse of the frequency of a term t_i among the emails in the whole space. This factor is usually referred as the inverse document frequency or the idf factor. The motivation for usage of an idf factor is that terms which appear in many emails are not necessarily useful for distinguishing a relevant email from non-relevant ones. idf can be written as

$$idf_i = \log \frac{N}{n_i} \tag{7}$$

Where N is the total number of emails in the system. Then $tfidf$ can be used to filter out common terms which have little discriminating power, as defined in the follows.

$$ifidf = tf_i \times idf_i \tag{8}$$

As our clustering algorithm has many iteration steps, in each iteration step the goal is to separate the existing collection of emails into two sets: the first one that is composed of emails related to the currently generated cluster and the second one is composed of emails not related it. Two main issues need to be resolved, intra-cluster similarity and inter-cluster dissimilarity. The quantification of intra-cluster similarity provides the features which better describe the emails in the currently generated cluster. Furthermore, the quantification of inter-cluster dissimilarity represents the features which better distinguish the emails in currently generated cluster. Therefore, intra-similarity is quantified by measuring the term frequency tf_i. Inter-cluster dissimilarity is quantified by measuring the inverse of the frequency idf_i.

3.3 Nonparametric Text Clustering Algorithm

Our new nonparametric text clustering algorithm has the following 7 steps.

1. Construct the data matrix with the vector space model;
2. Standardize the data matrix;
3. Compute the similarity matrix and input similarity matrix into the clustering procedure;
4. Select a seed for clustering;
5. Add or delete point into the currently generated cluster with Hubert's Γ statistic validity test;
6. Repeat step 5 until no point can be allocated;
7. Repeat step 4 to 6 until all the clusters are generated.

The key differences between our algorithm and traditional clustering algorithms such as hierarchical agglomerative algorithm and partitioning-based k-means algorithm [9] are first, there is no need to reconstruct the data or similarity matrix for each iteration, which can greatly save computational time; and second, it incorporates the validation part into to the clustering process, instead of putting the validation after all clusters are generated, which can optimize the quality of clustering all the time.

The clustering result does not depend on the selection of seed in step 4, although a good selection can speed up the clustering process. We use Euclidean distance measure to choose the seed, which has most neighbour points with the average Euclidean distances among points. The Euclidean distance measurement can be written as

$$d_{ij} = \left\{ \sum_{k=1}^{p} \left(X_{ik} - X_{jk} \right)^2 \right\}^{\frac{1}{2}} \tag{9}$$

Where X_{ik} is the value of the kth variable for the ith point. The average Euclidean distances then can be written as

$$\bar{d} = \frac{1}{n(n-1)/2} \sum_{i=1}^{n-1} \sum_{j=i}^{n} d_{ij} \tag{10}$$

3.4 Computational Simplification

The Hubert's statistic is robust because the inter-class and intra-class information is embedded into cluster evaluation. However, the original Hubert's statistic approach requires high computation load. Therefore, we make further simplification for (3) as follows.

$$\Gamma = \frac{\sum_{i=1}^{n-1}\sum_{j=i+1}^{n}\left(X(i,j)Y(i,j)-\bar{X}Y(i,j)-X(i,j)\bar{Y}+\overline{XY}\right)}{\sqrt{\sum_{i=1}^{n-1}\sum_{j=i+1}^{n}\left(X(i,j)-\bar{X}\right)^2}\sqrt{\sum_{i=1}^{n-1}\sum_{j=i+1}^{n}\left(Y(i,j)-\bar{Y}\right)^2}}$$

$$= \frac{\sum_{i=1}^{n-1}\sum_{j=i+1}^{n}X(i,j)Y(i,j)-\frac{\sum_{i=1}^{n-1}\sum_{j=i+1}^{n}X(i,j)}{n(n-1)/2}\sum_{i=1}^{n-1}\sum_{j=i+1}^{n}Y(i,j)-\frac{\sum_{i=1}^{n-1}\sum_{j=i+1}^{n}Y(i,j)}{n(n-1)/2}\sum_{i=1}^{n-1}\sum_{j=i+1}^{n}X(i,j)+\frac{\sum_{i=1}^{n-1}\sum_{j=i+1}^{n}X(i,j)\sum_{i=1}^{n-1}\sum_{j=i+1}^{n}Y(i,j)}{n(n-1)/2}}{\sqrt{\sum_{i=1}^{n-1}\sum_{j=i+1}^{n}\left(X(i,j)-\frac{\sum_{i=1}^{n-1}\sum_{j=i+1}^{n}X(i,j)}{n(n-1)/2}\right)^2}\sqrt{\sum_{i=1}^{n-1}\sum_{j=i+1}^{n}\left(Y(i,j)-\frac{\sum_{i=1}^{n-1}\sum_{j=i+1}^{n}Y(i,j)}{n(n-1)/2}\right)^2}} \tag{11}$$

$$= \frac{\left(\frac{n(n-1)}{2}\sum_{i=1}^{n-1}\sum_{j=i+1}^{n}X(i,j)Y(i,j)-\sum_{i=1}^{n-1}\sum_{j=i+1}^{n}X(i,j)\sum_{i=1}^{n-1}\sum_{j=i+1}^{n}Y(i,j)\right)}{\sqrt{\frac{n(n-1)}{2}\sum_{i=1}^{n-1}\sum_{j=i+1}^{n}X(i,j)^2-\left(\sum_{i=1}^{n-1}\sum_{j=i+1}^{n}X(i,j)\right)^2}\sqrt{\frac{n(n-1)}{2}\sum_{i=1}^{n-1}\sum_{j=i+1}^{n}Y(i,j)^2-\left(\sum_{i=1}^{n-1}\sum_{j=i+1}^{n}Y(i,j)\right)^2}}$$

From this formula we find many parts can be pre-calculated when the data and similarity matrix are given, which is before the iteration (from step 4 to 6) starts. If we can pre-calculate these parts, which are defined as follows, the computational time can be greatly saved.

$$A = \frac{n(n-1)}{2} \tag{12}$$

$$B = \sum_{i=1}^{n-1}\sum_{j=i+1}^{n}X(i,j) \tag{13}$$

$$C = \sqrt{\frac{n(n-1)}{2}\sum_{i=1}^{n-1}\sum_{j=i+1}^{n}X(i,j)^2-\left(\sum_{i=1}^{n-1}\sum_{j=i+1}^{n}X(i,j)\right)^2} \tag{14}$$

Then by substituting (12)(13)(14) into (11) we have

$$\Gamma = \frac{A\sum_{i=1}^{n-1}\sum_{j=i+1}^{n}X(i,j)Y(i,j)-B\sum_{i=1}^{n-1}\sum_{j=i+1}^{n}Y(i,j)}{C\sqrt{\frac{n(n-1)}{2}\sum_{i=1}^{n-1}\sum_{j=i+1}^{n}Y(i,j)^2-\left(\sum_{i=1}^{n-1}\sum_{j=i+1}^{n}Y(i,j)\right)^2}} \tag{15}$$

Therefore the actual computation needed in each iteration is for those parts with $Y(i,j)$.

4 Evaluation

4.1 Measurements

The performance of a text clustering algorithm can be evaluated in terms of computational time, and quality measure (high intra-cluster similarity and low inter-cluster similarity). We first use some unlabelled email data sets to test our algorithm on the first two measurements. We also compare our result with other two clustering algorithms, hierarchical agglomerative algorithm (using the nearest neighbour algorithm) and k-means algorithm. The quality of clustering is measured by using different measurements, Hubert's Γ statistic, simple matching coefficient, and Jaccard coefficient. Readers can find the definitions of simple matching coefficient and Jaccard coefficient in [9]. A higher value in these measurements indicates a higher clustering quality.

4.2 Data Sets

All the email data sets are from real life email collections in a university environment. Stop words are removed from the emails before performing clustering process. Suffix-stripping algorithm is also used to perform stemming. The data sets' details are shown in table 1.

4.3 Computational Time and Quality of Clustering

We compare our clustering results with other clustering algorithms. The numbers of main clusters produced by each algorithm are shown in table 2. Here we choose the clusters with email number greater than 5 as main clusters because grouping emails into even smaller clusters will require people's cognitive load to search through a large number of groups and therefore those clusters become useless. From this table we can see our algorithm can match the labelled data set 5 and 6 very well in terms of cluster number.

Table 1. Details of data set

Data Set No.	Labelled by human	Number of emails	Number of clusters	Number of words
1	No	1023	-	17650
2	No	1235	-	16432
3	No	2045	-	30215
4	No	3987	-	33442
5	Yes	342	7	2032
6	Yes	1126	12	7839

Table 2. Numbers of main clusters

Data Set	Nonparametric Text Clustering	Hierarchical agglomerative	K-means
1	14	16	10
2	13	15	10
3	15	17	12
4	16	15	15
5	7	12	7
6	12	13	12

Table 3. Computational time (seconds)

Data Set	Nonparametric Text Clustering	Hierarchical agglomerative	K-means
1	28.7	232	98.2
2	20.3	212	97.5
3	58.7	538	211
4	135	1207	484
5	9.21	101	42.1
6	22.2	215	103

Table 4. Hubert's Γ statistic

Data Set	Nonparametric Text Clustering	Hierarchical agglomerative	K-means
1	0.764	0.563	0.329
2	0.793	0.542	0.321
3	0.821	0.598	0.332
4	0.866	0.457	0.319
5	0.902	0.788	0.438
6	0.791	0.554	0.337

Table 3 shows the computational time of each algorithm. The time unit is second. From the table we can see our nonparametric text clustering algorithm performs much faster than both hierarchical agglomerative algorithm and k-means algorithm. For example, for data set 1, hierarchical agglomerative algorithm needs 808% of time of our algorithm to perform the clustering, and k-means algorithm needs 342% of time of our algorithm to perform the clustering. From the absolute computational time point of view, our algorithm also costs reasonably low. For example, when classifying data set 4 with 3987 emails, the computation time is 135 seconds (about 2 minutes), which is a reasonable response for a clustering system. We also find that k-means algorithm is faster than hierarchical agglomerative algorithm in all the runs, which conforms that k-means has lower time complexity than hierarchical agglomerative algorithm.

The average Hubert's Γ statistic of each algorithm is shown in table 4. From the table we can see for all the data sets, the Hubert's Γ statistic is higher than 0.764 if our clustering algorithm is used. Our algorithm outperforms others in this measurement, which means the clusters produced by our algorithm have higher intra-cluster similarity and lower inter-cluster similarity than other algorithms. Hierarchical agglomerative algorithm is better than k-means algorithm in terms of clustering quality measured by Hubert's Γ statistic.

The average simple matching coefficient of each algorithm is shown in table 5. Again we find our algorithm has better clustering quality measured by simple matching coefficient than both hierarchical agglomerative algorithm and k-means algorithm. The simple matching coefficient of k-means is lower than both our algorithm and hierarchical agglomerative algorithm.

The average Jaccard coefficient of each algorithm is shown in table 6. The Jaccard coefficient is often more sensitive than the simple matching coefficient sometimes the negative matches are a dominant factor. From the table we find our algorithm achieved above 0.821 Jaccard coefficients for all the data sets. Hierarchical agglomerative algorithm has slightly lower Jaccard coefficient than our algorithm from data set 1, 4, and 5. It has slightly higher Jaccard coefficient than our algorithm from data set 2, 3, and 6. K-means has much lower Jaccard coefficient than both our algorithm and hierarchical agglomerative algorithm.

From the above results we can clearly see our text clustering algorithm outperforms traditional hierarchical agglomerative algorithm and k-means algorithm in terms of computational time and clustering quality which is measured by Hubert's Γ statistic, simple matching coefficient, and Jaccard coefficient.

Table 5. Simple matching coefficient

Data Set	Nonparametric Text Clustering	Hierarchical agglomerative	K-means
1	0.978	0.912	0.839
2	0.974	0.923	0.856
3	0.964	0.918	0.832
4	0.939	0.921	0.813
5	0.991	0.985	0.903
6	0.971	0.922	0.847

Table 6. Jaccard coefficient

Data Set	Nonparametric Text Clustering	Hierarchical agglomerative	K-means
1	0.883	0.821	0.475
2	0.821	0.832	0.442
3	0.842	0.846	0.398
4	0.881	0.826	0.338
5	0.899	0.853	0.491
6	0.823	0.827	0.448

5 Related Work

Related work on techniques for managing email overload can be found in [4, 6, 12, 13]. We find that all existing email management systems heavily rellies on a user-created folder structure or user-defined input parameters, which have not essentially achieved the goal of automatically managing email overload.

6 Conclusion

Email overload problem has strongly affect people's usage of email as a knowledge management tool. We proposed a novel email clustering system to solve this problem. This system is essentially supported by a new automatic nonparametric clustering algorithm. By using this algorithm, emails users can get clustered emails easily without any input. The experiments show our algorithm has high efficiency and high clustering quality in terms of computation time and clustering quality measured by Hubert's Γ statistic, simple matching coefficient, and Jaccard coefficient.

References

1. IDC: IDC Examines the Future of Email As It Navigates Security Threats, Compliance Requirements, and Market Alternatives (2005), http://www.idc.com/getdoc.jsp?containerId=prUS20033705
2. Schultze, U., Vandenbosch, B.: Information Overload in a Groupware Environment: Now You See It, Now You Don't. Journal of Organizational Computing and Electronic Commerce 8, 127–148 (1998)
3. Schuff, D., Turetken, O., D'Arcy, J., Croson, D.: Managing E-Mail Overload: Solutions and Future Challenges. IEEE Computer 40, 31–36 (2007)
4. Schuff, D., Turetken, O., D'Arcy, J.: A Multi-attribute, Multi-weight Clustering Approach to Managing, E-Mail Overload. Decision Support Systems 42, 1350–1365 (2006)
5. Roussinov, D.G., Chen, H.: Document Clustering for Electronic Meetings: An Experimental Comparison of Two Techniques. Decision Support Systems 27, 67–79 (1999)
6. Mock, K.: An Experimental Framework for Email Categorization and Management. In: 24th ACM International Conference on Research and Development in Information Retrieval, pp. 392–393 (2001)
7. Whittaker, S., Sidner, C.: Email Overload: Exploring Personal Information Management of Email. In: ACM SIGCHI conference on Human Factors in Computing Systems, pp. 276–283 (1996)
8. Baker, F.B., Hubert, L.J.: Measuring the Power of Hierarchical Cluster Analysis. Journal of the American Statistical Association 70, 31–38 (1975)
9. Aldenderfer, M.S., Blashfield, R.K.: Cluster Analysis. Sage Publications (1984)
10. Tabachnick, B.G., Fidell, L.S.: Using Multivariate Statistics. Harper Collins College Publishers, New York (1996)
11. Baeza-Yates, R., Ribeiro-Neto, B.: Modern Information Retrieval. Addison-Wesley, Reading (1999)
12. Payne, T., Edwards, P.: Interface Agents that Learn: An Investigation of Learning Issues in a Mail Interface. Applied Artificial Intelligence 11, 1–32 (1997)
13. Kushmerick, N., Lau, T.: Automated E-Mail Activity Management: An Unsupervised Learning Approach. In: 10th International Conf. on Intelligent User Interfaces, pp. 67–74 (2005)

On the Routing Algorithms for Optical Multi-log$_2 N$ Networks

Yusuke Fukushima, Xiaohong Jiang, and Susumu Horiguchi

Graduate School of Information Sciences, Tohoku University, Japan
{yusuke,jiang,susumu}@ecei.tohoku.ac.jp

Abstract. Multi-log$_2 N$ networks architecture is attractive for construct-ing optical switches, and the related routing algorithms are critical for the operation and efficiency of such switches. Although several routing algo-rithms have been proposed for multi-log$_2 N$ networks, a full performance comparison among them is not available by now. Thus, this paper is com-mitted to such a comparison in terms of blocking probability, time com-plexity, hardware cost and load balancing capability. Notice that the load balance is important for reducing the peak power requirement of a switch, so we also propose in this paper two new routing algorithms for optical multi-log$_2 N$ networks to achieve a better load balance.

1 Introduction

It is expected that users of telecommunication services such as Internet, Web browsing, and tele-education will increase dramatically. This has greatly increased the demand for high-bandwidth and high capacity communication systems. All optical networks that work completely in the optical domain are expected to meet this demand. The optical switching networks (or switches), that can switch optical signals in optical domain with an ultra-high speed, will be the key supporting ele-ments for the operation and efficiency of future high-capacity optical networks. The multi-log$_2 N$ network architecture, which is based on the vertical stacking of multiple log$_2 N$ networks [1], has been attractive for constructing the optical switching networks due to its small depth, absolute loss uniformity, etc.

Since a multi-log$_2 N$ network consists of multiple copies (planes) of a log$_2 N$ network, so for routing each request (e.g., a connection request between an input-output pair) we have to select a plane based on a specified strategy. We call such a plane selection strategy as the routing algorithm for multi-log$_2 N$ networks. The routing algorithm is important for the operation and efficiency, since it di-rectly affects the overall switch hardware cost and also the switching speed. By now, several routing algorithms have been proposed for multi-log$_2 N$ networks, such as random routing [2,3,4], packing [2], save the unused [2], etc. It is notable that the available results on routing algorithms mainly focus on the nonblocking condition analysis when a specified routing algorithm is applied [1,2,5,6,7,8]. The recent results in [2] indicate that although some routing algorithms are apparently very different, such as save the unused, packing, minimum index,

K. Li et al. (Eds.): NPC 2007, LNCS 4672, pp. 91–100, 2007.

etc., they actually require a same number of planes to guarantee the nonblocking property of multi-$\log_2 N$ networks. The results in [2] also imply that a very high hardware cost (in terms of number of planes) is required to guarantee the nonblocking property, which makes the nonblocking design of multi-$\log_2 N$ networks impractical for real applications. The blocking design of multi-$\log_2 N$ networks is a promising approach to significantly reducing the hardware cost [3]. However, little literature is available on the performance of the available routing algorithms when they are adopted in the blocking network design [3,4]. In particular, no work is available on the detailed performance comparison among the available routing algorithms when they are applied to a blocking multi-$\log_2 N$ network (e.g., a multi-$\log_2 N$ network with a less number of planes required by its nonblocking condition). It is notable that the load-balancing capability of a routing algorithm is also important for the a multi-$\log_2 N$ network, since it directly affects the peak power requirement and power dispassion requirement (mainly determined by the maximum number of connections simultaneously supported by a plane). However, little available algorithms take into account the load-balancing issue in the routing process.

In this paper, to address the above two main issues, we will propose two routing algorithms which possess the load-balancing capability and also fully compare all routing algorithms in terms of blocking probability, hardware cost, complexity and load-balancing capability. The rest of this paper is organized as follows. Section II illustrates the structure and the features of multi-$\log_2 N$ networks. Section III introduces the available routing algorithms and our two routing algorithms. Section IV provides the comparison among the routing algorithms, and finally, the Section V concludes this paper.

2   Multi-$\log_2 N$ Networks

The multi-$\log_2 N$ network architecture was first proposed by Lea [1]. A multi-$\log_2 N$ network consists of multiple vertically stacked planes as shown in Fig. 1, where each plane of it is just a banyan class ($\log_2 N$) network [1,2,3,4,5,6,7,8] illustrated in Fig. 2. For the convenience of explanations, we use the notation $\text{Log}_2(N, m)$ to denote a multi-$\log_2 N$ network with m planes and we number its planes from the top to the bottom as $p_0, p_1 ..., p_{m-1}$ as shown in Fig. 1.

For a $\text{Log}_2(N, m)$ network, we define a request as an one-to-one (unicast) connection request and denote a request between input x and output y as $\langle x, y \rangle$. We further define a request frame as the set of all requests to the network and denote it as $\begin{pmatrix} x_0 \ x_1 \ \cdots \ x_{k-1} \\ y_0 \ y_1 \ \cdots \ y_{k-1} \end{pmatrix}$, where $0 < k \leq N$. An example of request frame in given in Example 1.

Example 1. *A request frame for $Log_2(16, m)$*

$$\begin{pmatrix} 0 & 1 & 5 & 7 & 12 & 15 \\ 1 & 13 & 10 & 2 & 8 & 0 \end{pmatrix}$$

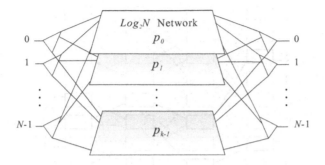

Fig. 1. A multi-log$_2 N$ network with m-planes. Each request will be routed in a plane selected from $p_0, p_1, ..., p_{m-1}$.

The multi-log$_2 N$ networks have several attractive properties, such as a small network depth and the absolute loss uniformity, which make them attractive for building the directional coupler (DC)-based optical switches, see, for example, [1, 3, 6]. Although the DC technology can support nano-second order switching speed [13] and can switch multiple wavelengths simultaneously, it may suffer from the crosstalk problem when two optical signals pass through a common DC at the same time. A simple and cost effective approach to guaranteeing a low crosstalk in DC-based optical multi-log$_2 N$ networks is to apply the node-disjoint (or DC-disjoint) constraint to all the connections in this network [3, 4, 8]. Thus, this paper focuses on the optical multi-log$_2 N$ networks with the node-disjoint constraint. It is notable that the above node-disjoint constraint will cause the node-blocking problem, which happens when two optical signals go through a common node (DC) at the same time and one of them will be blocked. Since link-blocking between two signals will definitely cause node-blocking between them, but the reverse may not be true. Thus, we only need consider the node-blocking issue in the routing process of optical multi-log$_2 N$ networks. For the requests of the request frame in Example 1, the node-blocking (blocking for short) scenario among them is illustrated in Fig. 2, where the blocking happens between $\langle 0, 1 \rangle$ and $\langle 1, 13 \rangle$, between $\langle 0, 1 \rangle$ and $\langle 7, 2 \rangle$ and between $\langle 0, 1 \rangle$ and $\langle 15, 0 \rangle$.

Notice that a plane of the multi-log$_2 N$ networks offers only one unique path to each connection, so the blocking will happen between two connections in the plane if their paths share a common node and the blocked one must be set up through another plane. For a set of requests to be set up, how to choose a plane for each request under the node-disjoint constraint requires a routing algorithm, as explained in the next section.

3   Routing Algorithms

In this section, we first introduce the seven available routing algorithms for a multi-log$_2 N$ network and then propose two new ones with a better load-balancing capability. For a given request frame and its set of requests, a routing

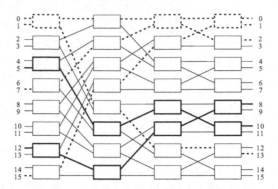

Fig. 2. A 16 × 16 banyan network with crosstalk set (even number of stages)

algorithm will try to route these requests one by one sequentially based on both the node-blocking constraint and a specified strategy (e.g., least occupied plane first, most occupied plane first, save the unused, etc.).

For a request, the random routing (R) algorithm [2,4] selects a plane randomly among all the available planes for this request, if any.

Based on the packing (P) routing algorithm [3, 9, 10, 11], we always try to route a request through the busiest plane first, the second busiest plane second, and so on untill the first available one emerges. The P algorithm has been well-known as an effective algorithm to reduce the request blocking probability, but it may introduce a very heavy traffic load (in terms of number of requests) to a plane.

The minimum index (MI) algorithm [2] always try to route a connection through the first plane p_0 first, second plane p_1 second and so on untill the the first available plane appears.

To route a request based on the save the unused (STU) algorithm [2], we do not select the empty plane(s) unless we can not find an occupied plane that can route the request.

The cyclic static (CS) algorithm [2] always keep a pointer to last used plane [2]. To route a new request, it checks the pointed plane first, then follows the same manner as that of the MI algorithm. The difference between the MI and CS is that starting point of latter is not fixed and it depends on the last used plane.

The cyclic dynamic (CD) algorithm [2] is almost the same as CS algorithm, and the only difference is that the CD algorithm always check the next plane of the pointed one first.

It is interesting to notice that although the above six routing algorithms are apparently different, a recent study in [2] revealed that they actually require a same number of planes to guarantee the nonblocking property of a multi-$\log_2 N$ network. The results in [2] also imply that the nonblocking design of multi-$\log_2 N$ networks is not very practical since it requires a very high hardware cost (in terms of number of required planes).

Danilewicz *et, al* (*D*) [6] recently proposed an novel routing algorithm for multi-log$_2 N$ networks to guarantee the nonblocking property with a reduced number of planes. The main idea of this algorithm is to select plane that new connection will block the fewest number of future requests of all planes. It is notable, however, the time complexity of this algorithm is significantly higher than the above six routing algorithms.

Notice that the blocking design of multi-log$_2 N$ networks is a promising approach to dramatically reducing their hardware cost [3] without introducing a significant blocking probability. However,the available study on the above seven algorithms mainly focus on their corresponding nonblocking conditions analysis and little literature is available on the performance of these routing algorithms when they are adopted in the blocking network design [3, 4]. It is an interesting question that although the nonblocking conditions of the first six routing algorithms are the same, whether their performance is still the same when that they are applied to a blocking multi-log$_2 N$ network (e.g., a multi-log$_2 N$ network with a less number of planes required by its nonblocking condition.) To answer this question, in the next section we will conduct a detailed performance comparison among the available routing algorithms in terms of blocking probability, hardware cost, complexity and load-balancing capability.

It is notable that the load-balancing capability of a routing algorithm is also important for the multi-log$_2 N$ network, since it directly affects the peak power requirement and power dispassion requirement (mainly determined by the maximum number of connections simultaneously supported by a plane). We will see in the next section that although the most available algorithms for multi-log$_2 N$ networks can achieve a low blocking probability, they usually result in a very uneven load distribution among all planes. To provide a better load balance among all planes of a multi-log$_2 N$ network, we propose here two new routing algorithms, namely the load sharing (*LS*) algorithm and low-load minimum index (*LMI*) algorithm as follows.

The main idea of the *LS* algorithm, as contrasted to the *P* algorithm, is to route request in the least occupied plane first, the second least occupied plane and so on until the first available one emerges.

The *LMI* algorithm will route a request in the least occupied plane number first, the second least occupied plane second and so on until the first available one emerges. The purpose of the *LMI* algorithm is also the same as the *LS* algorithm, however, the *LMI* algorithm do not need the sorting operation of the connection loading table.

4   Experimental Results

In this section, we will conduct an extensive simulation study to compare the performance of above nine routing algorithms in terms of their blocking probability, time complexity, hardware cost and load balancing capability. Our simulation program consists of two main modules: a request frame generator and a request router. The request frame generator generates request frames based on the occupancy probability r of each input or output port (e.g.,r is the probability that an input/output port is busy) and the order of all requests in a frame is determined randomly. For a request frame, the request router module will apply a specified routing algorithm to route the requests in the frame one by one sequentially according their order. Our simulation program is implemented in C on a cluster workstation - Opteron 2.0 GHz cluster and all together 10^7 request frames are generated in our simulation.

Following the tagged-path based analysis as that of the studies in [3,4,7], we will focus on a tagged-request in the blocking probability simulation. For each request frame, we define the tagged-request as the last request in the frame (e.g., for the frame in the Example 1, the tagged request is $\langle 15, 0 \rangle$).

4.1   Network Size Versus Blocking Probability

To compare the blocking probability of various routing algorithms, we simulated two network configurations, $Log_2(128, m)$ and $Log_2(256, m)$, for different m and workload (r). For reference, we also included in our simulation the upper bound and the lower bound on the blocking probability established in [3]. The corresponding results are summarized in the Fig. 3 and Fig. 4, respectively.

As mentioned earlier, we focus on the tagged request of each frame in the simulation of blocking probability, where the blocking probability (BP) is calculated as follows.

$$BP = \frac{\text{blocked times of the tagged request}}{\text{iteration times}} \qquad (1)$$

The results in both Fig. 3 and Fig. 4 indicate that all routing algorithms could be roughly divided into three groups based on their blocking probability. The group of algorithms with high BP, say g_h, consists of R, LS, LMI, CS and CD algorithms. The group of algorithms with middle BP, say g_m, consists of STU algorithm. The group of algorithm with low BP, say g_l, consists of MI, P and D algorithms. It is interesting to see from the above two figures that although the nonblocking conditions of the first six routing algorithms is the same, their blocking probability are very different. E.g., the BP of MI and P algorithms in g_l are very close to that of the D algorithm, which results in the lowest blocking probability among all algorithms, but the algorithms in g_m have a significantly higher BP than that of the g_l. It is notable, however, all the nine routing algorithms have a much lower BP than the upper bound established in [3].

4.2   Hardware Cost Versus Blocking Probability

When the upper limit on blocking probability is set as 10^{-6}, the minimum number of planes required by different algorithms are summarized in Fig. 5. For comparison, we also include in Fig. 5 the number of planes required by the nonblocking conditions [7]. It is interesting to notice the required hardware

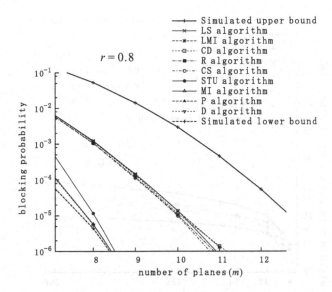

Fig. 3. Blocking probability of each algorithm on Log$_2$(128, m) networks (odd number of stages)

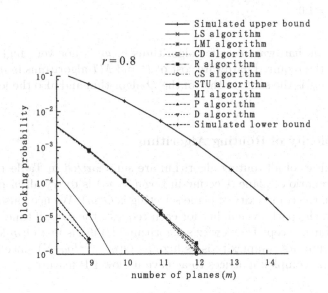

Fig. 4. Blocking probability of each algorithm on Log$_2$(256, m) networks (even number of stages)

cost (number of planes) of all routing algorithms is much less than that of the nonblocking condition even when a high requirement on BP is applied (BP is less than 10^{-6} here). We can also observe from the Fig. 5 the hardware cost of routing algorithms in g_m and in g_l are all similar and close to the lower bound.

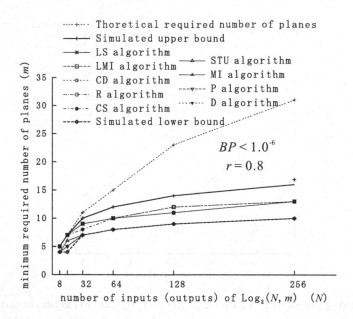

Fig. 5. Minimum number of planes for different size networks with blocking probability $< 1.0^{-6}$ on $r = 1.0$

In contrast, the hardware cost for algorithms in g_h is not very high. It is also notable that the required hardware cost of P and MI algorithms in g_l and STU algorithm in g_m is the same as that of the D algorithm and also the lower bound given by [3].

4.3 Complexity of Routing Algorithm

The complexities of all routing algorithm are summarized in Table 1. Since the worst case scenario of plane selecting in $Log_2(N, m)$ is to try all m planes for a request, thus, the complexity of plane selecting is $O(m)$. We need also $O(log_2N)$ time to check the path availability for each request, the overall time complexity of all algorithms, except Danilewicz's algorithm (D) [6], is just $O(m \cdot log_2N)$. For the D-algorithm, its complexity is as high as $O(m \cdot N^2 log_2N)$ since it needs to calculate many complex matrices to achieve its low BP feature .

Table 1. Complexity of routing algorithm for $Log_2(N, m)$

Algorithm	Complexity of Routing Algorithm
Danilewicz's algorithm (D)	$O(m \cdot N^2 log_2N)$
Otherwise	$O(m \cdot log_2N)$

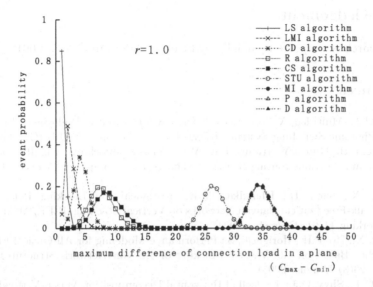

Fig. 6. Distribution of connection load on 128×128 multi-log$_2 N$ network with 10 planes, $r = 1.0$

4.4 Connection Load Distribution Versus Event Probability

Let C_{max} (C_{min}) denotes the maximum (minimum) number of connections in one plane, then the smaller the difference between C_{max} and C_{min} for a algorithm, the better load-balancing capability the algorithm has. Fig. 6 illustrates the load distribution ($C_{max} - C_{min}$) for each routing algorithm in a Log$_2$(128, 10) network with $r = 1.0$. We can see from the Fig. 6 that the LS and the LMI algorithms in g_h can achieve much better load-balancing capability than others. In contrast, the algorithms in g_l (e.g, P and D algorithm) may suffer from very heavy connection load.

5   Conclusion and Remarks

The blocking design of multi-log$_2 N$ networks is an attractive to reduce their hardware cost. In this paper, we fully compared the seven available routing algorithms and also two newly proposed algorithms for multi-log$_2 N$ networks in terms of blocking probability, complexity and load-balancing capability. We found that the routing algorithms which try to pack requests into few number of planes usually achieve a lower blocking probability, but such algorithms require high peak power supply and also advanced power dispassion. In contrast, our two newly proposed routing algorithms provide a good load-balancing capability but may result in a higher blocking probability. Thus, how to design a routing algorithm to achieve a nice trade-off between a low blocking probability and a good load-balancing capability is an interesting future work.

Acknowledgement

This research is supported partially by Scientic-Aid grant No.17300010, JSPS.

References

1. Lea, C.T.: Multi-$\log_2 N$ Networks and Their Applications in High-Speed Electronic and Photonic Switching Systems. IEEE Trans. Commun. 38(10) (October 1990)
2. Chang, F.H., Guo, J.Y., Hwang, F.K.: Wide-sense nonblocking for multi-$\log_d N$ networks under various routing strategies. Theoretical Computer Science (October 2005)
3. Jiang, X., Shen, H., Khandker, M.R., Horiguchi, S.: Blocking Behaviors of Crosstalk-Free Optical Banyan Networks on Vertical Stacking. IEEE/ACM Trans. Networking 11(6) (Decmeber 2003)
4. Jiang, X., Ho, P.H., Horiguchi, S.: Performance Modeling for All-Optical Photonic Switches Based on the Vertical Stacking of Banyan Network Structures. IEEE JSAC 23(8) (August 2005)
5. Lea, C.T., Shyy, D.J.: Tradeoff of Horizontal Decomposition Versus Vertical Stacking in Rearrangeable Nonblocking Networks. IEEE Trans. Commun. 39(6) (June 1991)
6. Danilewicz, G., Kabacinski, W., Michalski, M., Zal, M.: Wide-Sense Nonblocking Multiplane Photonic Banyan-Type Switching Fabrics With Zero Crosstalk. In: Proc. IEEE ICC 2006, June 2006, Istanbul, Turkey, pp. 11–15 (2006)
7. Vaez, M.M., Lea, C.: Strictly Nonblocking Directional-Coupler-Based Switching Networks Under Crosstalk Constraint. IEEE Trans. Commun. 48(2) (February 2000)
8. Maier, G., Pattavina, A.: Design of Photonic Rearrangeable Networks with Zero First-Order Switching-Element-Crosstalk. IEEE Trans. Commun. 49(7) (July 2001)
9. Ackroyd, M.H.: Call Repacking in Connecting Networks. IEEE Trans. Commun. com-27(3) (March 1979)
10. Jajszczyk, A., Jekel, G.: A New Concept - Repackable Networks. IEEE Trans. Commun. 41(8) (August 1993)
11. Mun, Y., Tang, Y., Devarajan, V.: Analysis of Call Packing and Rearrangement in a Multi Stage Switch. IEEE Trans. Commun. 42(2/3/4) (1994)
12. Yang, Y., Wang, J.: Wide-Sense Nonblocking Clos Networks under Packing Strategy. IEEE Trans. Computers 48(3) (March 1999)
13. Papadimitriou, G.I., Papazoglou, C., Pomportsis, A.S.: Optical Switching: Switch Fabrics, Techniques, and Architectures. Journal of lightwave technology 21(2) (February 2003)

Overall Blocking Behavior Analysis on Banyan-Based Optical Switching Networks Under Crosstalk Constraint

Chen Yu[1], Yasushi Inoguchi[2], and Susumu Horiguchi[3]

[1] School of Information Science, Japan Advanced Institute of Science and Technology, Japan
[2] Center for Information Science, Japan Advanced Institute of Science and Technology, Japan
[3] School of Information Sciences, Tohoku University, Sendai, Japan
{yuchen,inoguchi}@jaist.ac.jp, susumu@ecei.tohoku.ac.jp

Abstract. Vertically stacked optical banyan (VSOB) is an attractive architecture for constructing banyan-based optical switches. Blocking analysis is an effective approach to studying network performance and finding a graceful compromise among hardware cost, blocking probability and crosstalk tolerance; however, little has been done on analyzing the blocking behavior of VSOB networks under crosstalk constraint. In this paper, we study the overall blocking behavior of a VSOB network under various degree of crosstalk, where an upper bound on the blocking probability of the network is developed. The upper bound depicts accurately the overall performance behavior of a VSOB network as verified by extensive simulation results and it agrees with the strictly nonblocking condition of the network. The derived upper bound is significant because it reveals the inherent relationship between blocking probability and network hardware cost, by which a desirable tradeoff can be made between them under various degree of crosstalk constraint. Also, the upper bound shows how crosstalk adds a new dimension to the theory of switching systems. In particular, our bound provides network developers an effective tool to estimate the maximum blocking probability of a VSOB network in which different routing algorithms can be applied with a guaranteed performance in terms of blocking probability and hardware cost. An important conclusion drawn from our work is that the hardware cost of VSOB networks can be reduced dramatically without introducing significantly high blocking probability considering the crosstalk.

Keywords: Optical switching networks, banyan networks, blocking probability, vertical stacking optical banyan, degree of crosstalk.

1 Introduction

Optical mesh networks are considered increasingly capacity-efficient and survivable for serving as network backbone for the next generation Internet. All-Optical switches serve as key network elements in such an environment by automatically steering network traffic at an ultra-high speed. The basic 2×2 switching element (SE) in optical switching networks is usually a directional coupler (DC) [9], [13]. A DC can

K. Li et al. (Eds.): NPC 2007, LNCS 4672, pp. 101–113, 2007.

simultaneously switch optical flows with multiple wavelengths, and is one of the best candidates for serving as a SE for the future optical cross-connects (OXCs) to support Optical Burst Switching (OBS) and Optical Packet Switching (OPS).

Crosstalk is an intrinsic shortcoming of the DC. It is the effect of the undesirable coupling between the signals carried in the two waveguides of the coupler [9], [14]. When two optical signals meet at a DC, a small portion of the signal power will be directed to the unintended output channel. Crosstalk suppression becomes particularly important in networks, where a signal propagates through many nodes and accumulates crosstalk from different elements at each node from the system view. In order to obtain an approximate idea of the crosstalk requirements, suppose that a signal accumulates crosstalk from N sources, each with crosstalk level ε. This neglects the fact that some interfering channels may have higher powers than the desired channel. Networks are very likely to contain amplifiers and to be limited by signal-spontaneous beat noise. For example, if we have 10 interfering equal-power crosstalk elements, each producing intrachannel crosstalk, then we must have a crosstalk suppression of below 35dB in each element, in order to have an overall penalty of less than 1 dB [13]. Thus, crosstalk reduction is an important issue in designing the systems that are based on DC's. The crosstalk issue can be tackled at either the device level or the system level. The two methods complement each other. The focus of this paper is on the system-level approach. As shown by the analytical model, crosstalk adds a new dimension to the theory of building a nonblocking or a negligible blocking VSOB network.

Banyan networks [2], [6], [8], [10] are a class of attractive switching structures for constructing DC-based optical switches because they have a smaller and exact same number of SEs along any path between an input-output pair; therefore, an absolutely loss uniformity and smaller attenuation of optical signals are guaranteed. However, banyan networks are blocking networks, and a general approach to building banyan-based nonblocking optical switching networks is vertically stack the multiple copies of banyan [7], [12]. We use VSOB to denote the optical switching networks built on the vertical stacking of optical banyan networks. In this paper, we focus on the VSOB networks that are under various degree of crosstalk constraint c, where $0<c\leqslant \log N/2$[1] according to the real implementation.

Numerous results are available on the study of VSOB networks, such as [7], [11], [12], and their main focus has been on determining the minimum number of stacked copies (planes) required for a nonblocking VSOB network. These results indicate that the VSOB structure, although is attractive, usually requires either a high hardware cost or and a large network depth to achieve nonblockingness. Blocking behavior analysis of a network is an effective approach to studying network performance and finding desirable tradeoff between hardware costs and blocking probability. Some analytical models have been developed to understand the blocking behaviors of vertically stacked optical banyan networks under crosstalk-free constraint that do not meet the nonblocking condition (i.e., with fewer stacked copies than required by the nonblocking condition) [5], [15], [16]. To our best knowledge, however, no study has

---

[1] In this paper log means the logarithm to the base 2.

been reported for modeling and evaluating the performance behavior of VSOB networks under various degree of crosstalk constraint. Thus, this paper is committed to analyzing blocking probability of a VSOB network by deriving its upper bound with respect to the number of planes in the network. The model can guide network designers to evaluate the overall blocking behavior of a VSOB network adopting different routing strategies, in which a graceful compromise can be initiated between the hardware cost and the blocking probability. The model can also show clearly how the crosstalk add a new dimension in building VSOB networks and guide us in making the design tradeoff among the degree of crosstalk, the hardware cost and the blocking probability.

2 Preliminaries

A typical $N \times N$ banyan network has $\log N$ stages and one unique path between any input-output pair. One basic technique for creating multiple paths between an input-output pair is the vertical stacking, where multiple banyan networks are vertically stacked, as illustrated in Fig.1.

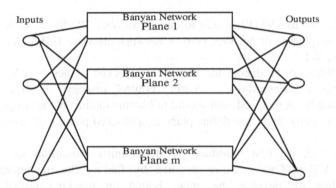

Fig. 1. Illustration of the vertical stacked optical banyan network

Due to their symmetry structures, all paths in a banyan networks have the same property in terms of blocking. We define the blocking probability to be the probability that a feasible connection request is blocked, where a feasible connection request is a connection request between an idle input port and an idle output port of the network. Without loss of generality, we chose the path between the first input and the first output (which is termed as the tagged path in the following context) for blocking analysis. All the SEs on the tagged path are called tagged SEs. The stages of SEs are numbered from left (stage 1) to right (stage $\log N$). For the tagged path, an input intersecting set I_i associated with stage i is defined as the set of all inputs that intersect a tagged SE at stage i. Likewise, an output intersecting set O_i associated with stage i is the set of all outputs that intersect a tagged SE at stage $\log N-i+1$.

When two light signals go through an SE simultaneously, crosstalk is generated at the SE. Such SE is referred to as a crosstalk SE (CSE). The degree of crosstalk of the switching system is defined as the number of CSE's allowed along a path. The crosstalk generated at each CSE can be found in the data sheet from the manufacturer.

A restricted SE (RSE) is a 2×2 SE which carries only one light signal at a time. Although crosstalk at an RSE is very small, it may not be entirely zero. For example, when a light signal passes through an RSE, a small portion of the signal will leave at the other unintended output channel. This stray signal can arrive at the input of the next stage SE and generate some crosstalk. Since crosstalk generated by the stray signal is much smaller than the regular crosstalk, we will ignore it in our analysis [11]. Following the typical assumption as in [15], [16] on probabilistic analysis of multistage interconnection networks, we neglect the correlation among signals arriving at input and outputs ports, and consider that the statuses (busy or idle) of individual input and output ports in the network are independent. This assumption is justified by the fact that the correlation among signals at inputs and outputs, though exists for fixed communication patterns, and becomes negligible for arbitrary communication patterns in large size networks, which is the trend of future optical switching networks that can switch huge data at high speeds.

3   Upper Bound on Blocking Probability

For simplicity, we use VSOB(N,m,c) to denote an $N \times N$ VSOB network that has m stacked copies (planes) of an $N \times N$ banyan network allows c CSEs along the path, where $0 < c \leq \log N/2$.

We take $NBP(N,c)$ to denote the number of blocked planes in a VSOB(N,m,c) network under a "conservative " routing control strategy, in which all these connections that block a tagged path should fall within distinct planes to guarantee the nonblocking property. Here, we define plane as a blocked plane if all its tagged paths are blocked.

In this section, we first introduce the deterministic condition for the strictly nonblocking VSOB(N,m,c) that is obtained by finding the maximum value of $NBP(N,c)$, then we develop the upper bound on blocking probability of a VSOB(N,m,c) network for the cases of even and odd numbers of stages, respectively.

3.1   Conditions for Strictly Nonblocking

Let the maximum value of $NBP(N,c)$ be max$\{NBP(N,c)\}$, then a VSOB(N,m,c) is strictly nonblocking if $m \geq 1 + max\{NBP(N,c)\}$[11]. Thus, we only need to evaluate max$\{NBP(N,c)\}$ for determining the nonblocking condition. The maximum value of $NBP(N,c)$ has been studied in [11]. Here, we study the maximum value of $NBP(N,c)$ from a different perspective. The method can be used to prove Theorem 1.

Lemmas 1: The maximum value of $NBP(N,c)$ is $(3/2)\sqrt{N} + \lfloor \sqrt{N}/(c+1) \rfloor$, if $0 < c \leq$ $(1/2)\log N$ when c is even. When c is odd, the maximum value becomes $\sqrt{2N} + \lfloor \sqrt{2N}/(c+2) \rfloor$, if $0 < c \leq (\log N - 1)/2$.

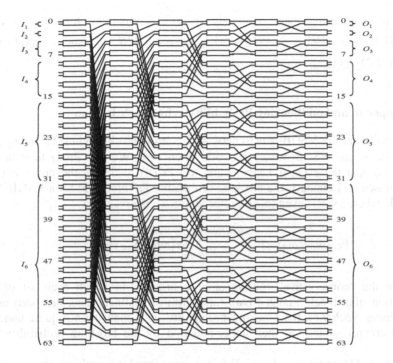

Fig. 2. 64×64 banyan network

Proof: As shown in Fig. 2, for the case when $\log N$ is even, we further define input set I_{even} and output set O_{even} as:

$$I_{even} = \bigcup_{i=1}^{\frac{1}{2}\log N} I_i \, , \quad O_{even} = \bigcup_{i=1}^{\frac{1}{2}\log N} O_i$$

Under the constraint of crosstalk c, the blocking behaviors on the tagged path consist of two parts: $L(N)$ regardless c and $C(N,c)$ regard c. The worst-case scenario of conflicts on the tagged path is when all inputs in set I_i are destined for the outputs in set $O_{(\log N-i+1)}$ and all outputs in set O_i are originated from the inputs in set $I_{(\log N-i+1)}$. Thus, the maximum number of conflicts with the tagged path is determined by both the connections from set I_{even} and the connections destined for set O_{even} which cause $L(N)$ and $C(N,c)$ separately.

Here, we focus on the maximum value of $NBP(N,c)$ when $c \geq 1$. Let $L(N)$ be the number of planes blocked by the connections from I_i $(1 \leq i \leq (1/2)\log N-1)$ and/or destined for O_i $(1 \leq i \leq (1/2)\log N-1)$. Then we have the $\max\{L(N)\}=|I_1|+...+|I_{(1/2)\log N-1}|+|O_1|+...+|O_{(1/2)\log N-1}|+(1/2)(|I_{(1/2)\log N}|+|O_{(1/2)\log N}|)= (3/2)\sqrt{N}$, and $\max\{C(N,c)\}= \left\lfloor \sqrt{N}/(c+1) \right\rfloor$. [11]

The proof for the case when $\log N$ is odd is the same as for the case when $\log N$ is even, after taking out all connections passing through the middle stage on the tagged

path and considering them separately from the remaining $\log N$-1 stages. The $\max\{L(N)\}=|I_1|+\ldots+|I_{(\log N\pm1)/2}|+|O_1|+\ldots+|O_{(\log N\pm1)/2}|=\sqrt{2N}$, and $\max\{C(N,c)\}=\left\lfloor\sqrt{2N}/(c+2)\right\rfloor$. [11]
QED.

3.2 Upper Bound on Blocking Probability When $\log N$ Is Even

The upper bound for VSOB($N,m,0$) network has been developed in [15]. In this paper, we focus on the VSOB(N,m,c) network when $c\geq1$. We use Pr(A) to denote the probability that the event A happens and use $\text{Pr}^+(A)$ to denote the upper bound of Pr(A). Based on Lemma 1, the blocking probability $\text{Pr}^+(blocking)$ for a VSOB(N,m,c) network, where $\log N$ is even (please refer to Fig. 2), is given by:

$$\text{Pr}^+(blocking)=1-\sum_{d=0}^{\min\left\{(3/2)\sqrt{N}+\lfloor\sqrt{N}/(c+1)\rfloor,m-1\right\}}\text{Pr}\big(NBP(N,c)=d\big) \qquad (1)$$

Since the "conservative" routing control strategy, in which each set of these connections that block a tagged path falls within a distinct plane, has been used in determining $NBP(N,c)$, the blocking probability of a connection request under any routing control strategy is then upper-bounded by the blocking probability given in (1).

Equation (1) indicates clearly that we only need to evaluate the probability Pr($NBP(N,c)=d$) to get the upper bound on blocking probability. To calculate Pr($NBP(N,c)=d$), we shall establish the following theorem.

Theorem 1: For a VSOB(N,m,c) network, the probability Pr($NBP(N,c)=d$) is given by:

$$\text{Pr}\big(NBP(N,c)=d\big)=\sum_{\substack{0\leq d_1\leq\min\left\{(3/2)\sqrt{N},d\right\}\\d_2=d-d_1}}\text{Pr}\big(L(N)=d_1\big)+\text{Pr}\big(C(N,c)=d_2\big)$$
$$-\text{Pr}\big(L(N)=d_1\big)\cdot\text{Pr}\big(C(N,c)=d_2\big) \qquad (2)$$

Proof: According to the definition of $L(N)$ and $C(N,c)$ in lemma1. The probability Pr($NBP(N,c)=d$)=Pr($L(N)+C(N,c)=d$) can be separated as the combination of two probabilities Pr($L(N)$) and Pr($C(N,c)$). Thus, we can easily get formula 2 as shown in theorem 1.

Theorem 1 shows clearly that the remain problems to get the upper bound on blocking probability are to calculate the probabilities Pr($L(N)=d_1$) and Pr($C(N,c)=d_2$) then we can get the probability of Pr($NBP(N,c)=d$). About the probabilities Pr($L(N)=d_1$) and Pr($C(N,c)=d_2$), given the case there t_1 connections from input set I_{even}-$I_{(1/2)\log N}$ and t_2 connections destined for O_{even}-$O_{(1/2)\log N}$ following the $L(N)$, among which there are k connections from I_{even}-$I_{(1/2)\log N}$ and destined for O_{even}-$O_{(1/2)\log N}$, we have the following lemma.

Lemma 2: For a VSOB(N,m,c) network, the probability $\Pr(L(N)=d_1)$ is given by:

$$\Pr(L(N)=d_1)=\sum_{t_1=0}^{\min\left\{d_1,\frac{\sqrt{N}}{2}-1\right\}}\sum_{t_2=0}^{\min\left\{d_1,\frac{\sqrt{N}}{2}-1\right\}}\sum_{k=\max\{0,t_1+t_2-d_1\}}^{\min\{t_1,t_2\}}\frac{\Pr(t_1,k)\cdot\Pr(t_2,k)}{\Pr(k)} \tag{3}$$

Where

$$\Pr(k)=\binom{\frac{\sqrt{N}}{2}-1}{k}\cdot\alpha^k\cdot(1-\alpha)^{\frac{\sqrt{N}}{2}-1-k} \tag{4}$$

$$\Pr(t_1,k)=\sum_{\substack{L_1+\cdots+L_{\log\frac{N}{2}-1}=k\\0\leq L_{i\leq}|I_i|,i=1,\ldots,(\log N/2)-1}}\sum_{\substack{T_1+\cdots+T_{\log\frac{N}{2}-1}=t_1-k\\0\leq T_{i\leq}|I_i|-L_i,i=1,\ldots,(\log N/2)-1}}$$
$$\left(\prod_{i=1}^{\frac{1}{2}\log N-1}\binom{|I_i|}{L_i}\cdot\binom{|I_i|-L_i}{T_i}\cdot\alpha^{L_i}\cdot\beta_i^{T_i}\cdot(1-\alpha-\beta_i)^{|I_i|-L_i-T_i}\right) \tag{5}$$

$$\Pr(t_2,k)=\sum_{\substack{L_1+\cdots+L_{\log\frac{N}{2}-1}=k\\0\leq L_{i\leq}|O_i|,i=1,\ldots,(\log N/2)-1}}\sum_{\substack{T_1+\cdots+T_{\log\frac{N}{2}-1}=t_2-k\\0\leq T_{i\leq}|O_i|-L_i,i=1,\ldots,(\log N/2)-1}}$$
$$\left(\prod_{i=1}^{\frac{1}{2}\log N-1}\binom{|O_i|}{L_i}\cdot\binom{|O_i|-L_i}{T_i}\cdot\alpha^{L_i}\cdot\beta_i^{T_i}\cdot(1-\alpha-\beta_i)^{|O_i|-L_i-T_i}\right) \tag{6}$$

Here, $\alpha=r\cdot\left(\sqrt{N}/2-1\right)/(N-1)$ is the probability that a connection from I_{even}-$I_{(1/2)\log N}$ blocks the tagged path and is destined for O_{even}-$O_{(1/2)\log N}$, and β_i is the probability that a connection from I_i but is not destined for O_{even}-$O_{(1/2)\log N}$.

Proof: Following the method of developing probabilistic model in [11], [15] (Omitted).

The evaluation of $\Pr(C(N,c)=d_2)$ is summarized in the following lemma.

Lemma 3: For a VSOB($N,m,0$) network, where $\log N$ is even, the probability $\Pr(C(N,c)=d_2)$ is given by the following formula:

$$\Pr(C(N,c)=d_2)=\sum_{s_1=0}^{\min\left\{d_2,\frac{\sqrt{N}}{2}+\left\lfloor\frac{\sqrt{N}}{c+1}\right\rfloor\right\}}\sum_{s_2=0}^{\min\left\{d_2,\frac{\sqrt{N}}{2}+\left\lfloor\frac{\sqrt{N}}{c+1}\right\rfloor\right\}}\sum_{l=\max\{0,s_1+s_2-d_2\}}^{\min\{s_1,s_2\}}\frac{\Pr(s_1,l)\cdot\Pr(s_2,l)}{\Pr(l)} \tag{7}$$

Where

$$\Pr(l) = \binom{\frac{\sqrt{N}}{2}}{l} \cdot \alpha^l \cdot (1-\alpha)^{\frac{\sqrt{N}}{2}-l} \tag{8}$$

$$\Pr(s_1, l) = \sum_{L_{\frac{\log N}{2}} + L_{\frac{\log N}{2}+1} = l} \sum_{T_{\frac{\log N}{2}} + T_{\frac{\log N}{2}+1} = s_1 - l}$$

$$\left(\prod_{i=\frac{\log N}{2}}^{\frac{1}{2}\log N + 1} \binom{|I_i|}{L_i} \cdot \binom{|I_i| - L_i}{T_i} \cdot \alpha^{L_i} \cdot \beta_i^{T_i} \cdot (1-\alpha-\beta_i)^{|I_i|-L_i-T_i} \right) \tag{9}$$

$$\Pr(s_2, l) = \sum_{L_{\frac{\log N}{2}} + L_{\frac{\log N}{2}+1} = l} \sum_{T_{\frac{\log N}{2}} + T_{\frac{\log N}{2}+1} = s_2 - l}$$

$$\left(\prod_{i=\frac{\log N}{2}}^{\frac{1}{2}\log N + 1} \binom{|O_i|}{L_i} \cdot \binom{|O_i| - L_i}{T_i} \cdot \alpha^{L_i} \cdot \beta_i^{T_i} \cdot (1-\alpha-\beta_i)^{|O_i|-L_i-T_i} \right) \tag{10}$$

Here, $\alpha = r \cdot \left(\sqrt{N}/2\right)/(N-1)$ is the probability that a connection from $I_{(1/2)\log N} \cup I_{(1/2)(\log N+1)}$ passing through the tagged SEs and is destined for $O_{(1/2)\log N} \cup O_{(1/2)(\log N+1)}$, and β_i is the probability that a connection from $I_{(1/2)\log N} \cup I_{(1/2)(\log N+1)}$ but is not destined for $O_{(1/2)\log N} \cup O_{(1/2)(\log N+1)}$.

Proof: (Omitted).   □

We can prove that the upper bound blocking probability derived above matches the strictly nonblocking condition of a VSOB network [11], as summarized in the following corollary.

Corollary 1: For a VSOB(N,m,c) network, where $\log N + x$ is even, the blocking probability $\Pr^+(blocking)$ given in (1) becomes 0 when $m > (3/2)\sqrt{N} + \lfloor \sqrt{N}/(c+1) \rfloor$ if $0 < c \leq (1/2)\log N$.

3.3 Upper Bound on Blocking Probability When logN Is Odd

Based on Lemma 1, the blocking probability $\Pr^+(blocking)$ for a VSOB(N,m,c) network, where $\log N$ is odd, is given by:

$$\Pr^+(blocking) = 1 - \sum_{d=0}^{\min\{\sqrt{2N} + \lfloor \sqrt{2N}/(c+2) \rfloor, m-1\}} \Pr(NBP(N,c) = d) \tag{11}$$

The probability $\Pr(NBP(N,x)=d)$ can also be evaluated based on the formula (3-10), in which the probability $\Pr(L(N)=d_1)$ is as same as Lemma 2 and the evaluation of $\Pr(C(N,c)=d_2)$ is summarized in the following lemma as Lemma 3.

Lemma 4: For a VSOB$(N,m,0)$ network, where $\log N$ is odd, the probability $\Pr(NBP(N,0)=d)$ is given by the following formula:

$$\Pr\big(NBP(N,c)=d\big)= \sum_{\substack{0 \le d_1 \le \min\{(3/2)\sqrt{N},d\} \\ d_2=d-d_1}} \frac{\Pr\big(L(N)=d_1\big)+\Pr\big(C(N,c)=d_2\big)}{-\Pr\big(L(N)=d_1\big)\cdot \Pr\big(C(N,c)=d_2\big)}$$

Proof: The Lemma can be also proved easily based on the model proposed in [15]. □

The following corollary indicates that, when $\log N$ is odd, the upper bound blocking probability we derived also matches the condition for a strictly nonblocking VSOB network [11].

Corollary 2: For a VSOB(N,m,c) network, where $\log N$ is odd, the blocking probability $\Pr^+(blocking)$ given in (11) becomes 0 when $m > \sqrt{2N} + \left\lfloor \sqrt{2N}/(c+2) \right\rfloor$ if $0 < c \le (\log N - 1)/2$.

4 Experimental Results

Simulation has been conducted to verify our model on blocking probability (also denoted by *BP* thereafter) of a VSOB network. Our network simulator consists of the following two modules: the request pattern generator and the request router. The request pattern generator randomly generates a set of connection request patterns for a VSOB network based on the occupancy probability r of an input/output port. To verify the upper bound on *BP*, the "conservative" routing strategy is used in the request router to route the connection requests of a connection pattern through the VSOB network. In the "conservative" routing strategy, we guarantee that all these requests that block a same tagged path will fall within distinct plans. In a VSOB(N,m,c) network, a plane is blocked if all its tagged paths are blocked. For a connection pattern, if no plane can satisfy the request of the tagged path using a routing strategy, the connection request pattern is recorded as a blocked connection pattern corresponding to the routing strategy. The blocking probability of a routing strategy is then estimated by the ratio of the number of blocked connection patterns to the total number of connection patterns generated. During the simulation, a certain workload is maintained. The workload is measured by the network utilization, which is defined as the probability that an input (output) port is busy.

4.1 Degree of Crosstalk, Blocking Probability and Hardware Cost

Fig. 4 illustrates the minimum number of planes estimated by our analytical model for negligible blocking probability (denoted by *BP* hereafter) under different degree of crosstalk constraint. For comparison, we also show in Fig.3 the minimum number of

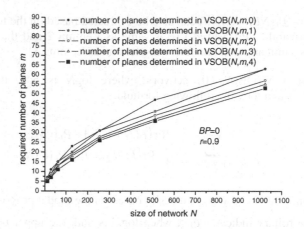

Fig. 3. Minimum number of planes for strictly nonblocking VSOB networks

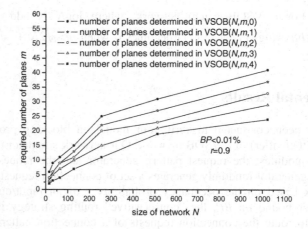

Fig. 4. Minimum number of planes for negligible blocking VSOB networks

planes given by the condition of a strictly nonblocking VSOB network ($c=0$) implemented by our simulator.

The results in Fig. 4 indicate that, for larger size networks, the hardware costs given by nonblocking condition are considerably higher than that given by the upper bound even for a high requirement of blocking probability. For a switching network with $N=512$, the minimum number of planes given by the nonblocking condition is 47, 41, 39, 37, 36 for $c=0$, 1, 2, 3 and 4 respectively, while the minimum number of planes given by the implementation are 31, 27, 23, 21, 19 for VSOB with BP <0.01%, so the (47-31)/47≅34%, (41-27)/41≅34%, (39-23)/39≅41%, (37-21)/37≅43% and (36-19)/36≅47% of the hardware can be reduced respectively while a very low blocking probability is guaranteed (BP<0.01%). It is interesting to note that by increasing the degree of crosstalk, the hardware cost will be more reduced when the same blocking probability constraint in the VSOB network. It is an efficient tool to find the relationship among hardware cost, blocking probability and degree of crosstalk.

4.2 Blocking Probability Versus Degree of Crosstalk

We have also examined two network configurations, $N=512$ and $N=1024$, for upper bound implementation. For each configuration and $r=0.75$, the blocking probabilities were generated under $c=1, 2, 3, 4$. The corresponding results are summarized in Table 1. The comparison results in Table 1 show clearly that the blocking probability is in sense of crosstalk. And we should note that our upper bound follows closely with the conditions of strictly nonblocking VSOB networks as shown in lemma 1. For $N=512$, the upper-bound blocking probability goes to zero at $m=47$ when $c=0$; goes to zero at $m=41$ when $c=1$; goes to zero at $m=39$ when $c=2$; goes to zero at $m=37$ when $c=3$ and goes to zero at $m=36$ when $c=4$. For $N=1024$, the upper-bound blocking probability goes to zero at $m=63$ when $c=0$. The results in Table 1 also indicate clearly that it is possible for us to dramatically reduce the hardware cost (number of planes) by tolerating a

Table 1. Blocking probability Versus Degree of crosstalk in 512×512 and 1024×1024 VSOB network

m	BP $(r=0.75\ N=512/1024)$			
	$c=1$	$c=2$	$c=3$	$c=4$
1	0.91949/0.96511	0.86818/0.96372	0.83512/0.92987	0.81375/0.91624
2	0.79915/0.92954	0.79197/0.91372	0.76228/0.89897	0.71953/0.86513
3	0.68799/0.89536	0.67316/0.87297	0.65537/0.81562	0.61462/0.78252
4	0.56308/0.81182	0.55117/0.79173	0.46531/0.77395	0.38752/0.71639
5	0.46889/0.77886	0.41892/0.72214	0.34973/0.68533	0.29542/0.61518
6	0.37765/0.63905	0.30593/0.59371	0.26184/0.45186	0.19837/0.29725
7	0.22063/0.54018	0.12063/0.48254	0.11597/0.30784	0.09896/0.16927
8	0.09251/0.27884	0.01747/0.11937	4E-5/0.09598	5E-6/0.00821
9	0.00283/0.09954	0.00184/0.01346	9E-7/4.95E-4	1E-9/3E-5
10	4.9E-4/0.00384	1.5E-4/3.1E-4	1E-10/2.1E-8	1E-10/1E-8
11	2E-5/7.4E-5	1.7E-7/6.9E-6	1E-10/1E-10	1E-10/1E-10
12	1E-10/2E-7	1E-10/8E-8	1E-10/1E-10	1E-10/1E-10
13	1E-10/2E-10	1E-10/1E-10	1E-10/1E-10	1E-10/1E-10
14	1E-10/1E-10	1E-10/1E-10	1E-10/1E-10	1E-10/1E-10
15	1E-10/1E-10	1E-10/1E-10	1E-10/1E-10	1E-10/1E-10

predictable and negligible blocking probability by increasing the degree of crosstalk. So our bound can initiates a graceful tradeoff between hardware cost and overall blocking probability.

5 Conclusions

In this paper, we have developed an analytical model for evaluating the upper bound on blocking probability of VSOB networks that under various degree of crosstalk constraint. The derived bound, which agrees with the strictly nonblocking condition of a VSOB network, is proved to accurately depict the overall blocking behavior of the VSOB network by extensive simulation results. The model provides network developers with a guidance of quantitatively determining the impacts of allowing crosstalk and reduction in the number of planes on the overall blocking behavior of a VSOB network in which different routing strategies may be applied. The numerical results of our model can also show how the crosstalk adds a new dimension on the VSOB networks and the effecting of crosstalk on hardware cost and blocking probability.

This analytical model can further help network designers to find the optimal VSOB structure for building an optical switching network with a specified constraint on blocking probability. An important conclusion drawn from our work is that the hardware cost of a VSOB network can be reduced dramatically while a negligible small blocking probability and reality crosstalk are guaranteed. We expect that modeling method employed in this paper will help deriving the upper bound on blocking probabilities of other types of optical switching networks.

Acknowledgments. This research is partly supported by the Grand-In-Aid of scienc research from Japan Society for the Promotion of Science (JSPS) and Strategic International Cooperative Program, Japan Science and Technology Agency (JST).

References

1. Jacobaeus, C.: A Study on Congestion in Link Systems. Ericsson Technics 51(3) (1950)
2. Kruskal, C., Snir, M.: The Performance of Multistage Interconnection Networks for Multiprocessors. IEEE Trans. Commun. COM-32, 1091–1098 (1983)
3. Lee, C.Y.: Analysis of Switching Networks. The Bell System Technical J. 34(6), 1287–1315 (1955)
4. Yu, C., Jiang, X., Horiguchi, S.: Performance Modeling for Vertically Stacked Optical Banyan Networks with Extra Stage. International Journal of Computational Science and Engineering (IJCSE) 2(1-2), 81–87 (2006)
5. Yu, C., Jiang, X., Horiguchi, S., Guo, M.: Overall Blocking Behavior Analysis of General Banyan-based Optical Switching Networks. IEEE Transactions on Parallel and Distributed Systems 17(9), 1037–1047 (2006)
6. Thomson Leighton, F.: Introduction to Parallel Algorithms and Architectures: Arrays, Trees, Hypercubes. Morgan Kaufmann, San Francisco (1992)
7. Maier, G., Pattavina, A.: Design of Photonic Rearrangeable Networks with Zero First-Order Switching-Element-Crosstalk. IEEE Trans. Commun. 49(7), 1268–1279 (2001)

8. Goke, G.R., Lipovski, G.J.: Banyan Networks for Partitioning Multiprocessor Systems. In: Proc. 1st Annu. Symp. Comp. Arch., pp. 21–28 (1973)
9. Hinton, H.S.: An Introduction to photonic Switching Fabrics. Plenum, New York (1993)
10. Patel, J.: Performance of Processor-memory Interconnections for Multiprocessors. IEEE Trans. Comput. C-30, 771–780 (1981)
11. Vaez, M.M., Lea, C.T.: Strictly Nonblocking Directional-Coupler-Based Switching Networks under Crosstalk Constraint. IEEE Trans. Commun. 48(2), 316–323 (2000)
12. Vaez, M.M., Lea, C.T.: Wide-Sense Nonblocking Banyan-Type Switching Systems Based on Directional Couplers. IEEE J. Select. Areas Commun. 16, 1327–1332 (1998)
13. Ramaswami, R., Sivarajan, K.N.: Optical Networks. Morgan Kaufmann, San Francisco, ISBN: 1-55860-655-6
14. Chinni, V.R., et al.: Crosstalk in a Lossy Directional Coupler Switch. J. Lightwave Technol. 13(7), 1530–1535 (1995)
15. Jiang, X., Shen, H., Khandker, M., Horiguchi, S.: Blocking Behaviors of Crosstalk-free Optical Banyan Networks on Vertical Stacking. IEEE/ACM Trans. Networking 11(6), 982–993 (2003)
16. Jiang, X., Shen, H., Horiguchi, S.: Blocking Probability of Vertically Stacked Optical Banyan Networks Under Random Routing. In: Xiaohong Jiang, H. (ed.) Proc. of GLOBECOM 2003, December 1-5, 2003, San Francisco, USA (2003)

SW-Uinta: A Small-World P2P Overlay Network*

Jie Xu and Hai Jin

Services Computing Technology and System Lab.
Cluster and Grid Computing Lab.
School of Computer Science and Technology
Huazhong University of Science and Technology, Wuhan, 430074, China
hjin@hust.edu.cn

Abstract. In this paper, we propose a new structured P2P overlay network, named SW-Uinta, where employs a non-deterministic caching strategy that allows for polylogarithmic search time while having only a constant cache size. Compared with deterministic caching strategies proposed by previous P2P systems, the non-deterministic caching strategy can reduce communication overhead for maintaining the routing cache table. Cache entries in the peer can be updated by subsequent queries rather than only by running stabilization periodically. A novel cache replacement scheme is used to improve lookup performance. We compare the performance of our system with that of other structured P2P networks such as Chord and Uinta. It shows that the SW-Uinta protocol can achieve improved object lookup performance and reduce maintenance cost compared with some other protocols.

1 Introduction

P2P systems are self-organizing distributed systems with no centralized control. Each peer in the P2P network has similar functionalities and plays the roles of a server and a client at the same time. These systems have recently gained much attention, primarily because of the great number of features they can offer to applications that are built on top of them, such as scalability, availability, fault tolerance, decentralized administration, and anonymity.

Current P2P systems can be classified into two types, namely unstructured and structured. Unstructured systems like Gnutella [1], KazaA [2] and Freenet [3] are constructed without any regularization on the connectivity among peers and the routing mechanism. For them, the emphases are on fast file retrieval, with no guarantee that files will always be located. In contrast, structured P2P systems such as Chord [4], CAN [5], Pastry [6] and Tapestry [7] follow a predetermined structure. They guarantee that the file will always be located at the cost of increased overhead for peers join/leave and maintaining the routing table. Therefore, the research issue of this paper is whether there exists a scheme such that each file can be located and maintenance cost can be reduced.

---

* This paper is supported by National Science Foundation of China under grant 60433040, and CNGI projects under grant CNGI-04-12-2A and CNGI-04-12-1D.

Most of the existing structured P2P systems adopt the deterministic caching scheme [8], where keys should be addressed in the cache of peer N is based on the key of peer N and cached index entries typically have expiration times after which they are considered stale. However, little attention has been given on how to maintain these caches during the lookup process. Therefore, communication overhead is high for maintaining the routing cache table.

In this paper, we propose a non-deterministic caching scheme to maintain routing cache tables in a structured P2P overlay network, named Uinta [9]. Our scheme is built on the structured system which can guarantee that each file can be located. The non-deterministic caching scheme builds of cache index entries after answering search queries which can reduce maintenance cost. The basic idea of our scheme is to arrange all peers along a ring-over-ring and equip them with some short distance contacts and long distance contacts. Short distance contacts are built when the peer joins the system with its immediate neighbors. Long distance contacts are built after the peer receives the reply that it requests for.

Assume that peer S initiates the query for key K which is in the cache of peer T. Upon receiving the answer from peer T, peer S caches the information of peer T which arrives with the reply. The traditional cache replacement scheme such as LRU, LFU, and FIFO can not result in the better lookup performance because they do not consider the network topology. In order to optimize the performance of global system, we use the intuition from the small world model [10-14] which says that the routing distance in a graph will be small if each peer has pointers pointing to its immediately neighbors and some chosen far away nodes.

Compared with our previous work [9], main contributions in this paper are:

(1) We propose a non-deterministic caching scheme to reduce maintenance cost for updating the routing cache table.
(2) We propose the SW cache replacement scheme with the small-world paradigm to further improve the performance of object lookup.

The rest of this paper is organized as follows. In Section 2, we give a brief background description of the small-world model and Uinta overlay network. In Section 3, we provide the method how to construct SW-Uinta overlay network. SW-Uinta routing algorithm is proposed and its complexity is given in Section 4. Experiments are discussed and results show the performance of SW-Uinta outperforms that of some other systems in Section 5. An overview of related works is presented in Section 6 and we conclude our research and propose future work in the last section.

2 Background

2.1 Small-World Model

The notion of small world phenomenon originates from social science research by Stanley Milgram [10]. He sought to determine whether most pairs of people in society were linked by short chains of acquaintances. Through some experiments, he concluded his research by showing that most pairs of people are joined by a median number of six steps, a so-called "six degrees of separation" principle.

A theoretical model for small-world networks by Watts and Strogatz [11] pictured a small world as a loosely connected set of highly connected sub-graphs. The edges of the network are divided into "local" and "long-range" contacts, which are constructed roughly as follows. One starts with a set V of n points spaced uniformly on a circle, and joins each point by an edge to each of its k nearest neighbors, for a small constant k. These are the "local contacts" in the network. One then introduces a small number of edges in which the endpoints are chosen uniformly at random from V — the "long-range contacts". However, according to the model of Watts and Strogatz, there is no decentralized algorithm capable of constructing paths of small expected length [13].

Kleinberg [13] defined an infinite family of network models that naturally generalized the model in [11] and then proved that there was exactly one model within this family for which a decentralized algorithm existed to find short paths with high probability. In this model, the probability of a random shortcut being a distance x away from the source is proportional to $1/x$ in one dimension.

Now, it has been observed that the small world phenomenon is pervasive in a wide range of settings such as social communities, biological environments, and data/communication networks. For example, recent studies [15] have shown that P2P networks such as Freenet may exhibit small world properties. Generally, small world networks can be characterized by average path length between two nodes in the network and cluster coefficient defined as the probability that two neighbors of a node are neighbors themselves. A network is said to be small world if it has small average path length (i.e., similar to the average path length in random networks) and large cluster coefficient (i.e., much greater than that of random networks). Studies on a spectrum of networks with small world characteristics show that searches can be efficiently conducted when the network exhibits the following properties: 1) each node in the network knows its local neighbors, called short range contacts; 2) each node knows a small number of chosen distant nodes, called long range contacts, with probability proportional to $1/x$ where x is the distance.

2.2 Uinta Overlay Network

P2P overlay networks, such as CAN, Chord, Pastry and Tapestry, lead to high latency and low efficiency because they are independent of underlying physical networks. A well-routed lookup path in an overlay network with a small number of logical hops can result in a long delay and excessive traffic due to undesirably long distances in some physical links. In these DHT-based P2P systems, each data item is associated with a key and the key/value pair is stored in the peer to which the key maps, not considering the data semantic. In [9], we propose an effective P2P routing algorithm, called Uinta, to adaptively construct a structured P2P overlay network. Uinta not only takes advantages of physical characteristics of the network, but also places data belonging to the same semantic into a cluster and employs a class cache scheme to consider the users' interest.

Construction of Uinta overlay network involves three major tasks: (1) forming peer clusters based on the physical topology of network; (2) assigning an identifier to a peer or a key to locate a peer in the peer cluster; (3) constructing an overlay network across peer clusters. The detail of Uinta overlay network can be found in [9].

3 SW-Uinta Overlay Network

3.1 Construction

Though experiments have shown that Uinta routing algorithm can improve P2P system lookup performance, a deterministic caching strategy is employed in it, which only achieves $O(logN)$ search time with $O(logN)$ cache size and maintenance cost for updating the routing table is $O(\log^2 N)$. P2P network is the high dynamic system so that too much maintenance cost will reduce the global performance of system. Now we construct an overlay network SW-Uinta to get $O((\log^2 N)/k)$ search time with $O(k)$ cache size. Maintaining the routing table need no additional cost.

In Uinta, each peer maintains two finger tables: c-finger table and l-finger table, and a class cache table. The deterministic caching strategy is employed for c-finger table and l-finger table and LRU replacement cache scheme is used for the class cache table. In SW-Uinta, each peer also maintains three cache tables. However, a non-deterministic caching strategy is proposed for two finger tables and a cache replacement scheme related to the small-world model is used for all three cache tables.

In the c-finger table of SW-Uinta, each peer maintains two short links: c-$successor$ which points to the first-joined peer in the next cluster and c-$predecessor$ which points to the first-joined peer in the previous cluster. Each peer maintains m long links c-finger[i] ($1<=i<=m$). In the l-finger table of SW-Uinta, each peer maintains two short links: l-$successor$ pointing to the next peer in the same cluster and c-$predecessor$ pointing to the previous peer in the same cluster. Each peer maintains m long links l-finger[i] ($1<=i<=m$).

If the cache size for peer P is m and its cache table is full, assuming that the cache table $CT=\{d_1, d_2, ..., d_m\}$ and d_m is the distance between the cache object and P, the cache object with distance d_i is replaced by the new object with the probability $\frac{1}{D} * \frac{1}{d_{m+1}}$ where $D = \sum_{i=1}^{m+1} \frac{1}{d_i}$ when a new object with distance d_{m+1} is received. We call this scheme SW cache replacement scheme.

Suppose that peer S gets the answer requested from peer T and there are no pointers to peer T in peer S.

(1) If peer S and peer T are in the same cluster and l-finger[i] is not full, peer S caches peer T in the l-finger table;

(2) If peer S and peer T are in the same cluster and l-finger[i] is full, SW cache replacement scheme is employed for l-finger[i];

(3) If peer S and peer T are in the different clusters and c-finger[i] is not full, peer S caches peer T in the c-finger table;

(4) If peer S and peer T are in the different clusters and c-finger[i] is full, SW cache replacement scheme is employed for c-finger[i].

Because users always retrieve data of a kind, which they are interested in, we store the data information based on data semantics in Uinta, which makes data of a kind placed in the same cluster in Uinta. After that, the user can utilize a *class cache table* to cache the identifier of peer where data of some kind searched recently store and the identifier of this kind. If the user searches data of this kind next, it can use the information of the cache table directly. It is obvious that P2P system workload has temporal and spatial localities just as that in the web traffic [16]. For example, a user who retrieves a song is likely to retrieve other songs in subsequential requests. A high class cache table hit rate can be expected, thus a reduced average number of routing hops and lower routing network latency can be achieved.

In Uinta, we used LRU as the cache replacement scheme, which could not improve the whole performance because the topology of network does not be considered in LRU. Therefore, in SW-Uinta, we also employ the SW cache replacement scheme. When peer S gets data D requested from peer T, the class identifier of data D and the IP address (and port number) of the first-joined peer in the cluster where T is will be stored in the class cache table if it is not full. Otherwise, SW cache replacement scheme is employed for the class cache table.

Cache tables are generally kept fresh by the traffic of requests traveling through peers. To handle pathological cases in which there are no lookups for a particular ID range, each peer refreshes any cache table to which it has not performed data lookup in the past hour. Refreshing means picking an entry in the cache table and performing a peer search for that ID. On the one hand, this scheme avoids the bottleneck of network traffic because all of the peers will not update at the same time. On the other hand, the peer can be responsible for the failure of some peers quickly. Maintenance cost for the routing table always goes with the lookup operation, which needs few other messages.

3.2 Peer Operation

Peer joins. When a new peer p joins the system, it sends a join message to a nearby peer q that is already a member of the system. This process can be done in different methods. We simply assume it can be done quickly (this is the same assumption as other DHT algorithms). Then peer p can get the information of landmark nodes from this nearby peer q and fulfill its own landmark table. It then decides the distance between itself and the landmark nodes and uses the distributed binning scheme to determine the suitable cluster P_p it should join. Then the identifier D_p of peer p can be gotten, i.e., $D_p=P_p*2^n+S_p$ (S_p is the hash value of IP address of peer p). Consequently, peer p connects the peer p' in the cluster P_p through the c-finger table of peer q and then is located in the cluster based on the suffix S_p. Assume that peer s is the l-successor of peer p and peer n is the original l-predecessor of peer s. Then, peer p acquires peer s as its l-successor and acquires peer n as its l-predecessor. Peer n acquires peer p as its l-successor and peer s acquires peer p as its l-predecessor. Other data structures needed by peer p are copied from peer s.

If peer p finds that c-$finger[i].identifier$ equals to P_p but the identifier prefix of c-$finger[i].node$ denoted as peer x does not equal to P_p rather than X_p in peer q, it shows peer p will form a new cluster whose identifier is P_p. Peer p acquires peer x as its c-successor and acquires peer q as its c-predecessor which is the original c-predecessor of peer x. Every peer in the cluster that peer x located, when notified by peer p, acquires peer p as its c-predecessor. Every peer in the cluster that peer q located acquires peer p as its c-successor. Both l-predecessor and l-successor of peer p point to itself. Other data structures needed by peer p are copied from peer s. Finally, keys between P_p*2^n and X_p*2^n are moved form cluster X_p*2^n to cluster P_p*2^n. Peer p joins the system successfully.

Peer leaves or fails. When a peer leaves the network, it checks whether it is the last peer in the cluster. If there are other peers in the cluster, this peer simply informs its leaving to its *l-predecessor* and *l-successor* and keys in it are moved to its *l-successor*. Otherwise, except for informing its leaving to its *c-predecessor* and *c-successor*, the key subspace of this cluster needs to be merged with one of its neighboring clusters. The peer of its neighboring clusters which is closest in the key space to the leaving peer takes over all of its keys. A failed peer is detected during routine operations such as search. If a peer detects a failure in one of its cache tables, it evicts this entry in the cache table.

4 SW-Uinta Routing Algorithm

SW-Uinta routing algorithm and its complexity are described in this section.

1) When peer p wants to obtain the file associated with a key k and a class c, it gets the class identifier P_k of the file hashed by SHA-1 with c;
2) Check whether exists an entry (P_k*2^n, q) for the class identifier P_k in the class cache table; if does, jump to peer q directly, then to 6); otherwise, to 3);
3) Check whether P_k falls between the P_p of p and the P_q of its *c-successor* q; if does, jump to q, then to 6); otherwise, to 4);
4) $x=p$;
   repeat
        Search peer x's *c-finger table* for peer q whose prefix of identifier P_q most immediately precedes P_k, $x=q$;
   until P_k falls between the P_x of x and the P_q of its *c-successor* q;
5) Jump to peer q;
6) Find a peer d through the *l-finger table* of peer q so as to make the suffix of key identifier S_k hashed by SHA-1 with k falls between S_x of x and S_d of its *l-successor* d;
7) Return the identifier of peer d and (key, value) pair searched to peer p; join the information of peer d to two finger tables of peer p and join (P_k*2^n, d) to the class cache table of peer p using the SW cache replacement scheme described above.

In SW-Uinta, the expected number of hops required to lookup an object is $O((\log^2 N)/k)$.

5 Performance Evaluation

5.1 Simulation Methodology and Performance Metrics

In our simulation, we use the GT-ITM [17] transit stub topology generator to generate the underlying networks, where the number of system peers N varies from 1,000 to 10,000. As far as the logical overlay is concerned, we build SW-Uinta and Uinta based Chord simulator. Each peer on the overlay is uniquely mapped to one node in the IP layer. We choose 4 landmarks placed at random and there is 3-level latency from landmarks to peers. 100*N pseudo file-ids that are classified 100 kinds are generated and distributed across all the peers in simulated networks. For each experiment, 100,000 randomly generated routing requests (including file-id and its class) are executed. To obtain a fair comparison, we keep the size of the cache table in SW-Uinta to $O(logN)$. We choose Chord as the platform because the ring geometry allows the greatest flexibility.

We consider four metrics to verify the effectiveness of SW-Uinta: (1) Routing hop: the average number of logical hops traversed by search messages to the destination; (2) Routing latency: the average time for search messages from the source to the destination; (3) Latency stretch: the ratio of the average latency on the overlay network to the average latency on the IP network; (4) Maintenance cost: the average number of messages incurred for each peer joins/leaves and for RT maintenance cost which is the average number of messages needed for maintaining the routing table to be up-to-date.

5.2 Routing Cost Reduction

The goal of simulation in this section is to show whether SW-Uinta can reduce the routing cost in P2P system just as Uinta. Fig. 1 shows the results of routing hops and routing latency evaluation. In this simulation, we compare the routing performance of Uinta-cache*logN*, SW-Uinta(LRU), and SW-Uinta(small-world) with Chord under different network size.

Fig. 1(a) shows the routing performance comparison result measured with the average number of routing hops. All of Chord, Uinta-cache*logN*, SW-Uinta(LRU) and SW-Uinta(small-world) have good scalability: as the network size increases from 1000 nodes to 10000 nodes, the average number of routing hops only increases around 33%, 32%, 36%, and 29%, respectively and the average number of routing hops is 6.07, 5.74, 6.24, and 5.24, respectively.

As a proximate metrics, the average number of routing hops cannot represent the real routing cost. The actual routing latency is highly depended on the average latency for each hop. Fig. 1(b) shows the measured results of the average routing latency in Chord, Uinta-cache*logN*, SW-Uinta(LRU), and SW-Uinta(small-world) algorithms. Although Uinta and SW-Uinta have the nearly equal average number of routing hops with that of Chord, they have smaller average routing latency which can represents the real routing cost. For Uinta-cache*logN*, SW-Uinta(LRU), and SW-Uinta(small-world), the average routing latency gets 24.3%, 18.0%, and 40.4% reduction respectively compared with Chord.

Obviously, the performance of routing hops and scalability for SW-Uinta(LRU) are worse than those of other algorithms, which shows the LRU cache replacement is not suitable for the P2P system. At the same time, because both the network characteristics and the network topology are considered in constructing the SW-Uinta(small-world) system so that the routing performance of SW-Uinta(small-world) is better than that of three other algorithms.

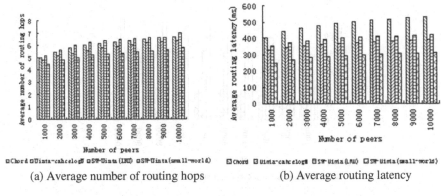

(a) Average number of routing hops   (b) Average routing latency

Fig. 1. Routing performance comparison for Uinta, SW-Uinta, and Chord

5.3 Stretch Reduction

Latency stretch is referred to the ratio of the average latency on the overlay network to the average latency on the IP network, which can be used to characterize the match degree of the overlay to the physical topology. Table 1 summarizes the stretch statistics in the case of a 10,000 peer network. From the table, we can find that stretch can be reduced using Uinta and SW-Uinta. This shows that using topology-aware and semantic-aware overlay construction, we can achieve significant improvement in the lookup performance. SW-Uinta(small-world) can get better performance than Uinta.

Table 1. Latency stretch result for Chord, Uinta, and SW-Uinta

Algorithm	Average routing latency	Latency stretch
Chord	531.51	4.40
Uinta-cache$logN$	366.68	3.04
SW-Uinta(LRU)	397.28	3.29
SW-Uinta (small-world)	289.31	2.40

5.4 Maintenance Cost

In this experiment, we show that SW-Uinta not only keeps the strengths of Uinta, but also is able to reduce maintenance cost. Maintenance cost here includes two parts: the number of messages incurred for each peer joins/leaves and RT maintenance cost. Maintenance cost is referred to the average number of messages for all maintaining operations such as peer joining, peer leaving and keeping the routing table to be up-to-date.

We assume that peer joins and leaves according to the Poisson process at rate $R=0.1$(minute^{-1}). RT maintenance period is an hour. Fig.2 depicts maintenance cost comparison for the Uinta-cache$logN$, SW-Uinta(LRU), SW-Uinta(small-world), and Chord schemes under different network size. Maintenance cost is around 16, 7, 6, and 21, respectively for the Uinta-cache$logN$, SW-Uinta(LRU), SW-Uinta(small-world), and Chord schemes. From this experiment, we know maintenance cost for SW-Uinta

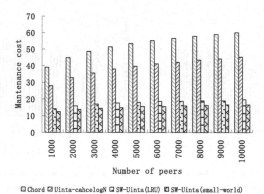

Fig. 2. Maintenance cost comparison for Uinta, SW-Uinta, and Chord

is lower than two other algorithms because there is no additional cost for the route table maintenance, that is RT maintenance cost, in SW-Uinta. Each searching operation can update the routing table, which needs no other operations to maintain the routing table to be up-to-date.

6   Conclusions and Future Work

In this paper, we propose a new overlay infrastructure SW-Uinta based on Uinta proposed by us in our previous study. SW-Uinta not only holds the strength of Uinta, which takes both the user's interest and the physical topology into consideration, but also considers the network characteristic so that the SW cache replacement scheme is proposed to further improve the performance of object lookup. Because the P2P system is a dynamic environment, maintenance cost for peer joining, peer leaving and routing state maintenance is very high. Therefore, we propose a non-deterministic caching scheme to reduce maintenance cost when peers join/leave and self-organization occurs. Simulations also show SW-Uinta can improve the lookup performance as well as it can reduce maintenance cost under the same size of routing table. Now, this infrastructure is only suitable for key-based retrieval and content-based retrieval is our next step of work.

References

[1] Gnutella: http://www.gnutellaforums.com/
[2] Leibowitz, N., Ripeanu, M., Wierzbicki, A.: Deconstructing the Kazaa Network. In: Proc. of 3rd IEEE Workshop on Internet Applications, Santa Clara, CA, pp. 112–120 (2003)
[3] Clarke, I., Sandberg, O., Wiley, B., et al.: Freenet: A Distributed Anonymous Information Storage and Retrieval System. In: Proc. of Workshop on Design Issues in Anonymity and Unobservability. ICSI, pp. 311–320 (2000)
[4] Stoica, I., Morris, R., Karger, D., Kaashoek, M.F., Balakrishnan, H.: Chord: A Scalable Peer-to-Peer Lookup Service for Internet Applications. In: Proc. of the ACM SIGCOMM, pp. 149–160. ACM Press, New York (2001)

[5] Ratnasamy, S., Francis, P., Handley, M., Karp, R., Shenker, S.: A Scalable Content-Addressable Network. In: Proc. of ACM SIGCOMM, pp. 161–172. ACM Press, New York (2001)

[6] Rowstron, A., Druschel, P.: Pastry: Scalable, Distributed Object Location and Routing for Large-scale Peer-to-Peer Systems. In: Proc. of the 18th IFIP/ACM International Conference on Distributed Systems Platforms, pp. 329–350. Springer, Heidelberg (2001)

[7] Zhao, B.Y., Huang, L., Stribling, J., Rhea, J., Joseph, S.C., Kubiatowicz, A.D.: A Resilient Global-Scale Overlay for Service Deployment. IEEE Journal on Selected Areas in Communications 22, 41–53 (2004)

[8] Sarshar, N., Roychowdhury, V.P.: A Random Structure for Optimum Cache Size Distributed Hash Table (DHT) Peer-to-Peer Design (2002),
http://www.ee.ucla.edu/~nima/Publications/opt_cache.pdf

[9] Jin, H., Xu, J., Zou, B., Zhang, H.: Uinta: A P2P Routing Algorithm Based on the User's Interest and the Network Topology. In: Fraigniaud, P. (ed.) DISC 2005. LNCS, vol. 3724, pp. 238–249. Springer, Heidelberg (2005)

[10] Milgram, S.: The Small World Problem. Psychology Today 2, 60–67 (1967)

[11] Watts, D., Strogatz, S.: Collective Dynamics of Small-World Networks. Nature 393, 440–442 (1998)

[12] Kleinberg, J.: Small-World Phenomena and the Dynamics of Information. In: Proceedings of Advances in Neural Information Processing Systems, pp. 14–25. MIT Press, Cambridge (2002)

[13] Kleinberg, J.: The Small-World Phenomenon: An Algorithmic Perspective. Cornell Computer Science Technical Report 99-1776 (2000)

[14] Iamnitchi, A., Ripeanu, M., Foster, I.: Small-World File-Sharing Communities. In: Proceedings of IEEE INFOCOM, pp. 175–186 (2004)

[15] Zhang, H., Goel, A., Govindan, R.: Using the Small-World Model to Improve Freenet Performance. In: Proceedings of IEEE INFOCOM 2002, pp. 1228–1237 (2002)

[16] Mahanti, A.: Web Proxy Workload Characterization and Modeling. Master Thesis. Department of Computer Science, University of Saskatchewan (1999)

[17] Zegura, E.W., Calvert, K., Bhattacharjee, S.: How to Model an Internet Work. In: Proceedings of INFOCOM'96, pp. 594–602 (1996)

Unmanned Navigation of the 1/10 Vehicle Using U-SAT

Su Yong Kim[1] and SooHong Park[2]

[1] Graduate student, Department of Mechanical Engineering, Pusan National University,
KumJung Ku, Pusan 609-735, Korea
syz2ang@hanmail.net
[2] Department of Mechatronics Engineering, Dongseo University,
Sasang Ku, Pusan 617-716, Korea
shpark@dongseo.ac.kr

Abstract. In order for a vehicle to follow a predetermined trajectory accurately, its position must be estimated accurately and reliably. In this paper, we propose new lateral control methods for unmanned vehicles and a positioning system using ultrasonic waves. The positioning problem is considered as an important issue of control problem for unmanned navigation of a vehicle. Dead Reckoning is widely used for positioning of vehicle. However this method has problems because it accumulates estimation errors. We propose a new method to increase the accuracy of position estimation using the Ultrasonic Satellite system. It is shown that we will be able to estimate the position of vehicle precisely, in which errors are not accumulated. We also propose new lateral control methods including a new path planning method and a heading angle modulator. The experimental results show that the proposed methods enable accurate vehicle trajectory tracking under various environmental factors.

Keywords: Ultrasonic satellite system (U-SAT), unmanned navigation, lateral control.

1 Introduction

In modern society, the road capacity is limited, but the number of vehicles is increasing continuously. Therefore, the smooth traffic of vehicles becomes difficult, which increases the threat to the safety of drivers. Under such circumstances, research is under way worldwide to develop unmanned navigation including ITS (Intelligent Transportation System), PATH (Partners for Advanced Transit and Highway) and AHS (Automated Highway System) [1], [2], [3].

The prerequisite for such unmanned navigation is the positioning of a vehicle. Only when the position of the vehicle is known, the vehicle could be drive associated with specific routes, which is generated using the general information needed for unmanned navigation. To this end, researchers have conducted various studies on INS (Inertia Navigation System), GPS (Global Positioning System), Vision System, and Ultrasonic System [4], [5]. In the case of INS, which uses an accelerometer or a gyroscope, there is no limitation regarding the recognition area. However, accumulative errors will occur with the passage of running hours, even though it is easy to construct a path planning. GPS guarantees precise positioning, but it created cost problems and limitations in recognizing environments. In the case of Vision

K. Li et al. (Eds.): NPC 2007, LNCS 4672, pp. 124–132, 2007.
© IFIP International Federation for Information Processing 2007

System, its image processing speed is improving, owing to the development of microprocessors, but it has failed to completely overcome the challenge of recognizing environments.

This paper proposes an Ultrasonic Satellite system (U-SAT) for the unmanned navigation of vehicles accordingly. One of the difficulties associated with the study of unmanned navigation, is to conduct a test to verify the algorithm using an actual car. To resolve such a difficulty, this study conducted unmanned navigation experiments indoors using a 1/10 vehicle and a U-SAT. In addition, overcome the limitation of the existing lateral control, this study suggests a new lateral control algorithm, in which the performance of the algorithm has been verified and evaluated.

2 Position Estimation Using Ultrasonic Waves

As shown in Fig. 1, the basic formulation of positioning using ultrasonic waves is to use Expression (1) in conjunction with Expression (2), to measure the Time of Flight (T.O.F), the gap between the time of transmission of ultrasonic waves (T_t) and the time receives of the waves (T_r). It is necessary to measure the T.O.F. precisely for exact positioning and, to this end, this study used the period detecting method [6]. Using the 40 kHz MA40BR/S ultrasonic sensor of Murata and the radio frequency (RF) transmitting-receiving module, the point of time of ultrasonic wave transmission

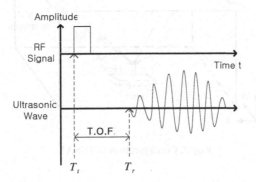

Fig. 1. Definition of T.O.F

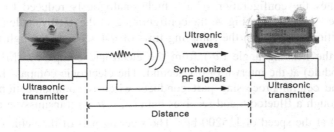

Fig. 2. Ultrasonic distance measurement system

is measured. This study also constructed a ultrasonic distance measurement system as shown in Fig. 2 [7].

$$d = c \times T.O.F \tag{1}$$

$$c = 331.5 + 0.60714T \tag{2}$$

Based on the ultrasonic distance measuring system shown in Fig. 2, this study constructed the U-SAT shown in Fig. 3. As shown in Fig. 3, the ultrasonic wave transmitter of Fig. 2 transmits ultrasonic waves and synchronized RF signals from four fixed positions. The ultrasonic receiver of Fig. 2 is attached on the moving object to receive ultrasonic waves and synchronized RF signals, as well as measuring the distances between ultrasonic transmitters and receivers. Based on this, the precise three-dimensional positions can be estimated through trilateration. In addition, ultrasonic waves are transmitted consecutively at the interval of 0.1 second in order to prevent interference of ultrasonic waves generated among each of the ultrasonic transmitters [8].

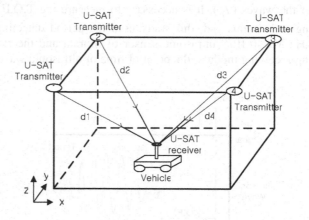

Fig. 3. Configuration of U-SAT

3   Configuration and Modeling of the 1/10 Vehicle

Fig. 4 indicates the configuration of a vehicle analogously reduced to 1/10 of an actual vehicle. As shown in Fig. 4, the configuration of the 1/10 vehicle acquires the absolute position (x, y) with the sampling time of 0.4 seconds through the U-SAT and obtains the heading angle (θ) from the electronic compass (CMP303-Robot Compass Module) at the interval of 0.1 second. The electronic compass has an error of about. The central processing part conducts wireless communications with the computer through a Bluetooth and receives data (x, y, θ, v) transmission and control inputs (δ, V) at the speed of 115200 bps. The steering part of the vehicle drives the HS 500 thermo motor of Hitec. The maximum right and left steering angle is $\pm 30°$.

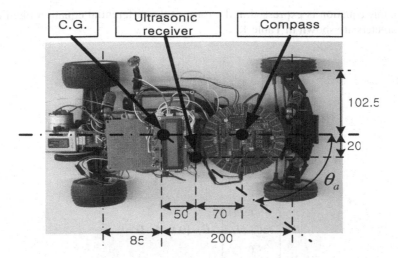

Fig. 4. Configuration of 1/10 vehicle (uint: mm)

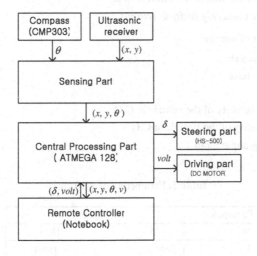

Fig. 5. Configuration of hardware

This study uses modeling that considers the look-down and actuator elements based on a bicycle model [4]. The bicycle model is a model that equalized two front wheels and two rear wheels as virtual wheels on the vehicle central line, respectively. This is to control steering and therefore, it ignores the vehicle roll and pitch movement. The premise is that the difference of angles in the small yaw rate and the longitudinal speed are maintained constantly. Linearization takes place under these conditions.

The dynamic equation is expressed in the form of the differential equation like Eq. 3. The parameters are shown in Table 1.

$$\begin{bmatrix} \dot{v} \\ \dot{r} \\ \dot{\theta} \end{bmatrix} = A \begin{bmatrix} v \\ r \\ \theta \end{bmatrix} + B\delta_f \tag{3}$$

$$A = \begin{bmatrix} -2(C_f + C_r)/mu & -u - l(aC_f - bC_r)/mu & 0 \\ -2(aC_f - bC_r)/I_{zz} & -2(a^2C_f + b^2C_r)/I_{zz}u & 0 \\ 0 & 1 & 0 \end{bmatrix}$$

$$B = \begin{bmatrix} 2C_f/m \\ 2aC_f/I_{zz} \\ 0 \end{bmatrix}, \ C = [0 \ 0 \ 1], \ D = 0$$

Where,

a	: Distance from the vehicle C.G. to front axle
b	: Distance from the vehicle C.G to rear axle
C_f/C_r	: front/rear tire cornering stiffness [N/rad]
I_{zz}	: yaw moment of inertia
l	: wheel base l= a+b
m	: vehicle total mass
r	: yaw rate
u	: longitudinal velocity of the vehicle at C.G
v	: side-slip velocity of the vehicle at C.G
δ_f	: front steering angle input

Table 1. Parameters of 1/10 car

Parameter	value	
m	2.105	[kg]
l	285	[mm]
a	200	[mm]
b	85	[mm]
C_f	0.191	[N/rad]
C_r	0.51	[N/rad]

4 Path Planning Method and Unmanned Navigation Algorithm

As indicated in Fig. 6, a new path planning method is generated in a point-to-point manner. First of all, the vehicle moves toward the target route point $P_p(i)$. When the

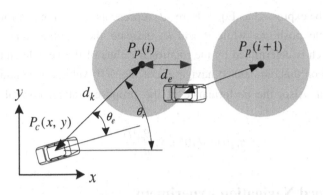

Fig. 6. Path planning, method and Lateral control algorithm

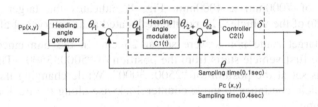

Fig. 7. Block diagram of feedback loop by using heading angle modulator

vehicle's center of gravity comes into a certain radius d_e of the target route point $P_p(i)$, the vehicle is considered to have reached the target route point. Then, the target point is converted to the next target route point $P_p(i+1)$ iteratively. Here, the purpose of the radius d_e is to facilitate natural movement to the next target route point. In this study, the vehicle speed is set at 40 cm/s and d_e at 25 cm in consideration of position errors.

Next, the lateral control algorithm controls the heading angle of the vehicle so that the error θ_e between the target route point $P_p(i)$ and the heading angle can be maintained at zero, as shown in Fig 6. As for the feedback loop, when the target route point $P_p(i)$ is given as shown in Fig. 7, the vehicle position $P_c(x, y)$ at that time is feedbacked to generate the target angle (θ_{r1}) of the vehicle. This angle is set as a basic input and the heading angle error (θ_{e1}) is made to converge at zero using the heading angle (θ) which comes in through the electronic compass. Then, the vehicle moves to the target route point P_p. The heading angle sampling time on the electronic compass is four times faster than the positioning sampling time of the U-SAT. Therefore, when the compensation is made simply by feedbacking the heading angle, $\theta_{e1} = \theta_{r1} - \theta$ is sent to zero. However, the vehicle can't realistically approach the target route point P_p. To overcome this problem, this study proposes a new lateral controller using the heading angle modulator $C_1(t)$, shown in Fig. 7. $C_1(t)$, as shown in Fig. 7 can be expressed as Eq. 4. Here, d_k represents the distance error between the current vehicle positions while P_c and K_r indicate the heading angle modulation gain. K_r, which is determined by the rotational radius of the vehicle and the distance to P_p. Based on this, unmanned navigation of the 1/10 vehicle is conducted through lateral control. Also, the performance of the proposed lateral control algorithm is verified.

$$\theta_{r2}(t) = \theta_{r1}(t) + K_r \frac{\theta_{e1}(t)}{d_k(t)} \tag{2}$$

5   Unmanned Navigation Experiment

The lateral control experiment of the 1/10 vehicle is conducted in an indoor space with an area of 7000mm x 4000mm. Fig. 8 indicates the target route points $P_p(i)$ ($i = 1, \cdots, 20$) of the vehicle. The points are located at an interval of 50 cm and the range of the target route points were set at 25 cm. In the unmanned navigation experiment, the first vehicle starts from the position of "5000, 3500". The first target route point   is set at the position of "2500, 3000". While changing its target route points, the vehicle continues to move counterclockwise along the track at a constant speed of 400mm/s.

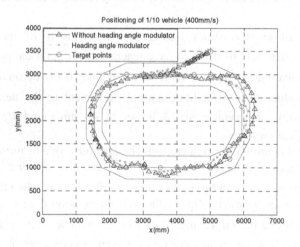

Fig. 8. Experiment result of unmanned navigation

Fig. 8 shows the result of an unmanned navigation experiment using the existing PID controller. They indicate that the vehicle travels in a relatively stable manner along the target points, but it deviates varies the route from time to time. To overcome such a problem, a lateral controller equipped with a heading angle modulator is employed. The experiment result is shown in Fig. 8. The experiment include the heading angle modulator, the vehicle follows the track well within an error range of

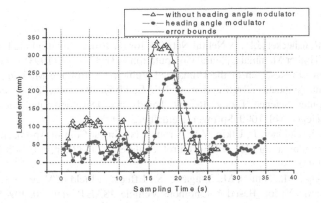

Fig. 9. Experiment result of lateral errors

250mm, which is the range of the target route points. The lateral errors of the experiments are shown in Fig. 24. In the case using the existing PID controller, the maximum error is 336mm and the average error is 109mm. The case include the heading angle modulator, however, the maximum error fell to 240mm and the average error to 61mm. The latter represents much more stable performances than the former. Its driving performance can be said to be stable since the maximum error range is below 250mm. Through the unmanned navigation experiment, this study can confirm that unmanned navigation was (is) possible with the application of the U-SAT and that the performance of the lateral control algorithm added with a heading angle modulator was better than that of the (the) existing method. In addition, the algorithm verification was conducted easily with the use of the 1/10 vehicle.

6   Conclusion

While overcoming the shortcomings of the existing positioning methods, this study suggests an U-SAT which enables precise positioning indoors, in addition to the configuration of the system. Based on this, the study used the U-SAT which is needed for the unmanned navigation of vehicles. In addition, this study has developed an unmanned navigation system for a 1/10 vehicle and propose a new lateral control algorithm which is suitable for the system. Also, we have applied the algorithm and evaluated the performances. Based on the experiment results, this study has verified the appropriateness of the proposed lateral control algorithm, making it possible to conduct more stable unmanned navigation. In addition, the 1/10 vehicle developed with the unmanned navigation system has removed the risks that can be found in actual vehicle experiments. As this vehicle enables various tests in an easier and more convenient way, it could be used as a pre-test vehicle applicable before actual car tests. With respect to the research challenges to be addressed in the future, the U-SAT shows rather large errors for high-speed vehicle driving and therefore, further research will be necessary on this matter.

References

1. Lappe, M., Raushecker, J.P.: A Neural Network for the Processing of Optic Flow from Ego-Motion and Higher Mammals. Neural Computation 5(3), 374–391 (1993)
2. Kim, S., Kim, J.: Research of the Unmanned Vehicle Control and Modeling for Obstacle Detection and Avoidance. Transactions of KSAE, 11(5), 183–192 (2003). van Leeuwen, J. (ed.): Computer Science Today. Recent Trends and Developments. Lecture Notes in Computer Science, vol. 1000. Springer, Heidelberg (1995)
3. Ackermann, J., Guldner, J., Utkin, V.I.: A robust Nonlinear Control Approach to Automatic Path tharcking of a car. In: IEEE control conference, (389), pp. 196–201. IEEE, Los Alamitos (1994)
4. Lappe Tanagiya, M., Tomita, M., Tsugawa, S.: Effects of Field of View on Lateral Control Performance in a Vision_Based Autonomous Vehicle. JSAE Review 20, 499–504 (1999)
5. Abbott, E., Powell, D.: Land-Vehicle Navigation Using GPS. Proceedings of the IEEE 87(1) (January 1999)
6. Lee, D.H., An, H.T., Baek, K.R., Lee, M.H.: A study on resolution Enhancement in the detection of ultrasonic signal. In: The KSAE Annual Fall Conference, Branch of Busan Ulsan Gyeongnam, pp. 95–102 (2003)
7. Arai, T., Nakano, E.: Development of Measure Equipment for Location and Direction(MELODI) using Ultrasonic Waves. Transactions of the ASME 105, 152–156 (1983)
8. Kim, S.Y., Lee, D.H., An, H.T., Lee, S.H., Koh, Y.H., Lee, M.H.: Analysis of UPS (ultrasonic positioning system) using DGPS. In: IECON 2004. 30th Annual Conference of IEEE, vol. 1, pp. 609–613. Industrial Electronics Society (2004)

Energy-Efficient Scheduling Fixed-Priority Tasks with Preemption Thresholds on Variable Voltage Processors

XiaoChuan He and Yan Jia

Institute of Network Technology and Information Security
School of Computer Science
National University of Defense Technology
Changsha, China 410073

Abstract. Slowdown factors determine the extent of slowdown a computing system can experience based on functional and performance requirements. Dynamic Voltage Scaling (DVS), which adjusts the clock speed and supply voltage dynamically, is an effective technique in reducing the energy consumption of embedded real-time systems. We address the problem of computing static and dynamic slowdown factors in the FPPT algorithm. In this paper, Sufficient constraints have been identified for the feasibility of the task set using slowdown factors. We formulate this problem of computing the static slowdown factors for tasks as an nonlinear optimization problem to minimize the total energy consumption of the system. Our simulation experiments show on an average 17%~53% energy gains over FPPT scheduling policy.

1 Introduction

Dynamic Voltage Scaling (DVS), which adjusts the supply voltage and its corresponding clock frequency dynamically, is an effective low-power design technique for embedded real-time systems. Since the energy consumption of CMOS circuits has a quadratic dependency on the supply voltage, lowering the supply voltage is one of the most effective techniques for reducing the energy consumption. There exist two primary ways of reducing the power consumption in embedded computing systems: *processor shutdown* and *processor slowdown*. Slowdown using frequency and voltage scaling has been shown to be effective in reducing the processor energy consumption [1], [2], [3].

It is known that preemptability is a necessary requirement to achieve higher processor utilization and optimal slowdown [2],[4]. However, preemptive scheduling has its additional costs as compared to non-preemptive scheduling. Though preemptive scheduling achieves higher utilization, it is not always required to preempt a lower priority task.

Fixed-Priority scheduling with preemption threshold (FPPT) [5],[6] allows a task to disable preemptions from tasks up to a specified preemption threshold priority. Tasks with a priority greater than the preemption threshold priority are

K. Li et al. (Eds.): NPC 2007, LNCS 4672, pp. 133–142, 2007.

still allowed to preempt. The preemption threshold scheduling model has been shown to reduce the run-time costs by eliminating unnecessary task preemptions. Furthermore, FPPT allows tasks to be partitioned into non-preemptive groups to minimize the number of threads [6] and the stack memory requirement [7], thereby leading to scalable real-time systems.

Fixed-Priority scheduling with preemption threshold (FPPT) eliminates unnecessary context switches, thereby saving energy. Slowdown using frequency and voltage scaling is more effective in reducing the energy consumption [4], [2], [8], [1]. In this paper, we integrate processor slowdown techniques with FPPT to enable scalable and energy efficiency real-time systems. Given task with predefined priorities and corresponding preemption thresholds, we propose an algorithm to compute the *static slowdown factors* by formulating the problem as a linear optimization problem. Furthermore, we consider the energy consumption of task set under different preemption threshold assignments. We gain as much as 17%~53% energy savings over the usual FPPT scheduling algorithm.

The remainder of the paper is organized as follows. The next section presents the assumed computation model. The related work is introduced in Section 2. Section 3 we formulate the computation of slowdown factors as an nonlinear optimization problem. The experimental results are given in Section 4. Finally, the conclusion is made in Section 5.

2 Preliminaries

In this section, we introduce the necessary notation and formulate the problem. We first describe the system model followed by the related works.

2.1 System Model

This study deals with the fixed priority preemptive scheduling of tasks in a real-time systems with hard constraints, i.e., systems in which the respect of time constraints is mandatory. The activities of the system are modeled by periodic tasks. The model of the system is defined by a task set Γ of cardinality n, $\Gamma = \{\tau_1, \tau_2, ..., \tau_n\}$. A periodic task τ_i is characterized by a 3-tuple (C_i, T_i, D_i) where each request of τ_i, called instance, has an execution time of C_i, a relative deadline D_i. T_i time units separate two consecutive instances of τ_i (hence T_i is the period of the task). Note that C_i is the worst case execution time (WCET) of the task at maximum speed, given that it is the only task running in the system. The system is said schedulable if each instance finishes before its deadline.

Each task is associated with a deadline D_i, that D_i may be arbitrarily large. This means that many instances of the same task can be active (in the ready queue) at the same time. We assume that the scheduler handles tasks with the same priorities using a FIFO rule. Hence an early instance of a task has priority over a later, and must be completed before the later instance is allowed to start.

We further assume that the total utilization of all tasks, U, is strictly less than 1. This will later be shown to be a necessary condition for the analysis.

Each task is assigned with a priority π_i and preemption threshold γ_i, and $\gamma_i \geq \pi_i$. The smallest number is given to the task with highest priority.

2.2   Variable Speed Processors

A wide range of processors like the Intel XScale [9] and Transmeta Crusoe [10] support variable voltage and frequency levels. Voltage and frequency levels are tightly coupled. The important point to note is when we perform a slowdown we change both the frequency and voltage of the processor. Given the minimum frequency f_{min} and the maximum supported frequency f_{max}, we normalize the speed to the maximum frequency to have discrete points in the operating range $[\eta_{min}, 1]$, where $\eta_{min} = f_{min}/f_{max}$.

The *slowdown factor* can be viewed as the normalized frequency. At a given instance, it is the ratio of the scheduled frequency to the maximum frequency of the processor.

2.3   Related Works

Previous investigations on the voltage scheduling problem have focused mainly on real-time jobs running under dynamic-priority scheduling algorithms such as the EDF (earliest-deadline-first) algorithm [4], [11], [12], [13]. For example, the problem of energy-optimal EDF scheduling has been well understood. For EDF job sets, the algorithm by Yao et al. [14] computes the energy-optimal voltage schedules in polynomial time. Although the EDF scheduling policy makes the voltage scheduling problem easier to solve, fixed-priority scheduling algorithms such as the RM (rate monotonic) algorithm are more commonly used in practical real-time systems due to their low overhead and predictability [15].

Most of the earlier work dealt with general fixed-priority task sets. Shin et al. [1] have computed uniform slowdown factors for an independent periodic task set. Jejurika and Gupta [3] proposed an algorithm to compute a near optimal constant slowdown factor based on the bisection method, and furthermore for the case of tasks with varying power characteristics, [3] develop the computation of near optimal slowdown factors as a solution to convex optimization problem using the ellipsoid method. Yao, Demers and Shanker [14] presented an optimal off-line speed schedule for a set of N jobs. An optimal schedule for tasks with different power consumption characteristics is considered by Aydin, Melhem and Mosse [4]. The same authors [2] prove that the processor utilization (at maximum speed) is the optimal slowdown factor when the deadline is equal to the period. Quan and Hu [16] [17] discuss off-line algorithms for the case of fixed priority scheduling.

Since the worst case execution time (WCET) of a task is not usually reached, there is dynamic slack in the system. Pillai and Shin [14] recalculate the slow-down to use the dynamic slack while meeting the deadlines. Low-power scheduling using slack reclamation heuristic is studied by Aydin et al. [2] and Kim et al. [12]. Scheduling of task graphs on multiple processors has also been considered. Luo and Jha [18] have considered scheduling of periodic and aperiodic task graphs in a distributed system. Non preemptive scheduling of a task graph on a multi processor system is considered by Gruian and Kuchcinski [19]. Zhang et al. [8] have given a framework for task scheduling and voltage scaling of dependent tasks on a multi-processor system. They have formulated the voltage scaling problem as an integer programming problem.

3 Static Slowdown Factors

We compute static slowdown factor for a system with an underlying fixed-priority with preemption threshold (FPPT) scheduler. For a task τ_i in FPPT, the kth instance of τ_i is denoted as J_i^k. Before J_i^k begin execution, the interference caused by other tasks with regular priority higher than π_i is possible; Once J_i^k starts actually, only the tasks with regular priorities higher than γ_i can preempt J_i^k. Thus the starting time of J_i^k play a necessary role in the analysis of FPPT, so a notation S_i^k is introduce to denote it, S_i^k is used to represent the starting point of J_i^k, F_i^k denote the finish time of J_i^k.

3.1 FPPT Scheduler

The existing schedulability analysis for FPPT [5], [20], [21]is based on the FPPT critical instant [21] which says that if a task meets its deadline whenever the task is requested simultaneously with requests for all higher priority tasks and the lower priority task that contribute the largest blocking time to it, furthermore all of the task instance in the level-i busy period must meets its deadline too, then the deadline will always be met for all task phrasings. The WCRT of a task τ_i can be derived through the following equations [20]:

$$B_i = \max_{\tau_j \in \Gamma} \{C_j | \pi_i > \pi_j \wedge \pi_i \leq \gamma_j\} \tag{1}$$

$$L_i = B_i + \sum_{\forall j, \pi_j \geq \pi_i} \lceil \frac{L_i}{T_j} \rceil \cdot C_j \tag{2}$$

$$S_i^k = B_i + k \cdot C_i + \sum_{\forall j, \pi_j > \pi_i} \left(1 + \lfloor \frac{S_i^k}{T_j} \rfloor \right) \cdot C_j \tag{3}$$

$$F_i^k = S_i^k + C_i + \sum_{\forall j, \pi_j > \gamma_i} \left(\lceil \frac{F_i^k}{T_j} \rceil - \left(1 + \lfloor \frac{S_i^k}{T_j} \rfloor \right)\right) \cdot C_j \tag{4}$$

$$R_i = \max_{k=0,1,2,\ldots,\lfloor \frac{L_i}{T_j} \rfloor} (F_i^k - k \cdot T_i) \tag{5}$$

In the course of schedulability analysis of FPPT, as for task τ_i, WCRT of τ_i, R_i can be derived. At the same time, the specific instance of τ_i which contribute this WCRT can be derived too. This instance is denoted as J_i^{kr}. Assuming the task are independent, let η_i be the slowdown factors for task τ_i. As we know, the allowably finish time of J_i^{kr} is $D_i + k_r T_i$, thus equation 4,3 is rewritten as following:

$$S_i^{kr} = \frac{B_i}{\eta_b} + k_r \cdot \frac{C_i}{\eta_i} + \sum_{\forall j, \pi_j > \pi_i} \left(1 + \lfloor \frac{S_i^{kr}}{T_j} \rfloor \right) \cdot \frac{C_j}{\eta_j} \tag{6}$$

$$D_i + k_r T_i = S_i^{kr} + \frac{C_i}{\eta_i} + \sum_{\forall j, \pi_j > \gamma_i} \left(\lceil \frac{D_i + k_r T_i}{T_j} \rceil - \left(1 + \lfloor \frac{S_i^k}{T_j} \rfloor \right) \right) \cdot \frac{C_j}{\eta_j} \tag{7}$$

In the equation 6,7, S_i^{kr} is calculated in the course of schedulability analysis, all of other terms are known already except for the *slowdown factors*, denoted as $\eta_i, i = 1, 2, ..., n$. From the combination of equation 6 and 7, the following theorem can be derived.

Theorem 1. *A task set of n independent fixed-priority periodic tasks, scheduled with preemption thresholds, is feasible at a slowdown factor of η_i for task τ_i if the following relations satisfy:*

$$D_i + k_r T_i \geq \frac{B_i}{\eta_b} + \frac{C_i}{\eta_i} +$$
$$\sum_{\substack{\forall j, \pi_j > \pi_i, \\ \pi_j \leq \gamma_i}} \left(1 + \lfloor \frac{S_i^{kr}}{T_j} \rfloor \right) \frac{C_j}{\eta_j} + \sum_{\forall j, \pi_j > \gamma_i} \left(\lceil \frac{D_i + k_r T_i}{T_j} \rceil \right) \frac{C_j}{\eta_j} \tag{8}$$

where τ_b is the blocking task which contribute to the longest blocking time to τ_i.

In the equation 8, term $\sum_{\forall j, \pi_j > \gamma_i} \left(\lceil \frac{D_i + k_r T_i}{T_j} \rceil \right) \frac{C_j}{\eta_j}$ represent the workload of the tasks with the regular priority higher than γ_i in the interval of $[0, D_i + k_r T_i]$, term $\sum_{\forall j, \pi_i < \pi_j \leq \gamma_i} \left(1 + \lfloor \frac{S_i^{kr}}{T_j} \rfloor \right) \frac{C_j}{\eta_j}$ represent the workload of the tasks with the regular priority higher than π_i before J_i^{kr} start the execution. once J_i^{kr} started actually, these tasks can not preempt J_i^{kr} again. The term $\frac{B_i}{\eta_b}$ represent the blocking time that the task with the priority lower than π_i contributes. The term $\frac{C_i}{\eta_i}$ represent the workload of J_i^{kr} itself.

3.2 Computing Slowdown Factors

Power Characteristics. The number of cycles, C_i that a task τ_i needs to complete is a constant during voltage scaling. The processor cycle time, the task delay and the dynamic power consumption of a task vary with the supply voltage V_{DD}. The power delay characteristics of the CMOS technology [21] are as given below.

$$P_d = C_{eff} V_{DD}^2 f \tag{9}$$

$$f = \alpha k' \frac{(V_{DD} - V_{TH})^\alpha}{V_{DD}} \tag{10}$$

where k' is a device related parameter, V_{TH} is the threshold voltage, C_{eff} is the effective switching capacitance per cycle and α ranges from 2 to 1.2 depending on the device technology. Since power varies linearly with the clock speed and the square of the voltage, adjusting both can produce cubic power reductions, at least in theory. Since the time needed to execute task τ_i is $t_i = C_i/f_i$, the energy consumption of the task executing for an interval of time I, is $E = P_d I$.

Linear Optimization Problem. We formulate the energy minimization problem as an optimization problem. The voltage and slowdown factors are normalized to the maximum values. We compute normalized voltage levels for the tasks such that the conditions in Theorem 1 are satisfied. Let $\bar{f} \in R^n$ be a vector representing the normalized frequencies f_i of task τ_i. The optimization problem is to compute the optimal vector $\bar{f}^* \in R^n$ such that the system is feasible and the total energy consumption of the system is minimized. Let P_d be the normalized energy consumption of task τ_i as a function of the normalized frequencies f_i (for the case of identical power characteristics $P_d = k'f^3$. The total energy consumption of the system E, a function of the voltage vector $\bar{f} \in R^n$, is given by Equation 11. Thus, we have the following optimization problem:
   minimize:

$$E(v) = \sum_{i=1}^{n} P_d \frac{C_i}{\eta_i} \frac{I}{T_i} \tag{11}$$

under the constraints:

$$i = 1, 2, ..., n \quad D_i + k_r T_i \geq \frac{B_i}{\eta_i} + \frac{C_i}{\eta_i} + \sum_{\substack{\forall j, \pi_j > \pi_i, \\ \pi_j \leq \gamma_i}} \left(1 + \left\lfloor \frac{S_i^{kr}}{T_j} \right\rfloor\right) \frac{C_j}{\eta_j} + \sum_{\forall j, \pi_j > \gamma_i} \left(\left\lceil \frac{D_i + k_r T_i}{T_j} \right\rceil\right) \frac{C_j}{\eta_j} \tag{12}$$

$$\forall i \quad \eta_{min} \leq \eta_i \leq 1 \tag{13}$$

Equation 12 ensures the feasibility when the tasks are independent. Equation 13 constraints the slowdown factor to be greater than or equal to the slowdown in the independent mode. The normalized slowdown factors are between the normalized minimum frequency η_{min} and 1. The optimization function depends on the power characteristics P_d of the task. If P_d is convex, the optimization function is convex. Thus we have a convex Quadratic minimization problem.

4   Experiments

We use randomly generated periodic task sets for our simulations. Each task is characterized by its computation time C_i, its period T_i, its deadline D_i. We vary three parameters in our simulations: (1) number of tasks *totaltasks*, from 5 to 15; and (2) maximum period for tasks *maxperiod*, from 200 to 800; and (3) utilization for task set, from 0.1 to 0.9. For any given pair of *totaltasks*, *maxperiod*, and utilization, we randomly generate 1000 task sets, and the expreiment result is the average value over these 1000 task sets.

A task set is generated by randomly selecting a period, a deadline, and computation time for each of the *totaltasks*. First, a period T_i is assigned randomly in the range $[1, maxperiod]$ with a uniform probability distribution function. Then,we assign a utilization U_i in the range $[0.1/totaltasks, 2.0/totaltasks]$, again with uniform probability distribution function. The computation time of the task is then assigned as $T_i * U_i$. Deadlines are assigned just as periods, and deadline of each task is unique. Considering an interval of time $I = 5,000$, the experiment calculated the energy consumption of task set in this time interval.

For the simplicity of description, the FPPT scheduling algorithm using slowdown factors is denoted as *ES_FPPT*. We note that our experiments are executed in the environment of Pentium 1.8G, 786M RAM, Redhat9 (linux-2.4.20-8, gcc-3.4.2, X11, SPAK-0.3).

Although different task might have varying power characteristics [4], we don't compute slowdown factors based on the task characteristics in this paper. k' is assumed to be 1. In other words, all tasks have the same power coefficient.

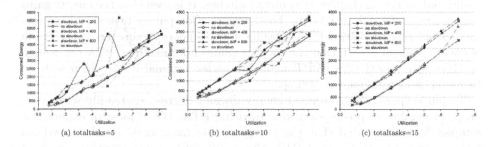

(a) totaltasks=5   (b) totaltasks=10   (c) totaltasks=15

Fig. 1. Average energy savings of ES_FPPT algorithm over the FPPT algorithm

In the first set of experiments, we guarantee the utilization of task set is unchanged when the respective slowdown factors of tasks are put in execution. Figure 1 shows the consumed energy of ES_FPPT scheduling algorithm in comparison with the FPPT scheduling algorithm. The energy consumption of both algorithms are collected in the time length of 5000ms, where figure 1(a), 1(b) and 1(c) describe respectively the experiment results of *totaltasks* is 5, 10 and 15. From the figure, it is seen obviously that the ES_FPPT algorithm performs more 13%~42% energy-saving than the FPPT algorithm. ES_FPPT assigns different slowdown factors for the tasks to have better energy gains. ES_FPPT performs up to low utilization of task set better than FPPT at high utilization. Since we compute continuous slowdown factors and assign them to the closest discrete voltage levels, there is run time slack even at worst case execution time. The complication workload demand analysis is required to implement the dynamically reclaim the run-time slack, which is the future working problem of our research.

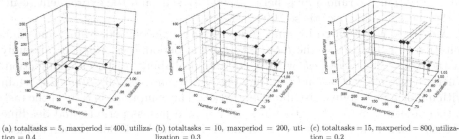

(a) totaltasks = 5, maxperiod = 400, utilization = 0.4

(b) totaltasks = 10, maxperiod = 200, utilization = 0.3

(c) totaltasks = 15, maxperiod = 800, utilization = 0.2

Fig. 2. Energy savings of ES_FPPT algorithm under different PTAs

In the second set of experiments, we allow the utilization can change after using slowdown factors. Figure 2 shows the energy consumption of the ES_FPPT
algorithm under different preemption threshold assignments(PTAs) [21]. With
the partial relations between the PTAs, which is defined in [21], It can be inferred that the smaller PTA, the more number of preemptions, and the more
additional energy dissipation of context switches. It is seen that the energy gains
increase with the different PTAs. Furthermore, Computing task slowdown factors considering the varied PTAs, results in more energy gains. From the graph
of energy gains, it is seen that the another gains under maximal PTA are as high
as 11%~46% over the ES_FPPT algorithm under minimal PTA, which adds up
to 2%~11% of total energy savings.

To our surprise, the consumed energy doesn't decreased steadily with some
drops in number of preemptions due to rising PTA. While most of experiment
samples have illustrated that the energy saving maximized by the slowdown
factors coming from maximal PTA, there still exist some exceptions, such as
figure 2(a) presents.

5   Conclusion

In this paper, we present algorithms to compute static slowdown factors under
FPPT scheduling policy. The sufficient constraints which slowdown factors must
satisfy to maintain the feasibility of FPPT task set are derived. Furthermore,
We formulate the computation of slowdown factors for tasks under different
preemption threshold assignments as an optimization problem. Experimental
results show that the computed slowdown factors save on an average 17%~53%
energy over the known techniques. The techniques are energy efficient and can
be easily implemented. This will have a great impact on the energy consumption
of embedded real-time systems.

We plan to further exploit the static and dynamic slack in the system to make
the FPPT algorithm more energy efficient. As a future work, we plan to compute
discrete slowdown factors for the tasks.

Acknowledgment

The authors wish to express their gratitude to ChuangGuo Guo, Yan Jia for useful discussions, and to the reviewers for their helpful comments on the paper.

References

1. Shin, Y., Choi, K., Sakurai, T.: Power optimization of real-time embedded systems on variable speed processors. In: 2000 International Conference on Computer-Aided Design (ICCAD '00), pp. 365–368 (2000)
2. Aydi, H., Mejia-Alvarez, P., Mosse, D., Melhem, R.: Dynamic and aggressive scheduling techniques for power-aware real-time systems. In: 22nd IEEE Real-Time Systems Symposium (RTSS'01), p. 95. IEEE Computer Society Press, Los Alamitos (2001)
3. Jejurikar, R., Gupta, R.K.: Optimized slowdown in real-time task systems. In: 16th Euromicro Conference on Real-Time Systems (ECRTS '04) (2004)
4. Aydin, H., Melhem, R., Mosse, D., Mejia-Alvarez, P.: Determining optimal processor speeds for periodic real-time tasks with different power characteristics. In: 13th Euromicro Conference on Real-Time Systems (ECRTS'01), p. 225 (2001)
5. Wang, Y., Saksena, M.: Scheduling fixed-priority tasks with preemption threshold. In: The Sixth International Conference on Real-Time Computing Systems and Applications, pp. 328–335. IEEE Computer Society Press, Los Alamitos (1999)
6. Saksena, M., Wang, Y.: Scalable real-time system design using preemption thresholds. In: 21st IEEE Real-Time Systems Symposium(RTSS'2000), pp. 25–34. IEEE Computer Society Press, Los Alamitos (2000)
7. Gai, P., Lipari, G., Di Natale, M.: Minimizing memory utilization of real-time task sets in single and multi-processor system-on-a-chip. In: 22nd Real-Time Systems Symposium, London, England (2001)
8. Yumin, Z., Xiaobo, H., Chen Danny, Z.: Task scheduling and voltage selection for energy minimization. In: 39th design automation conference (DMC), New Orleans LA, pp. 183–188 (2002)
9. Intel: Intel xscale processor (2000)
10. Transmeta: Transmeta crusoe processor (2000)
11. Inki, H., Qu Gang, M.M., Potkonjak, M., Srivastavas, M.B.: Synthesis techniques for low-power hard real-time systems on variable voltage processors. In: 19th IEEE Real-Time Systems Symposium, Madrid, Spain, pp. 178–187. IEEE Computer Society Press, Los Alamitos (1998)
12. Kim, S., Hong, S., Kim, T.: A dynamic voltage scaling algorithm for dynamic-priority hard real-time systems using slack time analysis. In: Fifth IEEE International Symposium on Object-Oriented Real-Time Distributed Computing. IEEE Computer Society Press, Los Alamitos (2002)
13. Pillai, P., Shin, K.G.: Real-time dynamic voltage scaling for low-power embedded operating systems. ACM SIGOPS Operating Systems Review 35, 89–102 (2001)
14. Yao, F., Demers, A., Shenker, S.: A scheduling model for reduced cpu energy. In: 36th Annual Symposium on Foundations of Computer Science (FOCS'95), pp. 374–382. IEEE Computer Society Press, Los Alamitos (1995)
15. Liu, J.: Real-Time Systems. Prentice Hall, Upper Saddle River (2000)

16. Quan, G., Hu, X.: Energy efficient fixed-priority scheduling for real-time systems on variable voltage processors. In: Annual ACM IEEE Design Automation Conference (38th conference on Design automation), Las Vegas, Nevada, United States, pp. 828–833 (2001)
17. Quan, G., Hu, X.: Minimum energy fixed-priority scheduling for variable voltage processors. In: Design, Automation and Test in Europe Conference and Exhibition (DATE'02), pp. 782–787 (2002)
18. Luo, J., Jha, N.K.: Power-conscious joint scheduling of periodic task graphs and a periodic tasks in distributed real-time embedded systems. In: 2000 International Conference on Computer-Aided Design (ICCAD '00), p. 357 (2000)
19. Kuchcinski, Gruian, F., Krzysztof.: Lenes: task scheduling for low-energy systems using variable supply voltage processors. In: The 2001 conference on Asia South Pacific design automation with EDA Technofair Design Automation Conference Asia and South Pacific (ASP-DAC), Yokohama, Japan, pp. 449–455. ACM Press, New York (2001)
20. Regehr, J.: Scheduling tasks with mixed preemtion relations for robustness to timing faults. In: 23rd IEEE Real-Time System Symposium, pp. 315–326. IEEE Computer Society Press, Los Alamitos (2002)
21. Chen, J.: Extensions to Fixed Priority with PreemptionThreshold and Reservation-Based Schedulin. PhD thesis, University of Waterloo (2005)

Estimation of Absolute Positioning of Mobile Robot Using U-SAT

Su Yong Kim[1] and SooHong Park[2]

[1] Graduate student, Department of Mechanical Engineering, Pusan National University,
KumJung Ku, Pusan 609-735, Korea
syz2ang@hanmail.net
[2] Department of Mechatronics Engineering, Dongseo University, Sasang Ku,
Pusan 617-716, Korea
shpark@dongseo.ac.kr

Abstract. This paper proposes a new method to find an absolute position by using ultrasonic sensors. In order to evaluate the performance of U-SAT (Ultrasonic Satellite system), the autonomous navigation performance of a mobile robot is tested. Experiments were performed in both cases that the mobile robot moves to the target point using relative positioning method in conjunction with U-SAT, which is, absolute positioning methods. The performance of U-SAT is evaluated accordingly with the results of the experiments. As a result, U-SAT could be effectively used as a pseudolites or pseudo-satellites to help a mobile robot navigate intelligently and autonomously in an indoor area.

1 Introduction

In terms of obstacle avoidance and path planning, it is a very significant issue for a mobile robot to identify its positions. Research on this issue has been actively conducted. Positioning can be largely divided into relative positioning and absolute positioning. Dead reckoning (DR) is widely used as a method of relative positioning. In this method, however, positioning errors are accumulated due to wheel sliding, mechanical errors and surface roughness, making it difficult to determine an actual position as the distance gets longer [1]. For this reason, it is only difficult for relative positioning to identify the accurate position of a robot that navigates a long distance. Accordingly, it is necessary to conduct absolute positioning and correct the positions. GPS (Global Position System) is widely used for absolute positioning, but GPS is expensive and cannot properly receive satellite signals indoors, which makes its indoor application to a robot difficult. Therefore, a great deal of research is underway in order to estimate absolute positions.

In a bid to estimate absolute positions indoors, much research is being conducted using CCD cameras, infrared rays and ultrasonic waves. First of all, the method using a CCD camera is expensive and requires complex signal treatment. It is also affected by camera correction and operating conditions [2,3]. Second, the system using infrared rays can be established easily and inexpensively but the coverage area is not

K. Li et al. (Eds.): NPC 2007, LNCS 4672, pp. 143–150, 2007.

wide and its performance level is lower than the other systems. In addition, it is greatly influenced by light [4]. Lastly, ultrasonic sensors are inexpensive and easy to use. They also consume less electricity than laser sensors or vision sensors and their signal handling devices are relatively simple.

This paper adopted a method in which the receiving part of an ultrasonic sensor receives ultrasonic waves from the ultrasonic transmitters located at a fixed position and estimates an absolute position [5,6]. In addition, this study proposed a method with a high degree of precision in the measurement of distances which separates the ultrasonic receiver and transmitter [7]. Based on this, a U-SAT (Ultrasonic Satellite system) of excellent performance has been developed to estimate a three-dimensional absolute position. Also, DR, which has been widely used for relative positioning, and a U-SAT have applied to a mobile robot to evaluate positioning and autonomous navigation performance.

2   Absolute Positioning of U-SAT

Distance measurement using ultrasonic waves makes use of the transmission speed and time information of ultrasonic waves. The time taken for the transmission of ultrasonic waves through air is called T.O.F. (Time of Flight), and it is defined as the difference between the time of transmission of the signal (t_t) and the time of its receipt (t_r). The distance (d) measured by ultrasonic waves can be expressed as follows:

$$d = c \times T.O.F \tag{1}$$

where, d_0 represents the distance offset caused by the vibrating plate position errors of the transmitter-receiver part, and c indicates the ultrasonic wave speed and is defined as follows for centigrade temperature T.

$$c = 331.5 + 0.60714T \tag{2}$$

Therefore, influence of temperature should be considered when measuring distances using ultrasonic waves.

In general, T.O.F. is determined by the time needed for the size of an ultrasonic signal to reach a certain threshold level after the ultrasonic receiver has received the ultrasonic signal. In this distance measuring method, however, it is difficult to determine a threshold of a proper size due to the influences of the media in the air, temperature, attenuation caused by a frequency increase and the absorption of ultrasonic waves by objects. The degree of precision decreases due to the sensitivity to noise. Therefore, this paper adopted T.O.F. measurement using the period detecting method [7]. With an increase in T.O.F., the amplitude of a transmitted signal is attenuated, with its period remains unchanged. Accordingly, if detection is made based on the period, the precision of distance measurement can be enhanced irrespective of the amplitude attenuation.

U-SAT can be composed as shown in Fig. 1. MURATA MA40BR/S of 40 kHz was used for the ultrasonic transmitter-receiver sensor. The ultrasonic transmitter discharges ultrasonic waves of 40 kHz as soon as it receives wire-carried synchronized signals from a synchronized RF-signal transmitter. At the same time, the synchronized RF-signal transmitter sends synchronized signals to the ultrasonic wave receiver, which calculates T.O.F. with the use of the time difference between the synchronized RF signals and the ultrasonic waves received. Using the T.O.F., the receiver also calculates the distance between the ultrasonic transmitter and receiver. With the outcome, the receiver can obtain its own three-dimensional coordinates. This is similar to the basic principles of GPS. In the case of GPS, a satellite transmits its starting signal and position information but U-SAT searches its starting point of time with synchronized RF-signals. The synchronized RF-signal transmitter is positioned together with transmitter #1. Synchronized signals are transmitted to transmitters #2, #3 and #4 by cable at certain intervals, controlling the transmission of ultrasonic waves one after another. Even though there are several receivers, they do not interfere with each other and can secure their own positions independently.

Fig. 2 shows a time diagram in which an ultrasonic receiver receives ultrasonic waves by synchronized RF signals. Based on the synchronized RF-signals, the ultrasonic receiver calculates T.O.F. of ultrasonic waves received from an ultrasonic transmitter, and it also calculates d1, d2, d3, and d4, which are the distances between the ultrasonic transmitter and receiver. After receiving synchronized RF-signals from an ultrasonic transmitter, the ultrasonic receiver should wait 100ms to receive next ultrasonic signal. Thus ultrasonic waves are transmitted at certain intervals to prevent interference between transmitters and reduce the influences of reflective waves.

Next, the positions of the ultrasonic receivers (x, y, z) can be expressed as in Eq (3) from the four fixed positions of the ultrasonic waves (x_i, y_i, z_i) and the distances between transmitters and receivers d_i $(i = 1, 2, 3, 4)$

$$(x_1 - x_2)x + (y_1 - y_2)y + (z_1 - z_2)z = \alpha$$
$$(x_2 - x_3)x + (y_2 - y_3)y + (z_2 - z_3)z = \beta \qquad (3)$$
$$(x_3 - x_4)x + (y_3 - y_4)y + (z_3 - z_4)z = \gamma$$

This can be changed to a matrix operation and is expressed as follows.

$$\begin{bmatrix} x \\ y \\ z \end{bmatrix} = A^{-1} \begin{bmatrix} \alpha \\ \beta \\ \gamma \end{bmatrix} \qquad (4)$$

Where, $A = \begin{bmatrix} (x_1 - x_2) & (y_1 - y_2) & (z_1 - z_2) \\ (x_2 - x_3) & (y_2 - y_3) & (z_2 - z_3) \\ (x_3 - x_4) & (y_3 - y_4) & (z_3 - z_4) \end{bmatrix}$,

$\alpha = \frac{1}{2}\{(x_1^2 - x_2^2 + y_1^2 - y_2^2 + z_1^2 - z_2^2) - (d_1^2 - d_2^2)\}$

$\beta = \frac{1}{2}\{(x_2^2 - x_3^2 + y_2^2 - y_3^2 + z_2^2 - z_3^2) - (d_2^2 - d_3^2)\}$,

$\gamma = \frac{1}{2}\{(x_3^2 - x_4^2 + y_3^2 - y_4^2 + z_3^2 - z_4^2) - (d_3^2 - d_4^2)\}.$

In Eq (4), if $\det A \neq 0$, (x,y,z) has a singular solution, making it possible to obtain three-dimensional coordinates in space.

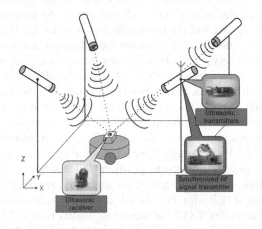

Fig. 1. Configuration of U-SAT

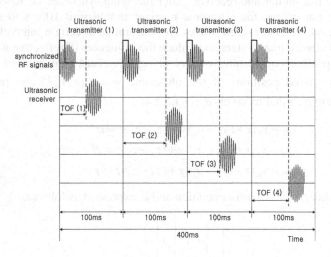

Fig. 2. Timing Diagram

3   Autonomous Navigation Algorithm of a Mobile Robot

The posture of a mobile robot driving on a two-dimensional plane can be shown as follows.

$$p = \begin{bmatrix} x \\ y \\ \theta \end{bmatrix} \tag{5}$$

where, θ represents the heading angle indicated counterclockwise from axis X. The kinematics of a mobile robot can be expressed by Jacobean matrix J as follows [8].

$$\begin{bmatrix} \dot{x} \\ \dot{y} \\ \dot{\theta} \end{bmatrix} = \dot{p} = Jq = \begin{bmatrix} \cos\theta & 0 \\ \sin\theta & 0 \\ 0 & 1 \end{bmatrix} q \ , \quad q = \begin{bmatrix} v \\ \omega \end{bmatrix} \tag{6}$$

where, v and ω represent the linear velocity and rotational velocity, respectively.

A mobile robot control system uses two positions of reference position $p_r = [x_r, y_r, \theta_r]^T$ and the current position $p_c = [x_c, y_c, \theta_c]^T$. In Fig. 3, the reference position is the position targeted by the mobile robot, and the current position indicates the position in which the mobile robot is actually located. When a position error between the reference position p_r and the current position p_c is defined as p_e, it can be expressed as follows.

$$p_e = \begin{bmatrix} x_e \\ y_e \\ \theta_e \end{bmatrix} = \begin{bmatrix} \cos\theta_c & \sin\theta_c & 0 \\ -\sin\theta_c & \cos\theta_c & 0 \\ 0 & 0 & 1 \end{bmatrix} (p_r - p_c) = T_e (p_r - p_c) \tag{7}$$

$$\text{Where, } T_e = \begin{bmatrix} \cos\theta_c & \sin\theta_c & 0 \\ -\sin\theta_c & \cos\theta_c & 0 \\ 0 & 0 & 1 \end{bmatrix}$$

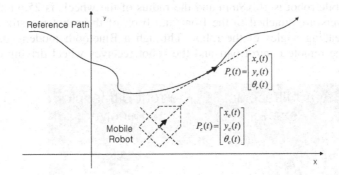

Fig. 3. Reference and current postures

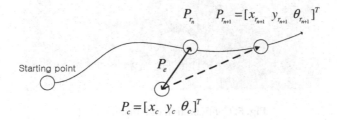

Fig. 4. Position estimation of a mobile robot

As shown in Fig. 4, when a position error p_e occurs between the current position p_c and the reference position p_{r_n} , it is difficult for a mobile robot to navigate to the accurate next reference position $p_{r_{n+1}}$ in the case of the autonomous navigation algorithm of a mobile robot. Therefore, it is necessary to calculate p_e after accurately measuring the current position p_c , estimated with U-SAT. When the error of the measured heading angle is above $\pm 3°$, it is necessary to reestablish the heading angle and the distance to the next reference position $p_{r_{n+1}}$. The robot should be driven along the trajectory in this way so that the errors may not be accumulated. Changing distances and heading angles can be calculated with the following equation.

$$D_p = \sqrt{(x_{r_{n+1}} - x_c)^2 + (y_{r_{n+1}} - y_c)^2} ,$$
$$\theta_p = \theta_{r_{n+1}} - \theta_c \tag{8}$$

where, D_p represents modified distance information, and θ_p indicates modified heading angle information.

4   Positioning Performance Experiment of a Mobile Robot

Fig. 5 shows the mobile robot used in this experiment. The right and left wheels of the mobile robot are driven by a stepping motor, and they rotate at 1.8 degrees per pulse. The movement and turn of the mobile robot are controlled by the two wheels. The width of the mobile robot is 100.8mm and the radius of the wheels is 25.6mm. Two ultrasonic receivers are attached to the front and back of the robot to estimate the positions and heading angles of the robot. Through a Bluetooth modem, data are transmitted to the remote control part and the robot receives wheel driving control

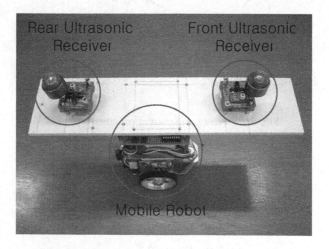

Fig. 5. Configuration of a mobile robot

orders. Using the algorithm proposed in the above and the positions and heading angles received from the ultrasonic receiver, the remote control part controls the robot. The remote control part was programmed using Visual C++.

Next, the positioning performance of the mobile robot is evaluated with use of the autonomous navigation algorithm suggested above. First, only DR was used to examine the state at the time when the mobile robot moved to the desired trajectory. Then, the autonomous navigation algorithm using U-SAT was applied to the mobile robot to evaluate the performance when the robot moved to the desired trajectory. In evaluating the positioning performance, the maximum speed was set at 300mm/s. For the experiment, four ultrasonic transmitters were installed to the rectangular satellites with a size of 7000x5000 mm attached to the ceiling.

Fig. 6 shows the results of the experiment in which the mobile robot autonomously navigated counterclockwise along a rectangular trajectory with a size of 2000x1000 mm. When positioning is conducted using DR only, the accumulated errors cannot be eliminated and therefore large accumulated errors occur when the mobile robot returns to the starting point. It was found that the errors between the first starting position and the position to which the robot returned after making a round were 117mm in the X direction and minus 209mm in the Y direction. Therefore, DR alone could not reduce the errors, making it difficult to properly perform autonomous navigation. Next, it was found that when autonomous navigation was conducted by estimating the position and heading angle using U-SAT, no accumulated errors occurred, and the robot was navigating in a stable manner within the position error range of ±30 mm. Unlike the previous results, it was found that when the mobile robot arrived at the final target point, the position errors were minus 2mm in the X direction and minus 14mm in the Y direction. Accordingly, when a mobile robot is navigated with absolute position estimations using U-SAT, accumulated errors can be decreased. Such positions may also apply to obstacle avoidance and path planning, giving a higher level of flexibility for working environments.

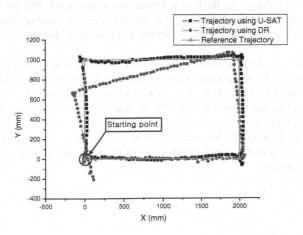

Fig. 6. Experimental result of the relative and absolute positioning performance

5 Conclusion

This paper has developed a U-SAT applicable indoors and tested the autonomous navigation performance of a mobile robot to evaluate the performance of U-SAT. To evaluate the positioning performance of a mobile robot using the proposed U-SAT, this paper examined two cases of autonomous navigation: the case in which a mobile robot conducted autonomous navigation only with relative position estimations and the case in which a mobile robot made autonomous navigation using absolute position estimations. The results showed that when relative position estimations were used, the robot could not navigate toward the desired position due to the accumulated errors but when absolute positions were estimated using U-SAT, the robot could autonomously navigate along the target trajectory in a stable manner. Therefore, the use of position estimations of U-SAT could greatly help a mobile robot navigate intelligently and autonomously. Further studies need to develop methods that can measure exact positions even when a mobile robot navigates at a faster speed.

References

[1] Kim, J.H., Seong, P.H.: Experiments on orientation recovery and steering of autonomous mobile robot using encoded magnetic compass disc. IEEE Transactions on Instrumentation and Measurement 45, 271–274 (1996)
[2] Wijesoma, W.S., Kodagoda, K.R.S., Balasuriya, A.P.: A laser and a camera for mobile robot navigation. In: ICARCV 2002. 7th International Conference on, Control, Automation, Robotics and Vision, pp. 740–745 (2002)
[3] Song, K.T., Tang, W.H.: Environment perception for a mobile robot using double ultrasonic sensors and a CCD camera. IEEE Transactions on, Industrial Electronics 43, 372–379 (1996)
[4] Arai, Y., Sekiai, M.: Absolute position measurement system for mobile robot based on incident angle detection of infrared light. In (IROS 2003). Proceedings. 2003 IEEE/RSJ International Conference on, Intelligent Robots and Systems, vol. 991, pp. 986–991 (2003)
[5] Tsai, C.C.: A localization system of a mobile robot by fusing DR and ultrasonic measurements. IEEE Transactions on, Instrumentation and Measurement 47, 1399–1404 (1998)
[6] Yi, S.Y., Jin, J.H.: Self-localization of a Mobile Robot Using Global Ultrasonic Sensor System. Journal of Control, Automation, and Systems Engineering 9(2), 145–151 (2003)
[7] Lee, D.H., An, H.T., Baek, K.R., Lee, M.H.: A study on resolution Enhancement in the detection of ultrasonic signal. In: The KSAE Annual Fall Conference, Branch of Busan Ulsan Gyeongnam, pp. 95–102 (2003)
[8] Kanayama, Y., Kimura, Y., Miyazaki, F., Noguchi, T.: A stable tracking control method for an autonomous mobile robot. In: Proc. IEEE Int. Conf. Robot and Automation, vol. 1, pp. 384–389 (1990)

A Collaborative Service Discovery and Service Sharing Framework for Mobile Ad Hoc Networks

Haidar Safa[1], Hassan Artail[2], Hicham Hamze[2], and Khaleel Mershad[2]

[1] Department of Computer Science
[2] Department of Electrical and Computer Engineering
American University of Beirut, Beirut, Lebanon
{hs33,hartail,hhh14,kwm03}@aub.edu.lb

Abstract. Service sharing and discovery play a relevant role in mobile ad hoc environments. Upon joining a self-organizing network, mobile nodes should be able to explore the environment to learn about, locate, and share the available services. In this paper, we propose a distributed and scalable service discovery and sharing framework for ad hoc networks. The proposed framework defines three types of nodes: service directories, service providers and requesting nodes. Service directory nodes act as mediators for lookup requests from requesting nodes. Joining service provider nodes register their services with the nearest service directory. A requesting node discovers the available services by submitting requests to its nearest service directory which determines the node providing the requesting service. The performance of the proposed model is evaluated and compared to the broadcast-based model that has been extensively studied in the literature.

Keywords: service discovery, mobile ad hoc networks, cooperative computing, ns2.

1 Introduction

Service discovery protocols like Service Location Protocol (SLP) of IETF [5], Sun's Jini [1], and IBM's Salutation [10] that have been developed to help applications discover remote services residing on machines in a wired network do not directly dwell on mobile ad-hoc network (MANET) environments where self-configurability is the key.

Several service discovery solutions for MANETs were recently proposed [2], [4],[6]. A distributed service discovery architecture that relies on a virtual backbone for locating and registering available services was presented in [6]. This architecture creates a mesh structure from a subset of a given network graph that includes the nodes acting as service brokers and also a subset of paths connecting them. Then it establishes sub-trees rooted at service requesting nodes and registering servers for efficient dissemination of the service discovery control messages. The disadvantage of this approach is that it totally relies on multicasting and broadcasting techniques for service discovery and registration. In [2] and

K. Li et al. (Eds.): NPC 2007, LNCS 4672, pp. 151–160, 2007.
© IFIP International Federation for Information Processing 2007

[4], two semantic-routing-based service discovery schemes were described and are called Group-based Service Discovery (GSD) and Candidate Node Pruning enhanced Group-based Service Discovery Protocol (CNPGSDP), respectively. In GSD, services are classified into several groups and each server periodically generates service advertisement packets that can be forwarded into the network. To restrict the spreading range of these packets, the maximum number of hops they can travel is limited (denoted as d). The service advertisement packet contains not only information about the service provided by the sender, but also about the groups to which the services provided the sender's d-hop neighbors belong. Each node maintains a cache called Service Information Cache (SIC), which is used to store service advertisement packet temporally. This makes a node know not only about the services provided by the servers in its d-hop neighbor set, but also about the groups to which these services belong. When a node needs services and there is no matched services in its SIC, the node constructs a service request packet and forwards the packet towards some elaborately selected nodes in unicast mode. When receiving a packet sent by a node, each selected node should forward the packet further, unless the packet is matched or exceeded its hop limit. If the node that receives a new request packet finds a matched service, it sends out a service reply packet in unicast mode directly to the sender of the service request packet. The reply packet will be relayed to the source of the service request packet using a traditional ad-hoc routing protocol (like AODV and DSDV [8]) or along the reverse path after retracing the path traversed by the request packet. As to the CNPGSDP protocol, it was proposed to enhance GSD by reducing the number of unicast messages using a techniqye called Broadcast Simulated Unicast (BSU) in which several unicast request packets are replaced with one request packet transmitted in broadcast mode with all unicast receivers enclosed. These semantic-routing-based approaches have several issues. First, when no service group finds a match in the service cache, the request would still have to be broadcasted to the whole network. Second, the selective forwarding process might result in false forwards, meaning the request might be forwarded to a region where the service is no longer available (due to mobility of nodes) or has the right group but not the exact service.

We observe that these proposed protocols are either request broadcast-based, advertisement-based, or a combination of both. The broadcast-based solution, in which a service discovery request is broadcast throughout the network and the node that contains the service responds with a service reply, suffers from several drawbacks [11]: 1)it scales poorly with increasing network diameter and size; 2)it utilizes resources and computation power on all nodes; and 3)it is heavy on network bandwidth. In the advertisement-based solution the services advertise themselves to all of the nodes [9] and each node interested in discovering services will cache the advertisements. The advertisements are matched with service requests and a result is returned. In this solution, the cache size increases with the number of services while many of the nodes may have limited memory that does not allow them to store all the advertisements. Similar to the broadcast method, this approach is also inefficient in terms of bandwidth usage, since the whole network has to be periodically flooded with advertisements.

In this work, we propose a scalable and distributed service discovery and sharing model (DSDSM) for self-organized networks. This model does not employ broadcasting for service requests and advertisements for service providers and as a result, avoids many of the issues that are associated with the above described approaches. The remaining part of the paper is organized as follows. Section 2 describes the proposed DSDSM model while Section 3 presents the simulations and analyses performed to evaluate the proposed model and describes the experimental results. Finally, Section 4 contains some concluding remarks.

2   Proposed Framework

2.1   Basic Concept

In the proposed Distributed Service Discovery and Sharing Model (DSDM) the network is composed of service directory nodes (SDs), service provider nodes (SPs), and requesting nodes (RNs). The main task of the Service Directory nodes (SDs) is to maintain a list of all the services provided by their nearby service provider nodes. We assume that every node that joins the network registers the services that it can provide with the nearest SD. A RN node that is requesting a service can discover the available services in the network by forming and submitting requests to its nearest SD node. SDs act as distributed indices for services by storing service description entries along with the addresses of the service provider. Service description includes information like type of service, signature, service provider, time to live (TTL). The RN can ask for a specific service (i.e., print service, scan service, internet service), a specific type of services (i.e., all music services, all food services), or all the services registered in the SD. If the SD receives a service discovery request and the requested service is not cached (i.e., a miss), the request is forwarded to the next nearest SD node to retrieve the required information. Upon receiving the response, the RN caches the service description so that the next time the node requests the same service it can retrieve the service description from its own cache.

Nodes can determine the nearest SD from the routing table assuming that table-driven proactive routing protocols such as DSDV are used [8]. Sending requests to or registering services with the nearest SD helps in minimizing delay and network congestion. If the contacted SD does not have the description for the requested service, it also forwards the request to its nearest SD that has not been visited yet by this request.

2.2   System Configuration

The SDs are the central component of the system and must be selected carefully. Preference is given to nodes with sufficient resources. Nodes summarize their capabilities by calculating a special score using the following parameters: availability time in the network ($TIME$), battery life (BAT), available bandwidth (BW), and available memory for caching (MEM). To be considered a candidate SD, the node must meet a minimum criterion in each category. That is,

$$\{D_k\}|R_k^x > \Theta_x, \forall x \in \{TIME, BAT, BE, MEM\} \tag{1}$$

where $\{D_k\}$ is the set of candidate devices, R_k^x is a resource for device k, and Θ_x an empirically-set threshold for resource X. If $\{D_k\}$ includes more than one device, then the one with the maximum weighted score is selected. That is, if device j is the selected one, then

$$SC_j = max\{SC_k\}|SC_k = \sum \alpha_x R_k^x \tag{2}$$

where SC_j is node k's score, k refers to one of the devices satisfying the condition in (1), and α_x is the weight associated with resource X such that $\sum \alpha_x = 1$.

2.3   System Formation and Operation

The system will start with one SD then add SDs on demand. When the network starts every node joins the network by broadcasting a HELLO packet that includes its score. Using the data from HELLO packets, each node will know about the scores of the other nodes. The node with the highest score will be considered as the first SD. Nodes meeting the conditions (1) and (2) will be considered as potential SD candidates. The first SD broadcasts a *DSDSM Information Packet* (DIP) that contains itself as the only SD in the list of SDs. the list of SDs is the main parameter in the DIP packet which is broadcast only when this list changes. Node that joins the network after forming the network broadcast a HELLO packet that includes its score and requests the list of SDs from a nearby node by sending a unicast *SDs List Request Packet* (SDLRP). The nearby node replies by sending a unicast DIP. When the number of nodes in the network increases, the last joining SD will start a timer and send a *SD Assignment Packet* (SDAP) to the SD candidate node with the next highest score to assume the role of SD. If the latter accepts the invitation it broadcasts a DIP message with its identifier added to the list of SDs. This message will be interpreted by the inviting SD as acknowledgment message. Otherwise, if the timer expires without receiving the DIP message, the next SD candidate on the row will be invited. Moreover, DSDSM depends on the table-driven proactive routing protocols to detect nodes going offline. If an SD goes offline, the candidate SD node with the highest score will broadcast a DIP to announce its new role as an SD. To protect for situations in which this or other candidates take no action, all candidates that meet the condition in (1) start a timer after detecting the departure of an SD. The second-highest-score candidate will wait a period of T and will assume the role of an SD and broadcast a DIP if it hears nothing. The third-highest candidate waits a period of $2T$ before it sends a DIP if it hears nothing, and so on. The service provider (SP) holds for each service the SDs that it registered its service with, thus allowing for rebuilding SD entries when an SD goes offline. Upon receiving the DIP from the replacement SD, the concerned SPs reply by sending a *SD Registration Packet* (SDRP) that contains the descriptions that were used to reference the lost SD. The DIP will also serve to inform nodes about the replacement and prompt them to update their SD lists. If an SP goes offline, the SDs will detect its departure when the routing protocol updates their routing tables, and will update their entries accordingly.

The message sequence diagram of the DSDM model is shown in Fig. 1. It consists of three phases. In the top *registration* phase each SP willing to share its services sends an SDRP to its nearest SD. In the *discovery* phase the RN asks its nearest SD for a specific service by sending a *Service Request Packet* (SRP) to its nearest SD. If this SD does not have a matching service, it adds its address to the SRP to indicate that it has been visited and then sends this modified SRP to the nearest SD that has not been checked yet. This continues until a hit occurs where the SD replies with a *Service Reply Packet* (SREP) that comprises the service description including the service provider address. In the bottom *invocation* phase, the RN sends a *Service Invoke Packet* (SINVK) to the SP node (SN) implementing the service. The RN gets the result from the SP via a *Service Response Packet* (SRESP).

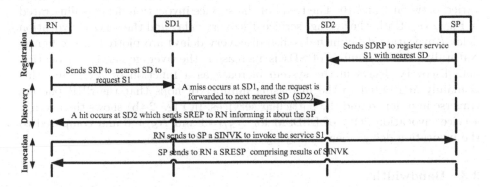

Fig. 1. Message sequence diagram in DSDM

3 Simulations

3.1 Simulation Parameters and Environment

To study the performance of the proposed approach, we have conducted several simulation scenarios and experiments using the network simulator ns-2 [7]. In these simulations, the distributed coordination function (DCF) of IEEE 802.11 is used as the underlying MAC protocol. The radio interface is based on Lucent's Wave LAN technology with 100 meters of nominal propagation range and 2 Mbps of nominal bit rate. The network topography is $1000 \times 1000 \ m^2$ in which 100 nodes were randomly deployed. The node speed (V_{max}) varied from 0 to 2 meters/sec using the Random way point model (RWP).

The duration of each simulation scenario is set to 1000 seconds. The first 150 seconds are given for the DSDV routing agents to populate the routing tables of each node. Then the mobile nodes that are willing to share their services starts registering them with their nearest service directory (SD) node by sending SDRP messages. We assume that 20 services are provided by a group of mobile nodes chosen randomly and the number of SDs (N_{SD})has been assigned in the network.

After the registration period is complete, the RNs start submitting SRP (service request packets) messages at a request rate (λ_i= 0.1 req/sec) per request node. These requests ask for diverse services using a Zipf-like access pattern, which has been used frequently to model non-uniform distributions [12]. In Zipf law, a service ranked i ($1 \leq i \leq n_s$) is accessed with probability $1/(i^{\Theta} \sum_{k=1}^{n_s} 1/K^{\theta})$ where Θ ranges between 0 (uniform distribution) and 1 (strict Zipf distribution). The access pattern is also location-dependent in the sense that nodes around the same location tend to choose the same set of services (i.e., have similar interests).

3.2 Delay Estimation

We studied the delay of the system as the number of service directories (N_{SD}) varied between 1 and 10. The trend of the service invocation delay is illustrated in Fig. 2 (a). Both, the average service discovery delay and the service invocation delay (invocation delay includes also discovery delay) are plotted in the figure. Naturally, as the number of SDs is increased, the average service invocation and discovery delays in the system increase as a function of N_{SD}, and this is mainly attributed to the increasing number of hops that the SRP packets traverse in order to find the particular services. In Fig. 2 (b) shows the average service invocation delay of DSDSM for N_{SD}=3 and N_{SD}=6 and compared to the invocation delay when employing a broadcast scheme.

3.3 Bandwidth

To study the traffic load on each SD, we assume that T_{SD_i} is the traffic traversing SD_i. T_{SD_i} is obtained by computing the number of each incoming and outgoing packets traversing the node SD_i. The average traffic for each SD is $\sum_{i=1}^{N_{SD}} T_{SD_i}/N_{SD}$ and is estimated simply by dividing the sum of such traffic by the number of service directories in the system, N_{SD}.

This process gets repeated for each value of N_{SD}. For each value of N_{SD}, averages of the results of 10 different trials were plotted in Fig. 2(c). Each trial lasted for 650 seconds and corresponds to a scenario in which a set of service providers were chosen randomly. Fig. 2(c) shows that as the number of service directories increases, the average traffic load at each SD decreases. This is because with multiple SDs, it is likely that the description of the desired service will be found at a closer SD. Fig. 2(d) shows that as the number of service directories increases, the traffic overhead incurred at each SD increases. This is can be justified since as the number of SDs increases, the average number of SDs that are traversed increases. Fig. 2(d) shows also that with more SDs the effect

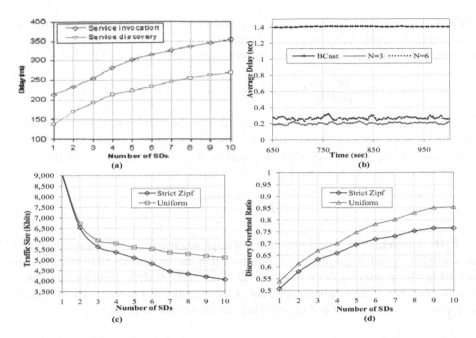

Fig. 2. (a) Service discovery delay and service invocation Delay versus N_{SD}, (b)Average service invocation delay, (c)SD Traffic versus N_{SD},(d) Overhead ratio

of the strict-Zipf distribution diminishes since popular services could be found across a growing number of SDs.

3.4 Estimating the Maximum Number of SDs

We observe that as the number of SDs in the system increases, the average delay to receive a response for a request will also increase. Intuitively, this is because the service request packet will traverse more SDs on average. It follows that a limit must be set on the number of SDs so as to prevent the number of SDs to increase indefinitely. One way to compute this limit is to set an upper limit on the average delay in the system $(E[\tau])$ and make this limit equal to the average delay of accessing a point at the corner of the topography and getting back the reply from it $(E[\tau_{corner}])$. Thus, the maximum number of SDs (N_{SD}^{max}) can be set as follows:

$$N_{SD}^{max} = max(N_{SD})|E[\tau] < E[\tau_{corner}] \tag{3}$$

We now have to derive several parameters that are involved in computing N_{SD}^{max}:
1) The expected number of hops between any two nodes in the network $(E[H])$,
2) The expected number of hops within the SDs system $(E[H_{SD}])$(different from $E[H]$ because of the nearest node selection), 3) The expected number of hops to the corner of the topography $(E[H_{CO}])$, and 4) The response time of the system.

To derive $E[H]$, we assume a rectangular topography with an area a×b (where $a < b$). Two nodes are capable of forming a direct link if the distance S between them is less than the node maximum transmission range r_0 . Using stochastic geometry, the probability density function (pdf) of x (x is a random variable denoting the straight line distance between two nodes) is given in [3] as

$$P_x(x) = \frac{4x}{a^2b^2}(\frac{\pi}{2}ab - ax - bx + 0.5x^2) \, For \, 0 \le x < a < b \tag{4}$$

It is concluded that if two nodes are at distance S_0 from each other, the number of hops between them when there is an infinite number of nodes would tend towards x_0/r_0. Hence, $E[H]$ is equivalent to dividing expected distance between two nodes $E[x]$ by r_0. E[H] is given in [3] as

$$E[H] = \frac{0.521a}{r_0} \tag{5}$$

$E[H]$ represents the expected number of hops when only one destination choice is available. Finding the expected number of hops to nearest SD node, is like selecting the minimum from a set of multiple independent random variables. Given N_{SD} random variables represented by a vector of random variables $X = (x_1, x_2, x_3, ..., x_{N_{SD}})$, the pdf of selecting the minimum of X is:

$$P_{min(x)} = \sum_{i=1}^{N_{SD}} P_X(x_i = r|x_j > r, \forall j \ne i) = N_{SD}P_{x_i}(x_i = r)\left(P_{x>r}(r)\right)^{N_{SD}-1} \tag{6}$$

Referring to the pdf in expression (4), the probability of the distance being greater than a value r is $P_{x>r}(r) = \int_x^\infty P_x(x)dx$. Hence, the expected distance to the nearest SD given N_{SD} choices is:

$$E[P_{min(X)}] = \int_0^\infty rP_{min(x)}(r)dr = N_{SD}\int_0^\infty rP_x(r)\left(\int_r^\infty P_x(r)dr\right)^{N_{SD}-1} \tag{7}$$

It follows that the expected number of hops to the nearest SD is $E[P_{min(x)}]$ divided by r_0 and given as

$$E[H_{SD_{nearest}}] = \frac{N_{SD}}{r_0}\int_0^\infty rP_x(r)dr\left(\int_r^\infty P_x(r)dr\right)^{N_{SD}-1} \tag{8}$$

To calculate the average number of hops to get to the SD with the desired service data from an RN, we multiply P_i, the probability that SD_i has the desired service data, with the average number of hops to contact each SD and then take the sum. For simplicity, P_i can be set to $\frac{1}{N_{SD}}$. Hence, the expected number of hops to get to the SD with the service data is:

$$E[H_{SD_{Data}}] = \sum_{i=1}^{N_{SD}} P_iE[H_{SD_{nearest}}] \tag{9}$$

To derive $E[H_{CO}]$, the expected number of hops to the corner of the topography, we calculate first the expected distance from a node to the corner of the topography, $E[S_{CO}]$, using tables of integration and the Mathematica software:

$$E[S_{CO}] = \int_0^a \int_0^a \frac{1}{a^2}\sqrt{x^2 + y^2}dxdy = \frac{1}{3}\left[\sqrt{2} + log(1 + \sqrt{2})\right]a = 0.7652a \quad (10)$$

Next, to get $E[H_{CO}]$ we divide $E[S_{CO}]$ by the transmission range r_0:

$$E[H_{CO}] = E[S_{CO}]/r_0 = 0.7652a/r_0 \quad (11)$$

With a topography of $1000 \times 1000m^2$ and a transmission range of $100m$, $E[H_{CO}]$ is therefore 7.65 hops.

To compute the average system delay $E[\tau]$, we assume that T_{in} is the average delay of transmitting packets between nodes in a MANET. For simplicity we assume that T_{in} takes into account factors such as node location, packet size, number of hops, and congestion. The delay for accessing a SD node that has the service description is $T_{in} \times E[H_{SDdata}]$, plus an additional delay of $T_{in} \times E[H]$ that is incurred to transmit the reply back to the RN. Then $E[\tau] = T_{in}(E[H_{SD_{Data}}] + E[H])$. Similarly, the delay for accessing a SD at the corner and getting back the reply is $E[\tau_{corner}] = T_{in}(2E[H_{CO}])$.

With the above information, we can now apply the expression in (3) to determine the value of N_{SD}^{max}. After substituting $E[\tau]$ and $E[\tau_{corner}]$ in (3) and plugging in the values of $E[H]$, $E[H_{SD_{Data}}]$, and $E[H_{corner}]$ using (5), (9) and (11) respectively, we get the inequality:

$$E[H_{SD_{Data}}] - 1.0094a/r_0 < 0 \quad (12)$$

The expression in (12) was evaluated for different values of N_{SD} using Matlab and plotted in Fig. 3. As illustrated in the figure, the upper bound of N_{SD}, N_{SD}^{max}, is 7 for the chosen threshold (i.e.,$E[\tau_{corner}]$).

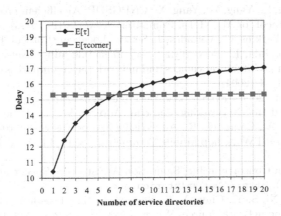

Fig. 3. $E[\tau]$ versus $E[\tau_{Corner}]$ for a $1000 \times 1000\ m^2$ topography with r_0 set to 100

4   Conclusion

This paper described a Distributed Service Discovery and Sharing Model baptized as DSDSM. In the proposed model, service provider nodes register their services with the nodes designated as service directories which act as mediators for lookup requests from requesting nodes. A node requesting a particular service contacts its nearest service directory which will in turn forward the request to another service directory in a sequential manner if it does not know who offers the service. Once the requesting node has the service description and the address of the service provider, it can invoke the service directly from the service provider. Both analytical and experimental performance evaluation were conducted to study the average response time and bandwidth consumption of the system, while focusing on the service discovery functionality. The performance of the proposed model was compared to that of the broadcast-based service discovery model that was proposed in the literature, and was found to outperform it by significant amounts.

Acknowledgments. This work was supported in part by a grant the Lebanese National Council For Scientific Research (no. 111135 022141, 2006/2007).

References

1. Arnold, K., Osullivan, B., Scheifler, R., Waldo, J., Wollrath, A.: The Jini Specification (The Jini Technology). Addison-Wesley, Reading, Mass (1999)
2. Chakraborty, D., Joshi, A., Yesha, Y., Fin, T.: Toward Distributed Service Discovery in Pervasive Computing Environments. IEEE Transactions on mobile computing 5(2), 97–112 (2006)
3. Bettstetter, C., Eberspacher, J.: Hop distances in homogeneous ad hoc networks. In: Proc. of the 57th IEEE semiannual Vehicular Technology Conf., pp. 2286–2290. IEEE Computer Society Press, Los Alamitos (2003)
4. Gao, Z., Wang, L., Yang, M., Yang, X.: CNPGSDP: An efficient group-based service discovery protocol for MANETs. Computer Networks (in Press)
5. Guttman, E., Perkins, C., Veizades, J.: Service Location Protocol. RFC 2165 (1997)
6. Kozat, U., Tassiula, L.: Service discovery in mobile adhoc Networks: an Overall perspective on architectural choices and network Layer support issues. Adhoc Networks 2(1), 23–44 (2004)
7. NS-2 simulator (2006), http://www.insi.edu/nsnam/ns
8. Perkins, C.: Ad Hoc Networking, 2nd edn. Addison-Wesley, Reading (2004)
9. Ranganathan, A., Campbell, R.: Advertising in a pervasive environment. In: Proc. Second ACM Int'l Workshop Mobile Commerce, pp. 10–14. ACM Press, New York (2002)
10. The Salutation Consortium Inc: Salutation Architecture Specification Part 1, Version 2.1 (1999), http://www.salutation.org
11. Tseng, Y.-C., Ni, S.-Y., Chen, Y.-S., Sheu, J.-P.: The broadcast storm problem in a mobile ad hoc network Source. Wireless Networks 8(2-3), 153–167 (2002)
12. Zipf, G.: Human Behavior and the Principle of Least Effort. Addison-Wesley, Reading (1949)

Proteus: An Architecture for Adapting Web Page on Small-Screen Devices

M.F. Caetano[1], A.L.F. Fialho[1], J.L. Bordim[1], C.D. Castanho[1], R.P. Jacobi[1], and K. Nakano[2]

[1] Department of Computer Science, University of Brasilia, Brasilia, 70910–900, Brazil
{caetano,alfoltran,bordim,carlacastanho,rjacobbi}@cic.unb.br
[2] Department of Information Engineering, School of Engineering, Hiroshima University 1-4-1 Kagamiyama, Higashi-Hirhoshima, 739-8527, Japan
nakano@hiroshima-u.ac.jp

Abstract. Reading the contents of Web page with a small-screen device, such as a PDA or cell-phone, is still far from being a pleasant experience. Owing to the device limitations, current mobile browsers cannot handle all HTML tags, such as tables, for instance. Thus, most mobile browsers provide a linearized version of the source HTML page, leading to a large amount of scrolling, not to mention the difficulty in finding the desired content. The main contribution of this work is to propose an architecture for adapting web page on small-screen devices. Among the features that our architecture offers, we can cite on-the-fly Web page adaptation and customization according to the user and device characteristics; text summarization; page blocks identification and content mapping to easy the task of locating user interests.

1 Introduction

Today, browsing the Web and reading emails while on the move has become common place. This has been possible due to cheaper and faster wireless network interfaces and the availability of mobile devices with augmented storage, memory, and battery capacity. Even though current cell-phones and PDAs have considerable processing power, their limited screen size and resolution makes it quite hard to visualize a Web page content. In general, Web pages are designed to be visualized on larger screens and, when one attempts to fit it on a small-screen device, most of its content is not visible. To better visualize a Web page content, the following approaches can be taken : create pages specially designed for the device or adapt them whenever needed. In the latter case, the content of a Web page could be adjusted, using a proxy-server for instance, to meet the device needs. The Wireless Application Protocol (WAP) [5] and i-Mode [7] work on the idea of creating Web content tailored for mobile devices. This, however, has a major drawback as most of the Web content is not available in such formats.

Recently, a number of works have explored solutions to improve the ways mobile devices with limited resources display Web content [3,4,11,2]. Among them, we can observe two different approaches: those who preserve the source page

K. Li et al. (Eds.): NPC 2007, LNCS 4672, pp. 161–170, 2007.

layout [4,2,6], and those who do not [12,10,11]. OperaMini [10], is an example of the latter which linearizes the entire content of a Web page. Although it is simple to implement and does not demand much processing at the client side, it leads to a large amount of vertical scrolling. Buyukkokten et al. [11], proposed to reduce the source Web page textual content through the use of text summarization techniques. On the same line, Schilit et al. [12], analyze the original page and have its content mapped to a previously established layout interface. As the above approaches modify the source page layout, users may have difficulty finding the information they are looking for. It is worth mentioning that most Web portals arrange the information to in a way that provide easy access to the topics with higher relevance. Also, when the user is familiarized with the page layout, s/he probably knows where to look for the information s/he wants.

Clearly, when one attempts to fit an HTML page into a mobile device display, most of its content is hidden from the user as the page is usually larger than the mobile display. A common way to provide means for users to actually visualize the entire Web page on a mobile device is to create a preview image of the original page. In this context, Chen at. al. [4] proposed to split the source page structure into blocks and associate each block to the corresponding area in the generated thumbnail. In the same direction, the work in [2] focused on the identification and delimitation of a page's regions to provide a two-level hierarchy.

In this work, we propose an architecture, named Proteus for adapting web page on small-screen devices. Proteus takes into consideration user preferences, such as image rate compression, thumbnail generation, text summarization preferences, mobile display size and topics of interest. The user preferences are stored in a profile. When a client requests an HTTP page to the Proteus server, the page is adapted based on the user's profile, and then delivered to the client. As we will describe in latter sections, the Proteus's adapted pages assist the user to identify relevant information even in a source page preview.

The rest of this paper is organized as follows. In **Section 2** we present an overview of the proposed architecture and **Section 3** presents the implementation details. Preliminary results are shown in **Section 4** and conclusions are drawn in **Section 5**.

2   Proteus Architecture

Proteus architecture is based on a client/server model. In our case, the client's function is basically to display the information provided by the server and implement ways to navigate through it. The benefits of using a proxy server include: (a) Better use of the client's battery resources; (b) Help reducing the communication cost and download time; (c) The adapted pages are well formed; (d) Allows to cache adapted pages for latter retrieval. In addition, with the use of a proxy server, it is possible to provide the user the possibility to inform parameters that will be analyzed and used during the treatment of the requested pages. For instance, the user can customize how the Web content will be delivered to his/her device, allowing the user adjust parameters to better suit his/her needs.

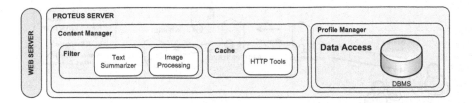

Fig. 1. The Conversion Server Architecture of Proteus Project

The works proposed in [12,2,4] also make use of a proxy server. The model presented by Schilit et al. [12] provides a type of conversion through a proxy known as *m-link service*. However, the provided service neither foresee the reuse of converted pages nor considers the users' preferences. The works in [2,4] only mention the possibility of using a proxy server but do not show its implementation details. The Proteus project's architecture is shown in Figure 1. In what follows, we will present in more details the component and services implemented by this architecture.

2.1 Web Page Analysis

On receiving a client request, the server tries to fetch the source HTML. When the page is successfully retrieved, the *content manager* parses the HTML to validate its code. In this phase, unnecessary information, like code remarks, is removed to avoid sending the user irrelevant data. After the validation, the page is represented in memory using the DOM (Document Object Model) structure [1]. After this preprocessing, co-related page blocks are identified, in a process similar to the one proposed in [2]. Next, each page block is analyzed and processed according to the user's profile.

2.2 Profile Manager

The *profile manager* is the module responsible for registering and managing the user profile. The profile information is used by the *content manager* during the page conversion process. Currently, the user profile can be accessed through the Web, where the user fills in an electronic form. In the form, the user customizes and selects the services s/he wishes to include in the conversion system. Among the conversion possibilities, we can cite:

- **Figures** - The user can choose to visualize only the textual contents. In this case, all the figures are withdrawn from the HTML source page;
- **Compression Rate** - Informs the compression rate that will be applied to the pictures in a Web page. This option will be disabled in case the user chooses not to receive figures;
- **Text Summarization Rate** - All text blocks of the source page will be summarized according to the stipulated rate;

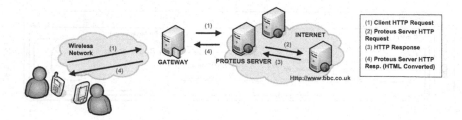

Fig. 2. Data flow involved from the moment the client makes a request until the answer is provided by the server

- **Content Highlight** - Highlights page regions that matches the user interests or preferences;
- **Subjects of Interest** - The user can inform the subjects of interest, which will be used by the content manager to identify the relevant areas on the accessed pages;
- **Thumbnail** - The converted page can be sent to the client as a thumbnail or conventional HTML text;
- **Diplay Size** - The size of the visualization area on the mobile device. This informartion is used to adapt requested pages to fit the user's device.

Based on the data provided by the user, the system will create an unique key that identifies which type of conversion should be performed by the content manager.

2.3 Content Manager

The *content manager* is responsible for the conversion, storage and retrieval of the converted pages. It is composed by a cache system and a filter system. After the identification and division of the page into blocks, the content manager uses the *filter system* to modify the blocks according to the user's profile. Concerning the content manager attributions, we can cite, among others: (*a*) Text summarization; (*b*) Identification of the user's degree of interest in each block; (*c*) Image resizing; (*d*) Identification and registration of new subjects of interest.

On a system that provides conversion services, it is important to implement strategies for conversion reuse, aiming to improve its performance. In our architecture, already converted pages are cached, which makes it possible to quickly retrieve them. More details concerning the content manager implementation and the techniques adopted will be presented in Section 3.

2.4 Data Flow

Figure 2 shows the data flow from the moment the user makes a request until an answer is provided by the server. Initially, the client submits an HTTP request to the Proteus Server for a specific URL. In case the client has a registered profile, his/her profile ID is sent, as cookie, along with the HTTP request. Otherwise, a standard profile is used. Suppose that the user issuing the HTTP request has a profile which specifies that a thumbnail should be generated from the requested page. At the time that the request is received, the server checks with the content manager whether there is a converted page according to the URL and the size of the user's mobile device display. If there is a hit, the thumbnail is retrieved, and the areas of user's interest (according to his profile) are highlighted and then sent to the client (the way the areas of interest are located in the stored thumbnail will be detailed in the next section). Otherwise, the server tries to fetch the source page. In case of success, the server goes on to analyze and convert the page, generate the thumbnail, and highlight areas of interest that matches the user profile. When the source page cannot be fetched, the server sends an appropriate message the client.

3 Implementation Details

3.1 Summarization

Recall that the Proteus goal is to adapt Web contents on-the-fly to better fit into a mobile device display. Hence, we considered summarization techniques with the following characteristics: language independent, fast, and able to generate summaries that express, with a reasonable degree, the essence of the original text. With that in mind, in this work we have focused our attention on *extraction* techniques. Among the existing extraction techniques, we have selected the *Keyword* [8] and *Term-Frequency Inverse Sentence Frequency – TF-ISF* [9].

In our tests, Keyword performed better with short texts while TF-ISF generates better results on larger inputs. In order to summarize the content of a Web page, we first have to parse the HTML file and extract its textual contents. It is important to note that HTML Tags may provide significant information about its contents as well. So, the text found in certain tags are retained during the parsing phase. Also, it is important to mention that words having the same radical should be counted as the same word. However, for doing so, it is necessary to find its root, thus eliminating prefixes, suffixes, and considering gender, number, tense, and case. For each text to be summarized, we first identify the number of words in the text. Based on this value, either Keyword or TF-ISF is used. With the help of the Keyword and TF-ISF, it is possible to allow users to define the desired degree of summarization. Also, as we are able to extract keywords from the accessed Web pages, one can use such information to enhance the accuracy of the system, as it will be shown latter. We will not go deeper into text summarization and extraction techniques here, for further details, we refer the reader to the references provide above and therein.

3.2 Web Page Content Mapping

Our architecture allows users to receive the requested HTML pages either in HTML format or thumbnail image. If an HTML format is to be received, the source page is adapted according to the information stored in the user's profile. When a reduced image is to be received, a thumbnail of the source page is created. In either case, while parsing the requested HTML page, a *blueprint* of the page is extracted. The blueprint will hold information concerning the source page structure, such as:

- Location of page blocks.
- Block content description.

The blueprint is cached along with the source HTML page. When a thumbnail is to be returned, the server uses the blueprint to identify the blocks that match to the user profile. Such blocks are highlighted to inform the user that its content matches the user preferences. According to the degree at which the contents match the profile, different colors, or shades, can be used to express the degree or relationship between the block and user preferences. When the user selects the block, its associated information is brought to the user. That is, on clicking on a thumbnail region, the HTML content of the region is displayed. This approach gives a two-level visualization: a reduced image on a first level, and the associated HTML content on a second one. Also, the user may define a rate for text summarization. In this case, the second-level will show a summarized text according to the rate defined in the user profile. The summarized text provides a link to see the entire content. Note that this latter approach introduces a three-level visualization.

3.3 Profile

In our architecture, each device has a profile which is stored on the server. The profile can be created and accessed via a mobile device itself or any another terminal. In any case, the user receives a key which shall be used when accessing the Proteus Server. The key will identify the device and users preferences, which will affect the ways the Web pages and its contents will be delivered to the mobile terminal. In case the user has no profile in the server, a standard one is used.

In the profile the user can define if s/he wants to receive the Web page in either thumbnail or HTML format. If s/he selects the thumbnail format, the navigation on the page relies on a two level visualization where the first level is the reduced image and the second level is the associated HMTL contents. The profile still permits the user to define the summarization rate of the text regions on the second level, introducing in fact a third layer of visualization. The profile also allows a user to specify the categories s/he is interested in, such as business, travel, etc. The Proteus Server will then create an association among the specified categories and the relevant keywords that match the selected categories. For example, consider a user with a previously stored profile connecting to the Proteus Server to request an HTML file. In this case, the requested page is treated by the server to identify regions, summarize text, generate the thumbnail and create the mappings (assuming these options match the user profile). Since the text summarization works by ranking keywords, if a match among the ranked keywords and the categories is found, the associated block receives a higher rank. We call this matching process as *static content matching*. In contrast to this, we also provide a *dynamic content matching*, which is described bellow.

In the dynamic content matching, the keywords that have obtained higher ranks during the summarization step, are stored in a database called *Dynamic Content Database – DCB*. When a user makes an HTTP request through the server, the system checks the higher ranked keywords on that page against the keywords stored in the DCB. If there is a match, the blocks containing the keywords are ranked higher, as in the static content matching. To prevent old keywords to have an impact on current pages, each keyword in the database is associated with a time stamp T_s, which is updated according to the user requests for Web content. When T_s expires, the associated keyword is removed from the DCB. Another point worth mentioning is that the DCB should not grow above a certain threshold as this has an impact on the server workload. For this reason, we have devised the following policy to update the DCB.

Let K_i denote the set of keywords stored in the DCB which are associated with the user profile P_i, where $0 < i \leq n$, and n denotes the number of users. Also, $|K_i| \leq \delta$, where δ is the maximum number of keywords allowed per user in the DCB. Now, suppose that a new set of keywords, call it S_i, have been obtained for user U_i. Then, the keywords satisfying $K_i \cap S_i$ have their time stamp T_s renewed in the DCB. The keywords in S_i may be incorporated in DCB up to the threshold δ.

3.4 Cache Module

As the mobile clients make HTTP requests to the server, the server caches information so that latter requests can be served in a faster way whenever there is a cache hit. As the mobile devices have different screen-size and resolution, we have organized them into categories, according to their characteristics. When a user requests to receive a preview of the original page, the generated thumbnail is stored in the appropriate category. Thus, when a user requests a page that has a cached thumbnail, the server checks whether the thumbnail matches the device category. If affirmative, the cached thumbnail is returned. Otherwise, a new thumbnail is created and returned. The Proteus cache module uses the LRU (Least Recently Used) replacement policy, which means old and least used cached information is removed when necessary.

4 Preliminary Results

4.1 Mapped Regions

Our first example illustrates how Proteus identifies the contents in a requested page that matches the user preferences. In this example we focus on static contents only. The user profile for this example is shown in Table 1. The profile shows that the user wishes to create a thumbnail of the original page, in a way

Table 1. Example of profile specified by the user

Description	Value
Keep Figures	Yes
Compression Rate	58%
Summarize Content	0%
Subject / Keywords	Games, Business
Highlight Content	Yes
Create Thumbnail	Yes
Size of the Display	470x770 pixels

that is applied to the figure a compression rate of 58%. Also, we can verify that the user has interest on subjects related to Games and Business. Using the keywords contained on the profile, the conversion server is capable of identifying, on the HTML page, which regions are of interest to the user. The identified regions are highlighted so that the user knows that they have information that matches his interests. By clicking over the region, the associated HTML is shown. The HTML content of other regions are reached in the same way.

Figure 3(a) shows the result obtained when the CNN site is submitted to Proteus Server under the profile presented in Table 1. The Proteus Server has identified four areas related to games (delineated in dashed-lines rectangles) and the two areas related to business (delineated in solid-lines rectangles). In the menu bar of the site, the option Business is circled. This options was ignored because it is located in the menu region, which is identified during the page analysis. On the bottom-left of the page, the figure Business2.0 was selected by the algorithm because its ALT tag contains a valid text which was identified. From the thumbnail, the user is able to see the whole page. However, s/he may not be able to identify, on a first level of visualization, the information that s/he is looking for. Highlighting areas of interest is a way of restraining the search area and avoid unnecessary zoom.

4.2   Summarization Results

This sub-section presents a combination of the region mapping and summarization. The profile selected for this example is shown in the Table 2. Here, the user requested an article published at the CNN website under the title: "MAC fans clamor for iPhone". The thumbnail result is shown in Figure 3(b), where the area delineated in dashed-line rectangle was identified by the content manager as an area of user interest. The highlighted text is composed of 789 words. By choosing this area, the content summarization will be applied. The result that is sent to the user is represented by the frame at the top of the page thumbnail. It contains an abstract with 21,68% of the original text. Should the user require the entire (original) text, s/he can access it via a link *more*, which is appended by the server. This approach is similar to the use of RSS feeds, in which a brief text is shown to allow the user to have a glance of the link contents.

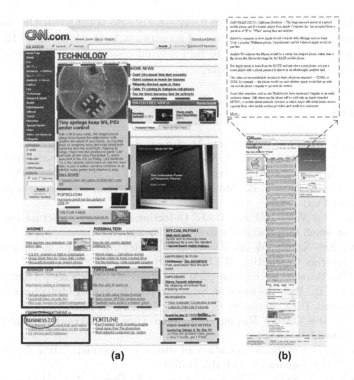

(a)   (b)

Fig. 3. (*a*):CNN website created from the profile presented in Table 1. *b*): Summarized text aaccessedfrom the Web page tthumbnail.

Table 2. Example of the profile specified by the user. The converted page is shown in Figure 3.

Description	Value
Keep Figures	Yes
Compression Rate	87,70%
Summarize Content	80%
Subject / Keywords	Technology
Highlight Content	Yes
Create Thumbnail	Yes
Size of the Display	124 x 320 pixels

5   Conclusions and Future Works

Up to this point, we have made a number of experiments, however, we have not made our architecture available to the general public. Before doing that, we plan to test our architecture with a selected number of users, so that their feedback may help us to fine tune and improve the system. Also, we are currently developping a mobile web browser that will have features to improve the ways the thumbnails are presented to the user. We are also considering the use of Web mining techniques and the extraction of semantic information of HTML pages as a mean to provide the possibility to find related contents on a page and suggest them as areas of interest to the user.

References

1. Apparao, V., Byrne, S., Champion, M., Isaacs, S., Jacobs, I., Hors, A.L., Nicol, G., Robie, J., Sutor, R., Wilson, C., Wood, L.: Document object model (dom) level 1 specification (second edition). Technical report, W3C (September 2000)
2. Cai, D., Yu, S., Wen, J.-R., Ma, W.-Y.: Vips: a vision-based page segmentation algorithm (2003)
3. Chen, Y., Ma, W.-Y., Zhang, H.-J.: Detecting web page structure for adaptive viewing on small form factor devices, pp. 225–233 (2003)
4. Chen, Y., Xie, X., Ma, W.-Y., Zhang, H.-J.: Adapting web pages for small-screen devices. Internet Computing, IEEE 9, 50–56 (2005)
5. Gellens, R.: Wireless device configuration (otasp/otapa) via acap (1999)
6. Hua, Z., Lu, H.: Web Browsing on Small-Screen Devices: A Multiclient Collaborative Approach. IEEE Pervasive Computing 5(2), 78–84 (2006)
7. Mobell. What is i-mode? Disponvel em: http://www.mobalrental.com/imode.asp (Accessed in 11/09/2006)
8. Luhn, P.H.: The automatic creation of literature abstracts. IBM Journal of Research and Development 2, 159–165 (1958)
9. Larocca Neto, J., Santos, A.D., Kaestner, C.A.A., Freitas, A.A.: Document clustering and text summarization. In: Proceedings of the 4th International Conference on Practical Applications of Knowledge Discovery and Data Mining, London, pp. 41–55 (2000)
10. Opera. Opera Mini. Disponvel em: http://mini.opera.com (Accessed in 11/09/2006)
11. Buyukkokten, O., Kaljuvee, O., Garcia-Molina, H., Paepcke, A., Winograd, T.: Efficient web browsing on handheld devices using page and form summarization. ACM Trans. Inf. Syst. 20(1), 82–115 (2002)
12. Schilit, B.N., Trevor, J., Hilbert, D.M., Koh, T.K.: m-links: An infrastructure for very small internet devices. In: MobiCom '01: Proceedings of the 7th annual international conference on Mobile computing and networking, New York, NY, USA, pp. 122–131. ACM Press, New York (2001)

EEGFGR: An Energy-Efficient Greedy-Face Geographic Routing for Wireless Sensor Networks*

Tao Zi-Jin, Wu Yi, and Gong Zheng-Hu

School of Computer, National University of Defense Technology,
Changsha 410073, China
taozj888@163.com, wuyi@nudt.edu.cn, gzh@nudt.edu.cn

Abstract. The geographic routing technology is good for the self-organizing and large-scale Wireless Sensor Networks(WSNs), and the energy-limited sensor nodes require the energy used for routing to be minimum. In this paper a new energy-efficient geographic routing algorithm is proposed and it is distributed and based on the geographic routing, the topology characteristics of the network and the wireless communication energy model. The algorithm is based on the planarized graph (GG) of the network, it deals with the routing void by saving more face neighbors in every node, and selects the most energy-efficient nexthop node by using the energy-saving technologies including the Minimum Energy One-hop Neighbor Path Selection and the Optimal Face-neighbor Selection. The theoretical analysis and simulations show that the algorithm is feasible and more energy-efficient than many existed geographic routing algorithms. In the end , the means of face information maintenance are proposed.

Keywords: geographic routing, minimum energy, face neighbors, routing algorithm, Wireless Sensor Networks(WSNs).

1 Introduction

Recent advances in micro-electro-mechanical systems (MEMS) and low power and highly integrated digital electronics have led to the development of micro sensors. Such sensors are generally equipped with data processing and communication capabilities. The Wireless Sensor Networks (WSNs) are composed of many sensor nodes , which are self-organizing and easy deployable. The routing techniques of the WSNs are the key of highly-efficient networking of these nodes. Now the Geographic Routing Technique based on the position of the sensor nodes is a feasible solution to the routing problem of WSNs, and is attracting much more attention.

The network graph G<V,E> can be planarized by the methods in [4]. In this paper the face neighbor information as well as the one-hop neighbor information is added to the node based on the face properties of the planar graph, and the node selects the the node based on the face properties of the planar graph, and the node selects the routing

---

* This paper is founded by the Chinese National 973 Natural Science Fund "Routing and Switching Theory of Next Generation Internet"(2003CB314802).

K. Li et al. (Eds.): NPC 2007, LNCS 4672, pp. 171–182, 2007.

path and the nexthop by the wireless communication model and the position of the neighbor stored in itself. The theoretical analysis and simulation show that the energy consumption expended by the data communication is greatly reduced by the added neighbor information which can be used to deal with the routing void. So the algorithm is very proper for the WSNs which are long-lifetime and of large volume of data to be transmitted.

2 Related Works

Most geographic routing algorithms belong to the type which uses only the face routing or the combination of greedy routing and face routing.

1) Compass Routing II[3]
Completed based on the face routing, every time the forwarding node chooses the face which is intersected the line formed by the source s and destination d , and traversing the face, if meeting the line (u,v) which is intersected by the line (s,t), the packet is routed around another face. This approach is very energy inefficient for the face traversing greatly increases the routing hops and many hops have no uses with respect to making the packet closer to the destination.

2) GPSR[4]
An early geographic routing algorithm combines the greedy and face routing. In this algorithm, the greedy mode is used if it is feasible, and if not the perimeter mode is used in which the packet traverses the face using the right-hand rule until the node which is closer to destination and the packet leave the local optimal node. GPSR is highly more energy-efficient than the Compass Routing II.

3) GOAFR+[5]
When meeting a void, the GOAFR+ selects a random forwarding direction to search, but it doesn't continuously forward the packet around a face, but uses an ellipse to restrict the search bound. When it meets the ellipse, it will search on the opposite direction.

4) GPVFR[6]
In GPVFR , the node stores some planar face neighbors which is within several hops and the number of the neighbors is adjustable. By the increased neighbor information the best forwarding direction will be chosen and the blindly search is avoided. The simulation shows it is more efficient that the GPSR and GOAFR+. The main disadvantage of the algorithm is neighbor number stored in the node is determined beforehand and randomly, and its performance can be improved more.

The above algorithms conquer the routing void with their own methods but their performance can be improved further and the energy metric has not been considered, so the routing path formed is not likely to be the most energy-efficient path. At the next section a new routing algorithm based on the greedy-face mode is proposed which not only considers the best way to overcome the routing void but also the energy factor at every forwarding phase. The analysis and simulations show that the energy efficiency of the algorithm exceeds the above algorithms.

3 Basic Idea and Model of EEGFGR

3.1 Basic Idea

As the above geographic routing algorithms, EEGFGR is also a distributive geographic routing algorithm in which the routing computation is completely dependent on the routing information stored in itself. EEGFGR added the face neighbors[10] as the candidate nexthop, so the node will see more neighbors closer to the target and have more opportunities to select an better neighbor in a reasonable way.

EEGFGR combines the greedy routing, face routing and perimeter routing and at every phase the energy metric is considered at the same time. So in every step of the algorithm the minimum energy path is selected.

When the face routing is used, the node has two directions to forward the packet: clockwise and counter-clockwise. The minimum hops routing metric may not be the most energy-efficient because the distribution of the nodes may not be uniform.

When the node which is closer to the target than the current node can not be found yet by the face routing, the perimeter mode is used as the GPSR uses.

3.2 Model of EEGFGR

There are many algorithms which can be used to planarize the graph, in EEGFGR we use the the same means as in [8] (GG)and [9](RNG). The WSNs' topology is described as a Graph G<V,E,E'>, V is the node set ,E is the set of all the communication link , E' is the set of the links which remains after planarization, $E' \subseteq E$. The communication link is represented as $\{v_1,v_2\}$, if $\{v_1,v_2\} \in$ E, then v_1,v_2 is a neighbor of v_2 and vice versa. If $\{v_1,v_2\} \in E'$, v_1 is a planar neighbor of v_2 and vice versa; if $\{v_1,v_2\} \in E - E'$, then v_1 is an non-planar neighbor of v2 and vice versa.

The face exploration usually uses the right-hand(left-hand) rule which can be represented as: if $v_1, v_2, v_3 \in V$, if the ray v_1v_2 rotate counter-clockwise around v1, when the ray meets the planar neighbor v_3, then right(v_1,v_2)=v_3. The concept face and face neighbor are given as following.

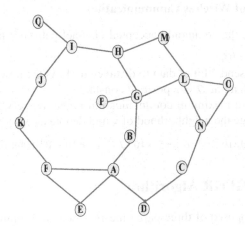

Fig. 1. The sketch map of the face

Definition 1. If F is a node sequence $(v_1, v_2, v_3, \ldots, v_{n-1}, v_n)$, if it satisfy the following condition , it will be called as a Face:

(1) $\{v_i, v_{i+1}\}$, $\{v_n, v_1\} \in E'$;

(2) $right(v_{i+1}, v_i) = v_{i+2}$, $right(v_n, v_{n-1}) = v_1$, $right(v_1, v_n) = v_2$; $(1 \leq i \leq n-1)$。

In Fig1, (A,E,F),(F,K,J,I,Q,I,H,G,P,G,B,A),(D,C,N,L,G, B,A) are the faces.
Below, F is defined to be the set of all the faces in G.

Definition 2
The face neighbors of the node v is a set of nodes that are contained in one face:

$$FN(v) = \{n | \exists f \in F , \text{ which satisfies } v \in f \; \text{且} \; n \in f \}$$

Definition 3
The one-hop neighbors of node v is defined as :

$$HN(v) = \{n | \{n, v\} \in E \} - \{v\}$$

The routing void can be avoided by using the face neighbor information, so it will shorten the routing hops. As shown in Fig.1 if node L want to send a packet to the node G, if using the one-hop neighbor greedy , the node G will send the packet to node P, but node P sees that all the one-hop neighbors are further than itself , so the packet enter a routing void and the perimeter mode is used. Then the path is G-P-G-B-A-F-K-J-I-Q, which has 9 hops. But if we use the face neighbors, G will see that node I is the node closest to node Q, and the path is G-H-I-Q which has 3 hops.

Subjected to the paper space, the detailed face discovery process is omitted here.

For the planar graph, the number of face neighbors can be estimated by the face number and the average number of nodes in the faces. As demonstrated in [10], the average size of a face is $O(\frac{2n_e}{n_e - n_v + 2})$, the average node degree is $O(\frac{2n_e}{n_v})$, so the number of the face neighbors is $O(\frac{2n_e}{n_e - n_v + 2} \cdot \frac{2n_e}{n_v})$. To the planar graph the size of n_e and n_v are at the same level, so the number of the face neighbors is acceptable.

3.3 Energy Model of Wireless Communication

In this paper, we use the commonly accepted channel path loss model, $\rho = a \times \delta^\gamma + b$, $Pt = l\alpha_{11} + l\alpha_2 (d)^2, P_r = l\alpha_{12}$

Pt is the power to send 1 bit of data to distance d , Pr is the power to receive 1bit of data. L is the packet length, α is a positive constant.

Each node, v, has a maximum communication range, range(v). We call the set of nodes within this range the neighborhood of v and denote as $N_v (\subseteq S)$.

$$\alpha_{11} = 50 \times 10^{-9} J , \quad \alpha_{12} = 50 \times 10^{-9} J , \quad \alpha_2 = 10 \times 10^{-12} (J/bit/m^2) 。$$

4 Details of EEGFGR Algorithm

The EEGFGR is composed of three parts: the first one is Minimum Energy One-hop Neighbor Path Selection Algorithm(MEONPSA, the name of the algorithm is

RouteInOneHopNeighbor for better memory), the second one is the Minimum Energy Face Path Selection Algorithm(MEFPA, the name of the algorithm is FacePath for better memory), and the EEGFGR full algorithm.

4.1 Minimum Energy One-Hop Neighbor Path Selection Algorithm (MEONPSA)

The algorithm is used to select a minimum energy path to the neighbor which is within the node's radio range, i.e., to find a best path to the one-hop neighbor, instead of sending the packet directly to the node.

Table 1. MEONPSA

RouteInOneHopNeighbor (d):
1. if d is very close to s, then d is select to be the nexthop; return;   *2. The radio range of s is R, its neighborhood set is the set of neighbors within the range and is represented as* N_{R_S} *. In order to limit the search range, a circle is constructed with the edge (s,d) as the diameter. The neighbors which is within the circle is represented as* N_{r_s} *, and for* $\forall v \in N_{r_s}$ *, we have* $(s,v)^2 + (v,d)^2 \leq (s,d)^2$ *, and if* $v_1, v_2 \in N_{r_s}, (v_1, v_2) \leq R$ *, i.e. there is an edge (v_1, v_2), and the set of the type of edges is represented as E_s.*   *3. For every edge* $e \in E_s$ *, label* l_e *represents the energy cost by the communication between two nodes. For any edge (v_1, v_2), the distance between v_1 and v_2 is represented as $d(v_1, v_2)$ and* $l_e \propto d(v_1, v_2)^2$ *.*   *4. In the neighborhood graph NGraph$_s$ = (N_{r_s}, E_s, l_e), we set s to be the source, d to be the destination , and the edge e's weight to be l_e, run the Shortest Path Routing Algorithm(Dijkstra Algorithm)*   *5. Record the shortest path after the algorithm completes as $P_{s,d}$=(s,v_1,v_2...v_{n-1},d), the path is the minimum energy path.*   **6.** *Return the nexthop node v_1 in $P_{s,d}$ as   MinE_nexthop, $P_{s,d}$ as MinE_Path。*

4.2 Dynamic Subdestination Adjust(Dyna_adjust)

After the node has got the minimum energy one-hop path with RouteInOneHopNeighbor, it send the packet to nexthop v_1, v_1 has two patterns to deal with the packet: one is to strictly send the packet to the next node which is denoted in $P_{s,d}$, this way is called Force mode; the other is v_1 recalculates a new minimum energy path and reselects a new subdestination based on its own neighborhood information, this way is called Dynamic Subdestination Adjust(Dyna_adjust) mode.

The Dyna_adjust will increase the energy efficiency of the routing algorithm, for every routing step the amount of energy consumed is less than that of the previous node calculates. But the Dyna_adjust may cause routing loop. But we have the follow theorem:

Theorem 1. If the Dyna_adjust satisfies $P_{s,d} \cap P_{s,d}{}' = \phi$, then the greedy algorithm with this method will not result in a routing loop.

Proof: If the Dyna_adjust will cause a routing loop, for $P_{s,d} \cap P_{s,d}{}' = \phi$, so the loop can only be caused after running the Dyna_adjust 2 or more times, and after running the algorithm many times, the routing path may have the same node. But in the greedy mode, the new subdestination will be closer than the previous one to the target and every node in the minimum energy path will be closer than the current node to the target, so these nodes must not have duplicate nodes. This contradicts the assumption.

4.3 Minimum Energy Face Path Selection Algorithm(MEFPSA)

When the packet is in the face routing mode, the minimum energy face path must be calculated when the packet traverses the face.

There are two ways for the node to select a nexthop from the face neighbors.

Mode 1: (The Most Greedy Mode, all-face-greedy)
The current node selects the face neighbor which is closest to the destination in all the face neighbors as the subtarget node.

Mode 2: (the face which is in the same direction with the line (u,t) fisrt, dir-face-greedy)
In this mode, the node u make a virtual line (u,t), if the face is intersected by the line, the face is called the face in the same direction(dir-face).If there exists that type of faces, the current node first selects the node which is closest to the destination in that face. If there are many that type of faces, then the first face that is intersected by the line (u,t) is selected.

It can be demonstrated that in GG(or RNG) graph, the dir-face must have node which is closer to the target than current node , and it is shown in below.

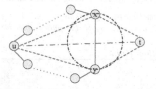 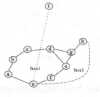

Fig. 2. The face which intersects the line (u,t) must has the node which is closer to the target

Fig. 3. The faces with and without the same direction with line (u,t) than the current node

Theorem 2. In GG graph, if there is a face which is intersected by the line (u,t), then that face must have a node which is closer than the current node to the target t.

Proof: (Omitted)

Table 2. MEFPSA

FacePath-all(v):
the node v constructs the face set which contains the node v, $FaceContain(v)$, $FaceContain(v) \subseteq Face(u)$, For each edge $e \in f$, $f \in FaceContain(v)$, computes the energy cost of every edge e, denoted as l_e; For each face $f \in FaceContain(v)$, compute the energy cost Ep_i of every path P_i from u to v in f, $Ep_i = \sum\limits_{j \in path_i} e_j$, if $Ep_k \leq (\forall i)Ep_i, i = 1,2,...n$, then the minimum energy face path MinEFacePath is P_k.

The reason to choose the dir-face is that generally the cost of traversing the face is high, so the face traversing should be finished as soon as possible. If the face is non-dir face, the face deviates from the target, even if the face has a better neighbor, the cost of traversing that face is higher than that of the dir-face. The dir-face example is shown in Figure 6, where node h is closer to t than the node d but the cost to get to node h is much higher than the cost to get to d.

If we adopt the dir-face first mode, then in the above algorithm we set the *FaceContain(v)* only contain the nodes in the set of the dir-face.

4.4 Detailed Description of EEGFGR

4.4.1 Symbols Used in EEGFGR
target: the destination node
pack: the packet received
e: in the Perimeter mode, the first edge that the packet enter the face, it is used to check whether the destination is unreachable.
Mode: the mode that the packet is in, 3 value is : EEGFGR-GREEDY, EEGFGR-FACE, EEGFGR-PERIMETER, the initial value is EEGFGR-GREEDY;
  n_1: the node which is closest to target   in the one-hop neighborhood set
  n_2: the node which is closest to the target in the face neighbors
  goal: the goal which EEGFGR-FACE mode want to arrive
  path: an array which elements are a lot of nodes, the index begins from 0
  now: the initial value is 0
  Neigh(u): the set that is composed of node u's one-hop neighbors
  Face(u): the faces which are stored in node u;
  FaceNeigh(u): the node set which is composed of the face neighbors of node u
  node(f): the node set which is composed of the nodes in face f, and edge(f) is used to represent the edges in face f;
  the distance between node u and node v is represented as d(u,v), the distance between the node u and the face f is represented as $d(u,f)=min(a,v)$, ($v \in node(f)$), and set the v_{uf} to be the node closest to node u in the face f.
  If $v_1, v_2 \in node(f)$, we define the Face distance of v_1, v_2, $D(v_1, v_2, f)$ to be the length of the minimum energy path in face f ;
  Face_Subgoal: the subdestination which the node u used to traverse the face;
  MinEFacePath: the minimum energy face path ($f_{v_0}, f_{v_1}, ..., f_{v_n}$) which is computed by the FacePath();
  RouteInOneHopNeighborNexthop: the nexthop node which is computed by RouteInOneHopNeighbor() algorithm
  RouteInOneHopNeighborPath: the minimum energy path ($v_0, v_1, v_2..., v_n$) which is computed by RouteInOneHopNeighbor()
  ForcedRoutingFlag: used to indicate the packet is in forced routing mode or dyna_adjust mode, 0 is for Dyna_adjust, 1 is for ForcedRouting.

4.4.2 Detailed Process of the Algorithm
  1. if u ==d, then the routing is successful, return;
  2. if ForcedRoutingFlag==1
  *If u != pack.RouteInOneHopNeighborNexthop /*Forced Mode, the current node is not the last hop in the Forced Path */*
    u ∈ RouteInNeighPath, if u =v_i, then nexthop=v_{i+1};goto 9;
  else / is the last hop in the Forced Path */*
  pack.ForcedRoutingFlag=0; goto 3;
  3. if pack.status = EEGFGR-PERIMETER and (d(n_1,t) < d(s,t) or d(n_2,t) < d(s,t))□then pack.status:= EEGFGR-GREEDY; pack.ForcedRoutingFlag=0; goto 5;
  4. if pack.mode = EEGFGR-FACE and u= pack.face_subgoal, then pack.mode:= EEGFGR-GREEDY; select step 5 or 6 or 7 based on the mode;

5. EEGFGR-GREEDY: /* the user may select 5.a or 5.b based on the greedy manner */

5.a) (one-hop neighbor first greedy) if $d(n_1,t) < d(u,t)$, then n_1 is set to be subdestination node; pack.subdest=n_1, nexthop = RouteInOneHopNeighbor (n_1), ForcedRoutingFlag =0;

Else, if $d(n_2,t) < d(u,t)$, /* the closer node is only situates in the face neighbors */, then select 5.a.1 or 5.a.2 according to the face greedy mode:

5.a.1) FacePath-all(n_2);

5.a.2) FacePath-dir(n_2);

Then we get the minimum energy path to n_2 MinEFacePath =($fv_0,fv_1,...,fv_k$), $fv_k=n_2$;

And the node u set:

ForcedRoutingFlag =1,

pack.mode=EEGFGR-FACE,

pack.path=MinEFacePath,

nexthop= RouteInOneHopNeighbor(MinEFacePath[1]),

and set the packet's path: pack.RouteInOneHopNeighborPath ;

pack.face_subgoal= n_2, pack.subdest= MinEFacePath[1],

pack.hops=1; /* the first hop when traversing the face */

else /* can't find closer node */

set pack.mode = EEGFGR-PERIMETER; goto 8;

5.b) (all-neighbor-greedy) if $d(n_1,t) \le d(n_2,t)$ && $d(n_1,t) < d(u,t)$ set n_1 to be subdestination:

pack.subdest=n_1, nexthop = RouteInOneHopNeighbor (n_1), ForcedRoutingFlag =0;

else if $d(n_2,t) \le d(n_1,t)$ && $d(n_2,t) < d(u,t)$, /* there is a closer node in face

neighbors */, then select 6.a or 6.b according to the face selection mode.;goto 6;

else /* there is no closer node in all neighbors */

pack.mode=EEGFGR-PERIMETER; goto 8;

6. Computing the minimum energy face path based on the face selection strategy, and record the result in the packet:

6.a) FacePath-all(n_2);

6.b) FacePath-dir(n_2);

and get a minimum energy face path to n_2 MinEFacePath =($fv_0,fv_1,...,fv_k$), $fv_k=n_2$;

the node u set the following values:

Pack.ForcedRoutingFlag =1,

pack.mode=EEGFGR-FACE,

pack.path=MinEFacePath,

nexthop= RouteInOneHopNeighbor (MinEFacePath[1]), and set pack.RouteInOneHopNeighborPath;

pack.face_subgoal= n_2, pack.subdest= MinEFacePath[1],

pack.hops=1; /* the first hop when traversing the face */

else /* can't find a closer node */ pack.mode=EEGFGR-PERIMETER; goto 8;

7. EEGFGR-FACE:

pack.hops = pack.hops+1,

pack.subgoal = pack.path[pack.hops];

nexthop= RouteInOneHopNeighbor (pack.subgoal), and set the pack.RouteInOneHopNeighborPath;

goto 8;

8. EEGFGR-PERIMETER: is the same as the PERIMETER mode in GPSR, ForcedRoutingFlag =1, using the right-hand rule to compute the nexthop: pack.subdest = RightHand_nexthop, nexthop= RouteInOneHopNeighbor (pack.subdest); and set the pack.RouteInOneHopNeighborPath;

9. send the pack to the nexthop。

5   Simulation Results and Evaluation

5.1   Simulation Environment

In order to learn the performance of EEGFGR, simulations have been run on the ns2 simulator, and Monarch wireless communication model[12] is used. GPSR and GPVFR are programmed according to [4] and [6]. The number of simulated nodes is 200-500, the increment is 50, and the nodes are randomly deployed in a 500m*500m area. For every node density, ten graphs are produced, the radio range of the node is 50m.

We randomly set a node pair in each graph which has a distance of 300m, and the length of the packet is set to 250 bytes. The energy model described in 3.3 are used. The total energy consumption are recorded in the packet header, and the mean value of the 10 results are used as the final result. The WSNs are usually powered by the battery, we assume each node has an initial energy of 2 Joule.

5.2 Energy Used for Face Neighbor Discovery

Compared with GPSR and GPVFR, EEGFGR has a complete face neighbor discovery process. In order to illustrate the feasibility of this method, we record the energy cost used for the face exploration, i.e., the total energy used by all face exploration messages.

It is shown in figure 9 that under each network density the energy used for face exploration is very low and on the whole it is below 0.0043 Joule which is a very little part of the node's initial energy. The reason is when the network is sparse, and node number of each face is high but the number of the face is high; when the network is dense, the number of the face is increased but the number of nodes in each face is decreased. At the same time, the face exploration is based on the one-hop neighbor information and avoids the blind broadcasts.

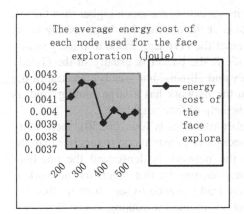

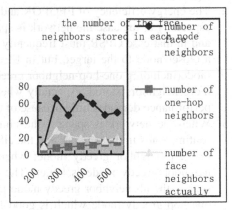

Fig. 4. The average energy cost of each node used for the face exploration

Fig. 5. The number of one-hop neighbors and face neighbors stored in each node

5.3 Number of Neighbors Stored in Each Node

In order to learn the storage cost for the face neighbors, we count the number of the face neighbors under each network density. In the topology, the outer face is composed of the nodes which locates at the network boundary and it has a great number nodes in it. But the outer face helps little to the routing, so the neighbors of the outer face may be discarded to decrease the storage cost.

It can be seen from the simulation that the number of face neighbors actually stored in each node is low and the peak value is reached when there are 250 nodes in the network.

5.4 Routing Performance of EEGFGR

The EEGFGR routing algorithm has many options, and in order to demonstrate the efficacy of the Minimum Energy One-hop Neighbor Path Selection strategy, we have used the strategy in GPSR. The following table illustrates the options of the algorithms.

Table 3. The Options of Each Algorithm

Name	Explanation
EEGFGR	MEONPSA(Dyna_adust), one-hop neighbor greedy, dir-face first
EEGFGR-II	MEONPSA(Dyna_adust), all-neighbor greedy, dir-face first
EEGFGR-III	MEONPSA(Dyna_adust), one-hop neighbor greedy
EEGFGR-IV	MEONPSA(Dyna_adust), all-neighbor greedy
GPSR-II	To improve the GPSR with MEONPSA, when the packet is in the greedy mode, the Dyna_adjust is used, and when the packet is in Perimeter mode, Forced mode is used

The experiments show that:

1. The energy cost is decreased as the network density is increased for each algorithm;
2. The energy efficiency of EEGFGR and its variations are much higher than GPSR, especially at the case the network is sparse or the network has large routing voids and in that case GPSR must frequently enter the Perimeter mode to blindly search a closer node to the target, but in EEGFGR the packet is usually in the Greedy mode(including one-hop-neighbor greedy and all-neighbor greedy) because of the more neighbors stored, especially when the network has a large routing void its performance degrades little because of the help of face neighbors.
3. When the network is sparse (the number of nodes is low, <=250), there more routing voids in the network and the all-neighbor greedy mode is superior than the one-hop-neighbor greedy mode; when the network is dense and the one-hop-neighbor greedy mode is better. The reason may be that when the network is sparse, the all-neighbor greedy mode may lead the node to see "further" than the one-hop greedy mode which is good for overcome the routing voids. When the network is dense, one-hop neighbor greedy is better because it leads to less face traversing manner which is energy expensive.
4. The Minimum Energy One-hop Neighbor Path Selection technology has some obvious effect in decreasing the energy consumption, which is shown in the graph when the GPSR has used that technology (GPSR-II), especially when the network is dense. About 5%-10% energy may be saved by the method.
5. Using the dir-face first technology is more energy efficient than not using that technology, which has an effect of decreasing the energy consumption by 3%-7%.

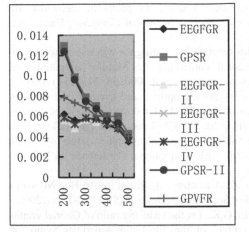

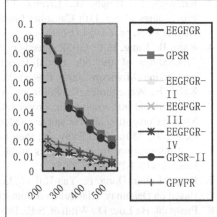

Fig. 6. The energy cost (Joule) of transferring the data from the source to destination when the nodes are normally distributed in the network

Fig. 7. When the network has been added an artificial routing void (100m*200m), the total energy cost (Joule) used for transferring the data from the source to the destination

6. The energy efficiency of GPVFR is similar as the EEGFGR, but the number of neighbors stored in GPVFR is less than EEGFGR. When the network is sparse more neighbors are good for avoiding the routing voids, so the energy efficiency of EEGFGR is still higher than the GPVFR.

6 Conclusion

We have presented EEGFGR, a new energy-efficient geographic routing algorithm based on the greedy-face technology, which achieves small per-node routing state, small routing protocol message complexity and good delivery guarantees as previous promoted geographic routing algorithms. Theoretic analysis and experiments show it has much higher energy-efficiency than previous ones, especially when the network has some large routing voids.

In the future work, we will check its performance in other planar graph, such as the UDel[13] graph, and improve the algorithm to fit for the practical communication environment[14].

References

1. Akyildiz, I.F., et al.: Wireless sensor networks: a survey. Computer Networks 38, 392–422 (2002)
2. Shigang, C., Guangbin, F., Jun-Hong, C.: Avoid Void in Geographic Routing for Data Aggregation in Sensor Networks. International Journal of Ad Hoc and Ubiquitous Computing (IJAHUC),Special Issue on Wireless Sensor Networks 2(1) (2006)

3. Kranakis, E., Singh, H., Urrutia, J.: Compass routing on geometric networks. In: Proceedings of the 11th Canadian Conference on Computational Geometry, Vancouver, August 1999, pp. 51–54 (1999)
4. Karp, B., Kung, H.T.: GPSR: greedy perimeter stateless routing for wireless networks. In: Proceedings of the 6th annual international conference on Mobile computing and networking (Mobicom 2000), Boston, Massachusetts, August 2000, pp. 243–254 (2000)
5. Kuhn, F., Wattenhofer, R., Zollinger, A.: Worst-case optimal and average-case efficient geometric ad-hoc routing. In: Proceedings of the 4th ACM International Symposium on Mobile Computing and Networking (MobiHoc 2003), ACM Press, New York (2003)
6. Leong, B., Mitra, S., Liskov, B.: Path vector face routing: Geographic routing with local face information. In: Proceedings of the 13th IEEE International Conference on Network Protocols (ICNP 2005) (2005)
7. Peng, H., Jian-Dong, L., Yan-Hui, C., Lei, Z.: A Routing Algorithm for Ad Hoc Networks Based on Delaunay Triangulation. Journal of Software(Chinese) 17(5), 1149–1156 (2006)
8. Prosenjit, B., Luc, D., William, S.E., David, G.K.: On the spanning ratio of Gabriel graphs and beta-skeletons. In: Sergio, R. (ed.) Proc. of the 5th Latin American Symp. on Theoretical Informatics, pp. 479–493. Springer, London (2002)
9. Toussaint, G.: The relative neighborhood graph of a finite planar set. Pattern Recognition 12(4), 261–268 (1980)
10. Qingfeng, H., Chenyang, L., Roman G.-C.: Reliable Mobicast via Face-Aware Routing. In: INFOCOMM 2004 (2004)
11. Heinzelman, W.R., Chandrakasan, A., Balakrishnan, H.: An Application-Specific Protocol Architecture for Wireless Microsensor Networks. IEEE Transactions on Wireless Communications 1(4), 660–670 (2002)
12. THE CMU MONARCH GROUP. Wireless and mobility extensions to ns-2, http://www.monarch.cs.rice.edu
13. Li, X.-Y., Calinescu, G., Wan, P.-J.: Distributed construction of a planar spanner and routing for ad hoc wireless networks. In: Proceedings of the 21st Annual Joint Conference of the IEEE Computer and Communications Society (INFOCOM'02), June 23-27, 2002, vol. 3, pp. 1268–1277. IEEE Computer Society, Los Alamitos (2002)
14. Kim, Y.-J., Govindan, R., Karp, B., Shenker, S.: Geographic routing made practical. In: Proceedings of USENIX Symposium on Network Systems Design and Implementation, May 2005, Boston, Massachusetts, USA (2005)

An Improved Bandwidth-Use Method on IEEE 802.11e Standard over Wireless LAN

Fang-Yie Leu, Yu-Hsin Chen, and Ching-Chien Kuan

Department of Computer Science and Information Engineering,
Tunghai University, Taichung, Taiwan
{leufy,g942825}@thu.edu.tw

Abstract. Currently, people can collect information and share resources on the Internet through WiFi. The Voice over Internet Protocol (VoIP) supported by wireless technology has made Internet access more versatile and flexible than before. However, the more sessions established for communication, the longer the transmission delay and the higher the packet dropping rate. In this paper, an improved bandwidth utilization approach developed on the IEEE 802.11e standard is proposed. Experimental results show that this approach significantly improves a system's throughput as compared with 802.11b and other schemes.

Keywords: VoIP, IEEE 802.11e, LCM, Bandwidth utilization.

1 Introduction

The rapid progress of scientific technology, e.g., merging different media, video, voice, images, and music, and the corresponding expansion of services, e.g., web and e-mail, will soon result in a fully digitalized world. Therefore, how to utilize the Internet technology to carry out high quality multimedia communication, especially with the human voice and video, has become one of the main challenges for research.

Due to its mobile convenience, wireless communication has become one of the focuses of researchers' attention. Several standards have been proposed, e.g., 802.11, 802.15 and 802.16. According to a report by eTForecasts [1][2], the number of people who access the worldwide network will approach 1,782 million by 2010, and the number of wireless network users is expected to rise to 779 million by 2010. One of the most compelling applications is VoIP. ON-World News [3] predicted that there will be more than 100 million VoIP users by 2011.

Traditional voice communication is provided by the Public Switched Telephone Network (PSTN), which deploys circuit switching to convey sound. PSTN is inefficient and expensive, whereas VoIP is efficient and inexpensive. Chen et al. [4] mentioned that today VoIP can provide all of the telephone services that traditional phone service provides. In fact, Session Initiation Protocol (SIP) [5] has been widely used in VoIP services to support call setup, call forwarding, voice mail and conference and multimedia calls. Researchers predict that SIP will be used in future all-IP mobile networks to deliver various services [6]. Wolff [7] noted that Skype membership reached 100 million at 1:12 p.m. on April 27, 2006. No other network software has reached this figure in the short span of two and a half years. The key

K. Li et al. (Eds.): NPC 2007, LNCS 4672, pp. 183–192, 2007.

reasons are that Skype membership simply requires a MIC and free access to the Internet. Courtney [8] reported that Skype was running at 30 billion Skype-to-Skype minutes a year, and predicted that the number would continue to rise. He speculated that one-tenth of a percent of those minutes go through Skype Prime. The minimum charge is $0.50 per minute.

Generally speaking, IEEE 802.11 is only designed for best effort service [9-10]. The lack of a built-in mechanism to support real-time services makes it very difficult to guarantee QoS for throughput-sensitive and delay-sensitive multimedia applications. Hence, modification of existing 802.11 standards is necessary. Although the 802.11e has supported QoS for WLAN applications [11-12], choosing the right set of MAC parameters and the QoS mechanism to provide predictable service quality remains a challenge for researchers.

In this paper, an improved bandwidth utilization approach based on a non-packet-dropping scheme developed on the IEEE 802.11e standard is proposed. It not only provides qualified transmission, but also increases communication channel utilization.

The rest of this paper is organized as follows. Section 2 introduces the related background. Section 3 describes the proposed scheme. Experimental results are described in section 4. Section 5 concludes this paper.

2   Background and Related Work

2.1   IEEE 802.11 MAC Protocol

IEEE 802.11 MAC provides two main access methods, Distributed Coordination Function (DCF) and PCF. Coordination Function is a mechanism that coordinates when a station can start transmitting data. DCF is a basic access method, which primarily deploys Carrier-Sense Multiple Access/Collision Avoidance (CSMA/CA) to enable a station to send and receive non-synchronous data. CSMA/CA can be used in Ad Hoc and WLAN infrastructures as well. PCF, a contention-free method, enables stations to send and receive time-bounded data; hence, no packet collisions occur. However, PCF can only be used in certain basic WLAN frameworks, e.g., WLANs containing AP.

2.2   VoIP

VoIP Internet phone is a type of voice transmission service that first digitizes a voice signal, and then encapsulates the result into data packets for transmission over an IP network. This technique can compensate for signal distortion, echo and data loss for packet transmission so as to reestablish the original voice data and improve communication quality. Thus, utilizing the Internet not only enables real-time voice transmission services, but also achieves global connectivity, providing users with an alternative to traditional PSTN for long-distance phone calls.

2.3   IEEE 802.11e

IEEE 802.11e [13-16] employs Hybrid Coordination Function (HCF) as its medium access protocol. HCF uses contention-based and controlled-channel accesses as its channel allocation strategies.   The former is an enhanced DCF and the latter an enhanced PCF.

The Point Coordinator (PC) of traditional PCF is only allowed to transmit data in contention-free periods, whereas the Hybrid Coordinator (HC, equivalent to PC) in HCF can transmit data or instruct stations to transmit data in both contention and contention-free periods. To minimize transmission delay and jitter and maximize medium transmission efficiency, IEEE 802.11e provides "packet bursting", which means that after being allowed access to a transmission medium, a station can transmit more than one frame within a certain time slot without requesting access to the transmission medium again.

2.4 Related Work

Using the contention approach to allocate channel access right is inadequate for transmitting real-time packets. Thus, PCF employs PC to allocate channel access right to stations. Even based on CSMA/CA, the MAC layer of IEEE 802.11b WLAN can still provide a real-time environment, but would result in less-than-optimal performance. Several solutions have been proposed [17-23]. Some give voice packets a higher priority over data packets to shorten VoIP packets' waiting time. Others suggest transferring voice packets under the DCF contention mode with special mechanisms to meet the real-time requirement. But most compromise their service quality through packet loss and delay.

PCF usually has lower channel efficiency owing to too many failed polls, especially when most stations do not attempt to transfer packets. In other words, neither PCF nor DCF is suitable for voice transmission.

3   The Proposed Scheme

To improve the quality of such transmission, we propose the following scheme: build a token buffer within AP, dynamically, establish a transmission polling list based on the parameters, and then follow the polling list to multi-poll stations.

3.1 Parameters

For each real-time station S, we use two parameters, r_c and δ, to represent its transmission characteristic. r_c is the packet transfer rate, and δ the maximum amount of jitter (i.e., packet delay variation) allowed for a specific packet. Transmitting voice data either too fast or too slow should be avoided. In other words, each packet of S should inherit r_c and δ from its voice source, i.e., S.

3.2 Theoretical Discussion

Assume there are n voice sources and their characteristic parameters are (r_{ci}, δ_i), $i = 1, 2, \cdots, n$. The maximum waiting time of a token T, from the time point T's corresponding packet P arrives at the transfer buffer to the time point P is delivered, is δ_i^*.

According to theorem 1, each packet can be delivered within δ_i.

Theorem 1[9]

Let $\delta_1^* = 2 \cdot \text{SIFS} + \text{CFPoll} + T_P + \text{ACK}$ (See Fig. 1), and

$$\delta_i^* = (2 \cdot \text{SIFS} + \text{CFPoll} + T_p + \text{ACK}) + \sum_{k=1}^{i-1} \left\lceil \frac{r_{ck}}{r_{ci}} \right\rceil \cdot (2 \cdot \text{SIFS} + \text{CFPoll} + T_p + \text{ACK}),$$

$i = 2, \cdots, n$

where T_p is the time required to transmit and receive a packet. If $\delta_i^* < \dfrac{1}{r_{ci}}$

and $\delta_i^* \le \delta_i$, $i = 2, \cdots, n$, then all voice packets of each session can be transmitted within their jitter constraints.

Theorem 2 [9]

Assume n voice sources are scheduled in the given priority order. The average waiting time is minimized for voice packets if $r_{ci} \le r_{cj}$ for all i<j.

3.3 Improvement in Multi-polling

Improvement in multi-polling is as follows:

(1) Our design is based on a hypothetically perfect environment. AP creates a polling list in its buffer to arrange the order and relative time of packet transmission, according to the parameters (r_{ci}, δ_i) of the packets that have arrived at AP's transfer buffer. It then broadcasts the polling list to all stations of the underlying Basic Service Set (BSS).

Theorem 3

Given n voice sources with r_{ci} and δ_i, i=1, 2, 3... n, there exists a cycle LCT = LCM

(The Least Common Multiple) $\left[\dfrac{1}{r_{c1}}, \dfrac{1}{r_{c2}}, \ldots\ldots\ldots, \dfrac{1}{r_{cn}} \right]$ within which the amount of

packets transmitted is $\sum_{i=1}^{n} (r_{ci} \bullet LCT)$. If two or more packets of different sessions

arrive at the same time point, based on theorem 2 a session with lower jitter has lower priority. This ensures a minimum total waiting time.

(2) In a BSS, stations normally follow their current polling list to transmit voice packets. AP and stations monitor whether the sequence is correct or not. If any discrepancy or collision occurs, e.g., a session is newly established or disconnected, or a station crashes or follows an out-of-date polling list, AP updates its polling list if needed and again broadcasts it to all stations which will then follow the new list. AP does not need to poll stations one by one, thus

saving a significant amount of polling time. AP resets the TPT field at any time token buckets are empty, and judges whether it has sufficient time to switch to contention mode to transmit ordinary data. If so, AP switches to DCF mode.

3.4 Bandwidth Utilization

In an LCM, several tokens can be generated at the same time. Lower-priority packets are then postponed without seriously affecting their sound quality. Attempting to send voice data D to another station, a station first partitions D into several packets when necessary and sends them with IEEE802.11e protocol. An AP at any given moment can deploy only one channel to transmit packets. However, due to transmission overhead and times when no packets are transmitted, the channel bandwidth is very often not completely used. The former can not be avoided except by using a modified 802.11e protocol, which is currently unavailable in the commercial market. However, if we can negotiate with some stations which, based on theorem 1, are not allowed to send packets at first, to reduce their $r_{c}is$ and extend their jitters, then many empty slots will be efficiently used and channel bandwidth utilization will be significantly improved. In the following subsection, two ways to increase bandwidth utilization are discussed.

3.4.1 The Ways to Improve Channel Utilization

Let $K = (k_1, k_2, k_3, \ldots, k_m)$ be empty slots in an LCM. Assume there is an arithmetic progression $Arip = \{k'_1, k'_2, \ldots, k'_p\}$ with a parameter c, where $c = k'_{j+1} - k'_j > 0$ for all j, $1 \leq j \leq p - 1$ and $k'_1 = (k'_p + c) \% p$, i.e., a circular arithmetic progression.

Approach 1 is applicable to the situation where elements of $Arip$ are all unallocated, i.e., for all $k'_i, k'_i \in K$, $1 \leq i \leq p$, and a station, e.g., STA_g, which is filtered out by theorem 1, agrees to reduce its r_c to $r'_c(= 1/(c * time\_of\_a\_slot))$, and changes its δ_c to $\delta'_c (= 1/r'_c)$. We then allocate $Arip$ to STA_g, which will send data with r'_c and δ'_c. As several such $Arips$ exist simultaneously, e.g., $Arip1$ with $c_1 = 3$ and $Arip2$ with $c_2 = 6$, the one with the smallest c is chosen since much more data can then be sent. However, when there are several such stations, the one with the greatest r_c will be negotiated with first.

Approach 2 is applicable to the situation where some elements (slots) of $Arip$ have been allocated, e.g., $KO = \{o_1, o_2, \ldots, o_w\}$ where $o_i \notin K$, $o_i \in Arip$, $i = 1, 2, \ldots, w$. However, for each o_i, there is at least one empty slot k'_b, located between $o_i(= k'_v)$ and k'_{v+1}, $1 \leq v \leq p - 1$, $k'_b \in K$. STA_g can then transmit a packet for STA_g at k'_b instead of at k'_v without violating STA_g's new jitter.

4 Simulations and Experiments

In the following, we evaluate the performance of the proposed scheme.

4.1 Simulation Environment

The basic assumptions of our simulation environment are as follows. Two types of traffic are considered.

(1) **Pure data.** The arrival of data frames from a station's higher-layer to the MAC sub-layer is Poisson. Frame length is assumed to be exponentially distributed with a mean length of 1024 octets.
(2) **Voice traffic.** We use the mio8380's [24] built-in audio codec based on the GSM610 format to generate voice traffic patterns. For each session, frames are sent every 10ms. Sessions are generated as exponentially distributed. Frames of voice traffic that are not successfully transmitted within their maximum jitter constraint are assumed to be lost.

4.2 Simulation Results

The simulation was performed based on the number of sessions that could successfully complete their communication. We generated a fixed number of session requests with the same r_c and jitter for each of the following groups: LCM multi-polling [9], LCM single-polling [9], 802.11b [17] [20-23], 802.11e [15-16][23], and scheduled the requests of a group in a sequence of time slots.

Fig. 1 shows that channel utilization of GCD (of course, LCM-based) was not as high as that of the IEEE 802.11b since GCD filtered out requests with theorem 1, but 802.11b did not. The GCD outperformed the LCMs since GCD dynamically adjusted sessions' jitters to make them acceptable to theorem 1. The bandwidth utilization was then improved.

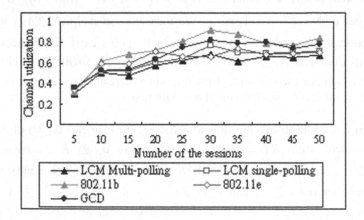

Fig. 1. Channel utilization for different sessions

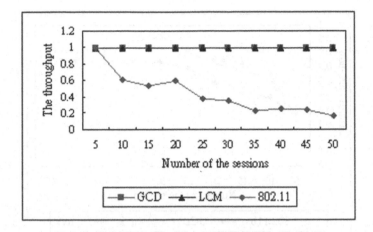

Fig. 2. Throughput for different sessions

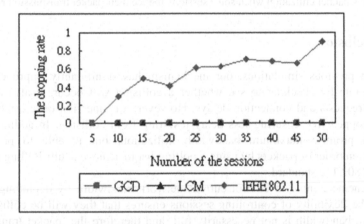

Fig. 3. Dropping rate for different sessions

We defined throughput as the ratio of successfully transmitted packets over total packets. In the IEEE 802.11 standard, all collided packets were dropped. Our mechanism will block all requests whose jitters can not be satisfied, hence dropping no packets in any sessions. The only side effect is that those stations will continuously request AP until their requests are accepted. Fig. 2 shows the simulation results.

Fig. 3 illustrates that the dropping rates of the GCD and LCM were significantly lower than that of the IEEE 802.11 standard. As stated above, both in single-polling and multi-polling, their values were zero.

Fig. 4 shows that GCD's channel utilization was not better than that of IEEE 802.11b. But when the r_c of the requests rejected by theorem 1 was reduced, GCD was better than IEEE802.11b.

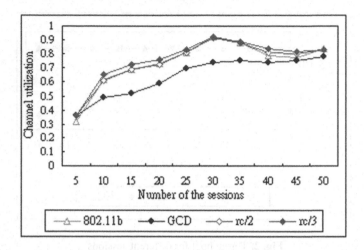

Fig. 4. Channel utilization when some sessions reduce their packet transmission rates r_c

5 Conclusion

Based on previous simulations, our mechanism has significantly improved packet dropping rate by checking to see whether a collision will occur. It also results in repeated requests and connection delays. However, a connection once established is packet-dropped free ensuring less delay resulting from collision. In addition, LCM does not promise maximum bandwidth utilization, but is able to predict the transmission order of packets by using a polling list to achieve Multi-Polling and meet the IEEE 802.11e standard.

Our scheme is able to control current network bandwidth by deploying a token buffer. The flexibility of controlling sessions ensures that they will be collision free. The actual bandwidth is not necessarily full, and therefore the 'packet transfer rate' and 'tolerated jitter' values become very important. Simultaneous small jitters of multiple sessions will cause a jam, thus forcing a token buffer to fill up much earlier. However, the bandwidth is not fully occupied, theoretically allowing more tolerated large-size jitters. Simultaneous large session jitters will also cause a jam, but as with small session jitters, our mechanism can increase the bandwidth by accepting more tolerated small-size jitters. In summary, the capacity of pairing the 'packet transfer rate' and 'tolerated jitter' values is a tradeoff but one of critical importance.

References

1. Worldwide Internet Users Top 1 Billion in 2005—USA Reaches Nearly 200M Internet Users, (January 3, 2006) http://www.etforecasts.com/pr/pr106.htm
2. Internet Users by Country, eTForecasts's Products.
   http://www.etforecasts.com/products/ES_intusersv2.htm

3. One Hundred Million Mobile VOIP Users in 2011 (May 23, 2006) http://www.onworld.com/html/newscmvoip.htm
4. Chen, J.J., Cheng, Y.L., Tseng, Y.C., Wu, Q.: A Push-Based VoIP Service for an Internet-Enabled Mobile Ad Hoc Network. In: The IEEE Asia Pacific Wireless Communications Symposium (2006), http://www.csie.nctu.edu.tw/ỹctseng/pub.html
5. Rosenberg, J., et al.: SIP:Session Initiation Protocol. IETF RFC 3261(June 2002)
6. Lin, Y.B., Huang, Y.R., Pang, A.C., Chlamtac, I.: All IP Approach for Third Generation Mobile Networks. IEEE Networks 16(5), 8–19 (2002)
7. Wolff, P.: Skype Achieves 100 Million Users (April 28, 2006), http://www.skypejournal.com/blog/archives/2006/04/ 100000000_or_so_skype_accounts_more_skyp_1.php
8. Courtney, J.: The Skype Prime Rates (March 07, 2007), http://www.skypejournal.com/blog/every_post/skype/
9. Leu, F.Y., Kuan, C.C., Deng, D.J., Chang, W.K.: Quality of Service for Voice over Wireless LAN by Deploying Multipolling in IEEE802.11e Standard. In: Proc. of International Symposium on Multimedia Over Wireless, June 2005, pp. 170–175 (2005)
10. Gu, D., Zhang, J.: QoS Enhancement in IEEE 802.11 Wireless Local Area Networks. IEEE Communication Magazine 41(6), 120–124 (2003)
11. Wang, Y., Bensaou, B.: Priority-Based Multiple Access for Service Differentiation in Wireless Ad-Hoc Networks. In: Proc. of Mobile and Wireless Communication Networks, pp. 14–31 (2000)
12. Chuang, P.H., Wu, H.K., Liao, M.K.: Dynamic QoS Allocation for Multimedia Ad Hoc Wireless Networks. In: Proc. of Computer Communications and Networks, pp. 480–485 (October 1999)
13. Ni, Q.: Performance Analysis and Enhancements for IEEE 802.11e Wireless Networks. IEEE Networks 19(4), 21–27 (2005)
14. Hwang, G.H., Cho, D.H.: New Access Scheme for VoIP Packets in IEEE 802.11e Wireless LANs. IEEE Communications Letters 9(7), 667–669 (2005)
15. Naoum-Sawaya, J., Ghaddar, B., Khawam, S., Safa, H., Artail, H., Dawy, Z.: Adaptive Approach for QoS Support in IEEE 802.11e Wireless LANs. In: Proc. of the IEEE International Conference on Wireless And Mobile Computing, Networking and Communications, vol. 2, pp. 167–173 (2005)
16. Lee, J.F., Liao, W., Chen, M.C.: A Per-Class QoS Service Model in IEEE 802.11e WLANs. Quality of Service in Heterogeneous Wired/Wireless Networks (QShine) (August 2005)
17. Sobrinho, J.L., Krishnakumar, A.S.: Quality-of-Service in Ad Hoc Carrier Sense Multiple Access Wireless Networks. IEEE Journal on Selected Areas of Communications 17(8), 1353–1368 (1999)
18. Xiao, Y.: Enhanced DCF of IEEE 802.11e to Support QoS. Proc. of Wireless Communication and Networking, pp. 1291–1296 (March 2003)
19. Eshghi, F., Elhakeem, A.K.: Performance Analysis of Ad Hoc Wireless LANs for Real-Time Traffic. IEEE Journal on Selected Areas of Communications 21(2), 204–215 (2003)
20. Deng, D.J., Chang, R.S.: A Priority Scheme for IEEE 802.11 DCF Access Method. IEICE Transactions on Communications E82- B(1), 96–102 (1999)
21. Chang, C.S., Chen, K.C., You, M.Y., Chang, J.F.: Guaranteed Quality-of-Service Wireless Access to ATM Networks. IEEE Journal on Selected Areas of Communications 15(1), 106–118 (1997)

22. Wang, W., Liew, S.C., Li, V.O.K.: Solutions to Performance Problems in VoIP over a 802.11 Wireless LAN. IEEE Transactions on Vehicular Technology 54(1), 366–384 (2005)
23. IEEE 802.11: The Working Group Setting the Standards for Wireless LANs, http://grouper.ieee.org/groups/802/11/
24. MiTAC International Corporation, "Mio8380" http://www.mitac.com/

Maximum Life-Time Localized Broadcast Routing in MANET

Ruiqin Zhao, Aijun Wen, Zengji Liu, and Peng Yue

State Key Lab. of Integrated Service Networks,
Xidian University, Xi'an 710071 China
rqinzhao@gmail.com, {ajwen,zjliu,pyue}@xidian.edu.cn

Abstract. Added delay strategy can be used to solve the broadcast storm problem of ordinary broadcast mechanism (OBM) and maximize network life-time. Available added delay strategies take into account the distance and/or the residual energy. In this paper, we propose a new added delay strategy—Maximum Life-time Localized Broadcast (ML^2B). As the node's number of neighbors that have not received the broadcast message (we call it coverage degree) can better describe the coverage rate, ML^2B takes the coverage degree rather than the distance into account. ML^2B also takes the residual energy into account as other strategies do. ML^2B only need one-hop neighbor information to find the coverage degree, so ML^2B is a distributed protocol and the overhead is small. Simulation results show that, as compared with OBM, ML^2B can save at least 50% rebroadcast, its maximum end-to-end delay is lower, its reachability is the same, and its network life-time is two times longer.

Keywords: Broadcast, life-time, localized, ML^2B, wireless ad hoc networks.

1 Introduction

The issue of energy-efficient communication in ad hoc networks has been attracting attention of many researches during last several years. Broadcasting is a common operation in ad hoc networks which is used not only for distributing the data among all network devices, but also for spreading the control information, e.g., for maintaining routes between devices and updating their states.

The straightforward way of broadcast in MANET is flooding which also is known as ordinary broadcast mechanism (OBM). OBM will cause serious broadcast redundancy, which is referred to as broadcast storm problem [1]. A satisfying broadcast strategy should be able to reduce the broadcast redundancy effectively, not only for the saving of bandwidth, but also for the saving of energy, as both bandwidth and energy are valuable resources in MANET.

With the aim of solving the broadcast storm problem and maximizing the network life-time, we propose an efficient broadcast algorithm—Maximum Life-time Localized Broadcast (ML^2B) for MANET, which possesses the following properties:

1. **Localized algorithm.** Each node makes the decision of rebroadcast according to its one-hop local information. ML^2B need not maintain any global topology information at each node, so the overhead is small.

K. Li et al. (Eds.): NPC 2007, LNCS 4672, pp. 193–202, 2007.

2. **Effective Coverage adaptive broadcast strategy.** To reduce the redundancy of rebroadcast, nodes with larger coverage degree are selected as forward nodes with higher priority. The coverage degree is the number of left neighbors that have not received the broadcast message, it describes the effective coverage rate of the broadcast node more accurately than the distance of the node, and reduces broadcast redundancy more effectively.

3. **Energy-efficient approach.** Small algorithm overhead and reduced broadcast redundancy result in the reduction of energy consumption. ML^2B also takes residual energy of the node into consideration when selecting rebroadcasting node to maximize network life-time,

2 Related Works

Various approaches have been proposed to solve the broadcast storm problem of ordinary broadcast mechanism, generally they can be classified into two categories: energy-saving methods and non energy-saving methods.

Non energy-saving methods are designed with the aim of alleviating the broadcast storm problem by reducing redundant broadcasts. As in [2]–[6], each node computes a local cover set consisting of as less neighbors as possible to cover its whole 2-hop coverage area by exchanging connectivity information with neighbors. Several methods [3], [5]–[8] require each node know its k-hop (k >=2) neighbor information. These non energy-saving methods need heavy overhead to maintain the fresh k-hop (k >=2) neighbor information and they consume much energy at each node. Some methods proposed in [1] select forward node based on probability, which cannot guarantee the reachability of the broadcast.

Most proposed energy-saving broadcast methods are centralized, which require the topology information of the whole network. They try to find a broadcast tree such that the energy cost of the broadcast tree is minimized. Methods in [9]–[12] are based on geometry information of the network, and others [13]–[16] are based on graph theory to compute the minimum energy tree. Since the centralized method will cause much overhead in MANET, some localized versions of the above algorithms have been proposed recently. [17] reduces energy consumption by taking advantage of the physical layer design. [18] finds the network topology in a distributed way, it requires every node to maintain the network topology, and the overhead is obviously more than a localized algorithm. The method proposed in [19] requires that each node must be aware of the geometry information within its 2-hop neighborhood. It results in more control overhead and energy cost than the thorough distributed algorithm that requires only one-hop neighbors' information.

3 System Model

The MANET can be abstracted as a graph $G(V, E)$, in which V is the set of all the nodes in the network and E consists of edges in the graph. We assume all links in the graph are bidirectional, and the graph is in a connected state. Given a node i, time t is 0 when it receives the broadcasted message for the first time. The residual energy of node i is $e(i,t)$. r is the radius of the coverage of the node. $nb(i)$ is the one-hop neighbor of node i, and $NB(i)$ is the set of all neighbors of node i. We assume each node knows its own position information by means of GPS or other instruments. It can obtain its one-hop neighbors' information like most location-aided routing [20] of MANET do. Residual energy is also known at each node locally.

For $\forall i \in V$, several variables are defined as follows:

- **Uncovered set** $UC(i,t)$, consists of one-hop neighbors that have not been covered by a certain forward node of the broadcasted message or the broadcast originator, before t.
- **Coverage Degree** $d(i,t)$, is the number of nodes belonging to $UC(i,t)$ at t. $d(i,t)$ implies the rebroadcast efficiency of node i. If $d(i,t)$ is below a threshold before its attempt to rebroadcast the broadcasted message, node i would abandon the rebroadcast.
- **Up-link forward node** $uf(i,t)$, is the $nb(i)$ that rebroadcasts or broadcasts the message which is received by node i at t $(0 \le t \le D(i))$. During the period of $0 < t \le D(i)$, it may receive several copies of the same broadcasted message from different up-link forward nodes ($D(i)$ is the added delay of node i).
- **Up-link forward set** $UF(i,t)$, is the set of all up-link forward nodes of node i before t. If it has received the same broadcasted message for k times before $t(t \le D(i))$, its up-link forward set can be expressed as:

$$UF(i,t) = \left\{ uf(i,t_0), uf(i,t_1), uf(i,t_2)...uf(i,t_{k-1}) \right\}, (k \ge 1) . \tag{1}$$

(where $t_0, t_1, t_2...$, and t_{k-1} $(t_{k-1} \le t)$ records the time node i receives the 1st, 2nd, 3rd ..., and k th copy of the same broadcasted message).

4 Maximum Life-Time Localized Broadcast (ML²B) Algorithm

4.1 The Length of Added Delay $D(i)$

Utilization of added delay in broadcast is to reduce the redundancy of nodes' rebroadcast and energy consumption. When node i receives a broadcasted message for the first time, it will not rebroadcast it as OBM. It defers a period of $D(i)$ before its attempt to do the rebroadcast. Even when $D(i)$ expires, the node will not rebroadcast it urgently until the node coverage degree $d(i, D(i))$ is larger than the abandoning threshold n. During the interval of $0 \le t \le D(i)$, $\forall$ node i could abandon its attempt to rebroadcast the message as soon as its node coverage degree $d(i,t)$ is equal to or below the threshold, thus reducing the rebroadcast redundancy and energy consumption largely.

Nodes with larger added delay have a higher probability of receiving multiple copies of a certain broadcasted message from different up-link forward nodes, before they attempt to rebroadcast. Each reception of the same message decreases the node coverage degree, thus making nodes with large added delay rebroadcast the message with little probability. However nodes with little added delay may rebroadcast the message quickly. We assign little added delay or no-delay to nodes with high rebroadcast efficiency and enough residual energy, large added delay to nodes with large rebroadcast redundancy. To formulate the rebroadcast efficiency, two metrics are presented as follows:

$$f_d(i) = \frac{a - d(i,0)}{a}, \qquad (0 \le f_d(i) \le 1) \ . \tag{2}$$

Formula (2) is the node coverage degree metric. a is the maximum node coverage degree. It can be induced from the formula that less $f_d(i)$ results in a higher rebroadcast efficiency.

To maximize the network life-time, we present the second metric—energy metric. If the residual energy at a node is smaller than an energy threshold E_T, it refuses to forward the broadcasted message. Otherwise, the node calculates the added delay based on formula (3), where E' is the maximum energy. E_T is used to prevent nodes with little energy from dying.

$$f_e(i) = \frac{E' - e(i,0)}{E' - E_T}, \qquad (E_T \le e(i,0) \le E') \ . \tag{3}$$

ML^{2}B first introduces a new metric $f(d(i,0), e(i,0))$ for the selection of rebroadcast node in MANET. It incorporates the two metrics presented above together to select rebroadcast nodes with goals of obtaining low rebroadcast redundancy, high reachability, limited latency, and maximized network life-time. We propose two different ways to combine node coverage degree and residual energy metrics into a single synthetic metric, based on the product and sum of the three metrics respectively. The synthetic product metric of delaying are given by formula (4). The sum metric is shown by formula (5) by suitably selected values of the two factors: α and β.

$$f^{pro}(d(i,0), e(i,0)) = f_d(i) f_e(i) \ . \tag{4}$$

$$f^{sum}(d(i,0), e(i,0)) = \alpha f_d(i) + \beta f_e(i) \ . \tag{5}$$

We compute the added delay with the following formula:

$$D(i) = D.f(d(i,0), e(i,0)) \ . \tag{6}$$

D defines the maximum added delay. $f\left(d(i,0),e(i,0)\right)$ is the synthetic metric shown by formula (4) or (5). Hence, based on formulas (2)–(6), we can get product and sum versions of the added delay are:

$$D^{pro}(i) = \frac{D[a-d(i,0)][E'-e(i,0)]}{(E'-E_T)a} . \tag{7}$$

$$D^{sum}(i) = D(\frac{\alpha[a-d(i,0)]}{a} + \frac{\beta[E'-e(i,0)]}{E'-E_T}) . \tag{8}$$

4.2 Algorithm Description

ML^{2}B is a thorough distributed broadcast routing protocol, in which each node requires only its one-hop local information to fulfill a broadcast task. The thorough distributed and localized nature of ML^{2}B could relieve the heavy overhead presented in most proposed energy-saving methods. The goal of a broadcast routing algorithm is to carry broadcasted messages to each node in network with as less rebroadcast redundancy as possible, satisfied reachability and maximized life-time of network. ML^{2}B is designed with the goal in mind. Let s be the broadcast originator, the algorithm flow for $\forall\ i \in \left(V-\{s\}\right)$ may be formalized as follows:

Step 0: Initialization: $j = -1, D(i) = D, UF(i,0) = \varnothing$.

Step 1: If node i receives the broadcasted message M_s, go to step 2; else if $j \geq 0$, go to step 7, else the node is idle, and stay in step 1.

Step 2: Check the node ID of the originator s and the message ID. If M_s is a new message, go to step 3; else, node i has received repeated M_s, then let $j = j+1$, and go to step 4.

Step 3: Let $t = 0$, and the system time begins. Let $j = 0$, where j indicates the times of the repeated reception of M_s. Let $UC(i,0) = NB(i)$. Thus, $d(i,0)$ equals the number of all neighbors. If $e(i,0)$ is smaller than an energy threshold E_T, node i abandons its attempt to rebroadcast, and go to step 9.

Step 4: Let $t_j = t$, and use p_{t_j} to mark the previous-hop node of M_s. p_{t_j} transmits M_s at t_j. We assume the propagation delay can be omitted. Then we get $uf(i,t_j) = p_{t_j}$, where p_{t_j} is the j th up-link forward node of node i. Add p_{t_j} to up-link forward set $UF(i,t)$ at last.

Step 5: Based on the locally obtained position of $uf(i,t_j)$, node i computes the geographical coverage range of $uf(i,t_j)$ which is expressed as $C(i,t_j)$. Then it updates $UC(i,t_j)$ by deleting nodes that locate in $C(i,t_j)$ from $UC(i,t_j)$, which is shown in Fig.1. Based on the updated $UC(i,t_j)$, node i could calculate its coverage

198   R. Zhao et al.

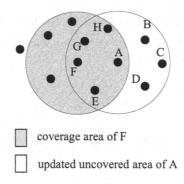

□ coverage area of F

□ updated uncovered area of A

Fig. 1. Node F rebroadcasts M_s at time t. When receives the message, node A updates its uncovered set by deleting node E, F, G and H which are covered by node F.

degree $d(i,t_j)$. If $d(i,t_j) \le n$, it abandons its attempt to rebroadcast, and go to step 9; else if $j > 0$, go to step 7.

Step 6: $j = 0$ means node i has received M_s for the first time. It calculates its added delay $D(i)$ based on two factors: $d(i,0)$ and $e(i,0)$. $d(i,0)$ has been computed in step 5, and $e(i,0)$ can be obtained locally. Then it calculates the added delay using formula (7) or (8).

Step 7: Check the current time t: if $t < D(i)$, go to step 1; else let $d(i,t) = d(i,t_j)$.

Step 8: If $d(i,t) \le n$, node i abandons its attempt to rebroadcast; else rebroadcasts M_s to all its neighbors.

Step 9: The algorithm ends.

5 Performance Evaluation

To verify the proposed ML^2B, we made lots of simulations with an 802.11 MAC layer, using NS-2 [21]. Nodes in MANET are placed randomly in a 2-D square area. For all simulation results, CBR streams are used, and each broadcast stream consists of packets of size 512 bytes. In the all simulations made in this paper, we use the formula (7) to calculate the added delay. The abandoning threshold and energy threshold used in our simulations are configured as: $n = b/5$, $E_T = E'/100$. b is the average number of neighbors of nodes.

5.1 Performance Metrics Used in Simulations

- **Saved rebroadcast (SRB):** $(x-y)/x$, where x is the number of nodes that receive the broadcasted message, and y is the number of nodes that rebroadcasts the message after their reception of the message. Therefore SRB of OBM is 0 under all scenarios.
- **Reachability (RE):** x/z, where z is the number of all nodes in the simulated connected network. So RE is also known as the coverage rate.

- **Maximum end-to-end delay (MED):** the interval form the time the broadcasted message is initiated to the time the last node in the network receiving the message.
- **Life-time (LT):** the interval from the time the network is initiated to the time the first node dies.

5.2 Simulation Results

5.2.1 Performance Dependence on the Network Scale

To study the influence of network scale on ML^2B, we maintain a same node density by placing randomly different number of nodes separately in square areas of different size. The packets generation rate here is 2 packets-per-second (pps). As illustrated in Fig.2, ML^2B achieves high SRB without sacrificing the RE and MED under varying network sizes. According to expectation, MED increases with the increased network scale.

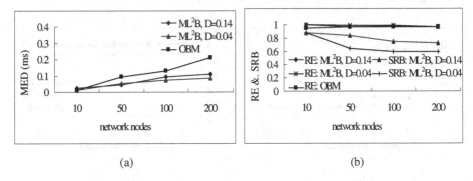

| (a) | (b) |

Fig. 2. Influence of network scale

5.2.2 Performance Dependence on Node Density

Many simulations were made to study the ML^2B performance. For the reason of limited pages, we give the results of the network consisting of 50 nodes, which is shown by Fig.3. The packets generation rate here is 2 pps. Results illustrated by Fig.3 shows SRB of ML^2B falls with the decrease of node density. That is because the theoretical

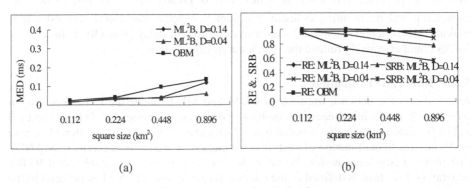

| (a) | (b) |

Fig. 3. Influence of node density

value of SRB depends upon the node density. Large density causes big SRB, and ideal SRB will be zero when the node density is below a certain threshold, which is not the main issue of this paper.

We also compare the performance of ML^2B with maximum added delay $D = 0.14$ s and $D = 0.04$ s. From Fig.2 and Fig.3, it is clear that the former outbalanced the latter in SRB and RE. And both of them have less MED than the OBM in all circumstances. Therefore, in the following experiments we set $D = 0.14$ s.

5.2.3 Performance Dependence on Packets Generation Rate

We study the influence of network load on network performance by varying the packets generation rate from 2 pps to 10 pps. Simulation results in Fig.4 show that increased network load incurs little impact on ML^2B, however leads to increased MED in OBM. ML^2B maintains nearly as high RE as OBM, and simultaneously achieves SRB with a value larger than 80%, which reveals the superiority of ML^2B over OBM.

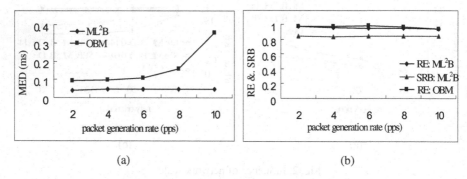

(a)   (b)

Fig. 4. Influence of network load

It can be summarized from the above simulations that, ML^2B achieves high SRB without sacrificing the RE and MED under all circumstances. It is beyond our expectation that ML^2B, which has delayed the rebroadcast for an interval of $D(i)$, obtains a smaller MED than OBM that has not delayed rebroadcast. Using the different $D(i)$ values for different nodes, ML^2B greatly alleviates and avoids the contention and its resulting collision problem that persecutes OBM seriously, thus making ML^2B achieve a smaller maximum end-to-end delay than OBM. In a word, ML^2B could effectively relieve the broadcast storm problem.

5.2.4 Life-Time Evaluation

Fig. 5 shows the network life-time of OBM and ML^2B under the same scenario, in which each node's initial energy is uniformly distributed between 0.5 J (Joule) and 1.0 J. The first and last node dies separately at 32.48 s and 33.62 s in OBM. After 33.62 s no node dies due to malfunction of the broadcast caused by the unconnectivity of MANET due to too many dead nodes. While in ML^2B, they happen at 73.05 s and 95.0 s separately. Life-time is defined as the interval from the time MANET is initiated to the

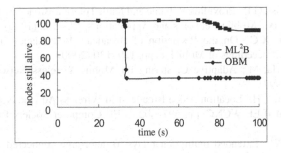

Fig. 5. Nodes still alive in the network of 100 nodes

time the first node dies. Obviously, ML^2B has more than doubles the useful network life-time compared with OBM.

We break the whole simulation time into many small time steps which also are called as rounds. Broadcast originator broadcasts each packet to other nodes in the network during each round. Table 1 shows the network life-time by rounds with different initial energy, which manifests ML^2B obtains much longer network life-time than OBM.

Table 1. Life-time using different amount of initial energy

Initial Energy(J/node)	Protocol	Life-Time (rounds)
0.25	ML^2B	192
	OBM	45
0.5	ML^2B	245
	OBM	91
1.0	ML^2B	407
	OBM	195

6 Conclusion

To solve the broadcast storm problem and maximize the network life-time, we propose an efficient broadcast protocol ML^2B for MANET. ML^2B is a novel added delay strategy, in which each node requires only its one-hop local information to fulfill a broadcast task. The thorough distributed and localized nature of ML^2B results in less overhead than ordinary broadcast methods. It is featured by the following properties: localized algorithm to cut down overhead, effective coverage adaptive to reduce broadcast redundancy and energy-efficient to maximize network lifetime. The effectiveness of ML^2B has been verified by simulations in NS-2.

References

1. Ni, S.Y., Tseng, Y.C., Chen, Y.S., Sheu, J.P.: The Broadcast Storm problem in a Mobile Ad Hoc Network. In: Proceedings of the 5th ACM/ IEEE Int. Conf. on Mobile Computing and Networking, pp. 151–162. IEEE, Seattle (1999)

2. Pagani, E., Possi, G.P.: Providing Reliable and Fault Tolerant Broadcast Delivery in Mobile Ad-hoc Networks. Mobile Networks and Applications, 175–192 (1999)
3. Peng, W., Lu, X.C.: On the Reduction of Broadcast Redundancy in Mobile Ad Hoc Networks. In: Proceedings of MobiHoc, pp. 129–130 (2000)
4. Lin, C.R., Gerla, M.: Adaptive Clustering for Mobile Wireless Networks. IEEE JSAC, 1265–1275 (1997)
5. Sun, M.T., Lai, T.H.: Location Aided Broadcast in Wireless Ad Hoc Network Systems. In: Proceedings of IEEE WCNC, pp. 597–602. IEEE Computer Society Press, Los Alamitos (2002)
6. Wu, J., Lou, W.: Extended multipoint relays to determine connected dominating sets in MANETs. In: Proceedings of SECON, pp. 621–630 (2004)
7. Katsaros, D., Manolopoulos, Y.: The Geodesic Broadcast Scheme for Wireless Ad Hoc Networks. In: Proceedings of WoWMoM'06 (2006)
8. Wu, J., Dai, F.: A generic distributed broadcast scheme in ad hoc wireless networks. IEEE TC 53, 1343–1354 (2004)
9. Wieselthier, J.E., Nguyen, G.D., Ephremides, A.: Algorithm for Energy-Efficient Multicasting in Static Ad Hoc Wireless Networks. Mobile Networks and Applications 6, 251–263 (2001)
10. Wieselthier, J.E., Nguyen, G.D., Ephremides, A.: On the Construction of Energy-Efficient Broadcast and Multicast Trees in Wireless Networks. In: Proceedings of IEEE INFOCOM, IEEE Computer Society Press, Los Alamitos (2000)
11. Wan, P.J., Calinescu, G.X., Li, Y., Frieder, O.: Minimum-Energy Broadcast Routing in Static Ad Hoc Wireless Networks. In: Proceedings of IEEE INFOCOM (2001)
12. Cheng, M.X., Sun, J., Min, M., Du, D.Z.: Energy Efficient Broadcast and Multicast Routing in Ad Hoc Wireless Networks. In: Proceedings of 22nd IEEE Int'l Performance, Computing, and Comm. Conf. (2003)
13. Egecioglu, O., Gonzalez, T.F.: Minimum-Energy Broadcast in Simple Graphs with Limited Node Power. In: Proceedings of PDCS, pp. 334–338 (2001)
14. Cagalj, M., Hubaux, J.P., Enz, C.: Minimum-Energy Broadcast in All-Wireless Networks: NP-Completeness and Distribution Issues. In: Proceedings of MOBICOM (2002)
15. Liang, W.: Constructing Minimum-Energy Broadcast Trees in Wireless Ad Hoc Networks. In: Proceedings of MOBIHOC (2002)
16. Li, D., Jia, X., Liu, H.: Minimum Energy-Cost Broadcast Routing in static Ad Hoc Wireless Networks. IEEE Transactions on Mobile Computing 3(2) (2004)
17. Agarwal, M., Cho, J.H., Gao, L., Wu, J.: Energy Efficient Broadcast in Wireless Ad hoc Networks with Hitch-hiking. In: Proceedings of IEEE INFOCOM, IEEE Computer Society Press, Los Alamitos (2004)
18. Song, W.Z., Li, X.Y., Wang, W.Z.: Localized Topology Control for Unicast and Broadcast in Wireless Ad Hoc Networks. IEEE Transactions on Parallel and Distributed Systems 17, 321–334 (2006)
19. Ingelrest, F., Simplot-Ryl, D.: Localized Broadcast Incremental Power Protocol for Wireless Ad Hoc Networks. In: Proceedings of IEEE ISCC, IEEE Computer Society Press, Los Alamitos (2005)
20. Mauve, M., Widmer, J., Hartenstein, H.: A Survey on Position-Based Routing in Mobile Ad Hoc Networks. IEEE Network 30–39 (2001)
21. NS-2 Network Simulator (2006), http://isi.edu/nsnam/ns/index.html

Modulation Multiplexing Distributed Space-Time Block Coding for Two-User Cooperative Diversity in Wireless Network

Rong Ran and Dongku Kim

Department of Electrical and Electronic Engineering, Yonsei University, Seoul, 120-749 Korea
{sunny_rr,dkkim}@yonsei.ac.kr

Abstract. In this paper, we propose a modulation multiplexing distributed space-time coding for two-user cooperative diversity in wireless network, in which the information of one user lies in the in-phase axis (**I** axis), while that of the other user lies in quadrature-phase axis (**Q** axis). Since two users share both time and frequency resource in cooperation sub-frame, the proposed scheme is more bandwidth efficient. We characterize performance of the proposed scheme in symmetric inter-user case. Simulation results show that the proposed scheme outperforms the amplify-to-forward cooperative system. Compared to the distributed space-time coding with time-division multiple accesses cooperative system, the proposed scheme achieves the same diversity gain but loses some coding gain. However, when the selection relay protocol is adopted for the proposed scheme, coding gain is also achieved.

Keywords: Distributed Space-Time Coded Cooperative diversity system, Alamouti structure, Modulation Multiplexing.

1 Introduction

In wireless networks, signal fading arising from multipath propagation is a particularly severe form of interference that can be mitigated through the use of diversity-transmission of redundant signals over essentially independent channel realizations in conjunction with suitable receiver combining to average the channel effects. Traditional space-time coded multi-antenna system exploits spatial diversity through multiple transmit or receive antennas. However, due to the size of mobile and carrier frequency constraints, achieving spatial diversity through multiple antennas may not be possible. In this case, a promising approach for achieving spatial diversity without multiple antennas is cooperative diversity. As there are many users in the wireless system, cooperative diversity allows sharing the resource (e.g., time, frequency) among cooperative users and each user can serve as a relay for the transmission of other user's information. Diversity is obtained from the relay transmission of other users in the system. The concept of cooperative diversity was introduced in [1], where the capacity region, outage probabilities, coverage area were derived and code-division multiple-access

K. Li et al. (Eds.): NPC 2007, LNCS 4672, pp. 203–211, 2007.

(CDMA) implementation was discussed. In [2] and [3], various cooperative diversity algorithms are developed for a pair of users based upon relays amplifying their received signals or fully decoding and repeating information. These algorithms are referred as amplify-and-forward and decode-and-forward, respectively. Distributed space-coded cooperative (DSTC) systems were introduced to combat fading in [4] and [5]. In these systems, a pair of users cooperates in order to construct the space-time coded transmission. Full spatial diversity benefits of these DSTC systems come at a price of decreasing bandwidth efficiency with the number of cooperation users, because each relay requires its own time or frequency resource to relay the partner's information. The analysis of these systems was given in [6], in which the outage probability is a performance measure. The idea of using distributed space-time coding has also been reported in [7].

In this paper, a situation that both users have information to send and they share the same frequency band is considered. Therefore, we propose a modulation multiplexing Distributed space time coding (DSTC-MM) for two-user cooperative diversity system. In this system, The information of one user lies in the in-phase axis (I axis), while that of the other user lies in the quadrature-phase axis (Q axis), which is to ensure that both users can share time and frequency resource in cooperation subframe so as to increase the bandwidth efficiency. We focus on a half-duplex transmission, i.e. the users cannot transmit and receive signal at the same time.

2   System and Signal Model

We consider a cellular system in which two cooperative users transmit their information to the same base station (BS) shown as in Fig.1. A single antenna is accommodated at each user and BS. The transmission frame structure and its associated transmissions and reception are shown in Fig.1. A total transmission frame is divided into three sub-frames. The first sub-frame belongs to the first user (U1). The second sub-frame belongs to the second user (U2). The cooperation sub-frame is shared by both users and used to relay each other's message to the destination. Compared with the distributed space-time coding with TDMA cooperative system [6], this partition is more bandwidth efficient since cooperation transmissions share both time and frequency resource. In order

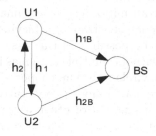

Fig. 1. System Model

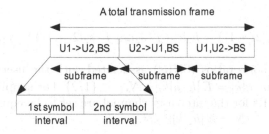

Fig. 2. Transmission frame structure

to apply space-time block code transmission, we assume each sub-frame includes two symbol intervals.

We assume that the inter-user channels and the user-destination channels are independent of each other. All channels experience quasi static flat fading, i.e., they are fixed during a sub-frame and change independently in the next sub-frame. With the above assumption, we consider a discrete-time model. In the first sub-frame, the first user broadcasts the signal vectors $s_1[i] = (s_1[2i], s_1[2i + 1])$ of equally probable MPAM sysbols lied in $\mathbf{I}$ axis. At BS, the received signal vector $\mathbf{r}_{1B}$ corresponding to the direct transmission path from the first user to BS $\mathbf{r}_{1B}[i] = (r_1[2i], r_1[2i + 1])$ is given as

$$\mathbf{r}_{1B} = \big(r_1[2i]\ r_1[2i + 1]\big) = h_{1B}[i] \cdot \big(s_1[2i]\ s_1[2i + 1]\big) + \big(n_{1B}[2i]\ n_{1B}[2i + 1]\big) \tag{1}$$

where the channel gain, $h_{mB}[i], m \in \{1, 2\}$, are associated with a transmission path from the mth user to BS at the ith sub-frame. $n_{mB}[k], m \in \{1, 2\}$, representing additive white noise and interference in the path from the mth user to the base station at the kth symbol interval, is modeled as independent circularly symmetric zero-mean complex Gaussian random variables with variances N. Meanwhile, the received signal vector for the second user $\mathbf{r}_{12}[i] = (r_{12}[2i], r_{12}[2i + 1])$ is given as

$$\mathbf{r}_{12} = \big(r_{12}[2i]\ r_{12}[2i + 1]\big) = h_1[i] \cdot \big(s_1[2i]\ s_1[2i + 1]\big) + \big(n_{12}[2i]\ n_{12}[2i + 1]\big) \tag{2}$$

where $h_m[i], m \in \{1, 2\}$, represents channel gain of the path from the mth user to its partner at ith sub-frame. And $n_{12}[k]$ represents additive white noise and interference in the path from the first user to its partner at kth symbol interval.

In the second sub-frame, the second user's information lies on the $\mathbf{Q}$ axis, i.e. $s_2[i] = (j \cdot s_2[2i], j \cdot s_2[2i + 1])$ and $j = \sqrt{-1}$. The roles of the first and second users are switched. Therefore, the received signal vector at BS and the first user are $\mathbf{r}_{2B}[i] = (r_2[2i], r_2[2i + 1])$ and $\mathbf{r}_{21}[i] = (r_{21}[2i], r_{21}[2i + 1])$ respectively. where

$$\mathbf{r}_{2B} = \big(r_2[2i]\ r_2[2i + 1]\big) = h_{2B}[i] \cdot \big(j \cdot s_2[2i]\ j \cdot s_2[2i + 1]\big) + \big(n_{2B}[2i]\ n_{2B}[2i + 1]\big) \tag{3}$$

and

$$\mathbf{r}_{21} = \big(r_{21}[2i] \; r_{21}[2i+1] \big) = h_2[i] \cdot \big(j \cdot s_2[2i] \; j \cdot s_2[2i+1] \big) + \big(n_{21}[2i] \; n_{21}[2i+1] \big) \tag{4}$$

The signal-to-noise ratios (SNRs) associated with the user-destination link are defined as $snr_{nB}[k] = E\,|h_{nB}[k]|^2 /N, n \in \{1,2\}$. For simplicity in the comparison, both SNRs for the inter-user channel are set to be equal and defined as $isnr[k] = E\,|h_1[k]|^2 /N = E\,|h_2[k]|^2 /N$.

3   Modulation Multiplexing DSTC(DSTC-MM)

During the cooperation sub-frame. The same amplify-and-forward protocol as that in [2] is applied in this paper. For the first user, the transmitted signal vector constructed by the relay information and its own information is given as follows

$$\begin{aligned}
\mathbf{s}_1[i+1] &= \big(s_1[2i+2] \; s_1[2i+3] \big) \\
&= \sqrt{\alpha_1} \cdot \big((|h_2[i]||s_1[2i] + \sigma_2 r_{21}[2i+1]) \; (|h_2[i]||s_1[2i+1] + \sigma_2 r_{21}[2i]) \big)
\end{aligned} \tag{5}$$

where $\sigma_i, i \in \{1,2\}$ is an automatic gain control (AGC) for a non-regenerative system, which is required at the relay mobile in order to prevent $r_{mn}[k]$ from saturating the relay amplifier. In this paper, we adopt an AGC that employs

$$\sigma_k = \frac{h_k^*[i]}{|h_k[i]|}, k \in \{1,2\} \tag{6}$$

for the second user, the transmitted signal vector is shown as follows

$$\begin{aligned}
\mathbf{s}_2[i+1] &= \big(s_2[2i+2] \; s_2[2i+3] \big) \\
&= \sqrt{\alpha_2} \cdot \big(|h_1[i]||js_2[2i] + \sigma_1 r_{12}[2i+1] \; |h_1[i]||js_2[2i+1] + \sigma_1 r_{12}[2i] \big)
\end{aligned} \tag{7}$$

These signals are transmitted by using the Alamouti-like structure. At the base station, the received signal vector is

$$\begin{aligned}
\mathbf{r}[i+1] &= \big(r_B[2i+2] \; r_B[2i+3] \big) \\
&= \begin{pmatrix} h_{1B}[i+1] \\ h_{2B}[i+1] \end{pmatrix}^T \begin{pmatrix} s_1[2i+2] & s_1[2i+3] \\ -s_2^*[2i+2] & s_2^*[2i+3] \end{pmatrix} + \begin{pmatrix} n_B[2i+2] \\ n_B[2i+3] \end{pmatrix}^T
\end{aligned} \tag{8}$$

By complex conjugation of the second element of $\mathbf{r}[i+1]$, the input/output relation can be reformulated as follows:

$$\begin{aligned}
\mathbf{r}[i+1] &= \begin{pmatrix} r_B[2i+2] \\ r_B^*[2i+3] \end{pmatrix} \\
&= \mathbf{H} \begin{pmatrix} s_1[2i] + j \cdot s_2[2i+1] \\ s_1[2i+1] + j \cdot s_2[2i] \end{pmatrix} + Noise
\end{aligned} \tag{9}$$

where

$$\mathbf{H} = \begin{pmatrix} \sqrt{\alpha_1}h_{1B}[i+1]|h_2[i]| & -\sqrt{\alpha_2}h_{2B}[i+1]|h_1[i]| \\ \sqrt{\alpha_2}h_{2B}^*[i+1]|h_1[i]| & \sqrt{\alpha_1}h_{1B}^*[i+1]|h_2[i]| \end{pmatrix} \tag{10}$$

and

$$Noise = \begin{pmatrix} \frac{\sqrt{\alpha_1}h_{1B}[i+1]h_2^*[i]n_{21}[2i+1]}{|h_2[i]|} - \frac{\sqrt{\alpha_2}h_{2B}[i+1]h_1^*[i]n_{12}^*[2i+1]}{|h_1[i]|} \\ \frac{\sqrt{\alpha_1}h_{1B}[i+1]h_2^*[i]n_{21}[2i+1]}{|h_2[i]|} + \frac{\sqrt{\alpha_2}h_{2B}[i+1]h_1^*[i]n_{12}^*[2i+1]}{|h_1[i]|} \end{pmatrix} + \begin{pmatrix} n_B[2i+2] \\ n_B^*[2i+3] \end{pmatrix} \tag{11}$$

The received signals in (9) are similar to those of the Alamout's scheme. The difference is an additive noise in (11). Therefore, the receiver detects

$$\hat{\mathbf{r}}[i+1] = \begin{pmatrix} \hat{r}_B[2i+2] \\ \hat{r}_B[2i+3] \end{pmatrix} = \mathbf{H}^H\mathbf{r}[i+1]$$

$$= \left(|h_{1B}[i+1]h_2[i]|^2a_1 + |h_{2B}[i+1]h_1[i]|^2a_2\right)\begin{pmatrix} s_1[2i] + js_2[2i+1] \\ (s_1[2i+1] + js_2[2i])^* \end{pmatrix}$$

$$+\mathbf{H}^H \cdot Noise \tag{12}$$

Since the symbols $s_1([k]$ and $js_2[k]$ are in **I** axis and **Q** axis respectively, we can decode them separately by considering the real and imaginary parts of (12), therefore, the following descriptions are obtained:

$$\hat{s}_1[2i] = Re\,(\hat{r}_B[2i+2])$$
$$\hat{s}_1[2i+1] = Re\,(\hat{r}_B[2i+3])$$
$$\hat{s}_1[2i] = Im\,(\hat{r}_B[2i+3])$$
$$\hat{s}_1[2i+1] = Im\,(\hat{r}_B[2i+2])$$

Furthermore, $r_{kB}[2i]$ and $\hat{s}_k[2i], k \in \{1,2\}$ do not share the same noise power, we use a Maximum Ratio Combiner (MRC) to optimally combine these two signals, and each branch of the MRC receiver is weighted by its respective complex fading gain over the total noise power on that particular branch. The output of the MRC is shown as follows

$$\tilde{s}_k[2i] = w_k[i+1]\hat{s}_k[2i] + w_k[i]r_{kB}[2i] \tag{13}$$

where

$$w_k[i+1] = \frac{2}{N}\frac{1}{|h_{1B}[i+1]|^2 + |h_{2B}[i+1]|^2 + 1}, w_k[i] = \frac{h_{kB}^*[i]}{N} \tag{14}$$

the result of (13) is quantized to ± 1 to obtain an estimation of $s_k[2i]$, similarly, $s_k[2i+1]$ also can be estimated by the same procedure.

4   Modulation Multiplexing DSTC with Selection Relay (S-DSTC-MM)

In the cooperative diversity system, the relaying protocol is a crucial component to achieve diversity. In [2], Selection Relay (SR) was proposed in which not all relay mobiles are allowed to transmit the relay signals. The permission to transmit the relay signals or not depends on the amplitudes of the fading gains between the user and its partner. If these values fall below a certain threshold, the relay user is not allowed to transmit the relay signal. In this paper, we also adopt SR as a relaying protocol, but the permission criteria is changed into the signal to noise ratio (SNR) at the output of the receiver. For easy description, we rewrite the received signal vector (9) based on several switching parameters $(\rho_1, \rho_2, \theta_1, \theta_2)$ as follows:

$$\hat{\mathbf{r}}[i+1] = \begin{pmatrix} \hat{r}_B[2i+2] \\ \hat{r}_B[2i+3] \end{pmatrix} = \left(|h_{1B}[i+1]\rho_2 h_2[i]|^2 a_1 + |h_{2B}[i+1]\rho_1 h_1[i]|^2 a_2\right)$$
$$\cdot \begin{pmatrix} \theta_1 s_1[2i] + \theta_2 j s_2[2i+1] \\ (\theta_1 s_1[2i+1] + \theta_2 j s_2[2i])^* \end{pmatrix} + \mathbf{H}^H \cdot Noise \qquad (15)$$

where

$$\mathbf{H} = \begin{pmatrix} \sqrt{\alpha_1} h_{1B}[i+1]\rho_2|h_2[i]| & -\sqrt{\alpha_2} h_{2B}[i+1]\rho_1|h_1[i]| \\ \sqrt{\alpha_2} h_{2B}^*[i+1]\rho_1|h_1[i]| & \sqrt{\alpha_1} h_{1B}^*[i+1]\rho_2|h_2[i]| \end{pmatrix} \qquad (16)$$

Based on these parameters, there exist three cases:

1. *only the first user transmit the relay information*: in this case, the first user acts as a relay and only transmits the relay information, and switching parameters are set as $\rho_1|h_1[i]| = 1, \rho_2 = 1, \theta_1 = 0$ and $\theta_2 = 1$. Hence the SNR at the output of the receiver for the second user is shown as follows:

$$SNR_1 = \frac{a_1|h_{1B}[i+1]h_2[i]|^2 + a_2|h_{2B}[i+1]|^2}{(a_1|h_{1B}[i+1]|^2 + 1) \cdot N} \qquad (17)$$

2. *only the second user transmits relay information*: in this case, the roles of the first user and second user is switched. Parameters are given as $\rho_1 = 1, \rho_2|h_2[i]| = 1, \theta_1 = 1$ and $\theta_2 = 0$ and the SNR for the first user is

$$SNR_2 = \frac{a_2|h_{2B}[i+1]h_1[i]|^2 + a_1|h_{1B}[i+1]|^2}{(a_2|h_{2B}[i+1]|^2 + 1) \cdot N} \qquad (18)$$

3. *both users transmit relay information*: both users act as relays and parameters are set as $\rho_1 = 1, \rho_2 = 1, \theta_1 = 1$ and $\theta_2 = 1$. The SNR for the ith user is shown as follows:

$$SNR_3 = \frac{a_u|h_{uB}[i+1]h_v[i]|^2 + a_v|h_{vB}[i+1]h_u[i]|^2}{(a_u|h_{uB}[i+1]|^2 + a_v|h_{vB}[i+1]|^2 + 1) \cdot N} \qquad (19)$$

where $u, v \in \{1, 2\}, u \neq v$.

The SR is applied by comparing these three SNRs at the base station. When SNR_i is the largest value among three SNRs, the corresponding case i occurs. Hence the optimum SNR is $SNR_{opt} = \max\{SNR_i\}, i \in 1, 2, 3$.

5   Results and Discussion

We assume users experience symmetric inter-user channel. Performance of the
proposed DSTC-MM system, the amplify-and-forward system (AAF) [3] and the
conventional DSTC system with TDMA [6] are evaluated.

5.1   DSTC-MM Without SR

In Fig.3, the DSTC-MM system achieves a performance gain over the AAF system [4]in the medium range of EbNo when the SNR of inter-user channel defined
as *isnr* is larger than 10dB . The DSTC-MM achieves the almost same diversity
gain as that of the DSTC system. However, it loses about 3-dB performance gain
compared with the conventional DSTC at BER of 10-3 whether isnr is 20dB or
30dB. Because the proposed scheme use the relay information and the user's
information to construct a 2MQAM signal but the conventional DSTC applies
MPAM modulation.

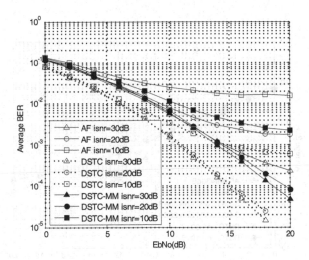

Fig. 3. BER comparison among the DSTC, the AAF and the DSTC-MM systems

5.2   DSTC-MM with SR (S-DSTC-MM)

It is important to establish how the selection relay affects the DSTC-MM system.
And the performance of the S-DSTC-MM system is shown in Fig.4. All BER curves
of the S-DSTC-MM system have the same slope as that of the DSTC-MM system,
which means that the S-DSTC-MM system achieves the same spatial diversity as
that of the DSTC-MM system. Moreover, the S-DSTC-MM system achieves 3dB
coding gain compared to the DSTC-MM system at the BER of 10^{-3}.

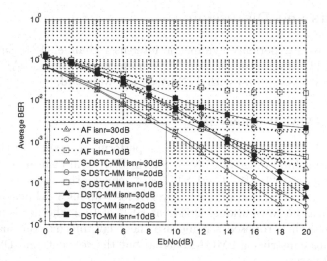

Fig. 4. BER comparison among the S-DSTC-MM, the AAF and the DSTC-MM systems

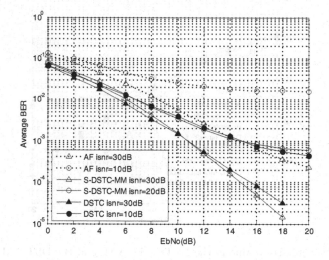

Fig. 5. BER comparison among the DSTC, the AAF and the S-DSTC-MM systems

Performances of the S-DSTC-MM and the conventional DSTC systems are evaluated in Fig.5. When $isnr = 10dB$, performances of the S-DSTC-MM system is as good as that of the DSTC system. When $isnr = 30dB$, the S-DSTC-MM system outperforms the conventional DSTC system at medium range of high EbNo. Furthermore, The S-DSTC-MM system achieves much better performance gain than the AAF system when the inter-user channel is bad such as $isnr = 10dB$.

6   Conclusion

In this paper, we propose a modulation multiplexing distributed space-time coding for two-user cooperative diversity system in wireless network. In the system, the information of the first user lies in **I** axis, while the information of the second user lies in **Q** axis, which ensures both users can share time and frequency resource during the cooperation frame and increases the bandwidth efficiency. We also adopt the selection relay protocol for the proposed system to improve the coding gain. Based on simulation results, we conclude that the proposed DSTC-MM system significantly outperforms the AAF cooperative system when inter-user channel SNR is high. Furthermore, the scheme achieves the same diversity as that of the DSTC cooperative system in [4]. However, around 3-dB coding gain is lost. By applying selection relaying, the S-DTSC-MM system outperforms the DSTC system at medium range of high EbNo.

Acknowledgments. This research was supported by the Brain Korea 21 project and also supported by the Institute Information Technology Assessment (IITA) of the Ministry of Information and Communication of Korea Government.

References

1. Sendonaris, A., Erkop, E., Aazhang, B.: User cooperation diveristy -Part I: system description. IEEE Trans. Commun. 51, 1927–1938 (2003)
2. Laneman, J.N., Tse, D.N.C., Wornell, G.W.: Cooperative diversity in wireless networks: efficience protocols and outage behavior. IEEE Trans. Inf. Theory 50(12), 3062–3080 (2004)
3. Laneman, J.N., Wornell, G.W.: Energy-efficient antenna sharing and relaying for wireless networks. Proc. of wireless communication and networking conference 1, 7–12 (2000)
4. Laneman, J.N., Wornell, G.W.: Distributed space-time coded protocols for exploiting cooperative diversity in wireless networks. In: Proc. of Clobal Telecom. conference, vol. 1, pp. 77–81 (2002)
5. Anghel, P.A., Leus, G., Kaveh, M.: Distributed space-time coding in cooperative networks. In: Proc. of Intenational Conference on speech and signal processing (April 2003)
6. Laneman, J.N., Wornell, G.W.: Distributed space-time coded protocols for exploiting cooperative diversity in wireless networks. IEEE Trans. Information Theory 49, 2415–2425 (2003)
7. Chang, Y., Hua, Y.: Diversity analysis of orthogonal space-time modulation for distributed wireless relays. In: Proc. of International conference on Acoustics, Speech and Signal Proc., May 2004, vol. 4, pp. 561–564 (2004)

Modified Widest Disjoint Paths Algorithm for Multipath Routing

Shangming Zhu[1], Zhili Zhang[2], and Xinhua Zhuang[3]

[1] Department of Computer Science, East China University of Science and Technology,
Shanghai, 200237, China
[2] Department of Computer Science, University of Minnesota, Minneapolis, MN 55455, USA
[3] Department of Computer Science, University of Missouri-Columbia, Columbia,
MO65211, USA
zhusm@ecust.edu.cn, zhzhang@cs.umn.edu, zhuangx@missouri.edu

Abstract. Widest Disjoint Paths (*WDP*) algorithm is a promising multipath routing algorithm aimed at selecting good paths for routing a flow between a source-destination pair, where their bottleneck links are mutually disjoint. Nevertheless, the complexity of *WDP* algorithm is relatively high due to the fact that the good path selection process considers all available paths. To reduce its complexity, This paper proposes a modified *WDP* algorithm, which uses only a subset of available paths based on shortest widest paths, thereby limiting the number of candidate paths considered. As a result, the number of iterations in the good path selection process is significantly reduced. Performance analysis shows the modified scheme is more efficient than the original algorithm in a large network. Simulation results demonstrate that, in comparison with the original *WDP* algorithm, the modified *WDP* algorithm leads to lower latency and faster packets transferring process as the number of available paths increases.

Keywords: Widest disjoint paths, multipath routing, candidate path, width of path set.

1 Introduction

Multipath routing is designed to optimize the operational performance of a network by routing simultaneously along multiple paths on demand. It improves QoS (Quality of Service) of a network in using multiple "good" paths rather a single "best" path in routing. Several multipath routing algorithms have been proposed for balancing the load across a network [1-3]. *WDP (Widest Disjoint Paths)* [1,2] and *LDM (Load Distribution over Multipath)* [4] schemes make routing decisions at the flow level. The *WDP* algorithm is based on two concepts: path width and path distance. Path width is used to detect bottlenecks in the network and avoid them if possible. Path distance is indirectly dependent on the utilization ratio of each constituent link of the path. The *LDM* algorithm attempts to find a minimal set of good paths based on two criteria: (a) the metric hop-count associated with each path kept as low as possible and (b) link utilization maintained inferior to a certain parameter. Schemes like

K. Li et al. (Eds.): NPC 2007, LNCS 4672, pp. 212–219, 2007.

ECMP (Equal Cost MultiPath) [5], *MPLS-OMP (Optimized MultiPath)* [6] and *MATE (MPLS Adaptive Traffic Engineering)* [7] perform packet level forwarding decisions. ECMP splits the traffic equally among multiple equal cost paths. But these paths are determined statically that may not reflect the congestion status of the network. It is always desirable to apportion the traffic according to the quality of each individual path. *MPLS-OMP* uses updates to gather link load information, selects a set of optimal paths and then distributes traffic among them. *MATE* does constant monitoring of links by using probe packets to measure link quality such as packet delay and packet loss.

The simulation results reported in [1] and [2] show that *WDP* is a promising multipath routing algorithm that can provide higher throughput and is capable of adapting to the changing network conditions at different time scales comparing to other schemes. In this paper, we attempt to improve the *WDP* algorithm in terms of computational efficiency.

2 Widest Disjoint Path Problem

The *WDP* algorithm is aimed at selecting good paths for routing a flow between a source-destination pair so that their bottleneck links are mutually disjoint. There are three tasks in the multipath routing: (a) dynamically select the candidate paths, (b) determine the good paths from the candidate paths and (c) proportion traffic among the good paths. This section lays out the basic assumptions for path selection.

In *WDP* algorithm, source routing is used and the network topology information is assumed available to all source nodes. One or multiple explicit-routed paths or label switched paths are set up statically between each source-destination pair using, e.g., MPLS. A flow is blocked when routed to a path whose bottleneck link has no bandwidth left.

Consider a network topology with N nodes and L links. Let s be a source node and d be a destination pair, and let r denote a path in the network, i.e., r is a set of links from a source to a destination. Let the maximum capacity of link l be $\hat{C}_l > 0$, which is fixed and known in advance.

Let $\hat{R}$ denote the set of all available paths for routing flows between the source and destination node. The set of good paths R is a subset of $\hat{R}$ selected by the good path selection algorithm for multipath routing. The *WDP* algorithm aims at computing a path set R for routing a flow between a source-destination pair such that all paths in R are mutually disjoint with regard to (w.r.t.) the bottleneck links.

3 Modified WDP Algorithm

The original *WDP* algorithm [1,2] compares all available paths against the width of the set of existing good paths for good path selection. To reduce its computation complexity, we modify the *WDP* algorithm in the following two aspects: (a) we use only a subset of available paths based on shortest widest paths rather than all available paths as the candidate paths; (b) we limit the number of candidate paths, hence, the number of iterations in good path computation.

3.1 Width of Path Set

To determine whether a candidate path is a good one and whether to include it in the existing good path set, the width W of a path set R is calculated as follows.

First, the difference $C_l = \hat{C}_l - v_l$ is defined as the average residual bandwidth on link l, where v_l is the average load on the link. The width and distance of a path r are defined as $w_r = \min_{l \in r} C_l$ and $d_r = \sum_{l \in r} 1/C_l$, respectively. Disjoint paths in a path set are recursively determined w.r.t. the bottleneck links, and the sum of their widths is used to calculate the width of the path set.

Initially, W is set to 0. The width w of each disjoint path r is added to the width W of path set R according to their widths and distances. In each iteration, only the shortest widest paths are considered. A subset R^* of paths with the widest width w^* is identified. There may be more than one path with the widest width w^*, from these widest paths, a path r^* with the shortest distance d^* is selected and the width w^* of shortest widest path r^* is added to the total width W by $W = W + w^*$.

To ensure the disjoint paths are only used to compute the width of set R, the residual capacities of all the links along each shortest widest path r^* is reduced by an amount w^* by $C_l = C_l - w^*$ and the path r^* is removed from the set R. The above iteration process is repeated until the set R becomes empty. The resulting W is considered to be the width of R. The narrowest path, i.e., the last path removed from the set R, is referred to as *Narrowest(R)*.

Based on the defined width of a path set, a new candidate path is added only if its inclusion increases the width of the set of good paths, and an existing good path is removed if its exclusion does not decrease the total width. When the number of good paths reaches a specified limit, a good path is replaced with another path if this change increases the width.

3.2 Modified Good Paths Selection

The success of *WDP* relies on how to efficiently select good paths. We observe that there is a significant overhead and high complexity in the original *WDP* algorithm because all available paths are considered. As the number of available paths increases, it becomes increasingly computational expensive to compute good paths.

To improve the efficiency of the original *WDP* algorithm and shorten the time for computing good paths, we use only a subset of available paths based on shortest widest paths, thereby reducing the number of iterations in good path computation. Our proposed good path selection algorithm is shown in Fig. 1.

First we exclude R from $\hat{R}$ to initiate candidate path set A, namely, $A = \hat{R} \setminus R$ (excluding R from $\hat{R}$). Different from the original *WDP* algorithm, we set up a parameter η_0 as the maximum of iterations in this procedure to reduce the number of candidate paths and limit the number of iterations.

In each iteration, rather than consider all available paths, our proposed approach considers only a subset of available paths based on shortest widest paths to compute good paths, namely, it only selects a candidate path r^+ with the widest width w^+ and

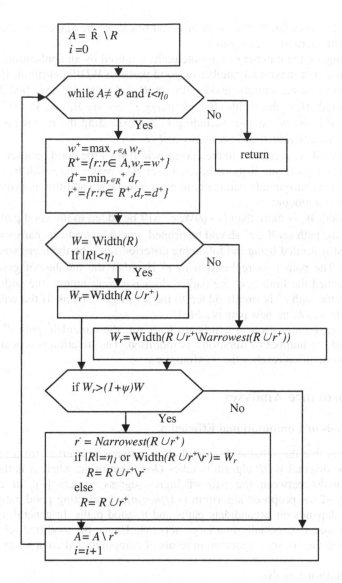

Fig. 1. Modified WDP algorithm

shortest distance d^+ to compute good paths. It is possible that many candidate paths may have the same widest width w^+. Among such paths, the path r^+ with the shortest distance d^+ is chosen.

Second, the procedure of adding a new path to good path set and removing an existing good path from good path set or replacing it with another path is similar to the original *WDP* algorithm.

The width of a set of paths before inclusion r^+ is defined as $W=Width(R)$. The function *Width()* that computes width of a path set has been discussed in III.A.

Inclusion of a candidate path r^+ is determined based on the number of good path set R and the width increase due to path r^+.

Depending on the number of multiple paths required by an application, a parameter η_1 is set up as the maximum number of good paths in *WDP* algorithm. If the number of good paths in the current good path set R is below the specified limit η_1, the resulting width W_r is the width after including r^+ among R, i.e., $W_r = Width(R \cup r^+)$; Otherwise, it is the width after including r^+ but excluding the narrowest path among $R \cup r^+$, i.e., $W_r = Width(R \cup r^+ \setminus Narrowest(R \cup r^+))$.

This width W_r is compared to the current width W of the good path set. A candidate path is made a good one if its inclusion in set R increases the width by a fraction ψ. Here $\psi > 0$ is a configurable parameter to ensure that each addition improves the width by a significant amount.

If the width W_r is more than $(1+\psi)W$, r^+ will be added to the good path set. Before adding r^+, the path set $R \cup r^+$ should be pruned, in other words, its narrowest path may be removed if needed using the following criterion Let r^- be the narrowest path in the set $R \cup r^+$. The path r^- is replaced with r^+ if either the number of good paths has already reached the limit η_1 or the path r^- does not contribute to the width of the set. Otherwise, the path r^+ is simply added to the set of good paths. If the width W_r is not more than $(1+\psi)W$, no new path is added.

After each computation of candidate path set, the candidate path r^+ is removed from A, and the number of iteration i is modified. The iteration is repeated until A is empty or its iteration reaches the maximum η_0.

4   Performance Analyses

4.1 Analysis of Computational Efficiency

It is obvious that the scheme described above always converges for all values of η_0 and η_1. The original *WDP* algorithm takes $O(n^3)$ iterations, where n is the number of available paths between the pair of ingress-egress routers [3]. In contrast, the complexity of our proposed algorithm is $O(\eta_0\eta_1 n)$, as selecting good paths from a set of n paths depends on η_0 candidate paths and η_1 good paths. In general, η_0 and η_1 are far smaller than n, especially in a large network. Hence the modified scheme is more efficient than the original algorithm in terms of computational complexity.

4.2 Simulation Results

In this section the performance of the modified *WDP* algorithm is studied through simulation experiments using NS2. The simulation environment we use is shown in Fig. 2. There are two types of links: solid and dotted. To simplify the simulation, all solid links have the same capacity with 2Mbps of bandwidth and all the dotted links have the same capacity with 3Mbps of bandwidth. We also ignore the propagation delay of each links. There are 18 nodes and 30 links in the topology. To analyze the performance of our modified *WDP* algorithm, node *1* is chosen as the source node and node *18* is as the destination node. The default values for the *WDP* parameters are $\psi=0.2$, $\eta_0=3$, $\eta_1=2$.

We use the *end-to-end packet delivery latency* (in short, latency) as a metric to evaluate the impact f the computational overheads of the modified *WDP* and the original *WDP* algorithm on the efficacy of multi-path routing. To measure the end-to-end packet delivery latency, the packet sending rate at the source node is set to 4.5Mbps.

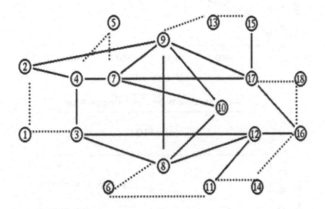

Fig. 2. Network model for the simulation

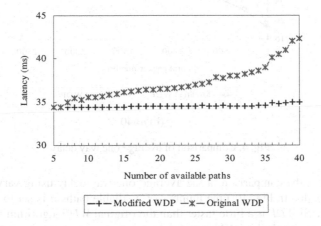

Fig. 3. Latency with variable numbers of available paths

Fig. 3 shows the latency variation as the number of available paths n is varied. It is seen that as the number of available paths increases, the modified *WDP* performs better than the original *WDP* algorithm. When the number of available paths is small ($n \leq 6$), there is not much difference of latency between the modified *WDP* and the original *WDP* algorithm; As the number of available paths increases, latency of the modified *WDP* varies slightly and is much lower than that of the original *WDP* algorithm.

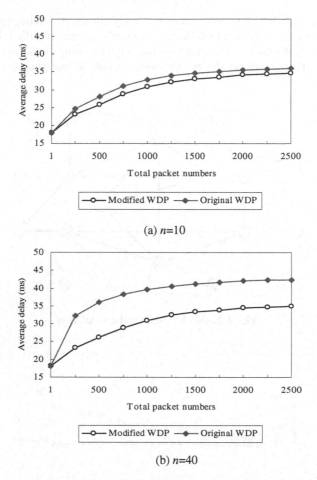

(a) $n=10$

(b) $n=40$

Fig. 4. Comparison of average one way delay

Fig. 4 shows the comparison of the average one way delay using varying numbers of available paths. In Fig. 4(a) the number of available paths n is set to 10; it is seen that the modified *WDP* is a little faster than the original *WDP* algorithm in the packets transferring process. In Fig. 4(b) n is set to 40; it is seen that the modified *WDP* is much faster than the original *WDP* algorithm in the packets transferring process because of its better computational efficiency.

5   Conclusions

In this paper we propose an improvement to the *Widest Disjoint Paths (WDP)* routing algorithm which performs good paths selection based on the computation of the width of the disjoint paths with regard to bottleneck links. To reduce the complexity of this algorithm and shorten the time for computing good paths, we develop a modified *WDP* algorithm by limiting the number of candidate paths and thereby reducing the number of iterations needed for good path computation. Our proposed approach only uses a subset of available paths based on shortest widest paths rather than all available paths to compute the good paths. Performance analysis shows the modified scheme is more efficient than the original algorithm in a large network. Simulation results demonstrate that the modified *WDP* algorithm leads to lower latency and faster packets transferring process as the number of available paths increases in comparison with the original *WDP* algorithm.

Acknowledgments. This work is supported in part by NIH, NSF, and the National Science Council (NSC) of Republic of China under grant number NIH DHHS 1 R01 DC04340-01A2, NSF EIA 9911095, and NSC-94-2213-E-006-068 respectively. This work was also supported by China Scholarship Council (CSC).

References

1. Nelakuditi, S., Zhang, Z.-L., Du, D.H.C.: On Selection of Candidate Paths for Proportional Routing. Computer Networks 44, 79–102 (2004)
2. Nelakuditi, S., Zhang, Z.-L.: On Selection of Paths for Multipath Routing. In: Wolf, L., Hutchinson, D.A., Steinmetz, R. (eds.) IWQoS 2001. LNCS, vol. 2092, pp. 170–184. Springer, Heidelberg (2001)
3. Lee, K., Toguyeni, A., Noce, A., Rahmani, A.: Comparison of Multipath Algorithms for Load Balancing in a MPLS Network. In: Kim, C. (ed.) ICOIN 2005. LNCS, vol. 3391, pp. 463–470. Springer, Heidelberg (2005)
4. Song, J., Kim, S., Lee, M.: Dynamic Load Distribution in MPLS Networks. In: Kahng, H.-K. (ed.) ICOIN 2003. LNCS, vol. 2662, pp. 989–999. Springer, Heidelberg (2003)
5. Moy, J.: OSPF Version 2, RFC 2328. Internet Engineering Task Force (1998), http://www.ietf.org/rfc/rfc2328.txt
6. Villamizar, C.: MPLS Optimized Multipath (MPLS-OMP). Work in Progress Internet-Draft, draft-villamizar-mpls-omp-01 (1999)
7. Elwalid, A., Jin, C., Low, S., Widjaja, I.: MATE: MPLS Adaptive Traffic Engineering. In: Proceedings of INFOCOM'2001, Alaska (2001)

Optimum Broadcasting Algorithms in (n, k)-Star Graphs Using Spanning Trees

Jinli Li[1], Manli Chen[2], Yonghong Xiang[3,4], and Shaowen Yao[3]

[1] Kunming Electric Power Supply Bureau, YNPG, Kunming, 650011, China
[2] Natioanl Computer network Emergency Response technical Team/Coordination Center-Yunnan Branch, Kunming, 650011, China
[3] Department of Computer Science, University of Durham, Science Labs, South Road, Durham, EH1 3LE, UK
[4] School of Software, Yunnan University, Kunming, 650091, China
{lonetimberwolf,chenmanliyn}@163.com, yonghong.xiang@durham.com

Abstract. In a multiprocessor network, sending a packet typically refers to start-up time and transmission time. To optimize these two times, as opposed to earlier solutions, a spanning tree and multiple spanning trees are constructed to solve four types of broadcasting problems in an (n, k)-star graph: one-to-all or all-to-all broadcasting with either one-port or all-port communication model, respectively. Since the proposed spanning tree has an optimal height, both one-to-all and all-to-all broadcasting algorithms achieve nearly optimal start-up time and transmission time under all-port model and one-port model, and optimal transmission time under one-port model. By using multiple spanning trees, both one-to-all and all-to-all algorithms achieve nearly optimal transmission time under all-port model and one-port model.

Keywords: (n, k)-star graph, a spanning tree, multiple spanning trees, one-to-all broadcasting, all-to-all broadcasting, all-port model, one-port model.

1 Introduction

As a new topology of interconnection networks, the (n, k)-star graph has attracted lots of attentions: it not only preserves many appealing properties of n-star: scalability, maximally fault tolerance, partitionability, node- symmetry, but also overcomes the practical drawback with the star graph in that only $\frac{n!}{(n-k)!}$ nodes are involved, compared with $n!$ nodes for an n-star. Some works have been done on this graph, such as basic properties[1],[2],[3], embeddability[3], broadcasting algorithms[4] ,and so on.

The tree structure has received much interest as a versatile architecture for a large class of parallel processing applications. Spanning trees in particular support communications in different networks: hypercube[5], star graph[6], and (n, k)-star graph[7], and (n, k)-arrangement graph[8].

In this paper, we study one-to-all and all-to-all broadcasting problems in an (n, k)-star graph using packet-switching technique, one-port and all-port communication capabilities are considered.

K. Li et al. (Eds.): NPC 2007, LNCS 4672, pp. 220–230, 2007.

2 Preliminaries

For simplification, denote the identity node $(12...k)$ as Id and set $\{1,2,...,n\}$ as $<n>$.

Definition 1. An (n, k)-star graph, denoted by $S_{n,k}$, is an undirected graph. Any node p is denoted by $\{p_1 p_2...p_k \mid p_i \in <n>\}$ and $p_i \neq p_j$ for $i \neq j$. Two nodes p and q are adjacent if q is obtained by swapping p_1 with p_i, where $2 \leq i \leq n$, that is, $q = S_i(p_1 p_2...p_i...p_k) = p_i p_2...p_1...p_k$.

$S_{n,k}$ is a regular graph of degree $n-1$ and $\frac{n!}{(n-k)!}$ nodes. The diameter is $2k-1$ for $1 \leq k \leq \lfloor \frac{n}{2} \rfloor$, and $k + \lfloor \frac{n-1}{2} \rfloor$ for $\lfloor \frac{n}{2} \rfloor < k < n$. $S_{4,3}$ is illustrated in Figure 1.

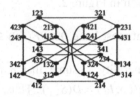

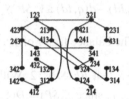

Fig. 1. $S_{4,3}$ **Fig. 2.** $SP(S_{4,3})$

Definition 2. If node p has a label of $p_1 p_2...p_k$, we may denote symbol p_i by $p[i]$. Given nodes p_1 and p_2, $dif(p_1, p_2)$ is the smallest $i > 1$ such that $p_1[i] \neq p_2[i]$.

Steps to correct node $p = p_1 p_2...p_k$ with α internal cycles and β external cycles are computed by the following formulas[1], [2].

For an internal cycle C_i ($1 \leq i \leq \alpha$) of m_i symbols:

$$steps(C_i, m_i) = \begin{cases} m_i - 1, \ p_1 \in C_i \\ m_i + 1, \ p_1 \notin C_i \end{cases} \tag{1}$$

For β external cycles of M' symbols totally:

$$steps(\beta, M') = \begin{cases} M' + \beta - 1, \ p_1 \in someC_j \\ M' + \beta + 1, \ p_1 \notin anyC_j \end{cases} \tag{2}$$

3 An Optimal Spanning Tree

Definition 3. Given any node p in $S_{n,k}$, the directed graph $SP(S_{n,k})$ is defined such that $V(SP) = V(S_{n,k})$; and for any node $s \in V(S_{n,k}) - \{v\}$, $E(SP)$ contains the directed edge $<s, v>$, where s is the parent of node v, defined by $s = G_\alpha(v)$, where

$$\alpha = \begin{cases} dif(v, Id), \ v[1] = Id[1] \\ i, v[1] = Id[1] \wedge 2 \leq i \leq k \\ d[j], \ v[1] = Id[j] \wedge k+1 \leq j \leq n \wedge e = 1 \\ \min\{D - d[j]\}, \ v[1] = Id[j] \wedge k+1 \leq j \leq n \wedge 2 \leq e \leq n-k \end{cases}.$$

Theorem 1 [7]. For an (n, k)-star graph, there must be a greedy spanning tree $SP(S_{n,k})$ of height $h(SP) = D(S_{n,k})$, and the result is optimal.

Corollary 1. Two nodes are adjacent in $S_{n,k}$, if they are at the same level or two consecutive levels of $SP(S_{n,k})$.

Proof. Suppose that two nodes p and q are adjacent in $S_{n,k}$, and they aren't neither at the same level nor two consecutive levels of $SP(S_{n,k})$. Let q be at the t, $0 \le t < D(S_{n,k})$, level of $SP(S_{n,k})$ and $d(p, Id) \ge d(q, Id)$. If $d(p, Id) - d(q, Id) \ge 2$, i.e. $d(p, Id) \ge d(q, Id) + 2 = t + 2$. Since $d(p, q) = 1$, $d(q, Id) + d(p, q) = t + 1 < t + 2$, that is, $d(p, Id) \ne d(q, Id) + 1$, which is a contradiction.

So, $0 \le d(p, Id) - d(q, Id) \le 1$. $SP(S_{4,3})$ is given in Figure 2.

Corollary 2. The balance factor of $SP(S_{n,k})$ is at most 1, i.e. $0 \le BF(SP) \le 1$.

Proof. Suppose that $BF(SP) \ge 2$. Without generality, assume that p and q are two leaves in $SP(S_{n,k})$, since $h(SP) = D(S_{n,k})$, let $d(p, Id) = D(S_{n,k})$. Thus, node p has to satisfy one of following three conditions. We will prove that the proposition that p and q are two leaves and $d(p, Id) - d(q, Id) = 2$ is false under any circumstance. Let e be an external symbol, i be an internal symbol, inv be an invariable symbol and $|x|$ be the size of x.

(1) For $1 \le k \le \lfloor \frac{n}{2} \rfloor$, $C(p)$ satisfies one of the following two[2]:

(1.1) $p_1 = 1$, and the other $k - 1$ symbols are external symbols;

(1.2) $p_1 \ne 1$, k symbols are external symbols.

For (1.1), informally, $p = (1e_1 e_2 ... e_{k-1})$. From formula (2), $steps(\beta, M') - steps(\beta - 1, M') = 2$. So if $d(p, Id) - d(q, Id) = 2$, q should satisfy that $q_1 \ne 1$, there are $k - 2$ external symbols and there is an invariant, that is, $q = (e_1 ... e_{x-1} e_x e_{x+1} ... e_{k-1})$, where $\exists x \in \{1, ..., k-1\}$, $e_x = inv$ and $|e_x| = 1$; $\forall y \in \{1, ..., k-1\} - \{x\}$, $|e_y| = 1$. By definition 3, $q = G_\alpha(e_x e_2 ... e_{x-1} e_1 e_{x+1} ... e_{k-2})$, so q isn't a leaf.

For (1.2), informally, $p = (e_1 e_2 ... e_k)$. If $d(p, Id) - d(q, Id) = 2$, q should satisfy that $q_1 = 1$, there are $k - 1$ external symbols and there is an invariant, i.e. $q = (1e_1 e_2 ... e_{x-1} e_x e_{x+1} ... e_{k-2})$, where $\exists x \in \{1, ..., k-1\}$, $e_x = inv$ and $|e_x| = 1$; $\forall y \in \{1, ..., k-1\} - \{x\}, |e_y| = 1$. By definition 3, $q = G_\alpha(e_x e_1 e_2 ... e_{x-1} 1 e_{x+1} ... e_{k-2})$ isn't a leaf.

(2) For odd n and $\lfloor \frac{n}{2} \rfloor < k < n$, $C(p)$ satisfies the following three[2]:

$p_1 = 1$, there are $n - k$ external symbols, and each of them forms a cycle of length 1, and the rest form internal cycles of length 2.

Same to (1.1), we have the result that $q = G_\alpha(e_x e_1 e_2 ... e_{x-1} 1 e_{x+1} ... e_{k-2})$ isn't a leaf.

(3) For even n and $\lfloor\frac{n}{2}\rfloor < k < n$, $C(p)$ satisfies one of the following two[2]:

(3.1) $p_1 = 1$, there are $n-k$ external symbols, and each of them forms a cycle of length 1; three symbols form one cycle of length 3, and the rest form internal cycles of length 2;

(3.2) $p_1 \neq 1$, there are $n-k$ external symbols, and each of them forms a cycle of length 1; and the rest form internal cycles of length 2.

Same to (1), we have the result that $q = G_\alpha(e_x e_2 ... e_{x-1} i_1 e_{x+1} ... e_{n-k-1})$ for (3.1) and $q = G_\alpha(e_x e_2 ... e_{x-1} i_1 e_{x+1} ... e_{n-k-1})$ for (3.2) are not leaves.

Thus, the conditions that $d(p, Id) - d(q, Id) \geq 2$ and p, q are two leaves can't be satisfied simultaneously. So, the corollary holds. Especially, $BF(SP(S_{4,2})) = 0$.

4 One-to-All Broadcasting Based on Optimal Spanning Tree

One-to-all broadcasting refers to the problem of sending a message from one source node to all other nodes in the network. In this section, we assume the packet-switching or store-and-forward model, thus, the latency to transmit a packet of b bytes along a link takes $T_s + bT_c$ time, where T_s is the time to start-up the communication link and T_c is the latency to transmit a byte. Under one-port model, a node can send and receive at most one packet at a time, while under all-port model, a node can send and receive packets along all $n-1$ ports simultaneously.

Lemma 1. A lower bound for one-to-all broadcasting in a store-and-forward $S_{n,k}$ is $\max\{ D(S_{n,k})T_s , \frac{m}{n-1}T_c \}$ under all-port model, and $\max\{ \lceil \log(n!/(n-k)!) \rceil T_s , D(S_{n,k})T_s, mT_c \}$ under one-port model, where m is the size of message M.

4.1 All-Port Model

In the proposed algorithm, time will be slotted by fixed length and all nodes perform broadcast synchronously. In each time slot each node transmits a packet of size $\frac{m}{p(n-1)}$, and p is an integer to be determined later. So each time slot is of length $T_s + \frac{m}{p(n-1)}T_c$.

Algorithm-Broadcasting(one-to-all, all-port)

(1) Slice message M evenly into $p(n-1)$ parts, each called a "message segment" and of size $\frac{m}{p(n-1)}$;

(2) In each time slot, node Id issues $n-1$ message segments to the network. A message segment is then propagated along the tree .In each time slot, each node helps propagating all message segments it received in the previous time slot to the subsequent nodes in the corresponding tree.

By theorem 1, $h = D(S_{n,k})$, the total times of all-port broadcasting are: $T = h(T_s + \frac{m}{p(n-1)}T_c) + (p-1)(T_s + \frac{m}{p(n-1)}T_c)$, where the former term is the time for the first packet to arrive at the bottom of the tallest tree and the latter term is due to the pipelined effect. Let the derivative of T with respect to p equal to 0,

$\frac{\partial T}{\partial p} = T_s - \frac{m(h-1)}{p(n-1)p}T_c \Rightarrow T_s - \frac{m(h-1)}{p(n-1)p}T_c = 0$, therefore, $p = \sqrt{\frac{m(h-1)Tc}{(n-1)Ts}} = O(\sqrt{\frac{m(h-1)Tc}{(n-1)Ts}})$.

Theorem 2. Under all-port model, one-to-all broadcasting can be performed in $S_{n,k}$ within time $O((D(S_{n,k}) - 1)T_s + \frac{m}{n-1}T_c + 2\sqrt{\frac{m(D(Sn,k)-1)TcTs}{n-1}})$.

Table 1. Comparison of One-to-All Broadcasting Algorithms

Model	Algorithm	Start-up Comp.	Trans. Comp.	Overall Complexity
All-port model	optimal	$O(D(S_{n,k})T_s)$	$O(\frac{m}{n-1}T_c)$	$\max\{ D(S_{n,k})T_s, \frac{m}{n-1}T_c \}$
	Y.S. Chen	$O((2D(S_{n,k})-1)T_s)$	$O(\frac{4m}{n-1}T_c)$	$O(2D(S_{n,k})-1)T_s + \frac{4m}{n-1}T_c)$
	a spanning tree	$O(D(S_{n,k})T_s)$	$O(\frac{m}{n-1}T_c)$	$O(D(S_{n,k})T_s + \frac{m}{n-1}T_c$ $+ 2\sqrt{\frac{m(D(Sn,k)-1)TcTs}{n-1}})$
	multiple spanning trees	$O((2D(S_{n,k})-1)T_s)$	$O(\frac{m}{n-1}(\frac{n!}{(n-k)!}-1)T_c)$	$O((2D(S_{n,k})-1)T_s$ $+(\frac{n!}{(n-k)!}-1)\frac{m}{n-1}T_c)$
One-port model	optimal	$\max\{ D(S_{n,k})T_s,$ $\lceil \log(n!/(n-k)!-1)\rceil T_s \}$	$O(mT_c)$	$\max\{ D(S_{n,k})T_s , mT_c ,$ $\lceil \log(n!/(n-k)!-1)\rceil T_s \}$
	Y.S. Chen	$O((2nk - n - k^2)T_s)$	$O(2mT_c +$ $\frac{m(n-k-2)(n-k+1)!}{n!}T_c)$	$O((2nk-n-k^2)T_s + 2mT_c +$ $\frac{m(n-k-2)(n-k+1)!}{n!}T_c)$
	a spanning tree	$O(nD(S_{n,k})T_s)$	$O(mT_c)$	$O((n-1)(D(S_{n,k})-1))T_s + mT_c$ $+2\sqrt{m(n-1)(D(S_{n,k})-1)T_cT_s}$
	multiple spanning trees	$O((n-1)(2D(S_{n,k})-1)T_s)$	$O(mT_c)$	$O((n-1)(2D(S_{n,k})-1))T_s + mT_c$ $+2\sqrt{m(n-1)(2D(S_{n,k})-1)T_cT_s}$

4.2 One-Port Model

A node with one-port communication capability can simulate the communication activity of an all-port node in one time slot using $n-1$ time slots. The simulation can be done as follows: in the first time slot, the one-port node simulates the all-port nodes activity along dimension 1; in the second time slot, the one-port node simulates the all-port nodes activity along dimension 2; etc. By simulation algorithm stated above at every one-port node in $S_{n,k}$, the following theorem is seen.

Algorithm-Broadcasting(all-to-all, one-port)

(1) Slice message M evenly into $p(n-1)$ parts, each called a "message segment" and of size $\frac{m}{p(n-1)}$;

(2) In each time slot, node Id issues $n-1$ message segments to the network. A message segment is then propagated along one of trees $SP(R_i(Id))$, $i = 1...n-1$. A message segment is then propagated along the tree it is issued. In each time slot, each node helps propagating all message segments it received in the previous time slot to the subsequent nodes in the corresponding tree;

(3) Repeatedly perform step 2 until all message segments have been broadcast.

Theorem 3. Under one-port model, one-to-all broadcasting can be performed in $S_{n,k}$ within time $O((n-1)(D(S_{n,k})-1)T_s + mT_c + 2\sqrt{m(n-1)(D(S_{n,k})-1)T_cT_s})$.

Table 2. Comparison of All-to-All Broadcasting Algorithms

Model	Algorithm	Start-up Comp.	Trans. Comp.	Overall Complexity
All-port	optimal	$O(D(S_{n,k})T_s)$	$O(\frac{m}{n-1}(\frac{n!}{(n-k)!}-1)T_c)$	$\max\{$ $D(S_{n,k})T_s$, $\frac{m}{n-1}(\frac{n!}{(n-k)!}-1)T_c\}$
	a spanning tree	$O(D(S_{n,k})T_s)$	$O(\frac{m}{n-1}(\frac{n!}{(n-k)!}-1)T_c)$	$O(D(S_{n,k})T_s + (\frac{n!}{(n-k)!}-1)\frac{m}{n-1}T_c)$
	multiple spanning trees	$O((2D(S_{n,k})-1)T_s)$	$O(\frac{m}{n-1}(\frac{n!}{(n-k)!}-1)T_c)$	$O((2D(S_{n,k})-1)T_s + (\frac{n!}{(n-k)!}-1)\frac{m}{n-1}T_c)$
One-port	optimal	$\max\{$ $D(S_{n,k})T_s$, $\lceil\log(n!/(n-k)!-1)\rceil T_s\}$	$O((\frac{n!}{(n-k)!}-1)mT_c)$	$\max\{$ $(\frac{n!}{(n-k)!}-1)mT_c)$, $D(S_{n,k})T_s$, $\lceil\log(n!/(n-k)!-1)\rceil T_s\}$
	a spanning tree	$O(n(n-1)D(S_{n,k})T_s)$	$O((\frac{n!}{(n-k)!}-1)mT_c)$	$O(n(n-1)D(S_{n,k})T_s + (\frac{n!}{(n-k)!}-1)mT_c))$
	multiple spanning trees	$O((n-1)(2D(S_{n,k})-1)T_s)$	$O((\frac{n!}{(n-k)!}-1)mT_c)$	$O((n-1)(2D(S_{n,k})-1)T_s + (\frac{n!}{(n-k)!}-1)mT_c))$

5   All-to-All Broadcasting Based on Optimal Spanning Tree

All-to-all broadcasting refers to the problem of sending a message from all source nodes to all other nodes in the network, which is $\frac{n!}{(n-k)!}-1$ copies of one-to-all broadcasting problem.

Lemma 2. A lower bound for all-to-all broadcasting in a store-and-forward $S_{n,k}$ is $\max\{$ $(\frac{n!}{(n-k)!}-1)\frac{m}{n-1}T_c$, $D(S_{n,k})T_s$ $\}$ under all-port model, and $\max\{$ $D(S_{n,k})T_s$, $\lceil\log(n!/(n-k)!-1)\rceil T_s$, $(\frac{n!}{(n-k)!}-1)mT_c$ $\}$ under one-port model.

5.1 All-Port Model

LC and *EC* schemes proposed by Tseng et al.[6] are used to design our all-to-all broadcasting such that each node in $S_{n,k}$ can use $n-1$ spanning trees.

Theorem 4. Under all-port model, all-to-all broadcasting can be performed in $S_{n,k}$ within time $O(D(S_{n,k})T_s + \frac{m}{n-1}(\frac{n!}{(n-k)!}-1)T_c)$.

Proof. Assume that in each iteration of time slot, all message segments can be combined into one packet and send at one time. Therefore, the start-up overhead times nearly $D(S_{n,k})T_s$. To propagate a message segment of size $\frac{m}{n-1}$ along a spanning tree of $\frac{n!}{(n-k)!}-1$ links, network bandwidth of $\frac{m}{n-1}(\frac{n!}{(n-k)!}-1)T_c$ is required. Totally, there are $(n-1)(\frac{n!}{(n-k)!}-1)$ message segments to be broadcast. Thus, the total network bandwidth required is $m(\frac{n!}{(n-k)!}-1)^2 T_c$. Since the network is evenly loaded at every time step, the bandwidth is evenly distributed to all $(n-1)(\frac{n!}{(n-k)!}-1)$ links in the network, Therefore, the transmission time is obtained.

5.2 One-Port Model

Theorem 5. Under one-port model, all-to-all broadcasting can be performed in $S_{n,k}$ within time $O(n(n-1)D(S_{n,k})T_s + (\frac{n!}{(n-k)!}-1)mT_c)$.

6 Multiple Spanning Trees

Node p can be also described as $p = p_1 p_2 ... p_i ... p_k [p_{k+1}...p_n]$ [4]. The congestion of a directed tree is defined to be the maximum number of times the links of these trees overlapping on same edges.

Definition 4. Given any node p , $R_i(p)$ is the node obtained from p by cyclically shifting the label of p to the right by i positions.

Theorem 6. The $n-1$ spanning trees $SP(R_1(Id))$, $SP(R_2(Id))$,... , $SP(R_n(Id))$ totally have an edge congestion of i in $S_{n,k}$, when $n \in (i*k, (i+1)*k]$, $i=1,2,...$.

Proof. The roots of multiple trees can be represented as $R_i(Id)$, $i \in \{1,2,...,n-1\}$, i.e. $R_1(Id) = n1...i-1...k-1[k..n-1]$, $R_2(Id) = n-1n..i-2...k-2[k-1...n-2]$,......, $R_n(Id) = 23...i..k-1[k...1]$ .For node $v = v_1 v_2 ... v_i ... v_k$, consider its in-degrees:

(1) $v_1 = R_i(Id)[1]$

Let $t = R_i(Id)[1]$, then, satisfying the first condition of definition 3 . So there exists an edge $<s_i, v>$ in $T(R_i(Id))$, where $s_i = G_\alpha(v)$ and $\alpha = dif(v, R_i(Id))$.

Since $i \in \{1,2,...,n-1\}$, there are $n-1$ edges. For any $i, j \in \{1,...,n-1\}$, $R_i(Id) \neq R_j(Id)$ for $i \neq j$, so there is no congestion among $n-1$ edges.

(2) $v_1 \neq R_i(Id)[1]$

If $v_1 \neq R_i(Id)[1]$, where $2 \leq i \leq k$, then, satisfying the second condition of definition 3. So there exists an edge $< s_i, v >$ in $T(R_i(Id))$, where $s_i = G_\alpha(v)$ and $\alpha = i$. Thus, there are $k-1$ edges and no congestion. When $k+1 \leq i \leq n$, discuss it by cases:

(2.1) $v_1 = R_i(Id)[n]$ and $n = k+1$

Since $n = k+1$ and $Id = 12...i...k[k+1]$, then, satisfying the third condition of definition 3. So there exists an edge $< s_i, v >$ in $T(R_i(Id))$, where $s_i = G_\alpha(v)$ and $v = tv_2...v_i...v_k$, t is the desired symbol of $R_i(Id)[n]$, so $t = d(R_i(Id)[n]) = R_i(Id)[1]$. Thus, there exists an edge of congestion 1 inevitably.

(2.2) $v_1 = R_i(Id)[j]$ and $k < j \leq n$

Since the desired symbol of an external symbol corresponds to one symbol in $< k >$, and the fourth condition of definition 3 is satisfied, thus, there are another $n-k$ number of edges. So the congestion is related to $n-k$, that is, Congestion$= i$, where $n \in (i*k, (i+1)*k]$, $i = 1,2,....$

Thus, the theorem holds. See figure 3 for example.

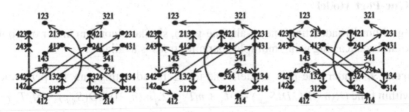

Fig. 3. Three Spanning Trees in $S_{4,3}$ Rooted as (412),(341),(234)

7 One-to-All Broadcasting Using Multiple Spanning Tree

Definition 5. Let $p_i : R_i(Id) \Rightarrow Id$ be the path in $T(R_i(Id))$ leading from $R_i(Id)$ to Id . Define $MT(R_i(Id))$ to be the directed graph obtained from $T(R_i(Id))$ by reversing the direction of all edges along the path p_i , where $i \in \{1,...,n-1\}$.

Theorem 7. $MT(R_i(Id))$, $i \in \{1,2,...,n-1\}$,is a spanning tree of height h , where $k + D(S_{n,k}) \leq h \leq 2D(S_{n,k})$.

Proof. Only edges along p_i , $i \in \{1,2,...,n-1\}$, in $T(R_i(Id))$ have reversed the direction, so $MT(R_i(Id))$ has $\frac{n!}{(n-k)!} - 1$ edges and all nodes are connected directly or indirectly, thus $MT(R_i(Id))$ is a spanning tree. The height is $D(S_{n,k})$ plus the length of p_i .Since p_i be the path leading from $R_i(Id)$ to Id , thus, $k \leq h(p_i) \leq D(S_{n,k})$, and

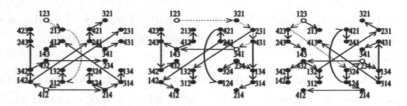

Fig. 4. Multiple Spanning Trees in $S_{4,3}$ Rooted as (123)

$T(R_i(Id))$ is of height $D(S_{n,k})$, so the height of $MT(R_i(Id))$ satisfies the condition that $k + D(S_{n,k}) \le h \le 2D(S_{n,k})$ .See Figure 4 for example.

7.1 All-Port Model

As Algorithm-Broadcasting(one-to-all, all-port), similar algorithm under all-port for one-to-all broadcasting using multiple spanning trees is available.

Theorem 8. Under all-port model, one-to-all broadcasting can be performed in $S_{n,k}$ within time $O((2D(S_{n,k})-1)T_s + \frac{m}{n-1}T_c + 2\sqrt{\frac{m(2D(Sn,k)-1)TcTs}{n-1}})$.

7.2 One-Port Model

As Algorithm-Broadcasting(one-to-all, one-port), similar algorithm under one-port for one-to-all broadcasting using multiple spanning trees is available.

Theorem 9. Under one-port model, one-to-all broadcasting can be performed in $S_{n,k}$ within time $O((n-1)(2D(S_{n,k})-1)T_s + mT_c + 2\sqrt{m(n-1)(2D(S_{n,k})-1)T_cT_s})$.

8 All-to-All Broadcasting Using Multiple Spanning Trees

Same to all-to-all broadcasting based on the optimal spanning tree, the following theorems are obtained.

Theorem 10. Under all-port model, all-to-all broadcasting can be performed in $S_{n,k}$ within time $O((2D(S_{n,k})-1)T_s + \frac{m}{n-1}(\frac{n!}{(n-k)!}-1)T_c)$.

Theorem 11. Under one-port model, all-to-all broadcasting can be performed in $S_{n,k}$ within time $O((n-1)(2D(S_{n,k})-1)T_s + (\frac{n!}{(n-k)!}-1)mT_c)$.

9 Conclusion

We have shown how to solve various versions of broadcast problems in an (n, k)-star graph by using a spanning tree and multiple spanning trees to simultaneously optimize both transmission time and start-up time.

Finally, we compare our results with other broadcasting algorithms. The numbers of start-up time, transmission time, and overall time complexity are presented in Table 1 and Table 2, respectively.

From Table 1, for one-to-all broadcasting, under all-port model, the algorithm based on an optimal spanning tree achieves nearly optimal start-up time $O(D(S_{n,k})T_s)$ and transmission time $O(\frac{m}{n-1}T_c)$, far lower than $O((2D(S_{n,k})-1)T_s)$ and $O(\frac{4m}{n-1}T_c)$ achieved by the Y.S. Chen's, also $O((2D(S_{n,k})-1)T_s)$ and $O(\frac{m}{n-1}(\frac{n!}{(n-k)!}-1)T_c)$ by using multiple spanning trees. Under one-port model, the algorithm based on an optimal spanning tree achieves start-up time $O(nD(S_{n,k})T_s)$ and nearly optimal transmission time $O(mT_c)$, Y.S. Chen's algorithm achieves start-up time $O((2nk-n-k^2)T_s)$ and transmission time $O(2mT_c+\frac{(n-k-2)(n-k+1)!}{n!}mT_c)$, the algorithm based on multiple spanning trees achieves start-up time $O((n-1)(D(S_{n,k})-1)T_s)$ and nearly optimal transmission time $O(mT_c)$.

From Table 2, for all-to-all broadcasting, under all-port model, the algorithm based on an optimal spanning tree achieves nearly optimal start-up time $O(D(S_{n,k})T_s)$, far lower than $O((2D(S_{n,k})-1)T_s)$ achieved by using multiple spanning trees, as for transmission time $O(\frac{m}{n-1}(\frac{n!}{(n-k)!}-1)T_c)$, both are nearly optimal. Under one-port model, the algorithm based on an optimal spanning tree achieves start-up time $O(n(n-1)D(S_{n,k})T_s)$, higher than $O((n-1)(2D(S_{n,k})-1)T_s)$ achieved by using multiple spanning trees, as for transmission time, both are nearly optimal.

From Table 1 and Table 2, we can see that it is a hard work to optimize both start-up time and transmission time simultaneously. So our algorithms based on an optimal spanning tree are asymptotically optimal. To the best of our knowledge, this is the first work reporting the possibility of embedding multiple $(O(n))$ spanning trees in an (n, k)-star graph, while keeping the edge congestion variable. But no more comparative broadcasting algorithms are available in $S_{n,k}$.

Acknowledgments

This work is supported by Natural Science Foundation of Yunnan Province, China, under Grant NO.2004F0006Q.

References

1. Chiang, W.K., Chen, R.J.: The (n, k)-star graph: A generalized star graph. Information Proc. Let. 56, 259–264 (1995)
2. Chiang, W.K., Chen, R.J.: Topological Properties of the (n, k)-star graph. International Journal of Foundations of Computer Science 9(2), 235–248 (1998)
3. Chang, J.-H., Kim, J.: Ring Embedding in Faulty (n, k)-star graphs. In: Proceedings of the Eighth International Conference on Parallel and Distributed Systems (ICPADS'01), pp. 99–106 (2001)

4. Chen, Y.-S., Tai, K.-S.: A Near-Optimal Broadcasting in (n, k)-star graphs. In: ACIS Int'l Conf on Software Engineering Applied to Networking and Parallel/Distributed Computing (SNPD'00), pp. 217–224 (2000)
5. Johnsson, S.L., Ho, C.T.: Optimal Broadcasting and Personalized Communication in Hypercubes. IEEE Trans. Computers 38(9), 1249–1268 (1989)
6. Tseng, Y.-C., Sheu, J.-P.: Toward Optimal Broadcast in a star graph Using Multiple Spanning Tree. IEEE Trans. Computers 46(5), 593–599 (1997)
7. Li, J.L., Xiang, Y.H., Chen, M.L., Zhou, Y.H.: An Optimal Spanning Tree in (n, k)-star graph Network. Microelectronics and Computer 23(9), 168–170 (2006)
8. Chen, Y.S., Juang, T.Y.: Efficient Broadcasting in an Arrangement Graph Using Multiple Spanning Trees. IEICE Tans. Fundamentals E83-A(1), 139–149 (2000)

Link Protocol Based on DS-CDMA with MUD for Decentralized All-Connected Wireless Network

Zhe Hu, Jun Zhang, and Huiyuan Zheng

Beijing University of Aeronautics and Astronautics
huzhe@ee.buaa.edu.cn

Abstract. To fulfill the application of wireless network in small area, this paper proposed a protocol for decentralized all-connected wireless network. This protocol is based on DS-CDMA with the ability of multi-user detection (MUD). And it has the characteristics of transmitting data in parallel, high network throughput and low communication error rate. In this paper, the process of the protocol is introduced, and an improved quasi-synchronous decorrelation multi-user detection algorithm is deduced in detail. And then, the protocol is simulated and the results are analyzed.

Keywords: Decentralized network, multi-user detection, DS-CDMA.

1 Introduction

Compared with centralized wireless network, decentralized wireless network architecture is more suitable to be used in this environment[9]. That is because decentralized network needs no station, nodes are more autonomous and the network is more robust[4]. And wireless link could be assumed as physically connected when nodes are within a short distance one another. Therefore, the network described above can be simplified as decentralized all-connected model[3]. This paper will propose a protocol to be used in this environment to accomplish a no delay, low power cost, high anti-interference wireless network.

Among common link protocols, such as ALOHA, Carrier Sense Medium Access (CSMA), Multiple Access With Collision Avoidance (MACA), Time Division Multiple Access (TDMA) and Code Division Multiple Access (CDMA)[4], CDMA system has the characteristics of strong anti-interference ability and good security[1]. Especially, the theory of Direct Sequence CDMA (DS-CDMA) system is simple, its power cost is low, and it is easy to be realized[1], so it is very suitable to be used in local quickly deployed temporary wireless network. However, in practical system, when using DS-CDMA strategy to realize multiplexing, the spreading codes used by transceivers could not be exactly in quadrature, which will lead to nonzero cross correlation. This cross correlation will produce multi address interference (MAI), and finally forms a near-far problem[6]. As in decentralized network, power control can be hardly realized[7], while MUD technique not only can eliminate or decrease MAI, but also its performance is far better than power control [8]. Therefore, MUD is a necessary technique to improve the performance of DS-CDMA network system.

K. Li et al. (Eds.): NPC 2007, LNCS 4672, pp. 231–241, 2007.

By analyzing the MUD DS-CDMA system, this paper designs a network protocol based on MUD DS-CDMA architecture. And then, a quasi-synchronous decorrelation MUD algorithm is promoted in this paper, according to the practical network characteristics. Finally, the protocol is simulated and its performance is analyzed.

2   The Process of the Accessing Protocol

2.1   Protocol Initialization

In the spread spectrum communication system, the transmitter spreads the signal spectrum by a spreading code that is independent of the signal. The receiver could only receive useful information by using the same spreading code as the transmitter to despread the signal, or else, the signal from the transmitter would be treated as noise. Meanwhile, in the all-connected network, link could be established between any two nodes, and then they can do operations like accessing and transmitting[9]. Considering the system characteristics listed above as well as the application requirements described in section one, the initial protocol is designed as follows:

a. Allocate two spreading codes, which are defined as transmitting code (TC) and receiving code (RC), for each known node. And each node in the network knows other nodes' spreading code information. In idle state, each node uses its own RC to despread signal, preparing to receive data. The dispreading code of each node is approximately in quadrature to make sure the independence of the channels in the communication process, so that multi-node-pairs can implement the protocol on the same spectrum at the same time.

b. All the nodes in the network communicate each other by using the allocated spreading codes to make sure that the channels are independent. Therefore each node can use its spreading code as its address code to accomplish the addressing operation without any other control orders.

c. The source and dest nodes check the occupation of the channel by specific handoff operations, during which the spreading code (addressing code) is exchanged between them. During the data transmission period, the source and dest nodes use specific information interaction and retransmission mechanism to check and protect the integrity of the received data, which is implemented according to the HDLC protocol[14]. After transmission, still use handoff operation to release the occupied spreading code and the channels are also released.

Based on the settings above, the operation flow of the link layer protocol is as follows:

2.2   Establishing Link Process

When node 1 wants to communicate with node2, it first changes its RC to TC2 to make sure that it does not response to other node's request, and listens in node 2 to judge whether it is transmitting or not. If not, node 1 uses RC2 to transmit its RTS (Request to Send) packet. As the spreading codes are in quadrature, only node 2 could receive this request. On receiving the RTS packet from node 1, node 2 changes its RC to TC1, preparing to receive data from node 1. Then, node 2 will use TC2 to reply CTS (Clear to Send) packet and transmit data to node 1. When node 1 receives CTS, it will use TC1 to transmit data.

When node 1 needs to send data to node 2, but node 2 is using TC2 to communicate with node 3, node 1 will receive the data from node 2, so it will not send RTS to node 2 in this case. Then, node 1 will set a timer and listen in node 2 until its transmission is over or the timer is expired. When the transmission of node 2 is finished, node 1 will send RTS to node 2 immediately and communicate with node 2. When the timer expires, node 1 will retreat for a while, and try again as the rule described above until the link is established. The process is shown in figure1.

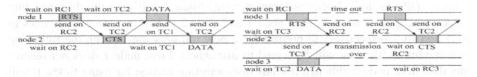

Fig. 1. The link establishment when dest node is idle (left) or under transmitting (right)

By the link establishment process described above, the hide and exposed terminal problems in wireless network could be solved[6]. By using the technique of channel listening, the idle waiting time in link establishment will be decreased. And the nodes use their own spreading code to connect, so multi nodes could establish links at the same time, which will increase the throughput of the network greatly.

2.3 Data Transmission Process

To improve the data validity and decrease the retransmission overhead of the network, sequence detection of data frames and partial retransmission mechanism are adopted in this paper. When the link between node 1 and node 2 is established, node 1 will send data to node 2 frame by frame in order. Node 2 will open a window to store a certain amount of received frames and check the serial number of the frame. When node 2 discovers that the frame with the expecting number is lost, it will request node 1 to retransmit the frame with the specific number. In another case, node 1 sends frames with request response (RR) information. When node 2 receives these frames, it will response the frame with its number in the response frame (RES). By doing this, node 1 could judge whether some frames are lost or node 2 is still active[14]. The transmission process is shown in figure 2, in which the window size is 3.

The design of the transmission process makes sure both the correction of transmission error and the data validity of transmission. Meanwhile, nodes in the

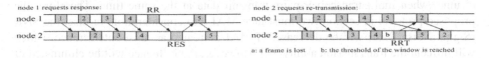

Fig. 2. Transmission process with sequence detection

network exchange control demands only when data validity is needed. By doing this, the overhead of control demands is decreased, and transmission efficiency is improved. What's more, this transmission protocol sets window length according to the channel quality, so the balance between checking rate and processing time is guaranteed.

2.4 Disconnection Process

After transmission, node pairs need a handshake to return to idle state, in order to release the occupied code division channel by releasing the communication spreading code. In normal state, if the link is started by node 1, node 1 will send disconnecting request (DIS) to node 2 after the transmission. Node 2 will send the disconnecting response (DISR) to node 1. Then node 1 and node 2 switch their receiving codes to RC1 and RC2 respectively to prepare for a new transmission. During the following two conditions, the link will be forced to disconnect. First, node 1 does not receive any data from node 2 although it sends disconnecting request for many times, it will disconnect unconditionally. Second, in the transmission process, if one node does not respond for a long time, the other one should be forced to disconnect. The disconnecting process is shown in figure 3.

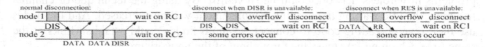

Fig. 3. Normal disconnection and forced disconnection processes

The design described above takes accessing interference, throughput, transmission validity, control command overhead and error operation time in to consideration. The final goal is to improve the performance of the whole network. The detail analysis of each factor listed above will be given in the fourth section. Before this, let's go back to focus on the quality of the physical communication channel based on DS-CDMA network in the next section.

3   Design of Ulti-user Detection Strategy

3.1   Introduction of Asynchronism DS-CDMA MUD

The code division isolation of channels ensures the ability of parallel transmission among transceivers and MAI is much stronger than other interferences arisen by channel when multi transceiver-pairs transmit data at the same time. Therefore, the proposed protocol in section two must take MAI into consideration, or else, the SNR (Signal Noise Rate) will be decreased if MAI is treated as noise interference, which will influent the transmission ability[10]. However, the influence will be eliminated or decreased if MUD technology is adopted to extract useful information from MAI.

Next, the asynchronism DS-CDMA de-correlation MUD model will be derivate in detail. Based on this derivation, a MUD algorism suited for decentralized all-connected wireless network is proposed.

In the all-connected network described in the second section, the received signals from multi transmitters are asynchronous. Therefore, asynchronous DS-CDMA model is adopted to describe signals at receivers in the network[11]. Assumed that there are K nodes in the network and the information length of node k is $N = 2M + 1$. Then base band spreading signal of node k is:

$$s_k(t) = \sum_{i=-M}^{M} \sqrt{2E_k} b_k(i) c_k(t - iT) \tag{1}$$

In which $b_k(i)$ is the i th information bit sent by node k, and $b_k(i) \in \{-1, 1\}$, $k = 1, 2, \cdots, K$, $i = -M, \cdots, M$, E_k is the receiving power of node k, T is the bit width of spreading code. So the base band signal of the receiver is:

$$r(t) = \sum_{k=1}^{K} s_k(t - \tau_k) + n(t) = \sum_{i=-M}^{M} \sum_{k=1}^{K} \sqrt{2E_k} b_k(i) c_k(t - iT - \tau_k) + n(t) \tag{2}$$

in which τ_k is the transmission delay of node k, and $\tau_1 \leq \tau_2 \leq \cdots \leq \tau_K$.

Assumed that the receiver uses matched filter for correlation dispreading, then for receiving signal, the ith bit of the client k of the matched filter's output is:

$$y_k(i) = \int_{iT+\tau_k}^{(i+1)T+\tau_k} r(t) c_k(t - iT - \tau_k) dt = \int_{iT+\tau_k}^{(i+1)T+\tau_k} \sum_{j=1}^{K} \sqrt{2E_j} b_j(i) c_j(t - iT - \tau_j) \cdot c_k(t - iT - \tau_k) dt$$

$$= \frac{1}{T} \int_{iT+\tau_k}^{(i+1)T} \sum_{j=1}^{K} \sqrt{2E_j} b_j(i) c_j(t - iT - \tau_j) \cdot c_k(t - iT - \tau_k) dt + \tag{3}$$

$$\frac{1}{T} \int_{(i+1)T}^{(i+1)T+\tau_k} \sum_{j=1}^{K} \sqrt{2E_j} b_j(i) c_j(t - iT - \tau_j) \cdot c_k(t - iT - \tau_k) dt + n_k(i)$$

$$= \sqrt{2E_k} b_k(i) + \left\{ \sum_{j<k} \sqrt{2E_j} b_j(i+1) \rho_{kj}(\tau_j - \tau_k) + \sum_{j<k} \sqrt{2E_j} b_j(i) \rho_{jk}(\tau_k - \tau_j) \right. \tag{4}$$

$$\left. + \sum_{j>k} \sqrt{2E_j} b_j(i) \rho_{kj}(\tau_j - \tau_k) + \sum_{j>k} \sqrt{2E_j} b_j(i-1) \rho_{jk}(\tau_k - \tau_j) \right\} + n_k(i)$$

In which the signal in the large bracket is the MAI of asynchronous DS-CDMA system. $\rho_{jk}(\tau_k - \tau_j) = \frac{1}{T} \int_{iT+\tau_k}^{(i+1)T} c_j(t - iT - \tau_j) c_k(t - iT - \tau_k) dt$ and $\rho_{kj}(\tau_j - \tau_k) = \frac{1}{T} \int_{(i+1)T}^{(i+1)T+\tau_k} c_j(t - iT - \tau_j) c_k(t - iT - \tau_k) dt$ represents the partial correlation function of the spreading code between client and client. $n_k(i) = \int_{iT+\tau_k}^{(i+1)T+\tau_k} n(t) c_k(t - iT - \tau_k) dt$ is the correlation noise. The matrix expression of formula (4) is[11]:

$$\mathbf{y}(l) = \mathbf{R}(-1) \mathbf{W} \mathbf{b}(l+1) + \mathbf{R}(0) \mathbf{W} \mathbf{b}(l) + \mathbf{R}(1) \mathbf{W} \mathbf{b}(l-1) + \mathbf{n}(l) \tag{5}$$

In which $\mathbf{W} = \mathrm{diag}\left(\left[\sqrt{2E_1}, \cdots, \sqrt{2E_K}\right]\right)$, $\mathbf{b}(l) = \left[b_1(l), \cdots, b_k(l)\right]$, $l = \{-M, \cdots, M\}$, $\mathbf{R}(0)$ and $\mathbf{R}(1)$ are $K \times K$ matrix, and element (j, k) is show in formula (7). So $\mathbf{R}(-1) = \mathbf{R}^T(1)$. After Z-transformation to formula (5), we get:

$$\mathbf{Y}(z) = \left[\mathbf{R}^T(1)z + \mathbf{R}(0) + \mathbf{R}(1)z^{-1}\right]\mathbf{Wb}(z) + \mathbf{n}(z) = \mathbf{H}(z)\mathbf{b}(z) + \mathbf{n}(z) \qquad (6)$$

As shown in formula (6), to use the asynchronous decorrelation DS-CDMA MUD system, the main point is to get the linear operator $\mathbf{L}$. Before this, the address of $\mathbf{R}(0)$ and $\mathbf{R}(1)$ should be acquired. And then compute the inverse of $\mathbf{H}$. Compared with synchronous DS-CDMA system[6], the complexity of computation is greatly increased, so a simplified method is needed.

$$\begin{aligned}
\mathbf{R}_{jk}(0) &= 1, \ j = k, \quad \rho_{jk}(\tau_k - \tau_j), \ j < k, \quad \rho_{kj}(\tau_j - \tau_k), \ j > k \\
\mathbf{R}_{jk}(1) &= 0, \ j \geq k, \quad \rho_{kj}(\tau_j - \tau_k), \ j < k
\end{aligned} \qquad (7)$$

3.2 Quasi-synchronous Decorrelation MUD Algorism

From formula (3) we can find out that in the case $\tau_1 \leq \tau_2 \leq \cdots \leq \tau_K \ll T$,

$\dfrac{1}{T} \displaystyle\int_{(i+1)T}^{(i+1)T+\tau_k} \sum_{j=1}^{K} \sqrt{2E_j}\, b_j(i) c_j(t - iT - \tau_j) \cdot c_k(t - iT - \tau_k)\, dt$ in formula (3) is far less than

$\dfrac{1}{T} \displaystyle\int_{iT+\tau_k}^{(i+1)T} \sum_{j=1}^{K} \sqrt{2E_j}\, b_j(i) c_j(t - iT - \tau_j) \cdot c_k(t - iT - \tau_k)\, dt$, so it could be ignored.

Therefore, formula (3) could be simplified as follow, in which $\tau_{x1} = \tau_x - \tau_1$.

$$\begin{aligned}
y_k(i) &= \frac{1}{T} \int_{iT+\tau_k}^{(i+1)T} \sum_{j=1}^{K} \sqrt{2E_j}\, b_j(i) c_j(t - iT - \tau_j) \cdot c_k(t - iT - \tau_k)\, dt \\
&= \frac{1}{T} \int_{\tau_{k1}}^{T} \sum_{j=1}^{K} \sqrt{2E_j}\, b_j(i) c_j(t - iT - \tau_{j1}) \cdot c_k(t - iT - \tau_{k1})\, dt
\end{aligned} \qquad (8)$$

This restriction of the simplifying can be reached, for example, all the transmitters use the same inter-clock (such as GPS timing clock) to ensure the time consistent of each chip transmitting. Then when the distance of nodes between each other is not far and transmission chip rate is not too quick, transmission delay of each node will differ little and far shorter than the chip length.

And formula (8) could be realized by this method: use the first peak correlation value of the matched filter as zero point to calculate delays of other peak correlation values, which is τ_x. Then calculate the summation of transmitters' partial correlation value. In this way, we can provide initial parameters for MUD. The error loss of correlation calculus will lead to the loss of output SNR, but latter analysis will show that this loss could be acceptable. By the simplifying process described above, formula (3) could be simplified as follows:

$$y_k(i) = \sqrt{2E_k}\, b_k(i) + \sum_{j<k} \sqrt{2E_j}\, b_j(i) \rho_{jk}(\tau_k - \tau_j) + \sum_{j>k} \sqrt{2E_j}\, b_j(i) \rho_{kj}(\tau_j - \tau_k) + n_k(i) \qquad (9)$$

So the linear decorrelation factor of quasi-synchronous MUD is $\left[\mathbf{R}(0)\right]^{-1}$ and the output of matched filter decision is $\hat{\mathbf{b}} = \text{sgn}\left(\left[\mathbf{R}(0)\right]^{-1}\mathbf{Y}\right)$. In this way, MAI is eliminated, but the computational complexity is much less complex than asynchronous system.

Based on the analysis given above, MUD method in quasi-synchronous DS-CDMA network is promoted. Compared with asynchronous MUD, the amount of computation is lowered (especially when the number of clients is large) which is meaningful to engineering realization. Meanwhile, by adopting MUD technology, the impact of MAI is eliminated, the detection ability of spreading code as address code is guaranteed, and parallel data transmission of transmitters is also realized. In this way, it provides support for protocol design that is based on this.

4 Protocol Simulation and Performance Analysis

4.1 Quasi-synchronous Decorrelation MUD Performance

Aimed at the quasi-synchronous decorrelation MUD algorism proposed in section three, bit error rate (BER) of nodes in the network is adopted to measure the channel quality, to ensure that the proposed MUD performance can satisfy the requirement of inhibiting MAI of the designed protocol.

Let background noise of channel be σ^2, element of the partial correlation matrix $\left[\mathbf{R}(0)\right]^{-1}$ is r_{ij}, the output noise power of node k after matched filter decision is $E_k = \sigma^2 \sum_{i=1}^{K} r_{ik}^2$. As for node k, the correlation time is shortened by τ_{k1}, so the output signal power decision is $(T - \tau_{k1}) E_k / T$. Then receiving BER of this node is:

$$\eta_k = Q\left(\sqrt{SNR_{out}}\right) = Q\left(\sqrt{(T - \tau_{k1}) E_k / T\sigma^2 \sum_{i=1}^{K} r_{ik}^2}\right) \tag{10}$$

In which: $Q(x) = 1/\sqrt{2\pi} \int_x^{\infty} e^{-u^2/2} du$.

Assuming $\sigma^2 = 1$, $E_1 = E_2 = \cdots = E_K = 15$ (output SNR is 11.8dB), using 31 bit Gold sequence as spreading code[12], $\tau_{k1} = (k-1)T/31K$. Then, according to reference [6], the BERs of synchronous decorrelation and the conventional receiver can be obtained, and BER of quasi-synchronous decorrelation can be calculated by formula (10). So BERs versus the change of node number is shown in figure 4.

From figure 4, it can be concluded that when there are fewer nodes, the performance of quasi-synchronous BER is worse than conventional single user receiver. This is mainly because that the influence of MAI is smaller than the influence of background noise at this time, while the process of decorrelation magnifies the background noise, therefore, the SNR is decreased. However, when there are more nodes, the BER performance of conventional receiver deteriorates

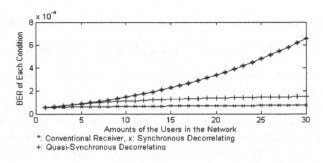

Fig. 4. BER comparing of different receiver

rapidly while the BER of quasi-synchronous decorrelation process is nearly smooth, and is similar to the performance of synchronous decorrelation process. The correlation time of quasi-synchronous process is shortened which leads to the BER difference between synchronous process and quasi-synchronous process. But the BER loss is acceptable. This can fully satisfy the proposed protocol's requirement for the performance of code division channel. Moreover, it is a better choice to take both realizability and MUD performance into consideration.

4.2 Network Simulation Model Description

To validate the implementation of the designed protocol, this paper uses OPNET to simulate it. The node model is comprised of sending process and receiving process, the state machine is shown in figure 5. In the sending process, state IDLE implements idle waiting and destination node selection operations. The state DETECT and CONNECT implement channel listening and link establishing operations. The state SEND implements data (information data and control data) transmission and reply request operations. At last, the state DISCONN implements link disconnection operation. The receiving process uses RECV state to implement information data and control data receiving operation, frame continuity detection operation and controlling the sending process to implement corresponding operation according to the state of the received data.

To validate the protocol performance in different cases, different simulation environments are established by OPNET based on the process models in figure 5. The

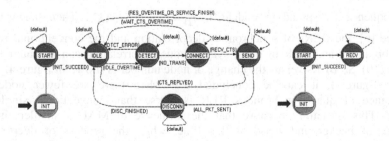

Fig. 5. Model of transmitting process (left) and model of receiving process (right)

simulation environment is described as follows: N nodes distribute uniformly on a 100 meters ×100 meters plane; the data transmission rate is 1000 packets/s; the length of each packet is 36 bits; each node selects destination node randomly; after link establishment, source and destination nodes transmit 100 packets respectively to each other, and a length L buffer window is used to detect the received data. During the process of data transmission, if there is one bit error in one packet, this packet will be requested to retransmit. The received packet is stored in the buffer window in sequence, and the one that is out of the sequence number will be dropped. After one data transmission, the source and destination nodes will be idle for $\bar{t} + \Delta t_{rand}$ (Δt_{rand} is a uniform distribution in [-0.02, 0.02], so $\bar{t}$ is the average idle period of each nodes), and then start new link and transmission. The transmission power of nodes in the network is set to 1.5W, and the background noise power is set to 0.1W. Because the network only overcasts a short range, the signal power loss during transmission could be ignored, so the SNR of each receiver is 11.8dB ($10\log(1.5/0.1)$). Therefore, the environment settings in OPNET of the receiving BER are the same as described in section 4.1. To be simple, we simulate the BER described in section 4.1 by Matlab, and modify the settings of pipeline stage in OPNET with the result. Based on the parameters settings above, by modifying the number of nodes N, average idle time and buffer window length L, simulated and compared the throughput of protocol adopting MUD with the throughput of the protocol without MUD and the throughput of CSMA/CD (CSMA with Carrier Detection) protocol[13] in different environments. Each simulation time of throughput is 5 minutes, and each simulation time of dropout rate is 30 minutes.

4.3 Analysis of Simulation Results

When $L = 1$, and $N = 25$, the curves of throughput changed with average idle time $\bar{t}$ is shown in figure 6(left). It is seen from the figure that the probability of collision during link establishment and invalid waiting time is reduced by adopting the link establishment mechanism of the proposed protocol. Therefore, when the business increases, after the throughput of the protocol using MUD reaches the peek value, it will then drop a little compared with the significant drop of the throughput of the protocol without MUD. This is mainly because, the numbers of nodes transmit at the same time increase with business, and the BER will also increase, which leads to the drop of throughput. However, after using MUD, the influence of BER will be reduced, so multi node pairs could communicate at the same time. Therefore, the throughput of the network using this protocol is far larger than the throughput of CSMA/CD which only one node pair could occupy the channel. And when $\bar{t} = 0.5$, $L = 1$, the curves representing the throughput changed with the number of nodes in the network is shown in figure 6 (right). In the same way, as this proposed protocol allows multi node pairs to transmit data at the same time, its throughput is much larger than CSMA/CD at the same condition. Moreover, with the influence of BER produced by users number increasing, after the throughput reaches the peak value, it also drops a little, compared with the significant drop of throughput of the protocol without MUD.

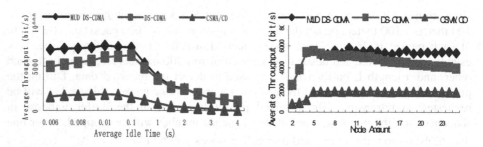

Fig. 6. Throughout comparing of MUD DS-CDMA, DS-CDMA and CSMA/CD in different network businesses (left) and in different network scale (right)

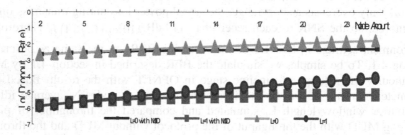

Fig. 7. Dropout rate comparing of MUD DS-CDMA and DS-CDMA at different length of transmission window

When $\bar{t} = 0.5$, $L = 0$, $L = 1$, the curves representing the dropout rate changed with nodes number changing are shown in figure 9. It can be seen that the dropout rate is greatly decreased by setting buffer window in the communication process and adopting the retransmitting mechanism proposed in this paper. This is because that with the checking window, only when there are successive error packets and it is beyond the window the packets will be dropped. Therefore, the retransmission and MUD mechanisms adopted in the protocol in this paper could decrease the dropout rate. However, with the increase of window length, the processing delay and complexity will be increased too. Therefore, both the dropout rate and window length should be considered in practical application.

5 Conclusion

By analysis of the performance of the proposed protocol, we can find that the designed link protocol and MUD methodology realizes the networking of a decentralized all-connected network, decreasing the accessing waiting delay, increasing the throughput and lowering the retransmitting rate and dropout rate. Therefore, it can fulfill the application requirement of quickly establishing temporary wireless network in a small area.

As the proposed network protocol in this paper is based on all-connected network, wide area application should still be researched. Meanwhile, the requirement of this protocol for MUD performance is strict, therefore, the processing complexity, detecting error performance and other aspects should be improved, for example, to adopt a better spreading code selection method to reduce the cross correlation of inter codes, and improve the MUD performance.

References

1. Sklar, B.: Spread Spectrum Technology. In: Digital Communication: Fundamentals and Applications, 2nd edn., pp. 547–608. Publishing House of Electronics Industry, Beijing (2005)
2. Ziemer, R.E., Peterson, R.L., Borth, D.E.: Characteristic of the m sequence. In: Introduction to Spread Spectrum Communications, pp. 124–143. Prentice Hall, Pearson (2006)
3. Xiao-cong, Q., Bao-yu, Z., Xian-jing, Z.: Throughput Study for Ad hoc Network with Multiuser Detection. Journal of Electronics & Information Technology 28(8) (August 2006)
4. Joa-Ng, M., Lu, I.-T.: Spread Spectrum Medium Access Protocol with Collision Avoidance in Mobile Ad-hoc Wireless Network. In: Eighteenth Annual Joint Conference of the IEEE Computer and Communications Societies, March 1999, vol. 2, pp. 776–783 (1999)
5. Weber, S., Yang, X., de Veciana, G., Andrews, J.G.: Transmission capacity of CDMA ad hoc networks. In: Global Telecommunications Conference, 29 November-3 December 2004 5 (2004)
6. Lupas, R., Verdu, S.: Linear Multiuser Detectors for Synchronous Code-Division Multiple-Access-Channels. IEEE Transactions on Information Theory 35(1) (January 1989)
7. Toumpis, S., Goldsmith, A.J.: Capacity Regions for Wireless Ad Hoc Networks. IEEE Transactions on Wireless Communications 2(4) (July 2003)
8. Weber, S., Andrews, J.G., Yang, X., de Veciana, G.: Transmission capacity of CDMA ad hoc networks employing successive interference cancellation. In: Global Telecommunications Conference, 29 November-3 December 2004, vol. 5, pp. 2838–2842 (2004)
9. Bao, J.Q., Tong, L.: A performance comparison between Ad hoc and centrally controlled CDMA wireless LANs. IEEE Transactions on Wireless Communications (2002)
10. Xiaobo, Y., Xin, Y., Luhong, F.: Multi-User Detection Technique for CDMA. Journal of UEST of China 32(4) (August 2003)
11. Lupas, R., Verdu, S.: Near-far resistance of multiuser detectors in asynchronous channels. IEEE Transactions on Communications 38(4) (April 1990)
12. Gold, R.: Optimal Binary Sequences for Spread Spectrum Multiplexing. IEEE Trans. Inform. Theory IT-13, 617–621 (1967)
13. Jereb, L., Marsan, M.A.: Transient performance analysis of nonpersistent CSMA and CSMA-CD protocols. In: Global Telecommunications Conference, November 1989, vol. 2, pp. 939–943 (1989)
14. International Standard: High-Level Data Link Control Procedures (July 2002)

A Small-World Optimization Algorithm Based and ABC Supported QoS Unicast Routing Scheme*

Xingwei Wang, Shuxiang Cai, and Min Huang

College of Information Science and Engineering, Northeastern University, Shenyang,
110004, P.R. China
wangxw@mail.neu.edu.cn

Abstract. In this paper, by introducing knowledge of fuzzy mathematics, probability theory and gaming theory, a QoS unicast routing scheme with ABC supported is proposed based on small-world optimization algorithm. Under inaccurate network status information and imprecise user QoS requirement, the proposed scheme uses the range to describe the user QoS requirement and the edge parameter, introduces the user satisfaction degree function, the edge evaluation function and the path evaluation function, trying to find a QoS unicast path with Pareto optimum under Nash equilibrium on both the network provider utility and the user utility achieved or approached. Simulation results have shown that it is both feasible and effective with better performance.

Keywords: NGI(Next Generation Internet), QoS(Quality of Service), Unicast routing, ABC (Always Best Connected), Small-world optimization algorithm, Nash equilibrium, Pareto optimum.

1 Introduction

Recently, with the growth and convergence of Internet, multimedia content and mobile communication technology, NGI (Next Generation Internet) is becoming an integrated network [1-4] converged seamlessly by heterogeneous multi-segment multi-provider sub-networks, such as terrestrial-based, space-based, fixed and mobile sub-networks, etc. Its backbone and access links become diversified. Several kinds of links may coexist on each hop for the user to choose along the end-to-end path. It is possible for the user to be ABC (Always Best Connected) [3-4] to NGI in the course of communication, that is, the user can connect with NGI anytime, anywhere in the currently best way and can switch to the better way adaptively and transparently whenever it comes forth, and thus the so-called global QoS (Quality of Service) roaming should be supported seamlessly [5].

In NGI, QoS routing is essential and ABC should be supported [4]. However, some characteristics of NGI, such as its heterogeneity and dynamics, influence of terminal and even network mobility, unavoidable message transfer delay and its uncertainty,

* This work is supported by the National High-Tech Research and Development Plan of China under Grant No. 2006AA01Z214; the National Natural Science Foundation of China under Grant No. 60673159; Program for New Century Excellent Talents in University; Specialized Research Fund for the Doctoral Program of Higher Education; the Natural Science Foundation of Liaoning Province under Grant No. 20062022.

K. Li et al. (Eds.): NPC 2007, LNCS 4672, pp. 242–249, 2007.

etc., make it hard to describe the network status used when routing in NGI exactly and completely. On the other hand, the user QoS requirements are affected largely by a lot of subjective factors and often can not be expressed accurately, therefore the flexible QoS description should be provided. ABC means a user can get the best available connection anytime, anywhere, however, 'best' itself is a fuzzy concept, depending on many factors, such as user QoS requirement, cost a user willing to pay, user preference, terminal ability and access network availability, etc. In addition, with the gradual commercialization of network operation, ABC is not a user's own wishful thinking and thus need to consider both the network provider profit and the user profit with both-win supported [6].

It has been proved that the problem of finding a path subject to constraints on two or more additive or multiplicative metrics in any possible combination is NP-complete [7]. There are already many heuristic and intelligent optimization algorithms used to solve this problem. In [8], the edges that do not meet with the bandwidth constraint are cut off from the graph at first, and then Dijkstra algorithm [9] is used to find the bandwidth-constrained least-delay path with delay as weight. In [10], a distributed heuristic algorithm is proposed, which constructs a delay vector and a cost vector for each node to help find the path. In [11], a comprehensive parameter that is the probabilistic combination of cost and delay is introduced and used when routing. In [12], QoS parameters are defined as path-correlative non-negative variables and are divided into two classes: QoS sensitive and non-sensitive, so that the routing computation can be simplified. In [13], a route pre-computation scheme is proposed based on Bellman-Ford algorithm [14], and the substantial improvement in terms of computational complexity has been achieved by quantizing the cost function. In [15] and [16], a distributed delay-constrained algorithm and a multi-constrained source routing algorithm are proposed respectively. In [17], several pseudo-polynomial time algorithms have been proposed to solve the delay-constrained least-cost routing problem. On the other hand, many optimization algorithms, such as genetic algorithm, ant colony algorithm, and simulated annealing algorithm, have been used to solve QoS routing problem in order to find the optimal or near-optimal QoS route [18-20].

However, the above proposed schemes do not consider sufficiently realizing a QoS unicast routing mechanism with both-win of the network provider and the user supported under imprecise network status and inaccurate user QoS requirement from ABC viewpoint. In this paper, by introducing knowledge of fuzzy mathematics, probability theory and gaming theory, a QoS unicast routing scheme with ABC supported is proposed. In order to deal with imprecise network status information and flexible user QoS requirement, it uses range to describe the user QoS requirement and the edge parameter and introduces the user satisfaction degree function, the edge evaluation function and the path evaluation function. Based on small-world optimization algorithm, it tries to find a QoS unicast path with Pareto optimum under Nash equilibrium on both the network provider utility and the user utility achieved or approached. Simulation results have shown that the proposed scheme is both feasible and effective with better performance.

2 Problem Description

In this paper, the adopted network model, routing request, edge parameter probability model, user satisfaction degree function, edge and path evaluation function, gaming analysis and mathematical model are the same as those in [21]. Due to limited space, please refer to [21] for their detailed descriptions.

3 Algorithm Design

Small-world optimization algorithm [22] optimizes its solution searching process based on small world phenomenon, regarding optimization process as information transfer from a candidate solution to the optimized solution in searching space. The proposed QoS unicast routing scheme based on small-world optimization algorithm is described as follows.

3.1 Basic Definition

In Small-world optimization algorithm, call a candidate solution as a transfer node. In this paper, s represents a transfer node and S represents a transfer node set, $s \in S$. $s = s_1 s_2 \cdots s_{|E|}$ adopts binary encoding, if one bit is 0, its correspond edge is in s, otherwise not in s. A node is generated randomly, that is, each bit of its codes is set to be 0 or 1 randomly.

The fitness function of s is defined as follows:

$$FT(s) = \frac{1}{EC_P(s)} \cdot \sum_{e_i \in P} \frac{NE_l}{PA_{xy}^l} .$$

(1)

$$NE_l = \begin{cases} 1 & \text{Nashequilibrim} \\ >1 & \text{otherwise} \end{cases} .$$

(2)

Obviously, the smaller its fitness value, the better the solution.

The information transfer target set is defined as follows:

$$T = \{s \mid (s \in I) \wedge (FT(s) = FT^*)\} .$$

(3)

Here, I is solution space, FT^* is the smallest fitness value of solutions in I.

Define the distance between two nodes as follows:

$$d(s_b, s_c) = \|s_b - s_c\| .$$

(4)

Here, $s_b, s_c \in S$, $\|s_b - s_c\|$ is the Hamming distance between s_b and s_c.

Define the set of solutions in its ℓ neighborhood of s_b as follows:

$$\zeta^\ell(s_b) = \{s_c \mid (s_c \in S) \wedge (0 < \|s_b - s_c\| \leq \ell)\} .$$

(5)

Then, use $\overline{\zeta^\ell(s_b)}$ to represent the set of solutions not in its ℓ neighborhood of s_b.

3.2 Local Short Conjunctive Search Operator

When ℓ is small, this operator is used to transfer information from $s_b(j)$ to $s_b(j+1)$ which is the closest to T in $\zeta^\ell(s_b(j))$, denoted as $s_b(j+1) \leftarrow \Psi(s_b(j))$. In this paper, take $N_{len}(j) < \left| \zeta^{\ell}(s_b) \right|$ nodes from $\zeta^{\ell}(s_b(j))$ randomly to construct a temporary local transfer network for local search. It is described in algorithm 3.1.

Algorithm 3.1 Set $N_{len}(j) < \left| \zeta^{\ell}(s_b) \right|$; $s_b(j+1) \leftarrow s_b(j)$

```
1:  c←0
2:  repeat
3:  s'_b(j) ← s_b(j)×0
4:  select  f(0<f≤ℓ) bits  from s'_b(j) randomly and set them
    to be 1
5:  s'_b(j) ← s_b(j)⌐2×(s_b(j)⊗s'_b(j))⊕s'_b(j)
6:  if  FT(s'_b(j))< FT(s_b(j+1))
7:  s_b(j+1) ← s'_b(j)
8:  endif
9:  c←c+1
10: until  c=N_len(j)
```

Here, j is the iteration times, $s_b(j) \times 0$ is to obtain a temporary string with each bit to be set 0, $\oplus$ represents "add bit by bit", $\neg$ represents "subtract bit by bit", and $\otimes$ represents "multiply bit by bit".

3.3 Random Long Conjunctive Searching Operator

When ℓ is large, this operator is used to select a node $s'_b(j)$ in $\overline{\zeta^{\ell}(s_b)}$ randomly by a preset probability as information transfer object node of $s_b(j)$, which is denoted as $S'(j) \leftarrow \Gamma(S(j))$. It is described in algorithm 3.2.

Algorithm 3.2 Set global long conjunctive probability p_{len} and ℓ

```
1:  b←0
2:  repeat
3:  s'_b(j) ← s_b(j)
4:  p←rand(0−1)
5:  if  p_len <p and s_b(j) is not the optimum in the current
node set
6:generate  two 'integers  μ and v randomly,  1≤μ<v≤len ,
|μ−v|>ℓ
7:  s_b(j) ← s'_b(j)|^v_μ
8:  endif
9:  b←b+1
10: until  b=N
```

In the above, the forth sentence is to generate a random number which is evenly distributed between 0 and 1, the seventh sentence is to reverse the bit order from the μth to the νth bit in $s'_b(j)$.

3.4 Algorithm Procedure

The procedure of the proposed QoS unicast routing algorithm is described as follows:

Step1: Set the node set size to be N ; set $p_{|E|}$ and ℓ .

Step2: Generate the initial node set $S(0) = \{s_1(0), s_2(0), \cdots, s_N(0)\}$ randomly according to section 3.1, i.e., generate N initial unicast paths.

Step3: For each node $s_b(0) \in S(0)$, compute the user utility and the network provider utility on each edge according to formula (23) and (25) in [21] , and play game according to section 2.4 in [21].

Step4: Compute $FT(s_b(0))$ for each node $s_b(0) \in S(0)$.

Step5: Judge whether $s_b(0)$ meets the constraints defined by formula (36)-(39) in [21] or not: if not so, regenerate it and go to Step4.

Step6: Record the best fitness value FT^b of the nodes in the current node set.

Step7: Set the iteration times to be Itr , set ε , $j = 0$.

Step8: If $j \le Itr$ and $\left| FT^* - FT^b \right| \le \varepsilon$ (termination criteria)is not met, go to Step9, otherwise go to Step17.

Step9: Construct the temporary node set $S'(j)$, $S'(j) \leftarrow S(j)$.

Step10: execute the algorithm 3.2, $S'(j) \leftarrow \Gamma(S'(j))$.

Step11: $b = 0$

Step12: execute the algorithm 3.1 to $s_b(j)$, $s'_b(j+1) \leftarrow \Psi(s'_b(j))$, $s'_b(j) \in S'(j)$.

Step13: If $FT(s'_b(j+1)) < FT(s_b(j))$, $s_b(j+1) \leftarrow s'_b(j+1)$, otherwise $s_b(j+1) \leftarrow s_b(j)$.

Step14: $b = b+1$. If $b < N$, go to Step12, otherwise go to Step15.

Step15: Update FT^b with the best fitness value of the nodes in the current node set.

Step16: $j = j+1$, go to Step8.

Step17: Output the optimal node as the problem solution, the algorithm ends.

Specially, when $0 < \left| FT^* \right| < 1$, termination criteria changes to $\left| FT^* - FT^b \right| < \varepsilon \left| FT^* \right|$.

4   Simulation Research

Simulations of the proposed QoS unicast routing scheme have been done on NS2 (Network Simulator 2)[23] and simulation results have shown that it has better performance when its main parameters are set to be the following values[22]: $\varepsilon=0.0005$, $k=2$, $\sigma_1=3$, $\sigma_2=3$, $\alpha_B=1/3$, $\alpha_D=1/3$, $\alpha_L=1/3$, $n=6$, $m=4$, $\delta=0.8$, $k_1=0.6$, $k_2=0.4$, $\lambda_1=0.6$, $\lambda_2=0.6$, $\rho=0.5$, $\alpha=0.5$, $\beta=0.5$.

Assume that there are three network providers providing satellite, cellular and fixed links respectively, that is, there are three kinds of links for a user to choose on each hop along the path. The proposed scheme, the proposed microeconomics based fuzzy unicast QoS routing scheme in [24], and the unicast routing scheme based on Dijkstra algorithm [8] have been simulated on some physical and virtual network topologies, called A, G and D schemes below for short. Compared with A scheme, G scheme takes imprecise network status and both-win of the network provider utility and the user utility into account but does not consider imprecise user QoS requirement and ABC. Simulation results have shown that A scheme has the better performance. Comparison results on QoS unicast routing request succeeded rate(RSR), user utility(UU), satellite link provider utility(SPU), cellular link provider utility(CPU), fixed link provider utility(FPU), network provider utility(NU=SPU+CPU+FPU), comprehensive utility(CU=UU+NU), Pareto optimum ratio under Nash equilibrium(PRN) achieved by A, G and D schemes over CERNET topology(T1), CERNET2 topology(T2), GÉANT topology(T3) and one virtual topology(T4, generated by Waxman2[25] with average node degree 3.5) are shown in Table 1. From Table 1, it can be concluded that the proposed scheme has the better performance, especially when topologies are complex.

Table 1(1). Comparison Results

Topology / Metrics	T1 A:G:D	T2 A:G:D
RSR	1.1624:1.1136:1.0000	1.1427:1.0848:1.0000
UU	1.1327:1.0816:1.0000	1.1029:1.0937:1.0000
SPU	1.0657:1.0411:1.0000	1.0531:1.0384:1.0000
CPU	1.1576:1.1295:1.0000	1.1465:1.1152:1.0000
FPU	1.1253:1.0773:1.0000	1.1187:1.0692:1.0000
NU	1.1369:1.0873:1.0000	1.1057:1.0632:1.0000
CU	1.1347:1.0866:1.0000	1.1036:1.0793:1.0000
PRN	4.4091:3.6819:1.0000	4.3519:3.7262:1.0000

Table 1(2). Comparison Results

Topology / Metrics	T3 A:G:D	T4 A:G:D
RSR	1.1935:1.1218:1.0000	1.2129:1.1694:1.0000
UU	1.1737:1.1033:1.0000	1.1859:1.1097:1.0000
SPU	1.0814:1.0548:1.0000	1.0894:1.0627:1.0000
CPU	1.1859:1.1348:1.0000	1.2065:1.1674:1.0000
FPU	1.1468:1.0961:1.0000	1.1722:1.1283:1.0000
NU	1.1562:1.1409:1.0000	1.1757:1.1376:1.0000
CU	1.1631:1.1274:1.0000	1.1991:1.1184:1.0000
PRN	4.8439:3.9644:1.0000	5.2161:4.2493:1.0000

5 Conclusion

In this paper, by introducing knowledge of fuzzy mathematics, probability theory and gaming theory, a QoS unicast routing scheme with ABC supported is proposed based on small-world optimization algorithm. Under imprecise network status and inaccurate user QoS requirement, it tries to search for a QoS unicast path to make both the network provider utility and the user utility achieve or approach Pareto optimum under Nash equilibrium. Simulation results have shown that the proposed scheme is both feasible and effective with better performance. In future, our study will focus on improving its practicality, developing its prototype system and extend it to multicast scenario.

References

1. Daoud, F., Mohan, S.: Challenges of Personal Environments Mobility in Heterogeneous Networks. Mobile Networks and Applications 8(1), 7–9 (2003)
2. Lu, W.W.: Open Wireless Architecture and Enhanced Performance. IEEE Communications Magazine 41(6), 106–107 (2003)
3. Gustafsson, E., Jonsson, A.: Always Best Connected. IEEE Wireless Communications 10(1), 49–55 (2003)
4. Fodor, G., Eriksson, A.: Aimo Tuoriniemi: Providing Quality of Service in Always Best Connected Networks. IEEE Communications Magazine 41(7), 154–163 (2003)
5. Zahariadis, T.B., Vaxevankis, K.G., Tsantilas, C.P., et al.: Global Roaming in Next-Generation Networks. IEEE Communications Magazine 40(2), 145–151 (2002)
6. Quan, X.T., Zhang, J.: Theory of Economics Game. China Machine Press, Beijing (2003)
7. Wang, Z., Crowcroft, J.: Quality of Service Routing for Supporting Multimedia Applications. IEEE Journal on Selected Areas in Communications 14(7), 1288–1294 (1996)
8. Wang, Z., Crowcroft, J.: QoS Routing for Supporting Resource Reservation. IEEE Journal on Selected Areas in Communications 14(7), 1228–1234 (1996)
9. Dijkstra, E.W.: A Note on Two Problems in Connection with Graphs. Numerical Mathematics 1 (1959)
10. Salama, H.F., Reeves, D.S., Viniotis, Y.: A Distributed Algorithm For Delay-Constrained Unicast Routing. IEEE/ACM Transactions on Networking 8(2), 239–250 (2000)
11. Kim, M., Bang, Y.-C., Choo, H.: New Parameter for Balancing Two Independent Measures in Routing Path. In: Laganà, A., Gavrilova, M., Kumar, V., Mun, Y., Tan, C.J.K., Gervasi, O. (eds.) ICCSA 2004. LNCS, vol. 3046, Springer, Heidelberg (2004)
12. Gelenbe, E.: An Approach to Quality of Service. In: Aykanat, C., Dayar, T., Körpeoğlu, İ. (eds.) ISCIS 2004. LNCS, vol. 3280, Springer, Heidelberg (2004)
13. Orda, A., Sprintson, A.: QoS Routing: the Precomputation perspective, pp. 128–136. IEEE Computer Society Press, Los Alamitos (2000)
14. Cormen, T.H., Leiserson, C.E., Rivest, R.L.: Introduction to Algorithms. MIT Press, Cambridge, MA (1990)
15. Shin, K.G., Chou, C.C.: A Distributed Route-Selection Scheme for Establishing Real-Time Channels. In: International Conference on High Performance Networking, pp. 319–329 (1995)
16. Chen, S., Nahrsted, K.: On Finding Multi-Constrained Paths. In: Proceedings of IEEE ICC'98, pp. 874–899 (1998)

17. Wang, X.W., Wang, Z.J., Huang, M., et al.: Quality of Service Based Initial Route Setup Algorithms for Multimedia Communication. Chinese Journal of Computers 24(8), 830–837 (2001)
18. Barolli, L., Koyama, A. (eds.): A Genetic Algorithm Based Routing Method Using Two QoS Parameters, vol. 8(1), pp. 7–11. IEEE Computer Society, Los Alamitos (2002)
19. Dorigo, M.: Ant Algorithms Solve Difficult Optimization Problems. In: Advances in Artificial Life: 6th European Conference, pp. 11–22. Czech Republic, Prague (2001)
20. Cui, Y., Wu, J.P.: A QoS Routing Algorithm by Applying Simulated Annealing. Journal of Software 14(5), 877–884 (2003)
21. Wang, X.W., Gao, N., Cai, S.X., Huang, M.: An Artificial Fish Swarm Algorithm Based and ABC Supported QoS Unicast Routing Scheme in NGI. In: Min, G., Di Martino, B., Yang, L.T., Guo, M., Ruenger, G. (eds.) Frontiers of High Performance Computing and Networking – ISPA 2006 Workshops. LNCS, vol. 4331, pp. 205–214. Springer, Heidelberg (2006)
22. Li, X.L., S, Z.J, Q, J.X.: An Optimizing Method Based on Autonomous Animals: Fish-swarm Algorithm. Systems Engineering-Theory & Practice 22(11), 32–38 (2002)
23. Xu, L.M., Pang, B., Zhao, R.: NS and Network Simulation, pp. 1–9. Posts & Telecom Press, Beijing (2003)
24. Wang, X.W., Hou, M.J., Wang, J.W., et al.: A Microeconomics-based Fuzzy QoS Unicast Routing Scheme in NGI. In: Yang, L.T., Amamiya, M., Liu, Z., Guo, M., Rammig, F.J. (eds.) EUC 2005. LNCS, vol. 3824, pp. 1055–1064. Springer, Heidelberg (2005)
25. Waxman, B.M.: Routing of Multipoint Connections. IEEE Journal on Selected Areas in Communications 6(11), 478–489 (1988)

Algorithms for the m-Coverage Problem and k-Connected m-Coverage Problem in Wireless Sensor Networks

Deying Li[1,2], Jiannong Cao[3], Dongsheng Liu[1], Ying Yu[4], and Hui Sun[1]

[1] School of Information, Renmin University of China, Beijing, China, 100872
[2] Key Laboratory of Data Engineering and Knowledge Engineering, MOE
[3] Department of Computing, The Hong Kong Polytechnic University, HongKong
[4] School of Information Engineering, University of Science and Technology of Beijing

Abstract. An important issue in deploying a wireless sensor network (WSN) is to provide target coverage with high energy efficiency and fault-tolerance. In this paper, we study the problem of constructing energy-efficient and fault-tolerant target coverage with the minimal number of active nodes which form an *m*-coverage for targets and a *k*-connected communication subgraph. We propose two heuristic algorithms for *m*-coverage problem, and get the performance ratio of one heuristic. Then two heuristic algorithms are further proposed to solve the *k*-connected *m*-coverage problem. The simulation results demonstrate the desired efficiency of the proposed algorithms.

Keywords: *k*-connected *m*-coverage, sensor networks, approximation algorithm, energy-efficient.

1 Introduction

Monitoring a geographical region or a set of targets and collecting the relevant data are very important tasks in wireless sensor networks. Since sensor nodes are often deployed in an arbitrary manner, one of the fundamental issues in the task of target monitoring is target coverage which reflects how well the deployed sensor nodes can monitor a set of targets. Meanwhile, the energy-efficiency is another important issue in WSNs. In general, sensor nodes are powered by very limited battery resources. Recent research has found that significant energy savings can be achieved by elaborate managing the duty cycle of nodes in WSNs with high node density. In this approach, some nodes are scheduled to sleep (or enter a power saving mode) while the remaining active nodes keep working.

Sensing is only one responsibility of a sensor network. To operate successfully, most sensor networks must also remain connected, i.e., the active nodes should not be partitioned in any configured schedule of node duty cycles. A sensor network must provide satisfactory connectivity so that nodes can communicate for data fusion and reporting the results to base stations. Single connectivity often is not sufficient for many sensor networks because a single failure could disconnect the network, and single coverage is also not sufficient. Therefore, maintaining sufficient sensing

K. Li et al. (Eds.): NPC 2007, LNCS 4672, pp. 250–259, 2007.
© IFIP International Federation for Information Processing 2007

coverage and network connectivity with minimal active nodes are critical requirements in WSNs.

In this paper, we study more general coverage problem--k-connected m-coverage problem: to find minimized number of active nodes to form a target m-coverage and meanwhile any pair of active nodes is connected by at least k disjoint paths. To solve the k-connected m-coverage problem, we first investigate an introductory problem, namely m-coverage problem that is to find the minimum number of active nodes ensuring that each target can be covered by at lease m distinct sensor nodes. We show that the m-coverage problem is NP-hard and then give one heuristic and an approximation algorithm accordingly. Next, based on the k-connected coverage problem [19], we propose two heuristic algorithms to solve the k-connected m-coverage problem.

The rest of the paper is organized as follows. In section 2 we present related works. Section 3 describes network model and problems studied in this paper. Section 4 and 5 propose two heuristics for m-coverage and k-connected m-coverage problem respectively . Section 6 describes the simulations and section 7 concludes the paper.

2 Related Works

There are many studies on the coverage problem ([1-5 etc.]) in WSNs. Different formulations of the coverage problem have been proposed, depending on the subject to be covered (area versus discrete points) [4,5], the sensor deployment mechanism (random versus deterministic [6]), as well as other wireless sensor network properties (e.g. network connectivity and minimum energy consumption). For energy efficient area coverage, the works in [7] and [8] consider a large population of sensors, deployed randomly for area monitoring.

Zhang and Hou [9] prove an important, but intuitive result that if the communication range Rc is at least twice the sensing range Rs, a complete coverage of a convex area implies connectivity of the working nodes. They further discuss the case of Rc > Rs. Wang et al [10] generalize the result in [9]. Wu and Yang [11] propose two density control models for energy conserving protocol in sensor networks, using the adjustable sensing range of several levels. Zhou et al [12,13] address the problem of selecting a minimum size connected k-cover.

The energy-efficient target coverage problem deals with the problem of covering a set of targets with minimum energy cost [1,6,14]. Cardei and Du [1] address the target coverage problem where the disjoint sets are modeled as disjoint set covers, such that every cover completely monitors all the target points. Cardei et. [14] propose an approach different from [1] by not requiring the sensor sets to be disjoint and by allowing sensors to participate in multiple sets, and design two heuristics that efficiently compute the sets, using linear programming and a greedy approach.

Alam[15] et al consider coverage and connectivity in 3-Dimensional networks. Liu [16,17,18] et al consider maximal lifetime scheduling for sensor surveillance systems with k sensors to 1 target. In these papers, they assume each sensor watch at most a target and each target is watched by at least k sensor.

In [19] we addressed the k-connected coverage problem for targets. In this paper we extend our work [19] to k-connected m-coverage problem. Our model is different from [16-18], in our model, a sensor may watch all targets in its sensing range.

3   Network Model and Problem Specification

In this section, we formulate the target m-coverage problem and the k-connected m-coverage problem addressed in this paper.

Let us assume that n sensors $v_1, v_2, \ldots v_n$ are deployed in a region to monitor t targets $I_1, I_2, \ldots I_t$. Each node v_i has a sensing region $S(v_i)$ and communication range R. Any target inside $S(v_i)$ is cover by v_i. v_i can directly communicate with v_j if their Euclidian distance is less than communication range R. Consequently, the sensor nodes in the communication network can form a undirected graph $G=(V, E)$, where $V = \{v_1, v_2, \ldots v_n\}$ is a set of sensor nodes and E is a set of edges (i, j). Without loss of generality, assume $T = \{I_1, I_2, \ldots I_t\}$ to be a given set of targets. For each sensor $v \in V$, there is a subset T_v of $T = \{I_1, I_2, \ldots I_t\}$, which is covered by v. Note that the targets are different from the sensor nodes.

The graph is k-connected if there are k node-disjoint paths between any pair of nodes. A set of sensors $C \subseteq V$ is said to be m-coverage if each target in T is covered by at least m distinct sensor nodes in C.

In order to reduce the energy consumption, our work is to minimize the number of sensor nodes.

Thus, the problem studied in this paper can be now formally defined as follows:

m-coverage problem: Given a graph $G=(V, E)$ and a set of targets T, we want to find a minimal number of sensor nodes in V, where these nodes form a m-coverage for targets.

k-connected m-coverage problem: Given a graph $G=(V, E)$ and a set of targets T, we want to find a minimal number of sensor nodes in V, where these nodes form a m-coverage for targets and the subgraph induced by these nodes is k-connected.

4   Approximation Algorithms to m-Coverage Problem

In this section, we will first investigate an introductory problem, namely m-coverage problem, of the k-connected m-coverage problem. This problem is NP-hard as it is a generalization of set cover, which is already known to be NP-hard. We present two heuristics for m-coverage problem. We first model the m-coverage problem as Integer Programming in section 4-A, and then use the relaxation technique to design a linear programming based heuristic in section 4-B. Next, we propose a heuristic based on duality rounding and give its approximation ratio in section 4-C.

A. Integer programming Formulation of the m-coverage problem

We formulate the m-coverage problem as follows:

Given:

n: The total number of sensor nodes; t: The total number of targets;

j: Indicator for sensor nodes, $j \in [1,n]$; i: Indicator for targets, $i \in [1,t]$.

$$a_{ij} = \begin{cases} 1 & \text{if target } i \text{ is covered by sensor } j; \\ 0 & \text{otherwise} \end{cases}$$

Variable:

$$x_j = \begin{cases} 1 & \text{if } j \text{ is selected for } m \text{ - coverage;} \\ 0 & \text{otherwise} \end{cases}$$

The m-coverage problem then can be formulated as 0-1 programming as follows:

ILP:

$$Z_1 = Min \sum_{j=1}^{n} x_j \tag{1}$$

subject to:

$$\sum_{j=1}^{n} a_{ij} x_j \ge m \quad i \in [1,t] \tag{2}$$

$$x_j = 0 \text{ or } 1 \quad j \in [1,n] \tag{3}$$

B. LP heuristic

This heuristic is a two-stage algorithm. At the first stage, an optimal solution for a linear programming (LP) relaxation of the ILP is computed. The obtained solution to LP may be fractional, so it may not satisfy the integer constraint (3). At the second stage, a greedy algorithm is employed to find an integral solution based on the optimal solution obtained at the first stage.

LP Heuristic:

Input: n sensor nodes and t targets

Output: m-coverage for targets

Formulate m-coverage problem as ILP, and relax ILP to LP

Compute an optimal solution $\{x_j^*\}$ and make an decreasing order $x_1^* \ge x_2^* \ge .... \ge x_n^*$;

For j=1 to n

$\quad x_j = 0$

For j=1 to n

$\quad$ If $\{v_1, v_2, ... v_{j-1}\}$ is not m-coverage, then

$\quad\quad x_j = 1$

$\quad\quad j = j+1$

We have seen that in the above heuristic, the optimal solution to a linear programming relaxation is employed to find out the priority of variables being assigned with 1. There is a disadvantage with this approach: Computing the optimal solution takes $O(n^{3.5})$ time for LP of n variables [20]. It is the main portion of the total computation time for this heuristic. In order to reduce the computational time and improve the quality of output solution, we will design another heuristic by applying rounding by duality.

C. Heuristic based on rounding by duality

To simplify the description of this heuristic, we consider the primal form of linear programming (PLP).

PLP

$$Z_2 = Min\sum_{j=1}^{n} c_j x_j \tag{4}$$

subject to

$$\sum_{j=1}^{n} a_{ij} x_j \geq b_i \qquad i \in [1,t] \tag{5}$$

$$0 \leq x_j \leq 1 \qquad j \in [1,n] \tag{6}$$

Where a_{ij} is 1 or 0, $b = (m,m,....,m)^T$ in which there are t's m. $c = (1,1,.....,1)$ in which there is n's 1. $x^T = (x_1, x_2, ..., x_n)$ is variable vector. The dual of the above linear programming is DLP, and $y^T = (y_1, y_2, ..., y_t)$, $z^T = (z_1, z_2, ..., z_n)$ are dual variable vector.

We use a two-stage algorithm to find an approximation solution for it. First, a feasible solution is obtained for the Dual Linear Programming problem (DLP). The corresponding solution for the Primal form (PLP) is obtained by the rounding procedure:

The formal description of the algorithm is given below:

Heuristic based on rounding by duality

```
Initially, set x⁰=0, (y⁰, z⁰)=(0,0), k=0 // x⁰ , y⁰, z⁰
                                          are vectors
```

While x^k is not prime feasible **do begin**

Set $J(k) = \{j \mid x_j^k = 0\}$;

Set $I(k) = \{i \mid \sum_{j=1}^{n} a_{ij} x_j^k \leq b_i - 1\}$;

Choose $r \in J(k)$ such that

$$\frac{c_r - \sum_{i=1}^{t} a_{ir} y_i^r}{\sum_{i \in I(k)} a_{ir}} = \alpha = \min_{j \in J}\left\{\frac{c_j - \sum_{i=1}^{t} a_{ij} y_i}{\sum_{i \in I(k)} a_{ij}} \mid c_j - \sum_{i=1}^{t} a_{ij} y_i \geq 0\right\}$$

Set $x_j^{k+1} = x_j^k$ if $j \neq r$ and $x_r^{k+1} = 1$;

Set $y_i^{k+1} = y_i^k + \alpha$ if $i \in I(k)$ and $y_i^{k+1} = y_i^k$ if $i \notin I(k)$

Set $z_j^{k+1} = \max(\sum_{i=1}^{t} a_{ij} y_i^{k+1} - c_j, 0)$;

$k \leftarrow k+1$;

end-while

Output x^k with $Z_{1A} = \sum_{j=1}^{n} c_j x_j^k$

Theorem. The performance ratio of heuristic based on rounding by duality is $f = \max_{1 \leq i \leq t} \sum_{j=1}^{n} a_{ij}$, and the time complexity is $O(n^2)$.

5 Approximation Algorithm for k-Connected m-Coverage Problem

In this section, we address the k-connected m-coverage problem which is NP-hard because m-coverage problem is NP-hard. We will design two heuristic algorithms. One is called as kmTS algorithm, the other is called kmReverse algorithm.

A. kmTS algorithm: The main idea of kmTS algorithm is that the algorithm includes two steps: the first step is to construct a m-coverage of targets; The second step is to increase small size nodes to this m-coverage such that the subgraph by these increased nodes and nodes of m-coverage is k-connected. For the first step, we may use the algorithms in section 4 to get an approximation for m-coverage problem. For the second step, we may use our algorithms [19] to get solution for k-connected m-coverage problem.

kmTS Algorithm: Construct an approximate solution for k-connected m-coverage

Input: Given $G = (V, E)$, a set T of targets, and $T_v, \forall v \in V$, which is a subset of T covered by v

Output: k-connected m-coverage for T

(1) Construct m-coverage C for T using m-coverage heuristic.

(2) Connect set C into k-connected subgraph, i.e. finding a subset X of $V-C$ to C such that $G[C \cup X]$ is k-connected subgraph and $|X|$ is minimized.

B. kmReverse algorithm: In the following, we will give another algorithm--reverse algorithm which directly apply Lemma[19]. The main idea of kmReverse algorithm is as follows: initially, each sensor node in the sensor network is active, then, change one active node to inactive node each time if it satisfies two conditions (1) deleting the node, the remain nodes also form a m-coverage (2) any two neighbours of the node has k-node disjoint paths in remain graph after deleting the node.

kmReverse algorithm: Construct an approximate solution

Input: Given $G=(V, E)$, a set T of targets, and $T_v, \forall v \in V$, which is a subset of T covered by v.

Output: k-connected m-coverage for T

1. $V^k := V$;

2. Sort all nodes in V in an increasing order of degree in T as $v_1, v_2, ... v_n$ such that $D_T(v_1) \le D_T(v_2) \le ... \le D_T(v_n)$, where $D_T(v) = |\{r_j \mid r_j \text{ is covered by } v\}|$

3. For $i=1$ to n,

   if $\forall u_1, u_2 \in N(v_i)$, u_1 is k-connected to u_2 in $G[V^k - \{v_i\}]$, and $V^k - \{v_i\}$ is a m-coverage for T, then

   $$V^k = V^k - \{v_i\}$$

   $$i := i + 1$$

6   Performance Evaluation

In this section we evaluate the performance of proposed algorithms. We simulate a stationary network with sensor nodes and target points randomly located in a 500×500 area. We assume the sensing range is equal for all the sensors in the network, and the communicating range is also equal for all the sensors in the network. In the simulation we consider the following tunable parameters:

- N, the number of sensor nodes, which varies between 40 and 80.
- M, the number of targets to be covered, which varies between 10 and 26.
- R, the communicating range which varies between 120 to 200.
- S, the sensing range, which varies between 70 and 110.

The simulation is conducted in a 500×500 2-D free-space by independently and uniformly allocating N nodes and M targets. All nodes have the same transmission range R. And all nodes have the same sensing range S. For any pair of nodes, if the distance between the two nodes is no more than the value of transmission range R, there exists an edge between the two nodes. For any sensor node and any target, if the distance between the sensor and the target is no more than the value of sensing range, the target is covered by the sensor node. We present averages of 100 separate runs for each result shown in figures. In each run of the simulations, for given N and M, we randomly place N nodes in the square, and randomly place M nodes as targets. Any topology which is not connected or targets are not covered by all sensor nodes is discarded.

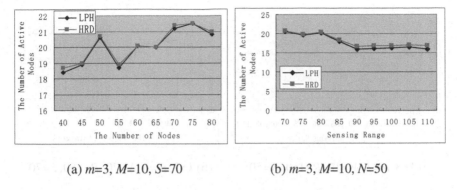

(a) $m=3$, $M=10$, $S=70$ (b) $m=3$, $M=10$, $N=50$

Fig. 1. The number of active nodes with the number of nodes, sensing range

In the first experiment, we simulate the proposed LP Heuristic (LPH) and Heuristic based on rounding by duality(HRD) for m-coverage problem. The results show the performances of the two heuristics are close from Fig.1 and Fig. 2.

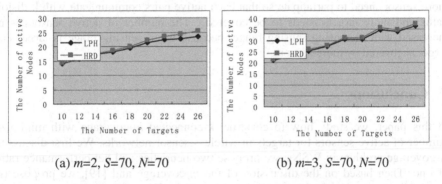

(a) $m=2$, $S=70$, $N=70$ (b) $m=3$, $S=70$, $N=70$

Fig. 2. The number of active nodes with number of targets

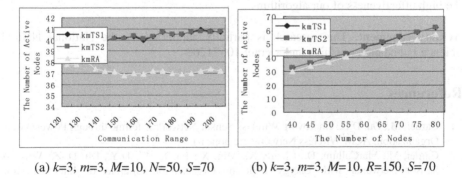

(a) $k=3$, $m=3$, $M=10$, $N=50$, $S=70$ (b) $k=3$, $m=3$, $M=10$, $R=150$, $S=70$

Fig. 3. The number of active nodes with comm. range, the number of nodes

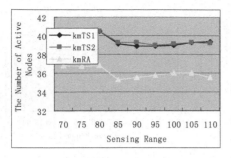
(a) $k=3$, $m=3$, $M=10$, $R=150$, $N=50$

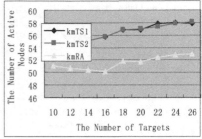
(b) $k=3$, $m=3$, $N=70$, $R=150$, $S=70$

Fig. 4. The number of active nodes with sensing range, the number of targets

In the second experiment, we simulate the proposed kmTS and kmRA and compare their performances. We call kmTS$_1$ and kmTS$_2$ when kmTS using LPH and HRD respectively. The simulation results are shown in Fig.3 and Fig.4. The number of active nodes increases with the number of sensors and the number of targets, as more sensors need to participate so that each active pairs communicate with k-disjoint paths and more targets needs to be covered. The number of active sensors is not increased with increasing sensing range, because when sensing range is larger each target is covered by more sensors.

7   Conclusions

In this paper, we study how to construct k-connected m-coverage with minimized number of active sensors for targets in wireless sensor networks. We first discuss the m-coverage problem in WSNs, we propose two heuristics and get performance ration of one. Then based on the discussion of the m-coverage and [19], we propose two heuristics to construct k-connected m-coverage. We also carry out extensive simulations for our algorithms and the obtained simulation results have demonstrated the high effectiveness of our algorithms.

Acknowledgement. This research is partially supported by the National Natural Science Foundation of China under grant 10671208.

References

1. Cardei, M., Du, D.Z.: Improving Wireless Sensor Network Lifetime through Power Aware Organization. ACM Wireless Networks (to appear)
2. Cardei, M., MarCallum, D., Cheng, X., Min, X., Jia, X., Li, D.Y., Du, D.-Z.: Wireless Sensor Networks with Energy Efficient Organization. Journal of Interconnection Networks 3(3-4), 213–229 (2002)
3. Cardei, M., Wu, J.: Energy-Efficient Coverage Problems in Wireless Ad Hoc Sensor Networks. Journal of Computer Communications on Sensor Networks (to appear)

4. Li, X., Wan, P., Wang, Y., Frieder, O.: Coverage in Wireless Ad-hoc Sensor Networks. IEEE Transactions on Computers 52(6), 753–763 (2003)
5. Meguerdichian, S., Koushanfar, F., Potkonjak, M., Srivastava, M.B.: Coverage Problems in Wireless Ad-hoc Sensor Networks. In: Proc. of INFOCOM'01, pp. 1380–1387 (2001)
6. Kar, K., Banerjee, S.: Node Placement for Connected Coverage in Sensor Networks. In: Proc. of WiOpt 2003 (2003)
7. Slijepcevic, S., Potkonjak, M.: Power Efficient Organization of Wireless Sensor Networks. In: Proc. of IEEE International Conference on Communications, vol. 2, pp. 472–476 (2001)
8. Huang, C., Tseng, Y.: The Coverage Problem in a Wireless Sensor Network. In: WSNA'03, September 19, 2003, San Diego, California, USA (2003)
9. Zhang, H., Hou, J.C.: Maintaining Sensing Coverage and Connectivity in Large Sensor Networks. In: NSF International workshop on Theoretical and algorithmic Aspects of sensor, Ad Hoc Wireless and Peer-to-Peer Networks (February 2004)
10. Wang, X., Xing, G., Zhang, Y., Lu, C., Pless, V., Gill, C.D.: Integrated Coverage and Connectivity Configuration in Wireless Sensor Networks. In: Proc. of the First ACM Conference on Embedded Networked Sensor Systems, ACM Press, New York (2003)
11. Wu, J., Yang, S.: Energy-Efficient Node Scheduling Models in Sensor Networks with Adjustable Ranges. International Journal of Foundations of Computer Science (February 2005)
12. Zhou, Z., Das, S., Gupta, H.: Connected K-Coverage Problem in Sensor Networks. In: ICCCN 2004, pp. 373–378 (2004)
13. Zhou, Z., Das, S., Gupta, H.: Fault Tolerant Connected Sensor Cover with Variable Sensing and Transmission Ranges. In: IEEE SECON 2005 (2005)
14. Cardei, M., Thai, M., Li, Y., Wu, W.: Energy-Efficient Traget Coverage in Wireless Sensor Networks. In: INFOCOM 2005 (2005)
15. Alam, S.: Coverage and connectivity in Three-Dimensional Networks. In: MobiCom'06, pp. 346–357 (2006)
16. Liu, H., Wan, P., Jia, X., Makki, S., Pissinou, N.: Maximal Lifetime Scheduling in Sensor Surveillance Networks. In: IEEE INFOCOM'05, Miami (March 2005)
17. Liu, H., Wan, P., Jia, X.: Maximal Lifetime Scheduling for Sensor Surveillance Systems with K Sensors to 1 Target. IEEE Trans on Parallel and Distributed Systems 17(12), 1526–1536 (2006)
18. Liu, H., Jia, X., Wan, P., Yi, C., Makki, S., Pissinou, N.: Maximizing Lifetime of Sensor Surveillance Systems. IEEE/ACM Transactions on Networking (Accepted)
19. Li, D., Cao, J., Liu, M., Zheng, Y.: K-connected Coverage Problem in Wireless Sensor Networks. In: COCOA2007 (2007)
20. Schrijver, A.: Theory of linear and integer programming (1985)

A Novel Multiple Access Protocol with QoS Support for Mobile Ad Hoc Networks

Dapeng Wang, Kai Liu, Lianzhen Cheng, and Yan Zhang

School of Electronics and Information Engineering,
Beijing University of Aeronautics and Astronautics, 100083 Beijing, China
bjwdp@sina.com, liuk@buaa.edu.cn, clz_tea@sina.com,
hiyanzy@yahoo.com.cn

Abstract. Based on the concept of random contention and collision resolution, a QoS-based multiple access (QMA) protocol for ad hoc networks is proposed to support multimedia service and multi-hop architecture. In this paper, the traffic is divided into two groups with different QoS requirements, namely real-time traffic and non real-time traffic. According to the protocol, nodes with real-time traffic have higher priority to access channel than those with non real-time traffic by broadcasting forecast bursts (FB) in earlier contention slots. Meanwhile, real-time traffic is scheduled according to its delay and the earliest deadline first (EDF) principle. Through simulations, it is shown that the QMA protocol outperforms the Carrier Sensing Multiple Access with Collision Avoidance (CSMA/CA) protocol in terms of throughput, message discard rate and average packet delay, and the QMA protocol can provide differentiated QoS guarantees for traffic in multi-hop networks.

Keywords: mobile ad hoc network, multiple access protocol, QoS, collision resolution, forecast burst.

1 Introduction

A mobile ad hoc network consists of a collection of mobile nodes without a fixed infrastructure, and it aims to set up and maintain a network for the nodes to communicate directly with each other. Medium access control (MAC) protocols are used for multiple nodes to share scarce bandwidth in an orderly and efficient manner.

Currently, there are many MAC protocols proposed for ad hoc networks, which can be classified into two categories: random access and on-demand assignment. In random access protocols, a node with data packets usually senses shared channel for a certain duration before packet transmission. If the channel is busy, the node waits for a random period and tries again at a later time. If the channel is idle, it makes an attempt to access the channel. A collision resolution mechanism is used to solve possible packet collisions in an orderly manner. Typical random access protocol is CSMA/CA coupled with request to send/clear to send (RTS/CTS) handshake in the distribution coordination function (DCF) of IEEE 802.11 MAC protocol [1]. Compared with the CSMA/CA without handshake, it decreases transmission collisions from the transmission time of long data packet to that of RTS mini-packet

K. Li et al. (Eds.): NPC 2007, LNCS 4672, pp. 260–266, 2007.

mostly due to hidden nodes, which are defined as nodes that are outside the communication range of the transmitter but inside the communication range of the receiver. However, its throughput still decreases drastically due to the increase of packet collisions when the total offered load is heavy [2, 3]. On the other hand, the on-demand assignment protocols generally use a central control point to assign channel resources for its neighbor nodes through reservation or polling mechanisms, such as point coordination function (PCF) of IEEE 802.11 protocol [1] and distributed packet reservation multiple access (D-PRMA) protocol [4]. However, their overhead and packet delay will increase when a large number of nodes have no packets to transmit.

To support multimedia traffic in fully distributed wireless ad hoc networks, quality of service (QoS) support in MAC layer is a very challenging issue. Generally, the existing QoS protocols achieve service differentiation by assigning different classes of traffic with different contention related parameters. For instance, enhanced distributed coordination function (EDCF) of IEEE 802.11e protocol [5] provides 4 access categories (AC) and 8 priorities, which are supported by assigning different contention window sizes and interframe spaces. However, the delay of high-priority packets is not bounded under heavy load in multi-hop networks, because high-priority packets may be blocked by alternate transmissions of low-priority packets within 2-hop range, and unbounded delay for initiating an RTS/CTS dialogue cannot guarantee the delay of all the real-time packets. To solve these problems, many improved protocols based on IEEE 802.11 series have been presented. Yang proposes an algorithm in [6] which adapts initial back-off window size to guarantee QoS requirements in the IEEE 802.11 one-hop networks. QPART [7] uses contention window adaptation parameters based on service differentiation to provide QoS-aware scheduling for multi-hop ad hoc networks, and ensures that the resource requirements of admitted real-time traffic are smaller than the network capacity. In [8] Collision Avoidance Interval (CAI) is defined instead of Network Allocation Vector (NAV) used in IEEE 802.11, because NAV is too short for a collision to be prevented in the carrier sensing zone. Besides IEEE 802.11 and its improved protocols, some new competition schemes have been proposed. In Hiperlan protocol [9], nodes broadcast bursts to contend in different slots according to the priority and delay of packets. According to Priority Binary Countdown (PBC) scheme [10], each node selects an appropriate competition number (CN) as signals to contend, which is composed of priority number part, random number part and ID number part. In each bit-slot of CN, a node whose CN value is 1 transmits a short signal, on the other hand, a node whose CN value is 0 keeps silent and senses channel whether there is any signal. If it finds the slot is busy, it loses the competition; otherwise, it survives and remains in the competition. So only the node that survives all the bit-slots is allowed to transmit control messages. However, the mechanism assumes all competing nodes are synchronized and start transmitting CN signal in the same slot. It is hard to realize in the distributed networks.

In order to meet the demand of efficient medium accessing in multi-hop ad hoc networks, we propose a QoS-based multiple access (QMA) protocol, which implements forecast bursts (FB) with priorities to achieve random contention access, collision resolution and the QoS guarantee for different traffic. The rest of this paper is organized as follows. In section 2, we provide the network model. The QMA protocol is presented in section 3. Section 4 discusses simulations and the results. We conclude the paper in section 5.

2 Network Model

The QMA protocol is based on carrier sensing networks. In [8], it states the range covered by the power necessary for transmitting a packet from a transmitter has two disjoint areas, named transmission range and carrier sensing zone. Within the transmission range, a node can sense and decode a signal correctly, whereas a node can sense but can not decode it correctly in the carrier sensing zone. Usually the carrier sensing range is more than twice of the transmission range. Therefore, a node can overhear the channel within its 2-hop transmission range by judging radio signal strength, in another word, the node in its MAC layer can judge whether the other nodes within its 2-hop range are transmitting or not to avoid a possible collision. As a result, the hidden terminal problem is solved in the QMA protocol.

3 Proposed QMA Protocol

In the QMA protocol, channel access cycle is divided into contention phase and transmission phase, and a node must sense the medium for a time interval T_{win} before accessing. If the channel is idle, the node is allowed to start contention phase; otherwise, it defers to wait for another attempt. The contention phase consists of $(n+m)$ mini slots, each T_{slot} ($T_{slot}<T_{win}$) long. Among them the former n slots are assigned to the nodes with real-time traffic to contend by broadcasting FBs ($T_{FB}=T_{slot}$), and the latter m slots are assigned to the nodes with non real-time traffic. Therefore, the nodes with non real-time traffic are allowed to broadcast FBs only on condition that all the former n slots for real-time traffic are idle. In this way, the requirements of real-time traffic are guaranteed prior to that of non real-time traffic. If a node senses the first B slots idle, it will start broadcasting k·FBs from the Bth slot in this contention phase. Otherwise, it stops contending and performs back-off. B is a random variable with a truncated geometric distribution. For the nodes that have real-time traffic, B is a random variable as follows:

$$\Pr(B=b) = \begin{cases} (1-q)q^b & 0 \le b < n \\ q^n & b = n \end{cases}$$

For the nodes that have non real-time traffic, B is a random variable as follows:

$$\Pr(B=b) = \begin{cases} (1-q)q^b & n \le b < n+m \\ q^m & b = n+m \end{cases}$$

In which, q is decided by the category and delay of the packet. The k is related to delay of packets according to the EDF principle, i.e., k is adjusted dynamically and the packet with earliest deadline has the largest k.

After broadcasting FBs, the node will sense the channel for the duration of T_{obs} ($T_{obs}=T_{slot}$). If the channel is sensed as busy during the T_{obs} interval, there must be at least one node with higher priority packet trying to access, so that the node has to perform back-off. Otherwise, if the channel is sensed as being idle, the node will win the contention and start transmission in the next transmission phase. The intended receiver will reply an acknowledgement (ACK) packet after receiving the packet correctly. As shown in Fig. 1, node A and B start broadcasting FBs in the same slot in the contention phase, while node C intends to start broadcasting FBs in the latter slot according to the priority and delay of its packet. Hence the node C senses the channel busy before it broadcasts FBs, and it stops contending and performs back-off. For the other two nodes, node A broadcasts more FBs than node B; therefore node A wins the contention and sends a packet in the transmission phase, while node B also performs back-off.

The above discussion illustrates that the nodes are allowed to broadcast FBs on condition that the channel is sensed as idle during first B slots in contention phase. This algorithm guarantees only the nodes which start broadcasting FBs in the same slot can become candidates in contention phase, and the node that broadcasts the most FB packets wins the contention and accesses the channel successfully. Since a packet with the highest priority and the earliest deadline results in the most FBs, the node with the packet will get to access the channel and transmit the packet at once.

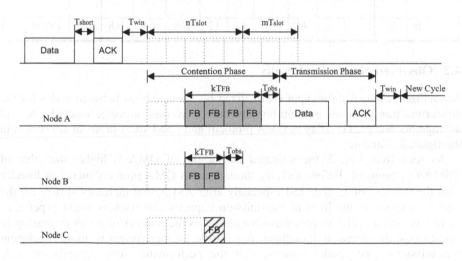

Tshort: short interval time Tslot: micro slot time Twin: sensing window time TFB: forecast burst time Tobs: observation time

Fig. 1. An Example of QMA Protocol

4 Performance Evaluation

4.1 Simulation Environment

To evaluate the effectiveness of QMA's QoS support, we compare the performance of QMA protocol with CSMA/CA protocol using the OPNET modeler. The simulation has modeled a network of N nodes randomly placed in an area named as A. The transmission radius is R, and hence, the receivers can sense the channel in a 2-hop transmission range (i.e., 2R). Assume that message generation process follows Poisson process with average arrival rate λ, and the number of data packets (PKT) per message follows truncated geometric distribution with the maximum number L_M and probability parameter q_{PKT}. The retransmission limit is L. Respectively, L_{FB} and L_{PKT} are the lengths of FB packets and data packets. The parameter q of random variable B is a constant for simplicity in simulations. The number of FB packets is k (0<k≤n), k∝D/D_{max}, in which D_{max} is the lifetime of the packet. The detailed parameters in QMA protocol simulations are set in Table. 1. Meanwhile, the simulation of CSMA/CA protocol is set in the same scenario with 40 nodes. For a good performance, the lengths of data packet and ACK packet in CSMA/CA are set to 4 kbits and 40 bits, and sensing interval is 0.1 ms.

Table 1. Simulation Parameters of QMA Protocol

Scenario		Channel	Message			Intervals					Packet		
A /km²	R /km	Data rate /(Mb/s)	L_M	q_{PKT}	m	n	T_{win} /us	T_{slot} /us	q	L_{FB} /bit	L_{PKT} /bit	L
50×50	10	2	40	0.95	12	12	268	64	0.8	128	18500	7

4.2 Observed Simulation Results

Normalized channel throughput (normalized by average hops between nodes for the concurrent transmissions in multi-hop networks), average message discard rate and average per hop packet delay of QMA protocol and CSMA/CA protocol are shown in the figure 2, 3 and 4.

As seen from Fig. 2, the saturated throughput of QMA is higher than that of CSMA/CA protocol. Before $\lambda<1$, the throughput of QMA protocol increases lineally with the increase of λ; after $\lambda>1$ especially after $\lambda>1.5$, that increases slowly for the load is reaching to the limit of transmission capacity and packets might experience more contention cycles or retransmissions. And as the number of nodes increasing in simulations, the saturated throughput rises a little for there might be more concurrent transmissions. The results illustrate that the performance also depends on node density in multi-hop networks.

In the Fig.3, the CSMA/CA protocol which uses shorter data packet has a lower average message discard rate than QMA protocol when offered load is low. With the increase of offered load, nodes in both protocols suffer from more collisions and more dropped messages due to overtime or the limit of retransmission times. Compared with CSMA/CA protocol, the QMA protocol has a better performance when offered load is high, because the contention of FB guarantees that only one node among many competitors can successfully get to access and transmit its packet without collision.

The Fig. 4 shows average per hop packet delay of real-time and non real-time traffic with different nodes. The CSMA/CA protocol has a better performance when

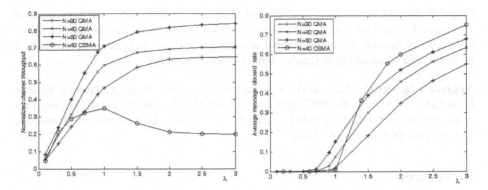

Fig. 2. Normalized Channel Throughput   **Fig. 3.** Average Message Discard Rate

$\lambda<1$, because nodes can send packets after sensing a short interval. However, the increase of collisions and back-off time deteriorates average packet delay drastically when offered loads become larger. In QMA protocol, even though the delay increases with load increasing, the delay of real-time packets is guaranteed and bounded in 1 s because the real-time packets access prior to non real-time packets in contentions. Before offered load reaching to the transmission capacity, the average delay of real-time packets remains very low while the delay of non real-time packets is increasing. In another word, the QMA protocol guarantees QoS of real-time packets with the price of the delay of non real-time packets.

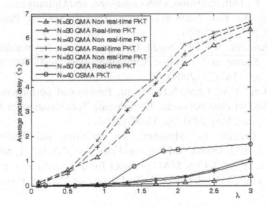

Fig. 4. Average per Hop Packet Delay

5   Conclusions

In this paper, the QMA protocol supporting multimedia service and multi-hop architecture is proposed for mobile ad hoc networks, which integrates the concepts of contention reservation and collision resolution. The nodes contend to access the channel by broadcasting FBs before packet transmission. Therefore, the QMA protocol can decrease the possibility of data packet collision and support QoS guarantee for the real-time traffic. The simulation results have shown that the QMA protocol can provide effective channel sharing for nodes compared with CSMA/CA protocol, and guarantee QoS requirements for different traffic.

Acknowledgements. This work was supported by the National Nature Science Foundation of China (No.10577005 and No.60625102), the National Defense Pre-Research Project (No.513250403), and the Innovation Foundation of Aerospace Science and Technology of China.

References

1. IEEE Standard for Wireless LAN Medium Access Control (MAC) and Physical Layer (PHY) Specifications (1999)
2. Chen, Y., Zeng, Q.A., Agrawal, D.P.: Performance analysis and enhancement for IEEE 802.11 MAC protocol. In: Proc. IEEE ICT 2003 vol. 4, pp. 860–867 (2003)
3. Xu, S., Saadawi, T.: Does the IEEE802.11 MAC protocol work well in multihop wireless ad hoc networks? IEEE Commun. Mag. 39(6), 130–137 (2001)
4. Yun, L.: D-PRMA: A Novel MAC Mechanism Supporting Resource Reservation for Wireless Ad Hoc Networks. Journal of Electronics & Information Technology 27(6), 967–972 (2005)
5. Hayoung, Y., JongWon, K., DongYun, S.: Dynamic Admission Control in IEEE 802.11e EDCA-based Wireless Home Network. In: Consumer Communications and Networking Conference, vol. V1, pp. 55–59 (2006)
6. Xiao, Y., Pan, Y.: Differentiation, QoS Guarantee, and Optimization for Real-Time Traffic over One-Hop Ad Hoc Networks. IEEE Transactions on Parallel and Distributed Systems 16(6), 538–549 (2005)
7. Yaling, Y., Kravets, R.: Distributed QoS guarantees for realtime traffic in ad hoc networks. In: Sensor and Ad Hoc Communications and Networks (IEEE SECON), October 2004, pp. 118–127 (2004)
8. Choi, W.C., Lee, Y.S., Rhee, S.H., et al.: End-to-end performance improvements for multi-hop ad-hoc wireless networks. In: Software Technologies for Future Embedded and Ubiquitous Systems, May 2004, pp. 53–57 (2004)
9. Anastasi, G., Lenzini, L., Mingozzi, E.: Stability and Performance Analysis of HIPERLAN. In: IEEE INFOCOM '98, San Francisco, CA, vol. 1, pp. 134–141 (1998)
10. Yeh, C.H., You, T.A.: A QoS MAC protocol for differentiated service in mobile ad hoc networks. In: The 2003 International Conference on Parallel Processing (ICPP'03), pp. 349–356 (2003)

Dual-Residue Montgomery Multiplication

Anding Wang, Yier Jin, and Shiju Li

College of Information Science & Engineering
Zhejiang University, Hangzhou, China
anding_704@hotmail.com, jinyier@gmail.com

Abstract. The paper introduces a new approach based on dual residue system to compute Montgomery multiplication. The novelty of this proposal is that we import an extra Montgomery residue system with new transformation constant beside the normal one. In this way, one of the multiplicand can be divided into two parts and both higher and lower parts are calculated in parallel to speed up computation. Then two implementations in hardware are proposed for the algorithm. In parallel architecture, the proposed algorithm can perform nearly twice speedup compared to normal Montgomery method. And in pipeline architecture, the computation speed can be even faster. Besides speeding up calculation the extra merit of our proposal is that the multiplier can partial replace Montgomery multiplier used nowadays without any changes on top architecture.

Keywords: Dual residue system, Montgomery algorithm, Parallelism.

1 Introduction

Modular multiplication is one of the basic computations which are widely used in public-key cryptography, especially in RSA algorithm [11], Diffie-Hellman key exchange algorithm [3], elliptic curve cryptography(ECC) and digital signature algorithm(DSA) [14]. Compared to other computation such as modular addition, modular multiplication costs much more time, so low-complexity algorithms and their high-efficient implementations both in hardware and software have been studied for a long time.

In the aspect of algorithm improvement, several methods are proposed to simplify divisions or to avoid trial divisions. Among them, two approaches are of major concentration: One is based on the interleaved modular multiplication algorithm, and the other is based on the Montgomery algorithm [5]. The former's strategy is to simplify the division by finding the quotient early and then to get modular result. Barrett modified this algorithm by getting approximate result first according to a finely selected radix $b = 2^L$ (L equals to two times of the length of modulus), and then subtract modulus in less than two times as Barrett's algorithm [2]. The latter's strategy avoids division by adding multiples of modulus in order to make lower bits of product zero. It leverages pre-computation which transforms operators into residue system to simplify the operation.

K. Li et al. (Eds.): NPC 2007, LNCS 4672, pp. 267–276, 2007.

Among these algorithms, it has been proved that the Montgomery method is better in most cases. However, each step in Montgomery Algorithm depends on the previous step's result that means this algorithm cannot be operated in parallel. Although Koc proposed a new architecture which can improve parallelism in reconfigurable hardware implementation, this modification just change the implementation form not the algorithm itself [16].

In this paper, we proposes a method that explores the parallelism of Montgomery algorithm itself to further boost speed. The point of this improvement in parallel comes from splitting normal residue system into dual-residue system modulo M. Since n-word modulus M is always an odd integer in cryptography application, an integer R which is coprime to M in normal Montgomery algorithm is often set $R_n = r^n$ where r is an s-bit word. Then we choose appropriate integers a and b which fulfill $a + b = n$. The novelty of our proposal is that we import an extra residue system with transformation constant $R_b = r^b$ beside the formal residue system where $R_n = r^n$. As $b < n$, the transformation constant R_b is less than the modulus M, similar to Kaihara and Takagi's new representation [5]. This extra residue system enables the splitting of one multiplier into higher part and lower part and each part can be computed in parallel. Both operations are processed under Montgomery algorithm except for different residues. Since parameters a and b can be chosen from 0 to $n - 1$, the variation of b covers all possibilities of the new residues with different performances. In the result showed below, we find when b is slightly larger than $\lceil n/2 \rceil$, the speed up is close to twice than that of normal Montgomery algorithm.

Further advantage is that the inputs and outputs on the top level of this new method are the same as normal Montgomery algorithm, so the implementation of this method no matter in hardware or in software can take place of Montgomery multiplier without any changes in high level. And even advanced, our proposal can make use of all improvements made for Montgomery algorithm up to date.

2   Montgomery Algorithm

Montgomery modular multiplication was first proposed by P.L. Montgomery in 1985 [4] and was a powerful modular algorithm to deal with arbitrary modulus M. It does not compute modular multiplication straightforward, instead, it leverage some pre-computation to transform multiplicands into residue system by a transformation constant R coprimed to modulus M. The M-residue representation of integers $A, B < M$ are defined as $X = A \cdot R \pmod{M}$, $Y = B \cdot R \pmod{M}$. Although this algorithm works for any R that is coprime to M and is larger than M, it is more useful when R is a power of 2 both in hardware and software implementation. To facilitate the implementation on word based system, we use s-bit word r as radix and let R be a power of r. Because M is often an odd integer in reality, the relative prime condition is fulfilled initially. Let $R = r^n$, the Montgomery multiplication algorithm computes

$$\begin{aligned} C = A \otimes_n B &= ABR^{-1} \bmod M \\ &= ABr^{-n} \bmod M \end{aligned} \tag{1}$$

for n-word integers satisfying the following condition:

$$0 \le A, B < M.$$

If the inputs are X, Y, the result will be

$$C' = XYR^{-1} = A \cdot R \cdot B \cdot R \cdot R^{-1} = ABR \bmod M.$$

The key idea of the Montgomery algorithm is to add an appropriate multiple of M to make the lowest n words of AB equal to 0. As $M = \sum_{i=0}^{n-1} m_i \cdot r^i$, $A = \sum_{i=0}^{n-1} a_i \cdot r^i$, $B = \sum_{i=0}^{n-1} b_i \cdot r^i$ and the word-level Montgomery multiplication algorithm is described below.

Algorithm 1. Word-level Montgomery Modular Multiplication	
Input	$A, B, M, (0 \le A, B < M),$ $(r^{n-1} < M < r^n), (R = r^n), m_0^{-1} (\bmod r)$
Output	$C = A \otimes_n B = ABr^{-n} \bmod M$
	$C := 0$ For $i = 0$ to $n - 1$ $\quad t_i = (c_0 + a_i b_0) m_0^{-1} \bmod r$ $\quad C = (c_i + a_i B + t_i M)/r;$ if $(C > M)$ then $C := C - M$ return C;

The transformation between normal representation and the M-residue representation can also be performed through Montgomery multiplication. X can be computed by multiplying A with $R^2 \bmod M$ in Montgomery algorithm as $X = A \otimes_n R^2 \bmod M = A \cdot R^2 \cdot R^{-1} \bmod M = A \cdot R \bmod M$. The backwards transformation can be performed between X and constant 1 which can be presented as $A = X \otimes_n 1 = A \cdot R \cdot R^{-1}$.

3   Dual-Residue Montgomery Algorithm

In order to speed up the Montgomery multiplication, a new fast method which improves the parallelism of this algorithm is proposed. The novelty of the new algorithm comes from the splitting of M-residue representation into a normal residue representation and a new residue representation. In the new residue representation, the constant R is less than modulus M, a situation that was forbidden in normal Montgomery algorithm. We denote the new constant as R_b which equals to r^b with $b < n$. The computation of modular multiplication can be processed in two residue systems in parallel to improve the processing speed.

According to the Montgomery modular multiplication of two integers with transformation constant $R = r^n$ mentioned in Section 2, the algorithm can be rewritten here with X, Y, the images of A, B, respectively:

$$X \otimes_n Y = XYr^{-n} \bmod M.$$

Our proposal is to achieve this goal with new method other than that in Algorithm 1. First, we split multiplier Y into two parts Y_H and Y_L according to a parameter a, $a < n$, i.e., $Y = Y_H \cdot r^a + Y_L$. Then we define another parameter b equal to $n - a$ to construct a new residue modulus M with transformation constant r^b. It is obviously that in this new residue system the constant r^b is less than modulus M as $b < n$ which is not the case required by Montgomery algorithm. However, we will show the effectiveness of the Montgomery computation in the new residue system later. With these pre-definitions, the Montgomery multiplication modulo M of images X, Y can be computed as follows:

$$X \otimes_n Y = (X \otimes_b Y_H + X \otimes_n Y_L) \bmod M \tag{2}$$

In Equation 2, the left term, $X \otimes_b Y_H$, is calculated using Montgomery algorithm where transformation constant is r^b. The right term, $X \otimes_n Y_L$, is calculated using Montgomery algorithm where the constant is r^n normally. These two calculations are performed in parallel. The split multiplicands Y_H and Y_L are both shorter than Y in length, so they can be performed faster than the NORMAL Montgomery method with unsplit operands. The computation details of $X \otimes_b Y_H$ and $X \otimes_n Y_L$ is described as follows and the computation process of the new Montgomery algorithm is shown in Figure 1.

The correctness of Equation 2 can be defined as following:

$$
\begin{aligned}
&(X \otimes_b Y_H + X \otimes_n Y_L) \bmod M \\
&= (X \cdot Y_H \cdot r^{-b} + X \cdot Y_L \cdot r^{-n}) \bmod M \\
&= X \cdot (Y_H \cdot r^{-n} \cdot r^a + Y_L \cdot r^{-n}) \bmod M \\
&= X \cdot (Y_H \cdot r^a + Y_L) \cdot r^{-n} \bmod M \\
&= X \cdot Y \cdot r^{-n} \bmod M
\end{aligned}
\tag{3}
$$

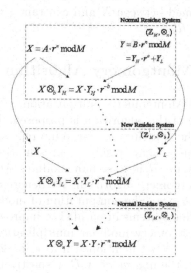

Fig. 1. The Computation process of New Montgomery Algorithm

Here we concentrate on the first term $X \otimes_b Y_H$ where the parameter b should fulfill $(X \cdot Y_H + m \cdot M)/r^b < 2M$, we have $X \cdot Y_H + m \cdot M < M \cdot r^{r-a} + M \cdot 2^b = M \cdot (r^b + r^b) = 2 \cdot M \cdot r^b$, so the only limitation of a and b is that $a + b = r$ and this condition is fulfilled initially.

Since the implementations of Montgomery algorithm can affect the computation performances and in our method, the operands are not of normal form, we pay attention to the selection of algorithms. In [9], Koc introduced several methods to compute Montgomery algorithm in word level and among these approaches, Coarsely Integrated Operand Scanning (CIOS) algorithm is proved to be least complex. Furthermore, CIOS algorithm is much more appropriate than others to implement our proposed dual residue Montgomery algorithm.

For the left term $X \otimes_b Y_H$, operand X is n words long, operand Y_H is b words long and the transformation constant is r^b. So we implement CIOS algorithm by reducing the iteration times in order to simplify the computation using the characteristic of short operand. The CIOS algorithm is showed in Figure 2.

Algorithm 2. CIOS Algorithm with constant r^b

Input	$X, Y_H, M, M'[0] = M^{-1}[0] \bmod r, r^b$
Output	$T = X \cdot Y_H \cdot r^{-b} \bmod M$

$$
\begin{aligned}
&For\ i = 0\ to\ b - 1\{ \\
&\quad C := 0 \\
&\quad For\ j = 0\ to\ n - 1\{ \\
&\quad\quad (C, S) := T[j] + X[j] * Y_H[i] + C \\
&\quad\quad T[j] := S \\
&\quad\} \\
&\quad (C, S) := T[s] + C \\
&\quad T[s] := S \\
&\quad T[s + 1] := C \\
&\quad C := 0 \\
&\quad m := T[0] * M'[0]\ \bmod\ r \\
&\quad (C, S) := T[0] + m * M'[0] \\
&\quad for\ j = 1\ to\ n - 1\{ \\
&\quad\quad (C, S) := T[j] + m * M[j] + C \\
&\quad\quad T[j - 1] := S \\
&\quad\} \\
&\quad (C, S) := T[s] + C \\
&\quad T[s - 1] := S \\
&\quad T[s] := T[s + 1] + C \\
&\}
\end{aligned}
$$

For the right term $X \otimes_r Y_L$, operand X is n words long, operand Y_H is a words long and the constant is r^n. Although one of the operand is shorter than normal operand in Montgomery algorithm, the constant remains r^n which means we cannot directly implement CIOS algorithm mentioned above because the normal form cannot strictly effectively make use of the short-operand and the improvement of speed will be quite restricted. If so, the parallelism of our algorithm will be consumed by poor performance of term $X \otimes_n Y_L$. To avoid this restriction, we modify CIOS algorithm to fit our proposal and the modified CIOS algorithm is listed in Algorithm 3.

Algorithm 3. Modified CIOS Algorithm with constant r^b

Input	$X, Y_L, M, M'[0] = M^{-1}[0] \bmod r, r^b$
Output	$T = X \cdot Y_L \cdot r^{-b} \bmod M$

$$
\begin{aligned}
&For\ i = 0\ to\ b - 1\{\\
&\quad C := 0\\
&\quad For\ j = 0\ to\ n - 1\{\\
&\qquad (C, S) := T[j] + X[j] * Y_L[i] + C\\
&\qquad T[j] := S\\
&\quad \}\\
&\quad (C, S) := T[s] + C\\
&\quad T[s] := S\\
&\quad T[s + 1] := C\\
&\quad C := 0\\
&\quad m := T[0] * M'[0] \bmod r\\
&\quad (C, S) := T[0] + m * M'[0]\\
&\quad for\ j = 1\ to\ n - 1\{\\
&\qquad (C, S) := T[j] + m * M[j] + C\\
&\qquad T[j - 1] := S\\
&\quad \}\\
&\quad (C, S) := T[s] + C\\
&\quad T[s - 1] := S\\
&\quad T[s] := T[s + 1] + C\\
&\quad \}\\
&For\ i = 0\ to\ a - 1\{\\
&\quad C := 0\\
&\quad m := T[0] * M'[0] \bmod r\\
&\quad (C, S) := T[0] + m * M'[0]\\
&\quad for\ j = 1\ to\ n - 1\{\\
&\qquad (C, S) := T[j] + m * M[j] + C\\
&\qquad T[j - 1] := S\\
&\quad \}\\
&\quad (C, S) := T[s] + C\\
&\quad T[s - 1] := S\\
&\quad T[s] := T[s + 1] + C\\
&\quad \}
\end{aligned}
$$

The complete computation of modular multiplication are listed below as Algorithm 4. In this algorithm, X and Y indicate the multiplicands of modular multiplication and Y_H, Y_L are higher and lower parts of Y, respectively. $TMP1$ and $TMP2$ are internal variables which are used to store partial products. $CIOS(X, Y_H)$ is a function whose detail is described in Algorithm 2 and $Modified\_CIOS(X, Y_L)$ make use of algorithm mentioned in Algorithm 3. The initial stage Step 1 transfers multiplicands from memory to register and flushes all the internal variables. Step 2 computes $TMP1$ and $TMP2$ in parallel. The complexity of our algorithm depends on this step and the parallelism depth decides the performance improvement of our proposal compared to normal Montgomery algorithm. Step 3 merges two internal variables together through a modular adder.

Algorithm 4. Dual Residue Montgomery Multiplication

Input	$X, Y, M, (0 \leq X, Y < M),$
	$(r^{n-1} < M < r^n), (R = r^n), M_0^{-1}(\text{mod } r)$
Output	$C = X \otimes_n Y = XYr^{-n} \bmod M$
step 1	$TMP1 := 0;\ TMP2 := 0;\ Y_H = Y/r^a;\ Y_L = Y \bmod r^a;$
step 2	$TMP1 = CIOS(X, Y_H, r^b)$
	$TMP2 = \text{Modified\_CIOS}(X, Y_L, r^n)$
step 3	$C = (TMP1 + TMP2) \bmod M;$

4 Hardware Implementation

4.1 Parallel Architecture

The diagram of multiplier with parallel architecture based on the new Montgomery algorithm are showed in figure 2. It includes six registers, two operation units(CIOS and Modified CIOS) and one modular adder. These six n-word long registers are used to store multiplicands X and Y, modulus M, internal variables $TMP1$ and $TMP2$ and final product C. The CIOS algorithm architecture can be find in [6], although we can make use of any other designs which may be of higher efficiency. In fact, this is one advantage of our algorithm that can make use of any available improvement of Montgomery algorithm no matter in hardware or in software. In the multiplier, input registers which store multiplicands X and Y, modulus M are all barrel registers of n-word width.

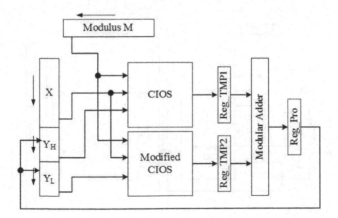

Fig. 2. The diagram of parallel architecture multiplier

In the aspect of area cost, this proposed multiplier requires one more Montgomery multiplier with CIOS architecture, two extra register for internal variables and a modular adder. As the CIOS architecture mentioned in [6] has an internal state machine and the hardware cost is less than other implementations, the extra hardware cost is insignificant.

Transformation between ordinary integers and their residue class representation is also performed in the same multiplier. The forward transformation is to compute modular multiplication of multiplicand A and $R^2(\mathrm{mod}M)$ which can be divided into higher and lower part to fit this multiplier. And backward transformation between X and constant 1 is less complex as the higher part is zero and only the lower part computation is required.

In reality, the division of multiplicand Y according to parameter a is case specific and the process element of CIOS algorithm architecture can be changed in variable environment. For example, the CIOS and Modified CIOS algorithm are of same radix and compute in same sequence, a should be set slightly smaller than $\lceil n/2 \rceil$ in order to achieve most significant performance speedup because the Modified CIOS algorithm requires more computation steps than CIOS algorithm. a should be chosen around $\lceil n/3 \rceil$ when CIOS algorithm runs at radix-2 while the Modified CIOS algorithm based on radix-4 [15].

This architecture is of high attractive when used in cryptography application such as public key cipher RSA. Because the use of our multiplier can reach nearly twice speedup with sequential output which cannot be produced through several independent Montgomery multipliers. Another advantage is that the product of our multiplier is the same as normal Montgomery algorithm although the computation process is different. That means our multiplier can partial replace Montgomery multiplier used nowadays without any change on top architectures. This characteristic provides significant flexibility on time and space trade-off. In the time critical paths, our multiplier can be used to speed up computation while in the area critical occasions normal Montgomery multiplier is used.

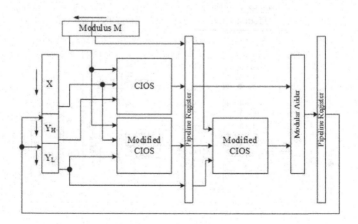

Fig. 3. The diagram of pipeline architecture multiplier

4.2   Pipeline Architecture

In other cryptography applications such as Elliptic Curve Cryptosystem(ECC) [14], the product of multiplier is not used in the next round immediately which differs from that in RSA system. In order to further improve multiplication speed, we introduce an two stages pipeline architecture showed in figure 3.

Compared to parallel architecture, the pipelined one require one more register as pipeline register. The modified CIOS algorithm is performed in two steps which is distributed in two stages. With this architecture, the bipartite multiplier can achieve even higher computation speed, i.e., we set a around $\lceil n/3 \rceil$, the time cost is only one third of normal Montgomery multiplication.

5   Conclusion

In this paper, we proposed a dual-residue method to compute Montgomery algorithm. In this approach, we define two residue systems with one normal transformation constant and another smaller one which assures the splitting of multiplicand and compute partial modular multiplication in parallel under CIOS algorithm or other Montgomery algorithms with low complexity. The implementation in hardware is then presented and two architectures are developed fit for different applications, in which the pipelined one can achieve three times speedup with little extra hardware cost. Further work will be concentrate on converting this method from GF(p) to $GF(2^m)$.

References

1. Knuth, D.E.: The Art of Computer Programming — Seminumerical Algorithm, 3rd edn., vol. 2. Addison-Wesley, Reading (1998)
2. Barrett, P.: Implementing the Rivest Shamir and Adleman public key encryption algorithm on astandard digital signal processor. In: Odlyzko, A.M. (ed.) CRYPTO 1986. LNCS, vol. 263, pp. 311–323. Springer, Heidelberg (1987)
3. Diffie, W., Hellman, M.E.: New Directions in Cryptography. IEEE Trans. Infomation Theory 22(11), 644–654 (1976)
4. Montgomery, P.L.: Modular multiplication without trial division. Mathematics of Computation 44(170), 519–521 (1985)
5. Kaihara, M.E., Takagi, N.: Bipartite Modular Multiplication. In: Rao, J.R., Sunar, B. (eds.) CHES 2005. LNCS, vol. 3659, pp. 201–210. Springer, Heidelberg (2005)
6. McLoone, M., McIvor, C., McCanny, J.V.: Coarsely integrated operand scanning (CIOS) architecture for high-speed Montgomery modular multiplication. In: IEEE International Conference on Field-Programmable Technology(ICFPT'04), pp. 185–191 (2004)
7. Walter, C.D.: Space/Time Trade-Offs for Higher Radix Modular Multiplication Using Repeated Addition. IEEE Trans. Computers 46(2) (1997)
8. Manochehri, K., Pourmozafari, S.: Modified radix-2 Montgomery modular multiplication to make it faster and simpler. In: International Conference on Information Technology: Coding and Computing(ITCC'04), vol. 1, pp. 598–602 (2005)

9. Ko ç, Ç.K., Acar, T., Kaliski Jr., B.S.: Analyzing and comparing Montgomery multiplication algorithms. IEEE Micro 16(3), 26–33 (1996)
10. Chiou-Yng, L., Jenn-Shyong, H., I-Chang, J., Erl-Huei, L.: Low-complexity bit-parallel systolic Montgomery multipliers for special classes of $GF(2^m)$. IEEE Trans. Computers 54(9), 1061–1070 (2005)
11. Rivest, R.L., Shamir, A., Adleman, L.: A method for obtaining digital signatures and public-key cryptosystems. Commum. ACM 21(2), 120–126 (1978)
12. Hars, L.: Long Modular Multiplication for Cryptographic Applications. In: Joye, M., Quisquater, J.-J. (eds.) CHES 2004. LNCS, vol. 3156, pp. 45–61. Springer, Heidelberg (2004)
13. Yanik, T., Savas, E., Koç, Ç.K.: Incomplete reduction in modular arithmetic. IEE Proceedings-Computers and Digital Techniques 149(2), 46–52 (2002)
14. IEEE Standard Specifications for Public-Key Cryptography, IEEE Std 1363-2000 (2000)
15. Tawalbeh, L.A., Tenca, A.F., Koç, Ç.K.: A radix-4 scalable design. IEEE Potentials 24(2), 16–18 (2005)
16. Tenca, A.F., Koç, Ç.K.: A Scalable Architecture for Modular Multiplication Based on Montgomery's Algorithm. IEEE Trans. Computers 52(9) (2003)

Design and Performance Analysis of CZML-IPSec for Satellite IP Networks

Zhan Huang and Xuemai Gu

Communication Research Center, Harbin Institute of Technology,
150001, Harbin, P.R. China
robbiehwang@yahoo.com.cn

Abstract. This paper analyzes the conflict between performance enhancing technology and IPSec in satellite IP networks, and proposes a solution called multilayer IP security with changeable zone (CZML-IPSec). It enables licensed intermediate nodes not only access TCP header, but also object links of upper layer in the form of HTML by converting static zone mapping to changeable dynamic mapping and building up composite security association correspondingly. A prototype is implemented to demonstrate the practical feasibility of CZML-IPSec. Measurements and performance analysis indicate that CZML-IPSec does not add unacceptable bandwidth overheads and delay, and it does not increase substantially processing hardware requirements. CZML-IPSec can help satellite IP networks provide both end-to-end security and performance enhancement.

Keywords: satellite IP networks, performance enhancing proxy, CZML-IPSec, HTTP accelerating proxy.

1 Introduction

Satellite channels are characterized by long propagation delays, large bandwidth-delay products and high bit error rates. These unfriendly features lead to TCP protocol performance degradation for satellite end-to-end reliable transmission in Internet application, which is widely utilized in terrestrial networks nowadays. Since TCP has been widely adopted by Internet hosts, many solutions have been proposed to overcome the problems of TCP over satellites, of which TCP performance enhancing proxy and HTTP accelerating proxy are comparatively efficient [1][2][3][4].

With the proposal of IP Security and adoption by the IETF, there are more and more IPSec-support services in Internet. IPSec is the most general way to supply end-to-end security at network layer for future full IP wireless networks. Therefore, it is considered suitable for data confidentiality and authentication in satellite IP networks. However, monolithic IPSec conflicts with TCP PEPs and HTTP accelerating proxies. To solve the problem, we analyze the collision among TCP PEPs, HTTP accelerating proxies and IPSec, propose the limitation of previous research, and present a compatible Multilayer IP Security with Changeable Zone (CZML-IPSec) scheme. The feasibility is validated by implementation. It proves that CZML-IPSec only adds marginal overhead and processing delay, and it can provide both network layer security and performance improvement for satellite IP networks.

K. Li et al. (Eds.): NPC 2007, LNCS 4672, pp. 277–286, 2007.

2 Analysis on IPSec Implementation in Satellite IP Networks

2.1 Conflicts Between IPSec and Performance Enhancement

IPSec is a standard mechanism for providing secure communications over the public Internet and its end-to-end model suits well in networks employing layer-architecture-packet like IP networks. However, IPSec's end-to-end mechanism conflicts with performance improvement methods in satellite IP networks. TCP PEPs and HTTP accelerating proxies operate on state information in IP header (IP destination and source addresses), TCP header (sequence number and flow identification), and upper layer data (objects following HTTP header). When TCP sessions are transmitted under the protection from IPSec ESP transport tunnel mode, in case of employing TCP snooping proxies, it is impossible to access TCP header and any information of upper layer data which are encrypted inside the ESP header at any intermediate nodes. If tunnel mode is in use, even original IP header can't be accessed. As far as TCP split connection proxies are concerned, IPSec transmission have to be split into two segments and IPSec packets ought to be checked and decrypted entirely at proxies, and then re-encrypted. In this case, a great deal of complicated data encryption and verification processing leads to loss of networks throughout. Furthermore, all data would exist in state of plaintext at one time or another. This is usually unacceptable by user's security policy. Similarly, HTTP accelerating proxies can't coexist with IPSec.

2.2 Related Solutions

The purpose of the study is to solve the conflicts between performance improvement and IPSec in satellite IP networks. So, we analyze the limitations of four existing related solutions.

2.2.1 Replacing IPSec with a Transport Layer Security Mechanism
Transport layer mechanism contains Secure Sockets Layer (SSL), Transport Layer Security (TLS), and so forth. They only encrypt TCP payload, so as to enable intermediate nodes to access plain TCP header and realize TCP performance enhancing function. However, permitting the entire TCP header to appear in plaintext exposes several vulnerabilities of the TCP session to a large amount of TCP protocol attacks, because the identity and transmission ports of sender and receiver would be visible without confidentiality protection. Additionally, SSL/TLS works only on TCP, but not on user datagram protocol (UDP), thus, the range of applications is more restricted than IPSec. Furthermore, HTTP accelerating function can't be implemented in this instance, because HTTP object zone is still encrypted.

2.2.2 Employing Transport Layer Friendly ESP (TF-ESP)
Transport layer friendly ESP format is proposed by Bellovin from AT&T Research [6]. It modifies the original ESP header to include some TCP header state information such as sequence numbers and flow identifications, in a disclosure header outside the encryption scope (but authenticated) for snooping purpose. However, TF-ESP lacks suitable integrity check verification protection, and disclosure state information is

easy to misuse by untrustworthy intermediate nodes. In addition, TF-ESP has not enough flexibility to support all of the upper protocols.

2.2.3 Tunneling a Transport Layer Security Mechanism Within IPSec

It is likely to adopt tunneling SSL/TLS within IPSec, in which SSL/TLS protects TCP payload segment and IPSec takes charge of protecting TCP header. Intermediate nodes can process TCP header related security affairs, and TCP performance enhancing can be realized accordingly, nevertheless TCP payload should be encrypted, authenticated, and decrypted twice, because IPSec treats TCP header and TCP payload as a whole. This is obvious an unnecessary waste of limited satellite networks resources.

2.2.4 Multiple Layer IPSec (ML-IPSec)

ML-IPSec improves standard IPSec by encrypting and authenticating data according to different zones on the basis of IP layers. Zone mapping and zone lists are defined in a composite security association (CSA). The former defines the coverage of zones, while the latter list all SAs. Compared with above three solutions, ML-IPSec is compatible with TCP snooping proxies, supplies limited, controllable access to upper layer data and supports IPSec end-to-end property. However, static zone mapping and inflexible CSA of ML-IPSec become the serious obstacles. In practical networks, IPSec zone coverage should be modified with the change of IP header and TCP header option's length, and encryption and authentication algorithm should be flexible according to the security requirement of the payload data. ML-IPSec couldn't function well, if the end nodes change the use of TCP or IP option, as the offsets and lengths of the headers change, causing the zone mapping to fail. ML-IPSec can't support HTTP accelerating proxies in addition, because it is not aware of the variable length of object links' information correctly in advance, in respect that the zone length is fixed in CSA.

Considering the limitation of above solutions, we propose multilayer IPSec with changeable zone (CZML-IPSec) by designing a novel IPSec ESP header and constructing a more reasonable composite security association. It enable TCP/IP header and TCP payload deserve efficient protection, meanwhile, TCP header and HTTP object links of variable length can be accessed by licensed TCP PEPs and HTTP accelerating proxies so that the performance of satellite IP networks is improved. In the following parts, the principle, design and implementation would be described in detail.

3 Design and Analysis of CZML-IPSec

3.1 Principle of CZML-IPSec

CZML-IPSec is characteristic of flexible dynamic zone mapping and modified composite security association (CSA). It enables each data packet has individual zone mapping to apply selective protection in different zones with different keys and algorithms. Zone mapping is defined in ESP header rather than SA, and transmitted within IP datagram. In the process of transmission, CZML-IPSec can adjust zone quantity and zone coverage according to the change of data information, security levels and user's security policies. A model of CZML-IPSec transport mode protection is given in Fig. 1, in which TCP payload is divided into two parts: HTML object links (length variable) and HTML basic page. HTML object links and TCP header make up of the first zone for TCP PEPs and HTTP accelerating proxies accessing at the intermediate nodes, while HTML basic page part is the second zone unavailable for any intermediate node.

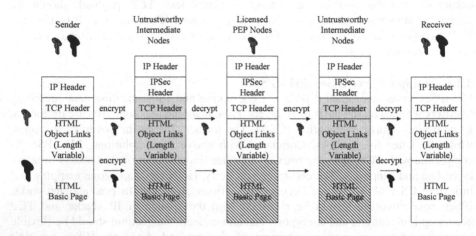

Fig. 1. CZML-IPSec transport mode protection model for TCP/HTTP

3.2 Design of CZML-IPSec

3.2.1 Dynamic Zone Mapping

Fig. 2 shows a two-zone CZML-IPSec ESP header format. Zone mapping information (4 octets) is located in the ESP header instead of original SA for dynamic mapping. The 4 octets contain zone quantity (1 octet), zone serial number (1 octet), and the length of the zone (2 octets). The zone quantity of IP datagram can be no more than the quantity in the CSA of the end nodes, because when processing bursting data of high security level, networks throughout would rather be lost to a certain extent than permission of any one of the intermediate nodes accessing HTTP segment or TCP header of the IP datagram under CZML-IPSec protection. In some special cases, CZML-IPSec can be transformed to original IPSec smoothly in the state of single zone. Zone serial number has the function of index, and it must conform to the SA number in CSA. Zone mapping information exists as plaintext in the entire process of IP datagram transmission, but it must be authenticated.

3.2.2 Composite Security Association

CZML-IPSec requires much more complex security relationship among sender, receiver and licensed intermediate nodes. So, CSA should be built to define the relationship for every zone of IP datagram. Zone mapping information is removed from CSA, and parameters are classed to two segments: mutual segment and individual

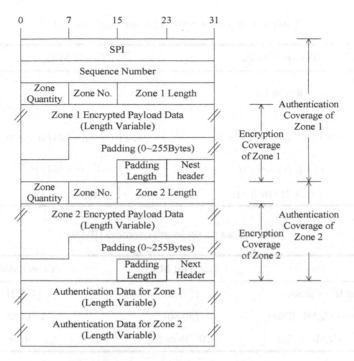

Fig. 2. Two-zone CZML-IPSec ESP header

segment. There are sequence number counter, anti-replay window, sequence counter overflow and security mode in the former one. The latter one consists of individual SA lifetime, keys of the encryption and authentication algorithms. Upon receipt of a packet contain ESP header, the receiver determine the appropriate SA based on destination IP address, SPI value and security protocol. Besides above three elements, zone serial number participates in CSA lookup for zone indexing.

3.2.3 Overhead Analysis

Overhead introduced by CZML-IPSec consists of the increase of IP data packet's length and processing loads. They are brought on by extra header information, multiple data padding and integrity check values. Zone mapping information adds 4 Bytes on the ESP header of CZML-IPSec. Individual encryptions and authentication for different zone lead to definite expansion on IP data packets due to separate padding and synchronization data. For example, a two-zone CZML-IPSec packet employing HMAC-MD5-96 would increase 12 Bytes except for data padding.

We assume the TCP/IP datagram contains two zone, 20-Byte IP header and 20-Byte TCP header without any option, the length of the HTML object links is m Bytes, and the length of the HTML basic page information is n Bytes. We calculate the overhead of IP datagram respectively under the CZML-IPSec protection of transport mode and tunnel mode and compare it with the origin IP and IPSec. Rijndael-CBC is assumed for encryption, and HMAC-MD5-96 is assumed for authentication. The results of six cases are summarized in Table 1 and Table2.

Table 1. Comparison on data packet length (Bytes)

	Transport Mode	Tunnel Mode
Origin IP	$40 + m + n$	$40 + m + n$
IPSec	$76 + \lceil (m + n + 6)/16 \rceil \times 16$	$92 + \lceil (m + n + 10)/16 \rceil \times 16$
CZML-IPSec	$112 + [\lceil (m + 6)/16 \rceil + \lceil (n + 2)/16 \rceil] \times 16$	$128 + [\lceil (m + 10)/16 \rceil + \lceil (n + 2)/16 \rceil] \times 16$

Table 2. Data packet length overhead (Bytes)

	Transport Mode	Tunnel Mode
Origin IP → IPSec	[27,42]	[47,62]
Origin IP → CZML-IPSec	[50,80]	[70,100]
IPSec → CZML-IPSec	20□36 or 52	20□36 or 52

It is concluded from Table 1 and Table 2 that, CZML-IPSec adds 36-Byte overhead on average compared with IPSec. CZML-IPSec adds 6.7%, if the average length of IP data packet is 536 Bytes. Employing HMAC-MD-32 at licensed intermediate nodes can bring overhead increase down to 5.3%. If Triple-DES-CBC (64-bit block) substitutes for Rijndael-CBC (128-bit block), the overhead increase is down to 3%.

4   CZML-IPSec Testbed Setup and Implementation

The testbed we setup for implementation of CZML-IPSec is shown in Fig. 3. CZML-IPSec is implemented in transport mode on Linux OS (kernel version 2.6) by modifying functions on free software FreeS/WAN (version 2.03). FreeS/WAN provides a base IPSec implementation on the base of which we can realize our design. We remove Linux kernel IPSec module, because it has combined original IPSec since version 2.5.47.

Cient   PEP   Server

192.168.1.2   192.168.1.1/192.168.2.1   192.168.2.2

Fig. 3. CZML-IPSec transport mode testbed

According to the principle of CZML-IPSec, We modify ESP header's data structures at KLIP part in FreeS/WAN, and realize CSA as shown in Fig.3. Apache Web Sever is built up at the server for HTTP service. However, we define the length of HTTP object links information by external commands instead of actual length for flexibility. The length parameter is transmitted to the zone mapping information of the ESP header as formal variable. So, the zone length can be changed flexibly so as to gain the relevant test results conveniently. Rijndael as AES winner and RC5 are introduced as encryption algorithms besides DES and Triple-DES still employed. RC5, developed by RSA Lab, is a fast symmetric block cipher fit for hardware or software implementations. The more rounds in RC5, the higher level of security is gained. The performance of RC5 is directly proportional to the quantity of the round, and is not affected by the key size. This flexibility of RC5 makes it ideal for our implementation of CZML-IPSec, as the tradeoff between speed (and hence throughput) and security can be balanced via appropriate parameter settings. A word size of 32 bits, a round number of 12, and a key length of 16 Bytes are recommended by RSA as the nominal choice of parameters for RC5. Manual keying is used for key exchange. It is assumed that TCP/IP datagram contains two zone, 20-Byte IP header and 20-Byte TCP header without any option.

For the purposes of timing measurements, the time stamp counter on Pentium chip is introduced. RDTSC (Read Time Stamp Counter) is a two-Byte assemble instruction, which returns the number of CPU clock cycles. Therefore, by reading this counter twice we can compute the number of cycles that have elapsed between the first and the second call. This provides us with a much more accurate and meaningful measurements of time, which are independent of the CPU clock speed. For TCP snooping proxies, we improve networks monitoring and analyses tool TCPdump to implement snooping function under Linux OS, and we enable it to access zone mapping length and check integrity in HMAC-MD5-96. So, we can calculate CPU clock cycles elapsing in authenticating and decrypting zone 1 of the inbound IP datagram under the protection of CZML-IPSec at intermediate nodes. All of the programs are complied by gcc3.4 with -O2 option. Each test section is repeated 10 times, and the results are averaged.

5 Test Results

5.1 IPSec Outbound Test Results

The performance of original FreeS/WAN with Rijndael and RC5 is tested firstly. Fig. 4 shows CPU clock cycles occupied by processing IPSec outbound through FreeS/WAN. The test involves eight combinations of encryption algorithms DES, Triple-DES, Rijndael, RC5, and integrity check algorithm HMAC-MD5, HMAC-SHA1.

As shown in Fig. 4, RC5 (32/12/16)-CRC + HMAC-MD5 and Rijndael-CBC + HMAC-MD5 are better choices with less CPU cycles. When data plaintext length is 64 Bytes, the advantage of RC5 +HMAC-MD5 is most obvious, 966.6 cycles fewer than Rijndael-CBC + HMAC-MD5. The block of RC5 is 32 Bytes, which make the padding overhead fewer than Rijndael. Taking flexible encryption parameter and processing speed into account, RC5-CBC + HMAC-MD5 is most suitable for Zone 1

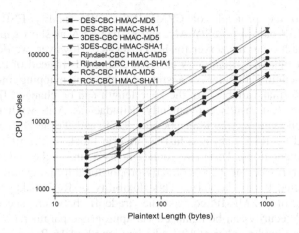

Fig. 4. CPU clock cycles occupied by processing IPSec through FreeS/WAN2.03

of CZML-IPSec with short and variable zone mapping. Hence, in the following test, it is adopted in Zone 1. Rijndael-CBC and HMAC-MD5 is used in Zone 2.

5.2 CZML-IPSec Overhead at End Node

It is assumed that TCP/IP datagram contains two zone, 20-Byte IP header and 20-Byte TCP header without any option. CPU clock cycles occupied by processing a single IP datagram with different zone mapping lengths under the protection of CZML-IPSec is listed in Table 3, where m is the length of the HTML object links in Byte, and n is the length of the HTML basic page information in Byte. The CPU cycles occupied by processing a single CZML-IPSec packet is 64.5 per Byte at most. It means that it requires CPU clock frequency at least $C\times64.5/8 = C\times8.225$MHz for a throughout of C Mbps CZML-IPSec connection. The test is under preshared manual keying, without considering key exchanging and key update, and CPU clock cycle is measured on Pentium chip, thus the estimation is not extremely accurate. So,

Table 3. CPU cycles occupied by processing single CZML-IPSec data packet in different zone length (Bytes) cases

n / m	20	40	64	128	256	512	1024
0	3416.6	4678.1	5419.6	8422.3	14548.0	28012.1	53884.9
20	5116.6	6378.1	7119.6	1012 2.3	16248.0	29712.1	55584.9
40	5827.3	7128.0	7624.3	10916.3	16697.9	30576.2	56181.2
64	7164.2	8242.1	9081.7	11959.5	18211.2	31701.8	57714.4
128	10014.5	11121.2	12074.1	15685.8	20994.2	34679.9	60852.0
256	16382.3	18094.9	18813.5	22514.5	28672.4	41354.8	67832.6
512	28464.6	29131.3	29744.9	33636.3	38743.6	52372.1	
1024	52938.0	53672.2	56759.4	59473.8	62624.5		

C×12MHz as the CPU clock estimation is recommended in practice. CPU clock of no less than 1.2GHz is required for 100Mbps CZML-IPSec transmission.

5.3 CZML-IPSec Overhead at Intermediate Nodes

Snooping CZML-IPSec packets at intermediate nodes, includes checking integrity, decryption, and analyses of Zone 1 by modified TCPdump. It is assumed that RC5-CBC + HMAC-MD5 are applied in Zone 1. CPU clock cycles occupied by processing are acquired by overhead test. Fig. 5 gives the test results, where l is the length of Zone 1, and the length of HTML object links is 20, 40, 64, 128, 256,512 Bytes.

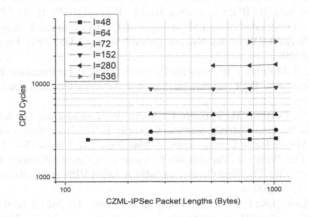

Fig. 5. Overhead measurement results at intermediate node

6 Conclusion

In satellite IP networks, the conflict is serious between end-to-end IPSec mechanism and performance enhancement techniques. In this paper, we have presented a multiple layer IPSec with changeable zone (CZML-IPSec) by designing a novel ESP header structure and constructing a more reasonable composite security association. It enable TCP/IP header and TCP payload deserve efficient protection, meanwhile, TCP header and HTTP object links of variable length can be accessed by licensed TCP PEPs and HTTP accelerating proxies so that the performance of satellite IP networks is improved. The overhead of CZML-IPSec is 6.7% greater than IPSec if Rijndael-CBC + HMAC-MD5-96 are employed. The feasibility is validated through testbed establishment and implementation. Moreover, it indicates how much overhead is added by CZML-IPSec module. It is concluded that CZML-IPSec can provide both network layer security and performance improvement for satellite IP networks. Future work would focus on automatic multiple key exchanges corresponding to CZML-IPSec, now that keys in this paper are preshared and set mutually.

Acknowledgments. This paper is supported by the grants from the National Natural Science Foundation of China [Project No. 60532030].

References

1. Border, J., Kojo, M., Griner, J.: Performance Enhancing Proxies Intended to Mitigate Link-Related Degradations, RFC 3135 (June 2001)
2. Balakrishnan, H., Padmanabhan, V., Seshan, S.: A comparison of mechanism for improving TCP performance over wireless links. In: IEEE/ACM Trans. Networking, December 1997, pp. 756–769 (1997)
3. Ehsan, N., Liu, M., Ragland, R.: Evaluation of Performance Enhancing Proxies in Internet over Satellite. Wiley Int'l. J. Commun. Sys. 16, 513–534 (2003)
4. Roy-Chowdhury, A., Baras, J.S., Hadjitheodosiou, M.: Security Issues in Hybrid Networks with A Satellite Component. Wireless Communications 12(6), 50–61 (2005)
5. Kent, S., Atkinson, R.: IP Encapsulating Security Payload (ESP). IETF, RFC 2406 (1998)
6. Bellovin, S.: Transport-friendly ESP (or layer violations for fun and profit). In: The Panel Talk 1999 Network Distributed System Security Symp. (NDSS' 99), February 1999, San Diego CA (1999)
7. Zhang, Y.: A Multilayer IP Security Protocol for TCP Performance Enhancement in Wireless Networks. IEEE Journal on Selected Areas in Communications 22, 767–776 (2004)
8. Ciccarese, G., DeBlasi, M., Patrono, L., Marra, P., Tomasicchio, G.: An IPSEC Aware TCP-PEP for Integrated Mobile Satellite Networks. In: IEEE Int. Symposium on Personal, Indoor and Mobile Radio Communications, May 2004, vol. 7, pp. 453–459 (2004)
9. Thompson, I.R., Waller, J.: Performance Enhancing Proxies and Security. In: IEE Seminar on IP over Satellite. The Next Generation: MPLS, DRM VPN and Delivered Services, vol. 2, pp. 1324–1331 (2003)
10. Karir, M., Baras, J.S.: Les: Layered Encryption Security. In: 3rd International Conference on Networking (ICN'04), Guadeloupe (French Caribbean), March 2004, pp. 382–388 (2004)

A Novel Group Key Management Based on Jacobian Elliptic Chebyshev Rational Map*

Qin Ke, Zhou Mingtian, Liu Naiqi, Hao Yujie, and Guo Jiandong

School of Computer Science and Engineering,
University of Electronic Science and Technology of China
Chengdu, 610054, P.R.C.
yuxuanqk@126.com,
{mtzhou,nliu}@uestc.edu.cn

Abstract. This paper proposes a novel scheme of group key management based on Jacobian Elliptic Chebyshev Rational Map, named Jacobian Group Key Management(JGKM). The scheme is more efficient than other group key managements since fewer re-keying messages are sent when group membership changes. Besides, it provides both forward and backward secrecy. Therefore, this proposal is helpful to deploy secure multicast over some networks with high latency or limited bandwidth such as wireless network. Furthermore, it fits both small-scale and large-scale groups.

Keywords: secure multicast, group key management, Jacobian Elliptic Chebyshev Rational Map.

1 Introduction

Encryption is one of the most effective access control mechanisms. All data are encrypted by keys and thus key materials should keep away from attacks. In the context of unicast, a pairwise secure channel is employed to update keys. Contrarily, secure multicast must deal with more complications. Many group key management schemes for secure multicast have been proposed in the past decade [1,2,3,4,5]. These schemes can be classified into three main classes, viz. centralized, decentralized and distributed. Centralized group key management schemes require a single or a small set of entities, named Key Server (KS), to generate or distribute share key to all group members via a secure channel. This kind of schemes can reduce both storage requirement and computational power remarkably. Respectively, decentralized key managements divide the whole group into smaller subgroups. Each subgroup is controlled by a single or several KSs. Distributed schemes allow each member to perform group key generation and the key generation can either be collaborative or done by a single member. However, no single one can uniquely determine what the key is. Each of the three schemes has its own advantages and disadvantages. No single scheme can fit all

---

* Supported by NSF 60473090.

K. Li et al. (Eds.): NPC 2007, LNCS 4672, pp. 287–295, 2007.

applications. For example, Centralized schemes have the risk of single-point-failure while distributed schemes must be weighed against its disadvantages: Many such schemes have a high complexity or a high computational cost. They are best suited for small-scale groups that have nodes with enough computational resources for group Diffie-Hellman key exchange and enough memory to store state information about all of the group's members. There also has to be a trusted mechanism to authenticate the membership join/leave events and the DH public keys.

Most of secure multicast key management schemes focus on decreasing computational and communication overhead [6,7,8]. In this paper, we introduce a novel approach based on Jacobian Elliptic Chebyshev Rational Map (JECRM) to minimize re-keying messages and computational cost.

JECRM has attracted many researchers from a variety of fields recently, of course cryptographist included[10,11,12,13,23,24,25,26,27]. Some encryption algorithms based on JECRM have been proven not secure[10,11,12,13]. In despite of utilizing the same property in this paper, attacks provided in [10] take no effect.

Here is the layout of our paper. Section 2 introduces Jacobian Elliptic Chebyshev Rational Map and its property. Section 3 illustrates Jacobian group key management detailedly. Security and complexity analysis are made in section 4 and 5. Finally, conclusions are drawn in section 6.

2   Jacobian Elliptic Chebyshev Rational Map

Jacobian Elliptic Chebyshev Rational Map satisfies chatic properties such as pseudo-random, sensitivity to tiny change of initial conditions, ergodicity, one-way iteration process and etc. All of these properties are interconnected with cryptography closely.

Definition 1. Let v be a variable taking value over the interval [-1,1], let $n \geq 2$ be an integer, Jacobian Elliptic Chebyshev Rational Map with modulus w is recursively defined by:

$$R_{n+1}(v, w) = \frac{2vR_n(v, w)}{1 - w^2(1 - v^2)(1 - R_n^2(v, w))} - R_{n-1}(v, w)$$

where $w \in [0, 1]$ and $R_0(v, w) = 1, R_1(v, w) = v$.

JECRM has two important features[24,25]:

Theorem 1. Jacobian Elliptic Chebyshev Rational Map is a One-way function in v.

Theorem 2. Jacobian Elliptic Chebyshev Rational Map satisfies the semi-group property when $r, s \geq 2$:

$$R_{rs}(v, w) = R_r(R_s(v, w), w)$$
$$= R_s(R_r(v, w), w)$$

There are also other functions that satisfy semi-group property, for example, mod-exp function

$$f_a(f_b(v)) = f_b(f_a(v)) = f_{ab}(v)$$

where $f_a(v) = v^a \mod p$.

The rest of the paper illustrates how to use JECRM to manage group keys in a secure group communication. The reason why we choose JECRM other than mod-exp function is explained in section 4.

3   Jacobian Group Key Managemen

The following notations will be used throughout this paper.

v	A secret seed selected by KS. None of other members knows v
w	A public share selected by KS
u_i	The ith user
r_i	A large random number selected by KS and delivered to member u_i. r_i can be either prime or composite. It makes no difference. Moreover, r_i is known to all members
k_i	A pre-placed key encryption key established between u_i and KS
k_{pri}	Private key of KS, It is used for signature
k_{pub}	Public key of KS. It is used for signature verification
k_{old}	The old group key before membership changes
k_{new}	The new group key after membership changes
$\{M\}_k$	M is encrypted by k

Here we make a reasonable assumption: k_{pub} is known to all group members. This can be done using PKI. k_i is a pre-placed key between KS and group members. This can be done using pairwise key k_{pub} and k_{pri}.

A group key management must provide re-keying mechanisms when membership changes. JGKM supports the following operations:

-Join: a new member is added to the group.
-Leave: a member is evicted from the group.
-Merge: a subgroup is added to the group.
-Partition: a subgroup is split from the group
-Re-key: the group key must be updated when any above operations occur.

3.1   Addition and Merge

Algorithm 1
At the beginning, there is no user in group. The first user is added by following steps.

Step 1. The first user u_1 sends joining request to KS.
Step 2. KS responses u_1 with $\{R_{r_1}(v, w)\}_{k_1}$, it can only be decrypted by u_1.
Step 3. u_1 selects $R_{r_1}(v, w)$ as the initial group session key.

Obviously, key distribution starting up needs for only two messages.

With the group growing, more and more users need to be added. JGKM consists of four steps.

Algorithm 2

Step 1. the newcomer u_{n+1} sends joining request to KS.

Step 2. KS responds u_{n+1} with $\{R_{r_{n+1}}(v,w)\}_{k_{n+1}}$. The cipher-text can only be decrypted by u_{n+1}.

Step 3. KS multicasts $\{r_1, r_2 \cdots r_{n+1}, w, cmd = addition\}_{k_{pri}}$ to all members. Each member can decrypt r_i ($i = 1, 2 \cdots n+1$) and w using k_{pub}. $cmd = addition$ indicates that each member should do addition computing after receiving this message. Here we should note that r_i and w are public. Everyone knows k_{pub} can decrypt r_i and w. Signature is used here to prove the source of multicast. This can prevent malicious attackers from sending mendacious r_i, w and cmd.

Step 4. Newcomer computes the new group key individually according to theorem 1:

$$k_{new} = R_{r_1 \cdots r_n}(R_{r_{n+1}}(v, w), w)$$
$$= R_{r_1 \cdots r_{n+1}}(v, w)$$

Old ones do addition computing, the same new group key is produced by

$$k_{new} = R_{r_{n+1}}(k_{old}, w)$$
$$= R_{r_{n+1}}(R_{r_1 \cdots r_n}(v, w), w)$$
$$= R_{r_1 \cdots r_{n+1}}(v, w)$$

Apparently, just three re-keying messages (from step 1 to step 3) are needed in JGKM when member added. Newcomers and old ones can compute new group key without too much interactions. This approach can be extended easily.

If m users, denoted as $u_{n+1}, u_{n+2}, \cdots, u_{n+m}$, will be added:

Algorithm 3

Step 1. $u_{n+1}, u_{n+2}, \cdots u_{n+m}$ send joining requests to KS.

Step 2. KS multicasts $\{R_{r_{n+1}}(v, w)\}_{k_{n+1}}$, $\{R_{r_{n+2}}(v, w)\}_{k_{n+2}}, \cdots$, $\{R_{r_{n+m}}(v, w)\}_{k_{n+m}}$. Each member choose the right part to decrypt.

Step 3. KS multicasts $\{r_1, r_2, \cdots, r_{n+m}, w, cmd = addition\}_{k_{pri}}$

Step 4. Newcomer u_{n+i} computes new group key by

$$k_{new} = R_{r_1 \cdots r_{n+i-1} r_{n+i+1} \cdots r_{n+m}}(R_{r_{n+i}}(v, w), w)$$
$$= R_{r_1 \cdots r_{n+m}}(v, w)$$

Old members compute the same group key by

$$k_{new} = R_{r_{n+1} \cdots r_{n+m}}(k_{old}, w)$$
$$= R_{r_{n+1} \cdots r_{n+m}}(R_{r_1 \cdots r_n}(v, w), w)$$
$$= R_{r_1 \cdots r_{n+m}}(v, w)$$

Here just $2m+1$ messages are needed. Now, we can draw a conclusion of JGKM.

Conclusion 1: The number of re-keying messages is irrelevant to current group size. It rests with the number of newcomers.

3.2   Eviction and Partition

It is easy to cope with member's eviction in JGKM. If member u_d should be evicted, KS multicasts one message:

Algorithm 4
Step 1. KS multicasts $\{u_d, r_d, cmd = eviction\}_{k_{pri}}$ to all members. $cmd = eviction$ indicates that each member should do eviction computing after receiving this message.
Step 2. The rest do eviction computing according below equation:

$$k_{new} = R_{r_1 \cdots r_{i-1} r_{i+1} \cdots r_{d-1} r_{d+1} \cdots r_n}(R_{r_i}(v, w), w)$$
$$= R_{r_1 \cdots r_{d-1} r_{d+1} \cdots r_n}(v, w)$$

The new group key contains no information of u_d. Simply, u_d has been removed since he knows nothing about v while v is a secret selected by KS. Security discussion will be shown in section 4.

It is also easy to extend this approach to fit m users' leaving. Assuming $u_{j_1}, u_{j_2} \cdots u_{j_m}$ leave the group.

Algorithm 5
Step 1. KS multicasts a combined message $\{(u_{j_1}, r_{j_1}), (u_{j_2}, r_{j_2}), \cdots, (u_{j_m}, r_{j_m}), cmd = eviction\}_{k_{pri}}$ to entire group.
Step 2. The rest do eviction computing and new group key is given by:

$$k_{new} = R_{r_1 \cdots r_{i-1} r_{i+1} \cdots r_n}(R_{r_i}(v, w), w), (i \neq j_1, j_2 \cdots j_m)$$

Similarly, the new group key contains no information of $u_{j_1}, u_{j_2}, \cdots, u_{j_m}$
Now, we have another conclusion:

Conclusion 2: Only one re-keying message is sent when someone evicted.

4   Security Analysis

The security of group key management protocols can be measured by:

-Backward secrecy: new members should not be able to read past traffic.
-Forward secrecy: Former members should not be able to read present and future traffic.
-Collusion attack: Evicted members must not be able to work together and share their individual piece of information to regain access to the group key.

From section 3, we know that JGKM's security bases on the secrecy of parameter v. JGKM provides both forward and backward secrecy grounding on the fact that $R_n(v, w)$ is one-way function in v and sensitive to initial condition v.

Considering an adversary u_d a group insider, he knows r_i $(i = 1, 2...n)$ and $R_d(v, w)$. He does not know v and $R_{r_i}(v, w), r_i \neq d$. The new group key has changed into k_{new} after its leaving.

Discussion 1: Section 3.2 indicates that

$$k_{new} = R_{r_1 \cdots r_{i-1} r_{i+1} \cdots r_{d-1} r_{d+1} \cdots r_n}(R_{r_i}(v, w), w)$$
$$= R_{r_1 \cdots r_{d-1} r_{d+1} \cdots r_n}(v, w)$$

This equation does not contain any information of u_d at all. If u_d want to regain the new group key, he must know r_i, v, w. But v is a secrecy selected by KS. u_d can't resolve v from $R_d(v, w)$ since $R_d(v, w)$ is a one-way function in v.

Discussion 2: At the same time, section 3.2 implies

$$k_{old} = R_{r_d}(k_{new}, w)$$

Obviously, k_{old} is also a one-way function in k_{new}, resolving k_{new} from above equation is a hard problem as well. Not any efficient method or quantitative measurement [21,22] have been found to finish this attack.

Similarly, If u_d is a newcomer, it is also impossible to recover k_{old} by

$$k_{new} = R_{r_d}(k_{old}, w)$$

However, we must point out that r_i should be restricted. Otherwise an adversary may recover group key without effort.

Restriction 1: $r_i \neq 1$

If $r_i = 1$, member u_i will receive $R_1(v, w)$ according to algorithm 1 and algorithm 2. On the other hand, according to definition 1, $R_1(v, w) = v$. This indicates member u_i receives the secret parameter v. That is forbidden.

Restriction 2: r_i must be larger enough, e.g. $r_i \geq 2^{32}$

According to definition 1, if r_i is very small, e.g. $r_i = 2$ or 3, it is possible to resolve v from $R_{r_i}(v, w)$. In order to enhance the security of JGKM, we choose random number $r_i \geq 2^{32}$.

Restriction 3

$$r_i \neq \prod_{\substack{j \in [1, n] \\ j \neq i}}^{l} r_j, \quad (l = 1, 2 \cdots n - 1)$$

If $r_n = r_1 r_2 \cdots r_{n-1}$, according to algorithm 2, u_n will receive KS's response R_{r_n}

$$R_{r_n}(v, w) = R_{r_1 \ldots r_{n-1}}(v, w)$$

which is the new group key after u_n's leaving.

Furthermore, restriction 3 also eliminates collusion attack.

Now, we will explain why JECRM is chosen other than mod-exp function. Although mod-exp function does satisfy semi-group property, it is a one-way function in n rather than v. That is , it is easy to resolve v from mod-exp function. Therefore, v can't be chosen as common secrecy. If mod-exp function is chosen, it is obvious that an attacker can recover k_{old} after his addition or regain k_{new} after his eviction.

5 Complexity Analysis

JGKM involves multiple floating-point operations. We employ unique decomposition theorem to improve JGKM's efficiency. According to unique decomposition theorem, an integer r can be uniquely decomposed to $r = p_1^{l1} p_2^{l2} \cdots p_n^{ln}$ where p_i are primes. If r is not decomposed, we must do r iterations in order to computer $R_r(v, w)$. On the other hand, according to following equation, at most $p_1 l_1 + p_2 l_2 + \cdots p_n l_n$ floating-point operations are needed.

$$R_r(v, w) = R_{p_1^{l1} p_2^{l2} \cdots p_n^{ln}}(v, w) = \underbrace{R_{p_1} \cdots}_{l_1} (\underbrace{R_{p_2} \cdots}_{l_2} (\underbrace{R_{p_n} \cdots R_{p_n}}_{l_n} (v, w), w), w)$$

For example, we choose $r = 7^5 17^3 31^4 67^{10} \approx 2^{128}$ (The key length of AES is 128 bits), thus computation of $R_r(v, w)$ need only $7 \times 5 + 17 \times 3 + 31 \times 4 + 67 \times 10 = 880$ other than 2^{128} floating-point operations. At present, Chinese Godson-2 can perform 2 billion single-precision floating-point and 1 billion double-precision floating-point operations per second. That is, Godson-2 perform $R_r(v, w)$ within $0.13ms$. It should be much faster in mainframe computers.

6 Summary

In this paper, we proposed a group key management based on Jacobian Elliptic Chebyshev Rational Map. On one hand, it has the structure of centralized schemes, on the other hand, it has the virtue of distributed schemes. Briefly, it has following features:

    -A Key Server is involved in performing initialization.
    -Each group member contributes its share r_i to group key.
    -Each member receives a secrecy from KS.
    -Each member make use of others' share and his own secrecy to compute new group key without interaction.
    -As the group grows, old members' secrecy remain unchanged. New members' secrecy are sent by pre-placed secret channel.
    -As the group shrinks, departing members' secrecy are removed from the new key.
    -JGKM does not need any auxiliary keys except for pre-placed keys.
    -JGKM is more efficient than other schemes[5,6,7,14,15]. The number of re-keying messages is irrelevant to current group size. Only $2m + 1$ re-keying messages are sent when group grows and only 1 re-keying messages are sent when group shrinks. This makes it differ from other schemes. Most of group key managements involve $2m + \log(n)$ re-keying messages where n is current group size.

Acknowledgment

We'd like to thank MSEC and RMT working group of IETF for their helpful discussions.

References

1. Ballardie, A.: Scalable multicast key distribution. RFC1949 (1996)
2. Hardjono, T.: Verisign. The Multicast Group Security Architecture. RFC3740. 2004
3. Wallner, D., Harder, E., Agee, R.: Key Management for Multicast: Issues and Architectures RFC2627 (June 1999)
4. Du, F., Ni, L.M., Esfahanian, A.-H.: Toward Solving Multicast Key Management Problem. Computer Communications and Networks, 232–236 (1999)
5. Rafaeli, S., Hutchison, D.: A Survey of Key Management for Secure Group Communication. ACM Computing Surveys 35(3), 309–329 (2003)
6. Duma, C., Shahmehri, N., Lambrix, P.: A Hybrid Key Tree scheme for Multicast to Balance Security and Efficiency Requirements. In: Proceedings of the Twelfth IEEE International Workshops on Enabling Technologies: Infrastructure for Collaborative Enterprises, pp. 378–383 (2003)
7. Pegueroles, J., Rico-Novella, F.: Reducing Latency in Multicast Group Re-keying using Eulers Theorem. IEEE Communication letters, April 2003, 6(4), 128–133 (2003)
8. Canneti, R.: Efficient Communication-Storage Tradeoffs For multicast Encryption. In: Advances in Cryptology-EUROCRYPT 1999, pp. 456–477 (1999)
9. Li, M., Poovendran, R., Berenstein, C.: Design of Secure Multicast Key Management Schemes With Communication Budget Constraint. IEEE Communications Letters 6(3) (March 2002)
10. Kocarev, L., Tasev, Z.: Public-Key Encryption Based On Chebyshev Mnnaps. Circuits and Systems (ISCAS'03) 3, 28–31 (2003)
11. Hong, Z., Jun, Y., Xie-Ting, L.: Design of chaotic feed forward stream cipher. Acta Electronica Sinica 26(1), 122–126 (1998)
12. Alvarez, G.: Security problems with a chaos-based deniable authentication scheme. arXiv:nlin. CD/0412023, 9 (December 2004)
13. Bergamo, P., D'Arco, P., Santis, A., Kocarev, L.: Security of Public Key Cryptosystems based on Chebyshev Polynomials. arXiv:cs.CR/0411030, vol. 10 (November 2004)
14. Steiner, M., Tsudik, G., Waidner, M.: Diffie-Hellman Key Distribution Extended To Group Communication. In: Proceedings of the 3rd ACM conference on Computer and communications security, New Delhi, India, pp. 31–37. ACM Press, New York (1996)
15. Amir, Y., Kim, Y., Nita-Rotaru, C., Tsudik, G.: On The Performance of Group Key Agreement Protocols. ACM Transactions on Information and System Security 7(3), 457–488 (2004)
16. Aiello, W., Bellovin, S.M., Mattblaze: Just Fast Keying: Key Agreement in a Hostile Internet. ACM Transactions on Information and System Security 7(2), 242–273 (2004)
17. Yang, T.: A survey of chaotic secure communication systems. International Journal of Computational Cognition 2(2), 81–130 (2004)

18. McGrew, D.A., Sherman, A.T.: Key Establishment in Large Dynamic Groups Using One-Way Function Trees, 29(5), 444–458. IEEE Computer Society, Los Alamitos (2003)
19. Ku, W.-C., Chen, S.-M.: An Improved Key Management Scheme for Large Dynamic Groups Using One-Way Function Trees. In: Proceedings of the 2003 International Conference on Parallel Processing Workshops, pp. 245–251 (2003)
20. Kim, Y., Perrig, A., Tsudik, G.: Simple and Fault-Tolerant Key Agreement for Dynamic Collaborative Groups. In: Proceedings of the 7th ACM Conference on Computer and Communications Security (ACM CCS 2000), pp. 235–244 (November 2000)
21. Abramowitz, M., Stegun, I.A.: Handbook of Mathematical Functions. Dover Publications (1970)
22. Wachspress, E.L.: Evaluating Elliptic Functions and Their Inverses. Computers and Mathematics with Applications (39), 230–236 (2000)
23. Carlson, B.C.: Jacobian elliptic functions as inverses of an integral. Journal of Computational and Applied Mathematics 174, 355–359 (2005)
24. Kato, A., Kohda, T.: Solvable 2-dimensional Rational Chaotic Map Defined by Jacobian Elliptic Functions. Circuits and Systems, 1477–1480 (2005)
25. Kohda, T., Fujisaki, H.: Jacobian elliptic Chebyshev rational maps. Physica D 148, 242–254 (2001)
26. Gotz, M., Kelber, K., Schwarz, W.: Discrete-Time Chaotic Encryption Systems Part I: Statistical Design Approach. IEEE Transactions on Circuits and Systems I: Fundamental Theory and Applications 44(10), 963–970 (1997)
27. Nam, J., Lee, J., Kim, S., Won, D.: DDH-based group key agreement in a mobile environment. The Journal of Systems and Software, 73–83 (2005)

Scheme of Defending Against DDoS Attacks in Large-Scale ISP Networks

Zhi-jun Wu and Dong Zhang

Communication Engineering Department, Civil Aviation University of China
Tianjin, 300300, P.R. China
caucwu@263.net, mymailbox66@sohu.com

Abstract. A scheme that defending against distributed denial of service (DDoS) attacks adopts the mechanism of Distribution-based Secure Overlay Nodes (DSON) to a large-scale ISP (Internet Service Provider) network is presented. The scheme uses local BPG announcement to divert traffic to the overlay network when experiencing high load, then filtering algorithm based on the technology of signal processing is applied to the diverted traffic. This algorithm detects and filters out DDoS attacks in frequency domain to allow targets to provide good service to legitimate traffic, with fast reaction and high energy ratio of legitimate to attacks traffic. DSON is implemented and installed on the monitor points of large-scale ISP network associated with the corresponding routers, edge router, border router, and core router, with no requirement for the modifying to network architecture, infrastructure, and protocol.

Keywords: Distributed Denial of Service (DDoS), Distribution-based Secure Overlay Nodes (DSON), China Education & Research Network (CERNET), Router, Large-scale ISP Network.

1 Introduction and Motivation

Distributed Denial of Service (DDoS) attack is a great threat to the quality of service (QoS) of Internet and large-scale Internet Service Provider (ISP) network [1]. In this paper, a network-based defense mechanism called Distribution-based Secure Overlay Nodes (DSON) is proposed to defend against DDoS attacks in large-scale ISP Networks. Since attacker hosts and victim under flood-type attacks are widely distributed, DSON takes a distributed approach to implement defense functions with the features: (i) secure overlay array nodes are installed at every edge or border router and managed by a management center (MC). (ii) no requirements of modifying the architecture, infrastructures, protocol, and routing strategy of existing ISP network, no additional routing path needed, and no physic routing link added.

2 Related Work

There are many network-based mechanisms of handling DDoS problem in large-scale ISP network. Secure overlay Services (SOS) [1] with the goal of routing only

K. Li et al. (Eds.): NPC 2007, LNCS 4672, pp. 296–305, 2007.

authenticated traffic can pass through the overlay network to the target sites, which accepts only packets from the servlets. Traffic that has not been confirmed to originate from a good client is dropped. Clients must use an overlay network, sitting on top of the existing network, to get authentication and reach the servers. Redirection-based defense mechanism [4] is a network-based defense mechanism that reduces the required number of defense nodes based on traffic redirection which allows the edge and border routers to divert suspicious packets to central defense nodes (C-DNs). Such traffic redirection requires an additional forwarding mechanism other than IP-destination-address-based forwarding since suspicious packets must be routed through a C-DN at all times before reaching a final destination. Traffic redirection using tunneling technique to set up tunnels between all the edge and border routers and C-DNs, and the packets destined for a victim are diverted to the C-DNs by configuring policy routing of the edge and border routers. D-ward [5] is a source network-based system aiming to detect attacks before or as they leave the network that the DDoS agent resides on. It is an inline system (transparent to the users on the network) that gathers two-way traffic statistics from the border router at the source network and compares them to network traffic models built upon application and transport protocol specifications, reflecting normal (legitimate), transient (suspicious), and attack behavior[6]. D-ward is a self-regulating reverse-feedback system collaborating with source router. The throttling component of D-ward generates and adjusts rate limit rules, then communicates them to the source router, which filters the attack traffic.

In general, approaches mentioned above depend on modifying the routing configuration policy and adding intelligent algorithm to routers. It is very difficult for a well-design and end-constructed existing large-scale ISP network to do these changes, which may degrade the network QoS, and bring other unexpected problems.

3   D-SON-Based DDoS Defense Mechanism

China Education & Research Network (CERNET) is a national-wide academic network platform. With more and more computers connected to CERNET, system security must be kept up with the increase in connectivity. Many secure measures have been implemented on CERNET with its scale expend. 42 monitor points (MPs) have been designed and installed on distributed 42 region and main network nodes to monitor, detect, and control the outgoing and incoming traffic.

D-SON is considered as the defense mechanism for CERNET to defend against flood-type attacks based on the experiences of handling DDoS attacks event, and analyzing flow connection and traffic data [4]. We assume all attack traffic is generated by some organized hosts on peer customer networks, or generated from other locations on the Internet and then routed over via neighboring ISPs. CERNET is an autonomous system (AS) constructed by inter-connected core routers forming the backbone network. The sub-networks are connecting to CERNET through border routers or access routers, while the other ISP networks connecting the CERNET through edge routers. The task for CERNET defending against DDoS attack focuses on two aspects: (i) Stop the CERNET suffering from DDoS attacks coming from outside networks. (ii) Prevent other ISP networks from DDoS attacks by coming from CERNET inside sub-networks.

The scheme for CERNET defending against DDoS attack adopts the distributed defense mechanism, which combining source-end defense with victim-end defense to protect the target inside CRNET from suffering DDoS attack and stop DDoS attack from CERNET to other ISP networks. SONs are installed on the CERNET associated with 42 distributed MPs. MC manages border routers, edge routers, and SONs. 42 MPs constitutes the monitor system of CERNET for detecting of anomaly traffic and attack flow. If MPs report DDoS attack events, MC turns to emergence status immediately and manages the border routers, edge routers, and SONs working together to defend against DDoS attacks.

Figure 1 gives an example of flood-type attacks from one ISP network and one CERNET sub-network. Attack detection is the task of monitor points are installed on the critical nodes of CERNET. The scene of normal and attack traffic flow in CERNET divides the network into three parts: (i) $CERNET_{BACKBONE}$ is backbone network of CERNET. (ii) $CERNET_{Sub1}$, $CERNET_{Sub2}$, and $CERNET_{Sub3}$ are three sub-networks of CERNET connect to $CERNET_{BACKBONE}$ through border routers. (iii) ISP_1, ISP_2, and ISP_3 are three neighboring ISP networks connected to CERNET through edge routers.

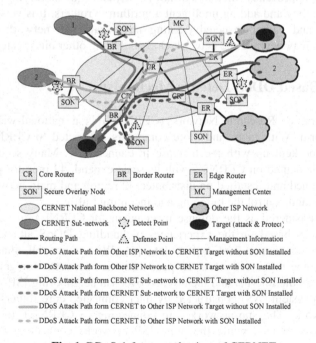

| CR | Core Router | BR | Border Router | ER | Edge Router |

| SON | Secure Overlay Node | MC | Management Center |

⬭ CERNET National Backbone Network   ⬭ Other ISP Network

⬤ CERNET Sub-network   ⬡ Detect Point   ⬤ Target (attack & Protect)

— Routing Path   △ Defense Point   — Management Information

═══ DDoS Attack Path form Other ISP Network to CERNET Target without SON Installed

● ● ● DDoS Attack Path form Other ISP Network to CERNET Target with SON Installed

═══ DDoS Attack Path form CERNET Sub-network to CERNET Target without SON Installed

● ● ● DDoS Attack Path form CERNET Sub-network to CERNET Target with SON Installed

─── DDoS Attack Path form CERNET to Other ISP Network Target without SON Installed

● ● ● DDoS Attack Path form CERNET to Other ISP Network with SON Installed

Fig. 1. DDoS defense mechanism of CERNET

Different roles of attacking and defending in Figure 1 are shown as followings:

(i) Two targets (attack and protect)

T_1 is the target located in the $CERNET_{Sub3}$, and T_2 is the target located in the ISP_1.

(ii) Three DDoS attack sources

A_1 is the DDoS attack launched by ISP_2 targeted the T_1 (outside attack)

A_2 is the DDoS attack launched by $CERNET_{Sub1}$ targeted the T_1 (inside attack)

A_3 is the DDoS attack launched by $CERNET_{Sub2}$ targeted the T_2 (inside attack)

(iii) Five defense points

The defense point with six angles means this point has the function of DDoS attack detecting and defending, while the point with triangle means this point only has defending function without detection.

D_{P1} and D_{P2} are the victim-end defense points without the detection function. The detection of DDoS attack is done by the Intrusion Detection System (IDS) installed on the sub-network or ISP network.

D_{P1}, D_{DP2}, and D_{DP3} are source-end defense points with both function of detection and defense.

(iv) Three attack paths

Two defense points are designed for every attack path, one source-end and one victim-end. Each attack path is denoted in two lines, the solid is the real attack path, the while dashed is the path through defense points.

$P_{ISP2-Sub3}$ is the attack path from ISP_2 to $CERNET_{Sub3}$ passing D_{P1} and D_{DP1}.

$P_{Sub1-Sub3}$ is the attack path from $CERNET_{Sub1}$ to $CERNET_{Sub3}$ passing D_{P1} and D_{DP2}.

$P_{Sub2-ISP1}$ is the attack path from $CERNET_{Sub2}$ to ISP_1 passing D_{P2} and D_{DP3}.

Note that in practical application of large ISP networks, the attack targets and sources are changeable, resulting in the change of attack path. In this case, each defense point has the function of both source-end and victim-end defense.

The differences between DSON and redirection-based defense mechanism are that: (i) Redirection modifies router configuration to change the routing policy, while DSON uses diverting algorithm to change the traffic normal path. (ii) Redirection uses Manager Node (MGR) to reconfigure the routing polics of edge and border router, while DSON adopts MC to manage the distributed SONs. The distinguished difference between DSON and D-ward is the executor for traffic limiting. The former is SON, the latter is router. D-ward has the function of traffic observation and rule-based traffic limiting, while SON not only monitors the traffic, also has the ability to remove malicious packets.

4 Design of SON

SON working together with an associated router as Riverhead [8]. If a DDoS attack is detected, all traffic destined to the target (protected and attacked) is then diverted off normal path through the SON, which applies filtering rule (algorithm) and judges guide-line to identify and eliminate malicious packets, allowing legitimate transactions to pass. Traffic to target is diverted to SON, which works in two operation modes depending on its two main functions: (i) *Defend*: SON actively filters out attack traffic and forwards legitimate traffic to the target. (ii) *Statistic*: if there no attack detected, SON sniffs at the traffic and extracts the data for statistic analysis. This helps SON to learn the normal behavior of every connection and client to establish a standard model. When the standard model is built, SON monitors the traffic behavior. Two situations will make SON switch from *Statistic* mode to *Defend* mode automatically: (i) If SON notices a deviant traffic behavior, which does not match the standard model. (ii) When an alert coming from the MP associated with current SON [8]. The working process of SON is divided into three steps: (i) Charging the target's traffic diverted from the associated router. (ii) Removing malicious packets. (iii) Returning legitimate to router and forwarding them to target.

Three kinds of SONs are designed for cooperation with different routers according to the throughput: (i) Intel network processor platform IXP 2800 is used for first kind of SON, with throughput of 2.5G (test at 256 bytes packet length, at 64 bytes the throughput is 0.75G). (ii) Intel network processor platform IXP 1200 is used for second SON, with throughput of 1G (test at 256 bytes packet length, at 64 bytes the throughput is 0.32G). (iii) AMD 64bits server is used for third SON, with throughput of 0.1G (test at 256 bytes packet length, at 64 bytes the throughput is 0.05G).

5   Key Technologies of SON

In statistic mode, traffic is diverted through the DSON so it could learn the normal behavior of different connections and clients to establish a baseline profile. Once the profile is built, the operator interacts with the DSON and may adjust or accept any of the suggested parameters.

(i) Traffic divert

When an attack has been detected, diversion is achieved by the SON sending out an iBGP announcement, the traffic should be routed to the Label Switching Protocol (LSP) path that ends at the SON's loop-back interface. To ensure that the BGP announcements will not propagate into all the backbone routers' routing tables, no-advertise and no-export BGP is applied on the community strings. As a result, only associated router will receive the BGP announcements about the target, with next hop to the corresponding SON loop-back interface [8].

(2) Detection approach

The detection of DDoS attacks adopts the technology of signal processing based on the frequency-domain characteristics from the autocorrelation sequence of Internet traffic streams [9]. The arrivals of network packet are expressed in a packet process: $\{X(t), t = n\Delta, n \in N\}$, where Δ is the constant interval. N is number of packet. X(t) represents the total number of packet arrivals at one router in $(t - \Delta, t]$ [10][11]. Take a single TCP flow plus one constant rate UDP flow with a rate of 300Kb/sec as the attack flow (Figure 2). The attack flow is destined to the target together with normal traffic. In this case, Δ =5ms.

In order to detect the attack flow from the normal flow, the packet arrivals are converted into frequency domain by adopting Discrete Fourier Transform (DFT):

$$DFT(x(n),k) = \frac{1}{N}\sum_{n=0}^{N-1} x(n)e^{-j2\pi kn/N} \qquad (1)$$

Where, $k = 0,1,2……N$-1. Equation (1) generates the amplitude spectrum of packets arrivals (Figure 3).

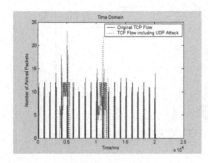
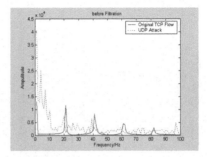

Fig. 2. TCP flow and UDP attack   **Fig. 3.** The amplitude of TCP flow and UDP attack

PSD implies the frequency-domain characteristics from the autocorrelation sequence of Internet traffic streams. The normalized cumulative PSD (NCPSD) curve of autocorrelation function of packet process is shown as Figure 4.

It shows that more than 85% of the packet process's energy distributes in frequency band [0, 50] Hz if the traffic contains a DDoS stream. By contrast, if there is no DDoS stream contained, the energy located in this low frequency band is less than 35%. This implies that NCPSD is a robust criterion in detecting whether current sampled traffic contains shrew streams [10][11].

To detect DDoS attack is to find out the frequency point, called detection point F_D, where the biggest distance between the NCPSD curve of TCP flow and UDP attack occurs. In this case, F_D =50Hz, which corresponds to cutting point where NCPSD=0.6. An optimal tradeoff is made between detection probability PD, false negative alarm rate PFN, and false positive alarm rate PFP during tests. The tests result is shown in Table 1 [10][11].

Table 1. Detection test result

Items	Threshold	NCPSD	F_D	P_D	P_{FN}	P_{FP}
Result	5.45	0.618	50Hz	0.902	0.098	0.154

(3) Filtering algorithm

The filtering algorithm is to design the finite impulse response (FIR) filter $H(\omega) = \sum_{i=1}^{N} H_i(\omega)$ for filtering the illegitimate frequencies in frequency domain and improve the LAR (Legitimate traffic to Attacked traffic Ratio). Where $H_i(\omega)$ is the filter for i^{-th} TCP flow, N is the total number of TCP flow. Based on the result of

DDoS attack detection, the attack and noise flows of network traffic will be filtered out when each packet passing through $H(\omega)$. The filtering result is shown as Figure.5.

Calculate the energy of TCP flow and UDP attack individually; the energy ratio of TCP to UDP is noted as *ERTU*. Test result shows the ERTU increases about 10dB (Table 2).

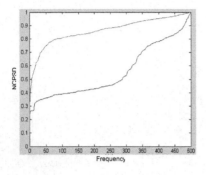

Fig. 4. The NCPSD curve   **Fig. 5.** Filtering result

Table 2. Test result (dB)

Item	Original	Filtering
ERTU	-19.3121	-10.8417

6 Performance Test with CERNET Data

The test of DSON performance is conducted by using the data that collected for CERNET.

(1) Flood-type DDoS attack to CERNET
Reports from CERNET NOC and CERNET Computer Emergency Response Team (CCERT) show that many mission-critical web sites of CERNET experienced many times flood-type DDoS attacks. Traffic Accounting record of CERNET show that a DDoS attack happened from AM 6:25 to 8:15, July 14, 2005, congestion in the rush hour is so serious (max traffic up to 453,667kpps) that lead to a lot of packets (Legitimate and attack) dropped, the traffic accounting of inbound and outbound descended shapely. Obviously, this attack causes big economy loss to CERNET [7], because this attack leads to a wrong traffic account.

At PM 1:10, Mar. 28, 2005, monitor center of CERNET record the detail information about one important Web page server of CERNET suffer from TCP SYN flood attack. This attack directs about 100 of compromised zombie hosts, all IP are spoofed. It adopts TCP protocol, average packets length is 60 Bytes [7].

Table 3 shows the records for 4 zombie hosts (in shorten, only list 4 of 100 zombie hosts' records). Table.4 is the analysis result to one zombie host. For privacy purpose, the destination (target) IP and source IP is omitted. These data of attack traffic are collected and stored in disc array storage for future testing of DSON performance.

Table 3. Records of four zombie hosts (4 sources IP) TCP SYN flood attack

Protocol	Bandwidth (Mbps)/Percent	Packets/sec/Percent	Average packet (Bytes)
TCP	12.43 (1.45%)	27161 (7.56%)	60
TCP	7.55 (0.88%)	16496 (4.59%)	60
TCP	7.13 (0.83%)	15589(4.34%)	60
TCP	6.63 (0.78%)	14497(4.04%)	60

Note: Percent in bandwidth means every attack TCP link occupies in total practical bandwidth 857.9 Mbps, and percent in packets expresses the packets of every attack TCP link sending occupies in total practical packets 359390.

Table 4. Analysis result to one zombie host(Single source IP)

Src_port	Dst_port	Protocol	Bandwidth (Mbps)	PPS	Average packet (Bytes)
329	80	6 (TCP)	0.033	72	60
718	80	6 (TCP)	0.032	70	60
851	80	6 (TCP)	0.032	69	60
833	80	6 (TCP)	0.031	68	60

(2) Defending against DDoS attack test

Every SON assigns an IP address. The management information of communication between SON and MC adopts the TCP/IP protocol. The former executing as a detector and the latter acting as a controller of the flood-type DDoS attack. MP detects the traffic destined to a certain network that are exceed "normal" levels, then SON examines the traffic of different port numbers, and/or different sources in order to detect the offending source or the characteristic port number. Experiment environment for testing the performance of DSON scheme is built by connecting to CERNET and TUNET (Tsinghua University Campus Network) as Figure 6.

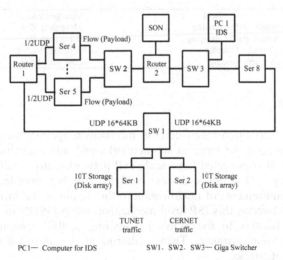

PC1— Computer for IDS   SW1、SW2、SW3— Giga Switcher

Ser1、Ser2—1U server with two giga network cards and 1CT disc array storage

Ser3、Ser4、Ser5、Ser7、Serv8—1U server with two giga network cards

Ser6—2U server with three giga network cards

Fig. 6. Test environment

The flows in this environment are composed of two kinds traffic: (i) Background flow come from the real flow of CERNET and TUNET. (ii) Attack flow is the playback of attack traffic, which is collected and stored in disc array. The background flow combines attack flow in the UDP (User Datagram Protocol) of 64KB in length. Each flow consists of 16 UDP packets.

In the experiment environment, router 1 and ser 4, 5 insert the payload to the packet and assign the flow to construct the attack path. Router 2 acts as the edge router cooperated with the SON to defend the attack. Ser 8 plays three roles: (i) Target for the attack. (ii) Indicator for the test result evaluation. (iii) Playback of attack scenery circularly for repeat testing.

Test result (Table 5) from the output of ser 8 shows that the SON has a good performance in filtering attack packets.

Table 5. Records of four zombie hosts (4 sources IP) TCP SYN flood attack survival

Protocol	Bandwidth (Mbps) /Percent	Packets/sec/Percent	Average packet (Bytes)
TCP	0.1864 (0.0217%)	407 (0.1133%)	60
TCP	0.0083 (0.0088%)	165 (0.0459%)	60
TCP	0.0071 (0.0083%)	156 (0.0434%)	60
TCP	0.0066 (0.0077%)	145 (0.0404%)	60

Statistics to the experiment result shows (Table 6) that the average ratio of legitimate traffic passing is more than 92%, legitimate traffic dropping is less than 8%, attack traffic filtering is more than 98.5%, and attack traffic passing is less than 1.5%.

Table 6. Test statistics result

Item	Average Percent
Legitimate traffic passing	More than 92%
Legitimate traffic dropping	Less than 8%
Attack traffic Filtering	More than 98.5%
Attack traffic passing	Less than 1.5%

7 Conclusion

In this paper, a distribution-based defense mechanism against flood-type attacks is proposed for protecting the targeted sub-networks and mission-critical Web sites of CERNT. For a well-constructed large-scale ISP networks, any small modification to the routing policy and network devices will lead to big troubles. Based on the principle of no requirements of modification to the topology and protocol of existing large-scale ISP networks, this ISP level mechanism using DSON to divert the traffic with suspicious packets to the SONs by sending a BGP announcement to the associated edge or border routers. Then, a filtering algorithm in frequency domain is applied to filter out attacks.

We will further study how to improve the accuracy of the malicious packet search process, develop the IP trace-back system to catch attacking source sites against a variety of attacks, and protect large-scale ISP network from vicious attacks to ensure business continuity.

Acknowledgement

The authors like to thank the CERNET NOC and CCRET for providing network data, and thank the anonymous reviewers for their hard works.

References

1. Keromytis, A.D., Misra, V., Rubenstein, D.: SOS: Architecture for Mitigating DDoS Attacks. Journal, IEEE Journal on selected areas in communications 22(1), 176–188 (2004)
2. Keromytis, A.D., Misra, V., Rubenstein, D.: SOS: Secure Overlay Services. In: Proc. of ACM SIGCOMM' 2002, August 2002, ACM Press, New York (2002)
3. Chen, S., Chow, R.: A New Perspective in Defending against DDoS. Distributed Computing Systems. In: FTDCS 2004. Proceedings. 10th IEEE International Workshop on Future Trends, 26-28 May 2004, pp. 186–90 (2004)
4. Hamano, T., Suzuki, R., et al.: A Redirection-based Defense Mechanism against Flood-type Attacks in Large-scale ISP Networks. In: Proceedings, 10th Asia-Pacific Conference on Communications and 5th International Symposium on Multi-Dimensional Mobile Communications, Taiwan, pp. 1–15 (2001)
5. Mirkovic, J., Prier, G., Reiher, P.: Attacking DDoS at the source. In: Proceedings, 10th IEEE International Conference on Network Protocols, Paris, France, November 2002, pp. 312–321. IEEE Computer Society Press, Los Alamitos (2002)
6. Mirkovic, J., Dietrich, S., Dittrich, D., Reiher, P.: Internet Denial Service: Attack and Defense Mechanisms. In: Prentic Hall Professional Technical Reference, Coirier in Stoughton, Massachusetts (December 2004) ISBN: 0-13-147573-8
7. Technical report, DDoS attack and defense of CERNET, CCERT, report, Network Research Center, Tsinghua University (March 2005)
8. DDoS Mitigation: Maintaining Business Continuity in the Face of Malicious Attacks, report, Technical Note, Riverhead, Cisco (2004)
9. Cheng, C.-M., Kung, H.T., Tan, K.-S.: Use of Spectral Analysis in Defense Against DoS Attacks. In: Proceedings, IEEE GLOBECOM (2002)
10. Chen, Y., Hwang, K., Kwok, Y.-K.: Filtering of Shrew DDoS Attacks in Frequency Domain. In: Proceedings of the IEEE Conference on Local Computer Networks, 30th Anniversary, 15-17 November 2005, pp. 786–793 (2005)
11. Chen, Y., Hwang, K., Kwok, Y.-K.: Collaborative Defense against Periodic Shrew DDoS Attacks in Frequency Domain. Journal, ACM Transactions on Information and System Security (TISSEC), 1–30 (May 3, 2005)

Security Analysis of the Authentication Modules of Chinese WLAN Standard and Its Implementation Plan*

Xinghua Li[1,2], Jianfeng Ma[1], and SangJae Moon[2]

[1] Key Laboratory of Computer Networks and Information Security(Ministry of Education),
Xidian University, Xi'an 710071, China
[2] Mobile Network Security Technology Research Center, Kyungpook National University,
Sankyuk-dong, Buk-ku, Daegu 702-701, Korea

Abstract. With the Canetti-Krawczyk (CK) model, we analyze the authentication module WAIs in the Chinese WLAN national security standard WAPI and its implementation plan respectively. The security weaknesses of WAI in the original WAPI are presented; then WAI in the implementation plan is proved secure in the CK model; at last we point out how the implementation plan overcomes the security weaknesses in the original WAPI.

Keywords: WLAN, WAPI, Key-agreement protocol, Canetti-Krawczyk model.

1 Introduction

The Chinese WLAN standard WAPI (GB 15629.11-2003) [1], the first issued Chinese standard in the field of WLAN, has been formally implemented since November 1, 2003. WAPI (WLAN Authentication and Privacy Infrastructure) is composed of two parts: WAI (Wireless Authentication Infrastructure) and WPI (Wireless Privacy Infrastructure). They realize the identity authentication and data encryption, respectively. In March of 2004, China IT Standardization Technical Committee drafted out a new version, WAPI implementation plan [2], which improves the original standard WAPI. Compared with the original standard, the greatest change the implementation plan made lies in the WAI module.

As a national standard which is about to be deployed and implemented in a big scale, its security is undoubtedly the focus. But as far as we know, up to now, there are no articles that systemically analyze the security of WAPI and its implementation plan, which is imperfect for a national standard. This contribution discusses the security of WAPI and its implementation plan with the Canetti-Krawczyk (CK) model [3]. It has three contributions. (1) The security weaknesses of WAI in WAPI are given. (2) The WAI module in the implementation plan is proved secure in the CK model. (3) How the implementation plan overcomes the security weaknesses of the original WAPI is

* Research supported by the National Natural Science Foundation of China (Grant No.90204012, No. 60633020), the National "863" High-tech Project of China (Grant No. 2002AA143021), the Excellent Young Teachers Program of Chinese Ministry of Education, the Key Project of Chinese Ministry of Education, and the University IT Research Center Project of Korea.

K. Li et al. (Eds.): NPC 2007, LNCS 4672, pp. 306–314, 2007
© IFIP International Federation for Information Processing 2007

pointed out. The analysis results can help us understand the necessity of the implementation plan and enhance the confidence of it. At the same time, as a case study, their analysis is helpful for the design of a secure key-agreement protocol.

The rest of the paper is organized as follows. In Section 2, we give an overview of the CK model. In Section 3, WAIs in the WAPI and its implementation plan are introduced. In Section 4, WAI in WAPI is analyzed and its security weaknesses are presented. We analyze WAI in the implementation plan in Section 5. In Section 6, we point out how the implementation plan overcomes the security weaknesses in the original national standard. This paper is concluded in Section 7.

2 The CK Model

At present, the CK model is a very popular formal methodology for the analysis of key-agreement protocols [4]. In this section, we give a brief description of the CK model.

A key-exchange (KE) protocol is run in a network of interconnected parties where each party can be activated to run an instance of the protocol called a session. A KE session is a quadruple (A, B, X, Y) where A is the identity of the holder of the session, B the peer, X the outgoing messages in the session, and Y the incoming messages. The session (B, A, Y, X) (if it exists) is said to be matching to the session (A, B, X, Y). Matching sessions play a fundamental role in the definition of security [3].

2.1 Attacker Model

The attacker is modeled to capture realistic attack capabilities in open networks, including the control of communication links and the access to some of the secret information used or generated in the protocol. The attacker, denoted $\mathcal{M}$, is an active "man-in-the-middle" adversary with full control of the communication links between parties. $\mathcal{M}$ can intercept and modify messages sent over these links, it can delay or prevent their delivery, inject its own messages, interleave messages from different sessions, etc. (Formally, it is $\mathcal{M}$ to whom parties hand their outgoing messages for delivery.) $\mathcal{M}$ also schedules all session activations and session-message delivery. In addition, in order to model potential disclosure of secret information, the attacker is allowed to access to secret information via session exposure attacks of three types: state-reveal queries, session-key queries, and party corruption [3].

2.2 Definition of Session-Key Security

In addition to the regular actions of the attacker $\mathcal{M}$ against a key-exchange protocol π, he can perform a *test session query*. That is, at any time during its run, $\mathcal{M}$ is able to choose, a *test-session* among the sessions that are completed, unexpired and unexposed at the time. Let k be the value of the corresponding session key. We toss a coin b, $b \xleftarrow{R} \{0,1\}$. If $b=0$ we provide $\mathcal{M}$ with the value k. Otherwise we provide $\mathcal{M}$ with a value r randomly chosen from the probability distribution of keys generated by protocol π. The attacker M is not allowed state-reveal queries, session-key queries, or party corruption on the test-session or its matching session. At the end of its run, M outputs a bit b' (as its guess for b).

An attacker that is allowed test-session queries is referred to as a KE-adversary.

Definition 1. Session-key Security: A key-exchange protocol π is called Session-key secure (or SK-secure) if the following properties hold for any KE-adversary M.

1. *Protocol π satisfies the property that if two uncorrupted parties complete matching sessions then they both output the same key; and*
2. *the probability that M guesses correctly the bit b(i.e., outputs $b'=b$) is no more than $1/2$ plus a negligible fraction ε in the security parameter. ε is called "advantage".*

3 WAIs in WAPI and Its Implementation Plan

WAI adopts port-based authentication architecture that is identical with IEEE 802.1X. The whole system is composed of mobile guest STA, Access Point (AP), and Authentication Service Unit (ASU).

3.1 WAI in WAPI

The interaction procedure of WAI in the original national standard WAPI is shown in Fig.1. From this figure, we can see that WAI is composed of two parts: certificate authentication and key agreement.

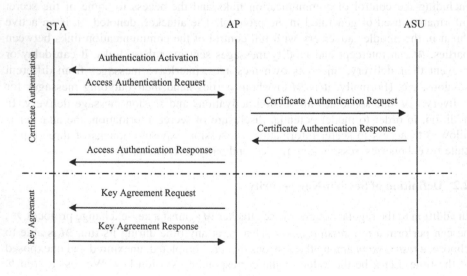

Fig. 1. WAI in WAPI

(1) Certificate authentication
In this process, STA sends its public key certificate and access request time to AP in the Access Authentication Request. AP sends its certificate, STA's certificate, STA's access request time and its signature on them to ASU in Certificate Authentication Request. After ASU validates AP's signature and the two certificates, it sends the certificates validation result, STA's access request time and ASU's signature on them to STA and AP.

(2) Key agreement
First, STA and AP negotiate the cryptography algorithms. Then, they respectively generate one random value r_1 and r_2. These random values are encrypted with the peer's public key and sent to each other. Both parties decrypt the encrypted random values and derive the session key $K=r_1 \oplus r_2$. The key agreement process is shown in Fig.2, where $ENC(\ )$ is the encryption function, PK_{AP} and PK_{STA} are AP and STA's public key respectively.

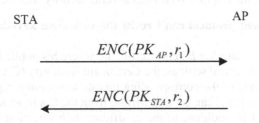

Fig. 2. The key agreement in the WAI of WAPI

3.2 WAI in the Implementation Plan

In the framework, WAI in the implementation plan is same as that of the original WAPI, and it is also composed of certificate authentication and key agreement. Compared with the original standard WAPI, the implementation plan remains unchanged in the certificate authentication, but makes rather big improvement in the key agreement. The new key agreement protocol is shown in Fig.3. It is different from the original one in the following points:

(1)   In the implementation plan, the Key Agreement Request has to be initiated by AP. At the same time, the secure parameter index SPI, AP's signature on the encrypted random value and SPI are included in this request. The signature algorithm is ECDSA.

(2)   In the Key Agreement Response, SPI and the STA's message authentication code on encrypted random and SPI are included. The message authentication code is computed through HMAC-SHA256 algorithm.

(3)   The keys derivation method is different. STA and AP first calculate the host key $k= r_1 \oplus r_2$, then extend k with KD-HMAC-SHA256 algorithm to get the session key k_d, the authentication key k_a and integration check key.

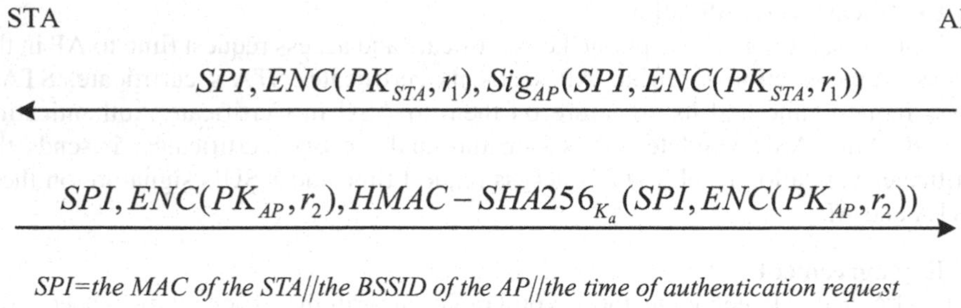

STA   AP

$$\xleftarrow{\quad SPI, ENC(PK_{STA}, r_1), Sig_{AP}(SPI, ENC(PK_{STA}, r_1)) \quad}$$

$$\xrightarrow{\quad SPI, ENC(PK_{AP}, r_2), HMAC - SHA256_{K_a}(SPI, ENC(PK_{AP}, r_2)) \quad}$$

SPI=the MAC of the STA||the BSSID of the AP||the time of authentication request

Fig. 3. The key agreement protocol in WAI of the implementation plan

4 The Security Weaknesses of WAI in WAPI

The WAI module in the original WAPI has several security weaknesses as follows.

(1) Its key agreement protocol can't resist the unknown key-share (UKS) attack [5, 6]

We assume that an attacker E gets a certificate where his public key PK_E is same as PK_{STA}. (In many practical settings, the Certificate Authority (CA) does not require a proof-of-possession of the corresponding private key from a registrant of a public key [7], so an attacker E can get a certificate from the CA in which his public key is same as STA's.) In addition, in the certificate authentication process, ASU just verifies the authenticity and validity of a certificate, so E also can pass the certification authentication. Then he can launch the unknown-key share attack in the key agreement. When STA sends the first message $ENC(PK_{AP}, r_1)$, E forwards this message to AP and claims that this message is from E. Then AP replies with $ENC(PK_E, r_2)$. E forwards this message to STA. When the protocol completes, STA thinks that he agreed upon a key with AP, while AP thinks that he negotiated a key with E. And these two keys are same. So, the attacker E succeeds in the unknown-key share attack.

Let's analyze this attack in the CK model. In the attack above, the KE-adversary chooses the session in STA as the test session and expose the session in AP (because these two sessions are not matching sessions, the session in AP can be exposed). Because STA and AP get a same session key, the KE-adversary can completely get the session key of the test session. According to Definition 1, this protocol is not SK-secure. And [8] can be referred to for the consequences of this attack.

(2) Its key agreement protocol can't resist key-compromise impersonation (KCI) attack

Let's analyze this attack in the CK model. First, we assume that STA's private key is compromised and the attacker chooses the session in STA as the test session after STA complete the matching sessions with AP. The attacker can first corrupt another mobile guest STA' and impersonates him to send message $ENC(PK_{AP}, r_1)$ to AP. We denote the session between STA' and AP as SID'. When AP receives this message from STA', he chooses another random value r_3 and responds with $ENC(PK_{STA'}, r_3)$. AP computes its session key of SID' $k' = r_1 \oplus r_3$. The attacker can expose this session and get k' (this session is not the matching session of the test session). In addition, the attacker can decrypt $ENC(PK_{STA'}, r_3)$ to get r_3. Thus he can get $r_1 = k' \oplus r_3$. In addition, the attacker can also decrypt $ENC(PK_{STA}, r_2)$ to get r_2. Then he can get the session key of the test session: $k = r_1 \oplus r_2$. Thus the attacker can impersonate AP to STA. According to Definition 1, this protocol is not SK-secure.

(3) It does not realize the explicit identity authentication of STA and perhaps lead to the faulty charge

From the WAI process, we can see that it does not realize the explicit identity authentication of STA to AP. An attacker can pass the certificate authentication and access the networks only if he gets a legal user's certificate, which will lead to the faulty charge if the networks charge the fee according to the access time.

5 The Security Analysis of WAI in WAPI Implementation Plan

In the certificate authentication, AP makes signature in the certificate authentication request, and ASU makes signature in the certificate authentication response. Both these signatures include STA's access request time which ensures the freshness of the signatures. Therefore ASU can authenticate AP's identity and STA can authenticate ASU's identity. In addition, STA trusts ASU. So STA can authenticate the identity of AP after the certificate authentication. At the same time, AP authenticates the certificate provided by STA.

The key agreement protocol in WAI of implementation plan is denoted by π. In the following, we will prove that π is SK-secure without PFS [9]. That is, the protocol is SK-secure, but does not provide perfect forward secrecy of the session keys. In order to prove that π is SK-secure, we define a "game". The game designed is very similar to the one in [11], therefore authors can refer to [11] for details.

5.1 Security Analysis of Key Agreement Protocol in WAI

According to Definition 1, in order to prove that π is SK-secure, we have to argue that it can meet two requirements. The first one is that STA and AP can get a same session key after they complete matching sessions. The second one is that $\mathcal{B}$ cannot distinguish the session key k_d from a random value with a non-negligible advantage. In the following, we will prove that π can meet these two requirements.

Lemma 1. *If the encryption scheme ENC is secure against the CCA2 attack, then at the end of protocol π, STA and AP will complete matching sessions and get a same session key.*[11]

Lemma 2. *If the encryption scheme ENC is secure against the CCA2 attack, the attacker cannot distinguish the session key k_d from a random value with a non-negligible advantage.* [11]

Theorem 1. *If the encryption scheme ENC adopted is secure against CCA2 attack, then* π *is SK-secure without PFS.*

Proof. According to Lemma 1, Lemma 2 and Definition 1, we can get that the protocol π is SK-secure.

In addition, if the private keys of STA and AP are compromised, the attacker can get the random values exchanged and can work out all the session keys that have been agreed about. Thus this protocol cannot provide PFS. So we can get that the key-agreement protocol is SK-secure without PFS. $\square$

6 The Implementation Plan Overcomes the Weaknesses of the Original WAPI

We know that WAI in the original WAPI has some security weaknesses. But WAI in the implementation plan is secure in the CK model, and according to [13], we get that the WAI module of the implementation plan can resist KCI attack and UKS attack. In the following, we will analyze how the implementation plan overcomes the security weaknesses in the original WAPI.

(1) The key agreement protocol in the implementation plan can resist UKS attack
In the implementation plan, even though the attacker $\mathcal{B}$ gets a certificate in which his public key is same as STA's or AP's, he cannot launch the UKS attack. Because the implementation plan requires that the key agreement request be sent by AP, STA just accepts the request from AP. So, $\mathcal{B}$ can just launch the UKS attack against the AP (i.e., AP thinks that he agrees upon a key with $\mathcal{B}$, but in fact he negotiates a key with STA, while STA correctly thinks that he negotiates a key with AP), that is, $\mathcal{B}$ just can forwards the key agreement request message for him to STA. But in this request, AP's signature includes SPI which includes the MAC address of the $\mathcal{B}$, so STA will not accept this request forwarded from $\mathcal{B}$. Therefore the key agreement protocol in WAI of implementation plan can resist the UKS attack.

From the analysis above, we can see that the essential reasons that WAI in the implementation plan can resist the UKS attack are that: (1) the implementation plan requires that the key agreement request be sent from AP; (2) AP's signature includes SPI which includes the destination entity's address.

(2) The key agreement protocol in the WAI of the implementation plan can resist the KCI attack
KCI attacks for the protocol π have two manners. The first one is that AP's private key is compromised and the attacker can impersonate STA to AP. The second one is that STA's private key is compromised and the attacker can impersonate AP to STA. In the following, we will discuss these two cases respectively.

If AP's private key is compromised, the attacker can decrypt $ENC(PK_{AP}, r_2)$ to get r_2. In order to get r_1, he just has two possible methods: (1) attacks the encryption algorithm ENC; (2) impersonates other entity to establish another session with STA, and sends $ENC(PK_{STA}, r_1)$ to STA, then the attacker exposes this session and gets r_1 through some computations. But neither of these two methods is feasible. For the first method, we know that if the encryption algorithm ENC is CCA2 secure, the attacker cannot get r_1 from the attack of this algorithm directly. As for the second method, the implementation plan requires the key agreement request be sent by AP, and the attacker cannot forge AP's signature, so the attacker cannot impersonate other entity to establish another session with STA. Therefore the attacker cannot get r_1. Then he still cannot get the host key k and session key k_d.

If STA's private key is compromised, the attacker can decrypt $ENC(PK_{STA}, r_1)$ to get r_1. In order to get session key r_2, he just has two possible methods: (1) attacks the encryption algorithm ENC directly to get r_2; (2) impersonates another mobile guest STA' to establish a new session with AP and sends it $ENC(PK_{AP}, r_2)$ in the key agreement acknowledgement. From the analysis above we get that the first method is infeasible. As for the second method, because r_2 and the host key k are just the ephemeral values, we assume that they are not the session states of AP. Therefore, the session states of the new session in AP are just the session key k_d^*, the message authentication key k_a^* and the message integration key. The attacker cannot get any information about r_2 from these session states because these three keys are the hash values of the host key k^*. Therefore the attacker cannot get r_2 either. (If the session key is not the hash value of k^*, the attacker can get k^*, futher can get r_2.) So the attacker still cannot get the host key k and the session key k_d.

As a whole, the essential reasons that the key agreement protocol can resist KCI attack are that: (1) the implementation plan requires that the key agreement request be sent by AP; (2) the session key in the implementation plan is derived through the hash function.

(3) The WAI module in the implementation plan realizes the mutual explicit identity authentication between STA and AP, which can withstand faulty charge
For AP, π is an explicit key authentication protocol [12]. So AP can authenticate the identity of STA at the end of WAI. At the same time, STA can authenticate the identity of AP in the certificate authentication. Therefore WAI in the implementation plan realizes the mutual explicit identity authentication between AP and STA. Therefore it can withstand faulty charge.

7 Conclusion

With the CK model, this paper analyzes the authentication module WAIs in the original WAPI and its implementation plan. The security weaknesses of WAI in the original WAPI are presented: its key agreement protocol cannot resist the UKS and KCI attacks; it does not realize the explicit identity authentication and can lead to the faulty charge. Then the WAI module in WAPI implementation plan is analyzed. We prove that if the encryption scheme ENC adopted is secure against the CCA2 attack, then the WAI module in the implementation plan is SK-secure without PFS. At last we analyze how the implementation plan overcomes the security weaknesses in the original WAPI. Compared with the original standard WAPI, the security of the implementation plan is improved greatly.

References

1. National Standard of the People's Republic of China. GB 15629.11-2003, Information technology-Telecommunications and information exchange between systems – Local and metropolitan area networks–Specific requirements – Part 11: Wireless LAN Medium Access Control (MAC) and Physical Layer (PHY) Specifications (2003)
2. National Standard of the People's Republic of China. Guide for GB 15629.11-2003, Information technology - Telecommunications and information exchange between systems-Local and metropolitan area networks- Specific requirements–Part 11: Wireless LAN Medium Access Control (MAC) and Physical Layer (PHY) Specifications and GB 15629.1102-2003, Information technology –Telecommunications and information exchange between systems–Local and metropolitan area networks–Specific requirements-Part 11: Wireless LAN Medium access control (MAC) and physical layer(PHY) Specifications: Higher-Speed Physical layer Extension in the 2.4 GHz Band (2004)
3. Canetti, R., Krawczyk, H.: Analysis of Key-Exchange Protocols and Their Use for Building Secure Channel. In: Pfitzmann, B. (ed.) EUROCRYPT 2001. LNCS, vol. 2045, pp. 453–474. Springer, Heidelberg (2001)
4. Boyd, C., Mao, W., Paterson, K.: Key Agreement using Statically Keyed Authenticators. In: Jakobsson, M., Yung, M., Zhou, J. (eds.) ACNS 2004. LNCS, vol. 3089, pp. 248–262. Springer, Heidelberg (2004)
5. Burton, S., Kaliski, J.R.: An unknown key-share attack on the MQV key agreement protocol. ACM transactions on Information and System Security 4(3), 275–288 (2001)
6. Blake-Wilson, S., Johnson, D., Menezes, A.: Key agreement protocols and their security analysis. In: Darnell, M. (ed.) Cryptography and Coding. LNCS, vol. 1355, pp. 30–45. Springer, Heidelberg (1997)
7. Krawczyk, H.: HMQV: A High-Performance Secure Diffie-Hellman Protocol. In: Shoup, V. (ed.) CRYPTO 2005. LNCS, vol. 3621, pp. 546–566. Springer, Heidelberg (2005)
8. Diffie, W., Oorschot, P.V., Wiener, M.: Authentication and authenticated key exchanges. Designs, Codes and Cryptography 2, 107–125 (1992)
9. Güther, C.G.: An identity-based key-exchange protocol. In: Quisquater, J.-J., Vandewalle, J. (eds.) EUROCRYPT 1989. LNCS, vol. 434, pp. 29–37. Springer, Heidelberg (1990)
10. Mao, W.: Modern Cryptography: Theory and Practice. Prentice Hall PTR, Englewood Cliffs (2003)
11. Li, X., Moon, S., Ma, J.: On the Security of the Authentication Module of Chinese WLAN Standard Implementation Plan. In: Zhou, J., Yung, M., Bao, F. (eds.) ACNS 2006. LNCS, vol. 3989, pp. 340–348. Springer, Heidelberg (2006)
12. Menezes, A., van Oorschot, P., Vanstone, S.: Handbook of Applied Cryptography. CRC Press (1996)
13. Li, X., Ma, J., Moon, S.: On the Security of Canetti-Krawczyk Model. In: Hao, Y., Liu, J., Wang, Y.-P., Cheung, Y.-m., Yin, H., Jiao, L., Ma, J., Jiao, Y.-C. (eds.) CIS 2005. LNCS (LNAI), vol. 3802, pp. 356–363. Springer, Heidelberg (2005)

Restoration Design in IP over Reconfigurable All-Optical Networks

Angela L. Chiu[1], Gagan Choudhury[1], Robert Doverspike[1], and Guangzhi Li[2]

[1] AT&T Labs Research, 200 Laurel Avenue, Middletown, NJ 07748, USA
[2] AT&T Labs Research, 180 Park Avenue, Florham Park, NJ 07932, USA
{chiu,rdd,gli}@research.att.com, gchoudhury@att.com

Abstract. Large IP backbone networks today are mostly deployed directly over sequences of point-to-point DWDM systems or chains of newer ROADM-based ultra long haul systems, interconnected by OEO regenerators. The next generation core optical network is moving toward an all-optical network architecture that is based on multi-degree ROADMs to reduce OEO regeneration cost as well as enabling automatic reconfigurability and dynamic restoration. In this paper, we study the restoration design in this new IP over reconfigurable all-optical network architecture to satisfy the resilience requirements for both IP and wavelength services. We propose two novel restoration schemes: 2-Phase Fast Reroute mechanism with optimized Traffic Engineering algorithm for restoring IP services and shared mesh restoration with standbys for restoring wavelength services. They both meet the requirement of sub-second restoration time and also maximize sharing among different failures with the objective of minimizing either overall capacity or overall cost. To further reduce the required restoration capacity in both IP layer and optical layer and address failures in both layers efficiently, we also propose an integrated IP-over-optical layer restoration strategy that enables sharing of restoration capacity among non-simultaneous failures across both IP and optical layers. Simulation results demonstrate significant improvements using our proposed schemes comparing with existing ones.

Keywords: IP-over-Optical, ULH, ROADM, reconfigurable all-optical network, IP service, wavelength service, fast reroute, traffic engineering, shared mesh restoration, restoration overbuild.

1 Introduction

After many years of research and industry efforts, ultra long haul (ULH) technologies for DWDM transport are maturing and carriers are deploying them for high capacity and capital savings [1, 2]. A first-generation ULH network typically consists of a set of point-to-point linear systems. Each linear system has two terminals. Between the two terminals, there are one or multiple reconfigurable optical add-drop multiplexers (ROADMs), where traffic can be added/dropped or expressed through optically (such an OADM is also called a degree-2 ROADM). With such a linear ULH system, a wavelength connection (also called a lightpath) is able to travel a long distance

K. Li et al. (Eds.): NPC 2007, LNCS 4672, pp. 315–333, 2007.
© IFIP International Federation for Information Processing 2007

(typically 1500km or longer) without requiring optical-electronic-optical (OEO) regeneration. This distance limit is called "ULH-reach". An OEO regenerator is needed when a connection length is longer than the ULH-reach or when it has to travel through two linear ULH systems even if its length is within the ULH-reach. Since the OEO regenerators are expensive devices, such a first generation ULH network is not inexpensive. They also complicate dynamic reconfiguration and restoration in the optical layer (OL).

In order to reduce the cost of OEO regeneration and enable automatic reconfigurability and dynamic restoration, next generation core optical networks are moving toward all-optical mesh networks from point-to-point linear ULH systems. This can be done via (1) converting the terminals and degree-2 ROADMs to higher-degree ROADMs to switch and route wavelengths optically [3, 4], also called as photonic cross connect (PXC), and (2) strategically placing OEO regenerators to reduce cost.

The next generation core IP network is the principal overlay network that is transported over the ROADM network, as shown in figure 1. All the middle SONET and Digital Cross-Connect System (DCS) layers are eliminated. Traditional sub-wavelength TDM private line service will be transported over the IP network via pseudo-wire circuit emulation with guaranteed minimum latency and quality of service (QoS) [5, 6]. Besides providing direct links for the IP layer, the optical network also provides wavelength services via optical connections that consist of one or multiple wavelengths. Both IP and wavelength services have very stringent quality requirements for their high priority traffic. One main requirement is resiliency against network failures including two main features: 1)The ability to restore within sub-second for high priority traffic for any single link/node failure; 2) For a small percentage of the traffic that is mission critical, the ability to restore from any double failures.

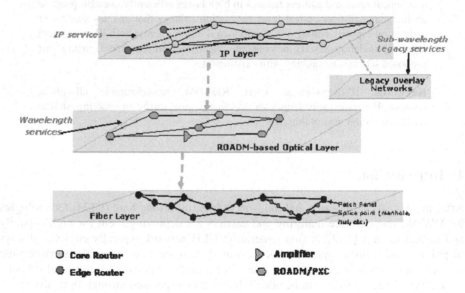

Fig. 1. IP over Reconfigurable All-Optical Network Architecture

The main challenge in reliable network design is to provide fast restoration while planning restoration capacity in a cost effective manner. After evaluating different IP-over-optical network architectures, we find that it is most cost effective to restore IP traffic in IP layer and restore wavelength traffic in optical layer since optical layer cannot restore failures that originate at the IP layer, such as router failures or router line card failures, unless some integrated method is used. However, the IP network is originally designed to support best-effort traffic and IP routing protocol re-convergence may take much longer than the sub-second restoration requirement. In this paper, we propose a novel 2-Phase Fast Reroute (FRR) mechanism with optimized Traffic Engineering algorithm to restore IP services. It meets the requirement of sub-second restoration time [7] and also maximizes sharing among single/double failures of links, routers and Shared Risk Groups (SRGs) and also among different phases of restoration with the objective of minimizing either overall capacity or overall cost. For wavelength service restoration, we propose to use shared mesh restoration (SMR) with standbys. Standbys are pre-cross-connected lightpaths providing connectivity between switching nodes (nodes with fiber link degree-2 or higher). It overcomes the problem of optical impairments for long connections, avoids today's wavelength power "balancing" delays, provides wavelength conversion for capacity efficiency and allows sharing of links across non-simultaneous failures.

Shared mesh restoration has been widely used in opaque optical networks such as AT&T's Intelligent Optical Network [8], where all restoration channels on each link are pre-installed and equipped with OEO regeneration at each end. They are thus optically isolated from other channels. When a failure is detected, a pre-planned restoration path will be dynamically established by cross-connecting unassigned channels. The whole process is automatic and rapid. In an all-optical ULH network, dynamically establishing a new restoration connection from scratch involves not only tuning the lasers and receivers to the appropriate frequencies and cross connecting the ROADMs/PXCs, but also triggering several feedback loop segments that are responsible for power equalization. This is because the new restoration wavelength(s) change the power profile on each link along the restoration path. The whole process can be slow and often unacceptable to large carriers. Furthermore, unlike an opaque optical network, an all-optical ULH channel does not necessarily have OEO regeneration at each end, thus extra OEO regenerators may be required in some nodes. Optimal regenerator placement becomes a critical problem in all-optical ULH network design. Because of these differences between electrical/opaque-optical networks and all-optical ULH networks, shared mesh restoration schemes [9, 10, 11] for opaque optical networks cannot be applied to all-optical ULH networks. Here, we propose using SMR with pre-configured (standby) lightpaths for restoring wavelength services in all-optical ULH networks.

To further reduce the required restoration capacity in both IP layer and optical layer and address failures in both IP and optical layers efficiently, we also propose to use an integrated IP-over-Optical restoration strategy that enables sharing of restoration capacity among non-simultaneous failures across layers. The basic idea is to install spare line cards on IP routers and automatically configure new IP links (or increase the capacity of existing IP links) via the optical layer after an IP-layer failure. Since component unavailability at the IP layer (e.g., failure/maintenance of a router line card or common equipment) and the optical layer (e.g., failure/maintenance of a transponder or amplifier) are generally statistically independent (i.e., nonsimultaneous with high probability), this is a clever method to pool spare capacity in the optical layer to cover failures at both IP and optical layers.

The remainder of the paper is organized as follows. Section 2 briefly reviews the assumed next generation core optical network architecture. Section 3 describes the proposed schemes for restoring IP and wavelength services. Section 4 presents numerical studies demonstrating performance advantages of the proposed schemes comparing with existing methods. The comparisons are based on simulations using a representative network. We conclude the work in section 5.

2   Next Generation Core Optical Network Architecture

The next generation core optical network consists of a set of ROADM-based network nodes interconnected by multi-wavelength fiber links with optical amplifiers (OA, also known as in-line amplifiers ILA) in a mesh topology [12]. The nodes are usually multi-degree ROADMs with wavelength blocking and/or wavelength switching capability. It also provides network operators a way to dynamically drop and add wavelengths at network nodes without having to manually balance optical parameters every time when distances traveled by individual wavelengths are changed. Figure 2 illustrates a state-of-art ROADM architecture with a broadcast-and-select switch fabric [13, 14, 15, 4, 16]: splitters send copies of each entering multi-channel signal to each output port. Nx1 wavelength selective switches (WSS's) are used to choose which of the input channels at each frequency to put on the output fiber. These devices can simultaneously provide power equalization at the channel level.

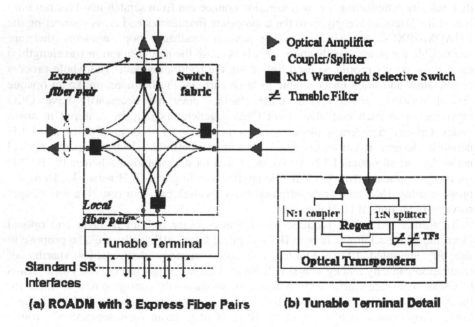

(a) ROADM with 3 Express Fiber Pairs   (b) Tunable Terminal Detail

Fig. 2. A Broadcast-and-Select ROADM Architecture

From the perspective of the switch fabric, the terminal used to add and drop channels is just another output port. It contains tunable lasers and filters that allow any wavelength at the terminal/switch fabric interface to be routed to any terminal transmit/receive port. It also contains regenerators that can do wavelength translation. Each wavelength can carry a 10Gbps or 40Gbps optical signal, and is moving towards 100Gbps rate in laboratory experiments. The optical signal is able to travel a long distance (typically 1500km or longer), i.e., the ULH-reach, without requiring OEO regeneration. Note that the ULH-reach is typically rate dependent. The main function of the reconfigurable all-optical network is to offer wavelength services as well as providing transport for links at the higher layers, mainly the IP layer, as shown in figure 1. In order to provide high resiliency for both IP and wavelength services, we examine the restoration design in the IP over reconfigurable all-optical network architecture.

The IP core network is built on top of the core optical network. We assume that the core IP routers are collocated at the same office as core optical ROADMs. IP links are wavelength connections in the optical network. Multiple IP links often share a common optical link. Thus a single optical layer failure would cause multiple simultaneous IP link failures. But there is a high probability that IP router/line card failures and optical layer failures are non-simultaneous. We take this observation and propose a novel integrated IP-over-optical layer restoration scheme.

3   Restoration Design in IP over Reconfigurable All-Optical Networks

3.1   IP Service Restoration: 2-Phase Fast Reroute with Optimized Traffic Engineering

A principal challenge for IP service restoration is to provide sub-second single-failure restoration for high-priority IP services while maintaining efficient bandwidth utilization. Two most prevalent methods for IP-layer restoration today are IP reroute and MPLS Fast Reroute (FRR) [17]. IP reroute is the default and the most common restoration method in large commercial IP networks today. It routes traffic along the shortest path using certain metric such as hop count, route mile. It uses Interior Gateway Protocol (IGP) protocols OSPF or IS-IS signaling for general topology discovery and updates and then re-computes paths upon a failure. Using default OSPF or IS-IS timer values, the re-convergence may take 10's of seconds. Currently, studies and experiments are being conducted to aggressively tuning down the timers so the re-convergence time can be reduced to a few seconds [18, 19]. MPLS Fast Reroute is an IETF standardized protocol [17] where primary and backup (restoration) Label Switched Paths (LSPs) are established for next-hop or next-next-hop MPLS FRR. When a failure is detected at the upstream router from the failure, the MPLS forwarding label for the backup LSP is "pushed" on the MPLS shim header at the upstream router and "popped" at the downstream or next-next-hop router. These labels are pre-calculated and stored in the forwarding tables, so restoration is very fast. However, in this scheme, IP flows stay routed over the backup paths until the failure is restored. Because these paths are segmental "patches" to the primary paths, the technique has poor capacity for restoring all traffic assuming that the backup paths follow the shortest paths. Algorithms for pure IP based Fast Reroute (without using MPLS signaling) have also been proposed and analyzed [18, 20].

For restoring IP services, we propose a novel 2-Phase Fast Reroute mechanism with optimized Traffic Engineering algorithm. It meets the requirement of sub-second restoration time and also maximizes sharing among single/double failures of links, routers and Shared Risk Groups and also among different phases of restoration with the objective of minimizing either overall capacity or overall cost. In phase 1, pre-computed next-hop or next-next-hop FRR tunnels would be used to restore only non-best effort traffic. Traffic switchover time has been measured in lab experiments at 50ms. Failed best effort traffic is not restored until the second phase. Note that best effort traffic that is on the backup path of the rerouted traffic is not guaranteed to have capacity, although for most failure states most flows would have enough capacity. However, this phase lasts only for a few seconds until OSPF/IS-IS or OSPF-TE/IS-IS-TE re-converges and provides a more optimal end-to-end path to be established for every primary LSP affected by the failure. During the second phase, where failed traffic is rerouted over an optimized end-to-end path, sufficient capacity is being planned for all traffic including all best effort traffic that has been indirectly affected by the failure. The failure information and Link Bandwidth availability information is obtained from IGP and its TE extension. Using this information, new end-to-end paths are established for all failed primary tunnels using a Constrained Shortest Path (CSPF) algorithm. After that all traffic flowing over the Next-Next-Hop FRR tunnels are switched over to the new and more efficient end-to-end primary tunnels. This phase lasts until the associated failure is repaired.

A key aspect of the 2-Phase FRR method is that an optimized traffic engineering algorithm is used during both phases of restoration that attempts to maximize sharing among all independent failure scenarios and attempts to minimize either the total capacity or total cost (including transport cost and IP port cost) or a linear combination of the two. Traffic Engineering algorithms have been proposed and analyzed in the past (e.g., see [21] and the references therein) but they have not been used in the past during two phases of Fast Reroute. Our proposed algorithm is distributed in nature. For each failure scenario, restoration traffic is routed using a Dijkstra shortest path algorithm where link weights along the path are chosen dynamically and depends on available and total capacity of the link, latency, and other cost measures such as IP port costs (during the operational phase this information is available through router provisioning and from OSPF-TE or IS-IS-TE Link State Advertisement packets). The algorithm reuses capacity already allocated for other independent failure scenarios as much as possible but also adds capacity, if needed, using a shortest path algorithm with dynamic link weights. Note that traditional IP routing based on OSPF/IS-IS uses static link weights and so is significantly less efficient than the proposed traffic engineering algorithm using dynamic link weights. The algorithm is also integrated with an algorithm for designing IP express links over the optical link topology with the objective of minimizing the sum of transport and IP port costs by choosing links along heavy-traffic paths while also minimizing the impact of Shared Risk Groups. The network design algorithm at first creates a large number of candidate IP express links (each one using one or more optical links) and ranks them according to the amount of working path traffic carried by them (in the numerical results section we will assume that working path uses shortest distance routing so as to minimize working path capacity, but this assumption can be relaxed to further reduce the overall capacity and cost). At any stage of the algorithm the next candidate link would typically be parts of many SRGs where SRG for a given failure scenario is defined as the set of links that fail together during that failure scenario. The size of the SRG affects the amount of restoration capacity needed during the failure scenario. The algorithm adds express links based on both the working path traffic carried by the express link (higher the better) and the maximum size of SRG group of which it is a member (lower the better). After adding the express link the entire restoration algorithm is repeated to identify if the overall network cost is reduced. Typically, as we add successive express links (using the two criteria mentioned above), the cost keeps decreasing, reaches a minimum and then increases. The 2-Phase method also works well with multiple failure scenarios.

The proposed 2-Phase Fast Reroute with optimized traffic engineering also ensures that in a dynamic environment the blocking probability requirement is met for many service classes each with its distinct arrival rate, holding time and bandwidth requirement and novel sharing arrangements based on trunk reservation, upper limit and guaranteed minimum policies [22].

3.2   Wavelength Service Restoration: Shared Mesh Restoration with Standbys

In a reconfigurable all-optical network, connections at the optical layer come from two major sources: 1) wavelength services and 2) links of higher layer network, such as IP network. In today's commercial IP networks, failure is usually restored in IP layer, i.e., IP links are usually provisioned as un-restorable connections in optical layer. Alternative solution would be integration of IP layer and optical layer restoration that will be discussed in the subsection on integrated IP/OL restoration. For restoring wavelength services when a failure occurs in the optical layer, 1+1 Tail-end switch is the only commercial available restoration form in all-optical networks today and is only used for a few priority circuits. The drawback is that it requires 1-to-1 dedicated backup connections for single failure protection and 2-to-1 dedicated backup connections for double failure protection, which usually result in 150-200% restoration overbuild of transport resources due to significantly longer diverse backup paths. P-cycle based restoration is a popular restoration topic in academic [23]. However, typically these methods only demonstrate significant capacity advantages under single optical failure scenario and, as such, virtually all such proposals avoid the issue of multiple failure scenarios. Furthermore, if designed for single-failure only, such a method can have serious complications during unplanned multiple-failures, where contention (two or more connections trying to use the same restoration capacity) can occur and has to be resolved in real-time.

In order to provide fast and cost effective restoration, we propose to use shared mesh restoration with standbys extended from our previous work [4, 24]. The standbys provide connectivity between switching nodes (nodes with fiber link degree-2 or higher). All-optical switching is used at the intermediate nodes along a standby's path. As in [4, 24], the standbys can be pre-configured using OEO regenerators at their two ends which send test signals continuously. This overcomes the problem of optical impairments for long connections, avoids today's wavelength power

322   A.L. Chiu et al.

"balancing" delays, provides wavelength conversion for capacity efficiency and allows sharing of links across non-simultaneous failures. Variations of "standby" schemes, including "hot standby", "cold standby" and "no-standby" proposed and analyzed in [24] provide tradeoffs between restoration speed and restoration capacity overbuild. To illustrate the concept of standby restoration, we illustrate a simple example in figure 3.

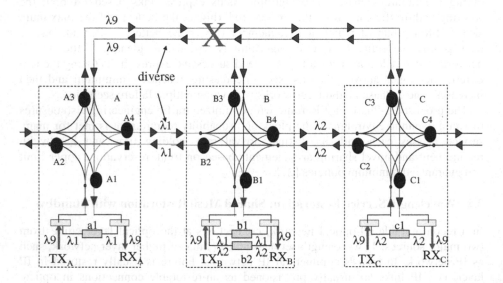

Fig. 3. An Illustration of Standbys

For an all-optical ROADM network, channels cannot be simply connected in series to create a restoration path due to wavelength continuity, ULH reach constraint, power equalization process. We propose to pre-place a few OEO regenerators strategically and pre-establish a set of "standby" optical connections between regenerators. During the restoration process, these "standbys" would be dynamically connected together in series to provide the desired restoration path. Since the "standby" connections are pre-established, i.e., the restoration wavelengths are actively present on the restoration paths, the optical transients associated with firing up their lasers would not be an issue at the point in time where restoration is needed. This will allow the restoration process to be done much more rapidly than it could otherwise be done. Those standbys are capable to be shared among multiple restoration paths via controlling the wavelength selective switches and tuning those regenerators. In figure 3, we assume that there is one service connection between node A and node C on wavelength λ9. There are two standbys pre-established: one between node A and node B on wavelength λ1 and the other between node B and node C on wavelength λ2. Note that there could be other nodes between node A and node C, node A and node B, node B and node C. If a fibre-cut between node A and node C brings down the working path, a pre-computed disjoint restoration path through the overlay route A-B-C is selected. Different from opaque optical networks where restoration channels are pre-installed on each network link, here the restoration channels are pre-reserved on pre-established standbys, which are restoration connections between OEO regenerators. In some sense, the standby restoration is performed on the standby overlay network bypassing the underlying transparent all-optical ULH network. Then all-optical network restoration time is equivalent to existing opaque optical network restoration time, which can achieve sub-second restoration on average using ROLEX-like signalling methodology [9].

To reduce network cost, the service providers would like to pre-establish as few restoration "standbys" as possible since standbys are reserved and not used to transfer traffic during network normal operation. To guarantee full restoration of any failure, the service providers need to pre-establish enough "standbys". Then the question is where and how many "standbys" the network should pre-establish, i.e., where and how many OEO regenerators the network should pre-placed in advance for restoration purposes.

There are many components in the restoration design of optical layer including service path selection algorithm, OEO regenerator placement, wavelength assignment [25], path based shared restoration with pre-cross-connected standbys, solution for dual failure restorable connections, as well as trap scenario avoidance for path selection. The detailed solutions are listed in following:

- Due to wavelength continuity constraint in all-optical networks, we select the service path to minimize the number of regenerators required with tie breaking of small number of hops. Once the number of regenerators is determined, we need to decide where to place the OEO regenerators considering the number of available wavelengths.
- Since the OEO regenerators separate the connection into multiple lightpaths, we can calculate the available number of wavelengths on each lightpath. One approach would be to maximize the sum of these available wavelengths over all separated lightpaths when all OEO placements are compared. However, if there is a choice of one OEO placement with 10 wavelengths available for either of two lightpaths and another OEO placement with 20 available wavelengths on one lightpath and only one available wavelength on the other lightpath, the maximum sum would vote for the asymmetric configuration. Obviously this is not a good idea to spend the last wavelength left on the second placement. So an improved approach should penalize a configuration which tries to spend the last few available wavelengths on their paths. Our proposed OEO placement solution would be to minimize the sum of the inverse of available wavelengths over all separated lightpaths, i.e., min $\Sigma 1/A(i)$, where $A(i)$ is the available wavelengths on lightpath i with OEO placement. This gives a high number for one of the lightpaths having only a few wavelengths still available. It tends to balance the number of available wavelengths on all lightpaths.
- Although there are many wavelength assignment schemes proposed in the literature, we choose first-fit wavelength assignment solution in this paper since it is simple and efficient. We order the wavelengths from 1 to W, where W is the maximum number of channels that the system supports, and select the smallest available wavelength along the lightpath. As we discussed before, with the help of regenerators, all optical connections are separated into lightpaths. Since

regenerator provides wavelength conversion capability, now wavelength assignment is on top of lightpaths instead of connections.

- With the concept of lightpath standbys and the help of regenerators, we can apply the path-based shared mesh restoration that was used in opaque optical networks [11] to all-optical networks. Specifically, the restoration channel sharing is on top of lightpath standbys instead of optical links only. We assume that each wavelength supports one OC-192 connection and each OC-192 demand is routed independently one at a time. To deal with optical signal reach constraints, we first create possible express links that are within the maximum optical signal reach distance on the network in two steps: (1) compute the potential path between any two nodes; (2) form an extended network by creating express links on these paths. Those express links are pre-established standbys candidates. To select the restoration path with minimum number of restoration wavelengths in the extended network for service path Ps, a matrix *failroute* is maintained where *failroute[i,j]* maintains how many standbys are needed on express link j if link i

  fails. Then $max_{i \in E}$ *failroute[i,j]* and $max_{i \in Ps}$ *failroute[i,j]* represent the total standby channels reserved on link j and the required standby channels required on link j if service path Ps fails, where E stands for the set of network original links.

  The difference, $S[j] = max_{i \in E}$ *failroute[i,j]* $- max_{i \in Ps}$ *failroute[i,j]*, would be the amount of sharable standby channels, and $max(0,1-S[j])$ would be the additional required channels on link j if path Ps fails. Thus, after service path Ps is selected, we reset link weights on the extended network as additional required channels and select the shortest new link weight path as the restoration path Pr, which should be the smallest number of channels required path. After Ps and Pr are selected, then the matrix *failroute* is updated. After all connections are routed

  on the network, each link j would have $max_{i \in E}$*failroute[i,j]* restoration channels and each restoration channel is a lightpath standby segment. Since each standby segment requires 2 unidirectional restoration regenerators, the total number of

  unidirectional restoration regenerators will be $H = 2*\Sigma_j(max_{i \in E}$*failroute[i,j]*$)$, where j includes express links.

- To deal with double failures, we would select two failure disjoint restoration paths, one for 1:1 restoration and the other for shared mesh restoration. To make sure enough capacity is reserved on the second restoration path no matter what order failure happens, we first select service path Ps, and dedicated restoration path Pr1, then we select the second restoration path Pr2 using SMR on extended network as we discussed above. The only difference is that in formula of

  sharable standby channels, $S[j] = max_{i \in E}$ *failroute[i,j]* $- max_{i \in \{Ps,Pr1\}}$ *failroute[i,j]*,we use Ps+Pr1 instead of Ps. The reason is that we want to reserve enough capacity for both scenarios either Ps fails first and Pr1 fails second or Pr1 fails first and Ps fails second. In this case, no matter what failure order, there is enough capacity reserved on the third restoration path.

- For path based restoration, one has to deal with trap scenario during path selection, i.e., although there are two or more failure disjoint paths between two nodes, a simple shortest path as service path may fail to find a failure disjoint restoration path. In this study, we use the following algorithm to avoid such cases: we first use maxflow-mincost algorithm to find 2 failure disjoint paths for single failure restorable connections and 3 failure disjoint paths for double failure restorable connections between the two ends of the connections via node splitting approach for node disjoint. Among the selected paths, we select the shortest path for service path. In this way, we guarantee the existence of single or double failure disjoint restoration paths.

3.3 Integrated IP-over-Optical Layer Restoration

As mentioned above in today's commercial IP networks, IP links are usually provisioned as un-restorable in the optical layer to satisfy minimum cost objectives and the restoration capacity is reserved in the IP layer. Again, this is mostly due to the presence of extra IP-layer capacity to restore failures that originate at the IP-layer plus the ability of the IP-layer to differentiate classes of service on a much finer scale than in the optical layer. However, as we explore the failure state space in more detail, we find that it is able to share some optical layer restoration capacity among non-simultaneous failures to restore or add some IP links via the optical layer. An innovative, yet practical method was developed by [26, 27, 28], which propose interaction between the IP and optical layers. By use of spare router line cards, this method optimizes network capacity by leveraging 1) the ability of the optical layer to make rapid OL connections and 2) the assumption that the optical layer requires extra restoration capacity (wavelengths) for restorable wavelength service and 3) except for extremely rare failure events, the non-simultaneity of failures between components in the IP and optical layers. Figure 4 shows a simple example to illustrate this concept, where dotted thick lines represent spare router line cards connecting to the ROADMs. Upon a router failure or router line card failure, those spare line cards will be used to restore failed IP links or add extra IP link capacity. A few key elements in this integrated method are described in the following:

- 1:N Interface Protection [27, 4]: The goal here is to provide rapid recovery from the failure of a router or ROADM line card or the connection between a router line card and the ROADM port. If one of the N working interfaces fails for whatever reason, the ROADM will rapidly switch the failed connection to the (spare) protection interface and (spare) line cards. This should be done locally at the node very rapidly and without involving either the remote router or any other ROADM. The benefits to the IP network of doing APS between the router and the ROADM are obvious when compared to the alternative, which is to have additional inter-router links. In addition, if done quickly enough the APS switch should hide the failure from the remote routers, thus eliminating disruptive IP layer convergence to a new forwarding table. A prototype demonstration that this is possible does exits using an opaque OXC [27]. It utilizes an extension of the OIF UNI together with enhancements to the router software. We will explore the usage of this fast protection in a transparent architecture.

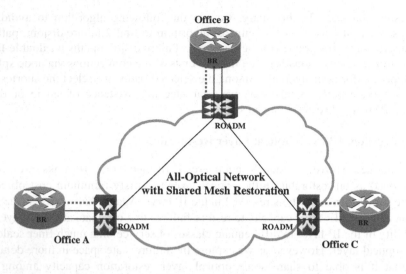

Fig. 4. Integrated IP-over-Optical Layer Restoration

- Restore from any single router failure or complete node failure [26, 28]: by use of spare router line cards, this method optimizes network capacity by leveraging 1) the ability of the optical layer to make rapid OL connections to add new IP link(s) or increase the capacity of existing IP links or virtual links (a logical link with 0 bandwidth). The latter will be faster since there is complex state information associated with each new IP router interface which would need to be dynamically associated with the backup interface.

- Restore IP links from OL failure(s) [28]: there are various options to restore IP links at the OL from OL failures. For bandwidth efficiency, composite IP link groups could recover with partial bandwidth to take advantage of the fact that there is no restoration requirement for significant part of the IP traffic – the best effort traffic. Another option is where IP links remain unprotected. Upon an OL failure, we reshape IP topology by making rapid OL connections to add new IP link(s) or by increasing the capacity of existing IP links or virtual links.

We propose to study the adaptation of theses schemes to the future IP over reconfigurable all-optical network and explore the cost advantages in future work.

4   Simulation Experiments and Results

4.1   Network and Traffic Models

We evaluate the performance of our proposed approaches via simulation on a hypothetical U.S. backbone network from [29] consisting of 28 nodes and 45 fiber links as shown in figure 5. The number over each link is the distance between two nodes in 10-mile unit. Each node consists of one router and one ROADM. Each fiber pair is assumed to support 100 wavelengths. There are two types of traffics generated

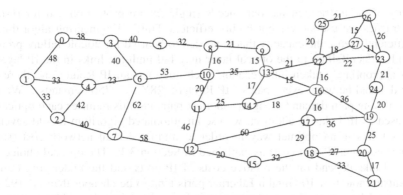

Fig. 5. A Hypothetical U.S. Backbone Network

at each node: IP traffic and wavelength traffic. All traffic demands are generated based on node traffic probability, which is proportional to the node degree. We randomly select a demand according to source node traffic probability and destination node traffic probability. For IP traffic, the bandwidth of each demand is uniformly generated from an interval (100, 1000) Mbps and there are 5000 such demands. Each IP demand flow has 40% chance to be best effort traffic and a small probability (up to 10%) requiring double failure restoration. For simplicity, the IP link bandwidths are assumed to be deployed in units of 10Gbps channels (the associated IP port may either be an OC192 port or a 10 Gigabit Ethernet port, the latter being usually cheaper). For each IP link the OSPF Administrative Weight metric is assumed to be distance plus 20 miles (this allows OSPF shortest path routing to be shortest distance routing as well in most cases but in the event of two nearly equal distance paths it chooses one with fewer hops). For wavelength traffic, we assume that each demand requires one wavelength and all demands need to be single failure protected at least. A small percentage of wavelength demands (up to 10%) needs to be double failure restorable. In our simulation, we assume wavelength demands arrive at the network one by one, and are never disconnected (or more realistically, have holding times in years), which is typical for commercial wavelength services. For both IP service and wavelength service restoration, we evaluate the performance of our proposals using restoration overbuild. It is defined as (total wavelength-mile for both service and restoration)/(wavelength-mile for service only) -1.

4.2 Results for IP Service Restoration

We will show results mainly for the 2-Phase Fast Reroute method with optimized Traffic Engineering. We will also provide comparison with pure shortest path routing (the most prevalent method in today's IP Networks) with and without Fast Reroute. In addition to single failure protection we also protect a subset of traffic under double failures (2 optical links or 1 node and 1 optical link, total of 2250 failure conditions). By pruning the failure state space, we reduced the number of cases significantly and we achieved further speed-up by using a very fast but less efficient pure shortest path routing algorithm for capacity allocation during multiple failure events. However, majority of the traffic demand only needs single failure protection and for restoring those traffics we use slower but highly efficient Traffic Engineering algorithm that can efficiently reuse the capacity that is needed to be used for double failure protected demands. Each failure in the optical layer may fail multiple links in the IP layer and that is appropriately taken into account. Each node has an IP Router and there is IP traffic demand between every pair of IP Routers (28X27 = 756 demands). We route all IP working path demand along the shortest path and this requires each optical link to be used as IP link. In addition, we use an automated algorithm to add several IP Express Links in an optimal way in order to minimize total network cost (sum of transport cost and IP port cost) as explained in Section 3.1. The optimal choice of IP Express Links depend on the relative costs of IP ports and the underlying transport mechanism (note that 10 Gigabit Ethernet ports tend to be cheaper than OC192 ports and newer Ultra Long Haul transport technology is cheaper than older technology). To illustrate this point we consider two cases. In Case 1 (Table 1) 10Gbps IP port cost is assumed to be equivalent to 100 miles of transport cost and in Case 2 (Table 2) 10Gbps IP port cost is assumed to be equivalent to 300 miles of transport cost (transport cost is assumed to be proportional to Route Miles in both cases). Both tables show the result of incrementally adding Express Links (all results are based on 2-Phase Fast Reroute with optimized Traffic Engineering which tries to minimize a linear combination of cost and capacity). The tables show that as the number of Express links increases, at first the cost decreases, reaches a minimum and then start increasing. However, the relative cost difference among the alternatives is significantly higher in Table 2 (higher IP port cost) compared to Table 1. Also the

Table 1. (IP Port Cost = 100 Miles of Transport Cost)

Alternative	# of IP Logical Links	Capacity in 1000 10Gbps-Miles		Restoration Overbuild	# of IP 10Gbps Physical Links (W. + Rest.)	Normalized Total Cost
		Working Path	Working Path + Restoration			
1	45	138.57	202.6	0.46	735	104.2
2	62	147.16	208.7	0.42	627	102.4
3	81	150.93	212.9	0.41	568	101.8
4	**92**	**157.46**	**213.0**	**0.35**	**520**	**100**
5	103	164.05	217.4	0.33	510	101.3

Table 2. (IP Port Cost = 300 Miles of Transport Cost)

Alternative	# of IP Logical Links	Capacity in 1000 10Gbps-Miles		Restoration Overbuild	# of IP 10Gbps Physical Links (W. + Rest.)	Normalized Total Cost
		Working Path	Working Path + Restoration			
1	45	138.57	203.2	0.47	731	120.7
2	81	150.93	211.2	0.40	539	106.5
3	103	164.05	216.3	0.32	475	102.5
4	**122**	**169.41**	**217.5**	**0.28**	**442**	**100**
5	130	171.69	220.4	0.28	456	102.0

optimal number of IP logical links is higher in Table 2. It is important to note that minimizing either the total capacity (working path + restoration) or the restoration overbuild does not necessarily translate to minimum cost. For example, Table 1 shows that Alternative 1 has the minimum total capacity and Alternative 5 has the minimum restoration overbuild, but Alternative 4 has the minimum cost (we choose this alternative for the rest of the study).

Under no failure condition and under the second and more permanent phase of Single Failure Fast Reroute the maximum IP link utilization is assumed to be 95%. During the rarer double failures and during the initial transient phase of Fast reroute (a few seconds) the maximum IP Link utilization is assumed to be 100%.

Table 3 below shows the impact of increasing the percentage of traffic that requires double failure protection.

Table 3.

Percentage of Traffic Requiring Double Failure Protection	0%	2.5%	5%	7.5%	10%
Restoration Overbuild	0.353	0.354	0.358	0.365	0.380

Table 4 below compares three IP design alternatives in terms of restoration overbuild and cost. Alternative 1 uses 2-Phase FRR with optimized Traffic Engineering and is the one we propose. Alternative 2 uses IP reroute using OSPF shortest-path routing (without Fast Reroute) and is the most common routing mechanism in today's IP network. Alternative 3 uses simple MPLS FRR, i.e., no Traffic Engineering and instead it uses shortest path routing during the two phases. Clearly, our proposed mechanism performs significantly better than the other two.

Table 4.

IP Routing alternative	# of IP Logical Links	Capacity in 1000 Wavelength-Miles		Restoration overbuild	# of IP 10 Gbps Physical Links (W + Rest)	Normalized Total Cost
		Working Path	Work. Path + Rest.			
1	92	157.46	213.0	0.353	520	100
2	92	157.46	305.87	0.943	675	140.9
3	92	157.46	335.81	1.132	752	155.1

4.3 Results for Wavelength Service Restoration

We compare our wavelength service restoration scheme with existing commercialized 1+1 for single failure protection and 1+2 for double failure protection. For shared mesh restoration with standbys, we use our proposed algorithm to select restoration paths. For 1+1 or 1+2 protection, we always use shortest disjoint restoration paths. To evaluate the impact of traffic size, we first fix the double failure restoration ratio as

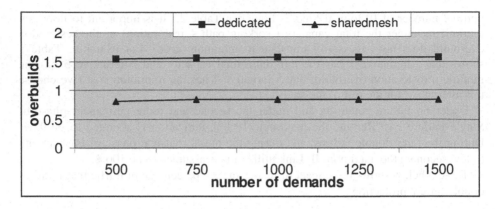

Fig. 6. Restoration Overbuild Comparison with a Fixed Double Failure Ratio (5%)

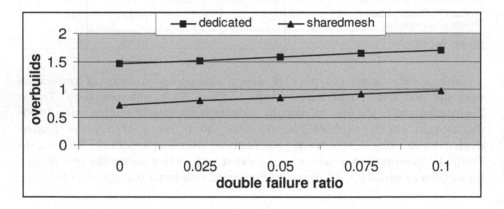

Fig. 7. Restoration Overbuild Comparison with a Fixed Number of Demands (1000)

5% and increase wavelength demands from 500 to 1500 with step size of 250. Then we fix the number of wavelength demands as 1000 and increase the double failure ratio from 0% to 10% in step size of 2.5% to evaluate the impact of demand double failure restoration requirement. In both cases, we compare restoration overbuilds of both schemes and leave the detail economic analysis for future study. Figure 6 and figure 7 show the simulation results.

Figure 6 shows that 1+1 protection results in very high restoration overbuild around 150% while our proposed shared mesh restoration with standbys demonstrates significant improvement by reducing the overbuild by 50% for all demand sizes studied.

Figure 7 shows that as we increase the double failure ratio from 0% to 10%, restoration overbuilds for both 1+1 protection and proposed shared mesh restoration with standbys increase steadily. Meanwhile, the improvements in restoration overbuild of our proposed scheme over 1+1 protection stay close to 50% for all double failure ratios.

We simulated both IP and wavelength service restoration solutions with different network topology and traffic patterns. On steady state, we observed similar levels of improvements comparing our proposed solutions and existing solutions. We omit to report them in this paper.

5 Summary

Large IP backbone networks today are mostly deployed directly over sequences of point-to-point DWDM systems or chains of newer ROADM-based ULH systems, interconnected by OEO regenerators. The next generation core optical network is moving toward an all-optical network architecture that is based on multi-degree ROADMs to reduce OEO regeneration cost as well as enabling automatic reconfigurability and dynamic restoration via wavelength switching and tuning. In this paper, we study the restoration design in this new IP-over-reconfigurable all-optical network architecture to satisfy the network reliability requirements for both IP and wavelength services. For restoring IP services, we propose a novel 2-Phase Fast Reroute mechanism with optimized Traffic Engineering algorithm. It meets the requirement of sub-second restoration and also maximizes sharing among single/double failures of links, routers and Shared Risk Groups and also among different phases of restoration with the objective of minimizing either overall capacity or overall cost. Simulation results have shown that the proposed restoration scheme provides significant savings comparing to existing IP reroute (e.g., OSPF or IS-IS) and MPLS Fast Reroute. In order to provide fast and cost effective restoration for wavelength services, we propose to use shared mesh restoration with pre-configured (standby) lightpaths. Simulation results demonstrate significant improvements in restoration overbuild using our proposed scheme when compared to existing 1+1 protection. To further reduce the required restoration capacity in both IP layer and optical layer and address failures in both layers efficiently, we also propose to use an integrated IP-over-optical layer restoration strategy that enables sharing of re storation capacity among non-simultaneous failures across both IP and optical layers. Detailed economical studies of the integrated method would be conducted in future work.

References

1. Wallace, A.F.: Ultra long-haul DWDM: network economics. In: OFC, vol. 2, TuT1-1 - TuT1-2, Anaheim (March 2001)
2. MCI Picks Ciena and Siemens for ULH,
   http://www.lightreading.com/document.asp?doc_id=48055.
3. Chiu, A., Yu, C.: Economic Benefits of Transparent OXC Networks as Compared to Long Systems with OADM's. In: OFC, Atlanta, pp. 411–412 (March 2003)
4. Strand, J., Chiu, A.: Realizing the Advantages of Optical Reconfigurability and Restoration with Integrated Optical Cross-Connects. Journal of Lightwave Technology 21(11) (November 2003)

5. Afferton, T., Doverspike, R., Kalmanek, C., Ramakrishnan, K.K.: Packet-Aware Transport for Metro Networks. IEEE Communications Magazine, 120–127 (March 2004)
6. Wei, J., Ramakrishnan, K.K., Doverspike, R., Pastor, J., Aguirre-Torres, L., Kalmanek, C., Afferton, T.: Convergence through Packet-Aware Transport. The Journal of Optical Networking, Special Issue on Convergence 5(4), 221–245 (2006)
7. Choudhury, G.: Models for IP/MPLS Routing Performance: Convergence, Fast Reroute, and QoS Impact. In: Keynote Speech, ITCOM's Conference on Performance, Quality of Service and Control of Next Generation Communication Networks II, Philadelphia, Pennsylvania, USA, pp. 1–12 (2004)
8. Cortez, B.: The Emerging Intelligent Optical Network: Now a Reality. In: OFC 2002 (2002)
9. Doverspike, R., Sahin, G., Strand, J.L., Tkach, R.W.: Fast Restoration in a Mesh Network of Optical Cross-connects. In: Proceedings of Optical Fiber Conference (OFC '99), San Diego, CA, February 1999 (1999)
10. Doshi, B., Dravida, S., Harshavardhana, P., Hauser, O., Wang, Y.: Optical Network Design and Restoration. Bell Labs Technical Journal, 58–84 (1999)
11. Li, G., Wang, D., Kalmanek, C., Doverspike, R.: Efficient Distributed Path Selection for Shared Restoration Connections. IEEE Conference on Computer Communication (INFOCOM) 2002, New York and Special Issue of IEEE Transactions on Networking 11(5), 761–771 (2003)
12. Simmons, J.: Network Design in Realistic All-Optical Backbone Networks. IEEE Communication Magazine 44(11) (November 2006)
13. Ranalli, E., et al.: Liquid-crystal based wavelength selectable crossconnect. In: ECOC, pp. 68–69 (1999)
14. Boskovic, A., et al.: Broadcast and Select OADM nodes: Application and Performance Trade-offs. In: OFC, TuX2, pp. 158–159 (March 2002)
15. Vasilyev, M., et al.: Broadcast and select OADM in 80 /spl times/ 10.7 Gb/s ultra-longhaul network. Photonics Technology Letters 15(2), 332–334 (2003)
16. Woodward, S.L., Feuer, M.D., Calvitti, J., Falta, K., Verdiell, J.: A High-Degree Photonic Cross-Connect for Transparent Networking, Flexible Provisioning & Capacity Growth. In: ECOC 2006, paper Th1.2.2 (2006)
17. Pan, P., Swallow, G., Atlas, A.: Fast Reroute Extensions to RSVP-TE for LSP Tunnels. In: IETF RFC 4090 (May 2005)
18. Choudhury, G.L.: IP Fast-Reroute: An Analysis of Applicability to a Core Network. In: NANOG 33 Conference, January 31 - February 1, 2005, Las Vegas, Nevada, USA (2005)
19. Francois, P., Filsfils, C., Evans, J., Bonaventure, O.: Achieving Sub-Second IGP Convergence in Large IP Networks. ACM SIGCOMM Computer Communications review 35(2), 35–44 (2005)
20. Ward, D., Atlas, A.: IP FRR: Overview and Things We are Struggling to Solve. In: NANOG 33 Meeting, January 31-February 1, 2005, Las Vegas, Nevada, USA (2005)
21. Kandula, S., Katabi, D., Davie, B., Charny, A.: Walking the Tightrope: Responsive yet Stable Traffic Engineering. In: SIGCOMM 2005, August 21-26, 2005, Philadelphia, PA, USA, pp. 253–264 (2005)
22. Choudhury, G.L., Leung, K., Whitt, W.: An Algorithm To Compute Blocking Probabilities In Multi-Rate, Multi-Class, Multi-Resource Loss Models. Advances in Applied Probability 27(4), 1104–1143 (1995)
23. Grover, W., Stamatelakis, D.: Bridging the ring-mesh dichotomy with p-cycles. In: DRCN 2000 (2000)

24. Li, G., Chiu, A., Strand, J.: Resilience Design in All-optical ULH Networks. Journal of Optical Networks (2006)
25. Zang, H., Jue, J.P., Mukherjee, B.: A Review of Routing and Wavelength Assignment Approaches for Wavelength-Routed Optical WDM Networks. Optical Network Magazine 1 (January 2000)
26. Chiu, A., Strand, J.: Joint IP/Optical Layer Restoration after A Router Failure. In: OFC2001, Anaheim, CA (March 2001)
27. Sebos, P., Yates, J., Li, G., Wang, D.: Ultra-fast IP link and interface provisioning with applications to IP restoration. In: IEEE OFC 2003 (2003)
28. Li, G., Wang, D., Yates, J., Doverspike, R., Kalmanek, C.: IP over Optical Cross-Connect Architectures. In: Optical Fiber Communications Conference (OFC 2004), Communication Magazine, vol. 45(2), pp. 34–39 (2007)
29. Xiong, Y., Mason, L.: Restoration strategies and spare capacity requirements in self-healing ATM networks., IEEE/ACM ToN, 7(1) (February 1999)

SIPS: A Stateful and Flow-Based
Intrusion Prevention System for Email Applications

Bo-Chao Cheng[1], Ming-Jen Chen[1], Yuan-Sun Chu[1],
Andrew Chen[1], Sujadi Yap[1], and Kuo-Pao Fan[2]

[1] Dept. of Electronic Engineering, National Chung-Cheng University, Taiwan
m9037@cn.ee.ccu.edu.tw, 94cheng@vlsi.ee.ccu.edu.tw
[2] Industrial Technology Research Institute of Taiwan

Abstract. In the fast-growing internet applications, email becomes more and more important in communication. SMTP attacks and spam have become one of the most serious problems. Particularly, the SMTP attacks and spam varies on email, for example spoofing address, illegal characters, sending in bulk, too many SMTP commands and so on. A single security technique is not enough to protect the system from these attacks and spam. In this paper, we propose a SMTP Intrusion Prevention System (SIPS) which bases on the concept of Stateful Protocol Anomaly Detection and Flow-based Inspection. SIPS is implemented by a finite state machine to inspect all coming email flows. It is according to the media type of email flow and their characteristics. On the test of a real email environment, our approach can prevent attacks on SMTP attack (mail bomb) average about 95.4% and spam average about 91.1%.

Keywords: Network Security, SMTP, SPAM, IPS, IDS, SIPS.

1 Introduction

In recent years, email has become more important in communication for most users on the internet. Due to the popularity and the importance of emails, many attackers try to launch SMTP attacks and spam. These problems often bother email users and administrators. Although some prevention techniques against SMTP attacks and spam are proposed respectively, these approaches usually focus on single threat. An integrated security technique is needed to resist these problems. According to the report by industry analyst firm IDC, the mark trend is changed from stand-alone threat management to Unified Threat Management (UTM). A stand-alone threat management is not enough to prevent more sophisticated email attacks. A UTM should include many security functionalities such as firewall, intrusion detection, anti-spam and so on. A robust Intrusion Prevention System (IPS) for email application must detect and prevent email attacks (SMTP attacks and spam).

SMTP attacks have become the top ten of internet security threat. Some various attacks on SMTP protocol and characteristics of spam flow [10] are as following: Buffer Overrun, Partial Message Attack, Probing Behaviors, Email Bombs, and HELO commands DoS attacks.

K. Li et al. (Eds.): NPC 2007, LNCS 4672, pp. 334–343, 2007.
© IFIP International Federation for Information Processing 2007

In order to effectively prevent both SMTP attacks and spam, we propose an integrated approach called SMTP Intrusion Prevention System (SIPS) which bases on the concept of Protocol Anomaly Detection (PAD) [2][3] and integrated with flow-based inspection to examine whether the email flows deviate from normal behavior.

The remaining of this paper is organized as following. Section 2 introduces the conventional anti-spam solutions and compares these solutions. Section 3 and section 4 describe the design concept and system architecture. In section 5, a test environment is built to evaluate the SIPS approach. And conclusion is given in section 6.

2 Background and Related Work

SMTP attacks and spam have become one of the most serious problems. In this section, we will introduce conventional anti-spam approaches and conventional prevention approaches of SMTP attacks.

2.1 Conventional Prevention Approaches of SMTP Attacks

Most of mail systems are vulnerable due to the openness of email standards and wide security holes. The attacks are including DoS (Denial of Service), buffer flow and so on. Many techniques have been developed in order to prevent such attacks. These techniques can be classified into two kinds of approaches:

A Signature-based Detection is commonly referred to the negative approach because it aims at the behavior known as "abnormal behavior" and assumes everything else as "normal behavior".

B Protocol Anomaly Detection is commonly referred to the positive approach because it detects "normal behavior" of the specific protocol. Protocol Anomaly Detection aims at protocol misusage.

2.2 Conventional Anti-spam Approaches

Conventional anti-spam approaches can be classified into three approaches [1]:

A Content-scanning approach Saito[6] identifies email messages by analyzing mail headers and contents using keyword matching or statistical analysis of the words to determine whether an email is spam. This technique could also be called spam filtering, such as Bayesian filtering and heuristic engines.

B List-based approach [8] determines a spam by inspecting the particular IP address or email address during mail transaction before the mail server receives the email. It requires DNS to lookup the database of IP addresses that are known to be a spam source.

C Flow-based approach Qiu[7] detects spam and abnormal email behaviors in the network according to the type of email flows and their characteristics.

Qiu's[7] flow-based concept is effective for email flows with small mail body or large amount of recipient, but it is unable to differentiate exterior and interior email behavior. Saito[6] sets a threshold according to IP address, Mail header and Mail

Body information. Spammer can deceive the system by modifying the mail header and body so that the system will not detect it (False Negative). On the other hand normal email may also be categorized as spam if it is above threshold (False Positive).

These approaches only aim at a single threat and do not have an integrated approach to prevent email attacks. We propose an integrated approach with stateful and flow-based inspection to prevent email attacks.

3 SMTP Behavior Analysis

Firstly we define the email flow and the record of an email flow for designing an integrated approach for preventing email attacks. And according to the analysis, we define the normal behaviors for an email flow.

3.1 Definitions of the Email Flow and the Record of Email Flow

An email flow is constructed of five tuple (source and destination IP, source and destination port and protocol type). As shown in Table 1, the flow record [9] is used to record behaviors of email flow (SMTP flow). It is for single direction from SMTP client to SMTP server and it holds values of attributes which interest in this flow.

According to the record of the email flow, we can analyze the behavior of an email between SMTP client and SMTP server. Based on the behavior observation, we can verify the normal or abnormal email with our finite state machine which is described in the following.

Table 1. An example for record of an Email Flow

Filed Name	Description
FlowID	ID number of each SMTP flow.
StartTime	SMTP Connection established time.
LastTime	The newest received network packet time of SMTP flow.
TotalFlowpkts	Total outbound network packet numbers.
ConnectionInfo	Source IP, Destination IP, Source Port, Destination Port, Protocol Type
TotalFlowsizes	Total outbound packet size.
BDFlowpkts	Outbound network packets numbers after receiving DATA command.
BDFlowsize	Outbound network packets size after receiving DATA command.
HeaderSizes	SMTP flow mail header size.
BodySizes	SMTP flow mail body size.
RcptCounts	Mail Recipients' number in a SMTP flow.
PlainFlag	Mail type in plain Mail.
HtmlFlag	Mail type in html Mail.
EmbeddedFlag	Mail with embedded resource.
AttachmentFlag	Mail with attachment files.
FormFlag	Mail with html form.
OutSideFlag	SMTP Client's IP address is Interior or Exterior.

3.2 Normal Email Behavior

Firstly we observe the behavior of a normal email by monitoring more than 300 emails transferred to a SMTP server. We specify that a normal email flow should have the following characteristics:

- In general, there are many differences between some MTA software, but a normal mail behavior usually follows RFC formats such as minimum implementation, general syntax principles and transaction model.
- A transmission of normal mail should not spoof the domain of SMTP client and make a guess on username.
- The same IP address of SMTP client sending emails should be in the regular cycle.
- The variation of the email flow size depends on the behavior of email flow mentioned above, the location of SMTP client and the media type of emails.
- An email flow that contains a mail transaction must be initialized by using EHLO command. A mail transaction includes several SMTP commands, which are MAIL, RCPT, DATA and QUIT. The SMTP client should send these commands to the SMTP server in order to expect QUIT command.
- By RFC2821 [5], the NOOP, HELP and VRFY commands can be used at any time during an email flow, but a normal mail mostly does not contain these SMTP commands.

Based on the normal email behavior, we can now design the SMTP Intrusion Prevention System based on stateful and flow-based inspection.

4   SMTP Intrusion Prevention System (SIPS)

Intrusion Detection System (IDS) has become an important part of network security system on most of business enterprises. Its function is like security alarm or surveillance system in our houses. If an intrusion is detected, it will alert the network administrator for further process. IDS could only passively detect an intrusion, but could not prevent it. It is insufficient for enterprises network requirement. Therefore a new generation of improved system is proposed, Intrusion Prevention System (IPS) with a feature to prevent an intrusion. In this paper we proposed a SMTP Intrusion Prevention System (SIPS) which can protect email servers from attacks.

4.1 System Architectures

We integrated SIPS with Snort[4] (Snort is an open source Network-based IDS), to aim at email attacks based on SMTP behaviors of practice and study of RFCs.

As shown Fig.1, a new preprocessor called "SMTP Inspection Preprocessor (SIP)" is implemented and integrated with Snort to realize our approach. The decoder resolves the protocol which is used by the given packet and matches the data against allowable behavior for packet of their protocol. After the packets are matched, the preprocessor will redirect the email flow to SIP, inspecting whether they are email attacks. And then the email flow will be taken into Detection Engine and compare it against the rules in Snort without verdict in SIP. It is the core part on signature-based NIDS.

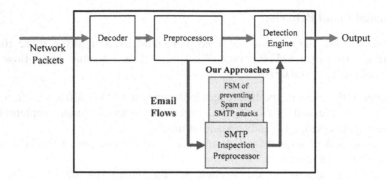

Fig. 1. SMTP Intrusion Prevention System, SIPS

4.2 SMTP Inspection Preprocessor (SIP)

SIP is constructed of two components as shown in Fig. 2. The first component is a finite state machine (FSM) for preventing email attacks whose states are mainly from RFC2821. It allows us to detect and prevent any deviation from the normal email behaviors we specified. The other component is the anomaly behaviors of email flows. It gives a feedback for administrators so that the administrators can re-specify the detection variables to reduce false positive.

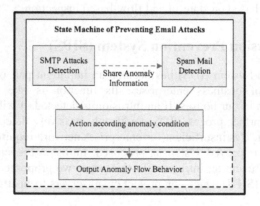

Fig. 2. SMTP Inspection Preprocessor

Protocol processes can be modeled as a collection of communicating FSMs. FSM of protocols must store some data value and synchronization messages [9] to maintain the temporal order of the event. In this paper, the SMTP communication behaviors are modeled as FSM based on the email flow. In order to check sizes, length, syntax and the order of SMTP commands and its parameters, each command is modeled as a state. It is constructed in a Moore machine, so that its output depends on the state and the input.

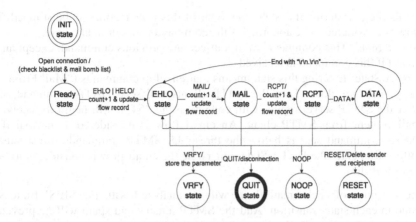

Fig. 3. The State Machine of Preventing Email Attacks

Fig. 3 shows the finite state machine of SIPS, the state transitions and prevention approach are described as following:

- Initial State: As SMTP connection is established, the system enters this state and checks whether the IP address is on blacklist and mail bomb list. The connection is categorized as normal if it is not on the list. The flow information will be stored and updated to flow records which are used to determine SMTP attack and spam.
- Ready State: After TCP 3-way handshake, the system enters this state that is waiting for HELO or EHLO command sent by SMTP Client. On this state the system sets a period of time Ta. The email flow is considered as normal if the number of connection is below the threshold N during Ta. Otherwise it is likely to be an email bomb, the system discard the email flow and record the source IP address in the mail bomb list for a dynamic and real-time prevention.
- EHLO State: According to RFC2821, the variable of HELO command must be a Full Qualified Domain Name (FQDN). In this state the SMTP client must send HELO/EHLO command with variable which follows FQDN. The length is limited under MaxCommandLength to prevent buffer overflow.
- MAIL State: The sender address must follow "<sender@domain>" format. And this domain must follow FQDN and checked for its existence. Attacker and spammer usually use false domain name to deceive SMTP server.
- RCPT State: The recipient address must follow "<recipients@domain>" format. The SMTP server will authenticate whether the sender or recipients is a legal user. If it is an illegal user, SMTP flow will be delayed 20 seconds, and if another illegal user is received, it will be delayed for another 30 seconds. If it keeps receiving illegal users, then this SMTP flow is considered to be abnormal.
- RESET State: The system enters this state if the previous mail transaction is canceled and the sender and recipients will be deleted. This flow is considered to be abnormal if the command is larger than 6 byte.
- VRFY State: If the number of failed user verification or VRFY command is sent more than the threshold, this SMTP flow is considered to be abnormal.

- QUIT State: Entering this state, the timer of this flow record can be stopped. This flow is considered to be abnormal if the command is larger than 6 byte.
- NOOP State: This command will not affect any previous command, except an OK is sent if this command is received.
- DATA State: Entering this state means that envelop commands ("Mail From" and "Rcpt To") are done. Then the SMTP clients will send DATA commands. And after the SMTP server replies with code message 354, it will begin to receive the mail content from SMTP client. An email flow is considered as normal if the DATA command sent is below the threshold. SMTP commands order must be followed to enter the DATA State, otherwise the email flow is considered to be an abnormal flow.

The behavior of each email flows will be analyzed with the SIPS' finite state machine in each state transition. And the SMTP attacks and spam will be prevented. In the next section, we will show our experimental results.

5 Experimental Results

We construct a real test environment shown in Fig. 4 to evaluate our approach.

On the left hand side, the senders (including normal sender, attacker and spammer) send emails to the Protected SMTP server on the right hand side. The SMTP Server on the right hand side is protected by our SMTP Intrusion Prevention System (SIPS) which uses stateful and flow-based method to detect SMTP attacks and spam. We evaluate performance of SIPS in term of false positive (FP) and false negative (FN) [14]. The attackers attack the SMTP server protected by SIPS through the SMTP client with open relay or free web mail service. And some sender sends normal email. Emails need to be inspected before sent to the protected SMTP server. In our testing, we use email bombs and spam to evaluate our approach correctly and efficiently. In evaluating spam, we compare SIPS with two papers Saito[6] and Qiu[7] mentioned in section 2.

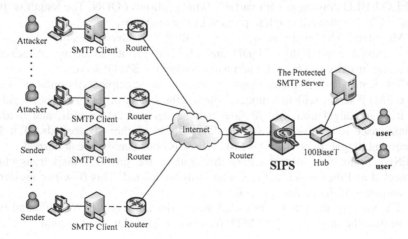

Fig. 4. Test Environment

Test of Mail Bomb

As shown in Table 2, we send 50, 100, 150, 200, 250, 300, 350 mail bombs with two IP addresses and 100 normal mails as the background traffic.

(100,50) denotes 100 normal mails and 50 mail bombs. As shown in Fig. 5, the ratio of FP is always below 5%. It is affected with a main factor: normal users might send a large number of mails and cause SIPS producing a false alarm. SIPS is still better than the existing security technology and the original Snort which can not detect and prevent any attacks of mail bombs. The ratio of FN is always below 10%. In "INIT state" and "Ready state", the FSM can detect and prevent the email bombs. FN of our approach is converged as the email bombs grow.

Table 2. Mail Bomb Test Traffic

Case	Normal Mails	Mail Bombs	Total
A	100	50	150
B	100	100	200
C	100	150	250
D	100	200	300
E	100	250	350
F	100	300	400
G	100	350	450

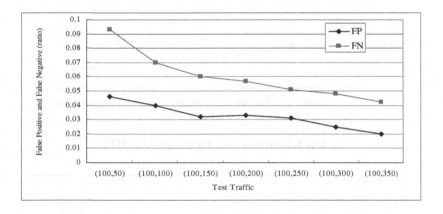

Fig. 5. SIPS Results on Mail Bombs Prevention

Test of Spam Mails

Our proposed approach can prevent spam according to normal behavior constructed by finite state machine. The results are shown in Table 3, Fig. 6, and Fig. 7.

As shown in Fig. 6, the FP of the approach proposed by Qiu[7] is worse than our approach, because it only determines spam by the flow size, there is no difference regarding interior or exterior email server. The same inspection for interior and exterior server makes the FP increasing. Qiu[7] approach also can not detect spoofing and defrauding during mail transactions.

The approach proposed by Saito[6] determine the email is spam when it receives large number of same mail header or mail body, or a large number of email from the same IP address in a period of time. But some of normal emails also have these characteristic so that it may lead to worse FP.

Table 3. Comparison of Preventing Spam

Normal	Spam	FP-SIPS	FN-SIPS	FP-Qiu	FN-Qiu	FP-Satio	FN-Satio
100	50	10.6%	5.3%	16%	8.7%	22%	14%
100	100	9%	9%	12%	12.5%	16%	18%
100	150	6.4%	11.6%	10.4%	14%	12%	18.4%
100	200	5.3%	12.3%	9%	14%	12%	18.6%
100	250	5.7%	12.9%	6.6%	14%	10%	18.9%
100	300	4%	14.3%	7.8%	15.8%	8.8%	18.8%
100	350	3.6%	15.1%	6.9%	16.7%	6.9%	18.4%
Average		6.3%	11.5%	9.8%	13.6%	12.5%	17.8%

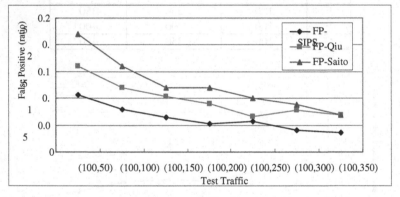

Fig. 6. Comparisons of Preventing Spam (FP)

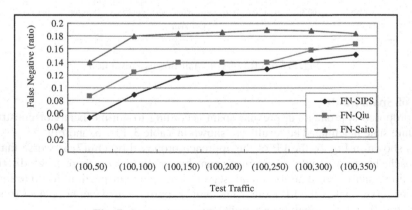

Fig. 7. Comparisons of Preventing Spam (FN)

As shown in Fig. 7 FN of the approach proposed by Qiu[7] is worse than our approach. It is because this approach does not record the state information. It only detects spam by quantity of the flow. Spammers usually change their identification within mail transaction so that their real identification will not be discovered.

Saito[6] approach is also insufficient to prevent spam because it uses IP header information. Nowadays, spammer usually sends spam by changing IP (SMTP client), header and body randomly. If spam has these characteristics, this approach will have worse FN.

SIPS uses stateful deep inspection on each email flow targeting various type of spam. The results show that SIPS is better than booth Saito[6] and Qiu[7] for the test traffic. The average ratio of FP in SIPS is 6.3% and 11.5% for the FN.

6 Conclusions

Since 1982 SMTP has become one of the most important internet applications, it has also become attacker's target. This paper proposes an approach to prevent spam on mail transactions using stateful and flow-based inspection on email flows. To blend a series of security solutions we also integrate Snort into IPS for email application. We evaluate our approach with real email environment. The average results are 3.2% for FP, 6% FN on mail bomb test and 6.3% for FP, 11.5% FN on spam mail test.

References

[1] Harris, D.: Drowning in Sewage: SPAM, the course of the new millennium: an overview and white paper. In: Spam Help, Available: http://www.spamhelp.org/articles/Drowning-in-sewage.pdf
[2] Das, K.: Protocol Anomaly Detection for Network-based Intrusion Detection. In: SANS, (August 13, 2001)
[3] CERT, State of the Practice of Intrusion Detection Technologies. Available: http://www.cert.org/archive/pdf/99tr028.pdf
[4] Snort, Available: http://www.snort.org
[5] Klensin, J.: Simple Mail Transport Protocol, RFC2821 (April 2001)
[6] Saito, T.: Anti-SPAM System: Another Way of Preventing SPAM. In: Proceedings. Sixteenth International Workshop on Database and Expert System Application. 22-66 August 2005, pp. 57–61 (2005)
[7] Qiu, X., Hao, J., Chen, M.: Flow-based anti-spam. In: Proceedings IEEE Workshop on IP Operations and Management, 11-13 October, 2004, pp. 99–103. IEEE Computer Society Press, Los Alamitos (2004)
[8] Park, J.S., Deshpande, A.: Spam Detection: Increasing Accuracy with a Hybrid Solution. Information System Management (2006)
[9] Brownlee, N.: Traffic Flow Measurement: Architecture, RFC2722 (October 1999)
[10] Bass, T., Freyre, A.: E-mail bombs and countermeasures: cyber attacks on availability and brand integrity, Network IEEE (1998)

Design and Evaluation of Parallel String Matching Algorithms for Network Intrusion Detection Systems

Tyrone Tai-On Kwok and Yu-Kwong Kwok*

Department of Electrical and Electronic Engineering
The University of Hong Kong, Pokfulam Road, Hong Kong
ykwok@hku.hk

Abstract. Network security is very important for Internet-connected hosts because of the widespread of worms, viruses, DoS attacks, etc. As a result, a network intrusion detection system (NIDS) is typically needed to detect network attacks by packet inspection. For an NIDS system, string matching is the computation-intensive task and hence the performance bottleneck, since every byte of the payload of packets must be checked against numerous predefined signature strings, which may occur arbitrarily in the payload. In this paper, we present the design and evaluation of parallel string matching algorithms targeting hardware implementation on FPGAs and software implementation on multi-core processors. Experimental results show that, on a multi-processor system, the multi-threaded implementation of the proposed parallel string matching algorithm can reduce string matching time by more than 40%.

1 Introduction

Network security is gaining more and more concern for Internet-connected hosts because of the widespread of worms, viruses, DoS attacks, etc. As illustrated in Figure 1, like hardware firewall systems, a network intrusion detection system (NIDS) can detect/prevent network attacks by packet inspection/filtering. However, unlike conventional firewall systems, which perform only protocol analysis by inspecting the header of packets, an NIDS also inspects the payload of packets. By adopting this kind of content-based security checking, an NIDS can significantly reduce much more security threats that cannot be detected by conventional firewall systems, such as buffer overflow attacks.

Snort [1] is an open source software NIDS that is widely adopted by the research community as a prototyping platform to investigate different intrusion detection techniques. As a lightweight and yet efficient NIDS, Snort is also used in small networks to detect various network attacks. To increase the security level of Internet-connected hosts, we can even install Snort on each host. Snort relies on a number of predefined rules to filter possible attack packets. For example, one of the signs of the Nimda worm attack is the occurrence of string "readme.eml"

---

* Corresponding author.

K. Li et al. (Eds.): NPC 2007, LNCS 4672, pp. 344–353, 2007.

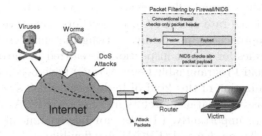

Fig. 1. Network intrusion detection scenario

in a packet. Then, a rule for the NIDS system might be to filter all packets having this particular string in the payload part. Figure 2 shows the actual Snort rule which filters incoming attack packets of the Nimda worm. The signature string "window.open|28 22|readme.eml|22|" is the string that Snort needs to check against every incoming packet (i.e., by performing a string matching on the signature string) so as to eliminate the Nimda worm attack. On the other hand, it should be emphasized that the signature string might appear arbitrarily in the payload of an attack packet, meaning that every byte of the payload must be checked against the signature string.

```
alert tcp $EXTERNAL_NET $HTTP_PORTS -> $HOME_NET any
(msg:"WEB-CLIENT readme.eml autoload attempt"; flow:to_client,established;
content:"window.open|28 22|readme.eml|22|"; nocase;
reference:url,www.cert.org/advisories/CA-2001-26.html;
classtype:attempted-user; sid:1290; rev:10;)
```

Fig. 2. The Snort rule for filtering incoming attack packets of the Nimda worm

At the time of writing, there are 8868 Snort rules like the one shown in Figure 2. Then, it follows that, for each packet, thousands of signature strings need to be checked against the payload of the packet. Thus, the string matching process is a computation-intensive task in Snort. In fact, on profiling the performance of Snort 1.6.3, it is found that 31% of the Snort processing is due to string matching [2], which is the bottleneck that new string matching algorithms should be developed so as to further increase the efficiency of Snort.

To increase the performance of Snort, various string matching schemes have been proposed for incorporation in Snort, for example, the classic Boyer-Moore [3] and Aho-Corasick [4] algorithms. Based on the ideas of the two algorithms, Coit *et al.* proposed a string matching algorithm that can improve the performance of Snort by 1.02–3.32 times when compared with the standard Boyer-Moore implementation [5]. The Wu-Mander multi-pattern matching algorithm [6] and the E^2xB algorithm [7] are another algorithms that have been implemented in Snort.

All the approaches mentioned above are software-based, and it is hardly that they can achieve a packet inspection rate on the order of Gb/s (in practice, a rate of about 750Mb/s is typically achieved [8]). In order to support fast packet inspection (e.g., at the rate of 10Gb/s), researchers have investigated different hardware-based approaches. Specifically, a string matching engine which implements the Snort rules for packet inspection is realized in hardware. In this regards, FPGAs (Field Programmable Gate Arrays) have become more and more popular in the realization of this kind of high-speed NIDS systems, because we can implement massively parallel circuits in FPGAs (FPGAs are computation-efficient), and more importantly, FPGAs can be dynamically reconfigured to incorporate new rules on-demand (FPGAs are flexible).

Knuth-Morris-Pratt algorithm (KMP) is an efficient string matching algorithm [9], and has been implemented in FPGAs by Baker *et al.* [10]. Other FPGA implementations of string matching algorithms are mostly based on hashing [11] or brute-force (i.e., using discrete comparators or NFAs/DFAs) [12] implementations. However, traditional string matching algorithms such as KMP and those based on hashing are designed based on the von Neumann load/store processor architecture, which cannot utilize the highly spatial parallelism of FPGAs. To this end of the problem, we propose that *cellular automata (CA)* [13,14], a highly parallel computational model as proposed by von Neumann as the *universal machine* [13], is desirable to tackle the string matching problem of NIDS systems.

Despite that current software-based implementation of Snort can hardly achieve a packet inspection rate on the order of Gb/s, we believe that the shortcoming is due to string matching algorithms adopted, not because of the performance of current processors. In fact, the power of current multi-core processors has not been fully harnessed, since the current implementation of string matching algorithms in Snort uses only one processor (i.e., single-threaded). Thus, we propose to design a parallel string matching algorithm with multi-threaded implementation. As multi-threaded programs can fully utilize a processor, we believe that such a multi-threaded implementation in Snort can achieve a packet inspection rate on the order of Gb/s.

The rest of the paper is organized as follows. In the next section, we present some preliminaries to help understand our proposed algorithms. In Section 3, we present the design and analysis of our proposed parallel multi-pattern string matching algorithms. Experimental evaluation is presented in Section 4. Finally, we conclude in Section 5.

2   Preliminaries

2.1   Multi-pattern String Matching Based on DFA

To recognize a set of string patterns, we can combine the patterns and form a string matching automaton, called deterministic finite automaton (DFA). Figure 3 shows the detailed process. As can be seen, the process is divided into two parts, construction of state transition table and pattern recognizing.

For simplicity, in Figure 3(a) we only illustrate with one pattern $((aab)^*ab)$ [1]. After a state transition table is constructed, as Figure 3(b) illustrates, the pattern recognizing unit (e.g., a processor) can use the table to recognize patterns in a text string (e.g., the payload of a packet). Specifically, each time a character (i.e., a byte) of the text string is taken, which is then used together with the current state of the pattern recognizing unit to look up the next state. If the next state is a final state, then we can know that a pattern is matched, and the pattern recognizing unit can stop or continue to find out other patterns in the rest of the text string.

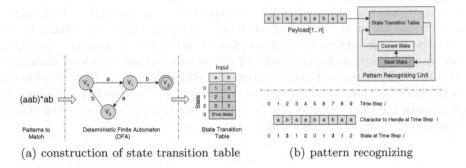

(a) construction of state transition table   (b) pattern recognizing

Fig. 3. The process of multi-pattern string matching based on DFA

2.2 One-Dimensional Cellular Automata (CA)

A one-dimensional cellular automaton consists of a linear array of identical cells, which can be regarded as some lightweight processing elements. Each cell can be in one of a finite number k of states. The state of cell i at time t is $s_t^i \in \Sigma = \{0, 1, ..., k-1\}$. As illustrated in Figure 4 [14], at each time step, all the cells update their state simultaneously according to a local update rule ϕ. This update rule takes as input the local neighbourhood configuration η^i of a cell, which consists of the states of the cell i itself and its $2r$ nearest neighbours, i.e., $\eta^i = (s^{i-r}, ..., s^i, ..., s^{i+r})$. Specifically, we can use the update rule ϕ to obtain the new state of cell i as follows: $s_{t+1}^i = \phi(\eta_t^i)$.

3   Design of Parallel String Matching Algorithms

3.1   Parallel Multi-pattern String Matching Based on CA

To recognize signature strings in the payload of a packet, each character of the payload is handled by a cell of a one-dimensional cellular automaton, and all the cells run in parallel and interactively, as illustrated in Figure 5(a). Specifically,

---

[1] The signature strings to be checked against by an NIDS are typically specified in a regular expression format, for example, $(aab)^*ab$. Then the NIDS alerts the user when it finds strings like "ab", "aabab" or "aabaabaabab" in a packet.

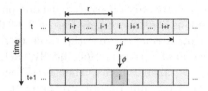

Fig. 4. The update process for cell i in a one-dimensional cellular automaton [14]

each cell (except the leftmost cell) gets the state of its left neighbour and uses this state information together with the character it is handling to look up the state transition table. After the table lookup, the state of the cell is updated and the new state is sent to the right neighbour of the cell. Algorithm 1 describes the update procedure for each cell i of the proposed string matching algorithm, Parallel Multi-Pattern Matching Based on Cellular Automata (CAMP). On the other hand, suppose that the payload of a packet is "*abaababaa*", Figure 5(b) illustrates the time evolution of the cellular automaton for recognizing strings belonging to the pattern $(aab)^*ab$.

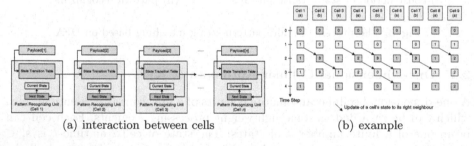

(a) interaction between cells   (b) example

Fig. 5. The working principle of the proposed multi-pattern string matching algorithm based on cellular automata

3.2   Multi-threaded Design of CAMP (MT-CAMP)

Handling each byte of the payload of a packet by a cell is the ideal case for CAMP, which can achieve the most efficiency. However, since the payload of a packet can have a length of around 1460 bytes, it is practically infeasible to create 1460 processing elements simultaneously on a processor-based system. To mitigate this problem, we develop a multi-threaded version of CAMP (MT-CAMP) for implementation on a multi-core-processor-based system. Algorithm 2 describes the details of the multi-threaded version of CAMP. Specifically, given that the length of payload is n and we want to create $threadNumber$ threads, then each thread implements $\frac{n}{threadNumber}$ cells (i.e., handles $\frac{n}{threadNumber}$ bytes of the payload). On the other hand, it should be noted that the $createThread()$ function in Algorithm 2 does not always create new threads for different packets. To reduce thread creation overhead, threads are reused. In actual implementation of MT-CAMP, we found that the performance is not satisfactory due to significant communication overhead between threads. We will discuss this issue in more detail in Section 4.

3.3   Parallel Multi-pattern String Matching with No Communication

The poor performance of MT-CAMP on a multi-processor system motivated us to develop a communication-less string matching algorithm, called Parallel Multi-Pattern Matching with Overlapping Region (ROMP). Figure 6 illustrates the idea of multi-threaded design of ROMP (MT-ROMP). Specifically, if there are *threadNumber* threads created, then the payload of a packet is divided into *threadNumber* regions, and each thread uses the DFA approach as mentioned in Section 2 to carry out string matching in its region. However, since a string belonging to a particular pattern can span across different regions of the payload, a thread will also perform string matching in its right neighbour's region. Hence, there is an overlapping region where two threads will perform string matching on it. As we will discuss in subsequent section, the length of this overlapping region is small when compared to the length of a payload. Algorithm 3 describes the string matching procedure in each thread of MT-ROMP.

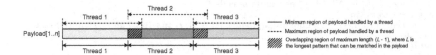

Fig. 6. Payload division in MT-ROMP

3.4   Performance Analysis and Comparison

Suppose that the longest pattern that can be matched in a payload is of length L, then the time complexity of CAMP is $O(L)$. The reason is that L cells are involved in order to recognize the pattern. Referring back to Figure 5(b), if the evolution process can stop at time step 2, then the longest pattern is "ab", meaning that $L = 2$. Similarly, if the evolution process has to stop at time step 4, then the longest pattern is "aabab" and $L = 5$. With a study of the Snort rules, the value of L is typically in the range $1 < L < 20$.

As for MT-CAMP, the time complexity is $O(\frac{n}{threadNumber} \cdot L)$, since each thread needs to implement $\frac{n}{threadNumber}$ cells and the cells within each thread are evolved one by one. The time complexity of MT-ROMP is $O(\frac{n}{threadNumber} + (L-1)) = O(\frac{n}{threadNumber} + L)$, as the longest pattern string can span across two regions of the payload. Table 1 shows the time complexity comparison of CAMP, MT-CAMP, and MT-ROMP with other existing algorithms.

Algorithm 1. CAMP—Update procedure for each cell i.

cellUpdate($payload[i]$, $transitionTable$)
```
 1: currentState ← stateLookup(payload[i], transitionTable) /* current state */
 2: newState ← NULL /* new state of the cell */
 3: leftNeighbourState ← NULL /* state of the cell's left neighbour */
 4: while (TRUE) do
 5:   leftNeighbourState ← getLeftNeighbourState()
 6:   newState ← stateLookup(payload[i], leftNeighbourState, transitionTable)
 7:   if (newState ≠ NULL and newState ≠ currentState) then
 8:     currentState ← newState
 9:     if (isFinalState(currentState, transitionTable)) then
10:       report("Matched at payload position i!")
11:     end if
12:   end if
13: end while
```

Algorithm 2. MT-CAMP—Creation of threads and update procedure of cells in each thread.

MTcreateThreads($threadNumber$, $payload[1..n]$, $transitionTable$)
```
 1: cellsPerThread ← n/threadNumber; head ← 1; tail ← 1
 2: while (head < n) do
 3:   tail ← head − 1 + ((head + cellsPerThread − 1 ≤ n)?cellsPerThread : (n − head))
 4:   createThread(MTcellsUpdate(payload[head..tail], transitionTable))
 5:   head ← head + cellsPerThread
 6: end while
```

MTcellsUpdate($payload[j..k]$, $transitionTable$)
```
 1: m ← k − j + 1 /* number of cells per thread */
 2: currentState[1..m] ← NULL /* current state of cells */
 3: newState[1..m] ← NULL /* new state of cells */
 4: for i = 1 to m do
 5:   currentState[i] ← stateLookup(payload[j + i − 1], transitionTable) /* initial state */
 6: end for
 7: while (TRUE) do
 8:   for i = 1 to m do
 9:     leftNeighbourState ← getLeftNeighbourState(i, currentState[1..m])
10:     newState[i] ← stateLookup(payload[j + i − 1], leftNeighbourState, transitionTable)
11:     if (newState[i] ≠ NULL and newState[i] ≠ currentState[i]) then
12:       currentState[i] ← newState[i]
13:       if (isFinalState(currentState[i], transitionTable)) then
14:         report("Matched at payload position (j + i − 1)!")
15:       end if
16:     end if
17:   end for
18: end while
```

Algorithm 3. String matching procedure in each thread of MT-ROMP.

MT-ROMP($payload[j..k]$, n, $transitionTable$)
```
 1: currentState ← stateLookup(payload[j], transitionTable) /* current state */
 2: newState ← NULL /* new state of the cell */
 3: for (i = j + 1; i <= n; i + +) do
 4:   if (i > k and currentState == NULL) then
 5:     break /* escape from the overlapping region */
 6:   end if
 7:   newState ← stateLookup(payload[i], currentState, transitionTable)
 8:   if (newState ≠ currentState) then
 9:     currentState ← newState
10:     if (isFinalState(currentState, transitionTable)) then
11:       report("Matched at payload position i!")
12:     end if
13:   end if
14: end for
```

Table 1. Time complexity comparison

Algorithm	Complexity
CAMP	$O(L)$
MT-CAMP	$O(\frac{n}{threadNumber} \cdot L)$
MT-ROMP	$O(\frac{n}{threadNumber} + L)$
Boyer-Moore [3]	$O(n)$
Aho-Corasick [4]	$O(n)$
KMP [9]	$O(n)$

4 Experimental Evaluation

To implement the ideal design of CAMP (i.e., each byte of the payload is handled by an individual processing element), a viable approach is to use FPGAs, since we can implement massively parallel circuits on FPGAs. More importantly, the communication overhead between cells will be insignificant since the communication is deterministic and at wire speed. On the contrary, the communication between threads is not deterministic, which accounts for the significant communication overhead. Currently, we have not implemented CAMP on FPGAs yet. In this section, we would like to evaluate the performance of MT-CAMP and MT-ROMP on a multi-processor system (particularly, a multi-core system) using multi-threaded implementation. Specifically, our focus is to study the scalability of the proposed parallel string matching algorithms, while maintaining a fast string matching rate.

Since the string patterns that we intend to match are the signature strings in Snort, the first step of evaluation is to convert the signature strings into a state transition table. This process can be carried out by an open source tool called JFlex [15], which is a lexical analyzer generator (or scanner generator). For performance evaluation, we do not use all the signature strings in Snort. In fact, we randomly choose 400 signature strings.

To evaluate the performance of our proposed parallel string matching algorithms, synthetic packets of payload of 1460 bytes are generated. Specifically, for each of the 400 string patterns chosen, we randomly put the string pattern in the payload, and the rest of the payload is filled with random bytes. Using this way, we generate 10 packets for each string pattern and the positions of the string pattern are different. Effectively, 4000 different packets are generated. For our experiments, these 4000 packets are duplicated 100 times to form a packet stream of 400K packets and the packets are stored in the main memory of the system under test.

As a comparison algorithm, the DFA string matching approach as mentioned in Section 2 is chosen. Since the DFA approach shares the same design mechanism as the Aho-Corasick algorithm [4], which is well-known to be a fast multi-pattern string matching algorithm, its speed is of the same grade as the Aho-Corasick algorithm.

First of all, we evaluated the performance MT-CAMP. Using a single thread, we found that MT-CAMP is about 16 times slower than the DFA approach. The deficiency of MT-CAMP comes from the fact that there is excessive communication overhead between cells. When using more threads, we also found that there is significant communication overhead in using thread-specific synchronization functions such as mutexes.

The poor performance of MT-CAMP motivated us to develop a communication-less parallel string matching algorithm for a multi-processor system, namely MT-ROMP. When inspecting the 400K packet stream under a Pentium D 3.4GHz system with Ubuntu Linux 6.10 installed, the DFA approach uses 3.40s, while MT-ROMP uses 4.08s and 2.06s [2] when one processor core and two processor cores are utilized, respectively. Hence, there is 40% reduction in string matching time when the two processor cores of the dual-core microprocessor are utilized. Since we were not able to obtain a quad-core system to study the scalability of MT-ROMP, we have resolved to evaluate its performance under an SMP machine with eight processors (Sun4u/Sparc with SunOS 5.9 installed). The results are shown in Figure 7. As can be seen from Figure 7(a), there is about 45% reduction in string matching time when two processors are used. This result is quite matched with that obtained from the dual-core machine. On the other hand, Figure 7(b) shows that the speedup is quite linear. However, the speedup is saturated when more than six processors are used. This is due to frequent context switching of the system.

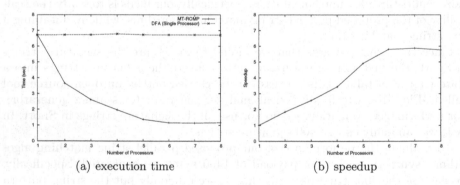

(a) execution time   (b) speedup

Fig. 7. Performance comparison of MT-ROMP and the DFA approach

The lesson learnt from our experience of designing a parallel string matching algorithm on a multi-processor system is that it is extremely important to reduce communication between threads. As discussed in detail in [16], the frequent use of mutexes, semaphores, monitors, etc., to achieve synchronization between threads has adverse effect on the performance of multi-threaded programs. With the emergence of multi-core microprocessors, if we expect parallel programming

---

[2] This corresponds to a string matching rate of about 2.1Gb/s. However, the actual value for real-life packet inspection should be lower than 2.1Gb/s, as the 400K packets are stored in the main memory of the system. We have not taken into consideration the preprocessing time of packets once they are received from the network interface.

to become mainstream, Lee suggested in [16] that we should construct parallel programming models that are much more predictable and understandable than threads.

5   Conclusions and Future Work

In this paper, we have presented the design and evaluation of several parallel multi-pattern string matching algorithms for an NIDS system. Our future work is to implement CAMP on FPGAs to investigate how fast string matching rate it can achieve in hardware implementation. As for MT-ROMP, we would like to integrate it with Snort, and then carry out more detailed performance evaluation with real-life network traffic.

References

1. Snort Official Web Site: http://www.snort.org/ (2007)
2. Fisk, M., Varghese, G.: Fast content-based packet handling for intrusion detection. Technical Report, CS2001-0670, University of California, San Diego (2001)
3. Boyer, R., Moore, J.: A fast string match algorithm. Communications of the ACM 20, 762–772 (1977)
4. Aho, A., Corasick, M.: Fast pattern matching: An aid to bibliographic search. Communications of the ACM 18, 333–340 (1975)
5. Coit, C.J., Staniford, S., McAlerney, J.: Towards Faster String Matching for Intrusion Detection or Exceeding the Speed of Snort. In: DARPA Information Survivability Conference and Exposition II, vol. 1, pp. 367–373 (2001)
6. Wu, S., Mander, U.: A fast algorithm for multi-pattern searching. Technical Report, TR-94-17, University of Arisona (1994)
7. Anagnostakis, K., Markatos, E., Antonatos, S., Polychronakis, M.: E^2xB: A Domain-Specific String Matching Algorithm for Intrusion Detection. In: The 18th IFIP International Information Security Conference (2003)
8. Norton, M.: Optimizing pattern matching for intrusion detection. White Paper, Sourcefire Inc. (2004)
9. Cormen, T.H., Leiserson, C.E., Rivest, R.L., Stein, C.: Introduction to Algorithms. MIT Press, Cambridge (2002)
10. Baker, Z.K., Prasanna, V.K.: Time and Area Efficient Pattern Matching on FPGAs. In: FPGA 2004, pp. 223–232 (2004)
11. Dharmapurikar, S., Krishnamurthy, P., Sproull, T., Lockwood, J.: Deep Packet Inspection using Parallel Bloom Filters. In: Symposium on High Performance Interconnects (HotI), pp. 44–51 (2003)
12. Sourdis, I., Pnevmatikatos, D.: Fast, Large-Scale String Match for a 10Gbps FPGA-based Network Intrusion Detection System. In: Cheung, P.Y.K., Constantinides, G.A. (eds.) FPL 2003. LNCS, vol. 2778, pp. 880–889. Springer, Heidelberg (2003)
13. Neumann, J.V.: Theory of Self-Reproducing Automata. University of Illinois Press (1966)
14. Hordijk, W.: Dynamics, Emergent Computation, and Evolution in Cellular Automata. PhD thesis, The University of New Mexico (1999)
15. JFlex—The Fast Scanner Generator for Java (2007), http://www.jflex.de/
16. Lee, E.A.: The problem with threads. IEEE Computer Magazine 39, 33–42 (2006)

Object-Based Storage Model for Object-Oriented Database*

Zhongmin Li[1] and Zhanwu Yu[2,**]

[1] State Key Laboratory of Information Engineering in Surveying,
Mapping and Remote Sensing, Wuhan University, Wuhan, Hubei, China, 430079
[2] Major Research Interests: Multimedia Communication, Massive Information Storage
{zhongmli,yzw2008}@gmail.com

Abstract. The current storage models for Object-Oriented DataBase (OODB), which organize data as objects according to the Object-Oriented Data Model (OODM), are mainly established on the block storage devices. In this way, the storage manager does not have detailed knowledge of the characteristics of the underlying storage devices, and the storage subsystem does not have the semantic knowledge of the data stored in the block storage devices, so it is very difficult to implement some workload-dependent tasks such as data layout and caching. Furthermore, the storage subsystem of OODB has to organize the objects in the pages, which is not well-suited to the objects storage. In this paper, we present an Object-Based Storage Model (OBSM) for OODB by using the recently-standardized Object-based Storage Device (OSD) interface. OSD offloads the storage management into the storage device itself and provides an object interface to data, which brings more intelligence into the storage subsystem. In the first glance at using OBSD in OODB, we explore the methods to map OODM to OBSM including direct mapping, mapping clustering to collection and declustering a large object to a series of sub-objects, and analyze the benefits to the storage subsystem of OODB by using OBSM such as providing storage functionalities offloading, providing objects sharing pool, providing integrative object persistence.

Keywords: object-oriented database, object-based storage, storage model, object-oriented data model.

1 Introduction

The storage subsystem is one of the kernel modules in database system, and its storage performance is of utmost importance for database applications. The standard interfaces to storage subsystem virtualize storage as a simple linear array of fixed-size logical blocks.

---

* Supported by the National Key Basic Research and Development Program of China (No.2004CB318206).
** Corresponding author.

K. Li et al. (Eds.): NPC 2007, LNCS 4672, pp. 354–363, 2007.

Most database systems use the N-ary Storage Model (NSM) as their low-level data layout. In the NSM, all attributes of a conceptual schema record are stored together. NSM organizes the table into fixed-size pages (e.g., 8KB) each containing a short range of full records, stores records contiguously starting from the beginning of each disk page, and uses an offset table at the end of the page to locate the beginning of each record, and the pages are stored sequentially on disk [1]. NSM is well-suited to workloads that access full records, which are always fetched into memory regardless of whether the query actually touches the data. In this way, it wastes memory capacity and, more importantly, disk bandwidth, so it is not well-suited to workloads that access partial records.

The Decomposition Storage Model (DSM) organizes a table in column major order by storing individual fields sequentially on the disk [2]. DSM gives good performance when accessing just one or a few fields from a relation, but suffers when reconstructing full records. In order to solve the problem, Ramamurthy et al suggested DSM stores two copies of each attribute relation: one copy is clustered on the value while the other is clustered on the surrogate [3]. To support the relational model, intermediate and final results need an N-ary representation. However, this technique needs double storage space and requires updating both copies of the relation.

To address the issue of low cache utilization in NSM, Ailamaki et al. introduce Partition Attributes Across (PAX), a new layout for data records [4]. Unlike NSM, within each page, PAX groups all the values of a particular attribute together on a minipage, and fully utilizes the cache resources during a sequential data access because only a number of the required attribute's values are loaded into the cache. However, compared with DSM, PAX doesn't optimize the I/O between disk and memory.

The Multi-resolution Block Storage Model (MBSM) stores records in a partitioned way in super-blocks, and then organizes super-blocks on disk into mega-blocks [5]. MBSM is most suitable for decision-support workloads that frequently execute table scans. Compared to NSM and PAX, MBSM requests fewer disk pages. Compared to DSM, MBSM's scan performance is comparable, and its cache performance is better. Furthermore, MBSM has better insert/update I/O performance, and doesn't require a join to reconstruct the records.

The Clotho Storage Model (CSM) allows the DBMS to construct in-memory data pages that contain only the data required for a given query [6]. CSM provides the desired tradeoff between full- and partial-record access to save memory and disk bandwidth. The Atropos disk array logical volume manager enables efficient two-dimensional access to relations stored on disk, allowing data pages to be filled efficiently, regardless of the query [7]. The combination of Clotho and Atropos uses knowledge of the relation's schema and the characteristics of the underlying disk storage to enable a geometry-aware storage model (GASM) with the desired tradeoff: the performance of NSM for full-record access, the performance of DSM for single-record access, and a near-linear tradeoff for partial-record access. Many studies [7, 8, 9, 10] have taken the view that a storage device can provide relevant characteristics to applications to allow for optimized I/O access. But the required information about detailed knowledge of the mechanical parameters and geometry of the disk drives in the storage subsystem can be measured empirically, so it is difficult and fragile in practice, making the realization of GASM problematic.

Schlosser uses Object-Based Storage (OBS) interfaces to allow the database storage manager to cleanly communicate its storage requirements to the storage subsystem, where more information is available to make low-level optimizations [11]. In this way, an entire table is stored as a single object, and the schema of the relation is expressed through attributes assigned to that object, so storage managers can take advantage of heterogeneous storage devices without being burdened with different device parameters. Using the Object-based Storage Devices (OSD) specification [12], data can be addressed at an object granularity, allowing the storage manager to access individual records and fields of the relation directly. Furthermore, object-based storage devices have much richer semantic information about the data that they store, allowing them to optimize their performance "under the covers" much more effectively than current storage devices. The database no longer needs detailed information about the storage subsystem, but still can take advantage of geometry-aware data placement techniques such as CSM.

Schlosser only discussed how to organize relational database tables into objects using OSD, which are mainly used in Relational Database (RDBM) and Object-Relational Database (ORDBM). Sometimes applications evolve to object-oriented software development to keep the promise of flexibility and extensibility. OODB is well-suited, since it provides homogeneous means to store and to manage complex structures very efficiently. As for Object-Oriented Database (OODB), it usually uses Object-Oriented Data Model (OODM) to store the hierarchical classes in the pages based on the block storage devices such as disks [1]. In this way, the storage subsystem needs manage two buffers: pages buffer and objects buffer, and frequently change the storage mode between them. Its storage performance is low, and it is difficult to realize multilevel persistent objects storage.

In this paper, we present an Object-Based Storage Model (OBSM) for OODB using OSD. We store the hierarchical classes as objects in the OSD devices by mapping OODM to OBSM. The rest of the paper is organized as follows: Section 2 briefly introduces the OSD model and its advantages. Section 3 summarizes the OODM and the methods to map OODM to OBSM. Section 4 analyzes the benefits to OODB by using OBSM. Section 5 gives a summary for the paper and future work.

2 Object-Based Storage

2.1 OSD Model

An object is variable-length and can be used to store any type of data, such as files, database records, medical images, or multimedia, even be used to store an entire file system or database [13]. The OSD object abstraction is designed to re-divide the responsibility for managing the access to data on a storage device by assigning to the storage device additional responsibilities in the area of space management [12]. Figure 1 shows the relationship between the OSD model and a traditional SBC-based model for a file system.

The user component of the file system contains such functions as hierarchy management, naming and user access control. The storage management component is focused on mapping logical constructs (e.g., files or database entries) to the physical organization of the storage media.

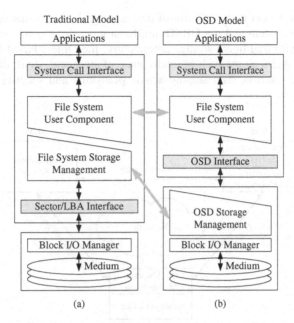

Fig. 1. Comparison of traditional and OSD storage models: (a) traditional storage model; (b) OSD storage model

In the OSD model, the logical constructs are called user objects, which are composed of data, user-accessible attributes, and device-managed metadata, and act as data containers that abstract the physical disk layout details under the object interface. A user object is the basic object type, and the root object, partition objects and collection objects provide additional navigational aids for user objects. Each object, regardless of its type, has a unique name or Object ID (OID), a set of object attributes, and some meta-data. There is only a root object on each Object-Based Storage Device (OBSD), which encompasses all the other objects. Each user object is a member of only one partition object which allows for efficient addressing, capacity and quota management, and security management of sets of user objects. Within each partition there may be zero or more collection objects that are used to group user objects for fast indexing and multi-object operations. A user object can be a member of zero or more collection objects at the same time.

In addition to mapping data, the storage management component maintains other information about the OSD objects that it stores (e.g., size, usage quotas, and associated username) in attributes. The user component may have the ability to influence the properties of object data through the specification of attributes by accessing the object interface. The difference between an OBSD and a block-based device is the interface, not the physical media [13]. The OBSD makes the decisions as to where to allocate storage capacity for individual data entities and managing free space.

2.2 OSD Advantages

Fig. 2 shows the architecture of the OSD. In order to separate access paths of control, management and data, the Client, the Metadata Server (MDS) and the OBSD are self-existent. The Client is the initiator of data access, the MDS manage the metadata of whole storage system and the OBSD are the storage devices to store objects [12]. In comparison with traditional storage architecture, the Object-based Storage System (OSS) possess some features such as intelligence of storage devices, distributed metadata, parallel data access, data sharing across platforms and security of data access [13,14].

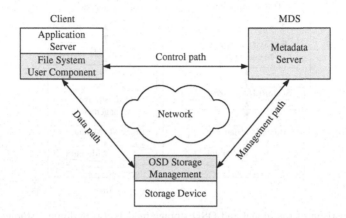

Fig. 2. OSD architecture

In the OSD model, the OBSD can understand some of the relationships between the blocks on the device, and can use this information to better organize the data and anticipate the storage requirements of whole system, because the object storage management component stands in the OBSD. The attributes of an object can contain static information about the object (e.g., creation time), dynamic information updated on each access (e.g., last access time), information specific to a storage application (e.g., filename, group, or user ids), and information specific to a current application. Attributes may also contain hints about the object's behaviors such as the expected read/write ratio, the most likely patterns of access (e.g., sequential or random), or the expected lifetime of the object [12, 13]. To access such various attributes enables the storage system to better store, organize and manage the data.

While separating the MDS, the Client can directly access the OBSDs, and 90% of the metadata management is offloaded from the metadata server to the OBSDs. In this way, it solves the bottleneck problem which results from using traditional network storage architectures, which are designed with a single monolithic metadata server. Each OBSD manages the layout and retrieval of the data that is presented to it. This brings improvement in an order of magnitude in the potential performance of the system's metadata management. Furthermore, adding more OBSDs to the system will not only increase the capacity of whole object-based storage system, but also increase the resources of the metadata management. This also improves scalability of clusters greatly since hosts no longer need to coordinate metadata updates.

Direct accessing the OBSD enables a high-performance solution, as there are no potential bottlenecks in the system between the hosts and the storage devices. Owing to intelligence built in the OBSD, there is no need for a file server to intermediate the transaction. Further, if the file system stripes the data across a number of OBSDs, the aggregate I/O rates and data throughput rates scale linearly.

Objects introduce a mechanism in the OBSD that allows the device treat storage applications or clients individually. With objects, since metadata is offloaded to the OBSD, the dependency between the metadata and storage system/application is removed. Attributes improve data sharing by allowing storage applications to share a common set of information describing the data, and are the key to giving storage devices an awareness of how objects are being accessed. In this way, OSD removes the biggest obstacle to data sharing.

Security is perhaps the single most important feature of object-based storage that distinguishes it from block-based storage. Although security does exist at the device and fabric level for SANs, objects provide a finer granular security at a much lower cost in the OSD model [13]. In order to realize secure data sharing, a credential-based access control system is running in the OSD model, which is very different to realize in the traditional network storage architectures. In this security architecture, every access is authorized, and the authorization is done without communicating with a central authority that may slow the data path. The security manager may authenticate the Client, but the OBSD does not authenticate the Client. It is sufficient for the OBSD to verify the credential sent by the Client. The credential-based access control system may ensure the Client to use more effective and more achievable network such as Ethernet.

3   OBSM for OODB

The common data model supported by ODMG [15] implementations is based on the OMG Object Model, which was designed to be a common denominator for object request brokers, object database systems, object programming languages, and other applications. Generally, OODM includes interface, class, and structure (literal) data types. An interface specifies the abstract behavior of its instances; a class specifies the abstract state and behavior of its instances; a structure type is defined with a name and a set of attributes, and will be called a named structure type [16]. An instance of a named structure type has no identifier but values of attributes. The ODMG Object Model defines atomic literal types such as short and string.

Logically, OODB consists of a class hierarchy represented by a Directed Acyclic Graph (DAG). Each node in the DAG represents a class, and classes are named and associated with each class that is a set of instance variables. The OODB consists of instances of these classes, and every instance in the OODB belongs to its home class. Since the hierarchy represents an ISA relationship among the objects, an instance belongs not only to its home class but to all the superclasses related to it, and has a unique identifier to distinguish it from every other instance in the OODB.

While using OSD to store the objects in OODB, the primary problem is how to map OODM to OBSM. There are several methods to map OODM to OBSM: (1) direct mapping a Logical Object (LO) based on OODM to a Storage Object (SO) in OBSD, (2) mapping LOs clustering to SOs collection, (3) declustering a large LO to a series of sub-objects (several SOs).

3.1 Direct Mapping

Primarily we map a LO to a SO in the object-based storage system. No need to change the structure of LO, just add a unique SO identifier (SOID), the length of LO and some storage attributes for the LO to construct a correlative SO (see Fig. 3). We also can add some other attributes to the end of SO. It is the general way to map a LO to a SO.

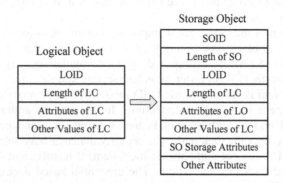

Fig. 3. Direct mapping

3.2 Mapping Clustering to Collection

Clustering is a container for the objects which attributes are similar such as all the instances of some class, and is the ability to store logically related objects close together. When applications access an object, applications can find the object or other correlative objects using clustering. Using OBSM, we can map a clustering to a Collection Object (CO) stored in the OBSD. In this way, each LO in the clustering is mapped to a relevant SO using the method described in 3.1, and the CO has its own unique object identifier and attributes (see Fig. 4). The SOs belong to the CO logically, but not the part of it. The common attributes of all the SOs can be drew out to become the part of the attributes of the CO. Each SO also has its own unique object identifier and attributes. Applications can access the CO, and also directly access any SO in the CO respectively.

3.3 Declustering a Large Object to a Series of Sub-objects

In the block storage device, a large logical object which size is bigger than one page must be stored in several pages using some strategy. In the OSD, a large logical object can be mapped to a SO using the method in 3.1. When the size of a large object is too big to affect the access efficiency mapping a SO stored in an OBSD, we can split the large logical object to several slices, and each slice is mapped to a relevant SO (see Fig. 5). In this way, we can use some strategies to distribute the series of sub-objects in different OBSDs to increase the access I/O bandwidth using the characteristic of parallel access of OSD. The procedure is hided in the object storage system, and the applications don't need to know the processing details. For applications, accessing a large object and accessing an average object are in the same way.

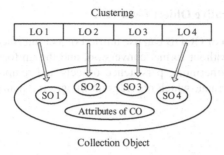

Fig. 4. Mapping clustering to collection

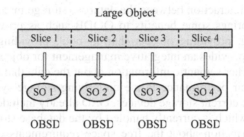

Fig. 5. Declustering a large object to a series of sub-objects

4 Benefits

In the OSD, the storage devices have the intelligence according to offloading the storage management component into the storage devices, which brings many benefits to the object management in the OODB.

4.1 Providing Storage Functionalities Offloading

Using OBSM, the storage management component of the storage subsystem is offloaded into the object-based storage devices. In this way, some functionalities of storage management can be offloaded into the object-based storage system, and the storage manager of OODB focuses on the transaction processing.

4.2 Providing Objects Sharing Pool

The object-based storage system can provide an objects sharing pool for OODB, and provide access control at object granularity. Synchronization of metadata is realized in the object-based storage system, so various OODBs can share the objects sharing pool to construct a parallel distributed Object-Oriented DataBase System (OODBS). The metadata server of the object-based storage system can provide a uniform DAG for all the OODBs.

4.3 Providing Integrative Object Persistence

The storage subsystem of OODB can use unified object interface to access the objects storage sharing pool without format conversion, and the uniform DAG provides efficiency navigation. Furthermore, persistence objects and temporary objects have the same object storage format, which provides an integrative management for objects in OODB.

5 Conclusion

In this paper, we introduce a new storage model called OBSM for OODM. We have explored the methods to store the objects of OODB by using object-based storage devices to improve the interaction between the database storage manager and the storage subsystem. OBSM brings some benefits to OODB such as providing storage functionalities offloading, providing objects sharing pool, providing integrative object persistence. OBSM provides an integrative management for objects in OODB.

OSD has much richer semantic information about the data that they store, allowing them to optimize their performance in the underlying storage system, so it is much more effectively than current storage devices. OSD already includes provision for free space management, which is currently handled by the database storage manager. With better semantic information about the free space requirements of the database, the storage subsystem could better optimize its layout and set aside free space for future inserts and deletes. Our future work focuses on investigating these opportunities for OODB applications.

Acknowledgments. This paper is supported by the National Key Basic Research and Development Program of China (No.2004CB318206). Every member in our project team has made contribution to this project. Especially thanks Dr. Sheng Zheng for his helpful advice.

References

1. Ramakrishnan, R., Gehrke, J.: Database management systems, 3rd edn. McGraw-Hill, New York (2003)
2. Copeland, G.P., Khoshafian, S.: A decomposition storage model. In: ACM SIGMOD International Conference on Management of Data, pp. 268–279. ACM Press, New York (1985)
3. Ramamurthy, R., DeWitt, D.J., Su, Q.: A case for fractured mirrors. In: International Conference on Very Large Databases, pp. 430–441. Morgan Kaufmann Publishers, Inc., San Francisco (2002)
4. Ailamaki, A., DeWitt, D.J., Hill, M.D., Skounakis, M.: Weaving relations for cache performance. In: Proceedings of VLDB Conference (2001)
5. Zhou, J., Ross, K.A.: A multi-resolution block storage model for database design. In: Proceedings of the Seventh International Database Engineering and Applications Symposium (IDEAS'03), Asunción, Paraguay (2003)

6. Schindler, J., Schlosser, S.W., Shao, M., Ailamaki, A., Ganger, G.R.: Atropos: A disk array volume manager for orchestrated use of disks. In: Conference on File and Storage Technologies, USENIX Association (2004)
7. Shao, M., Schindler, J., Schlosser, S.W., Ailamaki, A., Ganger, G.R.: Clotho: Decoupling memory page layout from storage organization. In: International Conference on Very Large Databases, pp. 696–707 (2004)
8. Schindler, J., Ailamaki, A., Ganger, G.R.: Lachesis: Robust database storage management based on device-specific performance characteristics. In: International Conference on Very Large Databases, pp. 706–717. Morgan Kaufmann Publishing, Inc., San Francisco (2003)
9. Schindler, J., Griffin, J.L., Lumb, C.R., Ganger, G.R.: Track-aligned extents: Matching access patterns to disk drive characteristics. In: Conference on File and Storage Technologies, USENIX Association, pp. 259–274 (2002)
10. VanMeter, R.: SLEDs: Storage latency estimation descriptors. In: IEEE Symposium on Mass Storage Systems. USENIX (1998)
11. Schlosser, S.W., Iren, S.: Database storage management with object-based storage devices. In: Proceedings of the First International Workshop on Data Management on New Hardware (DaMoN 2005), Baltimore, MD, USA (2005)
12. SCSI Object-Based Storage Device Commands-2 (OSD-2) (October 2004), http://www.t10.org
13. Mesnier, M., Ganger, G.R., Riedel, E.: Object-based Storage. IEEE Communications Magazine 41(8), 84–90 (2003)
14. Azagury, A., Dreizin, V., Factor, M.: Towards an Object Store. In: 20th IEEE Symposium on Mass Storage Systems, IEEE Computer Society Press, Los Alamitos (2003)
15. Cattel, R., Barry, D., Berler, M., Eastman, J., Jordan, D., Russel, C., Schadow, O., Stanienda, T., Velez, F.: The Object Data Standard: ODMG 3.0. Morgan Kaufgrnann, Publishers, Inc. (1999)
16. Li, L.: On ODMG Data Types. In: 39th International Conference and Exhibition on Technology of Object-Oriented Languages and Systems (TOOLS 39), pp. 219–228 (2001)

HPRD: A High Performance RDF Database

Liu Baolin and Hu Bo

Department of Computer Science and Technology, Tsinghua University,
Beijing 100084, P.R. China
lblin@cic.tsinghua.edu.cn

Abstract. In this paper a high performance storage system for RDF documents is introduced. The system employs optimized index structures for RDF data and efficient RDF query evaluation. The index scheme consists of 3 types of indices. Triple index manages basic RDF triples by dividing original RDF graph into several sub-graphs. Path index manages frequent RDF path patterns for long path query performance enhancement. Context index is optional for context oriented RDF data and temporal RDF data. In this paper, we describe the organization of index structures, show the process of evaluating queries based on the index structures, and provide a performance comparison with exist RDF databases through several benchmark experiments.

Keywords: Database, Index, RDF, Query.

1 Introduction

As the next generation of World-Wide-Web, the significant difference between Semantic Web[1] and traditional WWW is the quantity and quality of the metadata. In Semantic Web, by using metadata to describe the resources, it is possible to perform more intelligent machine-to-machine interactions, such as reasoning, deduction and semantic searches.

RDF[2] is defined as the standard of metadata description in Semantic Web. RDF, which is composed of RDF data model and RDF schema[3], is a framework to describe data and their semantics. In the RDF model, triple is the minimal unit to describe the relation of two resources.

In the near future, the quantity of data represented by RDF is increasing fast. As a result, the requirement of RDF database becomes important. A direct approach is using XML database to manage RDF data. However, this approach is not practical as the structure of RDF data model is different with XML data model.

Another way to implement an RDF database is to utilize the RDBMS. The normal method is dividing the RDF data to pieces and storing in a specific relational structure. The RDF query is transformed to the instructions in the RDBMS[4]. There are several methods already, such as RDFSuite[5], Jena[6] and Sesame[7]. But the emergency problem in these approaches is the performance.

In this paper, we propose HPRD which is a high performance RDF database. HPRD combines several database techniques into native RDF storage. By implementing a mixed index scheme, HPRD provides improved query answering performance

K. Li et al. (Eds.): NPC 2007, LNCS 4672, pp. 364–374, 2007.

and capabilities compared to current RDF storage systems. HPRD has the following novel combination of characteristics to improve the performance.

- An optimized index structure for RDF. The index scheme defined in HPRD consists of 3 types. The basic triple index manages all RDF triples by dividing original RDF graph. Path index is used to accelerate evaluation of queries with long path expression. Context index acts as an optional index for context oriented RDF and temporal RDF data.
- Workload aware path index. In HPRD, frequently used path expressions in query are extracted and managed by path index, so that the cost of complex path query processing can be improved significantly.

We implemented HPRD and conducted several experimental studies with both real-life and synthetic data sets. Experimental results show that the optimized index scheme improves the cost of query processing than existing RDF databases, especially for long path expressions with few constraints.

The rest of paper is organized as follows. Section 2 reviews the data model for RDF and the notion of queries. In section 3, related works about RDF database are analyzed. We present the optimized index scheme in Section 4 and describe how to perform query processing in Section 5. In section 6, we give the architecture and implementation of HPRD and show the experimental results. Section 7 concludes the paper.

2 Preliminaries

In this section we first give an example of RDF data from a real-life application and then define the data model and query language used in HPRD.

2.1 RDF Example

FOAF (Friend of a Friend) project is about creating web of machine-readable home-pages for describing people, the links between them and the things they create and do. FOAF[8] uses RDF as its fundamental data format, and is a good example for distributing data across the Semantic Web. Fig. 1 shows a small RDF graph describing a person and his relations.

2.2 RDF Data Model

We begin with defining the standard RDF data model as described in variousW3C Recommendations [9],[10].

Definition 1. (RDF Triple and RDF Node) Given a set of URI references R, a set of blank nodes B, and a set of literals L, a triple (s, p, o) $\in (R \cup B) \times R \times (R \cup B \cup L)$ is called an RDF triple, An element of an RDF triple is called an RDF node.

In such a triple, s is called the subject, p the predicate, and o the object.

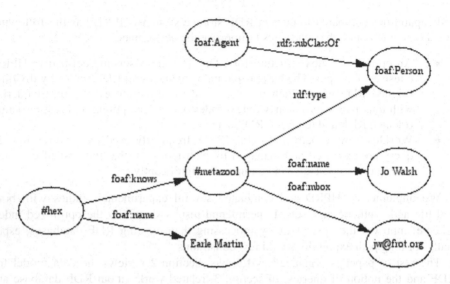

Fig. 1. A sample RDF graph

2.3 Context Oriented and Temporal RDF

Although the RDF specification itself does not define the notion of context[11], usually applications require context to store various kinds of metadata for a given set of RDF data.

The interpretation of context is depends on the application. For example, an RDF document repository may use the original RDF file name as the context, and the document version may also be used as the context to trace the changes.

Temporal RDF, which contains temporal information of triples, is a special use case of RDF context. Some studies already reveal that there are needs to use temporal RDF to address changes of ontology or apply temporal annotations to documents[12].

Definition 2. (Triple in Context) A pair (t, c) with t be a triple and c ∈(R∪B) is called a triple in context c. Usually a quad (c, s, p, o) is used to represent the triple.

2.4 RDQL

RDQL[13] is an evolution from several languages and is designed for RDF data query. An RDQL consists of a graph pattern, expressed as a list of triple patterns. Each triple pattern is comprised of named variables and RDF values (URIs and literals). An RDQL query can additionally have a set of constraints on the values of those variables, and a list of the variables required in the answer set.

An RDQL query treats an RDF graph purely as data and makes no distinction between inferred triples and ground triples.

Example 1. SELECT ?X WHERE
  (?X,   <http://www.w3.org/1999/02/22-rdf-syntax-ns#type>,
<http://example.com/someType>)

3 Related Work

Several RDF databases have already been proposed, most of which use relational databases as their underlying data storage[4],[5],[7]. We can make categorization of the ways relational schemas are designed. One approach flatly stores statements into a single relational table. The other creates relational tables for classes and properties that are defined in the RDF schema information, storing resources according to their classes (or properties). The latter approach is also referred as the generic scheme.

Flat approach stores statements flatly into a single relation; the generic schema represents the approaches that design relational tables for classes and properties based on RDF schema.

The problems of the conventional approaches are:

(1) Using the flat approach, it is difficult to perform schema queries because they do not make any distinction between schema information and resource descriptions. Thus, it is necessary to repeat queries composed from the previous answers;

(2) The schema approach is able to process queries about RDF schema. However, the approach cannot handle RDF data without RDF schema information because the relational schema is designed based on RDF schema information. Additionally, it is costly to maintain schema evolution because we have to change the relational schema depending on the changes of RDF schema;

(3) The capabilities of both approaches for processing complex queries are not sufficient.

4 Index Structure

The goal of index is to support evaluation of finding data that match the provided triple patterns and constraints. At the lowest level, the index structure enables efficient retrieval of triples.

4.1 Lexicon Lookup Processing

The lexicon lookup processing operates on the string representations of RDF nodes, and enables fast retrieval of object identifiers (OIDs) for RDF nodes. OIDs are represented and stored on disk as 64 bit longs. Since we reference RDF nodes in multiple indices the mapping from string values to OIDs saves space. Also, processing and comparing OIDs is faster than comparing strings.

Lexicon lookup consists of two types of search processing: mapping node to its OID, and vice versa.

A direct approach is using a hash function to compute the hash of the node and use the resulting number as an OID. However, hash functions with small probability of collisions such as MD5 produces at least 128bit keys, which is not convenient for further usage.

In HPRD, OIDs are assigned increasingly monotonically for each unique RDF node. An additional mapping table is maintained for OIDs to hash keys lookup. So a typical lexicon lookup is divided to two steps: first compute the hash value of the given node, then lookup the OID from the mapping table.

4.2 Triple Index

Triple index is used to lookup any combination of s, p, o directly, which means the index should be a data structure based on the notion of triple pattern.

Definition 3. A triple pattern is a triple where any combination of s, p, o is either a variable or specified. For example, the triple pattern (s, ?, o) denotes all triples where in each subject equals to s.

Therefore, the total number of triple pattern is 23 = 8. The following table shows all possible triple patterns:

Table 1. All triple patterns

No	Pattern	No	Pattern
1	(s, p, o)	5	(s, ?, o)
2	(?, p, o)	6	(s, ?, ?)
3	(?, ?, o)	7	(s, p, ?)
4	(?, ?, ?)	8	(?, p, ?)

A naive implementation would need 8 indices while one for each triple pattern. This approach results of expensive of index construction time and storage space usage.

To reduce the number of indices needed, B+-tree is used as the data structure of persistent indices. As B+-tree provides support for range or prefix queries, a single B+-tree based triple index can cover queries of several triple pattern. For example, an index on s, p, and o is able to support triple patterns 1, 4, 6, 7. Like pattern 7 (s, p, ?) can be resolved to a prefix query of s and p.

Therefore, HPRD uses 3 indices, which is listed in Table 2 including which triple pattern they cover.

Table 2. Indices and covered patterns

spo	po	os
(s, p, o)	(?, p, o)	(s, ?, o)
(s, p, ?)	(?, p, ?)	(?, ?, o)
(s, ?, ?)		
(?, ?, ?)		

As the later two indices need keep the remaining units of a triple in the form of linked list as the value part, HPRD implements the dual indices containing the full triple as their keys to simplify and speed up the search operations on triple patterns.

In order to take the semantic information provided by RDF schema, the original RDF graph is divided into several sub-graphs in HPRD. Four sub-graphs are defined and indexed as following: A schema index is maintained for the RDF schema data; to accelerate the processing of RDF class and property based queries, two sub-graphs are extracted and indexed for the class and property hierarchy; the graph data remained, which represented as general resources sub-graph, is indexed for the general path expressions.

4.3 Path Index

Triple index is efficient for simple triple pattern, but for some complex queries, it's still difficult to avoid expensive join instructions. In HPRD, path index is used to evaluate long path queries efficiently.

Given query P, if each triple can be linked head-to-tail and form a single chain, which is a path in the RDF graph, we call P is a path query.

The typical evaluation of path queries on triple index is lookup a certain triple pattern in the path query first. After getting an initial result set, search forward and backward to match other triple patterns. The evaluation time may be unacceptable while the initial result set is very large. Actually we use such query in our experimental study, and the result shows certain query can make some RDF database hang for a long time.

To perform long path query efficiently, a special index structure called path index is implemented in HPRD. For a given path query pattern, all matching data are extracted and stored in path index for fast evaluation. The extracted data are normally in the form of a long sequence of OIDs, and query evaluation can be transformed to a sub-sequence matching problem.

Definition 4. (Path pattern) A node sequence with each element is either a variable or specified by certain constraint is called a path pattern.

For example, (?, <http://example.org/arts/exhibited>, ?, <http://purl.org/dc/elements/1.0/title>, ?) represents any path in the original RDF graph which contains two specified relations.

HPRD uses a suffix array based path index to store and retrieval path data. Suffix array[14] is a widely used data structure in full-text retrieval applications for indexing one dimension data. Especially for textual data, by extracting all suffix sub-sequences of the text data and sorting in nature, an efficiency binary search can be applied for arbitrary sub-sequence queries.

In HPRD, path index is built manually for real-life application. User should pick up several frequently used query patterns and build path indices for them to accelerate the query processing.

4.4 Context Index

In order to support context oriented and temporal RDF data[15], the database should be able to manage the context and temporal information.

There are two mechanisms to archive this, labeling based approach and versioning based approach. The former consists in adding additional context label to triples. The latter is based on maintaining a snapshot of each state of the RDF data. For example on versioning mechanism, an RDF graph is marked temporal, each time some triples changes, a new version of the RDF graph is created, and the past state is stored somewhere separately.

Table 3. Indices and covered patterns for context index

cspo	spo	Poc	ocs	cp	so
(c, s, p, o)	(?, s, p, o)	(c, ?, p, o)	(c, s, ?, o)	(c, ?, p, ?)	(?, s, ?, o)
(c, s, p, ?)	(?, s, p, ?)	(?, ?, p, o)	(c, ?, ?, o)		
(c, s, ?, ?)	(?, s, ?, ?)	(?, ?, p, ?)	(?, ?, ?, o)		
(c, ?, ?, ?)					
(?, ?, ?, ?)					

Both approaches are implemented in HPRD, and should be specified manually in real-life applications. In summary, we believe that for common context oriented data, labeling based approach is better as it preserves the nature of RDF. And versioning is more effective in scenarios where changes are affecting most elements of the RDF data.

A new mapping table contains context (or version) to context (or version) id is conducted to manage the lexicon information of the context and version information.

In labeling approach, any context oriented triples are expanded to the form of quad (c, s, p, o). And triples with different context ids are stored in the same index store. It's similar to the implementation of triple index to construct a quad index. Table 3 shows the multiple indices for context index which is also based on B+-tree.

For versioning approach, each version of data is staying at their original triple form and stored in separate triple indices.

5 Query Evaluation

This section describes how to perform query evaluation on the index structure in HPRD.

5.1 Basic Lookup Operator

For any common queries, there are several atomic operations to lookup basic information from indices. Table 4 lists the basic operators defined in HPRD:

Table 4. Operator list

Operator	Function	Index/Lookup table
findOID findNode	Find the related OID or vice verse	nodeOID lookup table
findType	Find the <rdf:type> property of node	Schema sub-graph
findSubXXX findSupXXX	Find the related class or property hierarchy information	Class and property hierarchy sub-graph
findCID findContext	Find the related context id or vice cverse	contextID lookup table
findTriples findQuads	Iterator triples or quads based on the specified pattern	Triple index or context index
findSeqs	Iterator sequences for the specified path pattern	Path index

5.2 Index Lookup

Most queries can be evaluated step-by-step as following: first a preprocessing stage is performed to transform any node with specified value to its OID. Later is the query routing stage, the query pattern is analyzed and an optimized index lookup strategy is determined. Then the basic index lookup operation is performed to retrieve OID based data. For complex queries, lookup processing may involve multiple indices. Join instruction is performed to conjunct interval results. Finally the query results can be presented by OID to node lookup operation.

Consider queries that involve only one triple pattern, which involves looking up on a B+-tree based triple index. By constructing keys with lower and upper bounds to determine the result set, a range query is performed over the corresponding triple index to derive the matching triples. For example, a query is aimed to ask for all triples in which predicate is <http://example.org/arts/exhibited>. After the preprocessing stage, the corresponding OID 7 for the predicate is used to construct a set of keys with lower bound (vmin, 7, vmin) and upper bound (vmax, 7, vmax). Then, a range query is performed over po triple index.

As the path index is built on suffix array, a binary search over the index can be applied to perform a path pattern query. The required computational complexity is $O(\log_2(n))$.

5.3 Index Selection

For a given query, there are multiple index lookup strategies to get the same result. For example, consider query (?, p, o)(o, ?, ?) while p and o are specified nodes. The query can be performed by three different lookup operations: 1) Lookup (o, ?, ?) over spo triple index, then lookup over po triple index based on the yielded interval result set. 2) Reverse the lookup operation order, first po index then spo triple index. 3) If there is a path index conducted for path pattern (?, p, o, ?, ?), a single lookup operation over the path index can lead to the result.

The selection between the first two strategies is actually a join order selection problem. As we know, this is a NP-Complete problem[16]. In HPRD, a simple heuristic algorithm is used to determine the lookup order.

The basic idea behind the order selection is make the size of interval result set in the join processing as small as possible. In order to estimate the size of result set for a certain triple pattern, auxiliary statistic information is collected.

Table 5. Statistic information for triple pattern

Pattern	Count
(1, ?, ?)	12
(1, 5, ?)	3
(1, 5, 7)	1

Table 5 is a sample statistic information table for a simple RDF data. The occurrence count of any pattern is logged to help estimate result size fast.

Because counting and storing the occurrence count is an expensive processing, the update of the statistic table in HPRD is always performed after a batch data load processing and maintained background while the system is idle.

As path index is normally several times faster than join instruction over several triple indices, it's prior to choose path index if applicable. For a complex query, we first find if any sub-query can be evaluated on an existed path index, then perform join for other patterns.

6 System Architecture

The chief goal of HPRD is to build an efficient storage system for RDF data. And HPRD also offers a scalable access layer for real-life applications.

The architecture of HPRD is outlined in Fig. 2.

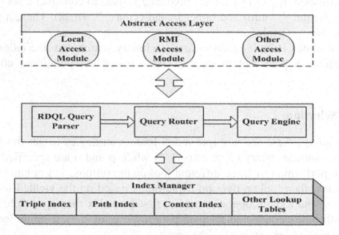

Fig. 2. The system architecture

The whole system is implemented in Java. A set of access APIs are defined in the abstract access layer and several access modules are provided to support both local and remote access application. All indices are managed by a module called index manager and provider all basic retrieval instructions to query module. RDQL queries are accepted by the query module, and transformed to the underlying indices.

7 Experimental Study

A modified version of LUBM is used to generate large scale RDF datasets for our performance experiment. The tool is referred as LUBM-R later. LUBM (Lehigh University Benchmark)[17] is original an OWL data generator, we modified it to remove incompatible data from OWL to RDF and add several RDF feature related data. We use the tool to generate a dataset contains 20 university information, which is composite of 2,449,810 triples.

Table 6. Test queries

No	Query
1	(?, <rdf:type>, <univ:GraduateStudent>)
2	(?X, <rdf:type>, <univ:Puglication>)
	(?X, <univ:publicationAuthor>, ?)
3	(?X, <univ:memberOf>, ?Z)
	(?Z, <univ:subOrganizationOf>, ?Y)
	(?X, <univ:undergraduateDegreeFrom>, ?Y)

As Sesame generally supersedes than Jena, we choose Sesame for evaluation. The two persistent storages (RDB and native repositories) provided by Sesame are evaluated.

Three queries are conducted to test different patterns and characteristics.

Table 6 lists the three queries. Each query was executed ten times against the chosen dataset to get the average query response time. The results are listed in Table 7:

Table 7. Query response time

No	Sesame RDB	Sesame Native	HPRD
1	9345.1	7122.0	265.1
2	9034.4	7006.1	1814.2
3	-	-	650.1*

For the first query, the matched data are fully schema data. In HPRD, the schema sub-graph is stored in a separated index; the lookup time is much shorter. Query 2 is a conjunction query with large output data size and reflects the difference of index structures. Since HPRD keeps complete triple indices, the lookup operation is much faster than single index mechanism.

Query 3 is a complex path query with large output size. Both Sesame implementations can't return the result in acceptable time. As each triple pattern derives to a very large result set, join on triple index is not efficient for this type of query. A path index is built to avoid expensive join instruction and the result proves our analysis.

We actually conducted more queries in the experimental study. The results we got shows that if a query involves multiple tables (RDB based approach) or multiple index lookup, HPRD is better in query performance. For certain complex path query, HPRD can produce a nice performance as the benefit of path index.

8 Conclusion

Query processing for RDF is an important issue for Semantic Web applications and we have determined a set of indices required for efficient RDF query processing. In comparison with many other RDF indexing approaches that index only for a restricted set of access patters, our approach provides indices for all triple patterns on RDF and maintain a path index for complex path queries. The experiment result shows that HPRD outperforms other RDF databases.

There are still some works can be improved in the future. First, the algorithm for index selection can be improved to gain a more optimized join order for real-life application. Second, the build of path index is manually in current implementation. Certain path pattern mining techniques[18],[19] can be used to find the most frequent sequence pattern from the data or the query log. The lack of full transaction support is another feature missed, we will try to find an efficient solution to manage and trace the update of RDF data.

References

1. World Wide Web Consortium: Semantic Web (2001), http://www.w3c.org/2001/sw/
2. World Wide Web Consortium: Resource Description Framework Model and Syntax Specification (1999), http://www.w3.org/TR/1999/REC-rdf-syntax-19990222/
3. World Wide Web Consortium: Resource Description Framework Schema Specification 1.0. (2000), http://www.w3.org/TR/2000/CR-rdf-schema-20000327/
4. World Wide Web Consortium: Survey of RDF/Triple Data Stores (2001), http://www. w3. org/ 2001/05/rdf-ds/DataStore
5. Alexaki, S., Christophides, V., Karvounarakis, G., Plexousakis, D., Tolle, K.: The RDFSuite: Managing Voluminous RDF Description Bases. Technical report, Institute of Computer Science, FORTH, Heraklion, Greece (2000), http://www.ics.forth.gr/ proj/isst/ RDF/RSSDB/rdfsuite.pdf
6. McBride, B.: Jena: Implementing The RDF Model and Syntax Specification. In: Proceedings of the Second International Workshop on the Semantic Web - SemWeb'2001, Hongkong (2001)
7. Sesame: A Generic Architecture for Storing and Querying RDF and RDF Schema, http://www.openrdf.org
8. FOAF: http://www.foaf-project.org/
9. Hayes, P.: RDF Semantics. W3C Recommendation (2004), http://www.w3.org/TR/rdf-mt/
10. Manola, F., Miller, E.: RDF Primer: W3C Recommendation (2004), http://www.w3.org/ TR/rdfprimer/
11. Guha, R.V., McCool, R., Fikes, R.: Contexts for the Semantic Web. In: Proceedings of the 3rd International Semantic Web Conference, Hiroshima (2004)
12. Visser, U. (ed.): Intelligent Information Integration for the Semantic Web. LNCS (LNAI), vol. 3159. Springer, Heidelberg (2004)
13. RDQL-A Query Language for RDF, http://www.w3.org/Submission/2004/SUBM-RDQL-20040109
14. Manber, U., Myers, E.: Suffix Arrays: A New Method for On-Line String Searches. SIAM. J. on Computing 5, 935–948 (1993)
15. Gutierrez, C., Hurtado, C., Vaisman, A.: Temporal RDF. In: Proceedings of European Conference on the Semantic Web (ECSW'05), pp. 93–107 (2005)
16. Ono, K., Lohman, G.M.: Measuring The Complexity of Join Enumeration in Query Optimization. In: Proceedings of 16th International Conference on Very Large Data Bases, Morgan Kaufmann, pp. 314–325 (1990)
17. SWAT Projects-The Lehigh University Benchmark (LUBM), http://swat.cse.lehigh.edu/ projects/lubm/
18. Agrawal, R., Srikant, R.: Mining Sequential Patterns. In: Proceedings of the 11th International Conference on Data Engineering, Taipei, pp. 3–14 (1995)
19. Garofalakis, M.N., Rastogi, R., Shim, K.: Spirit: Sequential Pattern Mining with Regular Expression Constraints. In: Proceedings of 25th International Conference on Very Large Data Bases, Edinburgh, pp. 223–234 (1999)

A Direction to Avoid Re-encryption in Cryptographic File Sharing

Lanxiang Chen, Dan Feng, Lingfang Zeng, and Yu Zhang

School of Computer, Huazhong University of Science and Technology,
Key Laboratory of Data Storage System, Ministry of Education, Wuhan, China
lxiangchen@gmail.com, dfeng@hust.edu.cn

Abstract. Almost all cryptographic file sharing systems need re-encryption when the sharing was revoked. These systems differ from each other only in the timing of re-encryption. As re-encryption is an expensive operation, it is significant to avoid re-encryption. The purpose of this paper is to advise a direction to avoid re-encryption and facilitate file sharing in cryptographic file sharing system. A Black-box model is set up to achieve this objective. In the model, FPGA or ASIC chips are used to act as the black-box as they have been extensively researched and applied in cryptography. Some applications of FPGA and ASIC in cryptography are detailed in this paper. Their feasibility to be functioned as the black-box is discussed. Also a software implementation on FPGA is attached with tested and effective performance.

Keywords: cryptographic file system, FPGA, ASIC, access control.

1 Introduction

It goes without saying the importance of information sharing. The rapid development of computer networks brings convenience for information sharing. As the computer network is open and pervasive, there are many security threats. How to securely share information? How to make you (adversary) can't 'see' the information even if you get the related data? One important way is to encrypt information before publishing. Only the authorized user can access the information. With this in mind, it gives birth to a set of cryptographic file sharing system.

Blaze's CFS [1] is the first cryptographic file system. But it was designed as a secure local file system, so it lacks features for sharing encrypted files among different users. The only way to share a protected file is to directly hand out keys for protected directories to other users. Compared to CFS, TCFS [2] makes file encryption transparent to users, provides data integrity, and enables file sharing between users of a group (UNIX group). There are similar systems such as SiRiUS [3] and SNAD [4]. All these systems need owner to provide file keys to share their files to others. Once owners want to revoke some users or the users leave their groups, owners have to re-encrypt their files as the keys have been exposed to the revoked users and distribute the new keys to the other un-revoked users. According to seven months of AFS protection server logs obtained from MIT, there were 29,203 individual revocations of

K. Li et al. (Eds.): NPC 2007, LNCS 4672, pp. 375–383, 2007.

users from 2,916 different access control lists (counting the number of times a single user was deleted from an ACL) [5]. Revocation will introduce masses of expensive cryptographic computation and key distribution to these systems.

To reduce the impact of aggressive re-encryption cost on performance, Cepheus [6] proposes the concept of lazy revocation which delays re-encryption to next file update. Plutus [5] exploits this concept. There are three types of re-encryption schemes when revocation:

1) Aggressive re-encryption – immediately re-encrypt data with a new key after a revocation.
2) Lazy re-encryption – delay re-encryption of the file to the next time it is updated or read. This saves encryption work for rarely-accessed files, but leaves data vulnerable longer.
3) Periodic re-encryption – change keys and re-encrypt data periodically to limit the window of vulnerability.

The difference of the three types of re-encryption is just the timing of re-encryption. All the above systems need re-encryption when revocation. There are systems that don't need re-encryption when revocation, such as NCryptfs [7]. NCryptfs file system is a stackable file system designed to provide kernel-level encryption services. Its file key is stored in the kernel memory, the user and the owner have to access files from the same machine. Since the encryption keys are always stored in the kernel's memory, it is never revealed to other users. Therefore, revocation of users does not require re-encryption. But the user has to (remember and) supply to the owner a hash of his password for every directory he wishes to access and the owner's machine must be online. Therefore, NCryptfs is quite inconvenient to use for distributed file sharing. As the key is pinned in memory, it is also vulnerable to attacks.

As discussed above, either system needs re-encryption or it needs not re-encryption but is inconvenient to file sharing. How to avoid re-encryption at the same time having convenient file sharing? In this paper a new direction is presented. Section 2 introduces the Black-box model. Section 3 will explain the technology which will be used to build the model. We will analysis feasibility in section 4 and conclude in section 5.

2 Model

To share files with others distributed everywhere, it is inevitable to transfer file data over network. Once data is on the wire, the best way to secure data is encryption. User can access the encrypted file only if he can decrypt the file: he must have the file key or some other special tools to complete. If the user has file key, when file owner doesn't hope him to access the file or the user leaves the group that is authorized to access the file, the file owner has to re-encrypt the file as the file key is exposed to the revoked user. How to share file with others without revealing key to them? The possible way is to access the shared file as NCryptfs, file key just only exists in owner's kernel memory. All users who want to access the file have to supply to the owner a hash of his password for every directory he wishes to access. First, it is quite inconvenient to use for distributed file sharing. Also, once owner is compromised, all users can't access files. Thirdly, as the key is pinned in memory, it is also vulnerable to attacks.

Is there a scheme to avoid re-encryption while having convenient file sharing?

We already know the requirements. It is to avoid re-encryption while sharing file with others conveniently. To avoid re-encryption, the only way is not to reveal file key to others while they can use the file key to decrypt the file. So the file key should be encrypted using their private key. User who can access file can get encrypted file and corresponding encrypted key. There are also other requirements such as the scheme is easy to configure, portable and low cost etc. A black box is supposed here. The encrypted file and encrypted key are the inputs of the black-box. And it outputs the decrypted file which we wish to get. Figure 1 is the illustration. The Black-box should be implemented utilizing existing technology and have preferable performance and is transparent to users.

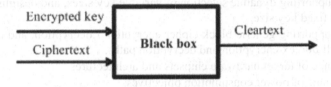

Fig. 1. Black-box model with inputs of encrypted key and ciphertext and it outputs cleartext

The Black-box may be implemented in many ways. But as Field Programmable Gate Array (FPGA) and Application-Specific Integrated Circuit (ASIC) technologies have been extensively researched and applied in Cryptography, we think they are the most suitable to act as Black-box. Along with avoiding re-encryption, hardware-based cryptographic solutions can provide significant security and performance improvements over software solutions.

3 The Application of VLSI in Cryptography

Very Large Scale Integration (VLSI) circuit is the field which involves packing more and more logic devices into smaller and smaller areas. Obeying Moore's law, the capability of an integration circuit has increased exponentially over the years, in terms of computation power, utilization of available area, yield. People can now put diverse functionality into the integration circuit, opening up new frontiers. Examples are embedded systems, where intelligent devices are put inside everyday objects, and ubiquitous computing.

The application of VLSI has been extensively researched in cryptography. These researches can be categorized into two types: the ASIC implementations and the FPGA implementations. The ASIC implementations have the advantage of fully optimized structure and thus resulted in smaller circuit area, higher speed of operation, and lower power consumption. But the design and implementation of ASIC is complex and time consuming and the cost is very high. The ASIC circuit can not be modified once it has been implemented. So it can not be adopted to often changed environment. Most of these designs were carried out on reconfigurable platforms. The reconfigurable platforms make use of the FPGA technology which combined the high speed of specialized hardware architecture and the agility of the software platform. And also the FPGA implementations cost much less than the ASIC.

Existing cryptographic algorithms utilizing ASIC and FPGA cover various fields, like AES [8], DES, SHA, HMAC and RSA [23]. For different design objectives and requirement, there are many design alternatives [9] as follows:

- Low area, low bandwidth designs, and high area, high bandwidth designs,
- Iterated architectures (frequent feedback), and fully unrolled pipelined architectures (zero feedback),
- Designs where part of the logic is executed using pre-computed SRAM operations, and designs where no pre-computed tables of SRAM are used,
- Designs with pre-computed key/round material, and designs with runtime generation of key/round material with the data to be encoded,
- Designs supporting dynamic selection of variable key sizes, and designs supporting a singular fixed key size,
- Designs supporting generic block-cipher encryption / decryption, and designs supporting full-duplex encryption and decryption paths,
- A wide range of target hardware chipsets and architectures,
- A broad range of power consumption objectives.

From the first ASIC implementation [10] of AES, there are serials of related implementation schemes [11, 12]. The best performance implementation of AES-ECB 128-bit on ASIC is Hodjat's [13]. It uses 473K gates with 606MHz clock frequency, and its highest speed is 77.6Gbps. The best performance implementation of AES-ECB 192-bit and 256-bit on ASIC is North Pole Engineering's [14]. It uses 26K gates with 323MHz clock frequency, and its highest speed is 41.3Gbps. The best performance implementation of AES-FEEDBACK on ASIC is Morioko's [15]. It uses 168K gates with 909MHz clock frequency and its highest speed is 11.6Gbps.

References [16-19] are some of the early implementations of the Rijndael algorithm before it was accepted as the Advanced Encryption Standard on FPGA. There are also serials of implementation schemes [20, 21].The best performance implementation of AES-ECB 128-bit on FPGA is Fu's [21]. It uses 17887 slices with 212.5MHz clock frequency, and its highest speed is 27.1Gbps. The best performance implementation of AES-ECB 192-bit and 256-bit on FPGA is North Pole Engineering's [14]. It uses 5840 slices with 100MHz clock frequency, and its highest speed is 12.8Gbps. The best performance implementation of AES-FEEDBACK on FPGA is Helion Tech's [22]. It uses 447 slices with 219MHz clock frequency and its highest speed is 25.48Gbps.

Implementations of RSA on ASIC refer to [24, 25] and implementations on FPGA can refer to [26, 27]. The best performance implementation of RSA is the implementation of McIvor [28].

Due to space limitations, the process of other related algorithms implementation won't be discussed.

4 Feasibility

Using FPGA and ASIC to act as the Black-box, they must satisfy following characteristics.

- User doesn't know the private key which is used to encrypt the file key. Usually, user should know their private key. As we can't expose the file key to user and the file key is encrypted with the private key. So each user's Black-box can generate public-private pair for user and submit the public part to user. As only Black-box knows user's private key, it can sign for user,
- User can't change Black-box data flow. Once the Black-box is distributed to users, they can't modify the Black-box,
- Convenience to file sharing. We will illustrate a FPGA scheme to show how to share files conveniently,
- Performance and cost. The Black-box should have preferable performance and acceptable cost.

As the ASIC circuit can not be modified once it has been implemented and FPGA is through configure file to set work pattern. The configure file is binary file and there isn't way to compile the file in reverse. How FPGA is organized is not known by anyone else except the designer. So they both satisfy characteristic two. As detailed above, the performance of ASIC and FPGA are excellent.

4.1 An FPGA Scheme

Figure 2 shows a simple architecture of the FPGA scheme. The files are stored to storage device by owners. File owner establishes ACL (Access Control List) according to local policy in which the owner defines who can access the file and uses whose public key to encrypt the file key. The encrypted file key is inserted to ACL and stored in storage device. The client who wants to access the file, he fetches file data and ACL from storage device. The ACL is signed by owner then client first verify the ACL. There is timestamp in ACL to avoid the client reuses the ACL. Client knows whether he can access the file from the ACL. He can fetch corresponding file key encrypted using his public key. Figure 3 illustrates the data flow between user and storage device.

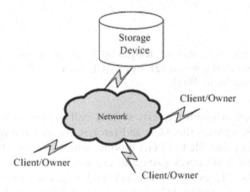

Fig. 2. Storage architecture

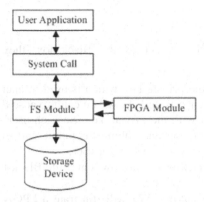

Fig. 3. Data flow between user and storage device

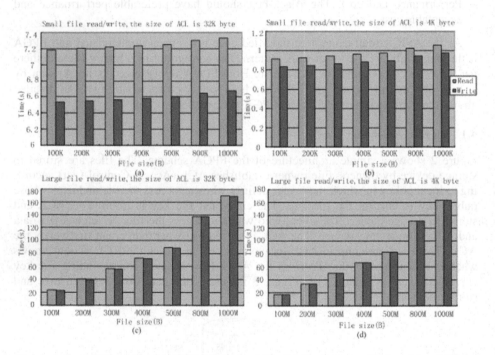

Fig. 4. (a)Small file read/write with a 32K bytes ACL. (b) Small file read/write with a 4K bytes ACL. (c) Large file read/write with a 32K bytes ACL. (d) Large file read/write with a 4K bytes ACL5 Conclusion and Future Work.

Client application program requests system call to read file from storage device. File system module verifies the ACL and fetches corresponding file key, then sends the encrypted file key and file to FPGA module which decrypts file key and encrypted file. A write request first causes system to create file key and establish ACL. Client system encrypts the file using the file key and requires FPGA module to sign the ACL, then attaches the signed ACL to encrypted file and sends to storage device. It only needs to provide file and file key for user and the rest work is transparently completed by FPGA module. As user doesn't know file key, it needs not to re-encryption when revoking the user. And this way authentication server or other center server can be eliminated, so it is well suitable to distributed file sharing.

4.2 Experimental Results

In this section, a software solution on XC4VLX200 is implemented. The read/write costs on FPGA are tested in Figure 4. The AES in 128-bit ECB mode and 1024-bit RSA are used and the size of ACL is limited to 32K bytes. The cost includes verification and decryption for a file read, correspondingly signature and encryption for a file write. The costs of small file read/write and large file read/write with small size ACL and large size ACL respectively are illustrated. Figure 4 (a) and (b) demonstrate the costs of small file read/write, and Figure 4 (c) and (d) demonstrate the costs of large file read/write. It indicates that read operation is slower than write and the size of ACL affects the costs of read/write greatly. It results from the operation of RSA which is time-consuming operation.

5 Conclusion and Future Work

In this paper, a direction is proposed which can avoid re-encryption when revocation in cryptographic file sharing system. As re-encryption is an expensive operation, it is significant to avoid re-encryption. We set up a Black-box model which is used to avoid re-encryption. In the model, FPGA or ASIC chips are used to act as the Black-box. The application of FPGA and ASIC in cryptography is detailed and their feasibility to function as the Black-box is discussed. We demonstrate the feasibility through a software implementation on FPGA with tested and effective performance.

The software implementation on FPGA just testifies that it is feasible, however it can't reflect the impact of avoiding re-encryption on performance. And the performance of software implementation on FPGA is far worse than hardware implementation. So we can't compare the performance of our scheme with other cryptographic file system described above. The future work is to evaluate the impact of re-encryption on performance quantitatively and compare the performance of our scheme using hardware implementation on FPGA with other cryptographic file system.

Acknowledgments. This work was supported by the National Basic Research Program of China (973 Program) under Grant No. 2004CB318201, and the National Science Foundation of China under Grant No. 60603048.

References

1. Blaze, M.: A Cryptographic File System for Unix. In: First ACM Conference on Communications and Computing Security, Fairfax, VA, November 1993 (1993)
2. Cattaneo, G., Catuogno, L., Persiano, P., Sorbo, A.D.: Design and implementation of a transparent cryptographic file system for UNIX. In: FREENIX Track: 2001 USENIX Annual Technical Conference (2001)

3. Goh, E.-J., Shacham, H., Modadugu, N., Boneh, D.: SiRiUS: Securing Remote Untrusted Storage. In: Proceedings of the Tenth Network and Distributed Systems Security (NDSS) Symposium, pp. 131–145 (2003)
4. Miller, E.L., Long, D.D.E., Freeman, W.E., Reed, B.C.: Strong security for network-attached storage. In: Proceedings of the 2002 Conference on File and Storage Technologies, Monterey, CA, pp. 1–13 (2002)
5. Kallahalla, M., Riedel, E., Swaminathan, R., Wang, Q., Fu, K.: Plutus: scalable secure file sharing on untrusted storage. In: USENIX File and Storage Technologies (2003)
6. Fu, K.: Group sharing and random access in cryptographic storage file system, Master's thesis, MIT (1999)
7. Wright, C.P., Martino, M.C., Zadok, E.: Ncryptfs: A secure and convenient cryptographic file system. In: USENIX Annual Technical Conference (2003)
8. National Institute of Standards and Technology (NIST), Advanced Encryption Standard (AES), Federal Information Processing Standards Publications, vol. 197 (2001)
9. Gittins, B., Landman, H., O'Neil, S., Kelson, R.: A Presentation on VEST Hardware Performance, Chip Area Measurements, Power Consumption Estimates and Benchmarking in relation to AES, SHA-256 and SHA-512 (14th November 2005)
10. Verbauwhede, I., Schaumont, P., Kuo, H.: Design and Performance Testing of a 2.29 Gb/s Rijndael Processor. IEEE J. Solid-State Circuits (JSSC 2003), 569–572 (2003)
11. Su, C.-P., Horng, C.-L., Huang, C.-T., Wu, C.-W.: A configurable AES processor for enhanced security. In: ASP-DAC, pp. 361–366 (2005)
12. Hodjat, A., Verbauwhede, I.: Area-Throughput Trade-Offs for Fully Pipelined 30 to 70 Gbits/s AES Processors. IEEE Trans. Computers 55(4), 366–372 (2006)
13. Hodjat, A., Verbauwhede, I.: Speed-area trade-off for 10 to 100 Gbits/s throughput AES processor. In: 2003 IEEE Asilomar Conference on Signals, Systems, and Computers (November 2003), http://www.ee.ucla.edu/āhodjat/AES/asilomar_paper_alireza.pdf
14. "AES Core", North Pole Engineering, http://www.northpoleengineering.com/aescore.htm
15. Morioka, S., Satoh, A.: A 10 Gbps Full-AES Crypto Design with a Twisted-BDD S-Box Architecture. In: IEEE International Conference on Computer Design (ICCD 2002) (2002)
16. Gaj, K., Chodowiec, P.: Fast Implementation and Fair Comparison of the Final Candidates for Advanced Encryption Standard Using Field Programmable Gate Arrays. In: Naccache, D. (ed.) CT-RSA 2001. LNCS, vol. 2020, pp. 84–99. Springer, Heidelberg (2001)
17. Ichikawa, T., Kasuya, T., Matsui, M.: Hardware Evaluation of the AES Finalists. In: Proc. Third AES Candidate Conf. (2000)
18. Gaj, K., Chodowiec, P.: Comparison of the Hardware Performance of the AES Candidates Using Reconfigurable Hardware. In: Proc. Third Advanced Encryption Standard Candidate Conf (AES3 2000), pp. 40–54 (2000)
19. Fischer, V.: Realization of the Round 2 Candidates Using Altera FPGA. In: Comments Third Advanced Encryption Standard Candidates Conf. (AES3 2000) (2000)
20. Rouvroy, G., Standaert, F.-X., Quisquater, J.-J., Legat, J.-D.: Compact and Efficient Encryption/Decryption Module for FPGA Implementation of AES Rijndael Very Well Suited for Small Embedded Applications. In: ITCC 2004, special session on embedded cryptographic hardware, vol. II, pp. 583–587. IEEE Computer Society, Los Alamitos (2004)
21. Fu, Y., Hao, L., Zhang, X., Yang, R.: ICESS 2005. LNCS, vol. 3820. Springer, Heidelberg (2005)
22. AES Core for FGPA and ASIC, Helion Technology, http://www. heliontech.com/core2.htm
23. Rivest, R.L., Shamir, A., Adleman, L.M.: A Method for Obtaining Digital Signatures and Public-key Cryptosystems. Communications of the ACM 21(2), 120–126 (1978)

24. M.-S., F.J., Kang.: A Novel Systolic VLSI Architecture for Fast RSA Modular Multiplication. In: Proceedings of the 2002 IEEE Asia-Pacific Conference on ASIC 2002, pp. 81-84 (2002)
25. Yeşil, S., İsmailoğlu, N., Tekmen, Ç., Aşkar, M.: Two Fast RSA Implementations Using High-Radix Montgomery Algorithm. In: 2004 IEEE International Symposium on Circuits and Systems, pp. 557–560 (2004)
26. Blum, T., Paar, C.: Montgomery Modular Exponentiation on Reconfigurable Hardware. In: Proceedings 14th IEEE Symposium on Computer Arithmetic, pp. 70–77 (1999)
27. Cilardo, A., Mazzeo, A., Romano, L., Saggese, G.P.: Carry-Save Montgomery Modular Exponentiation on Reconfigurable Hardware. In: Procs of the Design, Automation, and Test in Europe Conference (DATE 2004) (2004)
28. McIvor, C., McLoone, M., McCanny, J.V.: High-Radix Systolic Modular Multiplication on Reconfigurable Hardware. In: IEEE International Conference on Field Programmable Technology, pp. 13–19 (2005)

Exploit Temporal Locality of Shared Data in SRC Enabled CMP

Haixia Wang, Dongsheng Wang, Peng Li, Jinglei Wang, and XianPing Fu

Research Institute of Information Technology,
National Laboratory for Information Science and Technology,
Tsinghua University, Beijing, 100084, P.R. China
{hx-wang,wds}@tsinghua.edu.cn,
{p-li02,wjinglei00}@mails.tsinghua.edu.cn, fxp@dl.cn

Abstract. By run-time characteristic analysis of parallel workloads, we found that a majority of shared data accesses of parallel workload has temporal locality. Based on this characteristic, we present a sharing relation cache (SRC for short) based CMP architecture, saving recently used sharing relations to provide destination set information for following cache-to-cache miss requests. Token-SRC protocol integrates SRC into token protocol,reducing network traffic of token protocol.Simulations using SPLASH-2 benchmarks show that, a 16-core CMP system with token-SRC achieved average 15% network traffic reduction of that with token protocol.

1 Introduction

Multiple-processor systems, i.e. symmetric multiple processor systems and cluster systems are widely adopted in modern commercial and scientific computing infrastructures. Chip multiprocessor (CMP) [1,2,3], which integrates multiple processor cores into a single chip, is a promising technique that can efficiently exploit the inherent thread-level parallelism inside modern workloads. CMP systems share many critical design issues with traditional share-memory multiprocessor systems, especially the cache-coherence protocols.

For shared-memory multiprocessor systems, shared-bus offered a convenient solution to maintain cache-coherence with snooping mechanisms [4,5]. Although broadcast-based protocol is simple and easy to implement, shared-bus architecture serializes all messages in the system, limiting the system scalability.

Directory-based protocols [6,7] were proposed to solve the coherence problem in multi-processor system with unordered interconnection. They introduce a global directory keeping records of the locations and status of the cached copies. With determined destination set, network traffic of directory-based protocol will be much less than snooping protocol,which makes it applicable for large-scale shared-memory multiprocessor systems. Unfortunately, directory-based protocols suffer from long latency for cache-to-cache transfer misses.

K. Li et al. (Eds.): NPC 2007, LNCS 4672, pp. 384–393, 2007.

To avoid indirections for cache-to-cache misses of directory protocol and interconnect ordering of snooping protocol, token protocol [8,9] directly send broadcast on un-ordered interconnect, avoiding indirection for cache-to-cache miss in
directory-based protocol. Unfortunately, token protocol broadcasts request to
maximal destination set, which will incur heavy network traffic.

We proposed an efficient technique to reduce network traffic of broadcast-
based protocol, which was called sharing relation cache (SRC) [10]. The idea
came from the following characteristic that we found in the run-time characteristic analysis of parallel workloads: a majority of shared data accesses has
temporal locality. SRC integrates a sharing relation cache in each core to cache
directory information recently used sharing relations (that is of shared data),
providing destination set information for following cache-to-cache miss requests.
Different from directory, SRC keep only directory information of recently accessed shared data, not all directory information. Before issuing data requests,
SRC is lookup at first. If SRC hits, requests are sent to destination set pointed
by the SRC entry. Otherwise, requests are broadcast to all processor nodes in
the system.

In this paper, we integrated SRC technique in token protocol to reduce network traffic. We called this protocol token-SRC protocol. Preliminary evaluation
showed that running SPLASH-2 parallel benchmarks on 16-core CMP, token-
SRC protocol achieved an average 15% network traffic reduction of classical
token-protocol.

A related work on reducing network traffic of cache coherence protocol is
destination-set prediction technique [11]. It was invented to predict destination set for directory protocol. Destination-set prediction technique provides
three kinds of destination set choices for directory protocol: Owner node, in
which case read request is sent to owner node directly without looking up directory; Maximal set, in which case request is broadcast to all processor nodes
without looking up directory; and minimal set, in which case directory are
looked up and requests are sent to minimal destination set defined by directory
entry.

Destination set prediction in paper [11] yields minimal set by directory lookup.
In token protocol, there is no directory so that destination set prediction can
not find destination set for write requests. But in contrary, SRC technique may
generate a destination set that is close to minimal set, which reduces network
traffic of token protocol by avoiding broadcast.

The remainder of the paper is organized as followings. Section 2 defines the
quantitative analysis method on temporal locality of shared data, describes multiprocessor simulator and parallel workloads used in this study, and analyzes
experiment results on temporal locality characteristic of shared data. Section 3
addresses implementation of SRC in token protocol based system. Section 4 exhibits and analyzes the preliminary experiment results in 16-core CMP systems
with directory, token and token-SRC protocols. Finally, section 5 summarizes
the paper and discusses direction for future work.

2   Characteristic Analysis on Temporal Locality of Shared Data

2.1   Quantitative Analysis Method

When several processors accessed a shared data, a sharing relation was built on the shared data among those processors. The sharing relation is represented as a map ¡address, sharers¿. The address refers to the shared data, and the sharer field points out which processors own valid copies of the shared data, that is just like a directory entry.

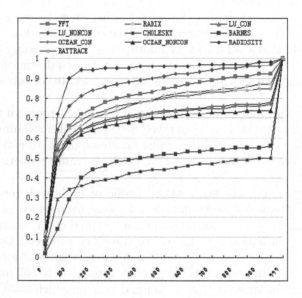

Fig. 1. Statistic of Distance Distribution

The time interval between twice continuous accesses of a shared data is defined as a sharing relation lifespan. During each sharing relation lifespan, the number of accesses on other shared data is called the distance of the sharing relation lifespan. If the distance of a sharing relation lifespan is small, the sharing relation is reused quickly. By counting all distances of any sharing relation lifespan, we could analyze the temporal locality characteristic of shared data.

2.2   Experiment Environment and Results

We simulate a 16-core CMP system with an open source multiprocessor simulator GEMS [12], which is developed by Wisconsin Multifacet project and built on the Virtutech Simics [13] full-system functional execution-driven simulator. GEMS simulator adds timing information of memory hierarchy and interconnection on simics. GEMS extends Simics with detailed processor, memory hierarchy and interconnection network models to compute execution times, enabling detailed simulation of multiprocessor systems, including CMPs. We choose a simple shared-bus MOSI snooping protocol to build the 16-core CMP system. To ensure that hardware architecture details do not affect program behavior analysis, perfect cache with infinite capacity is used in the simulated multiprocessor.

We use SPLASH-2 [14] parallel benchmark package as workload. SPLASH-2 provides a suite of shared-memory benchmarks for parallel systems and includes a set of kernel and application components. We select a representative subset of the SPLASH-2 as workloads,four kernel workloads and four application workloads.

For each SPLASH-2 workload and each given distance size, Fig. 1 illustrates the distribution of accesses whose distances are less than the given size. Between the 10 SPLASH-2 workloads, cholesky and barnes shows slightly lower temporal locality, only about 50% distances are less than 1000. Except for cholesky and barnes, the other 8 workloads have comparatively higher temporal locality of sharing relations, especially radiosity, about 90% distances are less than 100. The high temporal locality of the 8 workloads provides high hit rate of SRC with limited storage space.

3 Token-SRC Protocol

3.1 CMP Architecture

The sketch of CMP architecture with Token-SRC protocol is shown in Fig. 2. Each processor core owns a private SRC, which records directory information of recently accessed shared data.

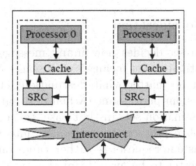

Fig. 2. Sketch of CMP architecture with Token-SRC protocol

On reading or writing, processor looks up its private caches firstly. If local cache misses, processor will send request to other processors or memory. Before issuing requests, token-SRC protocol looks up SRC for request destination set. If SRC hits, the processor will send request to destination set denoted by the SRC entry. Otherwise, the request will be broadcast to all processors.

An important optimization is to remove SRC lookup operation from critical path of memory access. SRC lookup process can be designed in parallel with normal data cache lookup process. When normal data cache completes lookup process, SRC lookup result should also be available. SRC is organized just like a normal data cache. Each entry of SRC has 3 fields: valid, tag and sharer. Sharer filed of SRC entry records identities of the processors which have valid copies of the shared data. The address lookup process of SRC is also as same as that of data cache.

3.2   Correctness Substrate

In broadcast-based protocol (such as snooping protocol, token protocol, and so on), destination sets of cache miss requests include all processor nodes, that is the maximal destination set. In directory-based protocol, destination sets of cache miss requests are minimal destination set, including one owner processor for reading request and all processors with valid cached copies for writing request.

Token protocol extended broadcast protocols from ordered network to unordered network while keeping safety property by enforcing the coherence invariant of a single writer and multiple readers. When data access conflicts, request may not be eventually satisfied(potential starvation), in which case token protocol initiates a persistent request, activates at most one persistent request and ensures all race requests be finally satisfied.

Based on the starvation solving mechanism, any definition of SRC entry is all right for token-SRC protocol. For example, if SRC presents an empty destination set to a write request, request processor will not get enough tokens, and then token protocol will reissue those requests, taking it as starvation case after timeout and solving it by issuing persistent requests.

3.3   Performance Consideration

The size of destination set decides how many messages are sent for a cache miss request. Small destination set means less messages and less network traffic. Although it is all right no matter what destination set are stored in SRC, it does degrade overall system performance when destination set of SRC are not superset of minimal destination set. In that case, token count requirement will not be satisfied and token protocol turns request into persistent request. The satisfy process of persistent requests is rather time-consuming. In token-SRC protocol design, it is better to be away from this case. Thus, for performance consideration, SRC entry should better be the superset of minimal destination set and be close to minimal destination set.

3.4   Token-SRC Protocol

To design cache controller of CMP system using Token-SRC protocol, we have to answer the following five questions: (1) Which states are used to describe a cache block? (2) What events incur cache state transition? (3) What does SRC record for each cache state? (4) How does cache state transit? (5) How is each event handled?

Firstly, we adopt MOESI protocol in token-SRC protocol design, which uses 6 states to describe a cache block. M (Modified) state means the cache block was modified. O (Owned) state means local processor owns the data block though other processor may have shared data copies. S (Shared) state means local processor has valid data copies. E (Exclusive) state means that only local processor has an exclusive data copies and not modified. I (Invalid) state means cache block in local processor is invalidated by other processors. NP (Not Present) state means that the data block does not remain in the cache, it is not a real state saved in cache block.

Secondly, we defined 4 kinds of events coming from local processor: cache read miss, cache write miss, data cache replacement, and SRC replacement. In dealing with local events, processor may generate 3 kinds of remote events: remote read request, remote write request, and remote data cache replacement. In the following cache state transition analysis, we only need to handle local events because the handling process includes remote events.

Thirdly, we give a definition on contents of SRC in Table 1. Data blocks in NP state did not exist in local cache, and SRC need not to save entries for that block. For data blocks in M or E state, reading or writing them always hit and SRC will not be searched for destination set. Reading data blocks in O or S state also hits, but writing those data blocks needs to invalidate other valid copies in the CMP system, at that time SRC can be used to denote destination set. Last, for data block in I state, read miss needs to request owner processor and write miss needs to invalidate all processors with valid cached copies. Based on definition in Table 1, SRC can helps to provide owner processor information for reading case, but no use to writing cases. Thus, writing data block in I state has to broadcast writing requests.

Fourthly, driven by each event, cache states may change. The state transition graph of token-SRC protocol is a traditional MOESI protocol.

Finally, For each cache state and each event from local processor, the event handling process consists of three continuous phases: requests sending process in local processor, requests responding process in remote processor and responses receiving process in local processor.

Compared with traditional token protocol, token-SRC protocol introduces new actions on SRC. (1) In request sending process of local processor, if SRC hits, request is sent to destination set denoted by SRC. Otherwise, request is broadcast. (2) In request responding process of remote processor, if remote processor is the owner of data block requesting, it searches its own SRC to get sharers, sending it back together with data and tokens. Otherwise, remote processor updates its SRC according to the request type and its own cache block state. (3) In response receiving process of local processor, local processor updates its SRC according to response message type and its own cache block state. Fig. 3 shows a general event handling process.

Table 1. Contents of SRC for Each Cache State

Cache State	Contents of SRC
M	None
O	All processors with valid cached copies
E	None
S	All processors with valid cached copies
I	Owner processor
NP	None

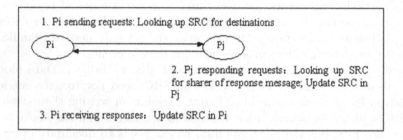

Fig. 3. General Event Handling Process of Token-SRC Protocol

4   Performance Evaluation of Token-SRC Protocol

4.1   Simulation Environment

We evaluate a 16-core SPARC CMP system using GEMS simulator. The CMP runs unmodified Solaris 8. Each processor core is a simple in-order processor with private 64KB L1 caches and 16MB L2 cache. Memory is 4GB and divided into 16 banks. We adopt 2D torus topology to interconnect 16 processor nodes, with on-chip link latency (processor-to-processor) 1 ruby cycle and out-of-chip link latency (processor-to-directory) 40 ruby cycles.

Token protocol and directory protocol has been implemented in GEMS, but we have to extend token protocol to integrate SRC. To compare directory, token and token-SRC protocol, their simulation machine use the same processor model, same cache organization and size, same unordered 2D torus interconnection network and latency parameters, and same peripherals outside core. Their cache coherence protocols have different state transition graph but with the same MOESI cache state description.

We use SPLASH-2 benchmarks as workloads. For fast simulation, we collect statistic result of parallel execution part instead of complete execution.

4.2   Network Traffic

We compare directory protocol, token protocol and token-SRC protocol in request traffic and network traffic. Network traffic is measured by the amount of information delivered in network per time unit. We calculate the amount of information delivered in network by total network message bytes, and time unit by cache miss. The size of request message is 8B, data response is 72B (64B data with an 8B header), and data response with sharer is 76B(64B data, 4B sharer with an 8B header) in Token-SRC protocol.

Fig. 4 shows evaluation result on request message number per cache miss for three protocols. Request message includes initial request, forwarded request (directory protocol), retried request and persistent request (token and token-SRC protocol). In the statistic process, if a request is send to k destination nodes, the message number of the request is set to k no matter how many requests exactly run through interconnection network.

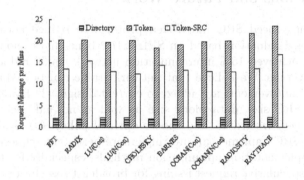

Fig. 4. Request Message per Miss(16p CMP)

As illustrated in Fig. 4, directory protocol issued 2.16 request messages per cache miss on average for 10 benchmarks. Token protocol has much higher bandwidth usage than directory protocol, issuing 20.27 request messages per cache miss on average(20.27 is greater than processor number 16, that is because the request may be reissued multiple times and turned into persistent request at last after time-out). Token-SRC protocol issues 13.85 request messages per cache miss on average. In contrast to token protocol, Token-SRC reduces request traffic by 32% in average.

Fig. 5 shows normalized network traffic per cache miss for three tokens. The network traffic of directory protocol is normalized to 1. From the figure, token protocol took about 66% more interconnection bandwidth on average than directory protocol, and token-SRC protocol used about 42% more interconnection bandwidth. Compared with token protocol, token-SRC achieved 15% network traffic reduction on average. Since 72B response message is much larger than 8B request message, it is easy to understand why token-SRC protocol issued 32% less requests than token protocol while incurred only 15% reduction in network traffic.

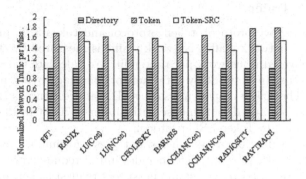

Fig. 5. Network Traffic per Miss (16p CMP)

5   Conclusions and Future Work

This paper introduced SRC into token protocol to reduce network traffic of token protocol. Evaluation based on SPLASH-2 benchmark shows that token-SRC protocol achieved 15% interconnection network traffic reduction of token protocol on average. We believe that network traffic can be reduced further if the following improvements are added to current design. (1) Evaluate how SRC organization, SRC size, data block size as well as normal cache replacement policy affects network traffic, and choose optimal policy. (2) Evaluate whether current token-SRC implementation brings more persistent requests and explore other SRC implementation optimization methods, especially for the write miss cases (3) Try speculative request issuing for broadcast case(for example, reading or writing an un-cached data block). (4) Optimize workload to improve temporal locality of shared data, achieving high SRC hit rate under limited cache space.

References

1. Hammond, L., Nayfeh, B., Olukotun, K.: A single-chip multiprocessor. IEEE Computer 30, 79–85 (1997)
2. Olukotun, K., Nayfeh, B., Hammond, L., Wilson, K., Chung, K.: The case for a single-chip multiprocessor. In: Int'l conf. Architectural Suppport for Programming Language and Operating System, pp. 2–11 (1996)
3. Hammond, L., Hubbert, B., Siu, M., Prabhu, M., Chen, M., Olukotun, K.: The Stanford Hydra. IEEE Micro, 71–84 (1996)
4. Goodman, J.: Using Cache Memory to Reduce Processor-Memory Traffic. In: Int'l Symp. on Computer Architecture, pp. 124–131 (1983)
5. Katz, R., Eggers, S., Wood, D., Perkins, C., Sheldon, R.: Implementing a Cache Consistency Protocol. In: 12th Int'l Symp. on Comp. Arch., pp. 276–283 (1985)
6. Tang, C.: Cache Design in the Tightly Coupled Multiprocessor System. In: AFIPS National Computer Conference, pp. 749–753 (1976)
7. Censier, M., Feautier, P.: A New Solution to Coherence Problems in Multicache Systems. IEEE Trans. on Computers 12, 1112–1118 (1978)

8. Martin, M., Hill, M., Wood, D.: Token Coherence: Decoupling Performance and Correctness. In: Int'l Symp. on Computer Architecture, pp. 182–193 (2003)
9. Marty, M., Bingham, J., Hill, M., Hu, A., Martin, M., Wood, D.: Improving Multiple-CMP Systems Using Token Coherence. In: Int'l Symp. on High-Perf.Computer Architecture, pp. 328–339 (2005)
10. Wang, H., Wang, D., Li, P.: SRC-based Cache Coherence Protocol in Chip Multi-processor. In: Japan-China Joint Workshop on Frontier of Computer Science and Technology, pp. 60–67 (2006)
11. Martin, M., Harper, P., Sorin, D., Hill, M., Wood, D.: Using Destination-Set Prediction to Improve the Latency/Bandwidth Tradeoff in Shared-Memory Multiprocessors. In: Int'l Symp. onComputer Architecture, pp. 206–217 (2003)
12. Martin, M., Sorin, D., Beckmann, B., Marty, M., Xu, M., Alameldeen, A., Moore, K., Hill, M., Wood, D.: Multifacet's General Execution-driven Multiprocessor Simulator (GEMS) Toolset. Computer Architecture News (2005)
13. Magnusson, P., Christensson, M., Eskilsson, J., Forsgren, D., Hallberg, G., Hogberg, J., Larsson, F., Moestedt, A., Werner, B.: Simics: A full system simulation platform. IEEE Computer 35, 50–58 (2002)
14. Woo, S., Ohara, M., Torrie, E., Singh, J., Gupta, A.: The SPLASH-2 Programs: Characterization and Methodological Considerations. In: Int'l Symp. on Computer Architecture, pp. 24–36 (1995)

Architectural Implications of Cache Coherence Protocols with Network Applications on Chip MultiProcessors*

Kyueun Yi and Jean-Luc Gaudiot

Department of Electrical Engineering and Computer Science
University of California, Irvine, CA 92697-2625, USA
{kyueuny,gaudiot}@uci.edu

Abstract. Network processors are specialized integrated circuits used to process packets in such network equipment as core routers, edge routers, and access routers. As predicted by Gilder's law, Internet traffic has doubled each year since 1997 and this trend is showing no signs of abating. Since all emerging network applications which require deep packet classification and security-related processing should be run at line rates and since network speed and network applications complexity continue increasing, future network processors should simultaneously meet two requirements: high performance and high programmability. Single processor performance will not be sufficient to support the requirements which will be imposed on future network processors. In this paper, we consider the CMP model as the baseline architecture of future network processors. We investigate the architectural implications of cache coherence protocols with network workloads on CMPs. Our results show that the token protocol which uses the tokens to control read/write permission of shared data blocks shows better performance than the directory protocol by a factor of 13.4%.

1 Introduction

Network processors are specialized integrated circuits used to process packets in such network equipment as core routers, edge routers, and access routers. Indeed, as predicted by Gilder's law, Internet traffic has continued doubling every year since 1997 [1]. Further, emerging network applications such as QoS, URL matching, virus detection, intrusion detection, and load balancing require deep packet classification processing [2] and security-related processing. The emerging deep packet classification processing and security-related processing are more computation-intensive than all other network applications [3]. Indeed, all network applications which require deep packet classification processing and security-related processing should be run at line rates. Since network

* This work is partly supported by the National Science Foundation under Grant No. CCF-0541403. Any opinions, findings, and conclusions or recommendations expressed in this material are those of the authors and do not necessarily reflect the views of the National Science Foundation.

K. Li et al. (Eds.): NPC 2007, LNCS 4672, pp. 394–403, 2007.

speeds and network applications complexity continue increasing, future network processors should simultaneously meet the two conflicting requirements of high performance and high programmability.

Since single processors will not be powerful enough to simultaneously reach high performance and high programmability [4], multiprocessors or multithreaded architectures have recently been proposed as the baseline architectures of network processors. Since modern processors have focused on exploiting Instruction-Level Parallelism (ILP), they have been quite successful at it and there is little room to exploit Instruction-Level Parallelism any longer. To overcome the limits of Instruction-Level Parallelism in wide-issue superscalar machines, two alternative microarchitectures have been proposed: Simultaneous MultiThreading (SMT) [5] and Chip MultiProcessor (CMP) [6] in order to exploit multiple threads (Thread-Level Parallelism - TLP).

Since the individual processor cores of CMPs are simple, CMPs can have low design complexity and achieve very high clock rates. Further, CMPs can efficiently reduce overall power consumption while maintaining the overall performance of them by increasing the number of processor cores and reducing clock rate of single-thread processor [7]. Since CMP provides performance scalability as well as programmability, CMP is an attractive candidate for future network processors. Indeed, single chip multiprocessors perform 50-100% better than wide-issue superscalar [6] with thread-level parallelism and multiprogramming workload. In this paper, we use the CMP architecture model as the baseline for future network processors.

When multiple processor cores are integrated on a single chip with shared cache, two different processor cores can have different values for the same location of the shared cache. This problem is called as the cache coherence problem. The architectural implications of cache coherence protocols such as the snooping protocol and the directory protocol have been investigated with commercial workloads, multiprogramming and OS workloads, and scientific/technical workloads [8,9]. Martin *et al.* have presented the Token Protocol which uses the tokens to control read/write permission of shared cache blocks. They have compared the performance of the token protocol with other cache coherence protocols such as the snooping protocol and the directory protocol with commercial workloads [10].

In this paper, we investigate the architectural implications of cache coherence protocols on CMP processors with network workloads. The performance of each protocol (the directory protocol and the token protocol) are measured against each other, as the number of processor cores is made to vary. The token protocol shows better performance than the directory protocol by 13.4%. As the number of processor cores is increased, the number of instructions used to complete the application is also increased due to multithreading mechanism and cache coherence protocol. The results will help to design single chip multiprocessors for network workloads.

The rest of this paper is organized as follows. Section 2 describes past research on architectural implications of network workloads on single thread as well as cache coherence protocols on CMP. Cache coherence protocols which are used in this paper are explained in section 3. Our simulation environment and methodology are presented in section 4. We present the architectural implications of network workloads on CMP in section 5. Finally, we summarize our observations in section 6.

2   Related Work

As an investigation of architectural implications with network workloads on CMP, Crowley *et al.* have compared the performance of different architectures such as a SuperScalar (SS) processor, a fine-grained multithreaded processor (FGMT), a single chip multiprocessor (CMP), and a simultaneous multithreaded (SMT) processor [11]. With equivalent processor resources and dynamically exploiting both instruction-level parallelism and thread-level parallelism, SMT shows better performance than CMP and better than FGMT and SS by a factor of two.

Nahum *et al.* have presented an experimental performance of packet-level parallelism on shared-memory multiprocessor [12]. They have found that limited packet-level parallelism exists within a single connection under TCP. However, an available packet-level parallelism is increased by using multiple connections.

The architectural implications of cache coherence protocols are investigated when the following parameters are changed: numbers of processors, cache size, and block size in the cache [8]. The snooping protocol and the directory protocol are evaluated with online transaction processing workload (OLTP) and scientific/technical workloads.

Martin *et al.* have measured and compared the performance of cache coherence protocols such as the snooping protocol, the directory protocol, and the token protocol with commercial workloads [10]. They have found that the token protocol is 25-65% faster than the snooping protocol and 6-18% faster than the directory protocol.

3   Cache Coherence Protocols

It is well known that if multiple processors share a cache, two different processors can have different values for the same location of the shared cache. This problem is referred to as the cache coherence problem. A cache is said to be coherent if any read of memory location returns the most recently written value of that data element. Cache coherence for multiple processors is maintained with cache coherence protocols which make all processors have a consistent view of the shared cache and manage the read/write of data in the shared cache.

A major role of cache coherence protocols is that of tracking the state of any shared data block. The MOESI coherence state model [13] is used to represent the state of shared cache data blocks in this paper. Each cache block has 5 states in MOESI coherence state model as follows:

- Modified state: No other processor has a copy of the data block. The copy of the data in main memory is incorrect.
- Owned state: Only one processor can be in the owned state. All other processors can have a copy of the most recent in the shared state. The copy of the data in main memory can be incorrect.
- Exclusive state: No other processor has a copy of the data. The copy of the data in main memory is also the most recent.
- Shared state: Other processors can also have copies of the data in the shared state. The copy of data in main memory is the most recent.

– Invalid state: Either main memory or another processor cache can have valid copies of the data.

The previously mentioned MOESI cache coherence state model can use different cache coherence protocols which track the sharing status of a copy of block of shared cache. Three kinds of cache coherence protocols are briefly explained below.

Snooping protocols: The cache of each processor has a copy of block of shared cache and a copy of the sharing status. Snooping protocols do not have a centralized location to maintain the states of cache blocks. All cache controllers in each processor continuously snoop on the bus to discover whether they have a copy of any block currently requested on the bus. The use of broadcast limits the scalability of bus-based snooping protocols.

Directory protocols: The sharing status of a block is maintained in the directory of the home node. The directory keeps information as to which caches have copies of the block, whether it is dirty, etc. Each access to a cache block of shared cache requires to first access the directory to find out the state of the cache block. Since directory protocols do not use the bus unlike snooping protocols, directory protocols do not need for all processors to watch the interconnection network.

The Token Protocol using broadcast: The token is the base unit which is used to control the read/write permissions to shared cache blocks in the token protocol. The token protocol [10] exchanges and counts tokens to control read/write permissions to the shared cache blocks. Each logical block of a shared cache has a fixed number of tokens. When each processor has at least one of the block's token, it can read the cache block. When each processor has all of the block's tokens, it can write the cache block.

4   Simulation Environment and Methodology

We present the simulator and benchmark programs which are used to investigate the architecture implications of cache coherence protocols with network workloads on CMP. There are 4 kinds of the options for CMP implementation [14], a conventional microprocessor, a simple chip multiprocessor, a shared-cache chip multiprocessor, and a multithreaded, shared-cache chip multiprocessor. In this paper, we used a shared-cache chip multiprocessor which has a private L1 data cache, a private L1 instruction cache, and a shared L2 unified cache.

4.1   Simulator

CMP is simulated with the Simics full-system functional execution-driven simulator [15] and Ruby of GEMS [16] as a cache simulator. The processor modeled is the Ultra-SPARC III. The simulated system runs an unmodified Solaris operating system version 9 and 1, 2, 4, and 8 processor-cores CMPs are simulated. Two cache coherence protocols, MOESI-directory and MOESI-token, are used to evaluate network workloads. The L2 cache is organized as a non-uniform cache architecture. The configuration of L1 I-cache and L1 D-cache is 16KB, 4-way and 3 cycles. The configuration of L2 shared cache is 16MB, 4-way and 6 cycles.

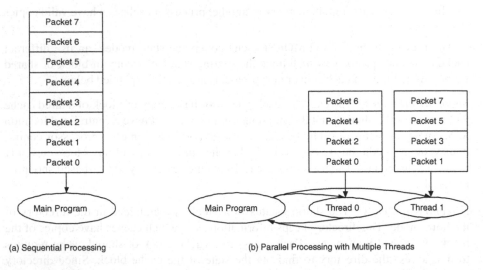

(a) Sequential Processing   (b) Parallel Processing with Multiple Threads

Fig. 1. Conversion single thread to multiple threads with packet-level parallelism

4.2 NetBench

NetBench is commonly used for the evaluation of network processors and composed of nine benchmark programs [17]. NetBench is a set of benchmarks used for single thread, generally not for multithreaded parallel applications with a shared memory. Since CMP architectures allow the exploitation of thread-level parallelism, in order to run NetBench on multiprocessors with shared memory, we need to modify NetBench to support multiple threads like SPLASH-2 [18] in which child processes share the same virtual address space as their parent process. To decompose a single thread into multiple threads, we exploited packet-level parallelism as shown in Figure 1. Figure 2 shows the implementation of Figure 1.

Among nine benchmark programs of NetBench, TL (Table Lookup), ROUTE, DRR (Deficit Round Robin), and NAT (Network Address Translation) works with the routing table. When these four benchmark programs are modified to have multiple threads, they require synchronization mechanisms to share the routing table among multiple threads. Since the synchronization mechanisms cause additional spinlocks, we do not use these four programs to investigate the architectural implications of cache coherence protocol with network workloads on CMP. The DH benchmark, Diffie-Hellman public-key encryption-decryption mechanism, does not require a packet trace. Thus, we used CRC (Cyclic Redundancy Check), MD5 (Message Digest), and URL (Uniform Resource Locator) to investigate the architectural implications of cache coherence protocols with network workloads on CMP. These three benchmarks are compiled with *gcc -O3* in SunOS 5.8. To warm up the cache, we ran these programs with 160 packets. Then we processed 5,000 packets. The simulation results are gathered between two MAGIC_BREAKPOINT instructions [19] as shown in Figure 2.

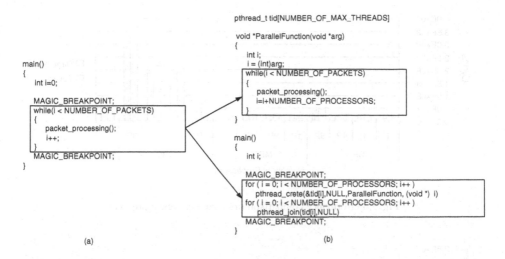

Fig. 2. Example codes to convert single thread to multiple threads with packet-level parallelism

The original NetBench uses the traces from Columbia University available in the public domain [20]. However, destination and source IP addresses of this trace are anonymized for privacy protection. Hence, for our purposes, we used other real packet traces [21].

5   Evaluation Results

We present the evaluation results of two cache coherency protocols, the directory protocol and the token protocol, with network workloads and investigate the architectural implications of these two cache coherence protocols on CMP.

Equation (1) shows the CPU time needed to execute a program. If two systems have the same clock cycle and run the same instructions per program, then the first term and the third term of Equation (1) are fixed and the CPU time depends on only the Clock cycles Per Instruction (CPI). Thus, to compare the performance of single processors which run single threaded and user-level programs, CPI (or IPC which is the inverse of CPI) is commonly used. However, CPI is inaccurate for multithreaded workloads running on multiprocessors. The inaccuracy is caused by the incorrect assumption that instructions per program is constant during execution of the programs. Multithreaded workloads running on multiprocessors can have different instruction paths which are caused by spinlocks and other synchronization mechanisms. The different instruction paths change the number of instructions to perform the same amount of work [22]. For this reason, we used as a measure the total number of cycles required to complete the programs for the performance comparison.

$$\text{CPU time} = \frac{\text{Seconds}}{\text{Program}} = \frac{\text{Instructions}}{\text{Program}} \times \frac{\text{Clock cycles}}{\text{Instruction}} \times \frac{\text{Seconds}}{\text{Clock cycle}} \qquad (1)$$

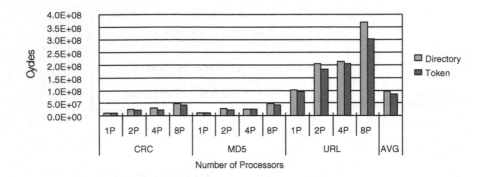

Fig. 3. Performance comparison of cache coherence protocols

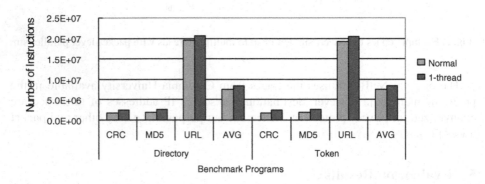

Fig. 4. Instruction overhead due to multithreading mechanism

5.1   Performance Comparison of Cache Coherence Protocols

As mentioned in related work, the token protocol showed better performance than the snooping protocol and the directory protocol in commercial workloads. Figure 3 shows the performance comparison between the directory protocol and the token protocol with 3 benchmark programs from NetBench. As shown in Figure 3, the token protocol shows better performance than the directory protocol by 13.4%.

As the number of processor cores is increased, the number of cycles required to complete the programs is also increased. This effect is due to the fact that the number of instructions needed to deal with multiple threads in an operating system is increased as the number of threads is increased. In the following subsection, we investigate the instruction overhead due to the multithreading mechanism.

5.2   Instruction Overhead Due to the Multithreading Mechanism

Since multithreading is used to exploit packet-level parallelism, the instruction overhead due to the multithreading mechanism is measured. To measure the instruction overhead due to multithreading mechanism, the numbers of instructions which are used to

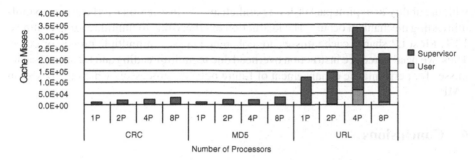

(a) Number of L2 cache misses in the directory protocol

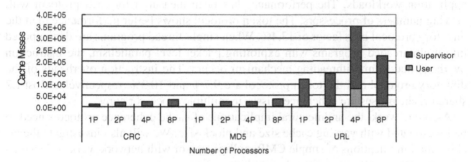

(b) Number of L2 cache misses in the token protocol

Fig. 5. Number of L2 cache misses

complete benchmark programs are compared two cases: normal program without multi-threading mechanism and multithreaded program with 1-thread. As shown in Figure 4, when multithreading mechanism is used, the numbers of instructions of the directory protocol and the token protocol are increased by 9.7% and 10.3%, respectively.

5.3 L2 Cache Misses

The performance of a shared cache is influenced by the cache misses which occur in the single processor and the coherence misses which arise from inter-processor communication in multiprocessors.

Figure 5 shows the number of cache misses in the L2 shared cache. As the number of processor cores is increased, the number of L2 cache misses is also increased. The reason for the increase in the number of L2 cache misses is the memory contention since the L2 cache is shared among all processors. Most L2 shared cache misses are coherence misses in the multiple processor cores as shown in (a) and (b) of Figure 5.

5.4 Architectural Implications

The token protocol shows better performance than the directory protocol by a factor of 13.4%. When a single-thread program is decomposed into a multithreaded program with the ability to exploit packet-level parallelism, the instruction overhead due to multithreading mechanism occurs. The instruction overhead due to multithreading is almost 10%. Most L2 shared cache misses are coherence misses in multiple processor cores. Thus, we need to reduce instruction overhead due to multithreading and L2 shared cache misses for performance enhancement of future network processors which are based on CMP.

6   Conclusions

The architectural implications of cache coherence protocols, the directory protocol and the token protocol, are investigated on the CMP processor model subjected to network application workloads. The performance has been measured for each protocol with varying numbers of processors. The token protocol shows better performance than the directory protocol by a factor of 13.4%. When single-thread programs are decomposed into multithreaded programs with exploiting packet-level parallelism, the instruction overhead due to multithreading mechanism occurs. The instruction overheads of the directory protocol and the token protocol are 9.7% and 10.3%, respectively. Most L2 shared cache misses are coherence misses in multiple processor cores.

As future work, the architectural implications of cache coherence protocols need to be investigated with varying cache size and block size. We will also investigate the architectural implications of simple CMP multiprocessor with network workloads which exploit multiprogramming instead of multithreading.

References

1. Odlyzko, A.M.: Internet traffic growth: Sources and implications. In: Proceesings of SPIE Optical Transmission Systems and Equipment for WDM Networking II, August 2003, vol. 5247, pp. 1–15 (August 2003)
2. Gebali, F., Rafiq, A.N.M.E.: Processor Array Architectures for Deep Packet Classification. IEEE Transactions on Parallel and Distributed Systems 17(3), 241–251 (2006)
3. Kant, K., Iyer, R., Mohapatra, P.: Architectural Impacet of Secure Socket Layer on Internet Servers. In: The Proceedings of the 2000 IEEE International Conference on Computer Design: VLSI in Computers and Processors, Austin, Texas, USA, September 2000, pp. 7–14. IEEE Computer Society Press, Los Alamitos (September 2000)
4. Lee, B.K., John, L.K.: NpBench: A Benchmark Suite for Control plane and Data plane Applications for Network Processors. In: Proceesings of 21st International Conference on Computer Design(ICCD'03), pp. 226–233 (2003)
5. Tullsen, D.M., Eggers, S.J., Levy, H.M.: Simultaneous Multithreading: Maximizing On-Chip Parallelism. In: Proceedings of 22nd Annual International Symposium on Computer Architecture, pp. 392–403 (1995)
6. Olukotun, K., Nayfeh, B.A., Hammond, L., Wilson, K., Chang, K.: The Case for a Single-Chip Multiprocessor. SIGOPS Operating System Reviev 30(5), 2–11 (1996)
7. Crowley, P., Franklin, M., Buhler, J., Chamberlain, R.: Impact of CMP Design on High-Performance Embedded Computing. In: Proceedings of the High Performance Embedded Computing Workshop (HPEC 2006), MIT Lincoln Laboratory, Lexington, MA (September 2006)

8. Hennessy, J.L., Patterson, D.A.: Computer Architecture A Quantitative Approach, 3rd edn. Morgan Kaufmann, San Francisco (2003)
9. Barroso, L.A., Gharachorloo, K., Bugnion, E.: Memory System Characterization of Commercial Workloads. In: ISCA '98: Proceedings of the 25th annual international symposium on Computer architecture, Washington, DC, USA, pp. 3–14. IEEE Computer Society Press, Los Alamitos (1998)
10. Martin, M.M.K., Hill, M.D., Wood, D.A.: Token Coherence: Decoupling Performance and Correctness. In: ISCA '03: Proceedings of The 30th Annual International Symposium on Computer Architecture, New York, NY, USA, pp. 182–193. ACM Press, New York (2003)
11. Crowley, P., Fiuczynski, M.E., Baer, J.-L., Bershad, B.N.: Characterization Processor Architectures for Programmable Network Interfaces. In: Proceedings of the 2000 International Conference on Supercomputing (2000)
12. Nahum, E.M., Yates, D.J., Kurose, J.F., Towsley, D.F.: Performance issues in parallelized network protocols. In: Operating Systems Design and Implementation, pp. 125–137 (1994)
13. Sweazey, P., Smith, A.J.: A Class of Compatible Cache Consistency Protocols and their Support by the IEEE Futurebus. SIGARCH Computer Architecture News 14(2), 414–423 (1986)
14. Olukotun, K., Hammond, L.: The future of microprocessors. ACM Queue 3(7), 26–29 (2005)
15. Magnusson, P.S., Christensson, M., Eskilson, J., Forsgren, D., Hallberg, G., Hogberg, J., Larsson, F., Moestedt, A., Werner, B.: Simics: A Full System Simulation Platform. IEEE Computer 35(2), 50–58 (2002)
16. Martin, M.M.K., Sorin, D.J., Beckmann, B.M., Marty, M.R., Xu, M., Alameldeen, A.R., Moore, K.E., Hill, M.D., Wood, D.A.: Multifacet's General Execution-driven Multiprocessor Simulator (GEMS) Toolset. SIGARCH Computer Architecture News 33(4), 92–99 (2005)
17. Memik, G., Mangione-Smith, W.H., Hu, W.: NetBench: A Benchmarking Suite for Network Processors. In: ICCAD '01: Proceedings of the 2001 IEEE/ACM international conference on Computer-aided design, Piscataway, NJ, USA, pp. 39–42. IEEE Press, Los Alamitos (2001)
18. Woo, S.C., Ohara, M., Torrie, E., Singh, J.P., Gupta, A.: The SPLASH-2 Programs: Characterization and Methodological Considerations. In: Proceedings of the 22th International Symposium on Computer Architecture, pp. 24–36 (1995)
19. Virtutech: Simics User Guide for Unix. 2.2.19 edn. (August 2005)
20. Passive Measurement and Analysis project, National Laboratory for Applied Network Research, http://moat.nlanr.net/Traces
21. Comer, D.E.: Computer Networks and Internets with Internet Applications, 4th edn. Prentice-Hall, Englewood Cliffs (2004)
22. Alameldeen, A.R., Wood, D.A.: IPC Considered Harmful for Multiprocessor Workloads. IEEE Micro 26(4), 8–17 (2006)

The SKB: A Semi-Completely-Connected Bus for On-Chip Systems

Masaru Takesue

Dept. Electronics and Information Engr., Hosei University, Tokyo 184-8584 Japan
takesue@ami.ei.hosei.ac.jp

Abstract. This paper proposes a semi-completely-connected bus, called *SKB*, to alleviate the long-wire and pin-neck problems against on-chip systems through a small diameter and dynamic clustering. Dynamic clustering allows to reduce the traffic to the per-cluster units such as the global interconnect interface, as compared with the static clustering fixed in hardware. We derive a 2^n-node *semi-complete (SK) graph* from a simple node-partitioning. An SKB is produced from the SK graph when we replace the links incident to a node by a single bus for the node. The diameter of SKB equals 1 (bus step), though the bus length is rather long, $O(\sqrt{2^n})$. Simulation results show that relative to the hypercube with the link delay of 1 clock, the SKB's bandwidth is about 0.97 and 0.14 assuming the bus delay of 1 and 8 clocks, respectively, that increases to about 4.57 and 0.71 with the dynamic clustering.

1 Introduction

With future LSI technologies, we will be able to put a large portion of a system in a single chip. However, the technologies have three problems above all: First, the signal delay due to long wires will dominate the clock cycle time of the system if the feature size of wires will scale with the same pace as for transistors [1].

Second, the design of a system on a chip (SoC) may be restricted by the power consumable in the chip. In the current high-performance microprocessors, interconnect power is over 50% of the total dynamic power, and its about 50% is consumed by global wires [2]. So a large-scale network on a chip (NoC) may limit the performance and/or power consumption against high-performance SoCs.

Third, on-chip multiprocessors (CMPs) in the near future will have on-chip caches and off-chip memory. Then a CMP design may be restricted by the number of available I/O pins. Although the number of pins per chip will increase, the number of transistors per chip will increase at a much higher rate [3]. So with the limited number of pins, we have to maintain a high traffic rate required between the on-chip caches and probably off-chip memory.

Static clusters fixed in hardware are effective to reduce the traffic to memory [12,13], and hence, to alleviated the pin-neck problem. However, the traffic concentrates on the per-cluster units such as the global interconnect interface and the cache coherence directory when the request rate is high in each cluster, leading to a long delay for the requests crossing the chip boundary.

K. Li et al. (Eds.): NPC 2007, LNCS 4672, pp. 404–414, 2007.

Good news with VLSI technologies is that a small node degree (i.e., the number of links incident to a node) is not necessarily a measure of good networks since almost all links of a network can be accommodated in the chip. Notice that a larger node degree generally leads to a smaller diameter but longer wires.

This paper proposes a *semi-completely-connected bus (SKB)* to cope with the long-wire and pin-neck problems mentioned above. We approach to the first problem by a small diameter, while to the second one by one set of dynamic clusters produced for *each target*, such as a memory block, of requests.

The small diameter with a large node degree may aggravate the long-wire problem, though it reduces the number of hops required in communications. So we assume a technology for very fast global wires, such as the transmission lines with a delay determined by an LC time constant [4], instead of an RC constant. Alternatively, we can assume a much larger number of metal planes than the current (about 10) to allow very fat and very sparse wires.

We derive a *semi-complete (SK)* graph by a simple partitioning of nodes. The SKB has the topology of a modified SK graph so that the links incident to a node are replaced by a single bus owned by the node. The diameter of the SKB is equal to 1 bus step. The layout pattern for the buses is very regular, but the maximum bus length of the 2^n-node SKB is rather long, i.e., $\mathbf{O}(\sqrt{2^n})$.

In the rest of paper, Section 2 introduces the simple partitioning and derives SK graph and its recursive version. Section 3 presents the structure, layout, routing, and clustering of the SKB. Section 4 shows the evaluation results. Section 5 describes related work, and Section 6 concludes the paper.

2 Semi-Complete Graphs

This section introduces the simple partitioning and defines the SK graph and its recursive version.

Let $\langle s_{p_1}, \ell_{k_1} \rangle$ denote an n-bit node address, where s_{p_1} and ℓ_{k_1} are the values of the upper p_1-bit and the lower k_1-bit ($p_1 + k_1 = n$) parts of the address. Moreover, let $P_{\langle s, \ell \rangle}$ be the partition represented by leader (i.e., the representative node) $\langle s, \ell \rangle$. Then the simple partitioning is defined as follows:

Definition 1. *The suit $S_{s_{p_1}}$ consists of 2^{k_1} leaders $\langle s_{p_1}, *_{k_1} \rangle$, and the partition $P_{\langle s_{p_1}, \ell_{k_1} \rangle}$ has 2^{p_1} members $\langle *_{p_1}, \ell_{k_1} \rangle$, where $*_b$ stands for b-bit don't care.*

With Definition 1, we can partition the n-bit address space in two ways: First we can produce 2^{p_1} suits $\mathcal{S} = \{ S_{s_{p_1}} \mid 0 \le s_{p_1} \le 2^{p_1} - 1 \}$ each of 2^{k_1} leaders. Second, with each suit $S_{s_{p_1}}$, we can obtain a set of 2^{k_1} partitions $\mathcal{P}_{s_{p_1}} = \{ P_{\langle s_{p_1}, \ell_{k_1} \rangle} \mid 0 \le \ell_{k_1} \le 2^{k_1} - 1 \}$ each of 2^{p_1} nodes and represented by leader $P_{\langle s_{p_1}, \ell_{k_1} \rangle}$, leading to a total of 2^{p_1} sets $\mathcal{P} = \{ \mathcal{P}_{s_{p_1}} \mid 0 \le s_{p_1} \le 2^{p_1} - 1 \}$.

This partitioning has the following interesting property: Members $\langle *_{p_1}, \ell_{k_1} \rangle$ of partition $P_{\langle s_{p_1}, \ell_{k_1} \rangle}$ are distributed to the all suits, and a member $\langle s'_{p_1}, \ell_{k_1} \rangle \in P_{\langle s_{p_1}, \ell_{k_1} \rangle}$ ($s'_{p_1} \neq s_{p_1}$) is the leader of partition $P_{\langle s'_{p_1}, \ell_{k_1} \rangle}$ when partitioned with suit $\langle s'_{p_1}, *_{k_1} \rangle$. Note that partition $P_{\langle s'_{p_1}, \ell_{k_1} \rangle}$ has also the members $\langle *_{p_1}, \ell_{k_1} \rangle$. We graphically represent this property by a *partition graph* $PG_n(p_1, k_1)$ that has a link between each member and the leader in every partition.

Property 1. The $PG_n(p_1, k_1)$ graph has 2^{k_1} complete graphs, K_{p_1}'s, each consisting of the 2^{p_1} nodes $\langle *_{p_1}, \ell_{k_1} \rangle$.

Example 1. The $PG_3(2,1)$ graph ($p_1 = 2$ and $k_1 = 1$) is shown in Fig. 1(a), where the node address $\langle s_{p_1}, \ell_{k_1} \rangle$ is denoted by $s_{p_1} \ell_{k_1}$. In this case, we can produce 4 ($= 2^{p_1}$) suits, S_0, S_1, S_2, and S_3, each of 2 ($= 2^{k_1}$) leaders. With any of the suits, we can obtain 2 ($= 2^{k_1}$) partitions each of 4 ($= 2^{p_1}$) members. For instance, with suit S_1, we can obtain the two partitions $P_{\langle 1,0 \rangle} = \{\langle 1,0 \rangle, \langle 0,0 \rangle, \langle 2,0 \rangle, \langle 3,0 \rangle\}$ and $P_{\langle 1,1 \rangle} = \{\langle 1,1 \rangle, \langle 0,1 \rangle, \langle 2,1 \rangle, \langle 3,1 \rangle\}$ with the leaders $\langle 1,0 \rangle$ and $\langle 1,1 \rangle$ in the suit. The members of each partition are scattered into the all suits and organizes a K_2. So the $PG_3(2,1)$ has 2 K_2 graphs each of 4 nodes (Property 1).

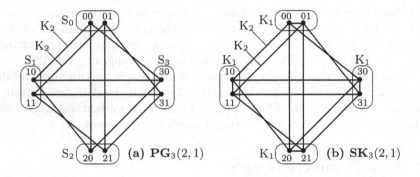

Fig. 1. (a) The $PG_3(2,1)$ graph for the partitioning when $p_1 = 2$ and $k_1 = 1$, and (b) the $SK_3(2,1)$ produced from the PG

We derive a *semi-complete (SK)* graph from a PG graph as described below. Then the obtained SK graph has the property presented next.

Definition 2. *An $SK_n(p_1, k_1)$ graph is obtained from the $PG_n(p_1, k_1)$ graph if we configure the 2^{k_1} leaders in each suit into the K_{k_1} graph, where $n = p_1 + k_1$.*

Property 2. The $SK_n(p_1, k_1)$ has 2^{p_1} K_{k_1} graphs (Definition 2), that are connected to each other by 2^{k_1} K_{p_1} graphs (Property 1).

Example 2. The $SK_3(2,1)$ shown in Fig. 1(b) is obtained from the $PG_3(2,1)$ (shown in Fig. 1(a)) by connecting the nodes in every suit with each other to produce, in this case, a K_1. So the $SK_3(2,1)$ has 4 K_1 (i.e., 2^{p_1} K_{k_1}) graphs connected with each other by 2 K_2 (i.e., 2^{k_1} K_{p_1}) graphs.

When n is large, the K_{k_1} and K_{p_1} may be too large to achieve short wires in organizing an SKB form the SK. To cope with this problem, we exploit a recursive SK graph. Let $SK_n^0(p_0, k_0) = K_n$ ($p_0 = 0$, $k_0 = n$) and $p_i + k_i = n_i = k_{i-1}$

$(1 \leq i \leq r)$, where $\sum_{i=1}^{r} p_i + k_r = n$. Then we produce an r-level recursive SK graph, $SK_n^r(p_1, \ldots, p_r, k_r)$, from the K_n by the recursive partitioning of each k_{i-1}-bit space to obtain an $SK_{n_i}^1(p_i, k_i)$ (i.e., $SK_{n_i}(p_i, k_i)$) as follows:

Definition 3. *An $SK_n^r(p_1, \ldots, p_r, k_r)$ is produced if we transform each $K_{k_{i-1}}$ in the $SK_n^{i-1}(p_1, \ldots, p_{i-1}, k_{i-1})$ to an $SK_{n_i}^1(p_i, k_i)$ to obtain the $SK_n^i(p_1, \ldots, p_i, k_i)$, for i from 1 to r.*

Example 3. We transform the initial K_4 into $SK_n^1(p_1, k_1) = SK_4^1(1, 3)$ (see Fig. 2(a)), and next obtain $SK_n^2(p_1, p_2, k_1) = SK_4^2(1, 1, 2)$ (see Fig. 2(b)) by converting each $K_{k_1} = K_3$ in $SK_4^1(1, 3)$ to $SK_{n_2}^1(p_2, k_2) = SK_3^1(1, 2)$ ($p_2 + k_2 = n_2 = k_1$).

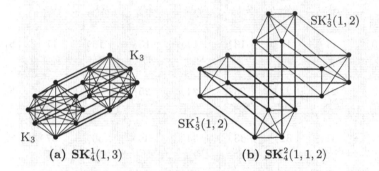

(a) **SK$_4^1(1, 3)$**   (b) **SK$_4^2(1, 1, 2)$**

Fig. 2. (a) The $SK_4^1(1, 3)$ produced from K_4 and (b) the $SK_4^2(1, 1, 2)$ obtained from $SK_4^1(1, 3)$

The number of links and the diameter of SK_n^r are equal to $2^{n-1} \sum_{i=1}^{r+1}(2^{p_i} - 1)$ (where $p_{r+1} = k_r$) and $r + 1$, respectively. Since the number of links in the K_n graph is $O(2^{2n-1})$, SK_n^r reduces the number by the factor of $O(2^{p_i}/2^n)$.

3   The Semi-Completely-Connected Bus: SKB

This section describes the structure, layout, routing, and dynamic clustering of the SKB. The effect of the clustering as applied to a memory hierarchy is also analyzed. For space, the description of recursive SKBs is omitted.

3.1   Structure of the SKB

The SKB_n is organized from the SK_n and is laid out as follows. The number of buses in SKB_n equals one per node and the diameter equals 1 (bus step).

Definition 4. *The $SKB_n(p_1, k_1)$ is obtained if we replace all links incident to a node of the $SK_n(p_1, k_1)$ by a single bus for the node, for all nodes in the SK_n.*

Definition 5. *We arrange the nodes of the $SKB_n(p_1, k_1)$ into a $2^{p_1} \times 2^{k_1}$ array and put node $\langle s, \ell \rangle$ at the position with array index (s, ℓ).*

Example 4. The layout of $SKB_6(3,3)$ is shown in Fig. 3. The BSK has 64 buses. The two-digit integer $s\ell$ in the node box stands for the node address $\langle s, \ell \rangle$. Each node has two sets of ports; one set for vertical lines, and the other for horizontal lines. For space, only even-numbered ports are shown. The bus for node $\langle s, \ell \rangle$ consists of a horizontal line along row s and a vertical line along column ℓ; the diamond ($\diamond$) at the cross point of the horizontal line and the stub to node $\langle s, \ell \rangle$ shows that the node is the owner of the bus. The bus of node, for instance, $\langle 2, 3 \rangle$ runs along row 2 and column 3 as shown by the bold line.

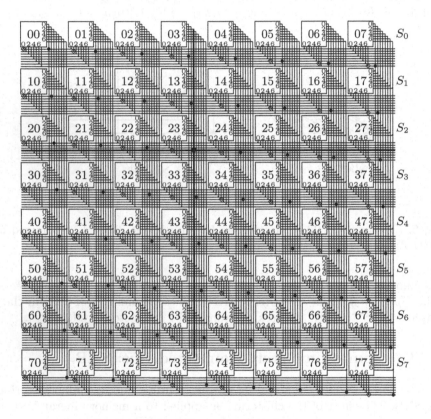

Fig. 3. The layout of $SKB_6(3,3)$

Let the unit length of the bus be equal to the distance between the adjacent nodes on the SKB_n layout, and the *bus length* be defined as the maximum of the distances for a signal to traverse for all buses. Then the routing distance is largest when the source and target are located at, for instance, the top-left and bottom-right corners of the array, respectively. Then the bus length of the $SKB_n(p_1, k_1)$ equals $2^{p_1} + 2^{k_1}$, that reduces to $2\sqrt{2^n}$ when $p_1 = k_1$.

3.2   Routing on the SKB

Let S-ports and L-ports of a node be the ports for choosing one of the suits and leaders, respectively, so are connected to the vertical and horizontal lines of the buses. Then S-port i of node $\langle s, \ell \rangle$ is connected to the bus of node $\langle i, \ell \rangle$, and L-port j to the bus of node $\langle s, j \rangle$ (see Fig. 3). Moreover, the bus of node $\langle s, \ell \rangle$ is connected to nodes $\langle s, *_{k_1} \rangle$ via the horizontal line. So the routing on the SKB is performed in the following way, and its diameter is given by the next theorem.

Definition 6. *To send a packet to the target node $\langle s_t, \ell_t \rangle$, the source node $\langle s, \ell \rangle$ puts the packet on its S-port s_t if $s \neq s_t$, or on its L-port ℓ_t otherwise.*

Theorem 1. *The diameter of $SKB_n(p_1, k_1)$ is equal to one bus step.*

Proof. When $s \neq s_t$, the S-port s_t of source $\langle s, \ell \rangle$ is connected to the bus of node $\langle s_t, \ell \rangle$ and that bus is connected with the target $\langle s_t, \ell_t \rangle$. Otherwise, the L-port ℓ_t of source $\langle s, \ell \rangle$ is connected to the bus of the target $\langle s, \ell_t \rangle = \langle s_t, \ell_t \rangle$. In both cases, the packet is sent from the source to the target in 1 bus-step.

Example 5. Assume the source node $\langle 2, 3 \rangle$ and the target node $\langle 7, 6 \rangle$ in Fig. 3. Then the source $\langle 2, 3 \rangle$ puts the packet on S-port 7. The port is connected to the bus of node $\langle 7, 3 \rangle$, and the bus is connected with the target $\langle 7, 6 \rangle$. When the target is $\langle 2, 7 \rangle$ for the same source, it sends the packet via L-port 7 connected to the target's bus. In both cases, the packet reaches the target in 1 bus-step.

3.3   Dynamic Clustering on the SKB

Suppose that a CMP consists of on-chip processing nodes and off-chip memory, and that the node has a processor, a level-1 (L1) cache, and a level-2 (L2) cache. *Dynamic clustering* of memory requests refers to the dynamic partitioning *only* of the nodes requesting for a specific memory block. So the size of a cluster is no more than the partition size 2^{p_1}.

Let M_s denote the off-chip shared memory unit consisting of memory blocks B_{s*} whose addresses $s*$ equal s in the upper p_1 bits. We associate unit M_s with suit S_s. When no copy of a memory block $B_{t\alpha} \in M_t$ is in the L2 cache of a node $\langle s, \ell \rangle$, we produce a set of dynamic clusters for block $B_{t\alpha}$, partitioning with suit S_t in the following way.

Definition 7. *In the dynamic clustering of the requests for a memory block $B_{t\alpha}$, a node $\langle s, \ell \rangle$ sends the request to the L2 cache of leader $\langle t, \ell \rangle$ in suit S_t.*

The L2 cache of leader $\langle t, \ell \rangle$ returns the copy of block $B_{t\alpha}$ if it has the copy. Otherwise, it produces a single request for the sake of the requests for block $B_{t\alpha}$ received in the cluster and sends it to unit M_t, crossing the chip boundary. The next theorem shows the effect of dynamic clustering.

Theorem 2. *The traffic to leaders for clustering memory requests reduces to at most $1/2^{p_1}$ of the traffic to the per-cluster units in the static clusters.*

Proof. Assume that the memory requests are uniformly distributed to all memory units. Then in the static clusters, the requests not satisfied in the L2 cache concentrate on a single per-cluster unit. On the other hand, with the dynamic clusters, the request is sent to one of the 2^{p_1} leaders depending on the address of requested memory block, so that the traffic to one leader reduces to one 2^{p_1}th of the traffic to the per-cluster unit.

When a miss occurs on block $B_{t\alpha}$ in the L2 cache of node $\langle s, \ell \rangle$, the copy of $B_{t\alpha}$ may be in some L2 caches in partition $P_\ell = \langle *, \ell \rangle$ and suit $S_t = \langle t, * \rangle$. To reuse the copy by an L2-L2 direct transfer, all L2 caches in P_ℓ snoop all memory requests issued in P_ℓ, while the L2 caches in S_t snoop the requests for the blocks in M_t. The clustering is performed only if P_ℓ and S_t have no copy of block $B_{t\alpha}$.

Example 6. Suppose in Fig. 3 that a miss on a memory block in unit M_0 (associated with S_0) occurs in the L2 cache of node $\langle 2, 3 \rangle$. Then the node puts the memory request on the bus of node $\langle 0, 3 \rangle$, that is snooped by the all L2 caches in partition P_3 and suit S_0. When no copy is found in those L2 caches, the clustering is performed with the L2 cache of leader $\langle 0, 3 \rangle$.

4 Evaluation

This section shows the results of evaluation on the 64-node SKB, comparing with the representative network, the 64-node hypercube.

4.1 Environments

We evaluate the SKB (denoted by SKB) and hypercube (Hyp) by a cycle-accurate simulator. They have the link- or bus-width of 1 byte, and perform wormhole routing. Hyp has simultaneously bidirectional links of which delay is fixed equal to one clock to use Hyp as the reference network. Let SKBd denote the SKB whose bus delay equals d clocks. We denote the SKB with dynamic and static clustering by appending D and S after the network notation, such as SKB4D and SKB2S.

Processing nodes simultaneously send 13-byte packets (header: 9 bytes, data: 4 bytes) to the individual target nodes chosen randomly in each node. The packet issue-rate in each node is varied from 1 packet per 1k clocks up to the rate at which the network's bandwidth saturates; the rate is fixed in one simulation run.

We simulate the 64-node networks; for SKB, we use SKB$_6(3, 3)$, so the cluster size equals 8. In the dynamic clustering, the leader produces a packet every time it receives the same number of packets as the cluster size and sends the produced packet to the target. We implement static clustering by fixing the leader to a specific node in each cluster independent of the target nodes.

We measure the total number of clocks required for sending 2048 packets per node to the targets and calculate the network's bandwidth relative to the Hyp's. We also calculate the average network delay from the source to the target.

4.2   Results

The bandwidth and network delay of SKBd (with no clustering) are shown in Fig. 4, where the bus cycle time d is varied from 1 to 4, and 8. The bandwidth of SKBd equals about 0.97, 0.53, 0.36, 0.28, and 0.14 respectively when d is equal to 1, 2, 3, 4, and 8, relative to the hypercube's. The network delay is then equal to about 18, 32, 45, 62, and 140 clocks respectively when the network are not saturated; the delay in Hyp equals about 24 clocks. Thus SKB1 and Hyp have almost the same performance. The performance of SKBd decreases almost proportional to d.

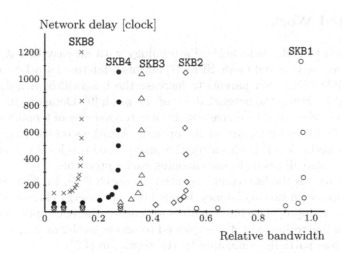

Fig. 4. Performance of SKBd relative to Hyp

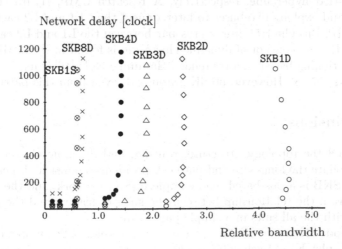

Fig. 5. Performance of SKBdD and SKB1S relative to Hyp

The dynamic clustering is effective to improve the performance of SKB as shown in Fig. 5. The relative bandwidth increases to about 4.57, 2.58, 1.89, 1.43, and 0.71 for SKB1 to SKB4, and SKB8, respectively; then the network delay decreases to 17, 30, 41, 55, and 117 clocks. This is because the packets issued in each cluster are sent to one of 8 leaders depending on the target address so that no traffic congestion on a specific leader occurs, though one extra-packet per 8 received packets is produced in each leader and is sent to the target.

On the other hand, static clustering SKB1S is not effective when the request rate is high: SKB1S decreases the SKB1's bandwidth of 0.97 to about 0.61 due to the traffic contention on the fixed leaders.

5   Related Work

One approach to NoCs is to achieve a topology with an easy layout and short wires, such as the tree and mesh. SPIN [7] adopts a fat-tree [8], where each node has four children and four parents to increase the bandwidth. A 2-dimensional torus is used to reduce the network delay of the mesh [9]. Octagon [10] exploits a recursive ring, where one recursive level is an extended ring of 8 nodes with extra links between the nodes located at the opposite locations on the ring. The hierarchical bus network [11] is also attractive since it reduces local communication overhead but also allows us to use snooping cache protocols.

An alternative is the interconnect-centric approach [5,6]. In [6], interconnects consist of wires with varying latency, bandwidth, and energy characteristics, and are mapped on appropriate interconnects for cache coherence operations. In [5], transmission line technology [4] is exploited to access level-2 on-chip caches. Our SKB study was partially stimulated by the results in [4,5].

To reduce memory traffic, the commercial multiprocessors (MPs), STiNG [12] and SGI Origin [13], adopt clusters connected to each other by the ring and the fat bristled hypercube, respectively. A research CMP, Hydra [14], has 4 processors and exploits two buses to interconnect their L1 and L2 caches, while another CMP, Piranha [15], uses a crossbar between the L1 and L2 caches for 8 processors. But no concept of dynamic clustering is found in those MPs.

The partitioning based on an extended Hamming code [16] is used to organize the networks [17,18]. However, no SK graph is derived from this partitioning.

6   Conclusions

We presented the topology, structure, routing, and dynamic clustering of the SKB to alleviate the long-wire and pin-neck problems against high-performance NoCs. The SKB is a bus-based semi-complete (SK) network, and the SK graph is derived from the relationship between the suits of leaders and the partitions produced with the all suits in a simple partitioning.

The 2^n-node SK graph, $SK_n(p, k)$ $(p+k = n)$, consists of 2^p number of 2^k-node complete graphs, K_k's. Each node in a K_k is connected to the nodes scattered in the other K_k graphs in such a way that those nodes together organize a complete graph K_p. The 2^n-node SKB, SKB_n, is obtained from the SK_n by replacing the links incident to a node by a single bus for the node.

We laid out the nodes of the SKB_n on the $2^p \times 2^k$ array. Then the buses have very regular wiring patterns and the maximum length of $O(\sqrt{2^n})$; it is expected that the delay of this rather long wire is alleviated by the transmission line technology or fat and sparse wires.

We evaluated the SKB_6 by a cycle-accurate simulator. The results show that relative to the bandwidth of the hypercube with the link delay of 1 clock, the SKB's bandwidth is about 0.97, 0.53, 0.36, 0.28, and 0.14 when the bus delay equals 1, 2, 3, 4, and 8 clocks, respectively. The bandwidths increase to about 4.57, 2.58, 1.89, 1.43, and 0.71 when the dynamic clustering is exploited.

We are designing an on-chip cache hierarchy and its coherence protocol so that we can evaluate the effects of dynamic clustering of memory requests.

References

1. Matzke, D.: Will Physical Scalability Sabotage Performance Gains. IEEE Computer 30, 37–39 (1997)
2. Magen, N., Kolodny, A., Weiser, U., Shamir, N.: Interconnect-Power Dissipation in a Microprocessor. In: Proc. of System Level Interconnect Prediction, pp. 7–13 (2004)
3. Huh, J., Burger, D., Keckler, S.W.: Exploring the Design Space of Future CMPs. In: Proc. Int. Conf. on Parallel Architectures and Compilation Techniques, pp. 199–210 (2001)
4. Chang, R.T., Talwalkar, N., Patrick, C.P., Wong, S.S.: Near Speed-of-Light Signaling Over On-Chip Electrical Interconnects. IEEE Jour. on Solid-State Circuits 38, 834–838 (2003)
5. Beckmann, B.M., Wood, D.A.: TLC: Transmission Line Caches. In: Proc. Int. Symp. on Microarchitecture, pp. 43–54 (2003)
6. Cheng, L., et al.: Interconnect-Aware Coherence Protocol for Chip Multiprocessors. In: Proc. 33rd Int. Symp. on Computer Architecture, pp. 339–350 (2006)
7. Guerrier, P., Greiner, A.: A Generic Architecture for On-Chip Packet-Switched Interconnections. In: Proc. Design and Test in Europe (DATE), pp. 250–256 (2000)
8. Leiserson, C.E.: Fat-Trees: Universal Networks for Hardware-Efficient Supercomputing. IEEE Trans. on Computer C-34, 892–901 (1985)
9. Dally, W.J., Towles, B.: Route Packets, Not Wires: On-Chip Interconnection Networks. In: Proc. Design Automation Conf. (DAC), pp. 683–689 (2001)
10. Karim, F., et al.: An Interconnect Architecture for Networking Systems on Chips. IEEE Micro 22, 36–45 (2002)
11. Kumar, R., Zyuban, V., Tullsen, D.M.: Interconnection in Multi-Core Architectures: Understanding Mechanisms, Overhead and Scaling. In: Proc. 32nd Int. Symp. on Computer Architectures, pp. 408–419 (2005)
12. Lovett, T., Clapp, R.: STiNG: A ccNUMA Computer System for the Commercial Marketplace. In: Proc. 23th Int. Symp. on Computer Architectures, pp. 308–317 (1996)
13. Laudon, J., Lenoski, D.: The SGI Origin: A ccNUMA Highly Scalable Server. In: Proc. 24th Int. Symp. on Computer Architectures, pp. 241–251 (1997)

14. Olukotun, K., et al.: The Case for a Single Chip Multiprocessor. In: Proc. 7th Int. Conf. on Architectural Support for Programming Languages and Operating Systems, pp. 2–11 (1996)
15. Barroso, L.A., et al.: Piranha: A Scalable Architecture Based on Single-Chip Multiprocessors. In: Proc. 27th Int. Symp. on Computer Architectures, pp. 282–293 (2000)
16. Takesue, M.: Ψ-Cubes: Recursive Bused Fat-Hypercubes for Multilevel Snoopy Caches. In: Proc. Int. Symp. on Parallel Architectures, Algorithms, and Networks (I-SPAN), pp. 62–67 (1999)
17. Takesue, M.: DC-Mesh: A Contracted High-Dimensional Mesh for Dynamic Clustering. In: Jin, H., Gao, G.R., Xu, Z., Chen, H. (eds.) NPC 2004. LNCS, vol. 3222, pp. 382–389. Springer, Heidelberg (2004)
18. Takesue, M.: The Psi-Cube: A Bus-Based Cube-Type Network for High-Performance On-Chip Networks. In: Proc 2005 Int. Conf. on Parallel Processing (ICPP) Workshops, pp. 539–546 (2005) (For the full version, see Parallel Computing, vol. 32, pp. 852–869, Elsevier B. V (2006))

An Instruction Folding Solution to a Java Processor

Tan Yiyu[1], Anthony S. Fong[2], and Yang Xiaojian[1]

[1] College of Information Science and Engineering, Nanjing University of Technology
NO.5 Xinmofan Road, Nanjing, China
[2] Department of Electronic Engineering, City University of Hong Kong
Tat Chee Avenue, Kowloon Tong, Hong Kong

Abstract. Java is widely applied into embedded devices. Java programs are compiled into Java bytecodes, which are executed into the Java virtual machine. The Java virtual machine is a stack machine and instruction folding is a technique to reduce the redundant stack operations. In this paper, a simple instruction folding algorithm is proposed for a Java processor named jHISC, where bytecodes are classified into five categories and the operation results of incomplete folding groups are hold for further folding. In the benchmark JVM98, with respect to all stack operations, the percentage of the eliminated P and C type instructions varies from 87% to 98% and the average is about 93%. The reduced instructions are between 37% and 50% of all operations and the average is 44%.

Keywords: Instruction folding, Java processor, Java virtual machine, Bytecode.

1 Introduction

As a result of its object-oriented feature and corresponding advantages of security, robustness and platform independence, Java is widely applied in network applications and embedded devices, such as PDAs, mobile phones, TV set-up boxes and Palm PCs [1]. Java programs are compiled into Java bytecodes, which are executed into the Java virtual machine. The Java virtual machine is a stack machine, where all operands, such as temporary data, intermediate results, and method arguments, are frequently pushed onto or popped out from the stack during execution. Thus some redundant load or store operations are performed, which results in the low execution efficiency and affects system performance, especially in embedded devices, where real-time operations and low power consumption are needed. For example, when the bytecode stream *"iload_0, iload_1, iadd, istore_2"* are executed in the Java virtual machine, firstly, the load type instructions *iload_0* and *iload_1*, push data from the local variable onto the top of the operand stack. Secondly, the instruction *iadd* pops data from the top of the stack, operates on them and stores the operation result onto the stack. Finally, the store type instruction *istore_2* moves the operation result from the top of the operand stack to the local variable. This execution procedure needs extra clock cycles to push or pop data from the operand stack. Moreover, operations are executed one at a time by using the operand stack, thus introducing a virtual data

K. Li et al. (Eds.): NPC 2007, LNCS 4672, pp. 415–424, 2007.

dependency between the successive instructions, which restricts instruction level parallelism and adversely affects system performance.

To address these shortcomings, Sun Microsystems introduced the notion of instruction folding [2][3], which was a technique to eliminate the unnecessary load or write-back operations to the stack by detecting some contiguous instructions and executing them collectively like a single, compound instruction. For example, to execute the bytecode stream mentioned above, the generated compound instruction may read data into ALU from the local variable directly, operate on them and write the operation result back to the local variable. Thus the intermediate operands and data do not need to push onto or pop out from the operand stack.

In this paper, a new folding algorithm is presented in jHISC, a Java processor for embedded devices. The rest of this paper is structured as follows. The previous work on instruction folding is summarized in Section 2. The jHISC instruction set is described in Section 3. Section 4 depicts our proposed folding algorithm, including bytecode type definitions and categories, folding rules, and system diagram. In Section 5, the performance estimation results based on JVM98 benchmarks are introduced. Finally, a summary is made in Section 6.

2 Related Work

In Sun Microsystems solution, the bytecodes were classified into six types and nine folding patterns were predefined. The Instruction Folding Unit (IFU) monitored the successive bytecodes to determine how many instructions were folded according to the folding patterns. N. Vijaykrishnan et al and L. R. Ton et al also proposed the similar folding algorithm to Sun Microsystems by introducing different folding patterns [4][5]. Although these folding algorithms are simple and easily implemented, only the continuous bytecodes that exactly match the predefined folding patterns are folded. If the bytecode stream does not match the folding patterns, the bytecodes will be executed in serial. Thus the folding is inefficient.

L. C. Chang proposed the POC folding algorithm [6] to improve folding efficiency, where bytecodes were classified into P (Producer), O (Operator), and C (Consumer) types according to the bytecode operation characteristics. The O type bytecodes were further divided into four subtypes: O_E, O_B, O_C and O_T. Recursive check was performed for every two consecutive instructions according to the POC folding rules. If the two checked instructions were foldable, they were marked with a new POC type, which was then checked with the following unfolded bytecode instructions until no folding was possible. The POC folding algorithm has no fixed folding patterns and can be implemented as finite automation through a state machine. But like the previous folding algorithms, it is only used to fold the consecutive instructions.

Based on the POC folding algorithm, A. Kim and M. Chang introduced the advanced POC folding algorithm by adding additional four discontinuous folding sequence patterns to fold the discontinuous bytecode instructions [7]. Different with the original POC folding algorithm, the O type bytecodes were further divided into two subtypes: Oc (Consumable operator) and Op (Producible operator), according to their operation results were written back onto the operand stack or not. This algorithm achieves higher folding efficiency with a relatively simple implementation circuitry. However, improper type definitions for each bytecode exist [8]. For example, the bytecode *lastore* should be *Oc* type according to its operation behavior, but it is defined to be *C* type in the advanced POC algorithm.

L. R. Ton et al presented the Enhanced POC (EPOC) folding algorithm by using a stack reorder buffer to hold the extra *P* type bytecodes and the incomplete folding groups for further folding [8]. The incomplete folding groups were treated as P types. M. W. El-Kharashi et al introduced an operand extraction-based algorithm by tagging the incomplete folding groups as *tagged producers* and *tagged consumers*, which were further used as *producers* or *consumers* in the following folding groups [9][10]. In the algorithm, bytecodes were classified into twelve types according to the way they handled the stack, and five folding pattern templates were defined. Although it claimed that 97% of stack operations and 50% of all operations were eliminated, the foldability check and bytecode type decoder are complicate to implement by hardware due to so many bytecode categories.

3   jHISC Instruction Set

In jHISC, the instruction set supports up to three operands. Each instruction is 32 bits in length with 8 bits for the opcode to define the instruction operation. T The operands may be registers or 11-bit, 16-bit, and 24-bit immediate data. The current local variable frame is accessed with 5-bit index, therefore addressing up to 32 general-purpose registers.

Seven groups of instructions are defined in jHISC. They are logical instructions, arithmetic instructions, branching instructions, array manipulation instructions, object-oriented instructions, data manipulation instructions and miscellaneous instructions. Excluding the instructions for floating-point operations, 94% of all bytecodes and 83% of the object-oriented related bytecodes are implemented in hardware directly [13]. Moreover, some quick instructions are provided to perform the operations of putting or getting variables after the first execution.

4   Proposed Instruction Folding Algorithm

4.1   Bytecode Categories

The Java virtual machine provides a rich set of instructions to manipulate the operand stack. In the original POC folding algorithm and its extensions (EPOC and the advanced POC), the O (Operator) type was defined as the bytecodes which popped data from the operand stack and perform operations. Thus some bytecodes, such as *getstatic*, which perform operations without popping data from the operand stack, are not O type. However, in the original POC folding algorithm and its later extensions, these bytecodes were defined as O type. In our proposed folding algorithm, they are defined as Tp or T type according to their behaviors of handling the operand stack. The other bytecode types and their definitions are similar to those in the advanced POC algorithm. The type definitions are presented as follows [11].

- **Producer (P):** instructions that get data from constant registers or local variables and push them onto the operand stack, such as *iconst_1*, *iload_3*.

- **Operator (O):** instructions that pop data from the top of the operand stack and perform operations. This type is further divided into two subtypes, namely **Producible Operator (O$_P$),** such as *iaload*, which pushes its operation result onto the operand stack, and **Consumable Operator (O$_C$),** which does not push the operation result, such as *if_icmpeq*.
- **Consumer (C):** instructions that remove data from the operand stack and store them back into local variables, such as *istore*.
- **Termination (T):** instructions that do not operate on the stack and some non-foldable bytecodes, such as *goto* and *return*. Such instructions contain table jump, multidimensional array creation, exception throw, and monitor enter and exit. They are more suitable to be emulated by software traps.
- **Temporary (Tp):** instructions that perform operations without popping data from the operand stack, but push the operation results onto it, such as *getstatic*.

4.2 Folding Algorithm

4.2.1 Folding Rules
The folding rules can be simply summarized and shown as follows.

(1) P type bytecodes are folded into the following adjacent C or O type bytecodes.
(2) C type bytecodes are folded into the previous adjacent P, Op or Tp type bytecodes.
(3) T type bytecodes cannot be folded.
(4) The intermediate results of incomplete folding groups are written into buffers and treated as P type bytecodes for further folding. When an Op or Tp type bytecode is directly followed by a C type bytecode, the C type bytecode, Op or Tp type bytecode, and the previous P type bytecode(s) form a complete folding group. If an Op or Tp type bytecode is not followed by a C type bytecode, the operation result is treated as a P type bytecode and the corresponding information is written into buffers for further folding.

In every folding group, there is a central instruction, which operates on the operand stack and modifies its contents. The central instruction, the necessary producer(s) and consumer instructions form a folding group. Typically, each folding group only has one central instruction, which may be an O or T$_P$ type instruction. When a consumer bytecode follows a producer instruction directly, it can also be a central instruction. In the generated jHISC instruction, the central instruction determines the opcode while the related producer and consumer instructions affect the operands.

4.2.2 System Diagram
The block diagram of instruction folding and translation unit is illustrated in Fig. 1. Bytecodes are fetched from the instruction cache or memory and stored into the Instruction Buffer. The Instruction Classifier classifies bytecodes according to their opcodes and the type definitions. The bytecode types, opcodes, operand types, the constant values and local variable indices are stored in different buffers, respectively.

The Folding Manager Unit checks the foldability and identifies the central instructions according to the bytecode types and folding rules. If some bytecodes can be folded, the Folding Manager Unit will generate the relevant jHISC opcode, foldable signal and folding length signal. The jHISC opcode is determined by the central instruction and the related operand type. The foldable signal is used to trigger the Operand Generator to generate the operands of jHISC instruction. The folding length signal is applied to update the pointer of the buffers. If a bytecode is not folded, it will be simply translated into a jHISC instruction in sequence.

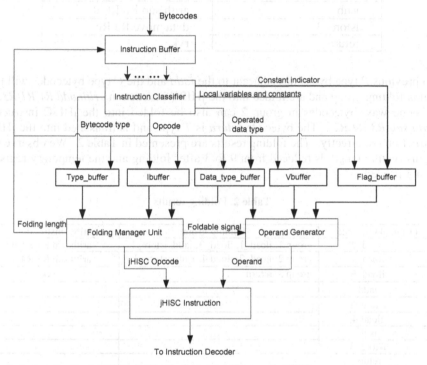

Fig. 1. Block diagram of instruction folder

4.2.3 Instruction Folding

In jHISC, the constant registers and local variable frames are implemented by register files. Typically, local variables are mapped into register files with the same index and all bytecodes are translated into jHISC instructions by one to one if no folding occurs. For example, if a bytecodes stream is *"iload_2, iload_1, iload_3, iadd, istore_1, iload_4, isub, istore_3, return"*, their corresponding types will be *"P, P, P, O_P, C, P, O_P, C, T"*. The one-to-one mapping results are shown in Table 1.

In the table, registers *Rb*, *Rc* and *Rd* are temporary registers allocated by the register file control engine. When bytecodes are fetched, the Folding Manager Unit will detect the first *O*, *T_P* or *C* type bytecode. Since it is *O_P* type (*iadd*), the Folding Manager Unit will check whether the next bytecode to the *iadd* is *C* type or not. The

Table 1. Mapping results by one to one

Bytecode	jHISC instruction
iload_2	data.move Rb R2
iload_1	data.move Rc R1
iload_3	data.move Rd R3
iadd	arith.add Rc, Rc Rd
istore_1	data.move R1 Rc
iload 4	data.move Rc R4
isub	arith.sub Rb Rb Rc
istore_3	data.move R3 Rb
return	rvk

two previous *P* type bytecodes adjacent to the *iadd* and the *C* type bytecodes will then form a folding group and are folded into the jHISC instruction *arith.add R1 R1 R3*. In the same way, bytecodes in group 2 can also be folded into the jHISC instruction (*arith.sub R3 R4 R2*). The bytecode *return* is *T* type and is translated into the jHISC instruction *rvk* directly. The folding results are presented in Table 2. We observe that the instruction length is reduced from 9 to 3 after folding and the temporary registers are not needed.

Table 2. Folding results

Original bytecodes	Folding group	jHISC instruction
iload_2	group 1: iload_1, iload_3, iadd, istore_1	arith.add R1 R1 R3
iload_1	group 2: iload_2, iload 4, isub, istore_3	arith.sub R3 R4 R2
iload_3	group 3: return	rvk
iadd		
istore_1		
iload 4		
isub		
istore_3		
return		

5   Performance Estimation

The proposed folding algorithm was evaluated based on the JVM98 benchmark trace analysis, which was a Java benchmark suit released by the Standard Performance Evaluation Corporation (SPEC) [14]. JVMTI profiler [12] was used to implement the proposed folding algorithm, trace bytecodes at run-time, and dump the executed bytecodes, the folding jHISC instructions and some other results. The analysis in this Section is based on these dumped results.

5.1   Folded P and C Type Bytecodes

Fig. 2 shows the percentages of the folded P and C type bytecodes relative to all operations and stack operations. With respect to all stack operations, the percentage of the eliminated P and C type instructions varies from 87% to 98% and the average is about 93%. However, the Sun's folding algorithm in PicoJava II folded up to 60% of all stack operations [2-3] [10]. The POC folding algorithm with 4-foldable strategy reduced up to 84% of all stack operations [6]. And the advanced POC folding algorithm claimed to eliminate about 93% of all stack operations in case load and store operations on array were mistaken to be treated as P and C type operations, respectively. Thus the actual folding ratio is smaller than 93%. With respect to all operations, the percentage of the eliminated P and C type instructions is from 42.2% to 51.8% and the average is 47% in the proposed folding algorithm.

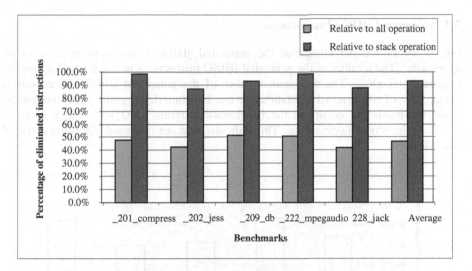

Fig. 2. Folded P and C type bytecodes

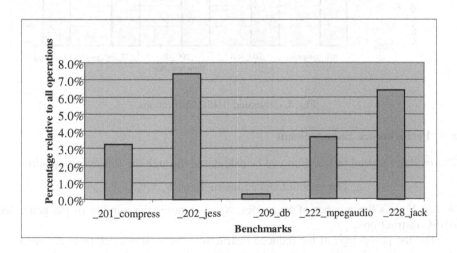

Fig. 3. Added data move operations

5.2 Added Data Move Operations

During instruction folding or translation, some data move operations are added because the two operated data may be 16-bit immediate value in Java bytecodes and the jHISC instruction is only 32 bits in length. For example, if two 16-bit immediate data precede a bytecode *iadd*, during instruction folding and translation, one immediate datum needs to firstly move to a register through a data move operation, and then the corresponding bytecodes are translated into the jHISC instruction *arith.addi*. The percentage of the added operations relative to all operations is shown in Fig. 3, which varies from 0.3% to 7.4%.

5.3 Generated jHISC Instructions

Fig. 4 shows the percentage of the generated jHISC instructions relative to all operations. The number of the generated jHISC instructions is much smaller than the original bytecodes. The minimum number of the generated jHISC instructions is about 50% of the original operations in the benchmark program _222_mpegaudio while the maximum occurs in the benchmark program _202_jess, which is about 63.7% of the original operations. This indicates that our proposed algorithm is useful and effective.

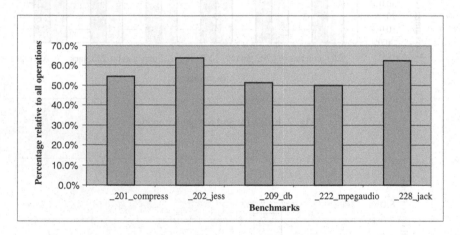

Fig. 4. Generated jHISC instructions

5.4 Performance Enhancement

The overall reduced instructions can be calculated through the following equation.

$$\text{The overall reduced instructions } N = N_{total} - N_{jHISC}$$

Where N_{total} is the number of bytecodes, N_{jHISC} denotes the number of the generated jHISC instructions.

Thus the percentage of the reduced instructions over all operations is obtained and shown in Fig. 5. The worst folding efficiency is in the benchmark program _202_jess, where the reduced instructions are about 37% of all operations. The best

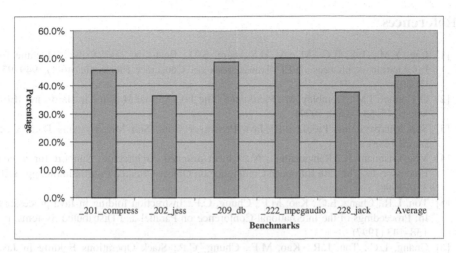

Fig. 5. Performance enhancement

folding efficiency appears in the benchmark program _222_mpegaudio, where more than 50% of all operations are reduced. And averagely, about 44% of all operations can be reduced in the benchmarks, which means that the actually executed instructions are only 56% of the original bytecode instructions before folding.

6 Conclusion

More and more complex Java programs are applied in embedded devices, such as complicate games, network application programs. These require processors in embedded devices to have good performance to run Java programs. To address this, a new instruction folding algorithm is presented to improve the performance of a Java processor. In this folding algorithm, all bytecodes are classified into five types according to their behaviors of handling the operand stack, and the intermediate results of incomplete folding groups are written into buffers and treated as P type bytecodes for further folding.

With respect to all stack operations, the percentage of the eliminated P and C type instructions varies from 87% to 98% and the average is about 93% in the proposed folding algorithm. The overall reduced instructions are from 37% to 50% of all operations, and averagely, about 44% of all operations can be reduced in the benchmarks. Compared with other folding algorithms, the proposed algorithm has a great improvement on folding efficiency and system performance.

Acknowledgment

This work is partially supported by the City University of Hong Kong under Strategic Research Grant 7001847.

References

[1] Lee, Y.M., Tak, B.C., Maeny, H.S., Kim, S.D.: Real-time Java Virtual Machine for Information Appliances. IEEE Transactions on Consumer Electronics 46(4), 949–957 (2000)

[2] O'Connor, J.M., Tremblay, M.: PicoJava-I: The Java Virtual Machine in Hardware. IEEE Micro, 45–53 (March 1997)

[3] Sun Microsystems: PicoJava-II: Java Processor Core, Sun Microsystems Data Sheet (April 1998)

[4] Vijaykrishnan, N., Ranganathan, N.: Object-oriented Architecture Support for a Java Processor. In: The 12th European Conference on Object-Oriented Programming, pp. 330–354 (1998)

[5] Ton, L.R., Chang, L.C., Kao, M.F., Chung, C.P.: Instruction folding in Java processors. In: Proceedings of the International Conference on Parallel and Distributed Systems, pp. 138–143 (1997)

[6] Chang, L.C., Ton, L.R., Kao, M.F., Chung, C.P.: Stack Operations Folding in Java Processors. IEE Proc.-Comput. Digit. Tech. 145(5), 333–340 (1998)

[7] Kim, A., Chang, M.: Java Bytecode Optimization with Advanced Instruction Folding Mechanism. In: Valero, M., Joe, K., Kitsuregawa, M., Tanaka, H. (eds.) ISHPC 2000. LNCS, vol. 1940, pp. 268–275. Springer, Heidelberg (2000)

[8] Ton, L.R., Chang, L.C., Shann, J.J., Chung, C.P.: Design of an Optimal Folding Mechanism for Java Processors. Microprocessors and Microsystems 26, 341–352 (2002)

[9] El-Kharashi, M.W.: The JAFARDD Processor: A Java Architecture Based on Folding Algorithm, with Reservation Stations, Dynamic Translation, and Dual Processing. Phd. Dissertation, University of Victoria

[10] El-Kharashi, M.W., Elguibaly, F., Li, K.F.: A Robust Stack Folding Approach for Java Processor: an Operand Extraction-based Algorithm. Journal of Systems Architecture 47, 697–726 (2001)

[11] Yiyu, T., Hang, Y.C., et al.: Design and Implementation of a Java Processor. IEE Proceedings on Computer and Digital Techniques 153(1), 20–30 (2006)

[12] Sun Microsystems: JVMTM Tool Interface (JVMTI) Version 1.0. http://java.sun.com/ j2se/1.5.0/docs/guide/jvmti/jvmti.html

[13] Yiyu, T., Yiu, L.W., Hang, Y.C., et al.: A JAVA Processor with Hardware-Support Object-Oriented Instructions. Microprocessors and Microsystems 30(8), 469–479 (2006)

[14] SPEC: JVM98 benchmark suits. http://www.spec.org/jvm98/

HNDP: A Novel Network Distance Prediction Mechanism

Chang-you Xing and Ming Chen

Dep. of Computer, PLA Univ. of Science & Technology,
210007 Nanjing, China
{xcy,cm}@plaust.edu.cn

Abstract. Network distance is an important parameter in optimizing performance of network applications. Although there are a number of network distance prediction mechanisms, they all take no consideration of Internet structure, which has great influence on Internet distance characteristics. By analyzing the hierarchical structure feature of Internet, a hierarchical network distance predication mechanism called HNDP is proposed. HNDP divides Internet into many independent prediction regions, and predicts distance information between network nodes by accumulating distances in different predication regions, which can avoid the problem that short distance and long one cannot be accurately predicated simultaneously. To optimize the influence of landmark selection on HNDP prediction accuracy, a shortest distance cover landmark selection model is proposed, and then a tabu search algorithm called TS_Landmark is given to solve this model in HNDP. Finally, the simulation results under ns-2 show that TS_Landmark can select landmarks effectively, and HNDP provides more accurate results than traditional single layer ones.

Keywords: network distance, space embedding, hierarchical structure, predication region, landmark selection.

1 Introduction

Nowadays, new distributed network applications such as grid, CDN (Content Distribution Network) and online games evolve rapidly, which have a more strict QoS demands. In these applications, more than one node provides the same service. Thus, if client node can obtain the lower network performance information and choose a best server node based on this information, the application performance will be increased dramatically. For example, In P2P applications, network performance information will help a client find out which peer is the best one to download files from. Likewise, in a CDN, an optimized client can download Web objects from the particular mirror site to which it has the highest bandwidth.

However, IP network uses a best effort service model and does not provide any QoS guarantee to upper layer applications, and it also provides no network performance information. On the other hand, on-demand network measurements are expensive and time-consuming, especially when the number of possible communication peers is large. Thus, a suitable performance service model is needed to predict

K. Li et al. (Eds.): NPC 2007, LNCS 4672, pp. 425–434, 2007.

unknown network performances from a set of partially observed measurements. Among all kinds of network performance parameters, Round Trip Time (RTT, which we call it network distance here) is an important and easy to acquire one. Quite a number of network distance prediction mechanisms have been proposed now. The key of network distance prediction lies in that predicting the distance of arbitrary nodes in network accurately using as small number of measurement as possible.

One way to predict network distance is to embed the network into a finite-dimension geometric space, and assign each node a virtual coordinate in that space. The distance of any two nodes can be computed by their coordinates using distance computation function in that geometric space [1-5]. In this paper, we make the following contributions:

a) Combination with Internet hierarchical structure, we propose a Hierarchical Network Distance Prediction mechanism (HNDP), in which Internet is divided into different predication regions according to network nodes relationship, and the distance of two nodes is predicted by the accumulation of distances predicted in each related region. In this way, we take full use of Internet structure to avoid the interference of different predication regions during virtual coordinate space construction, and increase the prediction accuracy.
b) We give a shortest distance cover landmark selection model, and design a tabu search landmark selection algorithm called TS_Landmark to solve this model in HNDP. The analysis results show us that TS_Landmark can select landmark set effectively.

The rest of the paper is organized as follows. Section 2 presents a short survey of the embedding techniques. Section 3 presents a Hierarchical Network Distance Prediction mechanism HNDP and a shortest distance cover landmark election model. A tabu search landmark selection algorithm TS_Landmark is also proposed in this section to solve the landmark selection problem. Section 4 gives a theoretical analysis and simulation evaluation of the performance of HNDP and TS_Landmark. Finally, Section 5 summarizes our work.

2   Related Works

T. Ng firstly proposed a distance predication mechanism named GNP (Global Network Positioning) [1], in which the whole Internet is modeled as a Euclid space, and each node is assigned a coordinate in that space according to its distance to some special nodes (called landmarks). Then distances between any two nodes can be computed using distance computation function in Euclid space.

However, GNP treats Internet as a flat space, and each node in the space has an equal status, which is in conflict with the fact that today's Internet has a hierarchical structure. Therefore, short distances predicted by this mechanism always have a large relative error. R. Zhang gave a detailed research on Internet distance predication error [6]. Based on the fact that most distance predication mechanisms cannot reduce relative error of short distance and long distance simultaneously, they propose a hierarchical distance predication mechanism, in which the relationship between network nodes is divided into short and long according to their distances. When the distance between two nodes is shorter than a threshold, it uses short distance predication method; otherwise it uses long distance predication method. However, this model is still too simple to describe the Internet structure.

On the other hand, in order to solve problems brought by using Euclid Space as embedding space (such as distance triangle inequality, distance symmetry, and so on), IDES [12] assigned each network node two vectors: ingress coordinate vector and egress coordinate vector. Distance between two nodes is computed by the inner product of source node's egress coordinate vector and destination node's ingress coordinate vector. Virtual Landmarks [3] and Internet Coordinate System [4] are also two virtual coordinate based network distance predication mechanisms, but they use Lipschitz space embedding instead of Euclid space embedding.

The study of Costa showed that landmark selection criterion has a great influence on distance predication accuracy. Closest node selection criterion can increase short distance predication accuracy, but meanwhile it has negative influence on long distance predication accuracy [4]. They proposed a mixture landmark selection mechanism, which combined the random selection and closest selection criterion. However, in [6] R. Zhang showed that mixture landmark selection mechanism still lacked the ability to predict all kinds of distances accurately.

3 Hierarchical Network Distance Predication Mechanism

Actually, the Internet hierarchy can be divided into international backbones, national backbones, area networks and local networks. Nodes in an area network have a high connectivity with each other, which gives a large aggregation coefficient in the network. The highly aggregate area networks are connected sparsely by international backbones and national backbones [8]. Therefore, the core network is a mesh structure composed of high performance routers and high speed links, while the edge network is composed of tree-liked area networks. Edge network connects to core network using low rate links.

The area characteristics of Internet can help us handle one area with no influence on other areas. Meanwhile, its hierarchical structure results in the network performance asymmetric. For example, in edge network there are a large number of nodes, but network bandwidth is not very high, which causes the range and frequency of network delay variation is large. But in the core network, high performance routers connect to each other with dedicated high speed links, therefore network delay variation is stable. Most of today's network distance predication mechanisms treat Internet as a flat structure, and embed it into a single geometric space, therefore, much of the Internet structure information is lost during the embedding process, which leads to high predication error. In fact, the area and hierarchy characteristics of Internet affect not only network traffic distribution [9], but also the network distance predication accuracy. In this paper, we design a decentralized Hierarchical Network Distance Predication mechanism (HNDP), in which Internet is divided into different predication regions according to network nodes relationship, and the distance of two nodes is predicted by the accumulation of distances predicted in each related area. By this means, we take full use of Internet structure to avoid the interference of different predication regions during virtual coordinate space construction. Each predication region can choose coordinate update period according to its own network condition, therefore the network intrusion is reduced with guarantee to predication accuracy.

3.1 Definition of HNDP

In HNDP, based on the Internet topology characteristics, we divide the whole Internet into edge network and core network. Core network is embedded into a geometric space as a whole; while edge network is divided into small regions according to network distance and administrative relationship. Each small region is embedded into an independent coordinate space. To describe this mechanism accurately, we firstly give some definitions of HNDP as follows.

Definition 1: Region. An area that is composed of one or more ASes. It can be embedded into a virtual coordinate space independently.

Definition 2: Core. Region that is composed of tier-1 and tier-2 ISPs. This region is located in network core, and in HNDP, there is only 1 Core.

Definition 3: Edge. Regions that are composed of tier-3 and access ISPs. There is more than one Edge in HNDP, and different Edges have no intersection. Each Edge has one or more intersected nodes with Core according to its access relationship.

Definition 4: Dual. The set of intersected nodes between Core and Edges. They are embedded both into Core prediction region and its own Edge prediction region, thus have two different coordinates.

Definition 5: Prediction error:

Suppose d_{ij} is the measured distance between node i and node j, and $\hat{d}_{ij}$ is the predicted distance after assigning coordinate $(x_i, y_i, ..., u_i)$ and $(x_j, y_j, ..., u_j)$ to node i and node j. Thus, the error between predicted distance and measured distance is

$$error_{ij} = d_{ij} - \hat{d}_{ij} \tag{1}$$

In which

$$\hat{d}_{ij} = ((x_i - x_j)^p + (y_i - y_j)^p + ... + (u_i - u_j)^p)^{1/p} \tag{2}$$

For Euclid Space, here we have $p = 2$.

We define error function

$$error = \sum_{i,j} (d_{ij} - \hat{d}_{ij})^2 \tag{3}$$

Therefore using multi-dimension downhill simplex algorithm [10], we can find out $(x_i, y_i, ..., u_i)$ and $(x_j, y_j, ..., u_j)$ that minimize error, and these coordinates are the best coordinates for node i and node j.

The principle of HNDP can be seen from a simple network demonstration in Fig. 1, in which the network is divided into 5 prediction regions: An independent network structure in the center and its neighbor dual nodes are defined as Core; each edge network and its related dual nodes are defined as an independent Edge. Core shares one or more dual nodes with each Edge.

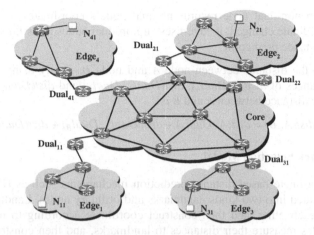

Fig. 1. Prediction region partition based on Internet hierarchical structure

Firstly, each prediction region is embedded into an independent Euclid Space, thus every non-dual node is assigned a coordinate, and every dual node is assigned two coordinates. When doing distance prediction, if two nodes i and j are in the same region, then their distance is computed directly using their coordinates; otherwise their distance is the distance from i to its dual nodes set plus the distance from j to its dual nodes set plus the distance between the two dual nodes sets.

When doing distance accumulation, each distance is computed in an independent coordinate space. An Edge may have more than one dual node, i.e., for node N_{21} in Fig. 1, we can see that it has two dual nodes $Dual_{21}$ and $Dual_{22}$. For this condition, we define the predicted distance is the smaller one among all possible ones. Due to the practical Internet structure, the number of each Edge network's dual nodes is limited. Therefore our definition above is meaningful.

3.2 Hierarchical Distance Prediction Mechanism

From the above discussion, we can give the flow of HNDP as follows.

Step 1. Initialization
   a) Dividing network into *Core*, *Edge* according to network topology, and determining *Dual* in network;
   b) Selecting landmarks in each prediction region using landmark selection model, which is discussed in the following section.

Step 2. Virtual coordinate computation
   a) Landmarks in each prediction region measure distances to each other, and then construct their coordinates $(x,y,...,u)$ in the embedded space by minimizing error between predicted distance and measured distance;
   b) Each non-dual node in the prediction region measures its distances to landmarks in the same prediction region, and then constructs its coordinate accordingly. Since dual nodes lie in both *Edge* and *Core*, they have two coordinates;

c)   Each non-dual node records its dual node's coordinates. If a dual node's coordinate changed, it advertises all non-dual nodes in its *Edge* to update.

Step 3. Distance prediction

To predict the distance between node A and node B, Firstly using coordinates to compute distances of $dist(A, Dual_A)$, $dist(Dual_A, Dual_B)$ and $dist(Dual_B, B)$, and then predicting the distance between A and B is:

$$dist(A, B) = dist(A, Dual_A) + dist(Dual_A, Dual_B) + dist(Dual_B, B). \qquad (4)$$

3.3   Landmark Selection Model

In virtual coordinate based distance prediction mechanisms such as HNDP, network nodes are divided into two kinds: landmarks and ordinary nodes. Landmarks measure distances to each other, and then construct coordinate according to measured data; Ordinary nodes measure their distances to landmarks, and then construct coordinate according to measured data and landmark coordinate. From some kind of view, when doing embedding from network distance space to other coordinate space, we firstly distill the basic feature of network distance space by landmark selection, and then determine ordinary nodes coordinates based on landmarks coordinates and the distances between them and landmarks. Thus, landmark selection has a vital influence on prediction accuracy. Firstly, the more landmarks we select, the more accurate distance prediction we get, but at the same time the more cost we have to pay; Secondly, if two landmarks are too close to each other, they nearly provide the same network distance information, thus we need only keep one of them to decrease the total cost.

Theoretically, each node in network can be selected as landmark, which means the number of possible solutions is terribly high for landmark selection. What's more, the relationship between landmark selection and distance prediction accuracy is very complex. As a result, the best landmark selection problem is relatively difficult to solve. The research of Costa showed that selecting closest nodes as landmarks can help improving short distance prediction accuracy, but it has negative effect on long distance prediction accuracy [4]. This phenomenon can be explained as follows. Each landmark contains distance information of its neighbor network with some scope, if a link lies in a landmark's scope, then the prediction accuracy will be high, otherwise the prediction accuracy will be low. Thus, landmark selection problem can be described in another way: How can we select a certain number of nodes that distribute in the network as uniformly as possible? Combined with the classical facility location problems in Math, we propose a shortest distance cover based landmark selection model, and then give a Tabu search approximation algorithm to solve that problem.

(1) Model Description

In a network with m nodes, suppose that

$N = \{N_1, N_2, \cdots, N_m\}, N_i (i = 1, 2, \cdots, m)$ is the set of nodes;

$L = \{L_1, L_2, \cdots, L_k\}, L_j (j = 1, 2, \cdots, k)$ is the set of landmarks;

d_{ij} is the shortest distance from landmark L_j to node N_i;

$D(L, N_i) = \min_{j \in L} d_{ij}$ represents distance landmark set to node N_i;

According to the analysis before, a good landmark set has the following aspect: the distance between landmark set and each node in the network should be as small as possible. Therefore, the landmark selection problem in network distance prediction can be described as follows: Given a network with m nodes, which k of them should be selected as landmarks, so that the distance of each node in the network to landmark set is minimized. Formally, the model is described as follows:

$$\min F(L) = \min \sum_{i \in N} D(L, N_i)$$

$$= \min \sum_{i \in N} \min_{j \in L} d_{ij}$$

(5)

(2) Tabu Search based Landmark Selection Algorithm TS_Landmark

The above problem is NP hard, and it's impossible to solve it in the whole Internet scale. However, in HNDP, we reduce the computation scale by prediction region partition, and prediction regions are also independent with each other, thus we can use this model on each prediction region and solve it with a suitable heuristic algorithm. Here we propose a Tabu Search based landmark selection algorithm TS_Landmark [13, 14], which is described as follows:

```
L: Random Selected Landmark Set.
L*: Best Landmark Set.
F(L*): Objective Function Value of Best Landmark Set.
A(s, L): Aspiration Function.
T: Tabu List.
Max-gen: Maximum Iteration Generation.

TS-Landmark(L, Max-gen) {
        T=null;
        L*=L;
        F(L*)=∞;
        A(s,L)= F(L*);
        gen = 1;
        while(gen < Max-gen) {
          for each i IN L {
            for each j (in neighbor(i) AND NOT in L AND T)
                    Si = Si + {j};
            L'= L'+best(Si);
          }
          if(F(L')<A(s,L)){
              A(s,L)=F(L');
              L=L';
          }
          if(F(L')<A(s,L))
              L*=L;
          gen = gen + 1;
        }
}
```

The algorithm uses search steps as stop condition, which can be set flexibly according to accuracy requirements. Obviously, if we set *Max-gen*=1 here, the algorithm regresses to a random selection algorithm.

4 HNDP Predication Accuracy Analysis

Firstly we give the definition of absolute prediction error and relative prediction error as follows:

$$error_{abs} = |\ predist - meadist\ | \tag{6}$$

$$error_{relative} = \frac{error_{abs}}{meadist} \tag{7}$$

In which *predist* stands for the predicted distance, and *meadist* stands for measured distance; with this two parameters we can justify the departure degree of different prediction mechanisms between predicted distance and measured distance.

To evaluate the performance of HNDP, we use Waxman random topology generation algorithm in BRITE [11] generate a 2 layer and 1000 nodes network, and the distances between network nodes are generated by BRITE randomly. Then we use this topology as ns2 simulation network.

Simulation scenario 1: Relative error of TS_Landmark algorithm.

Firstly we determine the ideal landmark set L_r based on network distance, and compute the sum of distances S_r from L_r to each node in the network. Then we use TS_Landmark select a landmark set L, and compute the sum of distances S from L to each node in the network. The relative error is

$$err = \frac{S - S_r}{S} \tag{8}$$

Obviously, here *err* is always larger than 0. During the simulation, we record the relative error *err* under different size of landmark set, and the curve is shown in Fig.2.

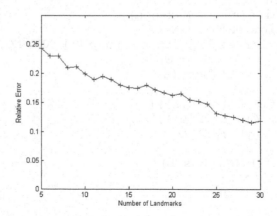

Fig. 2. Relative error of landmark selection

We can see that the relative errors of TS_Landmark are all less than 0.25 and larger than 0 in Fig. 2, and as the number of landmarks increases, the distance prediction relative error tends to become smaller. One reason for this phenomenon is that as the number of landmarks increases, the possibility that TS_Landmark selects good landmarks increases too, therefore the relative error between computed value and best value decreases accordingly. One extreme instance is that if we choose all nodes as landmarks, then the relative error will be 0.

Simulation Scenario 2: Distance Prediction Error Analysis.

To compare the relative prediction error of different distance prediction mechanisms, we use GNP, Random Landmark Selection based HNDP (Random HNDP) and Tabu Search Landmark Selection based HNDP (Tabu HNDP) to predict a given network separately, and the parameters used during simulation is shown as follows.

The cumulative distributions of three different distance prediction mechanisms' relative error is shown in Fig. 3.

Fig. 3 shows that both Random HNDP and Tabu HNDP are more accurate than GNP, which means that by partitioning Internet into different prediction regions the distance prediction accuracy can be increased. Meanwhile, Tabu HNDP is more accurate than Random HNDP. That is to say, by using TS_Landmark, better landmarks are selected, and thus the distance prediction accuracy is increased accordingly.

Table 1. Simulation parameters configuration

Parameters	GNP	Random HNDP	Tabu HNDP
Landmark Number	30	30	30
Landmark Selection	Random	Random	Tabu Search
Regions Number	1	5	5
Embedding Space	5D Euclid	5D Euclid	5D Euclid
Coordinate Algorithm	downhill simplex	downhill simplex	downhill simplex

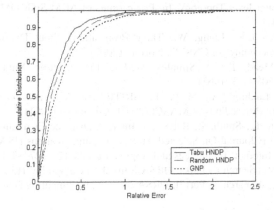

Fig. 3. Cumulative distribution of distance prediction relative error

5 Conclusion

Based on the hierarchical structure of Internet, a decentralized hierarchical network distance prediction mechanisms HNDP is proposed. In HNDP, Internet is divided into a Core prediction region and quite a number of Edge prediction regions. Each region is embedded into an independent geometric space. Thus the interfering problem of predicting precision between short distance and long distance is decreased, and the accuracy and flexibility of distance prediction is increased. The landmark selection has proven having the vital influence on HNDP prediction accuracy, so a shortest distance cover based landmark selection model is proposed, and a tabu search algorithm is also given to solve that model. The analysis and simulation results show us that both Random HNDP and Tabu HNDP have higher prediction accuracy than GNP.

References

1. Ng, T.S., Zhang, H.: Predicting Internet Network Distance with Coordinates-Based Approaches. In: Proceedings of IEEE INFOCOM'02, June 2002, New York (2002)
2. Lim, H., Hou, J.C., Choi, C.H.: Constructing an Internet Coordinate System Based on Delay Measurement. In: Proceedings of ACM IMC'03, October 2003, Miami (2003)
3. Tang, L., Crovella, M.: Virtual Landmarks for the Internet. In: Proceedings of ACM IMC'03, October 2003, Miami (2003)
4. Costa, M., Castro, M., Rowstron, A.: PIC: Practical Internet Coordinates for Distance Estimation. In: Proceedings of IEEE ICDCS'04, March 2004, Tokyo (2004)
5. Chen, Y., Katz, R.: Internet Iso-bar: A Scalable Overlay Distance Monitoring System. Journal of Computer Resource Management, Spring Edition (2002)
6. Zhang, R.M., Tang, C.Q., Hu, C.: Impact of the Inaccuracy of Distance Prediction Algorithms on Internet Applications. In: Proceedings of IEEE INFOCOM'06, April 2006, Barcelona (2006)
7. Zhang, R.M., Hu, C., Lin, X.J.: A Hierarchical Approach to Internet Distance Prediction. In: Proceedings of IEEE ICDCS'06, Lisboa, Portugal (2006)
8. Li, L., Alderson, D., Willinger, W.: A First Principles Approach to Understanding the Internet's Router-level Topology. In: Proceedings of ACM SIGCOMM'04, August 2004, Portland (2004)
9. Chen, M., Pei, L.B., Liang, W.: Three Propositions about Distributions of Network Traffic. In: Proceedings of CNS'07, Norfolk (2007)
10. Nelder, J., Mead, R.: A Simplex Method for Function Minimization. Computer Journal 8(7), 308–313 (1965)
11. Medina, A., Lakhina, A., Matta, I.: BRITE: An Approach to Universal Topology Generation. In: Proceedings of MASCOTS'01, Cincinnati (2001)
12. Mao, Y., Saul, L., Smith, J.: IDES: An Internet Distance Estimation Service for Large Networks. IEEE Journal On Selected Areas in Communications (JSAC), Special Issue on Sampling the Internet, Techniques and Applications 24(12), 2273–2284 (2006)
13. Glover, F.: Tabu Search — Part I. ORSA Journal on Computing 1(3), 190–206 (1989)
14. Glover, F.: Tabu Search — Part II. ORSA Journal on Computing 2(1), 4–32 (1990)

Analytical Model of IEEE 802.15.4 Non-beacon Mode with Download Traffic by the Piggyback Method

Tae Ok Kim[1], Jin Soo Park[2], Kyung Jae Kim[1], and Bong Dae Choi[1]

[1] Department of Mathematics and Telecommunication Mathematics Research Center,
Korea University, Seoul, Korea
{violetgl,kimkjae,queue}@korea.ac.kr
[2] USN Service Division, KT, Seoul, Korea
vtjinsoo@paran.com

Abstract. We analyze the MAC performance of the IEEE 802.15.4 LR-WPAN non-beacon mode with the piggyback method in non-saturated condition. Our approach is to model a stochastic behavior of one device as a discrete time Markov chain. We propose an analytical model describing the download behavior of a device using piggyback method. We obtain the performance measures such as throughput, packet delay, energy consumption and packet loss probability of a device. Numerical results and simulation results show that the piggyback method which removes a backoff procedure in the backoff method can reduce the delay, loss probability and energy consumption compared with backoff method. Our results can be used to find the optimal number of devices with some constraints on packet delay and packet loss probability.

Keywords: IEEE 802.15.4, Piggyback Method, Performance Analysis.

1 Introduction

IEEE 802.15.4[1],[2] is a standard toward low complexity, low power consumption and low data rate wireless data connectivity. Therefore IEEE 802.15.4 will play a key role as transmission protocol at WSN(Wireless Sensor Network) where energy consumption is an important factor.

Diverse applications for wireless sensor network based on IEEE 802.15.4 have generated interest in analytical models of access mechanism based on CSMA/CA. Pollin et al.[5] and Park et al.[6] proposed analytical model for upload traffic on IEEE 802.15.4 beacon-enabled mode under saturated condition where devices have always packets to send. In real environment, packets are generated in not too often, so that a device will have no packets to send or receive for significant periods. Therefore we need to investigate non-saturated case where a device does not have packets to send or receive for some period of time. Misic et al.[7] analyzed performance of IEEE 802.15.4 with both upload and download traffic in beacon-enabled mode under non-saturated condition.

K. Li et al. (Eds.): NPC 2007, LNCS 4672, pp. 435–444, 2007.

In non-beacon mode, for download data transfers, a device periodically sends a download request packet using CSMA/CA to its coordinator and the coordinator sends an acknowledgment packet to indicate the successful reception of the download data request. The standard of IEEE 802.15.4 specifies two ways to send download data packet. One way is to send download data packet by following backoff procedure using CSMA/CA (See Fig. 1(a)). Such a method is called the backoff method and is called the method with CSMA/CA in the standards. Other way is to send download data packet immediately after ACK packet is sent (i.e. without backoff procedure using CSMA/CA). Such a method is called the piggyback method in this paper, and is called the method without CSMA/CA in the standards. The piggyback method is obtained by removing the backoff period from the backoff method, the piggyback method can shorten the delay of download data packet and so can save the energy consumption. Another merit of piggyback method is that there is no loss of download data packet. We assume that all devices are synchronized, so that the slotted CSMA/CA is applied. Therefore, in order to protect acknowledge packets, implementation of two consecutive CCA (clear channel assessment) is assumed. Only these assumptions which are slotted CSMA/CA and two consecutive CCAs are different from the standard of IEEE 802.15.4 where unslotted CSMA/CA and only one CCA is used in non-beacon mode. Kim *et. al.*[4] analyzed the performances of IEEE 802.15.4 with backoff method under these assumptions.

In this paper, we investigate the performance of IEEE 802.15.4 with piggyback method and compare performance measures of the piggyback method and backoff method[3]. We model the stochastic behavior of a device with download traffic as a discrete-time Markov chain. First, we propose an analytical model describing the download behavior of a device using piggyback method. Then, we obtain the performance measures such as throughput, packet delay, energy consumption and packet loss probability of a device with download traffic. Numerical results and simulation results show that by removing a backoff procedure in the backoff method, the piggyback method can reduce the delay, loss probability and energy consumption compared with backoff method. Our results can be used for determining the optimal number of devices which can be admitted to the system while supporting the required QoS on the expected packet delay and the packet loss probability.

This paper is organized as follows. We describe the MAC procedure for download in Section 2. In the Section 3.1, we propose the analytical model of a device with download traffic only under non-saturated condition and obtain performance measures from our analysis. Numerical and simulation results for performance measures of the network with download traffic are presented in Section 4.

2   MAC Procedure for Download by Piggybacked Method

When the coordinator wishes to transfer data to a device, it stores the download data packet and waits until the appropriate device makes a contact and requests the data. A device may make contact by transmitting a download request packet

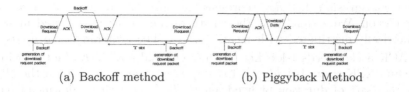

(a) Backoff method   (b) Piggyback Method

Fig. 1. Download procedure in a non-beacon network

using CSMA/CA periodically. The coordinator sends an acknowledgment packet which notifies the successful reception of the download request packet and information on whether there is a download data packet. If data are pending, the coordinator transmits the download data packet, without CSMA/CA (i.e. send download data packet immediately after ACK), to the device. The IEEE 802.15.4 standard[1],[2] allows transmission of download data packet without CSMA/CA. The communication sequences for these download methods are described in Fig. 1(b). After receiving the download data packet, the device sends an acknowledgment packet which notifies the successful reception of the download data packet.

3   Analysis for a Device with Download Traffic Only

Let n sensor devices be associated with the PAN coordinator. For download in IEEE 802.15.4 non-beacon mode, a device sends a download request packet to the PAN coordinator periodically to check whether there is a download data packet at the PAN coordinator. We assume that a device generates a download request packet after fixed number I of slots from the moment of the completion of download procedure (See Fig. 1(b)). We also assume that the PAN coordinator generates a download data packet destined to the tagged device according to Poisson process with rate λ_d and the PAN coordinator can accommodate only one packet for the tagged device. So, if the tagged device has a packet to transmit then arriving packet is discarded. This assumption is reasonable in the case of infrequent packet's arrival in practical applications. The MAC sublayer will retry backoff process to send the packet until the backoff stage reaches to $M(= macMaxCSMABackoffs - 1)$. At the Mth backoff stage, if one of two CCAs fails, the packet is discarded. We assume that if the transmitted packet suffers collision, it will restart from the 0th backoff stage.

3.1   Mathematical Model

Let $s(t)$, $0 \leq s(t) \leq M$, be the backoff stage and $b(t)$ be the backoff counter. Let $(s(t), b(t))_r$ denotes the backoff stage and backoff counter for download request packet. When the channel is idle at the first CCA, we define $b(t) = -1$. We assume that size of download request packet is fixed R in the unit of slots. Let $Tx_r[k]$, $1 \leq k \leq R$, represent the state of the kth slot of download request packet transmission. Let Rx_d represent the state of download data packet in transmission. We assume that the length of data packet measured in slots is geometrically distributed with mean $\frac{1}{1-P_{Rx,d}}$. The switching time needs 1slot and ACK packet needs 1slot. Let (-1, $Switch$) and (-1, ACK) be the switching state and ACK state. Let $idle[k]$, $1 \leq k \leq I$, represent the state of the kth slot from the start of duration of fixed length I for generating download request packet. Define $Y(t)$ at t by :

$$
Y(t) = \begin{cases}
idle[k], & \text{when a device is in the state before generating download request packet} \\
(s(t),b(t))_r, & \text{when a device is in the process of backoff for download request packet} \\
(s(t),-1)_r, & \text{when channel is idle at the first CCA for download request packet} \\
Tx_r[k], & \text{when a device transmits a download request packet} \\
(-1,Swithch)_r, & \text{when a device is waiting ACK for download request packet} \\
(-1,ACK)_r, & \text{when a device is receiving ACK for download request packet} \\
Rx_d & \text{when a device receives a download data packet} \\
(-1,Swithch)_d, & \text{when PAN coordinator is waiting ACK for download data packet} \\
(-1,ACK)_d, & \text{when PAN coordinator is receiving ACK for download data packet}
\end{cases}
\tag{1}
$$

Then $Y(t)$ is a discrete Markov chain with one-step transition probabilities described in Fig. 2 for download procedure. Let $\pi_{idle[k]}$, $\pi_{(i,j)_r}$, $\pi_{(i,-1)_r}$, $\pi_{Tx_r[k]}$, $\pi_{(-1,Switch)_r}$, $\pi_{(-1,ACK)_r}$, π_{Rx_d}, $\pi_{(-1,Switch)_d}$ and $\pi_{(-1,ACK)_d}$ be the steady-state probability.

Next we will calculate the probability α of channel being busy at the first CCA, the probability β of channel being busy at the second CCA and the probability P_s of successful packet transmission.

Since the probability of the channel being idle at the first CCA for the given device is equal to the probability that the all other $n - 1$ devices are

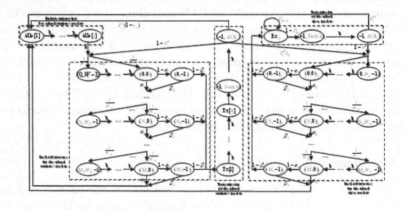

Fig. 2. Markov Chain for Download

not in the states of $Tx_r[k]$, $(-1, Switch)_r$, $(-1, ACK)_r$, Rx_d, $(-1, Switch)_d$ and $(-1, ACK)_d$. Therefore α is given by :

$$\alpha = 1 - (1 - \pi_d)^{n-1} , \tag{2}$$

where

$$\pi_d = \sum_{k=1}^{R} \pi_{Tx_r[k]} + \pi_{Rx_d} + \sum_{j=0}^{A} (\pi_{(-1,Switch)_r} + \pi_{(-1,ACK)_r} + \pi_{(-1,k)_d} + \pi_{(-1,ACK)_d}).$$

Note that in order to be eligible to sense the channel at the second CCA, the channel must be idle at the first CCA. So β is the probability that the channel is busy when the tagged device senses at the second CCA, given that the channel is idle at the first CCA, i.e,

$$1 - \beta = P\{\text{channel is idle at the second CCA} \mid \text{channel is idle at the first CCA}\}$$
$$= \frac{P\{\text{channel is idle at the first CCA, channel is idle at the second CCA}\}}{P\{\text{channel is idle at the first CCA}\}}$$
$$= \frac{\left(1 - \pi_d - \sum_{i=0}^{M} \pi_{(i,-1)_r}\right)^{n-1}}{1 - \alpha} \tag{3}$$

The successful transmission probability, P_s, can be represented by :

$$P_s = P\{\text{successful transmission} \mid \text{channel is idle at both the first CCA and the second CCA}\}$$
$$= \frac{\left\{1 - \pi_d - \sum_{i=0}^{M} \left(\pi_{(i,0)_r} + \pi_{(i,-1)_r}\right)\right\}^{n-1}}{\left(1 - \pi_d - \sum_{i=0}^{M} \pi_{(i,-1)_r}\right)^{n-1}} \tag{4}$$

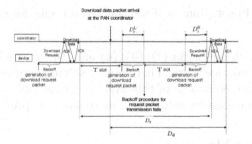

Fig. 3. Description of D_r^L, D_r^S D_r and D_d

Let e_d be the probability that there is a download data packet at the PAN coordinator when download request packet arrives at the PAN coordinator. This event occurs when download data packet arrives during the time duration, D_r, from the completion of one download procedure to the next arrival of download request packet at the PAN coordinator (See Fig. 3). The expected delay $E[D_r]$ are calculated by :

$$E[D_r] = \sum_{k=0}^{\infty}(P_{\text{loss}})^k(1 - P_{\text{loss}}) \cdot \{k(I \cdot \sigma + E[D_r^L]) + (I \cdot \sigma + E[D_r^S])\} + R \cdot \sigma \quad (5)$$

where P_{loss} is the probability of losing download request packet (given by (9)) and σ is the length of a slot. The expected delay $E[D_r^L]$ from the moment of generation of download request packet to the moment of discarding the packet and the expected delay $E[D_r^S]$ from the moment of generation of download request packet to the moment of beginning of download request packet transmission are calculated in Appendix. So, e_d is approximately calculated using $E[D_r]$.

$$e_d \approx 1 - e^{-\lambda_d \cdot E[D_r]} \quad (6)$$

To check the accuracy of the approximation (6), we simulated the system and it turns out that the approximation (6) is quite good (See Fig. 4).

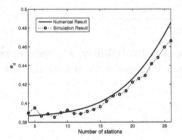

Fig. 4. Numerical and simulation results for e_d

Note that α, β, P_s and e_d in (2), (3), (4) and (6) express in terms of steady-state probability and vice versa. Therefore by solving nonlinear equation of (2), (3), (4), (6), balance equations of this Markov Chain and normalization condition, we obtain all necessary values such as steady-stae probability, α and β.

3.2 Performance Measures

In this subsection, we obtain several performance measures such as throughput, delay, loss probability and energy consumption.

Throughput. The normalized system throughput S, defined as the fraction of time the channel is used to transmit download data packet successfully, is given as follows.

$$S = n \cdot \pi_{Rx_d} \cdot P_s \quad (7)$$

Delay. The expected delay $E[D_d]$ from the moment of download data packet arrival at the PAN coordinator to service completion point is approximately calculated by :

$$E[D_d] \approx E[D_r] + \frac{1}{1 - P_{Rx,d}} + 2A - \frac{\int_0^{E[D_r]} x \cdot \lambda_d e^{-\lambda_d x} \, dx}{1 - e^{-\lambda_d E[D_r]}} \tag{8}$$

The last term in the right-hand side represents the average duration from the completion of previous download procedure to a arrival of next download data packet.

Packet Loss Probability. Let the probabilities of losing download request packet denoted by P_{loss}^r. Then we have

$$P_{loss}^r = \sum_{v=0}^{M} \sum_{w=0}^{v} {}_vC_w \alpha^w \{(1-\alpha)\beta\}^{v-w} (1-\alpha)(1-\beta)(1-P_s) P_{loss}^r$$

$$+ \sum_{w=0}^{M} {}_MC_w \alpha^w \{(1-\alpha)\beta\}^{M-w} \{\alpha + (1-\alpha)\beta\} \tag{9}$$

The general term in the first summation of (9) is the probability that the packet suffers loss after collision at the vth backoff stage in the first backoff procedure. Note that after collision the procedure starts from the 0th backoff stage again. The second term of (9) is the probability that the packet in the first backoff procedure suffers loss because channel is busy at the first CCA or the second CCA at the Mth backoff stage.

After a download data packet arrived in PAN coordinator waits until the download request packet is successfully transmitted from the tagged device and the download data packet is always successfully transmitted because the PAN coordinator transmits the download data packet without CSMA/CA.

Energy Consumption. Since power is quite critical in a sensor network, energy consumption is the most important performance measure. To obtain the total lifetime of a battery, we need a concept of average energy consumption E^{slot} per one slot(mJ/slot). Let E_{idle}, E_{Tx} and E_{Rx} be the energy consumption for idle slot, transmission slot and reception(or CCA) slot, respectively. Since energy consumption for reception slot and CCA slot are equal, we do not distinguish the valus. Let a^{idle}, a^{Tx} and a^{Rx} be the probabilities of slot being idle, being transmission, being reception(or CCA). Then,

$$a^{idle} = \sum_{k=1}^{I} \pi_{idle[k]} + \sum_{i=0}^{M} \sum_{j=1}^{W_i-1} \pi_{(i,j)_r}$$

$$a^{Tx} = \pi_{Tx[k]} + \sum_{j=0}^{A} \pi_{(-1,k)_d}$$

$$a^{Rx} = 1 - a^{idle} - a^{Tx}$$

Note that a device consumes E_{Rx} per one slot when it waits the download data from PAN coordinator.

The average energy consumption E^{slot} per one slot is obtained as follows.

$$E^{\text{slot}} = a^{\text{idle}} E_{idle} + a^{Tx} E_{Tx} + a^{Rx} E_{Rx} \tag{10}$$

4   Numerical and Simulation Results for Both Upload and Download Traffic

In this section, numerical results and simulation results for performance measures of the network in the same environments as in [4] are presented to compare the results of backoff method with one of piggyback method. For our numerical results, I is set to 500 backoff slots. The average length of a download data packet, $\frac{1}{1-P_{\text{Rx,d}}}$, is set to 4. Note that $\sigma = 0.32$ms in case of 250 Mbps, 2.4 GHz. N and M are 2 and 4, respectively. W_0 is set to $2^3 = 8$ in our experiment. The energy consumptions at T_x, R_x, and CCA states are 0.0100224mJ, 0.0113472mJ and 0.0113472mJ, respectively, [6]. A device consumes 0.000056736mJ during idle state.

Fig. 5(a) depicts the expected delay $E[D_d]$ for download traffic of backoff method and piggyback method. As the number of devices increases, $E[D_d]$ for two methods increase due to the exponential backoff by competitions of each other. Fig. 5(b) depicts the packet loss probability for download traffic of backoff method and piggyback method, respectively. Also P^d_{loss} for backoff method increases as the number of devices increases. As mentioned in 3.2, the download packet loss does not occur in piggyback method. Fig. 5(c) depicts the average energy consumption E^{slot} per one backoff slot of both backoff method and piggyback method. Fig. 5 shows that the numerical results and simulation results for performance measures differ slightly. This may be caused by the analytical model where two approximations (6) and (8) are used. Numerical results and simulation results show that by removing a backoff procedure in the backoff method, the piggyback method can slightly reduce the delay for download, loss

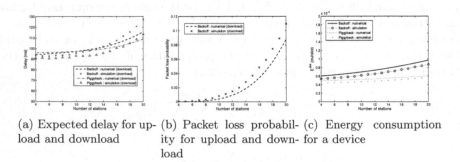

(a) Expected delay for upload and download

(b) Packet loss probability for upload and download

(c) Energy consumption for a device

Fig. 5. Numerical and simulation Results : Performance measures

probability download packet is prevented. Especially, the reduction of energy consumption is remarkable.

Finally, our results are used for determining the optimal number of devices which can be accommodated in the system while supporting the required QoS on the expected packet delay and the packet loss probability. For instance, with the requirements of $E[D_d] \leq 110ms$ and $P_{loss}^d \leq 2\%$, the optimal number of devices in the network is obtained as 20 in backoff method and 13 in piggyback method from Fig. 5(a) and Fig. 5(b). From these results, we can perceive that the new scheme which reduce the delay for download data packet is necessary. With this case, we obtain from Fig. 5(c) that the average energy consumption E^{slot} per one backoff slot is 7.1×10^{-4}mJ/slot in backoff method and 5.3×10^{-4}mJ/slot in piggyback method.

Acknowledgments. This research is supported by the MIC, under the ITRC support program supervised by the IITA.

References

1. IEEE 802.15.4, Wireless LAN Medium Access Control(MAC) and Physical Layer (PHY) specifications for Low-Rate Wireless Personal Area Network (LR-WPANs) (2003)
2. IEEE 802.15.4, Wireless LAN Medium Access Control(MAC) and Physical Layer (PHY) specifications for Low-Rate Wireless Personal Area Network (LR-WPANs) (2006)
3. Kim, T.O., Kim, H., Lee, J., Park, J., Choi, B.D.: Performance Analysis of IEEE 802.15.4 with Non-Beacon-enabled CSMA/CA in Non-Saturated Condition. In: Sha, E., Han, S.-K., Xu, C.-Z., Kim, M.H., Yang, L.T., Xiao, B. (eds.) EUC 2006. LNCS, vol. 4096, Springer, Heidelberg (2006)
4. Kim, T.O., Park, J., Choi, B.D.: Analytic Model of IEEE 802.15.4 with Download Traffic. In: Proceeding of The Second IEEE International Symposium on Pervasive Computing and Ad Hoc Communications (PCAC-07) (May 2007)
5. Pollin, S., Ergen, M., Ergen, S.C., Bougard, B., der Perre, L.V., Catthoor, F., Moerman, I., Bahai, A., Varaiya, P.: Performance Analysis of the Slotted IEEE 802.15.4 Medium Access Layer, draft-jwl-tcp-fast-01.txt (2005)
6. Park, T., Kim, T., Choi, J.Y., Choi, S., Kwon, W.: Throughput and Energy Consumption Analysis of IEEE 802.15.4 Slotted CSMA/CA. Electronics Letters (2005)
7. Misic, J., Shafi, S., Misic, V.B.: Performance of a Beacon Enabled IEEE 802.15.4 Cluster with Downlink and Uplink Traffic. IEEE Transactions on Paraller and Distributed systems 17(4) (April 2006)

Appendix: Delay for Download

In this section, we obtain the expected durations $E[D_r^L]$, $E[D_r^S]$ and $E[D_d*]$ (See Fig. 3). $E[D_r^L]$ is the expected time duration from the moment of generation of download request packet to the moment of discarding the packet, and $E[D_r^S]$ is the expected time duration from the moment of generation of download request packet to the moment of beginning of download request packet transmission. To obtain $\mathrm{E}[D_r^L]$ and $\mathrm{E}[D_r^S]$, let P^c be the probability that a packet suffers collision in a backoff procedure. Then,

$$P^c = \sum_{v=0}^{M} \sum_{r=0}^{v} {}_vC_r \alpha^r \{(1-\alpha)\beta\}^{v-r}(1-\alpha)(1-\beta)(1-P_s) . \tag{11}$$

Let $\mathrm{E}[D_{backoff}^T]$ and $\mathrm{E}[D_{backoff}^L]$ be the expected number of backoff slots that a packet experience until the moment of transmission attempt in a backoff procedure and the expected number of backoff slots that a packet experience until the moment of discarding in a backoff procedure, respectively. Then,

$$\mathrm{E}[D_{backoff}^T] = \frac{\sum_{v=0}^{M} \sum_{r=0}^{v} {}_vC_r \alpha^r \{(1-\alpha)\beta\}^{v-r}(\sum_{i=0}^{v} \frac{W_i-1}{2} + 2v - r + 2)}{\sum_{v=0}^{M} \sum_{r=0}^{v} {}_vC_r \alpha^r \{(1-\alpha)\beta\}^{v-r}} \tag{12}$$

$$\mathrm{E}[D_{backoff}^L] = \frac{\sum_{r=0}^{M} {}_MC_r \alpha^r \{(1-\alpha)\beta\}^{M-r}}{\sum_{r=0}^{M+1} {}_{M+1}C_r \alpha^r \{(1-\alpha)\beta\}^{M+1-r}}$$
$$\times \{\alpha(\sum_{i=0}^{M} \frac{W_i-1}{2} + 2M - r + 1 + (1-\alpha)\beta(\sum_{i=0}^{M} \frac{W_i-1}{2} + 2M - r + 2)\} \tag{13}$$

Note that a download packet is discarded when the CCA fails at the Mth backoff stage. So, the expected duration $\mathrm{E}[D_r^L]$ is given by :

$$\mathrm{E}[D_r^L] = \sum_{k=0}^{\infty} (P^c)^k (1 - P^c) \left\{ k \left(D_{backoff}^T + R + A\right) + D_{backoff}^L \right\} \sigma . \tag{14}$$

The general term in (14) is the expected duration for the case that a packet is discarded after the kth collision. Similarly, the expected duration $\mathrm{E}[D_r^S]$ is given by :

$$\mathrm{E}[D_r^S] = \sum_{k=0}^{\infty} (P^c)^k (1 - P^c) \left\{ k \left(D_{backoff}^T + R + A\right) + D_{backoff}^T \right\} \sigma . \tag{15}$$

The general term in (15) is the expected duration for the case that a packet is successfully transmitted after the kth collision.

A Novel Algorithm for Estimating Flow Length Distributions–LSM*

Weijiang Liu

School of Computer Science and Technology,
Dalian Maritime University, 116026, Dalian, Liaoning, China
wjliu@newmail.dlmu.edu.cn

Abstract. Traffic sampling technology has been widely deployed in front of many high-speed network applications to alleviate the great pressure on packet capturing.Increasingly passive traffic measurement employs sampling at the packet level. Packet sampling has become an attractive and scalable means to measure flow data on high-speed links. However, knowing the number and length of the original flows is necessary for some applications. This paper provides a novel algorithm, Least Square Method(LSM), that uses flow statistics formed from sampled packet stream to infer the absolute frequencies of lengths of flows in the unsampled stream. The theoretical analysis shows that the computational complexity of this method is well under control, and the experiment results demonstrate the inferred distributions are as accurate as EM algorithm.

1 Introduction

With the rapid increase of network link speed, packet sampling has become an attractive and scalable means to measure flow data. However, knowing the number and lengths of the unsampled flows remains useful for characterizing traffic and the resources required to accommodate its demands. Here are some applications: Resources Required for Collecting Flow Statistics: flow cache utilization and the bandwidth for processing and transmitting flow statistics are sensitive to the sampling rate, the number of flows, and flow lengths and duration; see [1,2]. Characterizing Source Traffic: the measured numbers of flows and the distribution of their lengths have been used to evaluate gains in deployment of web proxies [3], and to determine thresholds for setting up connections in flow-switched networks [4]. Sampling entails an inherent loss of information. We expect use statistic inference to recover information as much as possible.

* This work is supported in part by the National Grand Fundamental Research 973 Program of China under Grant No.2003CB314804; the National High Technology Research and Development Program of China (2005AA103001); the Key Project of Chinese Ministry of Education under Grant No.105084; the Jiangsu Provincial Key Laboratory of Computer Network Technology No. BM2003201; Jiangsu Planned Projects for Postdoctoral Research Funds.

K. Li et al. (Eds.): NPC 2007, LNCS 4672, pp. 445–452, 2007.

However, more detailed characteristics of the original traffic are not so easily estimated. Quantities of interest include the number of packets in the flow–we shall refer to this as the flow length–and the number of flows with fixed length.

1.1   Related Work

Kumar et al proposed a novel SCBF that performs per-flow counting without maintaining per-flow state in [5] and an algorithm for estimation of flow size distribution in [6]. Its disadvantage is that all packet must be processed due to not using sampling. Hohn and Veitch in [7] discussed the inaccuracy of estimating flow distribution from sampled traffic, when the sampling is performed at the packet level.

Although sampled traffic statistics are increasingly being used for network measurements, to our knowledge few studies have addressed the problem of estimating flow size distribution from the sampled packet stream. In [2], the authors studied the statistical properties of packet-level sampling using real-world Internet traffic traces. This is followed by [8] in which the flow distribution is inferred from the sampled statistics. After showing that the naive scaling of the flow distribution estimated from the sampled traffic is in general not accurate, the authors propose an EM algorithm to iteratively compute a more accurate estimation. Scaling method is simple, but it exploits the sampling properties of SYN flows to estimate TCP flow frequencies; EM algorithm does not rely on the properties of SYN flows and hence is not restricted to TCP traffic, but its versatility comes at the cost of computational complexity.

1.2   Some Elementary Concepts

This paper considers sampling some target proportion $p = 1/N$ of the packet stream. There are a number of different ways to implement this. Implementations include independent sampling of packets with probability $p = 1/N$, and periodic selection of every N^{th} packet from the full packet stream. In both cases we will call N the sampling period, i.e., the reciprocal of the average sampling rate. Although the length distributions by random and periodic sampling can be distinguished, the differences are, in fact, sufficiently small [8]. A flow is defined as a stream of packets subject to flow specification and timeout. When a packet arrives, the specific rules of flow specification determine which active flow this packet belongs to, or if no active flow is found that matches the description of this packet, a new flow is created. A TCP flow is a stream of TCP packets subject to timeout and having the same source and destination IP addresses, same source and destination port numbers. Similarly, a UDP flow is a stream of UDP packets associated with above specification. A general flow is a stream of packets subject to timeout and having the same source and destination IP addresses, same source and destination port numbers(not considering protocol). In this paper, we will use the term original flow to describe the above flow. A sampled flow is defined as a stream of packets that are sampled at probability $p = 1/N$ from an original flow.

1.3   Contribution and Outline

This paper presents a novel algorithm for estimation of flow size distributions from sampled flow statistics. Our method is available not only to TCP flows but also to general flows. We complete this work using four approaches. The first formalizes the probability distribution of original flow length of a sampled flow length j. The second classifies two types of flows based on their probability that no packet is sampled. A flow is labeled as small (S) when it's probability that no packet is sampled is more than ε and as large (L) when it's probability that no packet is sampled is less than or equal to ε. The third gives a simple estimation method for large flows. The fourth uses Least Square Method to estimate the full distribution of small flows.

The rest of this paper is organized as follows. In Section 2 we analyze the probability models of the original flow length distributions of a sampled flow. In Section 3, we classify two types of flows: small flow and large flow. Then we present different estimation methods for small flows and large flows, respectively. In Section 4 we discuss the computational complexity of our method. Furthermore, we compare our method with EM algorithm in estimation accuracy and computational complexity. We conclude in Section 5.

2   Probability Distribution of Original Flow length

For a specific original flow F, let X_F denote the number of packets in F, Y_F denote the number of packets in the sampled flow from F. The conditional distribution of Y_F, given that $X_F = l$, follows a binomial distribution $Pr[Y_F = k | X_F = l] = B_p(l, k) = \binom{l}{k} p^k (1-p)^{l-k}$. By the conditional probability formula,

$$Pr[X_F = x | Y_F = y] = \frac{Pr[Y_F = y | X_F = x]Pr[X_F = x]}{Pr[Y_F = y]} \tag{1}$$

and by the complete probability formula,

$$Pr[Y_F = y] = \sum_{i=y}^{\infty} B_p(i, y)Pr[X_F = i] \tag{2}$$

we assume that original flow length has a uniform *a priori* distribution. Thus,

$$P[X_F = k] = P[X_F = k+1] \ \ for \ k = 1, 2, \cdots.$$

How to prescribe the default *a priori* distribution has always been a controversial issue in statistics. It is however a widely acceptable practice to use uniform as the default when there are no obviously better choices. Assuming uniform as the default is reasonable also for the following reason. We use Pareto distribution as the default to calculate the probabilities, but we find that they is very close to the probabilities calculated with uniform distribution. However, computational complexity of Pareto is not desirable. So we select uniform as the default.

For fixed k, we sum for all $B_p(l,k), l = k, k+1, \cdots$:

$$\sum_{l=k}^{\infty} B_p(l,k) = \sum_{l=k}^{\infty} \binom{l}{k} p^k (1-p)^{l-k} = p^k \sum_{l=0}^{\infty} \binom{l+k}{k} (1-p)^l$$

$$= p^k \sum_{l=0}^{\infty} \binom{l+k}{k} q^l = p^k (1-q)^{-k-1} = 1/p = N$$

Hence,

$$Pr[Y_F = y] = \sum_{i=k}^{\infty} B_p(l,k) Pr[X_F = i] = Pr[X_F = y] \sum_{i=k}^{\infty} B_p(l,k) = \frac{Pr[X_F = y]}{p}.$$

Therefore,

$$Pr[X_F = x | Y_F = y] = \frac{Pr[Y_F = y | X_F = x] Pr[X_F = x]}{Pr[Y_F = y]}$$

$$= \frac{Pr[Y_F = y | X_F = x] Pr[X_F = x]}{Pr[X_F = y]/p} = p B_p(x,y).$$

We obtain

Lemma 1. *The probability that a sampled flow of length k is sampled from an original flow of length l is*

$$Pr[X_F = l | Y_F = k] = \binom{l}{k} p^k (1-p)^{l-k}, l = k, k+1, \cdots. \tag{3}$$

Lemma 2. *The mean and variance of the above probability distribution are $E\xi = N(k+1) - 1$ and $D\xi = (N+1)N(k+1)$, respectively.*

Let $a_1 = \frac{B_p(l,k)}{B_p(l-1,k)} = 1 + \frac{kN+1-l}{(l-k-1)N}$. For $l \leq kN$, since $a_1 > 1$, hence $B_p(l,k)$ is increasing as l increases. For $l > kN+1$, since $a_1 < 1$, hence $B_p(l,k)$ is decreasing as l increases. At $l = kN+1$, $a_1 = 1$ means that $B_p(l,k)$ is maximized at $l = kN$ and $l = kN + 1$. We have

Lemma 3. *The probability $Pr[X_F = l | Y_F = k]$ is maximized at $l = kN, kN+1$. It is increasing as l increases for $l < kN + 1$ and decreasing as l increases for $l > kN + 1$.*

In following section we will use this conditional probability to estimate large flow length distribution. To our knowledge no studies have addressed the problem of using conditional probability to estimate flow length distribution.

3   Estimation Method of Flow Length Distributions

3.1   Flow Classification: Large Flow and Small Flow

Let $g = \{g_j : j = 1, 2, \cdots, n\}$, where g_j is sampled flow frequencies of length j, be a set of sampled flow length frequencies, $f = \{f_i : i = 1, 2, \cdots, n, \cdots\}$ a set of original flow length frequencies to be estimated. Consider sampling the packets of an original flow of length Nj independently with probability $1/N$, the probability that no packet is sampled is $(1 - 1/N)^{Nj} = ((1 - 1/N)^N)^j$. $\{(1 - 1/N)^N\}$ is increasing in N and $\lim_{N \to \infty} (1 - 1/N)^N = 1/e < 0.37$. Thus for a given error ε, we require $(1 - 1/N)^{Nj} < (1/e)^j < \varepsilon$ and choose $j_{bord} \geq max(j(\varepsilon) = \lceil log(1/\varepsilon) \rceil, \alpha)$. For example, $j(0.01) = 5, j(0.001) = 7$. We classify two types of flows based on their probability that no packet is sampled. A flow is labeled as small (S) when it's probability that no packet is sampled is more than ε and as large (L) when it's probability that no packet is sampled is less than or equal to ε.

3.2   Estimation for Large Flows

For a sampled flow of length $j > j_{bord}$, by Lemma 3, the original flow length values of the $2N$ relatively large probabilities are $N(j - 1), \cdots, N(j + 1)$. We estimate the sampled flow is sampled from one of the $2N$ original flows. Then there are $\frac{g_j}{2N}$ sampled flows that are sampled from one of original flows of the above lengths in $g_j (j > j_{bord})$ sampled flows. Therefore, for all large flows of length $i > N j_{bord}$, we have

$$f_i = \frac{1}{2N}(g_j + g_{j+1}), where\ j = \lfloor (i - 1)/N \rfloor. \tag{4}$$

From Equation (4) we can observe that the number of original flows of length i is calculated by using the numbers of the sampled flows of two different lengths. In fact, this is maximum likelihood estimation for large flows. Since scaling method only use a sample flow length, so this method is more precise. Furthermore, in order to improve accuracy, we can extend the original flow length interval so that a sampled flow can be sampled from one of the more than $2N$ original flows, e.g. $3N$, $4N$. In this case, in order to estimate the number of original flows of a fixed length we need involve the more sampled flows. Since the probability increases, so the estimation is more reliable.

3.3   Least Square Method for Small Flows

For all small flows of length $i \leq N j_{bord}$, we estimate as follows:

$$g_j = \sum_{i=j}^{m} B_p(i, j) f_i, \quad j = 1, \cdots, N j_{bord} \tag{5}$$

where $m = \max\{i : f_i \neq 0\}$. For $i > Nj_{bord}$, substituting (4) into Equations (5):

$$\overline{g}_j = g_j - \sum_{i=Nj_{bord}+1}^{m} B_p(i,j)f_i = \sum_{i=j}^{Nj_{bord}} B_p(i,j)f_i, j = l, \cdots, Nj_{bord}. \qquad (6)$$

For the above some $\overline{g}_j \leq 0$, we replace it with $\delta\overline{g}_{j-1}, 0 < \delta < 1$. For example, we may take $\delta = 0.94$. Hence, we may assume that all $\overline{g}_j > 0$. Since some coefficients of Equations (6) are zero or very small, solving the equations directly may follow a large deviation. Therefore, we use the heavy-tailed feather of flow to reduce the number of the indeterminates of Equations (6).

For $i, l \in [8, Nj_{bord}], i > l$, we have:

$$f_i = (l/i)^k f_l \qquad (7)$$

Substituting Equation (7) into Equations (6):

$$\overline{g}_j = \sum_{i=j}^{l} B_p(i,j)f_i + \sum_{i=l+1}^{Nj_{bord}} B_p(i,j)(l/i)^k f_l, \quad j = 1, \cdots, Nj_{bord}. \qquad (8)$$

Now, we let the values of k increase from 0.5 to 5.0 by increment 0.1. Applying each concrete k of the above values to compute Equations (8), we obtain:

$$y_j^{(k)} = \sum_{i=1}^{l} x_{ji}^{(k)} f_i \quad j = 1, \cdots, Nj_{bord}. \qquad (9)$$

There are l indeterminates and Nj_{bord} equations in Equations (9) where $Nj_{bord} > l$. According to [9], we know least square estimate is unbias and its variance is least. Hence, we use least square method to solve Equations (9) and get the solutions $f_i^{(k)}$, $i = 1, \cdots, l$. If each $f_i^{(k)} > 0, i = 1, \cdots, l$, then let $m_k = \sum_{i=1}^{Nj_{bord}} (y_j^{(k)} - \sum_{i=1}^{l} x_{ji}^{(k)} f_i^{(k)})^2$. We find the value of k such that m_k is minimized in all positive solutions. Denoting the found value as $\overline{k}$, we substitute the corresponding $f_l^{(\overline{k})}$ into Equation (7). Finally, we obtain $f_i^{(\overline{k})}, i = 1, \cdots, Nj_{bord}$. We write our estimation of original small flows as $f_i^{(\overline{k})}, i = 1, \cdots, Nj_{bord}$.

4   Evaluations and Comparison

Computational complexity. Let i_{max} denote the maximum original flow length. The computation for binomial coefficients of Equations (5) is $O(Nj_{bord}i_{max})$. The computation for Least Square Method needs little time. We compare the computational complexity of our method against the best known EM algorithm in [8] for estimating flow distribution from sampled traffic. In [8] for all ϕ_i completing an EM iteration is $O(i_{max}^2 j_{size})$, where j_{size} denote the number of non-zero sampled flow length frequencies g_j. We collect all IP packet heads during a period of 300 minutes at Jiangsu provincial network border of China Education and Research Network (CERNET) (1Gbps) to do offline experiment. For

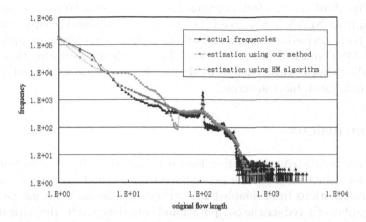

Fig. 1. Comparison of our method and EM algorithm at sampling period $N = 10$ for Jiangsu trace

Table 1. WMRD of our method and EM algorithm

trace	Sampling period	WMRD of our method	WMRD of EM algorithm
Abilence III	10	18%	29%
	30	23%	29%
	100	31%	34%
Jiangsu	10	15%	18%
	30	21%	19%
	100	34%	38%
Abilence I	10	13%	15%
	30	22%	23%
	100	31%	35%

IP header data during a period of 1 minute, sampling packets with $p = 1/10$, $i_{max} = 2000$, $j_{size} = 400$,in our method let $\varepsilon = 0.01$, then $j_{bord} = 5$, thus $(Nj_{bord})i_{max} = 2000 * 50 = 0.1 * 100^3$. However, $i_{max}^2 j_{size} = 2000 * 2000 * 400 = 1600 * 100^3$ in EM algorithm of [8].

Estimation accuracy: We adopt Weighted Mean Relative Difference (WMRD) as our evaluation metric. Suppose the number of original flows of length i is n_i and our estimation of this number is $\hat{n}_i$. The value of WMRD is given by: WMRD= $\frac{\sum_i |n_i - \hat{n}_i|}{\sum_i (\frac{n_i + \hat{n}_i}{2})}$.

We use three traces in our comparison experiments. The first trace is the first publicly available 10 Gigabit Internet backbone packet header trace from NLANR: Abilence III data set [10]. In our experiments , we used a minute of traffic from the trace. The second trace, which contains packets during a 5-minute period , was collected at Jiangsu provincial network border of China Education and Research Network (CERNET) on April 17, 2004. The backbone capacity is 1000Mbps; mean traffic per day is 587 Mbps. We call this trace as Jiangsu trace. The third trace, which contains packets during a 10 minute period, was obtained from NLANR: Abilence I [11]. Figure 1 compares the two estimators of Jiangsu trace derived by our method and EM algorithm of [8] at sampling period $N = 10$. Observe that they are so close. Table 1 shows the estimation accuracy of our algorithm is close enough to that of EM algorithm. In most cases, our algorithm is much more accurate.

5 Conclusions

Estimating the distribution of flow length is important in a number of network applications. In this paper we present a novel method for estimation of flow length distributions from sampled flow statistics. The main advantage is that it could significantly reduce the computational complexity. The theoretical analysis shows that the computational complexity of our method is well under control. The experimental results demonstrate that our method achieves an accurate estimation for flow distribution.

References

1. Duffield, N.G., Lund, C., Thorup, M.: Charging from sampled network usage. In: ACM SIGCOMM Internet Measurement Workshop, November 2001, pp. 245–256 (2001)
2. Duffield, N.G., Lund, C., Thorup, M.: Properties and Prediction of Flow Statistics from Sampled Packet Streams. In: ACM SIGCOMM Internet Measurement Workshop, November 2002, pp. 159–171 (2002)
3. Feldmann, A., Caceres, R., Douglis, F., Glass, G., Rabinovich, M.: Performance of Web Proxy Caching in Heterogeneous Bandwidth Environments. IEEE INFOCOM 99, 107–116 (1999)
4. Feldmann, A., Rexford, J., Caceres, R.: Efficient Policies for Carrying Web Traffic over Flow-Switched Networks. IEEE/ACM Transactions on Networking 6, 673–685 (1998)
5. Kumar, A., Xu, J., Li, L., Wang, J.: Space Code Bloom Filter for Efficient Traffic Flow Measurement. In: IEEE INFOCOM 2004, pp. 1762–1773 (2004)
6. Kumar, A., Sung, M., Xu, J.(Jim.), Wang, J.: Data streaming algorithms for efficient and accurate estimation of flow size distribution. In: ACM Sigmetrics 2004, pp. 177–188 (2004)
7. Hohn, N., Veitch, D.: Inverting Sampled Traffic. In: Internet Measurement Conference October 27-29, 2003, Miami Beach, Florida, USA (2003)
8. Duffield, N.G., Lund, C., Thorup, M.: Estimating Flow Distributions from Sampled Flow Statistics. IEEE/ACM Transation on Networking 13, 933–945 (2005)
9. Xuan, L.: Applied Statistics, pp. 80–89. Tsinghua University Press, Beijing (1999)
10. NLANR: Abilene-III data set, hppt://pma.nlanr.net/Special/ipls3.html
11. NLANR:Abilene-I data set, http://pma.nlanr.net/Traces/long/bell1.html

Performance Prediction for Mappings of Distributed Applications on PC Clusters

Sylvain Jubertie and Emmanuel Melin

Laboratoire d'Informatique Fondamentale d'Orléans (LIFO)
Université d'Orléans
{sylvain.jubertie|emmanuel.melin}@univ-orleans.fr
http://www.univ-orleans.fr/lifo

Abstract. Distributed applications running on clusters may be composed of several components with very different performance requirements. The FlowVR middleware allows the developer to deploy such applications and to define communication and synchronization schemes between components without modifying the code. While it eases the creation of mappings, FlowVR does not come with a performance model. Consequently the optimization of mappings is left to the developer's skills. But this task becomes difficult as the number of components and cluster nodes grow and even more complex if the cluster is composed of heterogeneous nodes and networks. In this paper we propose an approach to predict performance of FlowVR distributed applications given a mapping and a cluster. We also give some advice to the developer to create efficient mappings and to avoid configurations which may lead to unexpected performance. Since the FlowVR model is very close to underlying models of lots of distributed codes, our approach can be useful for all designers of such applications.

1   Introduction

Today, clusters are theoretically able to reach the performances needed by large simulations because they are extensible. This is an interesting property since it does not limit the simulation complexity or the amount of data to consider. However clusters bring new programming problems : it is more complex to produce efficient applications on distributed memory architectures than on shared memory ones. Several communication libraries like MPI or PVM provide point-to-point communications and synchronisations to program clusters efficiently. VR platforms were also ported to clusters to exploit their performances. For example the NetJuggler [7] environment allows to drive interactive applications with parallel simulations and a distributed rendering. These approaches are very interesting but are limited to simple applications assumed to run on homogeneous clusters. For example the model behind NetJuggler is too synchronous because the rendering rate is too dependant of the simulation rate [3].

Consequently we should add more asynchrony between the application parts. For example an interaction and a simulation code should be connected but not

K. Li et al. (Eds.): NPC 2007, LNCS 4672, pp. 453–465, 2007.

synchronized if we want to keep an interactive behaviour because the simulation often have lower frequencies than interaction devices. In this case, we want the simulation to receive interaction data asynchronously even if some are lost. We say that they are linked by *greedy communications*.

Once we have described how to synchronize the application parts, then we can map them on the cluster processors. Many choices are possible depending on the underlying nature of the cluster which may be composed of heterogeneous nodes, peripherals and networks. This mapping is not straightforward and affects the application performance. Consequently, we need a framework that eases mapping operations by catching the parameters of each application part and abstracting the architecture. This framework should also be associated with a performance model to tune efficient mappings.

The FlowVR library[2][4] was created to ease the development of distributed interactive applications and to permit greedy communication. But FlowVR does not offer a way to obtain the best application mapping on a given cluster nor any kind of performance information. Thus the developer should use his experiments and test several configurations to find a good mapping. But this task may become too complex for applications with many parts on heterogeneous clusters such as the application presented in [4] which integrates 5000 different objects.

We propose in this paper a unified approach to analyse at the same time synchronization, concurrency and network constraints. Thus the developer is able to associate performance information to his mappings. For example he can determine information like the frequency of each module, the load on each processor and the communication times for each connection.From these informations the developer can determine if its mapping is well suited and can run on the cluster. Otherwise our approach is able to detect and point out network bottlenecks and modules with low performance. Then the developer can detect parts of the application to optimize and adapt its mapping.

2   The FlowVR Framework

The FlowVR framework is an open source middleware used to build distributed applications. More details on FlowVR can be found in [2]. A FlowVR application is a set of modules which communicate via messages through a data-flow network. Each message is associated with lightweight data called *stamps* which contain information used for routing operations.

Modules are endless iteration which encapsulate tasks. Each module waits until it receives one message on each of its input port. This task is performed by a call to the FlowVR *wait* function. Then messages are retrieved by the *get* function and are processed by the module. Finally the module produces new messages and put them on its output ports with the *put* method.

The data-flow network describes the communication and synchronization schemes between module ports. Each communication is done with a point to point FIFO connection. Operations on messages like routing, broadcasting, merging or scattering are done with a special network component called a *filter*. Synchronization and coupling policy are performed with another network component called a *synchronizer*. Both filters and synchronizers are placed on connections between modules. A *synchronizer* only receives *stamps* from filters or modules. Then it takes a decision according to its coupling policy and sends new *stamps* to destination objects. This decision is finally performed by the destination filters or modules. With the use of synchronizers it is possible to implement the *greedy* filter. This filter allows to respectively write and read a message asynchronously. Thus the destination module always uses the last available message while older messages are discarded. A FlowVR application can be viewed as a graph $G(V, E)$, called the *application graph*, where each vertex in V represents a FlowVR objects like a module, a filter or a synchronizer, and each directed edge in E represents a connection between two objects.

3   Performance Prediction

We now present our approach to compute performance information for a FlowVR mapping on a cluster. Then the developer will be able to determine if his application runs as expected or to compare several mappings to find the best one.

3.1   Model Inputs

A mapping is a FlowVR network enriched with information on the location of modules in the cluster, and on networks used for communication. A cluster is defined as a set of nodes $Nodes$ and a set of networks $Networks$. To deal with SMP nodes, each node $n \in Nodes$ has a list of CPUs given by the function $CPUs(n)$. A node can also have several adapters connected to different networks. Thus each node n is associated to a list of networks $Nets(n) \subset Networks$. Each network $net \in Networks$ has a bandwidth $BW(net)$ and a latency $L(net)$. We assume networks with point-to-point connections in full-duplex handled by dedicated network adapters without CPU overload. We also assume that communication between objects mapped on the same node are costless since objects only exchange pointers to a shared memory. The FlowVR network is a graph G composed of a set of vertices V and a set of directed edges E. Each $v \in V$ represents a FlowVR object i.e. a module, a filter or a synchronizer. Each $e \in E$ represents a connection between a source objects $src(e)$ and a destination object $dest(e)$ with $src(e), dest(e) \in V$. To build a mapping the developer binds FlowVR objects and connections respectively to cluster nodes and networks. We denote the location of an object $v \in V$ by the function $node(m)$ which gives a node $n \in Nodes$. Note that the developer has to map modules on nodes but modules are then mapped on processors by the operating system scheduler. The network used by a connection e is given by the function $Net(e)$ which returns a network $net \in Networks$. If two connected objects are on the same nodes the connection is local: $Net(e) = \emptyset$. Otherwise the connection is associated to a network $net \in Networks$ such as $Net(e) = net$.

Our approach implies that the developer must give extra information on modules to compute performances. For each module $m \in V$ we need to know its execution time $T_{exec}(m)$ and its load $LD(m)$ on the host processor. The execution time $T_{exec}(m)$ is the time needed by a module m to perform one iteration when m is not synchronized with other modules and have no concurrent modules. The load $LD(m)$ is the percentage of $T_{exec}(m)$ used for the computation. The rest of $T_{exec}(m)$ is used for I/O operations. For each edge $e \in E$ we need to know the volume of data $Vol(e)$ sent by $src(e)$ through e during one sole iteration. If $src(e)$ is a module then $Vol(e)$ is equal to the amount of data sent by v through the output port connected to e. If $src(e)$ is a filter then $Vol(e)$ depends on the filter characteristics. For example the *merge* filter sends only one message built from all messages it received. If $src(e)$ is a synchronizer then for the sake of simplicity we assume that $Vol(e) = 0$. Indeed messages sent and received by synchronizers contain only stamps. Consequently their message sizes are negligible compared to the amount of data sent by modules. We also assume that filters and synchronizers have a negligible load compared to module loads. Indeed they only perform some memory operations on messages. The value of $Vol(e)$ is independent of the hardware and is statically determined from the module characteristics. Values of $T_{exec}(m)$ and $LD(m)$ can be determined in different ways. For example the developer can measure them by running each module separately on the target node. On the other hand, FlowVR allows to reuse modules from other applications and $T_{exec}(m)$ and $LD(m)$ may be already available.

3.2   Determining Performance

Performance of modules depend on synchronization and concurrency between them. Thus we need to determine for each module m its iteration time $T_{it}(m)$ and its concurrent execution time $T_{cexec}(m)$. We define $T_{it}(m)$ as the time between two consecutive calls to the FlowVR *wait* function. This definition characterizes the real frequency $F(m)$ of a module execution for a given mapping:

$$F(m) = \frac{1}{T_{it}(m)} \tag{1}$$

We define $T_{cexec}(m)$ as the execution time of m when several modules are running on the same node. Indeed, executions of concurrent modules are interleaved by the OS scheduler. Thus we always have $T_{cexec}(m) \geq T_{exec}(m)$. If m has no concurrent modules then:

$$T_{cexec}(m) = T_{exec}(m) \tag{2}$$

We determine $T_{cexec}(m)$ according to a scheduler policy. But this policy strongly depends on the time a module waits for I/O and is blocked in the FlowVR *wait* function. We first study the effects of synchronization on performances. Then we will evaluate how the concurrency between modules affects their performances.

Determining T_{it} from Synchronization. In this section we examine how synchronization between modules affect their iteration time. For a module m we define its input modules $IM(m)$ as the set of modules with edges connected to m. We distinguish two subsets of $IM(m): IM_s(m)$ and $IM_a(m)$ such as $IM_s(m) \cup IM_a(m) = IM(m)$ and $IM_s(m) \cap IM_a(m) = \emptyset$. The subsets $IM_s(m)$ and $IM_a(m)$ contain respectively the modules connected to m through FIFO connections and through *greedy* filters.

We first consider the effect of *greedy* connections on performance. A module m receiving data through *greedy* filters does not wait for messages from modules in $IM_a(m)$. Indeed a *greedy* filter always provide a message which is the last one available. This means that $T_{it}(m)$ does not depend on synchronizations with modules in $IM_a(m)$. Consequently m is like a module with only FIFO connections. Moreover if $IM_s(m) = \emptyset$ then $T_{it}(m)$ only depends on concurrency with other modules:

$$T_{it}(m) = T_{cexec}(m) \tag{3}$$

Thus to study the effect of synchronization on performance we can remove *greedy* filters from G. We obtain a new graph called G_{sync}. We note that G_{sync} may not be connected anymore and may be splitted into several synchronous components. Since components are not linked we can study each one independently.

We now consider each module m in a component $C \in G_{sync}$. If $IM_s(m) \neq \emptyset$ then m is synchronized with its input modules. To begin its iteration, m must receive messages from each module in $IM_s(m)$. If m is slower than its $IM_s(m)$ then $T_{it}(m) = T_{cexec}(m)$. Otherwise, it must wait for the slowest module in $IM_s(m)$ which determines its $T_{it}(m)$. Thus we have:

$$T_{it}(m) = max(max(T_{it}(i), \forall i \in IM_s(m)), T_{cexec}(m)) \tag{4}$$

If $IM_s(m) = \emptyset$ then m is not synchronized with other modules. We called these modules *predecessors* and we define $preds(C)$ as the set of *predecessors* in a component C. Their T_{it} is given by equation 3 since they are not synchronized. We can also have $preds(C) = \emptyset$. Indeed modules in C can be organized in synchronous cycles. In this case we have at least a predecessor cycle G_{pc} such as for each module m in G_{pc}, $IM_s(m) \in G_{pc}$. Note that we may have both predecessors and predecessor cycles in C. In the case of a predecessor cycle G_{pc}, each module $m \in G_{pc}$ waits only for other modules in G_{pc}. Consequently $T_{it}(m)$ depends on the T_{cexec} of other modules in G_{pc} and on the communication time between modules in G_{pc}. For each module $m_c \in G_{pc}$ we have:

$$T_{it}(m_c) = \sum_{m \in G_{pc}} T_{cexec}(m) + \sum_{\substack{e \in G_{pc} \\ Net(e) \neq \emptyset}} (\frac{Vol(e)}{BW(Net(e))} + L(Net(e))) \tag{5}$$

According to equations 3, 4 and 5 we need $T_{cexec}(m)$ for each m to obtain $T_{it}(m)$.

Determining T_{cexec} for Concurrent Modules. We turn to study consequences on concurrency on modules performances to compute their T_{cexec}. The behaviour of concurrent modules on a node n is determined by the OS scheduler. Our approach is based on the Linux scheduler policy [1][5] which gives priority to a module over others according to the time each concurrent module waits.

In this case the more a module waits, the higher priority it gets. Therefore to determine $T_{cexec}(m)$ for each module m we first need the time spent for I/O operations and for the FlowVR *wait* function. A predecessor pm is not synchronized and only waits for I/O operations according to its $T_{exec}(m)$ and $LD(m)$. For each predecessor pm, we define $T_{I/O}(pm)$ as follow:

$$T_{I/O}(pm) = T_{exec}(pm) \times (1 - LD(pm)) \qquad (6)$$

If $IM_s(m) \neq \emptyset$ then m If a module m is synchronized with its input modules then we define $T_{I/O}(m)$ as the time not used for the computation during an iteration:

$$T_{I/O}(m) = max(T_{exec}(m), T_{it}(i), \forall i \in IM_s(m)) - T_{exec}(m) \times LD(m) \qquad (7)$$

With $T_{I/O}(m)$ we can sort modules on each node n in a list $l(n)$ from the one with the highest $T_{I/O}(m)$ to the one with the lowest $T_{I/O}(m)$. Then we consider modules in the list order. Each module m is mapped on the most available CPU i.e. the CPU with the lowest load, and receives a concurrent load $LD_c(m)$ on this CPU according to its load $LD(m)$. Finally, we use the ratio between $LD(m)$ and $LD_c(m)$ to evaluate $T_{cexec}(m)$. Algorithm 1 describes this process. Note that some modules may have the same $T_{I/O}$, in this case the order between them is arbitrary. Our tests show that the scheduler can choose one possible order but if we run the application several times the scheduler can choose another possible order. Thus we have no performance garantee but we are able to detect when this case occur.

Algorithm 1. Computation of Tcexec

```
for all cpu ∈ CPUs(n) do
    CPULD(cpu) = 0
end for
while l(n) ≠ ∅ do
    m = head(l(n))
    l(n) = tail(l(n))
    load = 1
    for all cpu ∈ CPUs(n) do
        if CPULD(cpu) < load then
            p = cpu
            load = CPULD(cpu)
        end if
    end for
    LDc(m) = (1 − CPULD(p))) × LD(m)
    CPULD(p) = CPULD(p) + LDc(m)
    Tcexec(m) = Texec(m) × (LD(m)/LDc(m))
end while
```

In this approach $T_{I/O}(m)$ is determined from $T_{it}(i), i \in IM_s(m)$ from equation 7. But $T_{it}(i)$ may depend on $T_{cexec}(i)$ according to equations 3, 4 and 5. For example if i is a predecessor, $IM_s(i)) = \emptyset$, then $T_{it}(i)$ depends on $T_{cexec}(i)$ from equation 3. Then if m and i are mapped on the same node then we can not compute $T_{cexec}(i)$ since we have not yet determined $T_{I/O}(m)$ and $T_{I/O}(i)$ which depend on $T_{it}(i)$ from equation 7. Consequently, in this example we have an interdependency between equations 3 and 7. To detect interdependencies we first modify G_{sync} to represent concurrency between modules. Therefore we add bidirected edges between concurrent modules in G_{sync}. We obtain a new graph G_{dep} were each edge represents a dependency due to synchronization (directed edges) or concurrency (bidirected edges). If we detect a cycle in the graph then we can have an interdependency between modules in the cycle. We define a cycle as a path between a module and itself such as this path is not empty. Note that a cycle can contain the same bidirected edge twice but not the same directed edge.

We turn to present how to determine $T_{cexec}(m)$ and $T_{it}(m)$ for each module m in G_{dep}. Note that G_{dep} may not be connected, in this case G_{dep} has several components. Since there is no dependencies between components of G_{dep} we can study separately each one. A component C_{dep} can contain cycles of different nature and Directed Acyclic Graphs. We propose to extract cycles from C_{dep} to obtain a set D_{dep} of DAGs. Then we study cycles and DAGs independently.

If we consider a DAG d in D_{dep} then we have no concurrency between modules because we have no bidirected edges between them. Thus from equation 2 we have $T_{cexec}(m) = T_{exec}(m)$ for each module $m \in d$. If d contains a predecessor pm then from equations 2 and 3 we can determine $T_{it}(pm)$. Then we propagate this value to each module m such as $IM_s(m) = pm$ to determine $T_{it}(m)$ from equations 2 and 4. If, for a module m we have $IM_s(m) \not\subset d$ then it means that it is dependant of a module in a cycle. Consequently we must first study this cycle. Note that different kinds of cycles may be present in C_{dep}.

We first consider a cycle $C_{cycle} \subset C_{dep}$ with only bidirected edges i.e. all modules in C_{cycle} are on the same node and but from distinct components. If C_{cycle} contains only predecessors then we determine $T_{I/O}(pm)$ for each $pm \in C_{cycle}$ with equation 6. Otherwise if we have at least one non predecessor module m then we use equation 7. But we need to first study parts of the graph which contain $IM_s(m)$. If C_{cycle} contains only directed edges then C_{cycle} is a synchronous cycle. Moreover each module m within C_{cycle} has no concurrent modules. Consequently we have $T_{cexec}(m) = T_{exec}(m)$ from 2. If C_{cycle} is a predecessor cycle then we use equations 2 and 5 to obtain $T_{it}(m)$. Otherwise, for each module m in C_{cycle} with $IM_s(m) \not\subset C_{cycle}$ we first need to study parts with modules in $IM_s(m)$. Then we apply equation 4 to modules in C_{cycle}. We finally consider cycles with both directed and bidirected edges. In this case we have an interdependency and we can not sort modules. To solve this problem we propose to choose an order between modules. For example, we consider that modules in the same synchronous component C have the same iteration time. Indeed if we have $m \in C$ such as $T_{cexec}(m) > T_{it}(i), i \in IM_s(m)$ then m is slower than i. In this case messages from i are accumulated and generate a buffer overflow. Thus our hypothesis seems appropriate and desirable for the developer. But this single iteration time is not yet determined. We are nonetheless able to compare concurrent modules in the same component C. Indeed if we consider $m_1, m_2 \in C$ and $\in C_{cycle}$ with $node(m_1) = node(m_2) = n$ we have $T_{it}(m_1) = T_{it}(m_2)$ according to our hypothesis. If m_1 and m_2 are not predecessors of C we have from equation 7:

$$T_{I/O}(m_1) - T_{I/O}(m_2) = T_{exec}(m_2) \times LD(m_2) - T_{exec}(m_1) \times LD(m_1)) \qquad (8)$$

Consequently it comes to compare the time each module effectively uses the CPU. Note that, if we have a predecessor $pm \in C$, or a module m from another component, then we are not able to compare them. Consequently we distinguish two possible configurations. In the first one we have only modules from the same component on a node n. According to our hypothesis we are able to sort them and we can solve the interdependency. On the other hand if we have a predecessor pm, or a module m from a different component in C_{cycle}, then our hypothesis does not allow to compare them. In this case we propose to set $T_{cexec}(m) = T_{exec}(m)$ for each $m \in C_{cycle}$, just to define an order. Then we are able to determine $T_{cexec}(m)$ for each module m and then $T_{it}(m)$. At this step we can verify the order. If the order has changed we repeat the process but we can not guarantee that this process always converge. In this case our tests show oscillations of the execution time due to variations in the module order. This behaviour does not correspond to the one expected for performance, especially for interactive applications which performance has to be stable. Moreover this dynamic variation of performance due to the scheduling can be very difficult to detect and to analyse. Our method makes possible to detect when this behavior may occur and to precisely point out modules in these configurations. With this information the developer can change its mapping or can tune the scheduler to sort modules statically.

We now construct C_{dep} from these different parts. We first consider cycles and DAGs which are not dependent of others. The graph contains such parts since we have extracted cycles from it. For each module m in these "predecessor parts" we have determined $T_{cexec}(m)$ and $T_{it}(m)$. Then we merge parts which depends on these "predecessor parts" and we can compute $T_{cexec}(m)$ and $T_{it}(m)$ for each module m in them. We repeat the process for the other parts until we complete the graph. Once we have determined $T_{cexec}(m)$ and $T_{it}(m)$ for each $m \in G_{sync}$ we verify that $T_{cexec}(m) \leq T_{it}(i), i \in IM_s m$. If this is not the case for a module m then we predict a buffer overflow on $node(m)$. The developer can remove the buffer overflow in different ways. For example he can distribute m on several nodes to decrease $T_{exec}(m)$ and consequently $T_{cexec}(m)$. If is also possible to map concurrent modules of m on other nodes to decrease $T_{cexec}(m)$.

We can now determine performance for a given mapping. We also provide to the developer a way to detect incorrect mappings. In this case our analysis point out modules which generates errors and propose a mean to solve them.

Networking. We now consider communication between FlowVR objects. We begin our study with a traversal of the application graph $G(V, E)$ to determine the frequency $F(f)$ of each filter f, and $Vol(e)$ on its output ports. When we consider a filter f then we assign it a frequency $F(f)$ according to its behaviour. For example a greedy filter f_{greedy} sends a message only when the receiving module m_{dest} asks it for a new data and we have $F(f_{greedy}) = F(m_{dest})$. We also determine $Vol(e)$ from the frequency and the behaviour of objects. Note that we can add additional edges to represent communication out of the FlowVR communication scheme, for example MPI connections. Then we can compute the bandwidth bw_s needed by a node n to send its data on a network net:

$$bw_s(n, net) = \sum_{\substack{\forall e \in E, \\ Net(e)=net, \\ node(src(e))=n}} Vol(e) \times F(src(e)) \tag{9}$$

If, for a node n, we have $bw_s(n, net) > BW(net)$ then messages can not be sent through the network thus we can predict a buffer overflow on n. We can also determine the bandwidth bw_r needed by n to receive its data by replacing $node(src(e)) = n$ by $node(dest(e)) = n$ in equation 9. If $bw_r(n, net) > BW(net)$ then too much data are sent to the same node, leading to a buffer overflow on nodes sending data to node n through network net. Our method gives the developer the ability to point out network bottlenecks in his mappings. Then it is possible to remove them by reducing the number of modules on the same node, by modifying the communication scheme, or by using other networks.

We now study the *latency* between modules. It represents the time an information needs to be processed and transported through the mapping. In VR applications the latency is critical for user interaction and visualization. We determine the latency between two modules m_1 and m_2 from the path P between them. The path P is provided by the developer and contains a set of FlowVR objects and edges between them. The latency is obtained by adding concurrent execution times of modules in P and communication times.

$$L(P) = \sum_{m \in P} T_{cexec}(m) + \sum_{\substack{\forall e \in P \\ Net(e) \neq \emptyset}} \frac{V(e)}{BW(Net(e))} + L(Net(e)) \qquad (10)$$

The developer can detect whether the latency corresponds to its requirements, for example if it is low enough for interactivity. If the latency is too high, the developer can minimize it by mapping several modules on the same node to decrease communication latencies. He can also create more instances of parallel modules to decrease execution times or to use a faster network.

4   Tests

In this section we present several tests to validate our performance prediction model on simple FlowVR applications. Then we apply our method to a real application. Tests are performed on a cluster composed of two sets of eight nodes linked with a gigabit Ethernet network. The first set (nodes 1 to 8) is composed of nodes with two Opteron processors, each one with two cores. The second one (nodes 11 to 18) is composed of nodes with dual Pentium4 Xeon processors.

4.1   Test Application

We first verify our model on simple FlowVR applications.We first determine for each module m its $T_{exec}(m)$ by running independently each module on the destination host. Then we run the applications to compare predictions to results.

Synchronizations. We first consider a greedy connection between two modules m_1, m_2 mapped on different nodes. Results are shown in table 1 and confirm that greedy connections do not affect module performance. Then we replace the greedy connection by a FIFO connection. Results are shown in table 2. As expected $T_{it}(m_2) = T_{it}(m_1)$. Finally we invert the FIFO connection between m_1 and m_2. In this case we predict a buffer overflow since $T_{exec}(m_2) > T_{it}(m_1)$. Our tests confirm that the application exists with a buffer overflow error.

We turn to consider three modules organized in a synchronous cycle. Since each module waits for the others, two modules can not run at the same time. Thus we predict that $T_{cexec} = T_{exec}$ for each module if they are mapped on the same node. But we should have a higher T_{it} if modules are mapped on distinct nodes since we have network communications. We first map modules on distinct nodes. Each module sends 5MB per iteration through a gigabit network (BW=100MB/s) thus we expect that each communication will take around 50ms. We assume that the network latency is negligible compared to this communication time. We have three connections in the cycle so we add 150ms to the execution times in equation 5. Results shown in table 3 are close to predictions even with a simple estimation of the network parameters. If we map modules on the same node then we only sum the execution times to obtain the T_{it} of modules in the cycle from equation 5. Results in table 4 show that T_{it} is correctly predicted by our approach. We note that communication through the shared memory does not add extra latency.

Concurrency. In this test we consider four different modules m_1, m_2, m_3 and m_4 mapped on a dual processor node. These modules are not synchronized to avoid interdependencies since we want to validate our scheduling model. We apply our approach to determine $T_{cexec}(m)$ for each module m. Results in table 5 are close to our predictions. Nonetheless we note that the scheduler gives the higher priority to m_2 and m_4 but does not give them the necessary load.

4.2   The FluidParticle Application

We now apply our approach on our FluidParticle application which is used to observe typical fluid phenomena like vortices. It contains the following modules:

- *fluid:* this is an MPI version [6] of the Stam's fluid simulation [9].
- *particles:* this is a parallel module which stores a set of particles and moves them according to a force field.
- *viewer:* it converts the particles positions into graphical primitives.

Table 1.

Module	Nodes	LD	T_{exec}	T_{it} pred.	T_{it} real
m_1	1	1	37	37	37
m_2	2	0.5	18	18	18

Table 2.

Module	Nodes	LD	T_{exec}	T_{it} pred.	T_{it} real
m_1	1	1	37	37	37
m_2	2	0.5	18	37	37

Table 3.

Module	Nodes	LD	T_{exec}	T_{it} pred.	T_{it} real
m_1	1	1	37	234	240
m_2	2	0.5	26	234	240
m_3	3	0.5	21	234	240

Table 4.

Module	Nodes	LD	T_{exec}	T_{it} pred.	T_{it} real
m_1	1	1	37	84	84
m_2	1	0.5	26	84	84
m_3	1	0.5	21	84	84

Table 5. (Times are given in ms)

| Mod. | Node | T_{exec} | LD | | Prediction | | Measure | |
				$T_{I/O}$	T_{cexec}	LD_c	T_{cexec}	LD_c
m_1	1	20	1.00	0	48	0.42	36	0.55
m_2	1	16	0.30	11	16	0.30	19	0.25
m_3	1	10	0.50	5	14	0.35	17	0.44
m_4	1	51	0.58	20	51	0.58	56	0.52

– *renderer:* it displays informations provided by the viewer modules. In our study we use a display wall with four projectors thus we use four renderer modules on four distinct nodes.
– *joypad:* it is the interaction module which allows the user to interact with the fluid by adding forces.

Our goal is to obtain an interactive application. We focus our study on synchronization and concurrency effects on performance. A complete example of network performance analysis can be found in [8]. We first determine $T_{exec}(m)$ and $LD(m)$ for each module m (table 6). We note that the *joypad* module has load under 1% and is connected to simulation modules through *greedy* filters to allow an asynchronous interaction. Consequently it can not involve performance penalties and we choose to ignore it.

We now describe communication and synchronization between modules. The *fluid* module is connected synchronously with the *particles* module. The *particles* module is also connected synchronously with the *viewer* module. Finally the *viewer* and the *renderer* modules are connected through a *greedy filter*. This allows to change the user point of view and to update data from the *viewer* module asynchronously. If we remove greedy connections then the graph is splitted into two components. The first one contains the *fluid*, the *particles* and the *renderer* modules while the second one contains the *renderer* modules.

We turn to study synchronization and concurrency between modules for two mappings. We first propose a mapping with the *fluid*, *particles* and *renderer* modules on the same dual processor nodes. In this case we detect an interdependency since we have a cycle with a directed edge between the *fluid* and the *particles* modules, and a bidirected edge between the *renderer* and the *fluid* modules. The *particules* module is synchronized with the *fluid* module and have a lower execution time. The *renderer* module is the single module in its component and is consequently a predecessor. Since both the *renderer* and the *fluid* modules have a load of 97%, the *particles* module always have the highest priority. Consequently *renderer* or the *fluid* module will be mapped with the *particles* module on the same processor. But we can not order these two modules. Thus the scheduler may change their mapping on the two processors dynamically. Indeed our tests confirm that their T_{cexec} vary. We now propose a different mapping.

To obtain an interactive visualization we should map the *renderer* modules on dedicated processors. We also need to avoid concurrency for the *fluid* module to obtain the fastest simulation. Thus we propose to map modules as described in table 6. In this mapping we use nodes 1 to 8 for the simulation and we distribute

Table 6. (Times are given in ms)

Module	Nodes	LD	T_{exec}	Prediction			Measure		
				T_{cexec}	T_{it}	LD_c	T_{cexec}	T_{it}	LD_c
fluid	1, ..., 8	0.97	70	70	70	0.97	73	73	0.97
particles	15, ..., 18	0.97	20	20	70	0.28	21	73	0.30
viewer	15, ..., 18	0.97	28	28	70	0.40	28	73	0.38
renderer	11, ..., 14	0.97	57	57	57	0.97	60	60	0.97
joypad	1	<0.01	<1	0	0	0	0	0	0

four modules on each node to take advantage of the four processors. Then we map the *renderer* module on four nodes connected to four projectors to visualize the simulation on our display wall. Four nodes, with two processor on each one, are still available for the *particles* and *viewer* modules. Consequently we distribute them on these nodes to reduce their execution time. In this last case we have a cycle with only modules from the same synchronous component on each one of these nodes. Moreover we do not have a predecessor mapped with them. Thus we are able to determine their T_{it}. Results of this mapping are shown in table 6. We note that it confirms the predicted performance. However in this mapping each module is mapped on a dedicated processor to avoid interdependencies. We note that, if we want to optimize the use of the cluster, we can bind modules on processor to avoid interdependencies. Moreover, we have $T_{exec}(particles) + T_{exec}(viewer) < T_{it}(fluid)$. This means that each message from the *fluid* module is processed by the *particles* module which then sends a message to the *viewer* and waits for a new message. Then the message is processed by the *viewer* module which then waits for a new message from the *particles* module. But a new message is not yet available from the simulation. Consequently the next *particles* iteration can not start before the end of the *viewer* iteration. Thus the *particles* and the *viewer* modules are never concurrent and we can bind them to the same processor. We propose to modify the previous mapping by moving the *particles* and *viewer* modules to nodes 1 to 4 and to bind them on the second processor to avoid an interdependency with the *renderer* module. Our tests confirm that we obtain the same performance with this mapping.

We have applied successfully our approach on our interactive simulation. In each case we take into account synchronization and concurrency to determine performances of modules. We also detect mappings with poor performance.

5 Conclusion

We have shown in this paper that our approach is able to predict performances for distributed FlowVR applications. Thus the developer can determine if its mapping offers for each module the frequency he expected. He can also compare the execution time of a module to the concurrent execution time and then observe the effects of concurrency between modules. For each node we are able to compute the load of each processor. If the developer needs more performances our approach allows to point out modules which could be optimized. Then he can choose to map modules on nodes with lower processor loads or to distribute a module on several nodes. But this can generate more communications on the network. Nevertheless our method allows to determine consequences of such choices. We can point out modules which generates buffer overflow due to synchronizations. We can also locate bottlenecks on network links.

This approach brings to the FlowVR model a way to abstract the performance prediction from the code. Nevertheless it is not limited to FlowVR applications and is sufficiently general to consider applications developed with other distributed middleware. The next step in our approach is to enhance the scheduling of concurrent modules to improve performance. We also plan to provide automated tools based on our model to assist the developer in his mapping creation and optimization.

Acknowledgment

This work is supported by the Region Centre.

References

1. Aas, J.: Understanding the linux 2.6.8.1 cpu scheduler,
   http://citeseer.ist.psu.edu/aas05understanding.html
2. Allard, J., Gouranton, V., Lecointre, L., Limet, S., Melin, E., Raffin, B., Robert, S.: Flowvr: a middleware for large scale virtual reality applications. In: Danelutto, M., Vanneschi, M., Laforenza, D. (eds.) Euro-Par 2004. LNCS, vol. 3149, Springer, Heidelberg (2004)
3. Allard, J., Gouranton, V., Melin, E., Raffin, B.: Parallelizing pre-rendering computations on a net juggler pc cluster. In: Proceedings of the IPT 2002, Orlando Florida, USA (March 2002)
4. Allard, J., Ménier, C., Boyer, E., Raffin, B.: Running large vr applications on a pc cluster: the flowvr experience. In: Proceedings of EGVE/IPT 05, October 2005, Denmark (2005)
5. Bovet, D.P., Cesati, M.: Understanding the Linux Kernel, 3rd edn., Ch. 7, Oreilly (2005)
6. Gaugne, R., Jubertie, S., Robert, S.: Distributed multigrid algorithms for interactive scientific simulations on clusters. In: ICAT (2003)
7. Allard, E.M.J., Gouranton, V., Raffin, B.: Parallelizing pre-rendering com-putations on a Net Juggler PC cluster. In: IPTS 2002 (2002)
8. Jubertie, S., Melin, E.: Multiple networks for heterogeneous distributed applications. In: Proceedings of PDPTA'07, Las Vegas (to appear, 2007)
9. Stam, J.: Real-time fluid dynamics for games. In: Proceedings of the Game Developer Conference (March 2003)

Communication–Prediction of Scouting Switching in Adaptively-Routed Torus Networks

F. Safaei[1,3], A. Khonsari[1,2], M. Fathy[3], N. Talebanfard[4], and M. Ould-Khaoua[5,6]

[1] IPM School of Computer Science, Tehran, Iran
[2] Dept. of ECE, Univ. of Tehran, Tehran, Iran
[3] Dept. of Computer Eng., Iran Univ. of Science and Technology, Tehran, Iran
[4] Faculty of Mathematical Sciences, Shahid Beheshti Univ., Tehran, Iran
[5] Dept. of Electrical and Computer Eng., Sultan Qaboos Univ., Al-Khodh, Oman
[6] Dept. of Computing Science, Univ. of Glasgow, UK
{safaei,ak}@ipm.ir, {f_safaei,mahfathy}@iust.ac.ir,
mohamed@dcs.gla.ac.uk

Abstract. The switching technique determines how messages are propagated from source to destination, and has a great impact on network performance. Traditional flow control mechanisms such as Wormhole Switching (WS) realize very good performance, but prone to deadlock in the vicinity of faults. While techniques such as adaptive routing can alleviate the problem, it cannot by itself solve the problem. This has motivated the development of different switching techniques. The Scouting Switching (SS) has been suggested as an efficient switching method for reconciling the conflicting demands of communication performance and fault-tolerance in computer networks. In this paper, we present a novel mathematical model to predict communication delay of SS coupled with virtual channels and fully adaptive routing in 2-D torus networks. We have carried out extensive simulation experiments, the results of which are used to validate the proposed analytical model.

1 Introduction

In large-scale parallel computers, tasks are executed by a set of intercommunicating nodes or processors. The communication is usually carried out by means of passing messages from one node to another over the interconnect network. The performance of the inter-processor communication depends largely on the network *topology*, the *switching* technique, and the *path selection* technique. The topology of a network defines how the nodes are interconnected and is generally modeled as a graph in which the vertices represent the nodes and the edges denote the channels. The torus has become a widely accepted communication network due to its desirable and powerful topological properties [1].

The switching technique determines how messages are propagated from the source to the destination, including the hardware protocols for transmitting data across a physical channel and for buffering data at a router. Modern interconnect networks feature the use of message pipelining coupled with virtual channels to improve network performance and insure deadlock freedom [1, 2]. Messages are broken into

K. Li et al. (Eds.): NPC 2007, LNCS 4672, pp. 466–475, 2007.

small units called flits or flow control digits. In Wormhole Switching (WS), data flits immediately follow the header flit into the network. Network buffers and channels are committed as soon as they become available. This nature of WS leads to high network performance and low average message latencies. However, in the vicinity of faults, this behavior can lead to situations where the header can become blocked, no longer making progress, and hence cause the network to become deadlocked. While techniques such as adaptive routing can alleviate the problem, it cannot by itself solve the problem. This has motivated the development of different switching techniques [1, 2]. Scouting Switching (SS) is a hybrid message flow control mechanism that can be dynamically configured to provide specific trade-offs between fault-tolerance and performance. In SS, the first data flit is constrained to remain K (is referred as the *scouting distance* or *probe lead*) links behind the routing header. When $K = 0$, the flow control is equivalent to WS, while large values can ensure path set-up prior to data transmission (if a path exists). Every time a channel is successfully reserved by the header, it returns a *positive acknowledgement*. If the header message encounters blocking/faulty situation at an intermediate node, it is forced to backtrack to the preceding node and must send a *negative acknowledgement*. For performance reason, when $K = 0$, no acknowledgements are sent across the channels (realizing close to WS performance). By statically fixing the value of K, we fix the trade-off between network performance (overhead of positive and negative acknowledgements) and fault-tolerance (the ability of the header to backtrack and be routed around faults). Moreover, by dynamically modifying K, we can gain improved run-time trade-offs between fault-tolerance and performance [2].

Path selection technique is concerned by selecting a path from the source node to the destination node. The term "routing" usually refers to the algorithm that is used to select the routing path. Routing in interconnect networks which belongs to the network layer of the OSI model is used to map communications to hardware resources [3]. The routing algorithm is generally classified as being either *deterministic* or *adaptive* [1]. If the path between every pair of source and destination is fixed, the routing is called deterministic. For better system performance, it is preferable that the routing algorithm adapts itself to the traffic congestion in network. Adaptive routing overcomes the performance limitations of deterministic routing by enabling messages to explore all available paths. Furthermore, this strategy can also be efficiently implemented with SS because unlike in other switching methods (such as WS), message deadlock cannot arise since all seized channels are released when blocking occurs.

There have been a few studies that have considered the performance of switching methods, e.g., [2-5]. However, they have been conducted mainly through software simulation. Analytical models are cost-effective and versatile tools for evaluating system performance under different design alternatives. The significant advantage of the analytical approach over simulation is that the analytical models can be used to obtain performance results for large systems, which are infeasible by simulation due to the excessive computation demands on conventional computers. Although SS has been around for a number of years, and can greatly benefit from adaptive routing as it reduces blocking in the network, there has been hardly any attempt to provide an analytical model for SS in interconnect networks when fully adaptive routing along with virtual channels is used. In an effort to fill this gap, this paper proposes a new analytical model to capture the message latency of SS in adaptively-routed 2-D torus networks coupled with virtual channels. The model uses an M/G/1 queuing system [6] to calculate the average waiting time that a message experiences at the source node before entering the network. The validity of the model is demonstrated by comparing analytical results with those obtained through flit-level simulation experiments.

The rest of the paper is structured as follows. In Section 2, some preliminaries are given. Section 3 describes the analytical model of SS for 2-D torus networks. Section 4 validates the proposed analytical model through simulation experiments. Finally, Section 5 concludes this study.

2 The Torus Topology

The topology we have chosen to investigate is the 2-D torus (k-ary 2-cube). This is a topology which has become increasingly popular among researchers and has been implemented in a number of existing machines [1]. A k-ary 2-cube is a direct network with $N = k^2$ nodes; k is called the radix. Links (channels) in the torus can be either uni- or bi-directional. In this paper, we will focus on 2-D torus with bi-directional links as they have been more popular in parallel systems. Each node can be identified by a 2-digit radix k address (a_1, a_2). Nodes, with address (a_1, a_2), (b_1, b_2) are connected if and only if $a_1 = (a_2 + 1) \bmod k$ or $b_1 = (b_2 + 1) \bmod k$. In order to allow processors to concentrate on computational tasks and permit the overlapping of communication with computation, a *router*, is used for handling message communication among processors, and is usually associated with each processor. Consequently, each node consists of a Processing Element (PE) and router. A node is connected to its neighboring nodes via the input and output channels. The *injection/ejection* channel is used by the processor to inject/eject messages to/from the network.

3 Analytic Modeling

In this section, we describe an analytical model to assess the performance of SS in an adaptively-routed 2-D torus. The most important performance metric in our model is the average message latency.

3.1 Assumptions

The model is based on the following assumptions, which are accepted in the literature [7-11], and are listed below.

- Nodes (processors) generate traffic independently of each other, following a Poisson process with an average rate of λ_g messages/ cycle.
- Message destination nodes are uniformly distributed across the network.
- The message length is M flits, each of which requires one cycle to cross from one router to the next.
- The local queue at the injection channel in the source node has infinite capacity. Messages at the destination node are transferred to the local PE one at a time through the ejection channel.

- $V \, (\geq 1)$ virtual channels per physical channel are used. When there are more than one virtual channels available that bring a message closer to its destination, one is chosen at random.
- Messages are assumed to always follow shortest paths in the absence of faults. Further, when the header message encounters a busy link because all the required virtual channels are occupied, it is forced to backtrack to the preceding node and send a negative acknowledgement.

In the subsequent section, we derive the mathematical model that approximate the behavior of 2-D torus communication system using SS flow control mechanism.

3.2 Communication Analysis

The average message latency is composed of the average network latency, $\bar{S}$, which is the time to cross the network and the average waiting time seen by the message in the source node, $\bar{W}_s$, before entering the network. However, to capture the effects of virtual channels multiplexing, the mean message latency has to be scaled by a factor, say $\bar{V}$, representing the average degree of virtual channels multiplexing, that takes place at a given physical channel. Therefore, the average message latency can be approximated as [7]

$$Average \; Message \; Latency = (\bar{S} + \bar{W}_s)\bar{V} \qquad (1)$$

In what follows, we will describe the calculation of $\bar{S}$, $\bar{W}_s$, and $\bar{V}$.

3.2.1 Calculation of the Mean Network Latency

Under the uniform traffic pattern, the average number of channels that a message visits along a given dimension and across the network, $\bar{k}$, $\bar{D}$ respectively, are given by Agarwal [8]

$$\bar{k} \approx k/4 \; , \; \bar{D} = 2\bar{k} \qquad (2)$$

Fully adaptive routing allows a message to use any available channel that brings it closer to its destination resulting in an evenly distributed traffic rate on all network channels. The mean arrival rate, λ_c, on a given channel is determined as follows. When the header that has made i hops is blocked, it sends a negative acknowledgement, backtracks to the preceding node, and makes a new attempt to set-up a connection. Given that the probability of blocking is Pb_i (determined later by Eq. (9)), the header visits, on average, $\bar{D} + \sum_{i=0}^{\bar{D}-1} iPb_i$ channels before it successfully establishes a connection. Since a node generates traffic at a rate of λ_g messages/cycle and a router has 4 output network channels, we can write the rate of traffic on a channel, λ_c, as

$$\lambda_c = \lambda_g \left(\bar{D} + \sum_{i=0}^{\bar{D}-1} iPb_i \right) \Big/ 4 \qquad (3)$$

The average network latency, $\overline{S}$, consists of two parts: the average time to set-up a path, $\overline{C}$, and the actual message transmission time. Given that a message makes, on average, $\overline{D}$ hops to reach its destination, $\overline{S}$ can be written as

$$\overline{S} = \overline{C} + \overline{D} + M \tag{4}$$

where M and K indicate the message length and the scouting distance, respectively.

The average time to set-up a path, $\overline{C}$, is derived as follows. Consider the header message that is currently at a node being i hops away from the source. Let Pb_i be the probability that the header experiences blocking situation because all the required virtual channels are occupied at an intermediate node. Let $\overline{C}_{i,j}^t$ denote the expected duration time for the header to reach the destination from the current node that is i hops away from the source and has backtracked j times before reaching the current state. If the header succeeds in reserving the required virtual channel and advances to the next node, the residual expected duration time becomes $\overline{C}_{i+1,j}^t$. This case occurs with probability $1 - P_j^t Pb_i$; where P_j^t is the probability denoting that the header has backtracked j times. On the other hand, if the header message encounters blocking and backtracks to the preceding node, the residual expected duration time is $\overline{C}_{i-1,j+1}^t$. Given that the header requires one cycle to move from one node to the next, the above argument reveals that the expected duration $\overline{C}_{i,j}^t$ fulfils the following difference equations

$$\overline{C}_{i,j}^t = \begin{cases} (1 - Pb_0)(\overline{C}_{1,j}^t + 1) + Pb_0 \overline{C}_{0,j}^t & i = 0 \\ (1 - P_j^t Pb_i)\overline{C}_{i+1,j}^t + P_j^t Pb_i \overline{C}_{i-1,j+1}^t + 1 & 0 < i < \overline{D} \\ 0 & i = \overline{D} \end{cases} \tag{5}$$

Let us proceed to compute the quantity of P_j^t which is denoted as the probability that the header message has backtracked j times over in a single source-destination path. We use two important facts that correspond to the header actions to cross the network. First, the gap between the header and the first data flits can grow up to $2K - 1$ hops while the header can make forward progress. Second, when there is no available output channel at a router to select, due to it being busy, the header can backtrack over the previous links up to K hops. To simplify our model, we assume that the number of consecutive channels that the header message will be forced to backtrack is limited to the scouting distance (i.e., $t \leq K$). If $j = t$ no more backtracks could happen and thus $P_j^t = 0$. Assume that $j < t$. When the header at a node being i hops away from the source, there has occurred j backtracks and hence the header has to backtrack $t - j$ times along on its $\overline{D}$-hop path. Each backtrack could be made, on average, along $\overline{D}$ places. We can conclude that the number of ways that $t - j$ backtracks can be distributed among $\overline{D}$ places is equal to $\begin{pmatrix} t-j+\overline{D}-1 \\ \overline{D}-1 \end{pmatrix}$. We can also examine that, the number of ways that $t - j$ backtracks can be distributed among $\overline{D}$ places such that a specific place contains at least one backtrack is $\begin{pmatrix} t-j+\overline{D}-2 \\ \overline{D}-1 \end{pmatrix}$. Thus, the probability P_j^t can be obtained as

$$
P_j^t = \begin{cases} \dfrac{\begin{pmatrix} t-j+\overline{D}-2 \\ \overline{D}-1 \end{pmatrix}}{\begin{pmatrix} t-j+\overline{D}-1 \\ \overline{D}-1 \end{pmatrix}} & j < t \\[4mm] 0 & j = t \end{cases}
\tag{6}
$$

Noting that the average path set-up time is at most $\overline{C}_{0,0}^t + 2K - 1$, solving the above equations yields the expected time, $\overline{C}_{0,0}^t$ needed for the header to reach the destination starting from the source. As a result, the average time to set-up a path, $\overline{C}$ with the SS flow control mechanism can be expressed as

$$
\overline{C} = \frac{\sum_{t=0}^{K}(\overline{C}_{0,0}^t + 2K - 1)}{K+1}
\tag{7}
$$

Examining the Eqs. (3) and (5) reveals that the probability of blocking, Pb_i, is required to calculate $\overline{C}$. The probability that the header message is blocked at a given channel depends on its current network position. This is because the number of alternative paths that the header can take to progress is determined by the number of hops made by the header, and the way that these hops are distributed among the dimensions [11]. In order to calculate the probability Pb_i, that the header is blocked after making i hops, we need to enumerate the number of ways to distribute i hops among two dimensions. To do so, let Θ_i^m be the probability that the header message has entirely crossed m $(0 \le m \le 1)$ dimensions after making i hops. The details of calculation of Θ_i^m have been developed elsewhere [7]. We recollect briefly here the main equations for the calculation of Θ_i^m. The number of channels, and thus the number of virtual channels, that the header can select at a given hop depends on the number of dimensions still to be visited. When the header has made $i \left(0 \le i \le \overline{D} - 1\right)$ hops, these hops can be a combination of (x, y) hops, with x and y being the number of hops achieved in the X and Y dimensions respectively, where $(x + y = i), \left(0 \le x, y \le \overline{k}\right)$. To determine the probability that the header message has crossed all the channels of one dimension, two cases need to be considered:

(1) When $\left(0 \le i < \overline{k}\right)$, the header has not yet crossed any dimension since it has to make $\overline{k}$ hops along each dimension. Therefore, the header can choose among virtual channels of both dimensions.

(2) When $(\bar{k} \leq i < \bar{D} - 1)$, the number of ways to distribute these hops along the two dimensions is $(\bar{D} - i + 1)$. In only two cases, $(x = \bar{k}, y = i - \bar{k})$ and $(x = i - \bar{k}, y = \bar{k})$, the header has crossed all channels of one dimension and thus, all the remaining hops have to be made in other dimension.

So, when the header has made i hops, the probability that there remains only one dimension to be crossed, P_{φ_i}, can be written as

$$
P_{\varphi_i} = \begin{cases} 0 & 0 \leq i < \bar{k} \\ \dfrac{2}{\bar{D} - i + 1} & \bar{k} \leq i < \bar{D} - 1 \end{cases} \tag{8}
$$

When the header arrives at the i-th hop channel, it has already made $(i - 1)$ hops and has entirely crossed, say, m $(0 \leq m \leq 1)$ dimensions. At its next hop, the header message can select any available $(2 - m)V$ virtual channels from the remaining $(2 - m)$ dimensions. Blocking occurs when all possible virtual channels at the remaining dimensions to be visited are occupied. If P_V (is given by Eq. (12)) denotes the probability that V virtual channels at a given physical channel are busy, the probability Pb_i, that the header is blocked is given by

$$
Pb_i = \sum_{m=0}^{1} \Theta_i^m (P_V)^{2-m} \qquad 0 \leq i \leq \bar{D} - 1 \tag{9}
$$

where Θ_i^m is the probability that the header has entirely crossed m dimensions along on its i-hop path and is given by

$$
\Theta_i^m = \begin{cases} 1 - P_{\varphi_i} & m = 0 \\ P_{\varphi_i} & m = 1 \end{cases} \tag{10}
$$

3.2.2 Calculation of the Average Waiting Time at the Source Node

In this section, we compute the average waiting time at the source node $(\bar{W}_s)$. We assume that, messages have an arbitrary (but known) length or service distribution. However, the arrival process will be taken to be Poisson, a single server is assumed, and the queue buffer size is taken to be infinite. Such a queue is called M/G/1 queue, using Kendal notation [6]. Since a message in the source node can enter the network through any of the V virtual channels, the average arrival rate to the queue is λ_g / V.

Using adaptive routing under the uniform traffic pattern results in the average service time seen by messages at all source nodes being the same, and equal to the average network latency, i.e., $\bar{S}$ [7]. When the header message does not encounter any blocking during the path set-up stage, the minimum network latency seen by the message is $M + (2K - 1) + \bar{D}$. Applying the Pollaczek-Khinchine (P-K) mean value formula [6] with an approximated variance $\left(\bar{S} - M - (2K - 1) - \bar{D}\right)^2$ [9] yields the average waiting time seen by a message at the source node as

$$\bar{W}_s = \frac{\lambda_g \left(\bar{S}^2 + (\bar{S} - M - (2K - 1) - \bar{D})^2\right)}{2\left(V - \lambda_g \bar{S}\right)} \tag{11}$$

3.2.3 Calculation of the Average Degree of Virtual Channels Multiplexing

The probability, P_v $(0 \le v \le V)$, that v virtual channels at a given physical channel are busy can be determined using a Markovian model (details of the model can be found in [7, 10, 11]). In the steady state, the model yields the following probabilities [10].

$$P_v = \begin{cases} Q_0 = 1 \\ Q_v = Q_{v-1}\lambda_c\bar{S} & (0 < v < V) \\ Q_v = \dfrac{Q_{v-1}\lambda_c}{1/\bar{S} - \lambda_c} & (v = V) \\ P_0 = \left(\sum_{l=0}^{V} Q_l\right)^{-1} \\ P_v = P_{v-1}\lambda_c\bar{S} & (0 < v < V) \\ P_v = \dfrac{P_{v-1}\lambda_c}{1/\bar{S} - \lambda_c} & (v = V) \end{cases} \tag{12}$$

When multiple virtual channels are used per physical channel they share the bandwidth in a time multiplexed manner. The average degree of virtual channel multiplexing, that takes place at a given physical channel, can be estimated by [10]

$$\bar{V} = \frac{\sum_{l=1}^{V} l^2 P_l}{\sum_{l=1}^{V} l P_l} \tag{13}$$

4 Simulation Experiments

To further understand and evaluate the performance issues of the SS flow control mechanism, we have used a discrete-event simulator that operates at the flit level. The simulator uses the same assumptions as the analysis, and these assumptions were detailed in Section 3.1. Extensive validation experiments have been performed for several combinations of network sizes, message lengths, scouting distance, and virtual channels. However, for the sake of specific illustration, we have conducted our simulations for the following cases only:

- Network size $N = 64$, and 256 nodes.
- Number of virtual channels $V = 1$, and 6 per physical channel.

- Message length $M = 32$, and 64 flits.
- Scouting distance $K = 0, 1, 3,$ and 6.

The average message latencies obtained from the simulation and analytical results plotted in Fig. 1. The x-axis in this figure represents the traffic rate injected by a given node in a cycle (i.e., λ_g) while the y-axis shows the average message latency (in terms of flit cycles). The figure reveals that the simulation results closely match those predicted by the analytical model in the steady state regions. However, due to the approximations that have been made in the analysis to ease the model development, some discrepancies (of at most 15% error) are apparent around the saturation point. The approximations which are made to compute the variance of service time distribution and those made for determining the traffic rate on network channels are the factors of the model inaccuracy. Since the independence assumptions are essential in ensuring a tractable model, and given that most evaluation studies concentrate on network performance in the steady state regions, it can be concluded that the present analytical model constitutes a cost-effective evaluation tool for assessing the performance behavior of fully adaptive routing algorithms in torus networks.

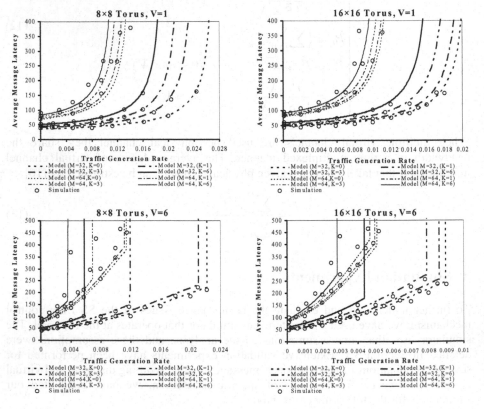

Fig. 1. Comparing the analytical model and flit-level simulation experiments in the 8×8 and 16×16 torus networks using Scouting Switching with message length M=32, 64 flits, Scouting distance K= 0,1,3,6, and V=1, 6 virtual channels per physical channel

5 Conclusions

This paper has presented a novel mathematical model to assess the relative performance merits of Scouting Switching (SS) in 2-D tori when adaptive routing and virtual channel flow control are used. The proposed analytical model is general and can easily be extended to other topologies. Results from flit-level simulation experiments have revealed that the latencies captured by the analytical model are in good agreement with those obtained through simulation. Our next step in this work is to extend our suggested modeling approach to consider the performance behavior of SS in the presence of failures.

References

1. Dally, W.J., Towles, B.: Principles and practices of interconnection networks. Morgan Kaufman Publishers (2004)
2. Dao, B.V., Duato, J., Yalamanchili, S.: Dynamically configurable message flow control for fault-tolerant routing. IEEE Transactions on Parallel and Distributed Systems 10(1), 7–22 (1999)
3. Theiss, I.: Modularity, Routing and Fault Tolerance in Interconnection Networks, PhD thesis, Faculty of Mathematics and Natural Sciences, University of Oslo (2004)
4. Colajanni, M., Dell'Arte, A., Ciciani, B.: Performance evaluation of message passing strategies and routing policies in multicomputers. Simulation Practice and Theory 6(4), 369–385 (1998)
5. Gaughan, P.T., Yalamanchili, S.: A family of fault-tolerant routing protocols for direct multiprocessor networks. IEEE Transactions on Parallel and Distributed Systems 6(5), 482–497 (1995)
6. Kleinrock, L.: Queuing Systems, vol. 1. John Wiley, New York (1975)
7. Ould-Khaoua, M.: A Performance model for Duato's adaptive routing algorithm in k-ary n-cubes. IEEE Trans. Computers 48(12), 1–8 (1999)
8. Agarwal, A.: Limits on interconnection network performance. IEEE Transactions on Parallel and Distributed Systems 2(4), 398–412 (1991)
9. Draper, J., Ghosh, J.: A comprehensive analytical model for wormhole routing in multicomputers systems. Journal of Parallel and Distributed Computing 32, 202–214 (1994)
10. Dally, W.J.: Virtual channel flow control. IEEE Transactions on Parallel and Distributed Systems 3(2), 194–205 (1992)
11. Min, G., Ould-Khaoua, M.: A Comparative Study of Switching Methods in Multicomputer Networks. Journal of Supercomputing 21, 227–238 (2002)

Communication–Prediction of Scouting Switching in Adaptively-Routed Torus Networks

F. Safaei[1,3], A. Khonsari[1,2], M. Fathy[3], N. Talebanfard[4], and M. Ould-Khaoua[5,6]

[1] IPM School of Computer Science, Tehran, Iran
[2] Dept. of ECE, Univ. of Tehran, Tehran, Iran
[3] Dept. of Computer Eng., Iran Univ. of Science and Technology, Tehran, Iran
[4] Faculty of Mathematical Sciences, Shahid Beheshti Univ., Tehran, Iran
[5] Dept. of Electrical and Computer Eng., Sultan Qaboos Univ., Al-Khodh, Oman
[6] Dept. of Computing Science, Univ. of Glasgow, UK
{safaei,ak}@ipm.ir, {f_safaei,mahfathy}@iust.ac.ir,
mohamed@dcs.gla.ac.uk

Abstract. The switching technique determines how messages are propagated from source to destination, and has a great impact on network performance. Traditional flow control mechanisms such as Wormhole Switching (WS) realize very good performance, but prone to deadlock in the vicinity of faults. While techniques such as adaptive routing can alleviate the problem, it cannot by itself solve the problem. This has motivated the development of different switching techniques. The Scouting Switching (SS) has been suggested as an efficient switching method for reconciling the conflicting demands of communication performance and fault-tolerance in computer networks. In this paper, we present a novel mathematical model to predict communication delay of SS coupled with virtual channels and fully adaptive routing in 2-D torus networks. We have carried out extensive simulation experiments, the results of which are used to validate the proposed analytical model.

1 Introduction

In large-scale parallel computers, tasks are executed by a set of intercommunicating nodes or processors. The communication is usually carried out by means of passing messages from one node to another over the interconnect network. The performance of the inter-processor communication depends largely on the network *topology*, the *switching* technique, and the *path selection* technique. The topology of a network defines how the nodes are interconnected and is generally modeled as a graph in which the vertices represent the nodes and the edges denote the channels. The torus has become a widely accepted communication network due to its desirable and powerful topological properties [1].

The switching technique determines how messages are propagated from the source to the destination, including the hardware protocols for transmitting data across a physical channel and for buffering data at a router. Modern interconnect networks feature the use of message pipelining coupled with virtual channels to improve network performance and insure deadlock freedom [1, 2]. Messages are broken into

K. Li et al. (Eds.): NPC 2007, LNCS 4672, pp. 466–475, 2007.
© IFIP International Federation for Information Processing 2007

small units called flits or flow control digits. In Wormhole Switching (WS), data flits immediately follow the header flit into the network. Network buffers and channels are committed as soon as they become available. This nature of WS leads to high network performance and low average message latencies. However, in the vicinity of faults, this behavior can lead to situations where the header can become blocked, no longer making progress, and hence cause the network to become deadlocked. While techniques such as adaptive routing can alleviate the problem, it cannot by itself solve the problem. This has motivated the development of different switching techniques [1, 2]. Scouting Switching (SS) is a hybrid message flow control mechanism that can be dynamically configured to provide specific trade-offs between fault-tolerance and performance. In SS, the first data flit is constrained to remain K (is referred as the *scouting distance* or *probe lead*) links behind the routing header. When $K = 0$, the flow control is equivalent to WS, while large values can ensure path set-up prior to data transmission (if a path exists). Every time a channel is successfully reserved by the header, it returns a *positive acknowledgement*. If the header message encounters blocking/faulty situation at an intermediate node, it is forced to backtrack to the preceding node and must send a *negative acknowledgement*. For performance reason, when $K = 0$, no acknowledgements are sent across the channels (realizing close to WS performance). By statically fixing the value of K, we fix the trade-off between network performance (overhead of positive and negative acknowledgements) and fault-tolerance (the ability of the header to backtrack and be routed around faults). Moreover, by dynamically modifying K, we can gain improved run-time trade-offs between fault-tolerance and performance [2].

Path selection technique is concerned by selecting a path from the source node to the destination node. The term "routing" usually refers to the algorithm that is used to select the routing path. Routing in interconnect networks which belongs to the network layer of the OSI model is used to map communications to hardware resources [3]. The routing algorithm is generally classified as being either *deterministic* or *adaptive* [1]. If the path between every pair of source and destination is fixed, the routing is called deterministic. For better system performance, it is preferable that the routing algorithm adapts itself to the traffic congestion in network. Adaptive routing overcomes the performance limitations of deterministic routing by enabling messages to explore all available paths. Furthermore, this strategy can also be efficiently implemented with SS because unlike in other switching methods (such as WS), message deadlock cannot arise since all seized channels are released when blocking occurs.

There have been a few studies that have considered the performance of switching methods, e.g., [2-5]. However, they have been conducted mainly through software simulation. Analytical models are cost-effective and versatile tools for evaluating system performance under different design alternatives. The significant advantage of the analytical approach over simulation is that the analytical models can be used to obtain performance results for large systems, which are infeasible by simulation due to the excessive computation demands on conventional computers. Although SS has been around for a number of years, and can greatly benefit from adaptive routing as it reduces blocking in the network, there has been hardly any attempt to provide an analytical model for SS in interconnect networks when fully adaptive routing along with virtual channels is used. In an effort to fill this gap, this paper proposes a new analytical model to capture the message latency of SS in adaptively-routed 2-D torus networks coupled with virtual channels. The model uses an M/G/1 queuing system [6] to calculate the average waiting time that a message experiences at the source node before entering the network. The validity of the model is demonstrated by comparing analytical results with those obtained through flit-level simulation experiments.

The rest of the paper is structured as follows. In Section 2, some preliminaries are given. Section 3 describes the analytical model of SS for 2-D torus networks. Section 4 validates the proposed analytical model through simulation experiments. Finally, Section 5 concludes this study.

2 The Torus Topology

The topology we have chosen to investigate is the 2-D torus (k-ary 2-cube). This is a topology which has become increasingly popular among researchers and has been implemented in a number of existing machines [1]. A k-ary 2-cube is a direct network with $N = k^2$ nodes; k is called the radix. Links (channels) in the torus can be either uni- or bi-directional. In this paper, we will focus on 2-D torus with bi-directional links as they have been more popular in parallel systems. Each node can be identified by a 2-digit radix k address (a_1, a_2). Nodes, with address (a_1, a_2), (b_1, b_2) are connected if and only if $a_1 = (a_2 + 1) \mod k$ or $b_1 = (b_2 + 1) \mod k$. In order to allow processors to concentrate on computational tasks and permit the overlapping of communication with computation, a *router*, is used for handling message communication among processors, and is usually associated with each processor. Consequently, each node consists of a Processing Element (PE) and router. A node is connected to its neighboring nodes via the input and output channels. The *injection/ejection* channel is used by the processor to inject/eject messages to/from the network.

3 Analytic Modeling

In this section, we describe an analytical model to assess the performance of SS in an adaptively-routed 2-D torus. The most important performance metric in our model is the average message latency.

3.1 Assumptions

The model is based on the following assumptions, which are accepted in the literature [7-11], and are listed below.

- Nodes (processors) generate traffic independently of each other, following a Poisson process with an average rate of λ_g messages/ cycle.
- Message destination nodes are uniformly distributed across the network.
- The message length is M flits, each of which requires one cycle to cross from one router to the next.
- The local queue at the injection channel in the source node has infinite capacity. Messages at the destination node are transferred to the local PE one at a time through the ejection channel.

- $V \; (\geq 1)$ virtual channels per physical channel are used. When there are more than one virtual channels available that bring a message closer to its destination, one is chosen at random.
- Messages are assumed to always follow shortest paths in the absence of faults. Further, when the header message encounters a busy link because all the required virtual channels are occupied, it is forced to backtrack to the preceding node and send a negative acknowledgement.

In the subsequent section, we derive the mathematical model that approximate the behavior of 2-D torus communication system using SS flow control mechanism.

3.2 Communication Analysis

The average message latency is composed of the average network latency, $\bar{S}$, which is the time to cross the network and the average waiting time seen by the message in the source node, $\bar{W}_s$, before entering the network. However, to capture the effects of virtual channels multiplexing, the mean message latency has to be scaled by a factor, say $\bar{V}$, representing the average degree of virtual channels multiplexing, that takes place at a given physical channel. Therefore, the average message latency can be approximated as [7]

$$Average \; Message \; Latency = (\bar{S} + \bar{W}_s)\bar{V} \qquad (1)$$

In what follows, we will describe the calculation of $\bar{S}$, $\bar{W}_s$, and $\bar{V}$.

3.2.1 Calculation of the Mean Network Latency

Under the uniform traffic pattern, the average number of channels that a message visits along a given dimension and across the network, $\bar{k}$, $\bar{D}$ respectively, are given by Agarwal [8]

$$\bar{k} \approx k/4 \; , \; \bar{D} = 2\bar{k} \qquad (2)$$

Fully adaptive routing allows a message to use any available channel that brings it closer to its destination resulting in an evenly distributed traffic rate on all network channels. The mean arrival rate, λ_c, on a given channel is determined as follows. When the header that has made i hops is blocked, it sends a negative acknowledgement, backtracks to the preceding node, and makes a new attempt to set-up a connection. Given that the probability of blocking is Pb_i (determined later by Eq. (9)), the header visits, on average, $\bar{D} + \sum_{i=0}^{\bar{D}-1} iPb_i$ channels before it successfully establishes a connection. Since a node generates traffic at a rate of λ_g messages/cycle and a router has 4 output network channels, we can write the rate of traffic on a channel, λ_c, as

$$\lambda_c = \lambda_g \left(\bar{D} + \sum_{i=0}^{\bar{D}-1} iPb_i \right) \Big/ 4 \qquad (3)$$

The average network latency, $\bar{S}$, consists of two parts: the average time to set-up a path, $\bar{C}$, and the actual message transmission time. Given that a message makes, on average, $\bar{D}$ hops to reach its destination, $\bar{S}$ can be written as

$$\bar{S} = \bar{C} + \bar{D} + M \qquad (4)$$

where M and K indicate the message length and the scouting distance, respectively.

The average time to set-up a path, $\bar{C}$, is derived as follows. Consider the header message that is currently at a node being i hops away from the source. Let Pb_i be the probability that the header experiences blocking situation because all the required virtual channels are occupied at an intermediate node. Let $\bar{C}_{i,j}^t$ denote the expected duration time for the header to reach the destination from the current node that is i hops away from the source and has backtracked j times before reaching the current state. If the header succeeds in reserving the required virtual channel and advances to the next node, the residual expected duration time becomes $\bar{C}_{i+1,j}^t$. This case occurs with probability $1 - P_j^t Pb_i$; where P_j^t is the probability denoting that the header has backtracked j times. On the other hand, if the header message encounters blocking and backtracks to the preceding node, the residual expected duration time is $\bar{C}_{i-1,j+1}^t$. Given that the header requires one cycle to move from one node to the next, the above argument reveals that the expected duration $\bar{C}_{i,j}^t$ fulfils the following difference equations

$$\bar{C}_{i,j}^t = \begin{cases} (1 - Pb_0)\left(\bar{C}_{1,j}^t + 1\right) + Pb_0\bar{C}_{0,j}^t & i = 0 \\ \left(1 - P_j^t Pb_i\right)\bar{C}_{i+1,j}^t + P_j^t Pb_i\bar{C}_{i-1,j+1}^t + 1 & 0 < i < \bar{D} \\ 0 & i = \bar{D} \end{cases} \qquad (5)$$

Let us proceed to compute the quantity of P_j^t which is denoted as the probability that the header message has backtracked j times over in a single source-destination path. We use two important facts that correspond to the header actions to cross the network. First, the gap between the header and the first data flits can grow up to $2K - 1$ hops while the header can make forward progress. Second, when there is no available output channel at a router to select, due to it being busy, the header can backtrack over the previous links up to K hops. To simplify our model, we assume that the number of consecutive channels that the header message will be forced to backtrack is limited to the scouting distance (i.e., $t \leq K$). If $j = t$ no more backtracks could happen and thus $P_j^t = 0$. Assume that $j < t$. When the header at a node being i hops away from the source, there has occurred j backtracks and hence the header has to backtrack $t - j$ times along on its $\bar{D}$-hop path. Each backtrack could be made, on average, along $\bar{D}$ places. We can conclude that the number of ways that $t - j$ backtracks can be distributed among $\bar{D}$ places is equal to $\binom{t-j+\bar{D}-1}{\bar{D}-1}$. We can also examine that, the number of ways that $t - j$ backtracks can be distributed among $\bar{D}$ places such that a specific place contains at least one backtrack is $\binom{t-j+\bar{D}-2}{\bar{D}-1}$. Thus, the probability P_j^t can be obtained as

$$
P_j^t = \begin{cases} \dfrac{\binom{t-j+\bar{D}-2}{\bar{D}-1}}{\binom{t-j+\bar{D}-1}{\bar{D}-1}} & j < t \\[4mm] 0 & j = t \end{cases}
\tag{6}
$$

Noting that the average path set-up time is at most $\bar{C}_{0,0}^t + 2K - 1$, solving the above equations yields the expected time, $\bar{C}_{0,0}^t$ needed for the header to reach the destination starting from the source. As a result, the average time to set-up a path, $\bar{C}$ with the SS flow control mechanism can be expressed as

$$
\bar{C} = \frac{\sum_{t=0}^{K}\left(\bar{C}_{0,0}^t + 2K - 1\right)}{K + 1}
\tag{7}
$$

Examining the Eqs. (3) and (5) reveals that the probability of blocking, Pb_i, is required to calculate $\bar{C}$. The probability that the header message is blocked at a given channel depends on its current network position. This is because the number of alternative paths that the header can take to progress is determined by the number of hops made by the header, and the way that these hops are distributed among the dimensions [11]. In order to calculate the probability Pb_i, that the header is blocked after making i hops, we need to enumerate the number of ways to distribute i hops among two dimensions. To do so, let Θ_i^m be the probability that the header message has entirely crossed m ($0 \leq m \leq 1$) dimensions after making i hops. The details of calculation of Θ_i^m have been developed elsewhere [7]. We recollect briefly here the main equations for the calculation of Θ_i^m. The number of channels, and thus the number of virtual channels, that the header can select at a given hop depends on the number of dimensions still to be visited. When the header has made i $\left(0 \leq i \leq \bar{D} - 1\right)$ hops, these hops can be a combination of (x, y) hops, with x and y being the number of hops achieved in the X and Y dimensions respectively, where $(x + y = i), \left(0 \leq x, y \leq \bar{k}\right)$. To determine the probability that the header message has crossed all the channels of one dimension, two cases need to be considered:

(1) When $\left(0 \leq i < \bar{k}\right)$, the header has not yet crossed any dimension since it has to make $\bar{k}$ hops along each dimension. Therefore, the header can choose among virtual channels of both dimensions.

(2) When $(\overline{k} \leq i < \overline{D} - 1)$, the number of ways to distribute these hops along the two dimensions is $(\overline{D} - i + 1)$. In only two cases, $(x = \overline{k}, y = i - \overline{k})$ and $(x = i - \overline{k}, y = \overline{k})$, the header has crossed all channels of one dimension and thus, all the remaining hops have to be made in other dimension.

So, when the header has made i hops, the probability that there remains only one dimension to be crossed, P_{φ_i}, can be written as

$$P_{\varphi_i} = \begin{cases} 0 & 0 \leq i < \overline{k} \\ \dfrac{2}{\overline{D} - i + 1} & \overline{k} \leq i < \overline{D} - 1 \end{cases} \tag{8}$$

When the header arrives at the i-th hop channel, it has already made $(i - 1)$ hops and has entirely crossed, say, m $(0 \leq m \leq 1)$ dimensions. At its next hop, the header message can select any available $(2 - m)V$ virtual channels from the remaining $(2 - m)$ dimensions. Blocking occurs when all possible virtual channels at the remaining dimensions to be visited are occupied. If P_V (is given by Eq. (12)) denotes the probability that V virtual channels at a given physical channel are busy, the probability Pb_i, that the header is blocked is given by

$$Pb_i = \sum_{m=0}^{1} \Theta_i^m (P_V)^{2-m} \qquad 0 \leq i \leq \overline{D} - 1 \tag{9}$$

where Θ_i^m is the probability that the header has entirely crossed m dimensions along on its i-hop path and is given by

$$\Theta_i^m = \begin{cases} 1 - P_{\varphi_i} & m = 0 \\ P_{\varphi_i} & m = 1 \end{cases} \tag{10}$$

3.2.2 Calculation of the Average Waiting Time at the Source Node

In this section, we compute the average waiting time at the source node ($\overline{W}_s$). We assume that, messages have an arbitrary (but known) length or service distribution. However, the arrival process will be taken to be Poisson, a single server is assumed, and the queue buffer size is taken to be infinite. Such a queue is called M/G/1 queue, using Kendal notation [6]. Since a message in the source node can enter the network through any of the V virtual channels, the average arrival rate to the queue is λ_g / V.

Using adaptive routing under the uniform traffic pattern results in the average service time seen by messages at all source nodes being the same, and equal to the average network latency, i.e., $\overline{S}$ [7]. When the header message does not encounter any blocking during the path set-up stage, the minimum network latency seen by the message is $M + (2K - 1) + \overline{D}$. Applying the Pollaczek-Khinchine (P-K) mean value formula [6] with an approximated variance $\left(\bar{S} - M - (2K - 1) - \bar{D}\right)^2$ [9] yields the average waiting time seen by a message at the source node as

$$\bar{W}_s = \frac{\lambda_g \left(\bar{S^2} + (\bar{S} - M - (2K - 1) - \bar{D})^2 \right)}{2 \left(V - \lambda_g \bar{S} \right)} \tag{11}$$

3.2.3 Calculation of the Average Degree of Virtual Channels Multiplexing

The probability, $P_v \ (0 \leq v \leq V)$, that v virtual channels at a given physical channel are busy can be determined using a Markovian model (details of the model can be found in [7, 10, 11]). In the steady state, the model yields the following probabilities [10].

$$P_v = \begin{cases} Q_0 = 1 \\ Q_v = Q_{v-1} \lambda_c \bar{S} & (0 < v < V) \\ Q_v = \dfrac{Q_{v-1} \lambda_c}{1/\bar{S} - \lambda_c} & (v = V) \\ P_0 = \left(\sum_{l=0}^{V} Q_l \right)^{-1} \\ P_v = P_{v-1} \lambda_c \bar{S} & (0 < v < V) \\ P_v = \dfrac{P_{v-1} \lambda_c}{1/\bar{S} - \lambda_c} & (v = V) \end{cases} \tag{12}$$

When multiple virtual channels are used per physical channel they share the bandwidth in a time multiplexed manner. The average degree of virtual channel multiplexing, that takes place at a given physical channel, can be estimated by [10]

$$\bar{V} = \frac{\sum_{l=1}^{V} l^2 P_l}{\sum_{l=1}^{V} l P_l} \tag{13}$$

4 Simulation Experiments

To further understand and evaluate the performance issues of the SS flow control mechanism, we have used a discrete-event simulator that operates at the flit level. The simulator uses the same assumptions as the analysis, and these assumptions were detailed in Section 3.1. Extensive validation experiments have been performed for several combinations of network sizes, message lengths, scouting distance, and virtual channels. However, for the sake of specific illustration, we have conducted our simulations for the following cases only:

- Network size $N = 64$, and 256 nodes.
- Number of virtual channels $V = 1$, and 6 per physical channel.

- Message length $M = 32$, and 64 flits.
- Scouting distance $K = 0, 1, 3$, and 6 .

The average message latencies obtained from the simulation and analytical results plotted in Fig. 1. The x-axis in this figure represents the traffic rate injected by a given node in a cycle (i.e., λ_g) while the y-axis shows the average message latency (in terms of flit cycles). The figure reveals that the simulation results closely match those predicted by the analytical model in the steady state regions. However, due to the approximations that have been made in the analysis to ease the model development, some discrepancies (of at most 15% error) are apparent around the saturation point. The approximations which are made to compute the variance of service time distribution and those made for determining the traffic rate on network channels are the factors of the model inaccuracy. Since the independence assumptions are essential in ensuring a tractable model, and given that most evaluation studies concentrate on network performance in the steady state regions, it can be concluded that the present analytical model constitutes a cost-effective evaluation tool for assessing the performance behavior of fully adaptive routing algorithms in torus networks.

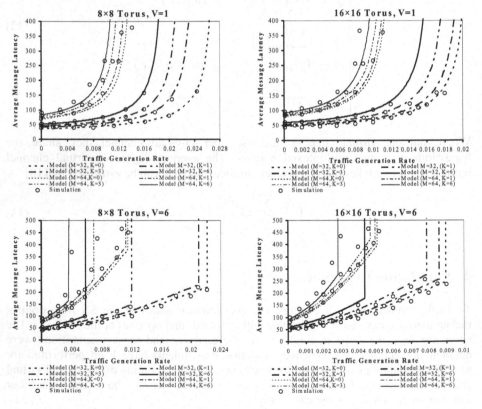

Fig. 1. Comparing the analytical model and flit-level simulation experiments in the 8×8 and 16×16 torus networks using Scouting Switching with message length M=32, 64 flits, Scouting distance K= 0,1,3,6, and V=1, 6 virtual channels per physical channel

5 Conclusions

This paper has presented a novel mathematical model to assess the relative performance merits of Scouting Switching (SS) in 2-D tori when adaptive routing and virtual channel flow control are used. The proposed analytical model is general and can easily be extended to other topologies. Results from flit-level simulation experiments have revealed that the latencies captured by the analytical model are in good agreement with those obtained through simulation. Our next step in this work is to extend our suggested modeling approach to consider the performance behavior of SS in the presence of failures.

References

1. Dally, W.J., Towles, B.: Principles and practices of interconnection networks. Morgan Kaufman Publishers (2004)
2. Dao, B.V., Duato, J., Yalamanchili, S.: Dynamically configurable message flow control for fault-tolerant routing. IEEE Transactions on Parallel and Distributed Systems 10(1), 7–22 (1999)
3. Theiss, I.: Modularity, Routing and Fault Tolerance in Interconnection Networks, PhD thesis, Faculty of Mathematics and Natural Sciences, University of Oslo (2004)
4. Colajanni, M., Dell'Arte, A., Ciciani, B.: Performance evaluation of message passing strategies and routing policies in multicomputers. Simulation Practice and Theory 6(4), 369–385 (1998)
5. Gaughan, P.T., Yalamanchili, S.: A family of fault-tolerant routing protocols for direct multiprocessor networks. IEEE Transactions on Parallel and Distributed Systems 6(5), 482–497 (1995)
6. Kleinrock, L.: Queuing Systems, vol. 1. John Wiley, New York (1975)
7. Ould-Khaoua, M.: A Performance model for Duato's adaptive routing algorithm in k-ary n-cubes. IEEE Trans. Computers 48(12), 1–8 (1999)
8. Agarwal, A.: Limits on interconnection network performance. IEEE Transactions on Parallel and Distributed Systems 2(4), 398–412 (1991)
9. Draper, J., Ghosh, J.: A comprehensive analytical model for wormhole routing in multicomputers systems. Journal of Parallel and Distributed Computing 32, 202–214 (1994)
10. Dally, W.J.: Virtual channel flow control. IEEE Transactions on Parallel and Distributed Systems 3(2), 194–205 (1992)
11. Min, G., Ould-Khaoua, M.: A Comparative Study of Switching Methods in Multicomputer Networks. Journal of Supercomputing 21, 227–238 (2002)

Service Process Improvement Based on Exceptional Pattern Analysis

Bing Li and Shuo Pan

School of Information Technology & Management Engineering
University of International Business and Economic
Chaoyang District, Beijing, China (100029)
lb0501@126.com, shuopan@126.com

Abstract. The continual improvement of service process is one of the most important factors for improving service process management level. But it is very difficult to identify the real causes of service fault executing service process improvement. Aiming at the problem, this paper proposed a service fault recognition & improvement method based on association rules mining. The method provides a new approach for enterprises to improve effectively service process fault.

1 Service Fault Analysis Based on Association Rules

In the present complicated and fierce competitive circumstance, it is increasingly important to improve the management of service process so as to improve enterprise's service effectively and quickly satisfy the customers' needs. Therefore, many scholars, domestic or foreign, have done lots of research in this area and attained abundant achievements. For instance, many companies and scholars have studied the improvement of service process in terms of 6σ management [1,2,3] and then use method DMAIC to achieve the optimization and improvement of service process. However, these methods need to be measured, analyzed and improved by the professional statistical means and specialists, which is comparatively difficult because of professional obstacles. Moreover, sometimes the real reasons for faults generated in service are too complicated to be improved, or even, be identified by these methods related above. In order to realize the dynamic optimization of service process, Yushun Fan and Fabio Casati[4,5] have proposed the framework of a real-time business process performance management(RTBPPM) and a toolbox of business process intelligence(BPI). Both of them have the common features as the real-time monitor of service process, which is efficient and convenient as well. J.Leon Zhao and Edward Stohr[6] have proposed a method of service time assessment based on workflow management and have put forward control strategy of service process. Besides, Cheung.C.F[7,8] has proposed multi-perspective knowledge-based system(MPKBS), which integrates case inference technique and time sequence model, predicts service quality, navigates automatically, and assesses service performance by analyzing customers' rights or conditions of customers and staffs. Although these service-oriented implementations and optimizations are effective, we still lack a good

K. Li et al. (Eds.): NPC 2007, LNCS 4672, pp. 486–494, 2007.

method to improve the service. It is undoubtedly beneficial for enterprise's management to find a better method to improve services based on the research mentioned above. Considering this demand, this paper proposes the method of service fault recognition and improvement which utilizes the historical records of service process, analyzes exceptional past events, discovers and fixes the imperfect links, and elevates the management level of service process.

Service faults are always the effects of several causes. The way to analyze service faults is to scan mass historical logs about service faults. Owing to masses of historical information generated in enterprise service process, one discovers that it is difficult to find out the causes of faults both by traditional cause-effect method and 6σ management. Therefore, we will use association analysis belonging to data mining technique to analyze the association between the service faults and their causes.

1.1 Basic Concept

Association analysis, proposed by Agrawal from IBM Almaden Research Center, America, in 1993, is a simple but practical method in data mining. From mass business records, we use it to get association rules which show us the interesting associations among items.

Here are some explanations about the related concepts. Let $I = \{i_1, i_2, \cdots, i_m\}$ be the set of m different transaction databases. We assume that task-related data D is the set of transactions in database and every transaction T is the set of items, which satisfies $T \in I$. The corresponding identifier of every transaction is TID. An association rule is a consequence of implication such as $A \Rightarrow B$, therein A, B are attributes(items) of the transaction record respectively, as well as $A \cap B = \Phi$.

Usually, Support and Confidence are used to measure an association rule. For an association whose form likes $A \Rightarrow B$, (and "=>" means "lead to") Support is the percentage of the transactions in which both item A and item B occur in all transactions, recorded as $\sup(A \Rightarrow B) = p(A \cup B)$ .Confidence is the conditional probability which B occurs in these transactions in which A occurs, and recorded as $conf(A \Rightarrow B) = p(B \mid A)$. Generally, only these association rules above both minimum threshold of Support ($\min\_ \sup$) and minimum threshold of Confidence ($\min\_ conf$), can be regarded as meaningful.

The algorithm "Apriori" by Rakesh Agrawal is the core algorithm of association rules mining; though many improved algorithms have followed, they are all based on "Apriori". It contains two parts: first, find out every combination of data items which satisfies the $\min\_ \sup$, called frequent itemset, and second, generate the rules which satisfy $\min\_ conf$ from every frequent itemset.

However, in the process of generating rules, many lengthy, unintelligible, and redundant rules and information will be mined out and reduce complexity of algorithm. In order to solve these problems mentioned above, R.Srikant, Robertor J and Bayardo J[9-11] proposed association mining methods based on constraints. Aimed at different problems, many scholars, at present, are researching on association mining based on constraints from different aspects. Based on this train of thought, this paper will try to bring constraint-based association mining to identify the causes for service faults.

1.2 Association Analysis of Service Fault Based on Constraint

When enterprises analyze service faults, the "possible cause---fault" records in historical logs can be utilized to find out association rules underlying general faults and their causes. When these rules' Support and Confidence reach or surpass the minimum threshold, we consider them as strong associations which, correspondingly, reflect the obvious weak links in service process. Therefore, by analyzing the rules afterwards, finding out the weak links, and improving the main process, we can effectively elevate service process management.

In order to reduce the complexity of algorithm and decrease the generation of needless or incomprehensible rules, we brought in some antecedent constraints (service fault reasons) according to features of a certain service, and then a consequent-fixed, antecedent-constrained association rules mining was formed. Besides, we added some evaluations about rules' Novelty to keep the incremental mining process run better.

First, in order to sharply decrease the number of generated rules, specialist could preliminarily sift the reason set $A = \{reason\_i \mid i \in N\}$ which causes a certain kind of faults, to ascertain the reasons which have little influence with the fault and create the following constraints for exclusive combination from the reasons and fault.

We introduced the following constraint:

$$reason\_i \Rightarrow !result\_j$$

And $reason\_i$ ------ The reason i in rules antecedents

$result\_j$ ------ The kind of fault j in rules consequents

This is a concise constraint, which can effectively decrease the number of frequent 1-itemset in the mining process. When we applied in the first scanning of historical service records, it indirectly decreased the number of frequent n-itemsets and increased the generation of rules, and of course the thresholds are decided by special application and real mining work.

Secondly, although there are many reasons leading to faults in service process, only a few frequently occurring factors contribute to the discovery of the faults' origin. So, we can proceed to add the following constraint in order to avoid the redundancy of antecedent rules.

We used the following constraint:

$$count(antecedent) \leq max\_antecedent$$

And $count(antecedent)$ ------ the number of rule antecedents

$max\_antecedent$ ------the maximum number of antecedents

This is an anti-monotone constraint, which prevents the generation of long-scheme rules, reduces the times of database scanning and effectively shortens the runtime.

Thirdly, according to the consequent-fixed rules, some complicate rules (the one has longer antecedent) barely offer any useful information, for example:

$$B_1, B_2 \Rightarrow C \quad (confidence = 80\%) \quad \text{(Rule 1)}$$
$$B_1 \Rightarrow C \quad (confidence = 85\%) \quad \text{(Rule 2)}$$

Rule 1 means that there is 80% probability of generating fault C, when B_1 and B_2 occur at the same time. We generally regard Rule 1 as a meaningful one, because it reflects the universality of reasons generating fault C. But comparing with Rule 2, the meaning of Rule 1 becomes dull.

Robertor and Bayardor J from IBM Almaden Research Center proposed the concept of Improvement [11] in the research of constraint-based rule mining in large, dense database. The Improvement of a rule is, in the condition of rule consequent fixed, the minimum difference between the Confidence of one rule and its sub-rule's Confidence, for instance, according to $C \Rightarrow A$, its improvement is:

$$imp(C \Rightarrow A) = \min\left(\forall C' \subset C, conf(C \Rightarrow A) - conf(C' \Rightarrow A)\right) ,$$

and due to the characteristics of dense database, the Improvement defined in that paper should be above 0. Here, we introduced Improvement to eliminate some rules which are not so meaningful.

Finally, since association rules include prior knowledge, we need to compare the new-generated rules with the old rules to estimate its Novelty. Because the whole mining process is an incremental process, we should find out the variances between the new and the old, and we consider the new ones with large variances as the novel, the new-mined knowledge which deserves our attention and preservation. Aimed at the analysis of service fault, on account of fixed rule consequents, we mainly pay attention to the difference of antecedents between the new rules and the old.

Assume S_1 represents the set of new-generated rules and S_2 the set of old rules. The number of rules in S_1, S_2 are $count(S_1)$ and $count(S_2)$ comparatively. w_{ij} is used to measure the difference between Rule r_i in S_2 and Rule r_j' in S_1, which is actually the Novelty. To estimate Novelty of rules in S_1 is, in fact, to find the Cartesian product $S_1 \times S_2$.

w_{ij} is calculated by the formula as follows:

$$w_{ij} = \begin{cases} 0 & r_i \in S_2, \text{or } r_i \text{and} r_j' \text{ have different consequents.} \\ \\ \sum_{h=1}^{m} f_h \cdot diff_h & \begin{array}{l} \text{other conditions}, h = 1, 2, \cdots, m \text{ is the number of attributes} \\ \text{in a rule antecedent.} \end{array} \end{cases} \quad (1)$$

Therein, f_h represents the weight value of h, $diff_h$ stands for the different degree between attributes h in r_i and its counterpart in r_j' according to the same language variable. For one attribute, we could disperse its value into several intervals marked with (an) ordinal numbers, in which the minimum is 1 and the maximal is the number of intervals. We define the difference of two continuous intervals as 1.

The novelty of Rule r_i, comparing with S_2, is the sum of all w_{ij}.

$$W_i = \sum_{j=1}^{count(S_2)} w_{ij} \qquad (2)$$

In this way, we can find all the novelty of rules in S_1. In practical, for rules which have the same consequent, we can set a minimum threshold θ according to the practical situation. When a rule satisfies $W_i > \theta$, we regard it as a novel one, and preserve it for following analysis, or else, we delete this rule. In this way, we can decrease the number of rules generation once more.

Based on the theory above, we designed the improved algorithm of service faults analysis based on association mining ("IApriori") as follows:

Algorithm: IApriori

input: min_sup (minimum   Support),   min_conf (minimum   Confidence), max_antecedent(maximum number of antecedent), exclusive constraint, min_imp(minimum Improvement), all the novelty thresholds of rules , database D

output: All rules which satisfy the constraint including min_sup, min_conf, max_antecedent_count , min_imp, θ

```
begin:
Put all transactions in D into temporary table D';
    if (consequent is frequent) then
        add consequent to L₁;
    else
        return;
 L₁= L₁+find_frequent_1-itemsets(D'); //generates
frequent 1-itemset
 delete T where not contain L1 ;
 while (L_{K-1}≠φ and k<= Antecedent+1)
 { C_K=apripri_gen( L_{K-1},min_sup);//generates K-itemset
     L_K=subset(C_K,D');//generates frequent K-itemset
 gen_rules(k, L_K, L_{K-1}) //generates rules with fixed
consequent}
```

```
for each r_i in new rules table

    θ_i=novelty( r_i )    // calculate novelty

    if  θ_i>θ_i'    //estimate whether its novelty satisfies
the novelty threshold of old rules which has same consequent
with it

    output the rule r_i; return;

procedure gen_rules(k, L_K, L_{K-1})

for each c in L_K

    if consequent∈c

    {conf=sup(c)/sup(c-consequent);

        conf>=min_conf   then

            {  max_subconf=0;

                for all (k-1)-subset s in (c-consequent)

                    if (conf(s)> max_subconf ) then
                            max_subconf=conf(s);

                    if (conf-max_subconf)≥ min_imp then

                        output the rule
                            c − consequent ⇒ consequent with

                            confidence=conf and
                                support=sup(c);

            }

    }

    return;
```

2 Improvement of Service Fault Based on Constraint

According to a series of analysis above, we used the following steps to realize service process improvement based on association analysis.

Step 1:

After a certain period of system running, decision center analyzes the log of exceptional events which are stored in data warehouse and then create tables of exceptional events and reasons (Table 1). The reasons of exceptional events include internal reason (such as employee's illness), external reason (such as delayed stock of component) and improper service model and etc.

Step 2:

In order to find out the degree of frequency that exceptional events and its corresponding reasons occur at the same time, we use "IApriori" to mine out rules formed as follows:

$$causes(X, "R1") \wedge \cdots \wedge causes(X, "Ri") \Rightarrow occurs(X, "Ej")$$

$$[\text{support} = x\%, \text{confidence} = y\%]$$

Step 3:

According to the generated rules above, companies can improve bottlenecks and improper process path to optimize the service process.

Table 1. Transaction Data of Exceptional Event Reasons

Exceptional event ID	Reason ID list
E100	R1，R2，R3，……
E200	R2，R5，…….
…….	……

3   Algorithm Analysis

According to the algorithm we proposed, we have done an experiment to validate it. With IBM data generator, we generated simulate historical logs for test, showed in Table 2. Experimental circumstance as follows: Pentium 1.4 PC, Memory 512M, Windows XP.

Table 2. Testing Parameter

Record number	Transaction number	Item number	Minimum Support	Minimum Confidence
10080条	860个	125个	0.1	0.1

As test data, we analyzed it with "IApriori" and brought several simulate constraints into our experiment. As a result, concise constraint had sharply decreased the rules number and runtime, and the influences of improvement and Novelty are also obvious. The average runtime of the association rule algorithm gets reduced only from 189 sec to 107 sec, which is less than half, and we can see it had not been reduced comparatively like generated rule number. So maybe it is important for us to advance the relativity between runtime and rule number in the future. We compared our algorithm with the traditional "Apriori". The comparison results are shown in Table3:

Table 3. Comparison of Algorithm

	Test times	Average rules number	Average runtime
Traditional Apriori	15	152	189.454 s
IApriori	15	19	107.117s

4 Conclusion

In this paper, to realize the service fault recognition & improvement, we proposed a service fault recognition & improvement method based on association rules mining, and it could become a new approach to correct the faults generated in enterprises service process effectively. In the future, we will use practical data to validate our method further, and then try to improve it and make it work better in practical business.

References

1. yi-qun, L.: The fifth special topic of BMG's Six Sigma: Six Sigma process design. China quality (12), 26 (2003)
2. xiao-fen, L., Tisheng, S.: Sigma management & supply chain management. Market Modernization 12, 29–30 (2004)
3. jing, C., lanying, D.: Six Sigma Management in Logistics Enterprise. Logistics Technology 4, 15–17 (2004)
4. Fan, Y., Bai, X.: Real-Time Business Process Performance Management. In: IEEE International Conference on E-Commerce Technology for Dynamic E-Business, 13-15 September 2004, pp. 341–344 (2004)
5. Casati, F., Dayal, U., Sayal, M., Shan, M.-C.: Business Process Intelligence (2002), http://www.hpl.hp.com/techreports/
6. Zhao, J.L., Stohr, E.: Temporal Workflow Management in a Claim Handling System. In: WACC'99, Sancisco, CA, USA, pp. 187–195 (1999)
7. Cheung, C.F., Lee, W.B., Wang, W.M., Chu, K.F., To, S.: A multi-perspective knowledge-based system for customer service management. Expert Systems with Applications 24(4), 457–470 (2003)
8. Ludwig, H.: Analysis framework of complex service performance for electronic commerce. In: Proceedings. Ninth International Workshop on Database and Expert Systems Applications, 26-28 August 1998, pp. 638–643 (1998)
9. Srikant, R., Vu, Q.: Mining Association rules with Item Constraints [A]. In: Proc. Of the Third Int'l Conf. On Knowledge Discovery in Databases and Data Mining [C], pp. 67–73 (1997)

10. Ng, R.T., Lakshmanan, V.S., Han, J., Pang, A.: Exploratory mining and pruning optimizations of constrained association rules [A]. In: Proc. Of the 1998 AACM-SIGMOD Int'l Conf. On Management of Data [C], pp. 13–24 (1998)
11. Robertor, J., Bayardo, J., Agrawal, R.: Constraint-based rule mining in large, dense database [A]. proc. Of the 15th int'l Conf. On Data Engineering [C], pp. 188–197 (1999)
12. Fu-dong, W., Bing, L., Jin-song, X., Yun-long, Z.: Constraint-based Association Rule Mining in CRM. Computer Integrated Manufacturing Systems 10(04), 465–470 (2004)

An Improved Fuzzy Support Vector Machine for Credit Rating

Yanyou Hao[1,2], Zhongxian Chi[1], Deqin Yan[3], and Xun Yue[1]

[1] Department of Computer Science and Engineering,
Dalian University of Technology, Dalian, 116024, China
[2] Dalian Branch of CCB, Dalian, 116001, China
[3] Department of Computer Science, Liaoning Normal University,
Dalian, 116029, China
haoyanyou@gmail.com

Abstract. In order to classify data with noises or outliers, Fuzzy support vector machine (FSVM) improve the generalization power of traditional SVM by assigning a fuzzy membership to each input data point. In this paper, an improved FSVM based on vague sets is proposed by assigning a truth-membership and a false-membership to each data point. And we reformulate the improved FSVM so that different input points can make different contributions to decision hyperplane. The effectiveness of the improved FSVM is verified in credit rating; the experiment results show that our method is promising.

Keywords: Fuzzy support vector machine (FSVM), fuzzy membership, vague sets, credit rating.

1 Introduction

Support vector machine (SVM) is based on the statistical learning theory (SLT) developed by Vapnik [1]. The formulations of SVM embody the structural risk minimization (SRM) principle and VC dimensions theory. Due to their high generalization ability SVMs have attracted many attentions and have been accepted widely [2, 3]. Credit risk is the primary risk facing commercial banks. With the proposed guidelines under the New Basel Accord, financial institutions will benefit from better assessing their risks. Statistical methods have been used to estimate credit rating, which typically require large data to build the forecasting model. However, there are not large data to use in real-life. Huang and Wang have shown that SVMs achieved better performance than traditional statistical methods in the field of credit rating assessment [4] [8].

The aim of SVM is to provide good generalization ability. The optimal hyperplane can be determined by only few data points that are called support vectors (SVs). Accordingly, SVMs can provide a good generalization performance for classification problems despite it does not incorporate problem-domain knowledge. There are some advantages of SVMs as follows. The training of SVMs is relatively easy and has no local optimal like neural networks. And SVMs scales relatively well to high dimensional data and tradeoff between classifier complexity and error. But there are

K. Li et al. (Eds.): NPC 2007, LNCS 4672, pp. 495–505, 2007.

some disadvantages in SVMs which need a "good" kernel function and the overfitting problem like neural network. These disadvantages impact the generalization ability of SVMs in many real applications.

As remarked in [5, 6, 7], SVMs are very sensitive to outliers and noises. The FSVMs proposed in [5, 6] treat the training data points with different importance in the training process. Namely, FSVMs fuzzily the penalty term of the cost function to be minimized, reformulate the constrained optimization problem, and then construct the Lagrangian so that the solutions to the optimal hyperplane in the primal form can be found in the dual form. The key part of FSVM is how to construct the membership model in the training data set. However, there is no general rule to determine the membership of each data point now. Wang proposed the Bilateral-weight fuzzy SVM (B-FSVM) to evaluate the credit risk [8]. This method treats each instance as both of positive and negative classes, but assigned with different memberships.

In this paper, we propose an improved fuzzy SVM based on the vague sets. We assign a truth-membership and a false-membership for each data point in training data set, and reformulate the FSVM. The experiment results show this approach improve the generalization performance of traditional SVM.

The rest of this paper is organized as follows. A brief review of the theory of FSVMs, B-FSVMs and Vague Sets will be given in Sections 2. Section 3 presents an improved FSVM based on vague sets. Section 4 reports the experiment results and analysis. Section 5 presents conclusions and future work.

2   Fuzzy Support Vector Machines and Vague Sets

2.1   Fuzzy Support Vector Machines

SVM has some merits such as multi-local minima and overfitting in neural networks seldom occur in SVM and it has a solid theoretical foundation. However, there are still some problems in SVM. All training points of one class are treated uniformly in the theory of SVM. As shown in [5,6], due to overfitting, the training process is very sensitive to those outliers in the training dataset which are far away from their own class.

FSVM is proposed in order to decrease the effect of those outliers. The main idea of FSVM is that we can assign a fuzzy membership to each data point, In other words, FSVM treats the input data unequally such that different data points can have different effects in the learning of the separating hyperplane. We can treat the noises or outliers as less importance and let these points have lower fuzzy membership. It is also based on the maximization of the margin like the traditional SVM, but FSVM uses fuzzy memberships to prevent some points from making narrower margin. This equips FSVM with the ability to train data with outliers by setting lower fuzzy memberships to the data points that are considered as noises or outliers with higher probability [9].

We give a briefly introduction about FSVM that are proposed in [5, 6] as follows. Suppose we are given a set of labeled training data sets with associated fuzzy membership (y_i, x_i, m_i). Each training point $x_i \in R^N$ is given a label $y_i \in \{-1,1\}$ and a fuzzy membership $\varepsilon \leq m_i \leq 1$ with $i = 1,2,...,N$, and sufficient small $\varepsilon > 0$. Since the fuzzy membership m_i is the attitude of the corresponding point x_i toward one class and the parameter ξ_i is a measure of error in SVM, the term $m_i \xi_i$ is a measure of error with different weighting. Then the optimal hyperplane problem is regarded as the solution to

$$\min \frac{1}{2} w^T \cdot w + C \sum_{i=1}^{N} m_i \xi_i \ , \tag{1}$$

Subject to: $\begin{array}{l} y_i (w \cdot x_i + b) \geq 1 - \xi_i \\ i = 1,...,N; \quad \xi_i \geq 0 \end{array}$

Where C is a free parameter that controls the tradeoff between the maximum of margin and minimum of classification error. It is noted that a smaller m_i reduces the effect of the parameter ξ_i in problem (1) such that the corresponding point is treated as less important. We obtain the following decision function

$$f(x) = sign(w \cdot x + b) = sign\left(\sum_{i=1}^{N} \alpha_i y_i K(x_i \cdot x) + b \right) . \tag{2}$$

$$0 \leq \alpha_i \leq m_i C . \tag{3}$$

Wang proposed the Bilateral-weight fuzzy SVM (B-FSVM) and presented a new approach to improve the FSVM [2]. This new method treats every data point in the training dataset as both positive and negative class but with different memberships. Memberships are assigned to both classes for every data point. This means it increases the number of training data points from the original N to $2*N$. i.e. from $\{x_i, y_i\}$ to $\{x_i, 1, m_i\}, \{x_i, -1, 1-m_i\}$. The classification problem is modeled by the following programming

$$\min \frac{1}{2} w^T w + C \sum_{i=1}^{N} [m_i \xi_i + (1-m_i)\eta_i] \ , \tag{4}$$

Subject to: $\begin{array}{l} [w^T \phi(x_i) + b] \geq 1 - \xi_i, i = 1,...,N \\ [w^T \phi(x_i) + b] \leq -1 + \eta_i, i = 1,...,N \\ \xi_i \geq 0, for \quad i = 1,...,N \\ \eta_i \geq 0, for \quad i = 1,...,N. \end{array}$

The problem can be transformed into its dual form

$$\max_{\alpha_i, \beta_i} \sum_{i=1}^{N} \alpha_i + \sum_{i=1}^{N} \beta_i - \frac{1}{2} \sum_{i=1}^{N} \sum_{j=1}^{N} (\alpha_i - \beta_i)(\alpha_j - \beta_j)\phi(x_i)^T \phi(x_j) \ , \tag{5}$$

$$\sum_{i=1}^{N} \alpha_i = \sum_{i=1}^{N} \beta_i,$$

Subject to: $0 \leq \alpha_i \leq Cm_i, i = 1,...,N,$
$0 \leq \beta_i \leq C(1-m_i), i = 1,...,N.$

Let $K(x_i, x_j) = \phi(x_i)^T \phi(x_j)$. In order to transform this into a quadratic programming problem, we let $\gamma_i = \alpha_i - \beta_i$. The previous optimization becomes

$$\max_{\beta_i, \nu_i} \sum_{i=1}^{N} \gamma_i + \sum_{i=1}^{N} 2\beta_i - \frac{1}{2}\sum_{i=1}^{N}\sum_{j=1}^{N} \gamma_i \gamma_j K(x_i, x_j) , \qquad (6)$$

$$\sum_{i=1}^{N} \gamma_i = 0.$$

Subject to: $0 \le \beta_i + \gamma_i \le Cm_i$ for $i = 1,...,N$.

$0 \le \beta_i \le C(1 - m_i)$ for $i = 1,...,N$.

After solving this quadratic programming problem, we obtain the following classifier

$$f(x) = sign(w^T \phi(x_i) + b) = sign(\sum_{i=1}^{N} (\alpha_i - \beta_i)K(x, x_i) + b). \qquad (7)$$

2.2 Vague Sets

Since the theory of fuzzy sets was proposed in 1965 by Zadeh [10], it has been used for handling fuzzy decision-making problems and the study of the aggregation processes.

Definition 1 (Fuzzy Set). Let U be the universe of discourse, $U = \{x_1, x_2,...,x_n\}$. A fuzzy set

$$A = \{(x, \mu_A(x)) \mid x \in A, \mu_A(x) \in [0,1]\}$$

The grade of membership of an element x_i in a fuzzy set is denoted as $\mu_A(x_i)$, $x_i \in U$. It is represented by a real value between zero and one. Fuzzy sets assign each object a single value. This single value combines the evidence for $x_i \in U$ and the evidence against $x_i \in U$, without indicating how much there is of each. The single number tells us nothing about its accuracy.

Vague set theory, introduced by Gau and Buehrer in 1993 [11], extends and improves fuzzy set theory. The membership ranging between zero and one in fuzzy set theory is extended to a continuous subinterval of [0, 1].

Definition 2 (Vague Set). Let U be the universe of discourse, with a generic element $x_i \in U$. A vague set V in U is characterized by a truth membership function t_V and a false membership function f_V , $t_V(x_i)$ is a lower bound on the grade of membership of x_i derived from the evidence for x_i , and $f_V(x_i)$ is a lower bound on the negation of x_i derived from the evidence against x_i . $t_V(x_i)$ and $f_V(x_i)$ both associate a real number in the interval [0,1] with each point in U , where $t_V(x_i) + f_V(x_i) \leq 1$.

This approach bounds the grade of membership of x_i to a subinterval [$t_V(x_i)$, 1 - $f_V(x_i)$] of [0, 1]. The vague value can be divided into three parts: the truth-membership part $t_V(x_i)$, the false-membership part $f_V(x_i)$, and the unknown part $1 - t_V(x_i) - f_V(x_i)$.

3   FSVM Based on Vague Sets (VS-FSVM)

A vague set is a further generalization of a fuzzy set. Instead of using point-based membership as in fuzzy sets, interval-based membership is used in a vague set [12]. The interval-based membership in vague sets is more expressive in capturing uncertainty and vagueness of data. In this paper, we use vague sets to define the membership in FSVMs.

Given a training datasets $\{x_i, y_i\}$, $for \quad i = 1, ..., N$, $y_i \in \{-1, 1\}$, we transform the original data sets into a new training datasets

$$\{x_i, 1, t_i\}, \{x_i, -1, f_i\}, \quad for \quad i = 1, ..., N .$$

t_i is the truth-membership of each data point in the training datasets with positive class.

f_i is the false-membership of each data point in the training datasets with negative class.

$t_i \leq 1, f_i \leq 1$ and $t_i + f_i \leq 1$.

Let $m_i = 1 - t_i - f_i$, which is the unknown part indicating the probability of each data point without positive class or negative class in the training datasets.

We propose an improved fuzzy SVM based on vague sets and deduce the formulation as follows.

$$\min_{w, b, \xi, \eta, \theta} \frac{1}{2} w^T w + C \sum_{k=1}^{N} [t_i \xi_i + f_i \eta_i + m_i \theta_i] , \tag{8}$$

Subject to: $\begin{aligned} & w^T x_i + b \geq 1 - \xi_i - \lambda \theta_i, for \quad i = 1, ..., N \\ & w^T x_i + b \leq -1 + \eta_i + (1 - \lambda) \theta_i, for \quad i = 1, ..., N \\ & \xi_i \geq 0, for \quad i = 1, ..., N \\ & \eta_i \geq 0, for \quad i = 1, ..., N \\ & \theta_i \geq 0, for \quad i = 1, ..., N . \end{aligned}$

Where θ_i is a slack variable of m_i , λ is a free parameter less than 1 which segments the unknown part, we process it with experiential value .To solve the previous optimization problem, letting the corresponding Lagrange multipliers to the condition be $\alpha_i, \beta_i, \mu_i, \nu_i$ and τ_i , we construct the Lagrangian function

$$L(w,b,\xi,\eta,\theta) = \frac{1}{2}w^T w + C\sum_{i=1}^{N}[t_i\xi_i + f_i\eta_k + m_i\theta_i]$$

$$- \sum_{i=}^{N}\alpha_i(w^T x_i + b - 1 + \xi_i + \lambda\theta_i) + \sum_{i=1}^{N}\beta_i(w^T x_i + b + 1 - \eta_i - (1-\lambda)\theta_i)$$

$$- \sum_{i=1}^{N}\mu_i\xi_i - \sum_{i=1}^{N}v_i\eta_i - \sum_{i=1}^{N}\tau_i\theta_i \tag{9}$$

And we find the saddle point of L, where $\alpha_i \geq 0, \beta_i \geq 0, \mu_i \geq 0, v_i \geq 0$ and $\tau_i \geq 0$. These parameters must satisfy the following conditions

$$\frac{\partial L}{\partial w} = w - \sum_{i=1}^{N}\alpha_i x_i + \sum_{i=1}^{N}\beta_i x_i = 0. \tag{10}$$

$$\frac{\partial L}{\partial b} = -\sum_{i=1}^{N}\alpha_i + \sum_{i=1}^{N}\beta_i = 0. \tag{11}$$

$$\frac{\partial L}{\partial \xi_i} = Ct_i - \alpha_i + \mu_i = 0. \tag{12}$$

$$\frac{\partial L}{\partial \eta_i} = Cf_i + \beta_i + v_i = 0. \tag{13}$$

$$\frac{\partial L}{\partial \theta_i} = Cu_i - \lambda\alpha_i + (1-\lambda)\beta_i - \tau_i = 0. \tag{14}$$

From the Kuhn-Tucker Theorem, the following conditions are also satisfied

$$\alpha_i(w^T x_i + b - 1 + \xi_i + \lambda\theta_i) = 0. \tag{15}$$

$$\beta_i(w^T x_i + b + 1 - \eta_i - (1-\lambda)\theta_i) = 0. \tag{16}$$

$$\mu_i\xi_i = 0, v_i\eta_i = 0, \tau_i\theta_i = 0. \tag{17}$$

$$\xi_i \geq 0, \eta_i \geq 0, \theta_i \geq 0, \alpha_i \geq 0, \beta_i \geq 0,$$
$$\tau_i \geq 0, \mu_i \geq 0, v_i \geq 0, i = 1,...,N. \tag{18}$$

According to (10), we obtain

$$w = \sum_{i=1}^{N}(\alpha_i - \beta_i)x_i. \tag{19}$$

We define E and F as

$$E = -\sum_{i=1}^{N}\alpha_i(w^T x_i + b - 1 + \xi_i + \lambda\theta_i). \tag{20}$$

$$F = \sum_{i=1}^{N} \beta_i \left(w^T x_i + b + 1 - \eta_i - (1-\lambda)\theta_i \right). \tag{21}$$

Apply E and F into (9)

$$L = \frac{1}{2} w^T w + C \sum_{i=1}^{N} [l_i \xi_i + f_i \eta_k + m_i \theta_i] + E + F - \sum_{i=1}^{N} \mu_i \xi_i - \sum_{i=1}^{N} v_i \eta_i - \sum_{i=1}^{N} \tau_i \theta_i. \tag{22}$$

From (15) and (16), we get $E=F=0$, and (22) be transformed into

$$
\begin{aligned}
L &= \frac{1}{2} w^T w + \sum_{i=1}^{N} (Ct_i - \mu_i)\xi_i + \sum_{i=1}^{N} (Cf_i - v_i)\eta_i + \sum_{i=1}^{N} (Cm_i - \tau_i)\theta_i \\
&= \frac{1}{2} w^T w + \sum_{i=1}^{N} (\alpha_i \xi_i + \beta_i \eta_i) + \sum_{i=1}^{N} [\lambda \alpha_i + (1-\lambda)\beta_i] \quad .
\end{aligned}
\tag{23}
$$

Taking the difference between the sum of (15) and (16) from $i=1$ to N, we obtain

$$\sum_{i=1}^{N} (\alpha_i \xi_i + \beta_i \eta_i) + \sum_{i=1}^{N} [\lambda \alpha_i + (1-\lambda)\beta_i] = -\sum_{i=1}^{N} (\alpha_i - \beta_i) w^T x_i + \sum_{i=1}^{N} (\alpha_i + \beta_i). \tag{24}$$

Apply (24) into (23), we obtain

$$L = \frac{1}{2} w^T w - \sum_{i=1}^{N} (\alpha_i - \beta_i) w^T x_i + \sum_{i=1}^{N} (\alpha_i + \beta_i). \tag{25}$$

Apply (19) into (25), we obtain

$$L = \sum_{i=1}^{N} (\alpha_i + \beta_i) - \frac{1}{2} \sum_{i=1}^{N} \sum_{j=1}^{N} (\alpha_i - \beta_i)(\alpha_j - \beta_j) x_i^T x_j. \tag{26}$$

The original classification problem can be transformed into its dual form

$$\max \sum_{i=1}^{N} (\alpha_i + \beta_i) - \frac{1}{2} \sum_{i=1}^{N} \sum_{j=1}^{N} (\alpha_i - \beta_i)(\alpha_j - \beta_j) x_i^T x_j, \tag{27}$$

$$\sum_{i=1}^{N} \alpha_i = \sum_{i=1}^{N} \beta_i$$

Subject to: $0 \le \alpha_i \le Ct_i + \lambda m_i, \quad i=1,...,N.$

$0 \le \beta_i \le Cf_i + (1-\lambda)m_i, \quad i=1,...,N.$

Let $K(x_i, x_i) = x_i^T x_j$, in order to transform (27) into a quadratic programming problem, we let $\gamma_i = \alpha_i - \beta_i$. The previous optimization becomes

$$\max \sum_{i=1}^{N} \gamma_i + 2 \sum_{i=1}^{N} \beta_i - \frac{1}{2} \sum_{i=1}^{N} \sum_{j=1}^{N} \gamma_i \gamma_j K(x_i, x_j), \tag{28}$$

$$\sum_{i=1}^{N} \gamma_i = 0$$

Subject to: $0 \le \alpha_i \le Ct_i, i=1,...,N$

$0 \le \beta_i \le Cf_i, i=1,...,N$

$0 \le \lambda \alpha_i + (1-\lambda)\beta_i \le Cm_i, i=1,...,N$

After solving this and substituting $w = \sum_{i=1}^{N}(\alpha_i - \beta_i)\phi(x_i)$ into the original classification problem, we obtain the following classifier:

$$y(x_i) = sign(w^T \phi(x_i) + b) = sign\left(\sum_{i=1}^{N}(\alpha_i - \beta_i)K(x \cdot x_i) + b \right). \tag{29}$$

4 Experiments Results and Analysis

4.1 Data Sets and Criteria

We used real life home loan data to conduct the experiment and selected one thousand sample data from a major commercial bank of China. The attributes of these data consisted of the customer information and the other information of the loan application form. There are 16 attributes listed in Table 1.

Table 1. Samples' Attributes

Index	Attributes
A01	Year of birth
A02	Number of children
A03	Number of other dependents
A04	Is there a home phone
A05	Education Level
A06	Applicant's Occupation
A07	Spouse's income
A08	Applicant's income
A09	Applicant's employment status
A10	Residential status
A11	Value of home
A12	Mortgage balance outstanding
A13	Monthly repayment of mortgage
A14	Year of Mortgage
A15	Outgoings on loans
A16	Outgoings on credit cards

In order to construct a two-class classification task, "good" customer and "bad" customer were taken into consideration. The "good" customer is the borrower who repayment on time. The "bad" customer is the one that did not pay one instalment over a period of three months. The "good" customer is labeled "1" and the "bad" customer is labeled "–1". These data is typically from a sample of applicants who have been granted bank credit already.

The estimation of loan defaults is a two-class classification task. Accuracy is the typical performance measure for two-class classification schemes. However, two learning algorithms can have the same accuracy, but the one which groups the errors near the decision border is the better one.

In order to appraise the performance of the classifier, Default Accuracy and Normal Accuracy are selected as standard criteria. We define them as follows

$$\text{Default Accuracy} = \frac{\text{default samples classified}}{\text{total default samples}} \tag{30}$$

$$\text{Normal Accuracy} = \frac{\text{normal samples classified}}{\text{total normal samples}} \tag{31}$$

The advantage of the default accuracy and normal accuracy is that they are a good indicator of whether the errors are close to the decision border or not. Given two classifiers with the same accuracy, the one with high default accuracy and normal accuracy is the better one. This definition is equivalent to the definitions of False Alarm and Miss Rate in [13].

4.2 Generating Vague Memberships

The key step of our experiment is to generate vague membership from the result of the loan classification system which is adopted in Chinese commercial banks widely. The loan classification system which is a risk-based approach provides a five-classification management on loan quality. The loans are classified into five categories, that is, pass, special-mention, substandard, doubtful and loss, the last three categories are recognized as non-performing loans (NPLs). The definitions of the five categories are as follow [14].

Pass: borrowers can honor the terms of the contracts, and there is no reason to doubt their ability to repay principal and interest of loans in full and on a timely basis.

Special-mention: borrowers are still able to service the loans currently, although the repayment of loans might be adversely affected by some factors.

Substandard: borrowers' ability to service loans is apparently in question, cannot depend on their normal business revenues to pay back the principal and interest of loans and certain losses might incur even when guarantees are executed.

Doubtful: borrowers cannot pay back principal and interest of loans in full and significant losses will incur even when guarantees are executed.

Loss: principal and interest of loans cannot be recovered or only a small portion can be recovered after taking all possible measures and resorting to necessary legal procedures.

The five-category classification of loan records all status in the management process of loans. The special-mention category is a transitional status between performing loan and non-performing loan. We use the results of five-category classification of loan to generate the vague membership. Then the truth-membership of a borrower is the pass category (performing loan) in proportion to all his loans classifications. The false-membership of a borrower is the non-performing loan category (i.e. substandard, doubtful and loss) in proportion to all his loans classifications. And the special-mention category indicates the unknown part.

4.3 Experiment Results

To decrease the bias due to the choice of split between training datasets and test datasets, we randomly divide the original data into two sub-datasets evenly, one half for training and the other half for testing, this is referred to as 50-50 split experiment. The training dataset includes 500 samples with 120 "bad" customers and 380 "good" customers.

We compare our VS-FSVM with the traditional SVM, FSVM and B-FSVM on the same training dataset. Then we predict the same test dataset using their classification model respectively. Table 2 shows the comparison of the predicting result of these algorithms.

Table 2. The comparison of predicting result

Classification Algorithm	Normal Accuracy	Default Accuracy	Overall Accuracy
SVM	88.95%	69.17%	84.20%
FSVM	89.47%	70.83%	85.00%
B-FSVM	90.26%	72.50%	86.00%
VS-FSVM	91.84%	75.00%	87.80%

It is obvious in Table 2 that total accuracy of VS-SVM is better than other SVMs, that is, the predicting accuracy can increase just 2%. Our future direction of the research will focus on how to improve the Default Accuracy especially in the test dataset.

5 Conclusions

In this paper, we propose an improved FSVM based on vague sets by assigning a truth-membership and a false-membership to each data point. And we reformulate the improved FSVM so that different input points can make different contributions to decision hyperplane. In order to verify the performance of the improved FSVM, we apply it to credit assessment. The experiment results show that our method is promising. Our future direction of the research will focus on how to improve the default accuracy. We believe that deeper data preprocessing and more suitable parameters selection will improve the performance of generalization. Extending the two-class classification to multi-class classification is also our future research work.

References

1. Vapnik, V.N.: The Nature of Statistical Learning Theory. Springer, New York (1995)
2. Cortes, C., Vapnik, V.N.: Support vector networks. Machine Learning 20, 273–297 (1995)
3. Burges, C.: A tutorial on support vector machines for pattern recognition. Data Mining and Knowledge Discovery 2(2) (1998)

4. Huang, Z., Chen, H.: Credit rating analysis with support vector machines and neural networks: a market comparative study. Decision Support Systems 37, 543–558 (2004)
5. Lin, C.-F., Wang, S.-D.: Fuzzy Support Vector Machines. IEEE Transactions on Neural Networks 2, 464–471 (2002)
6. Huang, H.P., Liu, Y.H.: Fuzzy Support Vector Machines for Pattern Recognition and Data Mining. International Journal of Fuzzy Systems 4, 826–835 (2002)
7. Zhang, X.: Using class-center vectors to build support vector machines. In: Proc. IEEE NNSP'99, pp. 3–11 (1999)
8. Wang, Y.-Q., Wang, S.-Y., Lai, K.K.: A New Fuzzy Support Vector Machine to Evaluate Credit Risk. IEEE Trans. On Fuzzy Systems 13(6) (2005)
9. Lin, C.-F., Wang, S.-D.: Training algorithms for fuzzy support vector machines with noisy data. In: IEEE XIII Workshop on Neural Networks for Signal Processing, pp. 517–526 (2003)
10. Zadeh, L.A.: Fuzzy sets. Information and Control 8(3), 338–353 (1965)
11. Gau, W.-L., Buehrer, D.J.: Vague sets. IEEE Transactions on Systems, Man and Cybernetics 23(2), 610–614 (1993)
12. Lu, A., Ng, W.: Vague Sets or Intuitionistic Fuzzy Sets for Handling Vague Data: Which One Is Better? In: Delcambre, L.M.L., Kop, C., Mayr, H.C., Mylopoulos, J., Pastor, Ó. (eds.) ER 2005. LNCS, vol. 3716, pp. 401–416. Springer, Heidelberg (2005)
13. Drucker, H., Wu, D., Vapnik, V.: Support Vector Machines for Spam Categorization. IEEE Transactions on Neural Networks 10(5) (1999)
14. The People's Bank of China, Guidelines on Risk-Based Loan Classification (2001), http://www.pbc.gov.cn/english//detail.asp?col=6800&ID=46

A Cost-Aware Parallel Workload Allocation Approach Based on Machine Learning Techniques

Shun Long[1], Grigori Fursin[2], and Björn Franke[3]

[1] Department of Computer Science, Jinan University,
Guangzhou 510632, P.R. China
long.shun@gmail.com
[2] Member of HiPEAC, ALCHEMY Group, INRIA Futurs and LRI,
Paris-Sud University, France
grigori.fursin@inria.fr
[3] Member of HiPEAC, Institute for Computing Systems Architecture,
The University of Edinburgh, UK
bfranke@inf.ed.ac.uk

Abstract. Parallelism is one of the main sources for performance improvement in modern computing environment, but the efficient exploitation of the available parallelism depends on a number of parameters. Determining the optimum number of threads for a given data parallel loop, for example, is a difficult problem and dependent on the specific parallel platform. This paper presents a learning-based approach to parallel workload allocation in a cost-aware manner. This approach uses static program features to classify programs, before deciding the best workload allocation scheme based on its prior experience with similar programs. Experimental results on 12 Java benchmarks (76 test cases with different workloads in total) show that it can efficiently allocate the parallel workload among Java threads and achieve an efficiency of 86% on average.

Keywords: parallelism, workload allocation, cost, instance-based learning.

1 Introduction

Parallelism is one of the main sources for performance improvement [4][11] in modern computing environment. This is particularly true in the area of high performance computing, where the cost of parallelism (on thread creation, scheduling and communication) is usually negligible when compared to heavy workload. However, the rapidly evolving hardware technology enables parallelization in most modern computing systems, for instance embedded devices. In many of these systems, the cost of parallelization becomes non-negligible when compared to workload. Moreover, inefficient workload allocation could even degrade the performance considerably, which is not acceptable. Therefore, it is vitally important to allocate the workload in a cost-aware manner in order to achieve optimal performance.

Java is a widely used programming language with multi-threading features. But the development of efficient parallel Java programs requires careful consideration to avoid performance degradation due to the cost of thread creation, scheduling and

K. Li et al. (Eds.): NPC 2007, LNCS 4672, pp. 506–515, 2007.

communication. This cost depends on many environment-specific factors (CPU, cache, memory, operating system, Java virtual machine, etc). The interaction of these factors is hard to model or predict in advance. In search for optimal performance in a given execution environment, it is expected that the compiler or virtual machines uses an adaptive workload allocation approach, so that the workload can be allocated among Java threads in a cost-aware manner. This can be achieved statically or in a dynamic manner via speculative parallelization, both approaches have their specific advantages and disadvantages as discussed in [12].

This paper presents a cost-aware parallel workload allocation approach based on machine learning techniques [15]. It learns from training examples how to allocate parallel workload among Java threads. When a new program is encountered, the compiler extracts its static program features for classification purpose, retrieves its prior experience with similar training examples, and uses this knowledge to decide the best parallel scheme for the new program. Experimental results suggest that this approach can effectively allocate workload among various numbers of threads and achieve optimal or sub-optimal performance.

The outline of this paper is as follows. Section 2 presents a Java multi-threaded framework, before demonstrating via some preliminary experiments the demand for a cost-aware parallel workload allocation approach. Section 3 presents our adaptive approach. Section 4 evaluates its performance and analyzes the results. Section 5 briefly reviews some related work, before some concluding remarks in section 6.

2 Motivation

We first present a Java multi-threaded framework which uses the class ExecutorService in package java.util.concurrent to parallelize a given *for* loop. For example, the sequential loop presented on the left of Table.1 can be parallelized as that on the right. The modification to the original code is given in bold font. Most of these modifications are loop-irrelevant and therefore can be implemented as a code template in advance. When a for loop is encountered, the compiler replaces the loop with the code template, copies the loop body into the run method of an inner class *Task*, before embedding Task into the class. The only question remains to be solved is the parallel scheme, i.e. how many threads should be used to share the workload in order to achieve optimal performance. Because this experiment aims to evaluate how a loop's performance varies under different schemes. They are decided in advance.

This framework is evaluated on a platform containing dual Xeon processors (each with two 2.80GHz cores) and 4G RAM, with Java Platform Standard Edition 1.5.0_02 running under Redhat Linux 2.6.12-1.1372_FC3cmp. Twelve benchmarks are chosen from the Java version of the DSPStone benchmark suite [22]. In total, there are 76 test cases derived from these benchmarks, each containing one *for* loop of a specific workload. *benchmark_n* is used to label the test case of benchmark with a workload of 2^n, and parallel level m is used to denote the scheme which allocates the workload evenly among 2^m threads. For simplicity concern, the experiment only considers workloads and thread numbers proportional to 2, so that the workload can be evenly distributed among threads. The discussion about more general workload sharing and load imbalance is left to future work.

Table 1. A sequential Java loop (*Example_Squential,* on the left) and its parallel version (*Example_Parallel,* on the right) via the Java multi-threading framework

```
public class Example_Sequential {          import java.util.concurrent.*;
int size;                                  public class Example_Parallel {
public static void main(                     static int size;
   String[] args)                            static int numberofThreads;
   throws InterruptedException {             static ExecutorService service;
      ...                                    public static void main(String[] args)
      for (int i = 0; i < size ; i++) {        throws InterruptedException {
         system.out.println(i));    }            ...
      ...                                      Service =
   }                                           Executors.newFixedThreadPool(
   ...                                            numberofThreads);
}                                              for (int i = 0; i<numberofThreads; i++)
                                               {   service.execute(new Task(i));    }
                                               service.shutdown();
                                                  ...

                                             }
                                             private static class Task
                                                implements Runnable {
                                                private final int id;
                                                private int lbound, ubound;
                                                public Task(int id) {
                                                   this.id = id;
                                                   lbound = id *    size
                                                          / numberofThreads;
                                                   ubound=
                                                   (id==numberofThread-1) ? size :
                                                      (id+1)*size/numberofThreads;
                                                }
                                                public void run() {
                                                   for (int i=lbound; i<ubound; i++) {
                                                      system.out.println(i);    }
                                                }
                                                ...
                                             }
                                             }
```

The impact of different parallel schemes on each benchmark is summarized in Fig.1. It demonstrates that parallelism can significantly improve the performance of most test cases. Take *Matrix_3* as an example, when parallel level *m* increases, there are more threads to share its workload. This results in a rising speedup, which reaches its highest (37.36) when the workload is shared among 2^5=32 threads. However, further increasing *m* means that more threads are created. This implies more time spent on thread creation and scheduling, which diminishes the performance improvement achieved via parallelism.

When applicable, all *for* loops in Java programs can be parallelized in the above manner. Due to different cost in thread creation, scheduling and communication, a program's performance may vary significantly when parallelized with different schemes (i.e. *numberofThreads*). In some cases, improper schemes may even degrade

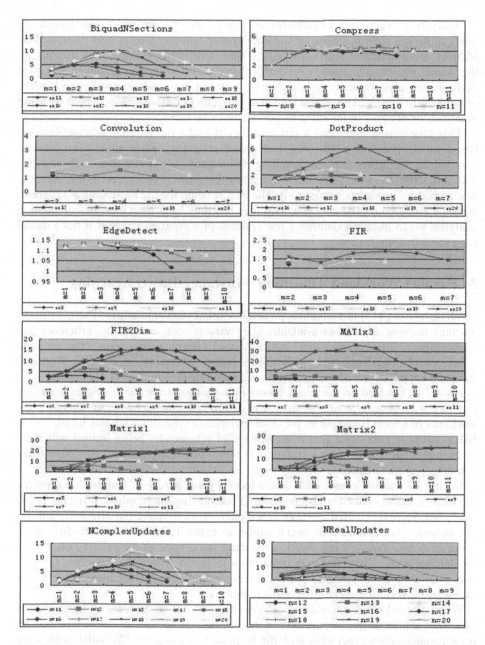

Fig. 1. Performance improvement via parallelism, over 12 benchmarks with different workloads (2^n) and different workload allocation schemes (2^m), where the speedup achieved is plotted against the number of threads used to share the workload

the performance. In search for higher performance via multi-threading, the compiler or virtual machine should decide the scheme in a cost-aware manner.

Analysis of experimental results reveals that *programs with similar workloads are likely to benefit from the same or similar parallel scheme*. This is best illustrated by *Matrix1* and *Matrix2* in Fig.1. Although coded in different manner, they actually do the same job, which results in performance curves almost identical. If good performance improvement can be achieved by using N threads to parallelize *Matrix1* of workload W, it is likely that a similar improvement can also be achieved by using N threads on *Matrix2* of the same workload, and vice versa.

This observation hints that a compiler could make the parallel scheme decision based on its previous experience with other programs. Each time a program is parallelized, the scheme and the resulting performance are stored in a database along with a description of the program. When a new program is encountered, this database is searched for programs similar to it. The best scheme for the most similar programs is then considered for the new one. This idea has long been used in static compilation analysis, which usually examines a few features of a program to see if it fits a model for a specific optimization.

3   Parallel Workload Allocation – Instance-Based Learning

Machine learning [15] is a natural approach to exploit such similarities. There are many machine learning approaches available. They vary in cost, complexity, efficiency and applicability. We believe that instance-based learning fits our objectives in effectiveness, timeliness and applicability better. Therefore, a Parallel Workload Allocation approach based on Instance-Based Learning (PWA-IBL) is developed.

PWA-IBL is based on the above observation that *programs with similar workload are likely to benefit from the same or similar parallel scheme*. It allocates the workload of a loop based on its previous experience with other similar loops. PWA-IBL consists of two steps: first it learns parallel schemes by being trained with a set of examples either carefully or randomly chosen; then it applies the knowledge when a new loop is encountered.

During the training phase, each time a loop is parallelized, its features are captured for classification. This can be considered as making an implicit estimate of its workload. Such an implicit estimate is not only easier to make but also sufficient for our purpose (as demonstrated later), whilst an explicit estimate is more difficult to achieve. A new category is created in the database if none of the existing ones has a similar workload. Then, the loop description is stored within the category, together with different parallel schemes and the corresponding performance improvement (for example, the resulting speedup or of other metrics).

When a new loop is encountered, PWA-IBL captures its features and classifies it. The most similar loop category within the database is identified. Then, based on its prior parallelization experience with the loops of this category, PWA-IBL selects the best scheme, before creating the threads and allocating the workload among them.

To implement PWA-IBL, the compiler must correlate loops, number of parallel threads and the resulting performance improvement in a systematic manner. In machine learning terms, the inputs or features of the problem are a description of the program and the workload allocation scheme, and the output is the performance improvement. These features not only reveal important details of the program but also help a compiler in classification. Therefore, they must be formally specified in order to enable instance-based learning.

PWA-IBL uses five program features for loop description and classification purposes. They are 1) loop depth; 2) loop size; 3) number of arrays used; 4) number of statements within the loop body, and 5) number of array references. It is understandable that not all program features play an equal role in workload estimation. Therefore, different weights are assigned to different features during classification, with higher weights given to feature 1), 2) and 4). Other features that can better describe the loop for PWA-IBL, but this set of features can be readily obtained from most compilers' internal representation of a program.

4 Evaluation

PWA-IBL is tested in the same environment as specified in section 2. The experiment aims to evaluate the impact of the training set selection on the performance of PWA-IBL, i.e. how enlarging the training set can improve its predictability. It is carried out in a cross-validation manner. For each *benchmark_n*, the size of training set is first decided, before the set itself is formed by selecting examples from the other 75 programs. For simplicity, only sizes 1, 5, 10, 15, 30, 45, 60 and 75 are considered, as it is unnecessary to increase the training set size by one each time. In addition, training examples are randomly chosen from all the other 75 programs. This is repeated for t times ($t=30$ in our test), each time with a different training set, before an average speedup is obtained.

For each *benchmark_n*, PWA-IBL applies its knowledge learned from a training set of a certain size s. If the chosen scheme cannot improve the performance, the resulting speedup is considered 0. Let r be the highest speedup achieved on *benchmark_n*. The performance of PWA-IBL with size s is defined as r'/r, where r' the average speedup achieved across t different training sets of size s. Take *DotProduct_20* as an example, when the training set size $s=30$, PWA-IBL achieves an average speedup of 5.36 over $t=30$ evaluations. Fig.1 shows that the highest speedup for *DotProduct_20* is 6.46 (when its workload is shared among $2^4=16$ threads), i.e. the performance of PWA-IBL is 5.36/6.46=83% with the training set size $s=30$.

Fig.2 summarizes the performance of PWA-IBL on all 76 test cases, where it is plotted against the training set size s. Take *DotProduct_20* as an example, when the training set size $s=1$, PWA-IBL is equivalent to a random algorithm, as it learns only from one randomly selected example. The average speedup it achieves is 3.81, and the resulting performance is 3.81/6.46 =59%. When $s=5$, the average speedup is 4.07 and its performance is 63%, and so on. When $s=75$, PWA-IBL learns from all the other 75 test cases. This is equivalent to the "leave one out" cross validation test. The best scheme (share the workload among $2^4= 16$ threads) from the one most similar to *DotProduct_20* is selected, resulting in a speedup of 6.46, when its performance reaches 100%. Similar results are found on most curves in Fig.2, which shows that as the training set size increases, the performance of PWA-IBL improves accordingly, because it can learn from more examples and therefore select better parallel schemes.

However, there are some surges in the PWA-IBL curves on some test cases which deserve further analysis. These test cases include *Convolution_17*, *EdgeDetect_8*, *EdgeDetect_10* when the training set size $s=5$, *MAT1x3_7* when $s=20$, and

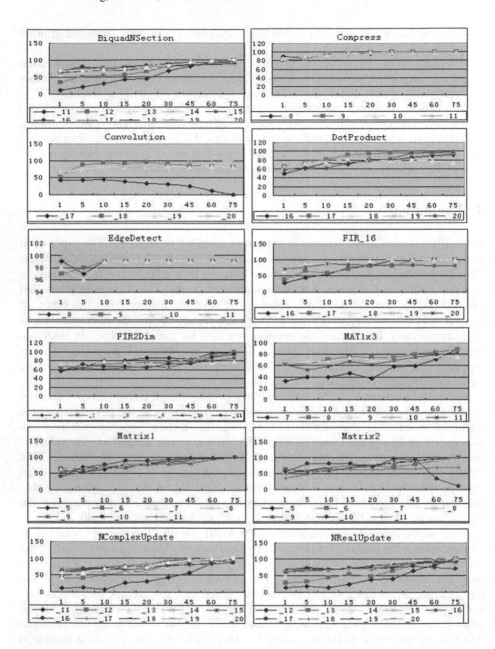

Fig. 2. The performance of PWA-IBL, where it is plotted against the size of training example set. The performance is defined as r'/r, where r' the average speedup achieved on a particular training set size s and r the highest speedup achieved on the given test case, regardless of training set size.

Matrix2_10 when $s>45$. In the case of *EdgeDetect_8* and *_10,* the surges are noise, as the actual variance is insignificant (between 96% and 98%), indicating that the training set selection has little impact on PWA-IBL performance. In the case of *MAT1x3_7*, a closer look at learning process shows that the training set contain many not-very-similar cases, which in turn affect the performance. Nevertheless, the highest speedup on *MAT1x3_7* is relatively modest at 1.74, with the variance less than 0.35.

Experimental results on *Convolution _17* show that speedup is achieved only with a scheme of $2^4=16$ threads. No other scheme can improve its performance. Because the training cases are randomly chosen, when *s* increases, it becomes less likely that PWA-IBL can effectively predict this scheme, and its performance decreases instead.

In the case of *Matrix2_10*, higher speedups can be achieved as the number of threads increases. It reaches the highest when there are $2^{10}=1024$ threads sharing the workload. A closer look at the raw experimental results show that besides *Matrix2_10* itself, only on *Matrix1_10*, *Matrix1_11* and *Matrix2_11* (all considered similar enough to *Matrix2_10*) similar speedup can be achieved with such a large number of threads. When the training set is small, the possibility is low for these programs to be included. PWA-IBL can only select a scheme of smaller number of threads, which results in a lower speedup. Therefore, the performance curve starts low. It starts rising when PWA-IBL is trained with a larger set of examples. When the size reaches a certain threshold (60 as indicated in Fig.2), it becomes more likely that one or more of these three programs be included in the training set. However, only on *Matrix1_10* the highest speedup is achieved with a scheme of 1024 threads, whilst on *Matrix1_11* and *Matrix2_11*, the highest speedup is achieved with $2^{11}=2048$ threads. Therefore, PWA-IBL reaches the highest speedup only when it correctly selects *Matrix1_10* as the one most similar to *Matrix2_10*. Otherwise, no speedup is found since sharing the workload among 2048 threads degrades the performance. For *Matrix1_10* and *Matrix1_11*, sub-optimal speedups are achieved when PWA-IBL decides that 1024 is the best parallel scheme from its prior experience from *Matrix2_10* and *Matrix2_11*.

In brief, PWA-IBL finds the optimal parallel schemes for 36 out of the 76 test cases and over 80% of the highest speedups on the other 33. On average, its efficiency over these 76 test cases is 86%. It shows that PWA-IBL should be trained with at least 30 training examples to achieve a reasonable accuracy, In addition, whenever possible, training examples should be selected as diverse as possible to cover most of the also be able to adapt to such cases.

It is worth noting that the current experiment only considers test cases with both thread numbers and workloads proportional to 2, where the workload is evenly distributed among the threads. We leave cases with arbitrary workload and thread numbers for the future work, though preliminary results show that PWA-IBL should also be able to adapt to such cases.

5 Related Work

Parallelism [4][11] is one of the main sources for performance improvement in modern computing environments. Key techniques for automatic detection of parallelism are discussed in [5]. A prototype compiler is presented in [3], where loop transformation and parallelization techniques are used to achieve high performance on numerical Java codes. Jikes[2] compiler uses runtime feedback to direct its adaptive optimization. Dynamic optimization is presented in [21] to measure the cost of thread creation and parallelize code insides a Jikes RVM at run time. The dynamic parallelizing compiler in [17] uses runtime feedback to adapt both application and operating system to the JAMAICA chip multiprocessor (CMP) architecture on the fly. Speculative techniques[9][16] are developed to exploit parallelism[14][17]. Jrpm[8] is a CMP-based runtime parallelizing JVM with thread-level speculation support. Most of these work focus on the search of parallelism opportunity, load balancing and thread migration[14][21], and give little concern to the cost of parallelism and its impact on performance[18]. PWA-IBL can be considered a complement to them in helping the compiler to decide how the workload should be allocated at the first place. It can accelerate the search for best parallel scheme.

Machine learning[15] has recently been introduced to compiler optimization at system level. Various learning approaches are used in iterative optimization[1][10] to explore a large optimization space. Machine learning is used in [6] to build a performance model based on a small number of evaluations. It first tests a small set of sample optimizations on a prior set of benchmarks, then analyzes the results in order to identify characteristic optimizations, based on which some further test runs are carried out on the target program. This technique significantly reduces the cost of evaluating the impact of compiler optimizations. Logistic regression is used in [7] to derive a predictive model that selects suitable optimizations to apply to each method based on code features. Instance-based learning is used in [13] to select suitable loop transformations within an optimization space of various loop re-ordering transformations.

6 Conclusion

This paper presents a fast and efficient machine learning based parallel workload allocation approach. It uses static program features to classify programs, before deciding the best workload allocation based on its prior experience with similar programs. It can decide, in a cost-aware manner, the best number of threads to share the workload of a given loop in order to achieve optimal performance via multithreading. Experimental results show that PWA-IBL can find the best parallel schemes for 36 out of the 76 test cases and over 80% of the best speedups on the other 33. On average its efficiency over these 76 test cases is 86%. Its performance improves when trained with more examples.

We plan to use PWA-IBL to achieve runtime adaptability, where features such as the hardware counter reading could be used to estimate not only program but also system workload. Portability of a PWA-IBL-enabled compiler could be achieved via the introduction of some architectural features. In addition, PWA-IBL shall be enhanced for more general code block and arbitrary workload. Methods could be developed to select better training examples, identify less representative ones and eliminate them when necessary.

References

[1] Agakov, F., Bonilla, E., Cavazos, J., et al.: Using machine learning to focus iterative optimization. In: Proc. of the 2006 International Symposium on Code Generation and Optimization (2006)
[2] Arnold, M., Hind, M., Ryhder, B.: Online feedback-directed Java optimization. ACM SIGPLAN Notices 37(11) (2002)

[3] Artigas, P., Gupta, M., Midkiff, S., Moreira, J.: Automatic loop transformation and parallelization for Java. In: Proc. of the 14th International Conference. for Supercomputing (2000)

[4] Banerjee, U., Eigenmann, R., Nicolau, A., Padua, D.: Automatic program parallelization. Proceedings of the IEEE 81(2) (1993)

[5] Blume, W., Eigenmann, R., Hoeflinger, J., et al.: Automatic detection of parallelism, a grand challenge for high performance computing. IEEE Parallel and Distributed Technology 2(3) (1994)

[6] Cavazos, J., Dubach, C., Agakov, F., et al.: Automatic performance model construction for the fast software exploration of new hardware design. In: Proc. of International Conference on Compilers, Architecture and Synthesis for Embedded Systems (CASES'06) (2006)

[7] Cavazos, J., O'Boyle, M.: Method-specific dynamic compilation using logistic regression. In: Proc. of ACM SIGPLAN Conferences on Object-Oriented Programming, Systems, Languages, and Applications (OOPSLA'06), ACM Press, New York (2006)

[8] Chen, M., Olukotun, K.: The Jrpm System for Dynamically Parallelizing Java Programs. ACM SIGARCH Computer Architecture News 31(2) (2003)

[9] Cintra, M., Martinez, J., Torrellas, J.: Architectural support for scalable speculative parallelization in shared-memory multiprocessors. In: Intl. Symp. on Computer Architecture (ISCA) (2000)

[10] Cooper, K., Subranmanian, D., Torzon, L.: Adaptive optimizing compilers for the 21st century. Journal of Supercomputing 23(1) (2001)

[11] Dongarra, J., Foster, I., Fox, G., Gropp, W., Kennedy, K., Torzon, L., White, A.: Sourcebook of parallel computing. Morgan Kaufmann, US (2003)

[12] Gupta, M., Nim, R.: Techniques for speculative run-time parallelization of loops. In: Proc. of Supercomputing '98 (1998)

[13] Long, S., O'Boyle, M.: Adaptive Java optimization using instance-based learning. In: P roc. of the 18th ACM International Conference on Supercomputing, France (2004)

[14] Marcuello, P., Gonzales, A., Tubella, J.: Speculative Multithreaded processors. In: P roc. of the 1998 ACM International Conference on Supercomputing (1998)

[15] Mitchell, T.: Machine learning. McGraw-Hill, US (1997)

[16] Oplinger, J., Heine, D., Lam, M.: In search of speculative thread-level parallelism. In: Malyshkin, V. (ed.) Parallel Computing Technologies. LNCS, vol. 1662, Springer, Heidelberg (1999)

[17] Wright, G., El-Mahdy, A., Watson, I.: Java machine and integrated circuit architecture, Java Microarchitecture. Kluwer, Dordrecht (2002)

[18] Yang, L., Schopf, J., Foster, I.: Conservative scheduling: using predicted variance to improve scheduling decisions in dynamic environments. Proc. of Scientific Computing (2003)

[19] Zhao, J., Kirkham, C., Rogers526, I.: Lazy interprocedural analysis for dynamic loop parallelization. In: Proc. of Workshop on New Horizons in Compilers, India (2006)

[20] Zhao, J., Rogers, I., Kirkham, C., Watson, I.: Loop parallelization for the Jikes RVM. In: Proc. of the 6th International Conference on Parallel and Distributed Computing, Applications and Technologies (PDCAT 2005) (2005)

[21] Zhu, W., Wang, C.L., Lau, C.M.: JESSICA2: a distributed Java virtual machine with transparent thread migration support. In: proc. of IEEE 4th International Conference on Cluster Computing (2002)

[22] Zivojnovic, V., et al.: DSPstone: a DSP-oriented benchmarking methodology. In: Proc. of Signal Processing Applications & Technology (1994)

A Hierarchical Programming Model for Large Parallel Interactive Applications

Jean-Denis Lesage and Bruno Raffin

INRIA, Grenoble Informatics Laboratory, France

Abstract. This paper focuses on parallel interactive applications ranging from scientific visualization, to virtual reality or computational steering. Interactivity makes them particular on three main aspects: they are endlessly iterative, use advanced I/O devices, and must perform under strong performance constraints (latency, refresh rate). In this paper, we propose an application description language based on a data flow and hierarchical component model to cope with the complexity of parallel interactive applications. It enables us to define highly generic components, enforcing the application maintainability and portability. An implementation on top of the FlowVR middleware is presented.

1 Introduction

An interactive application is an endless iterative process involving a user user interacting with a program through input and output devices. It is often referred to as a "human in the loop simulation". Today, an emerging class of interactive applications intends to associate virtual reality, scientific visualization, simulation and application steering. It leads to very complex applications coupling advanced I/O devices, large data sets, various parallel codes. To be interactive, they must perform under strong performance constraints, often measured in terms of latency and refresh rate. Examples of such applications are described in [1,2,3]. In this paper we focus on two issues faced when designing such application:

- Software engineering issues where multiple pieces of codes (simulation codes, graphics rendering codes, device drivers, etc.), developed by different persons, during different periods of time, have to be integrated in the same framework to properly work together.
- Hardware performance limitations bypassed by multiplying the units available (disks, CPUs, GPUs, cameras, video projectors, etc.), but introducing at the same time extra complexity. In particular it often requires to introduce parallel algorithms and data redistribution strategies, that should be generic enough to minimize human intervention when the target execution platform changes.

One challenge is to ensure the genericity and modularity of the application.

Scientific visualization applications are often developed with Modular Visualization Environments (MVE) like OpenDX [4], Iris Explorer [5] or VTK [6].

K. Li et al. (Eds.): NPC 2007, LNCS 4672, pp. 516–525, 2007.

These environments are usually based on a data flow model where processing tasks receive data and generate new ones. Most of MVEs support parallel executions. An application is basically a list of filters applied to the data set before rendering. The first natural level of parallelism is to distribute the different steps of the filter pipeline on different machines. Because the data set is read only, the pipeline can easily be duplicated and executed in parallel on sub parts of the data set [7]. Advanced parallel rendering algorithms exist, based for instance on specific parallel data structures and dynamic work balancing schemes. In this case they are implemented on their own, usually using classical parallel programming languages, because MVEs do not provide the necessary constructs.

In virtual reality, to ensure an efficient data redistribution between parallel algorithms that may run at different and varying frequencies, complex coupling schemes associating data re-sampling and collective communications are required. Dedicated environments like FlowVR [8], OpenMask [9] or COVISE [10] propose different approaches to support such features. However, the resulting application code tends to be difficult to maintained when reaching a certain size. Connectivity between processing tasks (communication channels) are expressed by direct links between the corresponding elements: it requires the concerned elements be directly visible one for each other, preventing attempts to strongly structure the code by encapsulating patterns in methods or functions.

Component models, like CCA (Common Component Architecture) or CCM (Corba Component Model), provide ADLs for the description of distributed applications. SCIRun, an environment dedicated to scientific visualization, is based on the CCA model [11]. Some extensions intend to enforce the support of parallel components and the associated coupling patterns [12]. But these models suffer from the same limitations as the systems mentioned earlier (FlowVR, Covise) regarding the modularity of parallel component coupling. Fractal [13] is a truly hierarchical component model. We are aware of one implementation of Fractal for parallel (grid) applications: ProActive [14]. A ProActive composite component can be a parallel component. But redistribution patterns are coded into the ports of the parallel components. A pattern cannot be modified without modifying the component, limiting application modularity. In this paper we propose to encode coupling patterns as standalone fractal components with a connectivity model between primitive components (processing tasks) that does impair this modularity.

We propose an application description language, called architecture description language or ADL following the uses of the component community, based on a data flow and hierarchical component model. We focus on interactive applications, instead of a general purpose language, relying mainly on their iterative nature, to restrain the domain of the language.

To enforce the genericity of the described application, components defer introspection and auto-configuration processes to controllers. A controller is local to a given component, but it may get extra data consulting the state of the neighbor components or through external data repositories. These controllers, that can generate new components for instance, are called recursively and repeatedly in a traverse process until reaching a fixed point. Traverse either leads to an error (missing data impair the traverse completion) or a success. This approach enables to define highly generic components, enforcing the application maintainability and portability. In particular, we can define arbitrarily complex and adaptive data redistribution components, for instance mixing collective communications and re-sampling. This is an important feature for interactive applications where these coupling mechanisms play an important role to enforce interactivity.

Section 2 presents our hierarchical model. Section 3 details our implementation on top of the FlowVR [15] middleware with a focus on the traverse process. Section 4 concludes the paper.

2   Programming Model

In this section, we describe our hierarchical component model inspired by Fractal[13] for large parallel interactive applications. Fractal is a component model based on a component hierarchy. This model enables to encapsulate components into high-level components. This encapsulation enforces reusability and modularity. We will also present another feature, named controllers, inspired by Fractal too. Theses objects enables dynamic reconfiguration and component introspection.

2.1   Components

A component has an interface defined by a set of ports. We distinguish two kinds of components:

Primitive components. A primitive component contains a loop. At each iteration, the component reads data from its input ports. It writes computation results on its output ports.

Composite components. A composite component contains other components (composite or primitive). We impose a strong encapsulation paradigm: a component cannot be directly contained into two parent components.

2.2   Port Typing

There are two types of ports: input and output ports. The input port receives data and output port sends data. We do not impose a strong typing. We simply require the input and output correspondence. Nevertheless, depending on the needs, the port typing can be extended. We plan a stronger typing based on the data type exchanged by the ports.

2.3   Example

Throughout this paper, we use a simple example (Fig. 1). It shows the classical structure of an interactive application. The goal of this application is to compute prime numbers and from these numbers compute a 3D image. The image is updated each time a new prime number is computed. A keyboard enables the user to change his point of view on the image.

The *Computes* composite component is a parallel component programed with MPI. It spawns n processes *Computes/0,..., Computes/n-1* seen as primitive components of *Computes*. Notice that n is only known once the application as been configured for an execution on a particular target machine.

The composite component *Renderer* is divided in two main parts (Fig. 1.b). The first one, *Visu* makes the rendering on a display. This display contains several screens. For each screen, a rendering process must be instanced. The *Visu* component contains all these rendering processes. The second one is the component *Capture*. It gets key events from user and sends them to the *Visu* component.

Two coupling components are dedicated to communication (Components *Connect* and *GreedyConnect*). The *Connect* component transmits data from *Computes* component to *Renderer* component. The *Connect* component contains a communication pattern. The *GreedyConnect* resamples messages from *Capture* for *Visu*.

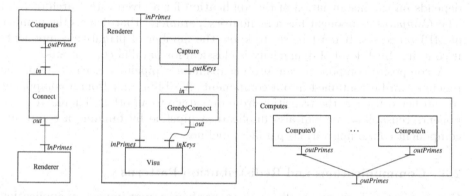

Fig. 1. a) The application : a composite component *Computes* generates primes numbers. They go through the *Connect* component to the renderer. **b)** The *Renderer* composite component contains two components *Render* and *Capture*. **c)** The *Computes* composite component is a MPI parallel component.

In this example, *Computes, Renderer* are examples of composite components. *Compute/0* and *Visu* are primitive objects. *outPrimes* from *Computes* is an output port. *inPrimes* from *Renderer* is an input port.

2.4 Links

Links are used to model data flows between ports. We distinguish two kinds of links. The parent link joins a port from a component to one of his children's port. The extremities of a parent link must have the same type. For example (Fig. 1.b), the *outPrimes* port on *computes* component has the same type as all its children (i.e. output port).

The second kind of links are called sibling links. They go from a component to an another. We assume that an object cannot share data with an another object without using a connection. So a sibling link must join an input port to an output port. Due to the strict encapsulation paradigm, a sibling link cannot directly connect two components that are not brothers (child of the same parent). A chain of sibling and parent links must be used to connect two non brother components.

The link between *outPrimes* port and *in* port of *Connect* in our example is a valid sibling link.

2.5   Parallel Components

A composite component can be a container for parallel application. For example, *Computes* is a parallel MPI code spawning when launched several processes, each one being a primite compenent. These primitive components are linked to the same parent port (Fig. 1.c). This kind of structure can express the data and task parallelism for instance. Notice that the number of processes spawned depends on the instanciation of the application for a given target architecture. The *Computes* component has a mandatory parameter that defines the number of MPI processes. It must be set to know the number of primitive components it contains. Such level of dynamicity is classical for parallel components.

A composite component can also encapsulate a pipeline. Each stage of the pipeline can be contained into a component. A sibling link from a component to another will make the transition from one stage to an other. Thanks to components reusability, we can also duplicate a pipeline by building a composite component containing various parallel pipelines.

2.6   Communications and Redistribution Patterns

Communication between parallel components have a huge impact on application performance. They need to be customisable and modular. A communication component is simply a component encapsulating a generic redistribution pattern. The simplest one is just a link transferring data from one output port of a primitive component to one input port of a primitive component.

In our example, a connection schema is implemented in the *MergeThenTree* component (Fig. 2). This component has a different implementation following the number of primitive components *Compute* and *Renderer* will spawn. Unlike the parallel components, user does not have to set the parameters of these dynamic components. These components get their mandatory parameters from their neighbors.

The simplest communication pattern is a simple connection. But it could be a merge tree and a broadcast tree with different arities. The order of merged messages could be customized. Communications may resample messages. Components can contain filters that operate on messages or enforce synchronizations between a set of components. Typically, filters are used to resample messages. Several filters can be synchronized to perform a coherent sampling, i.e. ensure they sample messages issued at the same logicial time.

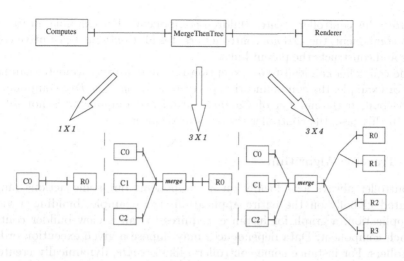

Fig. 2. Parallel compute component send data through a connection component to a parallel renderer. According to N and M parameters, a communication schemes is generated.

Some communication component parameters depends from the state of the neighbor components. In the example (Fig. 2), the shape of the communication pattern depends on the number of *Compute* and *Render* components connected at its extremities. For this reason, these components can create dependence relations between components.

Our model eases the development of generic communication patterns outside the context of an application. An implementation of this model can be associated for example with a library of $N \times M$ data redistribution components. Components provide modularity. A user is able to change a communication pattern for his application and see the impact on performance.

2.7   Controllers

Controllers are used for the configuration and the construction of dynamic components. Parallel and communication components are often dynamic. Parallel components can have a parameter to set the number of computational units (i.e. the degree of parallelism). Communication component parameters often depend on their neighbor states.

There are two types of controllers:

- Controllers getting data from a component (introspection)
- Controllers setting parameters (configuration)

A controller is associated to a component and a method. A main controller must be implemented for all new composite components. We named this controller *execute.* This controller creates children components. For example, in the *Computes* component, the *execute* controller creates all *Compute/i* primitive components and constructs the parent links.

The controller can lead to an exception if a mandatory parameter can not be set. For example, the communication pattern in *MergeThenTree* component can not be built if the number of *Compute* primitive components is not set (Sec. 2.6). In this case, the controller throws an exception.

2.8   Traverse Algorithm

A controller always acts locally on a component, but some actions must be executed globally on the entire application. For example, building a view of an application, a graph for instance, requires to call a view builder controller on each component. Data dependences may impose a given execution order on controllers. For instance some controllers, like *execute*, dynamically create new components. Connection components often have to be constructed after their neighbors. Most controllers have to be executed at most once by component to obtain the correct result. Consequently, the iteration algorithm is an important issue in our model. We named this algorithm the traverse algorithm. This algorithm must respect following constraints :

- Top-down iteration : a controller must be applied on the parent compoenent before to be applied to its children.
- A controller must be applied on a component at most once.
- Constraints on the execution order must be respected.
- The traverse algorithm stops if the controller cannot be called on any remaining component.

In the implementation section (Sec. 3), we will present an implementation of the traverse algorithm and some controllers.

2.9   Interactions with Traverse Algorithm

Due to traverse properties, when a traverse fails, the controller leads to an exception on the remaining components. Most programming languages enables exception catching. If exceptions provide enough details, user can know why controller cannot execute on these components. Often, a parameter is missing. In order to finish the traverse, the simplest solution is to ask the user to correctly set this parameter.

Indeed, the exception raised by component can be printed. User can give an appropriate answer to the algorithm. In case of an application with thousand components, we have made the interaction simpler with the use of a comma-separated-value file. This file can be read by a spreadsheet program. User can fill an automatic generated file with all parameters to be set with his favorite spreadsheet program.

Traverse algorithm can also interact with an other program. For example, for mapping issues, the choice of machines where a process must be mapped is a complex problem for a human. Mapping has a huge impact on performance like refresh rate or latency. A mapping program using a hardware description file could calculate a mapping solution efficiently.

This implementation could give the possibility to make dynamic reconfigurations. During execution, the entire application could be stopped. The system will proceed to a new instantiation of the application. The traverse algorithm can now use the log file to resolve exception raised during the traverse algorithm. This traverse algorithm could be done in parallel with the execution. A mapping algorithm could adapt the application to resource capacities at execution-time.

3   Implementation

3.1   Greedy Traverse Algorithm

The main issue in the model implementation is the traverse algorithm. This algorithm must iterate on components and respect several constraints. (Sect. 2.8). This algorithm must find a consistant order considering all constraints for the iteration through the components.

We make the traverse via a greedy algorithm. This algorithm manages a queue of non-executed components. For each components in this queue, the algorithm tries to execute the associated controller. If the controller was successfully executed, then all of its children are pushed in the queue. Otherwise, the algorithm makes a rollback operation on the component and push it at the end of the queue.

The traverse is done when the queue becomes empty. If the algorithm can not change the queue state, then a fixed point is reached. No new evolution can be performed to component states. To respect traverse properties, the algorithm must stop and signal its fail.

With this implementation of the traverse algorithm, there is no need to express constraints on components. But, this implementation may lead to unnecessary controller calls. We provide bounds on the number of controller calls for this algorithm:

Proposition 1. *Let N_{comp} the maximum number of composite components in an application. The maximum (resp. minimum) number of call of controllers performed by greedy traverse algorithm is $O(N_{comp}^2)$ (resp. $O(N_{comp})$).*

For sake of conciseness, the proof is omitted. The proof outline is to show that a controller can be called at most N_{comp} times by component.

The complexity of our algorithm is upper bounded by $O(N_{comp}^2)$ but we do not have to compute an order of iterations between components considering all constraints. The greedy traverse algorithm tries to iterate on components until it finds an acceptable order. Theses tries can lead to extra costs but computation of an acceptable order may involve complex algorithms. Our solution is a good tradeoff between scalability and complexity of the implementation.

3.2   Implementation on the Top of the FlowVR Middleware

We have built our model on the top of FlowVR [15,8]. This middleware is used to construct large parallel interactive applications. It eases the development of virtual reality applications that associates scientific visualization and simultations. For instance we developed applications involving a real time 3D modeling algorithm using data from a camera network, parallel simulations and multi-projector visualization with FlowVR.

FlowVR is based on four types of primitive components [8]:

Modules. User defined components. They make all computational issues in the application.

Connections. They transmit data from an output port to an input port.

Filters. They make treatments on messages. They are involved in communication schemes.

Synchronizers. They implement synchronization policies between components.

All these kinds of components have been implemented using our model. The second step of the implementation was to construct controllers dedicated to the middleware. The main controller specially developed for FlowVR builds a XML description of the application. When launching an application, FlowVR distributes order to FLowVR dameons running on the nodes of the target machines to load plugins, configure communications schemes, etc. These orders are describeexgtracted from an XML desctiption of the application. For each primitive component, we have created the controller that builds this XML description. Composite components just recusrively link children description into the XML tree.

All examples from the FlowVR suite have been redeveloped with the hierarchical model introduced in this paper. The example used in this paper (Fig. 1) was inspired from one of these applications. Mocing to the hierarchical model improved application modularity. For instance, an application can now be imported as a composite component in larger applications.

4   Conclusion

We presented an ADL for interactive applications based on the fractal component model. Our main goal was to ensure a high level of modularity for large applications involving parallel components and advanced coupling schemes. Configuration of components is deferred to controllers. It enables us to separate some aspects of a component from its core functional nature. An application is then configured by calling the controllers in a traverse process. This ADL has been implemented and validated on top of the FlowVR middleware. We expect to integrate it in the FlowVR distribution soon.

References

1. Tu, T., Yu, H., Ramirez-Guzman, L., Bielak, J., Ghattas, O., Ma, K.-L., O'Hallaron, D.R.: From Mesh Generation to Scientific Visualization: An End-to-End Approach to Parallel Supercomputing. In: Super Computing (2006)
2. Strehlke, K., Moere, A.V., Gross, O.S.M., Wuermlin, S., Naef, M., Lamboray, E., Spagno, C., Kunz, A., Koller-Meier, E., Svoboda, T., Gool, L.V., Lang, K.S.S., Moere, A.V., Staadt, O.: Blue-C: A Spatially Immersive Display and 3D Video Portal for Telepresence. In: Proceedings of ACM SIGGRAPH 03, San Diego (2003)
3. GrImage: website, http://www.inrialpes.fr/grimage/
4. Lucas, B., Abram, G.D., Collins, N.S., Epstein, D.A., Gresh, D.L., McAuliffe, K.P.: An architecture for a scientific visualization system. In: VIS '92: Proceedings of the 3rd conference on Visualization '92, Los Alamitos, CA, USA, pp. 107–114. IEEE Computer Society Press, Los Alamitos (1992)
5. Foulser, D.: IRIS Explorer: a framework for investigation. SIGGRAPH Comput. Graph. 29(2), 13–16 (1995)
6. Schroeder, W., Martin, K., Lorensen, B.: The Visualization Toolkit An Object-Oriented Approach To 3D Graphics, 3rd edn. Kitware, Inc. (2003)
7. Ahrens, J., Law, C., Schroeder, W., Martin, K., Papka, M.: A parallel approach for efficiently visualizing extremely large, Time-varying Datasets. Technical report, Los Alamos National Laboratory (2000)
8. Allard, J., Gouranton, V., Lecointre, L., Limet, S., Melin, E., Raffin, B., Robert, S.: FlowVR: a Middleware for Large Scale Virtual Reality Applications. In: Danelutto, M., Vanneschi, M., Laforenza, D. (eds.) Euro-Par 2004. LNCS, vol. 3149, Springer, Heidelberg (2004)
9. Margery, D., Arnaldi, B., Chauffaut, A., Donikian, S., Duval, T.: OpenMASK: Multi-Threaded or Modular Animation and Simulation Kernel or Kit: a General Introduction. In: Richir, S., Richard, P., Taravel, B. (eds.) VRIC 2002 Proceedings, pp. 101–110 (2002)
10. Wierse, A., Lang, U., Rhle, R.: Architectures of Distributed Visualization Systems and their Enhancements. In: Eurographics Workshop on Visualization in Scientific Computing, Abingdon (1993)
11. Zhang, K., Damevski, V., Venkatachalapathy, S.G., Parker, S.G.: SCIRun2: A CCA Framework for High Performance Computing. hips 00, 72–79 (2004)
12. Denis, A., Pérez, C., Priol, T.: PadicoTM: an open integration framework for communication middleware and runtimes. Future Generation Comp. Syst. 19(4), 575–585 (2003)
13. Bruneton, E., Coupaye, T.: Stefani, J.: The Fractal Component Model. Technical report, ObjectWeb Consortium (February 2004)
14. Baude, F., Caromel, D., Morel, M.: From distributed objects to hierarchical grid components. In: Meersman, R., Tari, Z., Schmidt, D.C. (eds.) CoopIS/DOA/ODBASE 2003. LNCS, vol. 2888, pp. 1226–1242. Springer, Heidelberg (2003)
15. Arcila, T., Allard, J., Ménier, C., Boyer, E., Raffin, B.: FlowVR: A Framework For Distributed Virtual Reality Applications. In: AFRV, Rocquencourt (November 2006)

Design of a Simulator for Mesh-Based Reconfigurable Architectures

Kang Sun[1,2], Jun Zheng[1,3], Yuanyuan Li[4], and Xuezeng Pan[1]

[1] College of Computer Science, Zhejiang University, Hangzhou, China
[2] IBM Global Engineering Solutions, GCG Delivery, Shanghai, China
swankong@126.com
[3] Zhejiang Institute of Communication and Media, Hangzhou, China
taurus-zheng@163.com
[4] Department of Computer Science, Shanghai Jiaotong University, Shanghai, China
brucelevy@163.com

Abstract. Reconfigurable computing has become a hot topic in research due to its high-performance and flexibility. In this paper we present a simulator called JRSim for mesh-based reconfigurable architectures. The purpose of this simulator is to provide a platform to evaluate new architectures, and to assist in analysis of algorithms as well as the visualization of their behavior. JRSim is a platform-independent tool which is implemented by Java. It supports flexible bus structure, user-defined function unit and dynamic reconfiguration. Case studies show that JRSim can simulate the behavior of mesh-based reconfigurable systems correctly and efficiently. This simulator can be used to evaluate reconfigurable system design, or demonstrate the ability of reconfigurable system in an educational environment.

Keywords: reconfigurable computing, reconfigurable mesh, simulator, dynamic reconfiguration.

1 Introduction

Reconfigurable computing is a new paradigm based on changing the hardware to reconfigure the computation and the communication structure [1]. One of the features of reconfigurable computing is spatial computation: the algorithms are directly mapped onto the reconfigurable architectures and the data are processed by spatially distributing the computations rather than temporally sequencing through a shared computational unit. The other feature is configurable data path: the function of the computational units and interconnection network can be changed by some configuration mechanism. Due to the high-performance and flexibility of reconfigurable hardware, it has become a new solution for high-performance computing.

With the rapid development of reconfigurable computing, various reconfigurable architectures have been developed by researchers and the industry [2], and all these systems form a very large design space. Designers are then facing the difficult choice of the target architecture which is critical since it can

K. Li et al. (Eds.): NPC 2007, LNCS 4672, pp. 526–535, 2007.
© IFIP International Federation for Information Processing 2007

strongly affect the final system's performance. Furthermore, the development of reconfigurable system CAD tools also requires a tool to help understand system properties in a way that leads to a better placing of data or utilization of available resources [3]. In general, a simulator developed in high level language is useful for the research on computing system architectures, because these architectures can be easily changeable with additional application specific function units or bus structures [4].

Currently, most reconfigurable system simulators are designed for dedicated systems (e.g. GARP Simulator [5]), and they are usually used for hardware functional verification. There is still a lack of research in development of general purpose reconfigurable architecture simulators which can be employed to assist the analysis of algorithms, perform design exploration, and evaluate CAD tools performance. Steckel et al. proposed a general purpose simulator for reconfigurable mesh architectures [6], but the processing element model in this simulator is based on RAM machine which only has a very limited instruction set and lacks extensibility. Furthermore, this simulator does not support the feature of dynamic reconfiguration. Vikram and Vasudevan designed a behavior simulator for hardware-software co-simulation of reconfigurable systems [7]. This tool is a hybrid system in which the reconfigurable array is designed by Verilog HDL and the micro-controller is implemented by integrating RSIM [8] - a C-based micro-processor simulator. A simulator designed by HDL usually needs EDA tool working environment, and the performance of most HDL simulation tools is too low for the performance analysis and design space exploration at the algorithmic and HW/SW partitioning level that we are planning to support [9]. In latest study results, Brito et al. introduced a dynamically reconfigurable FPGA simulator designed by SystemC [10].

In this paper, we propose JRSim - a 2-dimensional reconfigurable mesh architecture simulator. The advantages of JRSim include:

1. Both the processing element (PE) and the bus structure are scalable. Designer can add user-defined function unit, change data-path granularity, and define new bus structure in the system.
2. It supports the features of dynamically reconfigurable system.
3. JRSim is a platform-independent tool which is implemented by Java. Its user-friendly graphic user interface (GUI) improves the visibility of the system behavior.

2   JRSim Architecture

Fig. 1. shows JRSim system architecture. The simulation system consists of 3 components: configuration information, a simulation engine, and a graphic user interface (GUI). The configuration information includes (1) system architecture definition, and (2) system function configuration. Simulation engine is the core component of this simulation system: it analyzes configuration information and performs simulation task. The GUI is responsible for showing working procedure and simulation results of the system.

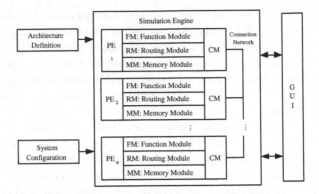

Fig. 1. JRSim system architecture

2.1   Hardware Architecture Definition

The target system of JRSim simulator is mesh-based reconfigurable architecture. Reconfigurable meshes usually contain a set of connected processing elements (PEs). They arrange their PEs mainly as a rectangular 2-D array with horizontal and vertical connections which support rich communication resources for efficient parallelism. Fig.2.(a). depicts a typical mesh-based architecture. In each PE, there are four ports at its north, east, west and south sides. These connection ports are used for implementing nearest neighbor connection (NN links) between PEs. Furthermore, additional communication resources can be provided by row or column buses. Each PE may be used to implement an operator and simultaneously to route data words through the array, as shown in Fig.2.(b).

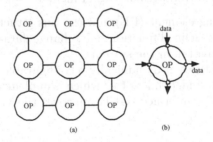

Fig. 2. Reconfigurable mesh architecture

This simulator uses special architecture definition information to describe the properties of hardware architecture, so that it can be applicable for various architectures. In architecture definition, 3 different architectural properties are specified:

1. The size of the reconfigurable array, which is the number of PEs in horizontal and vertical direction, respectively.

2. The connection resources in the reconfigurable array, such as the available repertory of nearest neighbor connections. Per side of the PE can be one or multiple unidirectional and/or bidirectional connections. Besides NN links, some systems may offer one or multiple buses as additional routing resources.
3. The PE operator repertory.

2.2   Processing Elements

A PE is a core information processing engine. It provides general purpose or application specific functions. As shown in Fig.1., each PE is constructed by (1) Function Module (FM), (2) Routing Module (RM), (3) Memory Module (MM), and (4) Communication Module (CM). Routing Module is responsible for implementing intra-PE communication, which is data transmission between inner ports of each PE. And Communication Module is responsible for controlling inter-PE communication, which is data transmission between different PEs.

Each PE is specified by four types of parameters:

1. Static parameter. Static parameter is some architecture definition information of PEs. Once defined, it cannot be changed before the completion of a simulation task. In JRSim, the static parameter is PE granularity, which is the data-path width of PE.
2. Function parameter. Function parameter is a set of functions which each PE can be configured to perform. So far each PE supports the integer operators provided by the programming language Java. JRSim also supports user-defined operation, which can simulate the behavior of some application specific function units. A further discussion about user-defined functions is presented in Section 2.3.
3. Cost parameter. Cost parameter defines the cost with different PE functionality, such as delay, power, etc.
4. Data transfer parameter. There are 2 types of data transfer parameter. One is transfer parameter for inter-PE connection, and the other is the parameter for intra-PE connection. In each PE, the function unit may need several operands. The operands are supplied by PE input ports or internal memory module. Thus, it is necessary to build a mapping table to maintain the correspondence among function unit's input ports, PE input ports, and internal memory module. Similarly the output data of each PE may directly come from its input ports, or from the output port of the function unit in PE. A mapping table is built to maintain the correspondence between PE output ports and possible output data sources. These two input/output tables record the transfer parameters for intra-PE connection.

2.3   User-Defined Functions

A simple description language is designed to describe user-defined functions in JRSim simulator. Fig.3. is an example of user-defined function declaration. The #DEFINE . . . #END_DEFINE statements define a block of function declaration statements. As shown in Fig.3., each function consists of four parts: function name (ACC), arguments (X, Y, Z), function body, and delay cost (delay=3).

User-defined function declaration is read and analyzed by the interpreter which is integrated in the simulator. Function objects will be constructed and stored in a hash table according to the declarations. Once a PE is configured as a user-defined operator and simulator runs into this operation clock cycle, the interpreter will read out corresponding function object from the hash table, execute this piece of code, and then output the result.

```
#DEFINE
ACC(X,Y, Z) {
    return X*Z+Y;
}

(delay=3)
#END_DEFINE
```

```
foreach clock cycle do
    foreach node m in system do
        if m.state == READY
            add m into ReadyList
        endif
    endfor
    foreach node n in ReadyList do
        sim(n)
        update state of n and n.child
    endfor
endfor
```

Fig. 3. Example of user-defined function   **Fig. 4.** Pseudo code of simulation process

3   The Implementation of JRSim

3.1   (Re)Configuration of Processing Elements

The simulator uses configuration information to configure the PEs. Configuration information includes PE architecture description, operator repertory, user-defined function declaration and connection resources. An object class is constructed in the simulator program code to record the status and properties of each PE during simulation. These properties include:

1. The position of each PE, which is the X and Y coordinates in the array.
2. The state of each PE. During simulation process, PEs will enter different states in different simulation stages. We will discuss the state transition of PE in Section 3.2.
3. The input/output ports of each PE, the attributes of the operands needed by the function unit, and the source of the operands.

3.2   System State Transition

We note the state of arbitrary PE $A_{i,j}$ at clock cycle t as s, and $s \in S = (Busy, Ready, Waiting, Idle, Null)$.

Busy - PE is executing some tasks.
Ready - PE is ready for running a new task.

Waiting - PE is waiting for some signal (or data) to get ready.
Idle - PE is configured, but there's no task to run immediately.
Null - PE is not used.

At the beginning of each clock cycle, all the PEs which are in *Ready* state will be placed in a queue named *ReadyList*. Then the task assigned to every PE in *ReadyList* will be executed and the corresponding PE's state will be updated. After this procedure, the PE which is in *Ready* state will be put into *ReadyList* in next clock cycle. This loop procedure will be repeated until the final result is produced and there's no more new input data. *ReadyList* is used for gathering all the PEs which should be processed in current clock cycle. Fig.4. is the pseudo code of simulation process.

In simulation process, the state transition of each PE $A_{i,j}$ at clock cycle t is determined by:

$$s_{i,j}(t) = F(t, PD_{i,j}, IN_{i,j}) \tag{1}$$

In formula (1), t is current clock cycle, $PD_{i,j}$ is a set of parent nodes of $A_{i,j}$, which have accomplished their task and generated output data, and $N_{i,j}$ is the number of effective input ports in $A_{i,j}$. If $PD_{i,j} = IN_{i,j}$, it means that all the input data needed by PE $A_{i,j}$ are available and $A_{i,j}$ is in *Ready* state. Otherwise, if $0 < PD_{i,j} < IN_{i,j}$, $A_{i,j}$ will be in *Waiting* state. $A_{i,j}$ will be in *Busy* state while executing a task. And if not used, its state will be *Null*. Fig.5. is the state machine of PE.

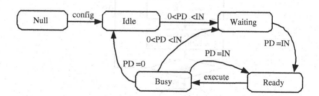

Fig. 5. State machine of reconfigurable PE

3.3   System Working Flow

As a synchronized reconfigurable system simulator, the behavior of JRSim is controlled by clock signal. The system work flow in each clock cycle is shown in Fig.6.

1. The system checks whether there are new input data or the system needs to be reconfigured. If some PEs get new input data, the system will update their states and put the PE whose state is *Ready* into *ReadyList*.
2. The system executes the simulation task. Each PE has two tables to record the correspondence between I/O ports and function unit. One is called operand table, where the input data indices are stored. $Operand[i] = j$ means that the ith operand of PE is $inVal[j]$. $inVal[j]$ is input port number or internal memory. The other is called output table. The output value is noted as $outVal[i]$. In (2), $outTab$ is output table. If $outTab[i] = -1$, it means that the output value of port i comes from FM (Function Module) in PE. And if $outTab[i]$ is between

0 and *inNum*, it means that the output value comes directly from input port. All the other values of *outTab*[*i*] are considered as error.

$$outVal[i] = \begin{cases} resofFM, & if \quad outTab[i] = -1, \\ inVal[outTab[i]], & if \quad 0 \leq outTab[i] \leq inNum, \\ Error, & else. \end{cases} \tag{2}$$

3. The system updates the status of each PE according to the state machine shown in Fig. 5.
4. When all the PEs finish their task and there's no new input data, the simulation process will terminate.

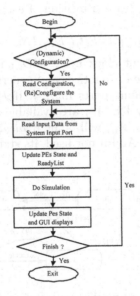

Fig. 6. The working flow of JRSim

3.4   Dynamic Reconfiguration

Reconfigurable technology includes static reconfiguration and dynamic reconfiguration [11]. In statically reconfigurable system, if the system needs to initiate a new configuration, it has to stop computation. But in dynamically reconfigurable system, it permits reconfiguration of a portion of the device while other portions of the device are still performing computations.

JRSim supports dynamically multi-context reconfigurable system modeling. The simulator stores multiple configuration information in memory. A series of configuration $C_i(0 \leq i \leq n)$ are queued in time sequence. At the beginning of each clock cycle, the system will check whether the configuration signal is valid or not. If valid, configuration C_i will be dequeued and the corresponding PEs and connecting networks will be reset and configured. During configuration, all other PEs will keep executing their own tasks.

4   Case Studies

JRSim is implemented by Java programming language, which owns the advantages of object-orientated and platform-independent features. Here we just use matrices multiplication as an illustrational example to demonstrate the effectiveness of the simulator.

Given an $m \times p$ matrix $\boldsymbol{A}$ and a $p \times n$ matrix $\boldsymbol{B}$, the production of $\boldsymbol{A} \times \boldsymbol{B}$ will be an $m \times n$ matrix which is noted as $\boldsymbol{C}$. $c_{i,j}$ represents the element in ith row and jth column of $\boldsymbol{C}$. $c_{i,j}$ can be calculated by equation (3).

$$c_{i,j} = \sum_{k=1}^{p} a_{i,k} \times b_{k,j} \quad (1 \le i \le m, 1 \le j \le n) \tag{3}$$

According equation (3), $c_{i,j}$ can be regarded as the inner product between ith row vector in $\boldsymbol{A}$ and jth column vector in $\boldsymbol{B}$. A recursive formula for computation of $c_{i,j}$ can be presented as (k is the number of inner product accumulation)[12]:

$$\begin{cases} c_{i,j}^{1} = 0, \\ c_{i,j}^{k+1} = c_{i,j}^{k} + a_{i,k} b_{k,j}, \quad i = 1, \dots, m; j = 1, \dots, n \\ c_{i,j} = c_{i,j}^{p+1}, \end{cases} \tag{4}$$

4.1   Algorithm Mapping

The multiplication algorithm can be mapped onto a mesh-based reconfigurable array. Fig.7 shows the mapping results. Each element in Fig.7. is a multiply-accumulator (MAC or ACC). Matrix $\boldsymbol{A}$ is preliminarily stored in the array and matrix $\boldsymbol{B}$ is inputted from the bus. After MAC operation, the results will be sent to the right-side adjacent PEs and the inputs from outside buses are also sent to next stage. The output of the PE in ith row and jth column is just the value of $c_{i,j}$. The two inputs of $PE_{i,k}$ are $c_{i,j}^{k}$ which is produced by $PE_{i,k-1}$ and $b_{k,j}$ which is

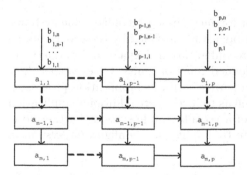

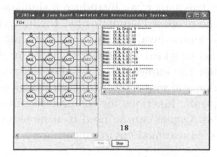

Fig. 7. Mapping matrices multiplication onto PE array

Fig. 8. JRSim runtime window

Table 1. The delay cost of each operation

Operation	Inner Product (ACC)	Multiplication (MUL)	Routing (RT)	Addtion (ADD)
Delay (Cycle)	3	2	0	1

received from *jth* bus input. $a_{i,j}$ is stored in $PE_{i,k}$. So $c_{i,j}^{k+1}$ can be computed by equation (5). After p times recursion of column i, we can get the result of $c_{i,j}$.

$$c_{i,j}^{k+1} = c_{i,j} + a_{i,k}b_{k,j} \tag{5}$$

4.2 Experiment Results

We used the two matrices shown in equation (6) to verify the simulator. In this experiment, the data-path width of each PE is 16-bit wide. The delay cost of each operation is listed in Table 1. ACC is MAC operation defined in Fig.3.

$$A = \begin{pmatrix} 1 & 3 & 5 & 8 \\ 7 & 9 & 11 & 4 \\ -3 & 9 & 6 & 10 \\ 0 & 6 & -4 & 5 \end{pmatrix}, B = \begin{pmatrix} 6 & 0 & 9 & -4 \\ -2 & 0 & 7 & 3 \\ -4 & 1 & 5 & -2 \\ 8 & -3 & -1 & 0 \end{pmatrix} \tag{6}$$

The simulation result is correct. The computation procedure consumes 19 clock cycles under circumstance that all multi-cycle operations are pipelined. Fig.8 is a runtime snapshot of the simulator. The red notes are working PEs.

The result shows that matrices multiplication algorithm can be mapped onto reconfigurable array to exploit the parallelism of PEs. The complexity of basic algorithm for multiplying two $n \times n$ matrices is $O(n^3)$. Strassen algorithm can reduce the time for matrices multiplication to $O(n^{lg7})$. But the time complexity of implementing matrices multiplication on reconfigurable hardware is only $O(n)$.

5   Conclusions

In this paper, we introduce a simulator for mesh-based reconfigurable systems. The proposed simulator has the integer operators provided by the programming language Java, and supports dynamic reconfiguration. Expansion interfaces are also provided by JRSim to add user-defined function units. Case studies show that the implemented simulator system is able to profile application processing time and waiting time of each PE, as well as to investigate additional application specific functions for the architecture of a reconfigurable system. Furthermore, this system can be used to demonstrate the ability of reconfigurable system in an educational environment.

Acknowledgments. This work was supported by Natural Science Foundation of Zhejiang Province, China (Grant No.Y105355), and special project of Zhejiang High-Tech Development Plan (Grant No.2006C11105).

References

1. Vaidyanathan, R., Trahan, J.L.: Dynamic Reconfiguration Architectures and Algorithms. Kluwer Academic Publishers, KAP (2004)
2. Compton, K., Hauck, S.: Reconfigurable Computing: A Survey of Systems and Software. ACM Computing Surveys 34(2), 171–210 (2002)
3. Duan, R., Fan, X.-Y., Gao, D.-Y., Shen, G.: Reconfigurable Computing Technology and Developing Trends (In Chinese). Application Research of Computers (8), 14–17 (2004)
4. Shinozaki, A., Shima, M., Guo, M., Kubo, M.: A high performance simulator system for a multiprocessor system based on a multi-way cluster. In: Jesshope, C., Egan, C. (eds.) ACSAC 2006. LNCS, vol. 4186, pp. 231–243. Springer, Heidelberg (2006)
5. Hauser, J.R., Wawrzynek, J., Garp, A.: A MIPS Processor with A Reconfigurable Coprocessor. In: Proceedings of 5th Annual IEEE Symposium on FPGAs for Custom Computing Machines, CA. USA, pp. 12–21 (1997)
6. Steckel, C., Middendorf, M., Elgindy, H., Schmeck, H.: A Simulator for The Reconfigurable Mesh Architecture. In: Rolim, J.D.P. (ed.) Parallel and Distributed Processing. LNCS, vol. 1388, pp. 105–110. Springer, Heidelberg (1998)
7. Vikram, K.N., Vasudevan, V.: Hardware-Software Co-simulation of Bus-based Reconfigurable Systems. Elsvier Microprocessors and Microsystems 29(4), 133–144 (2005)
8. Hughes, C.J., Pai, V.S., Ranganathan, P., Adve, S.V.: RSIM: Simulating Shared-memory Multiprocessors with ILP Processors. IEEE Computer 35(2), 40–49 (2002)
9. Rosa, A.L., Lavagno, L., Passerone, C.: A Software Development Tool Chain for A Reconfigurable Processor. In: Proceedings of International Conference on Compilers, Architecture, and Synthesis for Embedded Systems (CASE'01), Atlanta, GA. USA, pp. 93–98 (2001)
10. Britio, A.V., Melcher, U.K.M., Rosas, W.: An Open-source Tool for Simulation of Partially Reconfigurable Systems Using SystemC. In: Proceedings of IEEE Computer Society Annual Symposium on Emerging VLSI Technologies and Architectures, IEEE Computer Society Press, Los Alamitos (2006)
11. Sanchez, E., Sipper, M., Haenni, J.-O., Beuchat, J.-L., Stauffer, A., Perez-Uribe, A.: Static and Dynamic Configurable Systems. IEEE Transactions on Computers 48(6), 556–564 (1999)
12. Wu, S.-Q., Wang, Q., Xie, Y.-X.: Design and Implementation of Matrix Multiplier for Inverter Harmonic Elimination Model Calculation (In Chinese). Journal of South China University of Technology (Natural Science) 31(8), 1–5 (2003)

Personal Grid

Zhiwei Xu, Lijuan Xiao, and Xingwu Liu

Institute of Computing Technology, Chinese Academy of Sciences
100080 Beijing, China

Abstract. A long-term trend in computing platform innovation is the appearance of a new class of platform every 15 years or so, that drastically reduces barriers and expands user base. We have seen this trend in computer's 60-year history several times, with inventions like mainframe, personal computer (PC), Internet, and Web. To explore opportunities brought about by the new net infrastructure, we present a new computing paradigm called Personal Grid (PG). PG allows an individual user to own, control and use a personal server on the net, just as he owns 1a PC today. However, such a virtualized, net-centric server not only enables the user to utilize resources on the net, but also empower the user to contribute to the net and to share and collaborate with other users. We discuss the related emerging workloads and usage modes, the opportunity to lower barriers, the scientific and technical challenges, and research progress made by our Vega Grid Team.

1 Introduction

The 1960's and 1970's were a golden time in the history of computing system innovation. This wave of innovations helped expand the user population significantly, by reducing the *cost barrier*, the *control barrier*, and the *knowledge barrier* of computing platforms.

System cost was drastically reduced when the market mainstream shifted from mainframes to minicomputers and then microcomputers. Microcomputers coincided with personal computers (PC's), which simultaneously reduced all three barriers. In addition to reducing system cost, each PC is owned and managed (controlled) by a personal user, instead of an enterprise's IT department; and the knowledge required to operate a PC is much simplified compared to a mainframe.

As we enter the 21st century, the concept of computer has extended to cyber infrastructure, or grids. An opportunity exists to drastically lower the IT cost again, by enabling personally owned and controlled cyberinfrastructure, or personal grids. Cost reduction is possible due to sharing resources in a more efficient architecture. The control barrier can be lowered due to decentralization. The knowledge barrier can be lowered by abstractions and virtualization, and by utilizing man-computer society.

After presenting the personal grid paradigm and a PG architecture, we discuss the emerging workloads and usage modes, the opportunity to lower barriers, the scientific and technical challenges, and research progress made by our Vega Grid Team at Institute of Computing Technology (ICT), Chinese Academy of Sciences.

K. Li et al. (Eds.): NPC 2007, LNCS 4672, pp. 536–540, 2007.

2 Personal Computers, Net Services and Personal Grids

In addition to the obvious benefit of low system cost, a personal computer has two attractive properties: (1) a PC is a general-purpose computing *platform*, not a special-purpose solution such as a calculator; and (2) a PC is *personal*, meaning that it is controlled by a person (its owner), not an institution. The second property often leads to other properties. For instance, a PC is *dedicated*, in that a user's application execution on a PC cannot be slowed down by another user.

The net manifests its value to end users usually through various internet services, Web services, and grid services, in a number of overlapping forms:

- Traditional network services, such as email, BBS, and messages.
- Business web, such as salesforce.com.
- Consumer web, such as Amazon and eBay.
- Web 2.0 services, such as Wiki, MySpace, and YouTube.
- Grid services, such as Nanohub.

The current net services have the following characteristics: (1) they provide special-purpose solution services, not a general-purpose platform; (2) they are shared among many users, not for an individual's dedicated use; (3) they are operated and managed by an infrastructure or service provider. In other words, net services today are like the mainframes of the 1960's. They are *institutional*. The service providers are in control, and each user can only access the services predefined by the providers.

Personal grids combine the nice properties of personal computers and net services. A *personal net computing* (PNC) environment is shown in Fig. 1, where the PGs are the central piece. Five parties are present. The first layer consists of individual users. Each user uses a client device to access his personal grid.

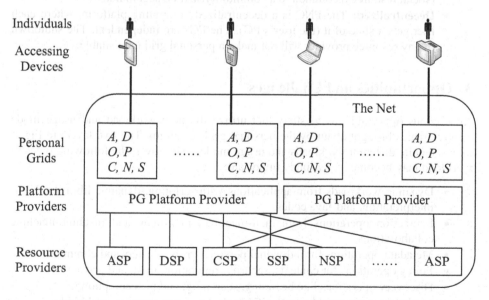

Fig. 1. Personal Net Computing Environment (PNC) Using Personal Grids

Each PG provides three levels of capabilities to the users. Hardware-level capabilities include computing capability (C), networking capability (N), and storage capability (S). System-level capabilities include operating system operations (O) and policies/contexts (P). Application-level capabilities include application software and services (A) and data (D).

There may be multiple PG platform providers, each providing PGs to the users. The resource providers provide hardware-level and application-level capabilities, usually through some form of net services. The resource types correspond to the capability types visible to the users via a PG. For instance, we have storage service providers (SSP) for the storage capability. Each platform provider can have multiple sources of the same type of resources. Each resource provider can provide for multiple platform providers.

From the user's viewpoint, a personal grid has the following characteristics:

- **Platform:** A personal grid manifests as a general-purpose computing platform, not a special-purpose solution. This is akin to comparing a personal computer to a calculator.
- **Personal:** A personal grid is owned and controlled by an individual user, and dedicated to his use.
- **Networked:** A personal grid is net-centric. Its resources come from the net, and can be shared by other parties on the net.
- **Sharing:** Users and PGs in a PNC can share the resources from the resources providers, as well as resources from other PGs. The sharing is controlled by the policies/contexts prescribed by each individual user.
- **Social:** Users and PGs interact and collaborate with one another. In addition to the "raw" resources from the resource providers, the individual users and their PGs can evolve into various clusters and communities, where social assets (social resources) common to a community will be accumulated.
- **Decentralized:** The PNC is a decentralized computing platform, where each user gets a slice of it (the user's PG). The PGs are independent. The shutdown of any resource provider will not make a personal grid unavailable.

3 Opportunities and Challenges

An obvious opportunity is to study and utilize the new workload and usage mode characteristics brought about by the personal grid paradigm. The five layers in Fig. 1 may see quite different workloads and usage modes. Moreover, the following types of workload may become increasingly important:

- Dynamic workloads from applications with scripting, dynamic libraries, XML interpretation, and Java codes.
- Interaction operations from man-machine, man-man, and machine-machine collaborations.
- Metadata operations for individual personal grids, clusters and communities.
- Policy operations for contexts, security, reputation, trust, and privacy.
- Discovery operations like browsing, searching, and tags computing.
- Market operations such as classified sales, recommendation, and bidding.

The second opportunity is to reduce the large amount of over-provisioning, redundancy, idleness, overhead, and other inefficiencies, thus lowering the per user cost. As each PG is a virtualized server on the net, resource over-provisioning can be avoided by on-demand, good-enough provisioning. There is also much space of improvement for individual requests, and still larger potential for improving multiple requests from many users and PGs. Our preliminary experiments show that fetching 10-byte data from a blog server takes 162 ms and 52 context switches at server side, where PHP scripts execution alone accounts for 96% of the total time. To call an empty Web service in Tomcat+Axis needs 15 ms. Calling a grid service with security needs 0.5-2 seconds. Such excessive overheads offer innovation opportunities.

Cost reduction may come from another source: the commoditization of resource providers. Solution-level net services of today, turned into capabilities, will become commodities, each type with multiple vendors. This will encourage competition and innovation. The same happened before for PCs. It is likely to happen with PGs. A loosely coupled architecture and standard interfaces are technical enablers.

The third opportunity lies in decentralization. The PGs and the resource providers are both decentralized. Thus independent innovation and advances are possible. The use and management of these two parties are also independent. The absence of architectural inter-dependency help lower the control barrier. Users and resource providers have more freedom in the control/use/provisioning of their own capabilities, and in how to integrate/collaborate with others. This is unlike many net services today, where users' data are tied to a specific application. Only limited interaction and integration are possible, via techniques such as mashup.

The fourth opportunity is the PG user interface, which is a key to reduce the knowledge barrier. The desktop and the browser metaphors may be augmented with new metaphors. In fact, a number of complementary metaphors may be created to support PGs. For instance, to manage a PG's capabilities, a *banking metaphor* may be appropriate. Each user (thus each PG) may have a capability portfolio, consisting of several personal accounts of different types of capabilities. A user may save cash capabilities for her current needs, invest excess capabilities, or borrow capabilities.

The opportunities are accompanied with many technical challenges. Consider the efficiency challenge. To lower the cost, the PNC architecture in Fig. 1 must be efficiently implemented and used, so that resources are efficiently utilized, with effective sharing and reuse.

A PG should have the responsiveness of a PC. Normal commands and interactive operations should have short response times (e.g., less than 0.25 seconds). However, a PG may need virtualization and high-level abstractions. User visible commands and operations of a PG thus may contain much more substance. As discussed above, even a small part of such a command will need hundreds of milliseconds to over a second. One reason is that such a "simple" operation needs to traverse a tall stack of layers, from application logic to WSDL, SOAP, XML, HTTP, TCP/IP to operating system calls. How to reduce layering overhead is a major technical challenge.

We also want a PG to be dedicated for a user. The performance should not be visibly affected when many users are using the underlying infrastructure and its resources. That is, we want PGs that are virtually dedicated to their individual owners, even though they may physically share resources. Simultaneously achieving such sharing and isolation for personal grids brings new challenges, especially considering that PNC is a decentralized environment. There is no centralized, omnipotent operating system kernel to help.

Users may access their personal grids via all kinds of devices with variant quality of network connection. How to tolerate transient disconnection and to enable offline operation are research issues. Data hoarding and proper client side running of PG applications are needed. Mining such workload characteristics could significantly improve user experience.

Another major challenge is to attract users and resource providers to join and stick with the personal grids (or the PNC). What are the proper incentives for them? Can these incentives be effectively implemented? Can the users and resource providers conveniently use such incentives? This is not only a business model question. There are technical and scientific issues involved.

From a scientific viewpoint, a very interesting research area has to do with emergent properties. PGs and PNC form a decentralized computing environment. Users and resource providers are highly autonomous. They make local decisions and have access to mostly local or community information. What global, emergent properties can arise? What are the necessary and sufficient conditions for "nice" emergent properties? Are there effective, constructive techniques that can implement such conditions?

4 Technology

At ICT, the following issues are being studied to realize personal grids:

Usage Classification. We have organized the PG usage modes into two classes of six types. The first class is for *personal use*, including three types of usage modes for *consumption, management* and *production* of resources. The second class is for *social use*, which includes three types of usage modes for *sharing, context* and *contribution* of resources, policies and contents.

System abstractions. We are developing a very small set of abstractions to support the common requirements of personal grids. For instance, each PG is implemented as a container of persistent handles, connecting to virtualized resources.

Virtualization. While each user sees a PG owned and controlled by herself, it is a virtualized set of capabilities, realized by resource providers. Techniques are being developed for efficient virtualization, such that direct (non-layered) execution is possible in most cases.

New forms of locality. We are exploring new locality phenomena, such as request locality (requests from independent users may hit the same resources) and social locality (e.g., locality in contexts, clusters, policies), to improve the efficiency of PGs.

Emergent properties. We are studying various potential emergent properties and the ways to achieve them, such as fair market and balanced utilization.

Acknowledgements. This work is supported in part by the National Natural Science Foundation of China (Grant No. 90412010, 60603004), the China National 973 Program (Grant No. 2005CB321807), and the Chinese Academy of Sciences Distinguished Scholars Fund (Grant No. 20014010).

On Parallel Models of Computation

Guang R. Gao

Department of Electrical and Computer Engineering
University of Delaware, USA

Abstract. The emerging trend on multi-core chips is changing the technology landscape of computing system in the scale that has not been witnessed since the Intel microprocessor chip commissioned in early 1970s. However, the implication of this technology revolution is profound: its success can only be ensured if we can successfully (productively) implement parallel computer architecture on a chip as well as its associated software technology.

Recently, a great deal has been said, studied, and written on the transaction memory model and its implementation as a promising solution for parallel programming/execution models and their architecture support – especially in the multi-core era. In this talk, we present a review on two types of memory events and their ordering in a parallel program - due to the data (or control) dependence and the mutual exclusion, respectively. We argue that the solutions based on the transaction memory model are intrinsically inefficient to support the fine-grain memory synchronization due to the data (or control) dependence in parallel programs in the scientific computation domain. We then comment on some fundamental work on parallel models of computation that goes back to 1960s and early 1970s that should be freshly reviewed and extended to resolve the new challenges in parallel architecture and software models presented by the multi-core chip technology.

K. Li et al. (Eds.): NPC 2007, LNCS 4672, p. 541, 2007.
© IFIP International Federation for Information Processing 2007

Challenges in Dependability of Networked Systems for Information Society

Takashi Nanya

Research Center for Advanced Science and Technology
University of Tokyo, Japan

Abstract. As networked systems pervade every aspect of the modern information society, we are faced with serious threats to dependability due to problems caused by accidental events such as human mistakes and physical malfunctions or by intentional behavior being either malicious or non-malicious. In this talk, we discuss major challenges and give views of future directions in research on dependability of evolving networked systems toward an advanced information society.

K. Li et al. (Eds.): NPC 2007, LNCS 4672, p. 542, 2007.

Reference Architectural Styles for Service-Oriented Computing

Tharam S. Dillon, Chen Wu, and Elizabeth Chang

Digital Ecosystems and Business Intelligence Institute, Curtin University of Technology,
Perth 6845, Australia
dillon@cbs.curtin.edu.au
http://debii.curtin.edu.au

Abstract. Architecting service-oriented systems is a complex design activity. It involves making trade-offs among a number of interdependent design decisions, which are drawn from a range of concerns by various software stakeholders. In order to achieve effective and efficient SOC design we believe a careful study of architectural styles that can form the reference architecture is important. Hence, this paper provides a study of architectural styles for the reference architecture of SOC-based software systems. We propose a classification scheme for the architecture styles. These architectural styles are extracted from existing research projects and industry practices based on our classification scheme. For all those identified styles, we present an evolution trend driven by engineering principles for Internet-scale systems. As a result, this paper moves the first step towards creating a Reference Architecture that can be utilised to provide sensible guidance on the design of Web services application architecture

Keywords: Service-Oriented Architecture, Web Services, Software Architecture.

1 Introduction

The power and flexibility that Service-Oriented Computing (SOC) can offer to system integration are substantial. As the most promising realization of SOC [1], Web services have the potential to enable business-level integration across heterogeneous platforms. Due to its distributed nature, architecting Web services-based SOC applications is not a trivial task. It requires an experienced architect to make trade-offs amongst a number of interdependent design choices, each of which reflects various concerns demanded by numerous stakeholders from different organizations with disparate business goals and IT infrastructure. A recent survey [2] on Web services adoption, for example, shows that quality requirements such as system security, scalability, reliability, flexibility, and performance have become the most important criteria for a company to choose Web services solutions. Many factors influence the software quality, however, most of these quality requirements can be heavily influenced by the software architecture [3, 4]. Hence, a formal study of the fundamental architectures for Web services is necessary to deliver quality-assured SOC systems. Although several fundamental standards and related case studies have been reported

K. Li et al. (Eds.): NPC 2007, LNCS 4672, pp. 543–555, 2007.

for Web services design, the merit of rigorously architecting Web services applications has only been partially studied. Each quality requirement listed in [2] might lead to different concerns for that architecture design decision resulting in appropriate compromises [3] to suffice all these requirements. Such a compromise, [5], can be achieved through combining related architectural styles. It is essential to reference an array of well-identified Web services architectural styles with their corresponding rationales and business contexts. This paper examines and evaluates the existing Web services architectural styles, which constitute the reference architecture for SOC applications and elicits an appropriate reference architectural style.

2 Preliminary Concepts

A well-accepted definition of software architecture is given in [6]:

"The software architecture of a program or computing system is the structure or structures of the system, which comprise software elements, the externally visible properties of those elements, and the relationships among them".

Research into software architecture indicates that the various concerns inherent in a software architecture can be modelled as different abstract views, which can be further organized into distinct architectural levels [7]. [7] proposed a multi-level architectural model. (1) The Reference Architecture (RA) which captures both domain requirements and infrastructure requirements at the high level abstract level. (2) The Application Architecture (AA) and (3) The Implementation Architecture (IA). Our paper primarily investigates the Reference Architecture for general SOC-based software systems. Furthermore, RUP[1] defines the Reference Architecture as *"a predefined architectural pattern, or set of patterns, possibly partially or completely instantiated, designed, and proven for use in particular business and technical contexts..."*[8]. In this paper, we use the term *'architectural style'* to define a family of Web services systems in terms of a pattern of structural organization. Software architectural style encapsulates important decisions about the architectural elements. This paper uses the definition from [5] for the architectural style: *Definition: an architectural style is a coordinated set of architectural constraints that restricts the roles/features of architectural elements and the allowed relation-ships among those elements within any architecture that conforms to that style*. Constraints are often motivated by the application of a software engineering principle as to an aspect of the architectural elements.

3 The Classification Scheme

A classification scheme is presented to categorise the identified architectures styles into different groups as it helps to understand the common features, allows new styles to be added as they are developed, and provides a framework within which the evolution or future trend can be envisioned. We have found that most contemporary Web services architecture can be grouped into three basic families: Matchmaker Style,

---

[1] Rational Unified Process®.

Broker Style, and Peer-to-Peer style. For each family, we present the styles in a sequence where the fundamental style is introduced first and various derived styles are discussed one after another. These derived styles are examined in section 4 – 6. In addition to these three, we also consider two promising "Web-Oriented" Styles.

4   Matchmaker Styles

Early Web services architecture is based on matchmaker style, where a matchmaker component is defined as the 'middle agent that stores capabilities advertisements that can then be queried by requesters'[9]. In Web services architecture, a service provider registers with the UDDI registry its capability information and a service consumer contacts the registry to discover this service provider's detail so that it can bind and interact with it. Providers make their services available by publishing their interface and thus advertising their service.

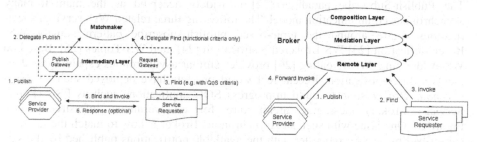

Fig. 1. Layered Matchmaker Style   **Fig. 2.** Layered Broker Style

Three classes of matchmaker styles can be distinguished, namely, (1) Layered (LM), (2) Hierarchical (HM), (3) Federated (FM). Service selection based on QoS requirements [10-12] adds an additional architectural layer (see Fig. 1) between the service requester/provider and the matchmaker to collect QoS data, and negotiate Qos requirements between them. Reliance on one single matchmaker can lead to a performance bottleneck and a single point of failure. Research in [13] thus proposed a framework with hierarchical structured registries, each of which maintains a specific business domain.All these registries are managed by one root registry .To address scalability issues, service replication or a federated architecture can be chosen. While [14] stated that "replication was chosen in UDDI because creating a scalable model for distribution of data is inherently difficult", recent researchers have attempted to tackle such distribution issues by introducing a *Federated Matchmaker* style [10, 14, 15].

5   Broker Styles

The major difference between a brokers and a matchmaker is that the broker is also involved in the transaction between requester (client) and provider (server).[16] defines a broker architectural pattern (style) as "a distributed software structure with decoupled components that interact by remote service invocation". They specify that the classical broker architectural style includes six major components. The most significant component is the broker component, which distributes client requests to the responsible server components and returns corresponding results.

Four broker-based styles can be distinguished and they are (1) Layered (LB), (2) Asynchronous (AB), (3) Hierarchical (HB), and (4) Federated (FB). LB and AB are illustrated in Figure 2 and 3 respectively. The broker style reduces the complexity involved in developing both service providers and requesters as it makes distribution transparent to the developers [16]. The layered-broker style [17] tackles such a challenge (see Figure 2). The virtual logistics network in [18] provides a real-world example of layered-broker architecture utilised in service-oriented logistics services.

Asynchronous communication provides temporal decoupling, which is crucial for Internet-scaled distributed systems and leads to scalability and resiliency. The *Asynchronous Broker* (see Figure 3) provides a callback mechanism through two Web services standards – the WS-Callback [19] and WS-Addressing [20] . This solves the problem that WS-* specifications have no standard concept for service references. The Publish-Subscribe paradigm [22] is widely accepted as the many-to-many asynchronous communication model. The following three related Web services specifications centre around the topic-based publish-subscribe pattern namely WS-BaseNotification [23] WS-Brokered Notification [24] ,and WS-Topics [25]. Based on WS-Addressing, WS-Eventing [26] provides similar asynchronous capability as does the WS-BaseNotification. Recent real world projects have deployed such an *Asynchronous Broker* style to build in-progress SOC applications such as PSB (Public Services Broker) messaging architecture for e-Government infrastructure.(see Figure 3). One issue with such an Asynchronous Broker is how to match the interests subscribed by service requester with the available notifications published by the service providers. At the time of writing, neither these WS-* specifications nor PSB[27] tackled this issue formatively and thoroughly. WS-Topics partly addresses this issue. The *Triple Space* architectural style, based on the *Asynchronous Broker*, proposes to solve this problem by utilizing semantic web technology. While the Hierarchical Broker style [28] solves the issue of service matching and interaction, and eases the management and complexity of each broker, its structure also brings about a number of shortcomings. Firstly the communication between brokers has to be facilitated by their parent brokers, which limits the flexibility and the velocity of broker interactions. Next, in hierarchical structure, sub-brokers are always controlled by the parent broker, and so are the services controlled by the intermediate broker. This makes it harder to perform dynamic re-organization. The most salient difference between Federated Broker and Hierarchical Broker is the autonomy of the child broker, and thus the flattening of the hierarchical structure. Brokers and services are organized into federations. Within a federation (a group of services facilitated by a single broker), a service gives up part of its autonomy to the broker.

6 Peer-to-Peer Style

Both matchmaker and broker architectural styles rely on a central control point in contrast to the peer-to-peer (P2P) architectural style. Thus the peer-to-peer Web services architectural style has no centralized registry to store the meta-data of service peers. For this P2P style based web service lifecycle, we discuss service discovery and service composition. P2P based service discovery relies solely on each individual peer's search capability to locate suitable service providers. The first approach to service discovery [29-32] leverages well-established P2P overlay discovery algorithms and places the Web services protocols on top of the native P2P protocols such as Gnutella and DHT [33], with WS-P2P adaptor to bridge the gap between the two protocols. The second approach[15, 34, 35] constructs the P2P communication protocol from the scratch using existing Web services protocols. For instance, [35] presented the PSI model to locate suitable services in a hybrid P2P registry network and the communication engine in each servant forms a Gnutella-compatible P2P network based on the proposed protocol – *probabilistic flooding*. Meanwhile, both of these approaches can also support semantic-based services discovery[29-31, 36].

As indicated earlier, P2P execution (P2PE) is a common means to invoke Web services in the matchmaker style. P2P composition can be classified into three substyles, namely (1) Static, (2) Mobile, (3) Hybrid. .In the Static Composition Style (P2PC-S) style[37] [38] [39], [40], the overall process specification (e.g. BPEL4WS²) is, at design-time, partitioned into smaller pieces and deployed to involved service providers and during run-time each local engine only obtains the partial copy of the whole process, and finally executes it at the local site where the invoked service resides. One problem here is that at run-time service providers cannot be changed, thus it will fail to fulfill the dynamic selection of service providers in an unreliable environment. In the Mobile Composition Style (P2PC-M) style[41,42], both the whole process specification and its related instances, which contain the state information of process execution, are dynamically brought to the next invoked service during run-time. [43] employed a combination of *Static Composition Style* to create a true P2P-based service process execution runtime environment and utilized the *Mobil Composition Style* to partition a process into a set of distributed execution units.

7 Web-Oriented Styles

We evaluate two architectural styles that are consistent with Web architectural principles [44]. Representational State Transfer (REST) [5] proponents argue that existing RPC-based Web services has serious weaknesses for the Internet in regards to scalability, performance, flexibility, and implementability[45]. REST specifically introduces numerous architectural constraints to the existing Web services architecture elements in order to: a) **simplify** interactions and compositions between service requesters and providers; b) **leverage** the existing WWW architecture wherever possible. We summarize as follows these constraints which form the fundamental REST-base ('RESTful' Web services) architectural style:

REST uses a resource identifier (URI) to provide an unambiguous and unique label for one particular web resource. In the RESTful architectural style, all resources are accessed with a generic interface resulting in a dramatic decrease in the complexity of the semantics of the service interface during the service interaction. Choosing these two styles in composing the business process can be found in [47].

---

² Business Process Execution Language for Web Services.

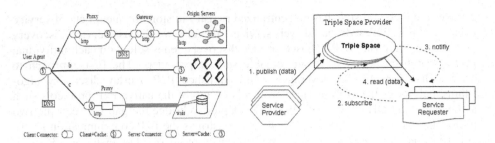

Fig. 5. REST Style. Source [5]   **Fig. 6.** TripleSpace

7.1 Triple Space

Triple Space Computing [48] is built on top of of several technologies: Tuple Space[49], Publish-Subscribe paradigm[22], Semantic Web and RDF [50] [46] Triple Space employs the "persistently publish and read" paradigm by leveraging the Tuple Space architecture and APIs. From an architecture perspective,Triple Space is, in effect, based on the natural confluence of *Asynchronous Broker* and *RESTful* styles.. The fundamental interaction among triple space architectural components is shown in Figure 6. The basic interactions between service provider and requester are rather straightforward : The service provider can "*write*" one or more triples in a concrete identified Triple Space. The service requester is able to "*subscribe*" triples that match with a template specified against its interests in a particular concrete Triple Space. Whenever there is an update in the spaces, the Triple Space will "*notify*" related service requesters indicating that there are triples available that match the template specified in its preceding subscription. The notified service requesters "*read*" triples that match with the template within a particular transaction or the entire concrete space, and further process the triples accordingly. It provides intelligent middleware(broker like), to manage the spaces without requesting each service provider and requester to either download or search through the entire space. Moreover, it needs to provide security and trust while keeping the system scalable and usage simple. Authors in [51] proposed a minimal architecture for such provider middleware. Authors in [48] identified a number of requirements for Triple Spaces (providers): Autonomy (including four basic forms of autonomy: time, location, reference, and data schema), Simplicily, Efficiency, Scalability, Decentralized Architecture, Security and Trust mechanisms, Persistent communications, and History. In order to overcome the lack of support for semantics-aware matching, Triple Space, utilizes RDF to represent and match the machine-processable semantics. It is a promising, if immature, Web services architectural style and may represent the future paradigm for designing and implementing a truly service-oriented architecture.

8 The Evolutionary CUBE

Based on previous related work[52-54], we have identified three general architectural design principles in an open environment such as the Internet – *Simplification, Decentralization*, and *Loose-coupling*. We believe these three should be equally considered in order to facilitate Internet-scaled Web services computing as they are a crucial prerequisite for any SOC-enabled applications. Each of them acts as an axis in one cubic dimension, which aligns a number of architectural styles in an order that the furthest end reflects the largest positive degree towards that principle. These three dimensions collectively constitute the 'evolutionary cube' as depicted in Figure 7, which provides an overview on current service-oriented computing reference architectural styles. The evolution starts from the *Basic Matchmaker (BM)*, which originates from the widely-accepted 'SOA triangle' architectural style. When both domain and infrastructure requirements become more complicated, the architecture of matchmaker itself becomes more intricate and difficult to design. Even if well designed, such a matchmaker might fail to scale properly in an Internet-wide business context due to its excessive complexity. Hence the appropriate simplification is crucial. The principle of simplification requires the architecture should not impose high barriers to entry for its intended adopters: each individual component in this architecture should be substantially less complex to be easier to understand and implement otherwise functionality of that component needs to be reallocated (by further decomposition or distribution). Under this principle, the *Basic Matchmaker* style moves up along the simplification axis, thus turning into two variant matchmaker styles: *Layered Matchmaker (LM)* and *Hierarchical Matchmaker (HM)*. The consequence of deploying these two variants is to reduce the complexity inherent in each complex matchmaker server, with each one being dedicated in one specific functional area (e.g. remote adaptor, execution, composition, etc.), domain, or geographic area. In other words, the simplification refers to the development and maintenance of each individual server, thus reserving simplicity of core architectural components, while pushing complexity into end systems across the Internet. REST [5] proponents pushed such a simplification trend further, and proposed the RESTful Web services style which only relies on

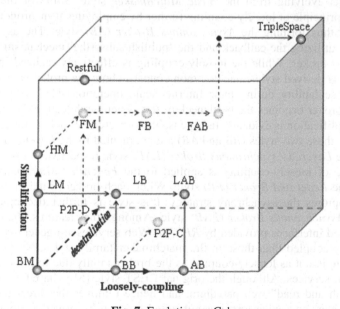

Fig. 7. Evolutionary Cube

the basic simple web protocol such as HTTP rather than creating so-called new WS-*
standards[45]. *RESTful* style is thus placed in the furthest point in the dimension of
simplification.

The principle of decentralization is based on the assumption that "the world will be
connected and widely distributed and that it will not be possible or desirable to leverage everything off a centralized, administratively managed infrastructure"[33]. In the
Internet environment,all the resources are distributed in their own preferred manner.
This principle motivates the architect to decentralize an existing architecture such as
matchmaker. This gives rise to, for example, the peer-to-peer based style. From *Basic
Matchmaker* style, this principle leads to the *P2P Discovery (P2P-D)* style. In the
case of the *Hierarchical Matchmaker*, the confluence of decentralization and simplification produces the *Federated Matchmaker (FM)* style, where a peer-to-peer communication mechanism is employed among separated yet cooperative matchmakers for
facilitating the federated service discovery. In addition, when the *basic broker* is to be
decentralized, one function – the service composition – is decentralized accordingly,
which results in the *P2P Composition (P2P-C)* style. The third principle – loosely-
coupling – refers to a very resilient relationship between two or more architectural
components – service providers and requestors in particular – that are communicating
via distant message transmission. Loosely-coupled systems are more likely to function well (e.g. without human intervention, or at low cost) when either side of the
interactions are subject to frequent changes – such as the system growth due to the
globalization, varying customer needs and requirements, unexpected network failures,
etc, which are always the case for Internet-scale systems. Realizing a loosely-coupled
architecture requires that few assumptions can be made about the detail (such as the
specific run-time platform, implementation, etc) of both service providers and requestors. Such a decoupled trend promotes *Basic Broker* styles (i.e. the facilitator
middle-agent) evolving from the *Basic Matchmaker* style. Some of these brokers
endorse the principle of loosely-coupling further by employing asynchronous message
interactions, thus forming the *Asynchronous Broker (AB)* style. The asynchrony is
achieved by utilizing the callback and the 'publish/subscribe' mechanism in such an
asynchronous broker. While the loosely-coupling is effectively realized in the *Basic
Broker* and its derived styles, one common concern about the broker style is its complexity and scalability during their Internet-scale operations [16]. Apparently, the
centralized broker becomes the bottleneck of the system architecture. Hence the principle of simplification is evidently indispensable to overcome such an intricacy. When
it is applied, these two styles (*BB* and *AB*) are augmented to the *Layered Broker (LB)*
style and the *Layered Asynchronous Broker (LAB)* style respectively. Likewise, when
the principle of loosely-coupling is applied to the *Federated Matchmaker* style, it
turns into the *Federated Broker (FB)* style. When each broker in the *Federated Broker* style captures the asynchrony strategy, this style is further decoupled into the
Federated Asynchronous Broker (FAB) style. Among other features, the constrained
and simplified interfaces provided by *RESTful* Web services are generally considered
more loosely-coupled than those in the matchmaker family styles. Nevertheless, the
RESTful style is not as loosely-coupled as the broker family due to its direct interaction between services. Although the original REST style [5] is based on the "persistently publish and read" web paradigm, and hence removes the direct link between
service providers and requestors, it is not suited for non-hypermedia applications that

are the case for the majority of Web services. Therefore, it appears natural to propose another style that can integrate the benefits of both RESTful and broker family styles. This gives rise to the *TripleSpace* style, which evolves from the *Federated Asynchronous Broker* style and meanwhile keeps the virtues of the canonical REST style. The *TripleSpace* style lies at the far end position of all the three dimensions. It is thus a highly desirable reference architecture for guiding the design of truly Internet-scale Web services applications.

9 Proposed Architecture

Based on the evolutionary cube, we propose the following architecture shown in figure 8 for the distributed Service-Oriented computing. Readers can refer to [60] for a comprehensive understanding of this architectural design and its associated styles.

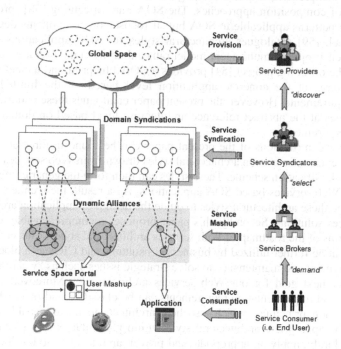

Fig. 8. Proposed Architecture

10 Conclusions

The right software architecture paves the way for the success of any software systems. However, producing a 'good' architecture design is always a very challenging task. Services-Oriented Computing applications realised by Web services are even more difficult to design since a) the core technology and related standards are still evolving; b) little experience is available from only a small number of existing successful SOA implementations. In order to design an effective and quality-assured software architecture, we found an abstract Reference Architecture (RA) can be extremely useful in guiding the architecture design at the application level. Aiming at providing fundamental reference architecture for Web services applications, this paper provides the first step towards creating such a RA by identifying and examining canonical architectural styles which are essential in composing the RA in accordance with domain and infrastructure requirements. The thirteen styles studied in this paper are all related in a manner that an evolution of these architectural styles is speculated based on three generic engineering principles for Internet-scale Web services-enabled SOA systems.

Architectural styles for web and network applications but not Web services-enabled systems are surveyed in [5]. Web services architectural patterns are defined and identified in [55],but these patterns are limited to e-business scenarios. For Web services discovery, [56] analyses contemporary Web services registries and provides comparison of these styles against attributes from the view-based framework . [57] provides a comprehensive understanding on service composition and identifies five categories of composition approaches. The SOA pattern catalog [58] presents thirteen design patterns applicable to SOA but it focuses on components design at fine-grained level. [59] catalogues architectural styles for SOC applications but bases these on their proposed multi-agent model rather than from the literature and industry practice. The on-going project [54] provides a SOA blueprint and a catalogue of normative patterns at the concrete application level based on the limited e-business specific requirements. However, the present paper catalogues these patterns and architectural styles at the abstract reference architecture level based on domain and infrastructure requirements.

The major contributions of the present paper can be found in three areas: firstly, it provides a review of common architectural styles drawn from Web services applications based on a classification scheme. These styles can then form the generic reference architecture for Web services-based SOA applications. As a result, the architect can eventually leverage these architectural styles to guide the design of application architecture for Web services solutions. Secondly, this paper proposes a comprehensible 'evolutionary cube' in terms of the roadmap of Web services architectural styles. This cube, if refined properly, can be further utilized by business consultants and CIOs as a blueprint during SOA deployment and maintenance to solve strategic issues such as "where are we now? What is our next goal for our Web services architecture?". Moreover, customer requirements and implementation requirements can be classified and mapped to the three major evolution principles, which also help architects to make sensible decisions in choosing the appropriate architectural style within particular business and technology contexts. Thirdly, applying appropriate and proven architectural styles drawn from the Reference Architecture significantly reduces the development time and increases the efficiency and adequacy of the Web services solution.

References

[1] Weerawarana, S., Curbera, F., Leymann, F., Storey, T., Ferguson, D.F.: Web Services Platform Architecture. Prentice-Hall, Inc. (2005)

[2] Cimetiere, J.C.: Web Services Adopt. and Tech. Choices, TechMetrix Research (2003)

[3] Lundberg, L., Bosch, J., Häggander, D., Bengtsson, P.: Quality Attributes in Software Architecture Design. In: Proc.3rd IASTED Conf. on Soft. Eng.& Applns., pp. 353–362 (1999)

[4] Bass, L., Clements, P.: Software Architecture in Practice. Addison-Wesley, Reading (2000)

[5] Fielding, R.T.: Architectural Styles and the Design of Network-based Software Architectures, PhD Dissertations, University of California, Irvine CA, USA (2000)

[6] Bass, L., Clements, P., Kazan, R.: Software Architecture in Practice. Addison Wesley, Reading (2003)

[7] Barber, K.S., Graser, T., Holt, J.: A Multi-Level Software Architecture Metamodel to Support the Capture and Evaluation of Stakeholder Concerns. In: ISAS-SCI, vol. 1 (2001)

[8] Artifact: Reference Architecture, v2006:1987-2003 Rational Software Corp (2003)

[9] Decker, K., Sycara, K., Williamson, M.: Middle agents for the internet. In: Proc.IJCAI (1997)

[10] Degwekar, S., Su, S.Y.W., Lam, H.: Constraint Specification and Processing in Web Services Publication and Discovery. In: IEEE Conf. on Web Services (ICWS'04) (2004)

[11] Wang, X., Yue, K., Huang, J.Z., Zhou, A.: Service Selection in Dynamic Demand-Driven Web Services. In: IEEE Conf. on Web Services (ICWS'04), IEEE Computer Society Press, Los Alamitos (2004)

[12] Yu, T., Lin, K.: Design of QoS Broker Algor. for QoS-Capable Web Serv., EEE'04 (2004)

[13] Papazoglou, M., et al.: Lever. Web-Services & P2P Networks. Springer, Heidelberg (2003)

[14] Pilioura, T., Kapos, G., Tsalgatidou, A.: PYRAMID-S: A Scalable Infrastructure for Semantic Web Service Publn. & Discovery. In: 14th Int. Wrksp. Rsch. Issues on Data Eng. (2004)

[15] Banaei-Kashani, F., Chen, C.-C., Shahabi, C.: WSPDS: Web Services Peer-to-peer Discovery Service. In: Int. Symp. on Web Services and Applns., USA, pp. 733–743 (2004)

[16] Buschmann, F., Meunier, R., Rohnert, H., Sommerlad, P., Stal, M. (eds.): Pattern-Oriented Software Architecture, a System of Patterns. J. Wiley and Sons, Inc., Chichester (1996)

[17] Piers, P., Benevides, M., Mattoso, M.: Mediating Heterogeneous Web Services. In: Symp. on Applns. and the Internet (SAINT' 03) (2003)

[18] Chang, E., Dillon, T.S., Gardner, W., Talevski, A., Rajugan, R.: A Virtual Logistics Network and an E-hub as a Competitive Approach for Small to Medium Size Companies. In: Web and Comm. Techn. and Internet-Related Social Issues – HSI, vol. 2003, Springer, Heidelberg (2003)

[19] Goland, Y., Nottingham, M., Orchard, D.: WS-CallBack Protocol (WS-CallBack) 0.91 (2003), http://dev2dev.bea.com/webservices/WS-CallBack-0_9.html

[20] Box, D., Curbera, F.: Web Services Addressing (WS-Addressing) (2004), http://www.w3.org/Submission/ws-addressing/

[21] Vinoski, S.: Web Services Notification. In: IEEE Internet Computing, pp. 86–90 (2004)

[22] Eugster, P.T., Felber, P.A., Guerraoui, R., Kermarrec, A.-M.: The Many Faces of Publish/Subscribe. ACM Survey 35, 114–131 (2003)

[23] Graham, S., Niblett, P.: Web Services Base Notification (2004), ftp://www6.software.ibm.com/software/developer/library/ws-notification/WS-BaseN.pdf

[24] Graham, S., Niblett, P.: Web Services Brokered Notification, ftp://www6.software.ibm.com/software/developer/library/ws-notification/WSBrokeredN.pdf

[25] Graham, S., Niblett, P.: Web Services Topics (2004), ftp://www6.software.ibm.com/software/developer/library/ws-notification/WSTopics.pdf

[26] Geller, A.: Web Services Eventing (WS-Eventing), Technical Specification (2004), http://www-106.ibm.com/developerworks/webservices/library/specification/ws-eventing/

[27] McGrath, S.: An overview of the Public Services Broker Architecture (2004), http://sdec.reach.ie/papers/psb-overview/psb-overview-v1.pdf

[28] Chang, S.-F., Fu, L.-C., Tsai, M.-Y.: Automatic Integration of Inter-Enterprise Process with Hierarchical Broker Framework, Bul. College of Eng., N.T.U., pp. 99–107 (2004)

[29] Ayyasamy, S., Patel, C., Lee, Y.: Semantic Web Services and DHT-based Peer-to-Peer Networks: A New Symb. Relnship. Pos. Ppr., Sch.Comp.& Eng. Uni.f Missouri (2003)

[30] Paolucci, M., Sycara, K., Nishimura, T., Srinivasan, N.: Using DAML-S for P2P Discovery. In: Int. Conf. on Web Services, ICWS (2003)

[31] Emekci, F., Sahin, O., Agrawal, D., Abbadi, A.: Peer-to-Peer Framework for Web Service Discovery with Ranking. In: IEEE Int. Conf. on Web Services (ICWS'04) (2004)

[32] Schmidt, C., Parashar, M.: A Peer-to-Peer Approach to Web Service Discovery, World Wide Web, pp. 211–229 (2004)

[33] Milojicic, D.S., Kalogeraki, V., Lukose, R., Nagaraja, K., Pruyne, J., Richard, B., Rollins, S., Xu, Z.: Peer-to-Peer Computing, Hewlett-Packard Report (2003)

[34] Wang, Q., Yuan, Y., Zhou, J., Zhou, A.: Peer-Serv: A Framework of Web Services in Peer-to-Peer Environment. In: Dong, G., Tang, C.-j., Wang, W. (eds.) WAIM 2003. LNCS, vol. 2762, pp. 298–305. Springer, Heidelberg (2003)

[35] Prasad, V., Lee, Y.: A Scalable Infrastructure for Peer-to-Peer Networks Using Web Service Registries and Intell. Peer Locators. In: Int. Symp. on Cluster Comp. and Grid, 216 (2003)

[36] Thaden, U., et al.: A Sem.Web based P2P Service Reg. Nwk., Rep. Uni. of Hanover (2003)

[37] Muth, P., Wodtke, D., Weissenfels, J., Kotz, D.A.: From Centralized Workflow Specification to Distributed Workflow Execution. J of Intell. Inf. Systems (JIIS), 10 (1998)

[38] Benatallah, B., Dumas, M., Sheng, Q., Ngu, A.: Declarative Composition and Peer-to-Peer Provisioning of Dynamic Web Services. In: Int/ Conf. on Data Engineering (2002)

[39] Nanda, M.G., Chandra, S., Sarkar, V.: Decentra. execution of composite web services. 19th ACM SIGPLAN Conf. on Object-oriented Progr., Systems, Lang., and Applns. (2004)

[40] Chafle, G., Chandra, S., Mann, V.: Decentralized Orchestration of Composite Web Services. In: Chafle, G., Chandra, S., Mann, V. (eds.) World Wide Web, New York, USA (2004)

[41] Haller, K., Schuldt, H.: Consistent Process Execution in Peer-to-Peer Information Systems. In: 15th Conf. on Adv. Info. Systems Eng (CAiSE), Klagenfurt/Velden, Austria (2003)

[42] Lakhal, N.B., Kobayashi, T., Yokota, H.: THROWS: an archi. for highly available dist. execution of Web services compositions. In: 14th Wkshp. on Res. Issues on Data Eng. (2004)

[43] Schuler, C., Weber, R., Schuldt, H., Schek, H.: Scalable Peer-to-Peer Process Management - The OSIRIS Approach. Int. Conference on Web Services (ICWS) (2004)

[44] Fielding, R.T., Taylor, R.N.: Principled Design of the Modern Web Architecture. ACM Trans. on Internet Technology (2002)

[45] Mitchell, K.: A Matter of Style: Web Services Arch. Patt. XML Conf & Exp. USA (2002)

[46] Vinoski, S.: Putting the "Web" into Web Services - Web Services Interaction Models, Part 2. IEEE Internet Computing, 90–92 (2002)

[47] Snell, J.: Resource-oriented vs. activity-oriented Web services, IBM developerWorks (2004), ftp://www6.software.ibm.com/software/developer/library/ws-restvsoap.pdf

[48] Bussler, C., Kilgarriff, E., Krummenacher, R., et al.: WSMX: Triple-Space Computing, SMO Working Draft (2005), http://www.wsmo.org/TR/d21/v0.1/20050613

[49] Gelernter, D.: Gen. Com. in Linda. ACM Trans. Prog. Lang. and Sys. 7(1), 80–112 (1985)

[50] Klyne, G., Carroll, J.J.: Resource Description Framework (RDF): Concepts and Abstract Syntax, W3C Recommendation (2004), http://www.w3.org/TR/rdf-concepts/

[51] Krummenacher, R., Hepp, M., Polleres, A., Bussler, C., Fensel, D.: WWW or What Is Wrong with Web Services. In: 3rd IEEE Euro. Conf. on Web Services, pp. 235–243 (2005)

[52] Austin, D., Barbir, A., Ferris, C., Garg, S.: Web Services Architecture Requirements. W3C Working Group Note (2004)

[53] Fielding, R.T., Taylor, R.N.: Principled Design of the Modern Web Architecture. ACM Trans. on Internet Technology (2002)

[54] MacKenzie, M., Amand, S.S.: Electronic Business Service Oriented Architecture. OASIA ebSOA Working Draft 047 (2004)

[55] Endrei, M., Ang, J., Arsanjani, A., Chua, S., Comte, P., Krogdahl, P., Luo, M., Newling, T.: Patterns: Service-Oriented Architecture and Web Services (2004)

[56] Dustdar, S., et al.: A View Based Anal. on Web Service Regist. Distr. & Para. DBs (2005)

[57] Dustdar, S., et al.: A survey on web services comp. Int. J. Web and Grid Services 1 (2005)

[58] Unknown: http://www.soaprpc.com/patterns/soa_pattern_catalog.html soaprpc.com (2005)

[59] Maximilien, E.M., Singh, M.P.: Toward Web Services Interaction Styles. In: 2nd IEEE International Conferences on Services Computing (2005)

[60] C.Wu, E. Chang, and T. Dillon.: A Semantic Grid Architecture. In: International Conference on Semantics, Knowledge and Grid 2007, Xi'an, China (to be presented)

Author Index

Lecture Notes in Computer Science

Sublibrary 1: Theoretical Computer Science and General Issues

Vol. 4599: S. Vassiliadis, M. Berekovic, T.D. Hämäläinen (Eds.), Embedded Computer Systems: Architectures, Modeling, and Simulation. XVIII, 466 pages. 2007.

Vol. 4598: G. Lin (Ed.), Computing and Combinatorics. XII, 570 pages. 2007.

Vol. 4596: L. Arge, C. Cachin, T. Jurdziński, A. Tarlecki (Eds.), Automata, Languages and Programming. XVII, 953 pages. 2007.

Vol. 4595: D. Bošnački, S. Edelkamp (Eds.), Model Checking Software. X, 285 pages. 2007.

Vol. 4590: W. Damm, H. Hermanns (Eds.), Computer Aided Verification. XV, 562 pages. 2007.

Vol. 4588: T. Harju, J. Karhumäki, A. Lepistö (Eds.), Developments in Language Theory. XI, 423 pages. 2007.

Vol. 4583: S.R. Della Rocca (Ed.), Typed Lambda Calculi and Applications. X, 397 pages. 2007.

Vol. 4580: B. Ma, K. Zhang (Eds.), Combinatorial Pattern Matching. XII, 366 pages. 2007.

Vol. 4576: D. Leivant, R. de Queiroz (Eds.), Logic, Language, Information and Computation. X, 363 pages. 2007.

Vol. 4547: C. Carlet, B. Sunar (Eds.), Arithmetic of Finite Fields. XI, 355 pages. 2007.

Vol. 4546: J. Kleijn, A. Yakovlev (Eds.), Petri Nets and Other Models of Concurrency – ICATPN 2007. XI, 515 pages. 2007.

Vol. 4545: H. Anai, K. Horimoto, T. Kutsia (Eds.), Algebraic Biology. XIII, 379 pages. 2007.

Vol. 4533: F. Baader (Ed.), Term Rewriting and Applications. XII, 419 pages. 2007.

Vol. 4528: J. Mira, J.R. Álvarez (Eds.), Nature Inspired Problem-Solving Methods in Knowledge Engineering, Part II. XXII, 650 pages. 2007.

Vol. 4527: J. Mira, J.R. Álvarez (Eds.), Bio-inspired Modeling of Cognitive Tasks, Part I. XXII, 630 pages. 2007.

Vol. 4525: C. Demetrescu (Ed.), Experimental Algorithms. XIII, 448 pages. 2007.

Vol. 4514: S.N. Artemov, A. Nerode (Eds.), Logical Foundations of Computer Science. XI, 513 pages. 2007.

Vol. 4513: M. Fischetti, D.P. Williamson (Eds.), Integer Programming and Combinatorial Optimization. IX, 500 pages. 2007.

Vol. 4510: P. Van Hentenryck, L.A. Wolsey (Eds.), Integration of AI and OR Techniques in Constraint Programming for Combinatorial Optimization Problems. X, 391 pages. 2007.

Vol. 4507: F. Sandoval, A. Prieto, J. Cabestany, M. Graña (Eds.), Computational and Ambient Intelligence. XXVI, 1167 pages. 2007.

Vol. 4501: J. Marques-Silva, K.A. Sakallah (Eds.), Theory and Applications of Satisfiability Testing – SAT 2007. XI, 384 pages. 2007.

Vol. 4497: S.B. Cooper, B. Löwe, A. Sorbi (Eds.), Computation and Logic in the Real World. XVIII, 826 pages. 2007.

Vol. 4494: H. Jin, O.F. Rana, Y. Pan, V.K. Prasanna (Eds.), Algorithms and Architectures for Parallel Processing. XIV, 508 pages. 2007.

Vol. 4493: D. Liu, S. Fei, Z. Hou, H. Zhang, C. Sun (Eds.), Advances in Neural Networks – ISNN 2007, Part III. XXVI, 1215 pages. 2007.

Vol. 4492: D. Liu, S. Fei, Z. Hou, H. Zhang, C. Sun (Eds.), Advances in Neural Networks – ISNN 2007, Part II. XXVII, 1321 pages. 2007.

Vol. 4491: D. Liu, S. Fei, Z.-G. Hou, H. Zhang, C. Sun (Eds.), Advances in Neural Networks – ISNN 2007, Part I. LIV, 1365 pages. 2007.

Vol. 4490: Y. Shi, G.D. van Albada, J. Dongarra, P.M.A. Sloot (Eds.), Computational Science – ICCS 2007, Part IV. XXXVII, 1211 pages. 2007.

Vol. 4489: Y. Shi, G.D. van Albada, J. Dongarra, P.M.A. Sloot (Eds.), Computational Science – ICCS 2007, Part III. XXXVII, 1257 pages. 2007.

Vol. 4488: Y. Shi, G.D. van Albada, J. Dongarra, P.M.A. Sloot (Eds.), Computational Science – ICCS 2007, Part II. XXXV, 1251 pages. 2007.

Vol. 4487: Y. Shi, G.D. van Albada, J. Dongarra, P.M.A. Sloot (Eds.), Computational Science – ICCS 2007, Part I. LXXXI, 1275 pages. 2007.

Vol. 4484: J.-Y. Cai, S.B. Cooper, H. Zhu (Eds.), Theory and Applications of Models of Computation. XIII, 772 pages. 2007.

Vol. 4475: P. Crescenzi, G. Prencipe, G. Pucci (Eds.), Fun with Algorithms. X, 273 pages. 2007.

Vol. 4474: G. Prencipe, S. Zaks (Eds.), Structural Information and Communication Complexity. XI, 342 pages. 2007.

Vol. 4459: C. Cérin, K.-C. Li (Eds.), Advances in Grid and Pervasive Computing. XVI, 759 pages. 2007.

Vol. 4449: Z. Horváth, V. Zsók, A. Butterfield (Eds.), Implementation and Application of Functional Languages. X, 271 pages. 2007.

Vol. 4448: M. Giacobini (Ed.), Applications of Evolutionary Computing. XXIII, 755 pages. 2007.

Vol. 4447: E. Marchiori, J.H. Moore, J.C. Rajapakse (Eds.), Evolutionary Computation, Machine Learning and Data Mining in Bioinformatics. XI, 302 pages. 2007.

Vol. 4446: C. Cotta, J. van Hemert (Eds.), Evolutionary Computation in Combinatorial Optimization. XII, 241 pages. 2007.

Vol. 4445: M. Ebner, M. O'Neill, A. Ekárt, L. Vanneschi, A.I. Esparcia-Alcázar (Eds.), Genetic Programming. XI, 382 pages. 2007.

Vol. 4436: C.R. Stephens, M. Toussaint, D. Whitley, P.F. Stadler (Eds.), Foundations of Genetic Algorithms. IX, 213 pages. 2007.

Vol. 4433: E. Şahin, W.M. Spears, A.F.T. Winfield (Eds.), Swarm Robotics. XII, 221 pages. 2007.

Vol. 4432: B. Beliczynski, A. Dzielinski, M. Iwanowski, B. Ribeiro (Eds.), Adaptive and Natural Computing Algorithms, Part II. XXVI, 761 pages. 2007.

Vol. 4431: B. Beliczynski, A. Dzielinski, M. Iwanowski, B. Ribeiro (Eds.), Adaptive and Natural Computing Algorithms, Part I. XXV, 851 pages. 2007.